EZRA POUND : POET

A Portrait of the Man and his Work

II : THE EPIC YEARS

1921–1939

A. DAVID MOODY

'Tout commence en mystique et finit en politique' (Péguy)

OXFORD
UNIVERSITY PRESS

OXFORD
UNIVERSITY PRESS

Great Clarendon Street, Oxford, OX2 6DP,
United Kingdom

Oxford University Press is a department of the University of Oxford.
It furthers the University's objective of excellence in research, scholarship,
and education by publishing worldwide. Oxford is a registered trade mark of
Oxford University Press in the UK and in certain other countries

First Edition published in 2014

Impression: 1

Published in the United States of America by Oxford University Press
198 Madison Avenue, New York, NY 10016, United States of America

British Library Cataloguing in Publication Data
Data available

Library of Congress Control Number: 2014933917

ISBN 978-0-19-921558-4

Printed in Italy by
L.E.G.O. S.p.A.—Lavis TN

FOR JOANNA

CONTENTS

ILLUSTRATIONS

View of Rapallo. Postcard sent by Pound to Olivia Shakespear,
6 March 1925, with note: 'arrows show flat, mostly roof' *endpapers*

ILLUSTRATIONS

TEXT ILLUSTRATIONS

PREFACE

One mistake of the political mind is to underestimate the diversity and discontinuity of the psyche. —Donald Hall, *Remembering Poets*

I could give you a verbal description of his character which would not be unjust to him, but what are such descriptions worth? A man's character is his whole life. —Goethe, *Italian Journey*

An artist's statement is made in and by his work. His work is his biography, and the better the artist the more this applies.

—Ezra Pound. 'Gaudier: A Postscript'

No critic has the right to pretend that he fully understands an artist.

—Ezra Pound, 'Brancusi'

A biographer—a novelist, on oath. —Leon Edel

Pound's middle years, the most productive of his career, coincided with the two decades between the 1914–18 'Great War', and the 'Second World War' of 1939–45. In the 1920s, and in Paris, Pound was among the leading figures of the avant-garde, along with Joyce, whose *Ulysses* was published there in 1922; and Picasso and Braque, and his more particular friends Brancusi and Picabia and Léger; and along with Stravinsky, and Satie, and Jean Cocteau. In that ambience he composed a musically inventive and emotionally intense opera, *Le Testament [de Villon]*; made an original contribution to the theory of harmony; and composed, following musical procedures, the first thirty cantos of his modern epic. Music was all important to him at that time. But so too was the imperative to promote advances in all the arts for the general betterment of society.

That concern was given a sharper focus by the severe economic depression brought on by the 1929 Wall Street Crash, a depression which continued, in America and Britain, through the 1930s. He found it infamous that the governments of those democracies should put saving the banks, and saving the financial system responsible for the crisis and the depression, before the welfare of their people. He held it as axiomatic that a democratic government should serve the interests of the whole people, not the interests of the few who controlled the nation's wealth; more, he held it to be criminally irresponsible for a government to allow the nation's credit to be in the hands of bankers and financiers who were free to use it for their private profit without regard for the public interest. At the same time, living now in Italy, he observed that Mussolini, in his Fascist and anti-democratic dictatorship, did provide for the welfare of his people, and did direct the banks to serve the nation's needs. That led him to endorse Fascism in and for Italy, while urging the United States to live up to its own democratic Constitution. The forty cantos which he composed in the 1930s were predominantly concerned with economic and social justice, and with historical instances of good and bad banking and good and bad government. One entire decad was devoted to the example of Confucian China, and another to John Adams, the mind behind the American Revolution and the founding of its democracy. Those two blocks of cantos, the 'China' and the 'John Adams', are the keystones of his epic, and the most developed working out of his economic and political commitments in the 1930s. Those cantos, and those commitments, have not been well understood; but the time may have come for a better appreciation of Pound's vision of the fundamental principles of a just society now that we are undergoing our own financial crisis and consequent economic and social 'austerity'.

Things were not simple, politically and socially, in the 1930s; and Pound himself was not simple. Hindsight simplifies, but rarely clarifies. Complexities, confusions, and contradictions have to be reckoned with, as features of the time and of Pound. The paradox of his endorsing Mussolini's Fascist economic programme, while taking his stand upon the Constitution of democratic America, might be matched by democratic America's maintaining an undemocratic and anti-social financial system. Another self-contradiction would be America's continuing discrimination against the descendants of its slaves while declaring that all men are born free and equal; and matching that might be Pound's deploying the anti-Semitism endemic in America and Europe, and already turning murderous in Hitler's Germany, as a weapon in his crusade for social justice. Altogether, Pound emerges in this account as a flawed idealist and a great poet caught up in the turmoil of his darkening time and struggling, often raging, against the current to be a force for enlightenment.

As I wrote in the preface to the first volume, Ezra Pound exists now in what he wrote, in his poetry, and also in all the thousands of pages of his published writings and the tens of thousands of pages of unpublished letters and drafts. That hoard is the form in which I have studied and contemplated him, and I have taken his words as the material and the medium of this portrait—as both what I have had to work from and what I have had to work with. Nearly everything that matters here has behind it some document—I have refrained from speculation, and I have ignored hearsay.

My interest has been to weave the varied threads of Pound's life and work into a patterned narrative, and to present the drama of this egregiously individual and powerful vortex in the stream of his language and culture.

A.D.M.

Alleins, June 2013.

CHRONOLOGY

1921   Jan., after two week in Paris to Saint-Raphaël; back to Paris 10 April. Works on opera *Le Testament de Villon*. Translates Remy de Gourmont's *Physique de l'amour*—published in 1922 as *The Natural History of Love*. Dec., *Poems 1918–21*, including cantos IV–VII, published in New York. EP and DP take studio at 70 *bis* rue Notre Dame des Champs, Paris VI.

1922   3 Jan., T. S. Eliot in Paris with *The Waste Land* 'in semi-existence'; EP edits the manuscript and transforms 'a jumble of good and bad passages into a poem'. Joyce's *Ulysses* published in Feb. by Shakespeare and Company in Paris. Pound's 'Eighth Canto', later revised as canto II, published in *Dial* in May.
Mar. begins 'Bel Esprit' scheme with Natalie Barney to raise a fund for Eliot and other writers.
Apr.–June, travelling in Italy; drafting canto 12 and 'Hell cantos'; early drafts towards Malatesta cantos.
Back in Paris begins affaire with Nancy Cunard; declares himself 'a Confucian' to John Quinn; meets William Bird, whose Three Mountains Press will publish several of his works.
30 Oct., Mussolini forms government following Fascist 'March on Rome'.
Nov., *The Waste Land* appears in *Dial*.

1923   Jan.–Apr., in Italy; walking tour there with Hemingway in Feb.; researching and writing Malatesta cantos, to be published as 'Cantos IX–XII of a Long Poem' in Eliot's *Criterion* in July.
Indiscretions published by Three Mountains Press.
In Paris, meets the violinist Olga Rudge (OR) in Natalie Barney's salon.
June, meets George Antheil, with whom he radically revises the score of *Le Testament*.
Transatlantic Review, edited in Paris by Ford with assistance by Basil Bunting—EP promotes and aids the journal.
Aug., walking tour in Dordogne with OR.
Oct., Bride Scratton, whom EP first met in London in 1910, divorces her husband, naming him as co-respondent.

1924   Jan.–May, EP and DP tour Italy looking for permanent home there.
June, William Carlos Williams in Paris.
Oct., EP and DP leave Paris for Italy, first to Rapallo, then in Dec. to Sicily until Feb.
Antheil and the Treatise on Harmony published by Three Mountains Press.

1925   Jan., *A Draft of XVI Cantos* published by Three Mountains Press.
Mar., EP and DP now settled in Rapallo.

9 July, birth of daughter Mary in the Italian Tyrol, child of EP and OR. Child to be fostered and brought up there in local farming family.

1926 June, *Le Testament* concert version performed in Paris.

10 Sept., birth of Omar Pound in Paris, son of Dorothy. Child to be fostered in Norland Nurseries and brought up in England.

Dec., *Personae, The Collected Poems of Ezra Pound* published in New York.

1927 EP begins to edit and publish his little magazine, *Exile* (four issues).

Oct., studying Guido Cavalcanti and his philosophical context.

1928 EP receives 1927 *Dial* award for poetry.

EP's translation of the Confucian *Ta Hio, or The Great Learning* published by the University of Washington Bookstore.

May, EP in Vienna for Antheil/OR concert; writes 'Mensdorf letter'.

July, EP's translation of Cavalcanti's 'Donna mi prega' with commentary in *Dial*.

Sept., *A Draft of The Cantos 17–27* published by John Rodker in London.

Oct., OR buys small house in Calle Querini, Dorsoduro, Venice.

Nov., *Selected Poems*, ed. TSE, published by Faber & Gwyer. W. B. Yeats takes apartment in Rapallo.

Dec., EP completes his edition of Cavalcanti.

1929 1 June, EP's parents sail from New York for London, then go on to Rapallo, where they decide to settle.

24 Oct., Wall Street Crash sets off the Great Depression of the 1930s.

1930 May, to Frankfurt for première of Antheil's opera *Transatlantic (The People's Choice)*; there meets Leo Frobenius.

Aug., *A Draft of XXX Cantos* published by Nancy Cunard's Hours Press. EP now working on cantos 31–5.

Nov., begins writing to US Senator Bronson Cutting.

OR begins renting upper floor of Casa 60, Sant' Ambrogio, above Rapallo.

1931 26, 27 Oct., BBC broadcasts *Le Testament*.

Dec., *How to Read* published by Desmond Harmsworth in London.

1932 Jan., EP's *Guido Cavalcanti/Rime* published by Edizioni Marsano, Genoa.

May, EP's *Profile/An Anthology collected in MCMXXXI* published by Giovanni Scheiwiller, Milan.

Aug., EP completes *Cavalcanti* ('a sung dramedy in 3 acts'). Begins to contribute to *Il Mare*, Rapallo's local newspaper. An *'Objectivists' Anthology*, ed. Louis Zukofsky, is dedicated 'To Ezra Pound who . . . is still for the poets of our time the most important'.

1933 30 Jan., EP granted interview with Mussolini.

30 Jan., Hitler becomes Reichschancellor of Germany.

Feb., EP writes *Jefferson and/or Mussolini*. Begins correspondence with Congressman George Tinkham of Massachusetts.

21–31 Mar., EP gives series of 9 lectures at Milan's Università Commerciale Luigi Bocconi, under general title 'An Historic Background for Economics', and beginning with 'Why or how a poet came to be drawn into economic discussion'; the fourth lecture was on 'Economic ideas of the early and constructive American presidents: Jefferson'; the fifth on 'John Quincy Adams'; and the sixth on 'Martin Van Buren'; the final lecture was on 'What literature has to do with it—The function of good writing in the State'.

Apr., *ABC of Economics*—'a concise introduction to "volitionist economics"'—published by Faber & Faber. [Not the text of the Milan lectures.]

June, first annual Rapallo concert series organized by EP.

July, OR becomes secretary to Accademia Musicale Chigiana in Siena.

Oct., EP's *Active Anthology* published by Faber & Faber.

Nov., starts writing to Senator William Borah of Idaho.

1934 Feb., EP as 'Alfie Venison', 'The Charge of the Bread Brigade', the first of the 'Alfred Venison' songs of social protest.

May, EP's *ABC of Reading* published by Routledge, London.

Aug., EP circulates his Volitionist Economics questionnaire.

Aug., Hitler proclaimed Führer.

Sept., EP's *Make It New/Essays* published by Faber & Faber.

Oct., *Eleven New Cantos/XXXI–XLI* published by Farrar & Rinehart, New York.

1935 Jan., EP's first radio broadcast to USA—next will be in Jan. 1941.

May, *Social Credit: An Impact* published by Stanley Nott, London.

July, *Jefferson and/or Mussolini/L'idea statale/Fascism as I have seen it/ . . . Volitionist Economics* published by Stanley Nott.

Sept., Nazi Germany promulgates 'Nuremberg Laws' depriving German Jews of their citizenship and further restricting their civil rights.

Oct., Italy invades Abyssinia.

1936 Jan., EP and OR promote Vivaldi revival.

Feb., canto 45, 'With Usura', published in English Social Credit magazine *Prosperity.*

July, Spanish Civil War begins.

Nov., Germany and Italy form their 'Axis'.

Dec., EP sends cantos 42–51 to Faber.

1937 Feb., EP's *Polite Essays* published by Faber.

Feb.–May, writes *Guide to Kulchur.* The first chapter published in June by Giovanni Scheiwiller in Milan as *Confucius/Digest of the Analects.*

June, *The Fifth Decad of Cantos* published by Faber.

July, Sino-Japanese war begun by Japan's invasion of northern China.

1938 Jan., EP elected to US National Institute of Arts and Letters.

Mar., Germany annexes Austria in the 'Anschluss'.

July, *Guide to Kulchur* published by Faber.

29 Sept., British, French, and Italian prime ministers (Chamberlain, Daladier, and Mussolini) meeting in Munich support Hitler's demand that Czechoslovakia's Sudetenland be ceded to Germany. Chamberlain boasts that this 'Munich Agreement' has bought 'peace in our time'.

2 Oct., death of Olivia Shakespear; EP in London for five weeks settling her affairs; Wyndham Lewis does his portrait now in the Tate.

9 Nov., Kristallnacht: Nazi pogrom in which hundreds of Jewish shops, houses, and synagogues are looted and burnt, and many Jews murdered. The Nazis decree that the Jews should collectively pay for the insured loss.

1939   28 Jan., death of W. B. Yeats at Cap Martin on the French Riviera.

Mar., Hitler invades and occupies the remainder of Czechoslovakia.

Apr., Italy annexes Albania.

Apr., EP's *What Is Money For* published by Greater Britain Publications.

Apr.–June, EP goes to America in hope of persuading President Roosevelt to keep USA out of the looming European war. Awarded honorary doctorate by Hamilton College.

26 June, death of Ford Madox Ford at Deauville, France.

Aug., EP contributing to *Meridiano di Roma*.

1 Sept., Germany invades Poland, thus setting off the Second World War.

Nov., EP declares 'my economic work is done', prepares to write his *paradiso*.

1940   Jan., *Cantos LII–LXXI* ['China'—'John Adams'] published by Faber.

PART ONE : 1921–1932

1 : A Year in Paris, 1921–1924

Pound would not settle in Paris. It was too 'northern' for him, with its menace of cold and dark that shut one in on oneself. He would go away for months at a time, and then for good at the end of 1924, to the more benign south of France and to Italy where he could leave all his senses open to the 'world of moving energies' around him. The light and warmth of the Mediterranean climate made not only for better health, he found, but also for increased intelligence and finer perceptions. He wanted to have just one 'solid year in Paris', he told Williams, though in the event he extended his 'year' over nearly four.

After crossing from London in early January 1921 Ezra and Dorothy spent only ten days in Paris, and for most of that time Ezra was in bed with flu. They got away by train on the 18th and went down to Saint-Raphaël on the coast near Cannes. The town, according to Baedeker, had a thriving port and was a favoured winter resort offering some 'well spoken of' hotels and an 'English Church (services in winter)'. The Pounds put up at one of the cheaper hotels near the station, l'Hôtel du Terminus et des Négociants. For the next three months Ezra 'for the first time in years...had a real rest' and wrote nothing, or so he told Ford. His typewriter was left behind in Paris. 'Palm leaf hut on the beach', he scrawled on a postcard to Alice Corbin Henderson in Santa Fe. His one duty was to write to Scofield Thayer telling him what he thought of each number of the *Dial* as it reached him, and offering unwanted suggestions and advice for future numbers. It is likely that his mind was on his *Villon* and his cantos, and that he did some composing of one or the other from time to time. But he admitted only to playing tennis, even to excess—'five hours on tennis court', and 'hand in sling' as a consequence. He made such an impression at the local tennis club that its members presented him with a silver ash tray when he was about to leave in April. Then it was 'Paris next week & a plunge into gawd knows wot.—certainly a change of life'.

By April 10th Dorothy and Ezra were established on the Left Bank in a high two-roomed studio with 'not much space' but a pleasant balcony, in

3

the Hôtel du Pas-de-Calais, 59 rue des Saints-Pères. Waiting for Ezra was a note from Thayer giving him his three months' notice as foreign agent for the *Dial*. He accepted without further comment this 'dismissal taking effect 1ˢᵗ July'. To Margaret Anderson of the *Little Review* he mentioned that the loss of the $750 a year salary would leave him with 'no means of support visible or predictable', but added that he remained grateful to Thayer for having 'paid my rent for 15 months'. He would loyally work out his three months, and would continue to contribute a bi-monthly 'Paris Letter' until February 1923; but after that Thayer's now settled hostility would put an end for some years to his connection with the *Dial*. The day after acknowledging his dismissal Pound resumed relations with the *Little Review*, and was soon planning 'a special summer number' to present 'the active element here'. 'There is the intelligent nucleus for a movement', he enthused to Ford, 'which there bloody well isn't in England'.

The leading intelligence in the vortex Pound now tried to stir up in Paris would have been the sculptor Constantin Brancusi, who struck him as living 'in his atelier as a Dordoigne cavern sculptor may conceivably have lived in his rock-fissure', content to do his work without apparently having any abstract ideas or theory about it. All his intelligence went into perfecting his creations. Pound, with his mind still running on the Vorticists, saw him 'doing what Gaudier might have done in thirty years time'; only 'Where Gaudier had developed a sort of form-fugue or form-sonata by a combination of forms', Brancusi was committed to a 'maddeningly more difficult exploration toward getting all the forms into one form'. His highly polished ovoids and birds were 'master-keys to the world of form', to the realm of pure geometric form freed from all accident; and to be caught up in contemplation of them was to approach 'the infinite *by form*, by precisely the highest possible degree of consciousness of formal perfection'. It was a *Paradiso* in sculpture, a revelation of 'the infinite beauty of the universe'. But the pleasure of it, Pound conceded, the world being as it was, would be 'the rare possession of an "intellectual" (heaven help us) "aristocracy"'.

After Brancusi Pound would have mustered an advance guard of those 'who have cast off the sanctified stupidities and timidities and are in defiance of things as they are'. Foremost among them he would have had Francis Picabia, as, in his *Dadaist* writings, 'a sort of Socratic or anti-Socratic vacuum cleaner' hoovering up 'fustian and humbugs'; and then there would be Cocteau, Paul Morand, Guy-Charles Cros, and Blaise Cendrars, all of them as working away, each in his own individual fashion, at the necessary *nettoyage*, clearing away the accumulated rubbish of 'the contemporary average mind' and contending against its tyranny over the individual intelligence. Pound hoped to combine the resisters into some sort of movement, some sort of 'civilization in the midst of the unconscious and semi-conscious gehenna'.

He wanted his special number of the now quarterly *Little Review*, 'this new Brancusi, Cocteau, Picabia, me. etc. number', to be 'a clean break. = a wholly new burst of something the public don't expect. = otherwise all my push goes to waste'. When it appeared as the 'Autumn 1921' number it included an essay on Brancusi by Pound, with twenty-four photo-illustrations of his sculpture; a translation, taking up nearly half the number, of Cocteau's poem 'Cap de Bonne Espérance'; a Dadaist essay by Picabia (who was named as Foreign Editor); and a squib from 'Abel Sanders', Pound's *Dada* persona. Pound's name was on the masthead along with those of Margaret Anderson and 'jh', and would remain there until 1925. But he did not appear again as a contributor, except fleetingly as 'Abel Sanders' the Dadaist, and his unpaid role was limited to advising, recommending, urging and criticizing. His influence and his agency were responsible in part at least for the more Parisian character the journal took on for a time, with Dada and Surrealism predominating, but it never became the organ of the 'movement' he had projected. Indeed his Paris vortex scarcely formed at all in the fast currents of that city's modernisms.

Though that effort had only a passing effect it provides a clear image of how Pound was seeing his world in the early 1920s. The 'average mind', Pound wrote in one of his 'Paris Letters', 'is our king, our tyrant, replacing [Creon] and Agamemnon in our tragedy':

It is this human stupidity that elects the Wilsons and Ll. Georges and puts power into the hands of the gun-makers, demanding that they blot out the sunlight, that they crush out the individual and the perception of beauty. This flabby blunt-wittedness is the tyrant.

And the individual who resisted that tyranny was in the predicament of Sophocles' Antigone, standing alone ultimately against the amorphous mass of a 'government' in which power is concentrated 'into the hands of the ignorant and the inept, the non-perceivers'. There, for Pound, was the basic struggle of the modern mind, the *agon* of its tragedy: 'the struggle of an hereditarily hampered and conditioned individual against the state'.

The individual, Pound recognized on this occasion, had little or no power to fight back against the imbecile state, whose 'power to do him evil... extends to his complete extermination'. (He would come to see his friend Upward's suicide in 1926 as one instance of that; and he himself would be close to being sentenced to death by the state in 1945.) 'Only by supreme genius', he went on, 'or more usually by luck, by the million to one chance can he do anything against *lo stato*.' Even to escape its pressures and bondage required an 'incalculable intensity of life, an intensity amounting to genius'; and, with that, a superlative awareness of 'the passion for τὸ καλόν, fighting against tyranny, against *lo stato*, if that *stato* is corrupt'.

That more or less was how Pound dramatized his situation as a poet in Paris. He would be the individual artist of genius with a passion for τὸ καλόν, the eternal order, and he would contend against the tyranny of the commonly accepted order of things. 'The function of poetry', he declared in an irritated response to a questionnaire in Harold Monro's *Chapbook*,

is to assert the existence of a world that Fleet Street cannot drop dung upon, over which the machinery of publishing has no control; into which usurers and manufacturers of war machinery cannot penetrate; into which the infamy of politicians, elected or hereditary, cannot enter and upon which expediency has no effect; against which the lies of exploiting religions, the slobberings of bishops, have no more influence than the bait of journalism or oppressions of the 'purveyors of employment'.

Or shall we say: To assert an eternal order ...

That tells us quite a lot about his hell, and nothing much about his *paradiso*. Yet it was a statement of his wholly serious intent to create in his epic, in its very different terms, his own version of Brancusi's 'universe ... [his] Platonic heaven full of pure and essential forms'.

In Brancusi's 'cavern of a studio' Pound could find 'a temple of peace, of stillness, a refuge from the noise of motor traffic and the current advertisements'. Otherwise he was compelled, as he put it for rhetorical effect, 'to move about in a world full of junk-shops', in the Paris of 'well-known and advertised clap-trap' with its 'galleries full of pictures made obviously for the market'. In fact of course Paris was also in a ferment of new and uncommercial creation in all the arts; and Pound, as ever, was eagerly keeping up with it all. In April he saw Braque, though only for two minutes, and liked what he saw; he 'met Picasso for first time on New Years eve'; by then he had moved to within a few doors from Fernand Léger and had come to know him and his work intimately. (Léger told him what the French soldiers thought of the recent war and he put that into canto 16.) Afternoons of high-voltage conversation 'at Picabia's with Cocteau and Marcel Duchamp' kept him *au fait* with whatever the *avant-gardes* were up to in music, ballet, theatre, and film, as well as in art and literature. Cocteau, whose friendship and conversation Pound valued above most, seems to have had a hand or a light finger in everything that was going on. He collaborated with Picasso, Satie, and Diaghilev in *Parade*, and with Stravinsky in *Oedipus Rex*; he helped found the Jockey Club Bar—Pound, in his best Left Bank beret and attitude, appears in a photograph of the 'founders'; he promoted the new music of Satie and 'Les Six', who included Georges Auric, Francis Poulenc, and Darius Milhaud. Pound measured his own music against theirs and was not daunted. 'Fortunately Satie's *Socrate* is damn dull', he confided to Agnes Bedford; and anyway he had a more 'definite system' than Les Six.

Probably his most privileged vantage-point for observing the artistic and intellectual life of Paris was at his good friend Natalie Barney's salon with its Grecian Temple de l'Amitié in the small enclosed garden.[1] There American wealth united with Parisian sophistication, stylish unconvention-ality was *de rigueur*, and the only taboo was against 'the average mind' and its conventions The great scholar Salamon Reinach could be seen there, and the great poet Paul Valéry and the great novelist Proust, along with Elisabeth de Gramont, Duchesse de Clermont-Tonnerre, one of Natalie's lovers, and Le Prince Edward de Polignac with his wife Winaretta, an heiress to the Singer Sewing Machine fortune. And there, in the autumn of 1922, Pound would meet the very gifted young violinist Olga Rudge.

Dr William Carlos Williams, when Pound took him to tea with Miss Barney, was unsettled by her lesbian entourage and had to keep up his morale as a 'primitive' American male by going out 'to take a good piss', standing up. Pound himself had no problem at all with the varieties of sexual behaviour, and felt no need to assert his manhood in her salon. He saw in Natalie Barney simply a woman with the courage, independence, and intelligence to be what she was to the utmost; one who, in her own words which he liked to repeat, 'got out of life, oh . . . perhaps more than was in it'. Their friendship extended to playing energetic tennis together.

Pound himself was much observed as he went about Paris, sometimes with insight and sympathy, often with little of either. Everyone saw 'the velvet jacket and the open-road shirt', the floppy artist's beret and the ebony cane, and many thought of Byron or of Whistler and the late Aesthetes, and thought no further. Margaret Anderson, meeting for the first time the *Little Review's* former foreign editor and longtime collaborator, sat in his studio for an hour in conversation and apparently took in not a word that he said. All she had to report from that meeting was 'his high Rooseveltian voice, his nervousness, his self-consciousness', and that 'Ezra's agitation was not of the type to which we were accustomed in America—excitement,

---

[1] Natalie Clifford Barney (1876–1972): born Dayton, Ohio; heiress to the fortune of the Barney Railroad Car Foundry; lived it up in Paris from the late 1890s, at 20 rue Jacob from 1909; a close friend of Remy de Gourmont, who named her 'L'Amazone'; by Mauriac she was called 'le pape de Lesbos' on account of her much celebrated Sapphic affaires and writings; she combined hedonism with high seriousness, was generous in support of artists and the arts, and kept up a famous social and intellectual salon.

pressure, life too high-geared'. For some he was always talking and talked too much. When he talked to Gertrude Stein about Japanese prints she was not amused and talked him down and later uttered her malicious *mot* that 'he was a village explainer, excellent if you were a village, but if you were not, not'. Then he fell out of her 'favourite little armchair' and broke it and she was furious and refused ever to see him again. But for Sylvia Beach 'he mended a cigarette box and a chair', skilfully, and did not talk about 'his, or, for that matter, anyone's, books'. She 'found the acknowledged leader of the modern movement not bumptious', and recorded that she 'saw Mr Pound seldom', because 'he was busy with his work and his young poets'. One of the young poets was E. E. Cummings, who would recall half a lifetime later how 'wonderfully entertaining' Pound had been, and how 'magically gentle', during the whole of a walk one night from the rue Castiglione to the Place Saint-Michel. To Sisley Huddleston also Pound was 'a good talker'. A *Times* correspondent and a connoisseur of the good life in Paris in the 1920s, Huddleston recorded 'a vivacious evening' in the restaurant next to the Bal Bullier at the top of the Boulevard Saint-Michel, one of many when 'Ford, Pierre Loving, Pound and myself gaily played with ideas for hours', with Pound 'the merriest spirit of the party'.

Pound was observed in yet another light by Nancy Cox McCormack, an American sculptor who was in Paris then. When she first met Pound he was 'accompanied by a slimly tailored, commanding young woman . . . [whose] entire personality bespoke the quality of an English lady'. Pound presented her as his wife, and she noticed that he 'seemed to address [Dorothy] in all his conversation "as if he were in the habit of crystallizing his thinking through the intellectual channels of their mutual understanding"'. That striking recollection was recorded after she had become a close friend of them both, and may owe something to friendship. Still, it must qualify the general impression one is given that Dorothy and Ezra were now leading fairly separate lives. Pound is usually seen among other men, or with other women, and Dorothy is rarely in the picture. It is said that she did not enjoy being in Paris; and she spent months back in England with her own family and friends, as well as the months away in Italy with Ezra. There are accounts of Pound dancing, wildly, to rhythms only he could hear, but there is no mention of his dancing with Dorothy.

But then how could they dance together, given the way he danced? Caresse Crosby gave a vivid account of a night out with Pound in Paris in 1930 when 'a brilliant band of Martinique players were beating out hot music':

As the music grew in fury Ezra avidly watched the dancers. 'These people don't know a thing about rhythm' he cried scornfully, and he shut his eyes, thrust forward his red-bearded chin and began a sort of tattoo with his feet—suddenly unable to sit still a minute longer he leapt to the floor and seized the tiny Martinique vendor of cigarettes in his arms, packets flying, then head back, eyes closed, chin out, he began a sort of voodoo prance, his tiny partner held glued against his piston-pumping knees.

The music grew hotter, Ezra grew hotter. One by one the uninspired dancers melted from the floor and formed a ring to watch that Anglo-savage ecstasy—on and on went the two, until with a final screech of [cymbals] the music crashed to an end. Ezra opened his eyes, flicked the cigarette girl aside like an extinguished match and collapsed into the chair beside me. The room exhaled a long orgasmic sigh—I too.

The sight of Pound dancing, according to Sisley Huddleston, was 'one of the spectacles which reconcile us to life'.

Nature, genius, and the state of the world

That genius is a force of nature, and that this force of nature is, or should be, the shaping power in human society, these were convictions Pound had long held. He had tried various ways of formulating them. He had invoked the myth of Isis and Osiris; he had invoked myth and science together to present *Imagisme* as the work of 'germinal mind' interpreting the vital universe and projecting its intellectual and emotional complexes into the minds of its readers; he had promoted Vorticism as manifesting the Dionysiac genius of the race in abstract forms which should have the same power to reveal order in the world as those of geometry or the equations of pure mathematics. Through all his various formulations he was seeking to bind together the creative workings of the mind and those of nature or the vital universe, and to conceive of them as not distinct the one from the other, but as driven by one and the same life force.

In 1921 he was speculating about a possible proof from natural science for his conviction that the mind was energized by the power of sex. He had previously found in de Gourmont's study of the reproductive mechanisms and habits of insects, birds, and beasts, *Physique de l'amour* (1903), a 'biological basis in instinct' for the conception, which he had drawn from the love poetry of the troubadours and of Dante and Cavalcanti, 'of love, passion, emotion as an intellectual instigation'. *Ingenium nobis ipsa puella fecit*, he repeated from Propertius, 'our genius is a girl's doing'; with the variation from the King of Navarre, 'science and beauty are from refining love', *De fine amor vient science et beauté*.

Some time after his return to Paris in 1921 he picked up a commission to translate *Physique de l'amour* for the New York publisher Horace Liveright, a 'rush order' carried through in June at the rate of '25 pages per diem'. 'If I do it quick enough it will pay the rent', he told Agnes Bedford; to Dorothy, then in London, he wrote on 23 July, 'Speak not evil of Jews. Liveright has paid up already.' As part of the commission he wrote 'a supplementary chapter for U.S. edtn', and this appeared at the end as 'Translator's Postscript' to *The Natural Philosophy of Love*.

In this 'Postscript' Pound took off from Gourmont's suggestion that 'There might be, perhaps, a certain correlation between complete and profound copulation and the development of the brain.' What if, he speculated, what if the 'genital fluid' of sexual reproduction functioned also as the 'cerebral fluid' of the image-making, form-projecting brain? 'The individual genius' might then be 'the man in whom the new access, the new superfluity of spermatozoic pressure (quantitive and qualitative) up-shoots into the brain, alluvial Nile-flood, bringing new crops, new invention'. He went on to note

the similarity of spermatozoides and ovules and brain cells in their capacity to contain or project a form. That is to say, the spermatozoide compels the ovule to evolve along certain predetermined lines; the ovule receives the pattern and evolves. The brain-cell also holds an image; a generalisation may be considered as a superposition of such images.

And 'creative thought', the projection of the brain's images and universal forms, 'is an act like fecundation, like the male cast of the human seed'. 'Genius', Gourmont had written, 'fecundates a generation of minds.' That is, by implication, it compels the individual minds or the society which receives its pattern ideas, its seed-*gestalten*, 'to evolve along certain predetermined lines'.

The science strikes us now as primitive. But had Pound known about DNA and the further advances in genetics he might well have used them in the same speculative fashion to underpin his argument that genius is a natural function and a function of nature, and that it acts as a formative, shaping power in its world. Behind his appeal to science, to Gourmont's natural philosophy in this case, was his conviction, dating back to 1912 at least, that the utility of the poet to the world's consciousness is 'scientifically demonstrable'. And behind that lies the fundamental, and still revolutionary, conception that there is one life in all things in our universe, and that 'mind' and 'body' are one as 'the human realm' and 'the natural world' are one.

By March of 1922 Pound was happy to dismiss most of the scientific or pseudo-scientific postulates of his 'Postscript' as 'various statements now antiquated' and 'speculations neither supported nor disproved'. He had discovered the relatively new science of the endocrine glands, and was speculating about a possible chemical basis of intelligence as suggested by Dr Louis Berman's book *The Glands Regulating Personality* (1922). In place of the 'genital fluid' he now postulated the pineal gland as the source of image-making intelligence and original thought. From Berman he learnt that the pineal gland contains 'cells filled with a pigment like that in the eye's retina, and little piles of lime salt crystals'. He took this to indicate that it had to do with the sense of light, and with intelligence developed from seeing, specifically with the power of orderly visualization. He termed it the 'gland of "lucidity"', of 'luminosity in vision'; and, again, the 'gland of metamorphosis, of original thought' and of 'the *new* juxtaposition of images'—at the same time seeking the physical cause in the secretion of the lime salt crystals, 'not as a slow effusion, but ejected suddenly into sensitised area [of the brain cells], analogy to the testes'.

These antiquated speculations are of interest now as background to Pound's next canto. But they serve also to show just how far Pound would go in search of a basis in natural science for his idea of creative intelligence; and they give a measure of how very far he was from associating, as Yeats would, a poet's inspiration with occult powers.

It must be noted in passing how Pound even while writing about originating genius was yet subject to the limited knowledge and the conventional prejudices of his time, for he held creativity, whether in sexual reproduction or in thought, to be the male function, and the female to be simply the passive receiver of his sperm or his intellectual gestalt. The female was allowed to be the conservatrix of useful instincts and traditions. But he could not see, though he did try to allow for a feminist view of the matter, that she was equipped for original creation. When he encountered original creativity in a woman, as in Marianne Moore or Mina Loy, or, initially, in H.D., he had to attribute it to the possibility that the ovaries did also have a 'male' function—something, he said, he could 'hardly be expected to introspect'—or else to the possibility that 'the ejection of lime salt particles in a female' would free her 'from the general confusions of her sex'.

Canto II: seeing the light

Pound's next canto was published in the *Dial* in May 1922 as 'Eighth Canto', but later, with a different lead-in, it was placed definitively as canto 'II'. Its centre is an epiphany, a visionary manifestation of Dionysos, the ancient Greek idea of the single force that drives all living things. As a son of Zeus Dionysos was associated with the divine light which is at once the light of life and the light of intelligence; and he was held to generate both the myriad forms of living beings and their powers to sense things and to make sense of their experience. He would figure then as the cause of our responsiveness to light and of the intelligence that is developed from seeing; thence of its power of orderly visualization, and of its further power of original thought ('the new juxtaposition of images'). He would be active in the 'germinal mind' interpreting his vital universe.

Dionysos first appears in the canto as 'a young boy loggy with vine-must', suggesting the most common perception of him as the god that is in wine, and hence, in the eye of the drinker, appearing as 'in his cups'. Later he is called 'Lyaeus' by the sailor who recognizes the god in him, a name given because wine (as Lemprière quaintly put it) 'gives freedom to the mind'. Dionysos was in fact held to be a force for every kind of liberation. Bringing forth new life was seen as a liberation; shape-shifting and metamorphosis, as in the transformation of flower to fruit or grub to butterfly, were seen as liberations; to be rapt in ecstasy, from honeyed wine or in a visionary trance, was to be liberated from one's ordinary self and the common world. In this latter aspect, as liberator from normal behaviour and custom and convention, he could change minds and perceptions and values and so threaten the established social order, sometimes comically, as in Pound's 'Salutation the Second', sometimes tragically, as in *The Bacchae* of Euripides. Generous and potentially violent *frère ennemi* to Apollonian reason, Dionysos represented the fluid, ever-changing, interacting, and uncontrollable energies that give rise to and sustain every living thing and are confined by none.

Everywhere present he is yet unseen by the mind in its everyday state. In the canto the piratical sailors who come upon him see just a lad they can seize and sell into slavery. In *The Bacchae* young King Pentheus, intent on keeping order in Thebes and seeing him only as a trouble-maker and a misleader of the women of his city, thinks to shut him away in prison and to ban his orgiastic rites. Blind Tiresias who sees what is hidden from ordinary sight tells Pentheus that this Dionysos is a powerful god not to be denied and that all Thebes, even the king himself, should join in his dance of life. 'You rely on force', he tells him, 'but it is not force that governs human affairs.' Pentheus of course does not believe that. Blinded by his own powers, he continues to oppose them, fatally, to the god's. His end is to be torn apart by the maenads, the god-possessed women led by his own mother. Euripides would have no one doubt that the god who liberates his followers and opens their eyes to his presence also destroys those who deny or resist his power.

Pound follows the emphasis of marvelling Ovid's version of the god's story, rather than that of moral Euripides. Instead of having Tiresias explain to Pentheus why he should recognize the god, he has Acoetes, the one sailor who saw the god in the young boy, attempt to make Pentheus see the danger he is in by reliving his own visionary experience. The wood of the ship comes alive in his telling—'where was gunwale, there now was vine-trunk, | And tenthril where cordage had been, | grape-leaves on the rowlocks'. The empty air becomes animate with crowding forms of Dionysos' wild cats, lynxes, panthers, and leopards—

> out of nothing, a breathing,
> hot breath on my ankles,
> Beasts like shadows in glass . . .
> fur brushing my knee-skin,
> Rustle of airy sheaths,
> dry forms in the aether

And the god thus manifest assures Acoetes that from now he may worship at his altars 'Fearing no bondage'. Pentheus, heedless of Acoetes' testimony will attempt to bind the god.

The canto does not go into Pentheus' doom. Its Dionysos, in this following the Homeric hymn and the archetypal idea, is the god of indestructible life. His law is not death followed by a possible transcendence but metamorphosis, unceasing change through successive forms of being. Thus his way of punishing the mindless greed of the sailors who think to catch and sell him is to transform them into fish—

> Medon's face like the face of a dory,
> Arms shrunk into fins . . .
> Fish scales over groin muscles

The 'John Dory' makes a fine-tasting dish and would be a much sought-after catch.

In its origins the story of Dionysos is archaic, as ancient and archaic as the tale of Odysseus calling up Tiresias from among the sunless dead. Pound said of the latter when discussing the *Odyssey* that 'it shouts aloud that it is older than the rest', that it belongs to 'that island, Cretan, etc., hinter-time'. This is equally true of Dionysos, and yet Pound's manner of treating the two stories could not be more different. In canto I he emphasized the remoteness of the rite, by intervening only as editor and translator, thus keeping his distance from it, and then by giving it a somewhat Anglo-Saxon stylization, as if placing it back in the heroic Dark Ages. But with Acoetes' story he does everything possible to make it an immediate experience, vividly actual, even contemporary. He is not now the mere editor and translator of another's book, but as it were Acoetes himself caught up in the very act of perceiving the god in his manifestations. In full sunlight he sees 'the godly sea' as Odysseus, in the dark of canto I, could not.

The entire canto, it now becomes apparent, is concerned with seeing the divine energies in the sea and elsewhere; or, to put it another way, it is concerned with the varieties of the visible and with the different kinds and degrees of vision. A seal is seen—'Seal sports in the spray-whited circles of cliff-wash, | sleek head . . . lithe daughter of Ocean'—and there the vision shifts from the seen to the intuited and the mythical. There is a further development with 'eyes of Picasso | Under black fur-hood', a doubling, shifting, unfixable image. There are the seal's eyes; and Picasso's that had about them the look of a seal's; and there is his artist's eye for the precise line of its object, so that for a moment the eyes might be his vision of the seal's. Thus sight comes alive to two or three different ways of seeing the world, with the archaic and the modern juxtaposed. Later, Tyro, in love with a river, is caught up by Poseidon—

> Twisted arms of the sea-god,
> Lithe sinews of water, gripping her, cross-hold,
> And the blue-gray glass of the wave tents them,
> Glare azure of water, cord-welter, close cover.

It may be merely a myth of divine possession and generativeness, yet it is so fully visualized and so much a vision of known natural phenomena that the mind's eye really sees and credits it, mythopoetically. In contrast, what follows is a naturalist's objective observation—'Snipe come for their bath, | bend out their wing-joints, | Spread wet wings to the sun-film'. Then the mind's associations come into play upon such observations, as in seeing a rock as 'Naviform', shaped like a ship; and still more in 'a wine-red glow in the shallows'. It may be only the algae that give that glow, but 'wine-red' to the responsive mind will suggest the hidden presence of Dionysos.

Between the visions of the 'lithe daughter of Ocean' and of Tyro there is a more extended passage presenting the very different vision the old men of Troy have of Helen, daughter of Zeus and cause of their war. Blind Homer, hearing their thin grasshopper voices, picks up their fear of her, their clear-sighted foreboding that Troy's holding her from the Greeks is dooming the city to destruction. This both parallels and contrasts with the central episode of the canto. In both cases the capture of the divine being proves disastrous, but for the old men there is to be no liberating revelation. They can see how 'like a goddess' Helen is in her face and moving, but they cannot worship, overcome as they are by a wholly justified fear. She will be the destruction of Trojans and Greeks alike, for both have regarded her as a possession and a prize.

There is another parallel and contrasting passage following on directly from the central episode. This time we are invited to look down from the 'naviform rock' and to see 'in the wine-red algae' and the rose-pale coral a face and a 'swimmer's arms turned to branches', and we are told that this was 'Ileuthyeria, fair Dafne of sea-bords', changed into coral as she fled some 'band of tritons'. In Ovid's *Metamorphoses* Daphne, daughter of a goddess, is pursued by Apollo and changed into a laurel tree as he seizes her. Here the depth of the violence against nature is encoded in the unknown name, 'Ileuthyeria'. It combines 'Eleutheria', Greek festivals of liberty, and 'Eileithyia', the Minoan goddess of childbirth—she who frees the child. It is as if an attempt to seize and ravish the life-force itself had turned her to stone.

The metamorphosis of 'Ileuthyeria' was Pound's own invention, an act as we say of pure imagination, and it is a triumph of dramatic visualization. But is it also, from a scientific viewpoint, doing violence to the real nature of coral, which lives and grows, after all, by its own metamorphic process? Does the moral of the tale turn back on the Apollonian imagination and convict it of wanting too much to have its own way with nature?

The canto's answer, if it gives one, is in its next moves. First there is this: 'And So-Shu churned in the sea, So-Shu also, | Using the long moon for a churn-stick.' So-Shu—'a Chinese mythological figure', or so Pound said for those who must ask—evidently imagines himself, possibly having drunk too much rice-wine, to be a divine being in a creation myth churning the sea into a butter from which to fashion earth and its creatures. That amounts to a drunken parody of the Dionysiac mystery. And the 'also' equates with it the imagination which would see, or half see, living coral as a fair Dafne in 'ivory stillness'. So-Shu's churning gives way to a variation upon the Tyro motif—

> Lithe turning of water,
> > sinews of Poseidon
> Black azure and hyaline,
> > glass wave over Tyro,
> Close cover, unstillness,
> > bright welter of wave-cords

The 'unstillness' and the energy in every detail there go against the imagined 'ivory stillness', and also against So-Shu's illusory churning.

The unfamiliar 'hyaline' can tease the mind's eye into discovering more in the natural phenomena than it had looked for. From the Greek for glass it is applied, in Greek poetry, to the crystalline sea; and in modern anatomy and biology to translucent sinew or cartilage, and also to the membrane and vitreous liquid of the eye. In the phrase 'Black azure and hyaline'—compare the earlier 'blue-gray glass', and think too of 'eyes of Picasso'—it seems that the sea is being seen, fleetingly, as itself an eye taking in and reflecting back the light of heaven. That reciprocity mirrors the reciprocity of a light-illuminated world and an intelligent eye reflecting back upon it what it is making of it. The process of perception is then, when it is precisely focused on its object, a continuation of the process of light-energies in nature.

The motif of the naturalist's observation is now repeated—'Sea-fowl stretching wing-joints'—and there is then a modulation, as the evening star is seen ('pallor of Hesperus'), into painterly discriminations against the fading light:

> Grey peak of the wave,
>> wave, colour of grape's pulp,
> Olive grey in the near,
>> far, smoke grey of the rock-slide,
> Salmon-pink wings of the fish-hawk
>> cast grey shadows in water

After that wonderfully interactive image as the light fails so too does the vision.

A discordant tower—it was explicitly a 'Church tower' when Pound drafted this passage at Sirmione—'like a one-eyed great goose | cranes up out of the olive-grove'. Its one eye may be a clock face which tells the time and knows nothing of the process it measures; or it may be the Church's dogma that there is only one God that makes it one-eyed. Either way, it is seen in the satiric mixed metaphor as if with double-vision. The canto closes in playful retort to monocular monotheism with the comedy of the double-natured fauns chiding Proteus, the shape-shifting sea-god, and then the once metamorphosed frogs 'singing against the fauns | in the half-light'. Fauns and frogs, variform though they are, seem to think that theirs is the only shape.

That coda looks back to the canto's (revised) introduction:

> Hang it all, Robert Browning,
>> there can be but the one "Sordello".
> But Sordello, and my Sordello?
> Lo Sordels si fo di Mantovana.
> So Shu churned in the sea.

The mock-protest encapsulates the painful lesson of his apprenticeship to Browning; while the rhetorical question would save his dignity by positing other possible Sordellos, the 'real Sordello' and the one he might invent. 'Lo

Sordels', from 'a manuscript in the Ambrosian library at Milan', might be taken to settle the matter with a statement of fact: Sordello was from Mantua. That might satisfy the scholar-historian; and it might be as illusory as So-Shu's trying to solidify the ocean. Are there not now as many Sordellos as there are perceivers of him; and is not Sordello compounded of all the recorded perceptions? It will be the burden of the canto that the One is manifold and that we need to be many-minded to comprehend it.

The canto, which at first sight can appear a simple succession of fragments, can now be seen to be organized as a musical composition. It has a main theme, and a counter-theme, both of them developed through a series of variations around the extended central episode. Simply stated, the theme has to do with the different modalities of seeing the sea of being and all that is in it; while the counter-theme has to do with the errors of false or one-eyed perception which can arise from and lead to possessiveness, repression, rape. In the development through the variations of the main theme there is a progression from myth, which opens the mind to what there might be in life, towards precise observation and analysis of its manifestations. The light and life-in-process of the universe, it is implied, are not occult but are evident to illuminated sense, as in the 'Salmon-pink wings of the fish-hawk'.

'Le Testament' or Pound's Villon: in the dark

Canto (meaning, in Italian, 'I sing' as well as 'a chant or song') signals an aspiration to compose words into music, and certainly canto II is as musical as words alone can be. Its method of composition is that of music, and so too is its way with words. In the dimension of the meanings and resonances of words and images it works as music does by accords and dissonances and progressions. In the dimension of sound it makes melodies of the tones of vowels, while the consonants, shaping the weights and durations of the syllables, help define the tempo and rhythm. Most striking to the ear is the recurrent double-beat, coming twice or even three times in many lines, and pulsing at varying intensities throughout the canto. It sets a definite overall measure, and yet each line has its own measure, so that a seemingly complete freedom for change and variation coexists with that constant though shifting pulse, rather as in an Indian *raga*.

Pound had been working intensively on the music in words in the months before completing that canto. He had brought with him to Paris some preliminary draft settings of Villon's poetry, and in April of 1921 he resumed work on composing his opera, *Le Testament*. 'Will probably send you my first scrawls sprawls, for criticism in a few days,' he wrote to Agnes Bedford on 5 May. By the 16th he had 'done 116 pages of something that looks, at 1st glance, like an orchestral score'. But he was having to ask elementary questions. 'Cello is I believe written in same clef as the troubadour stuff in original mss.??? No.? That clef is only half tone lower than mod. treble??' And again, 'have a vague suspicion that cello ought to be about three notes lower than voice to sustain it, and that bass viol ought to be about an octave below...possibly it should be two octaves, save that I want to use that cellarage for definite purposes'.

He needed Agnes Bedford's trained musicianship because he didn't know how to write down music as it was then written; but at the same time the music he had in his head was not that of a modern trained musician and he did not want it to sound as if it were. It was more nearly related to the modes of Arab and of Provençal and medieval music than to Satie or Stravinsky. 'My ignorance is deeper than Erebus, and really my chief hope,' he told Bedford, meaning that it would leave him free to stick to his own principles. Foremost among those was to admit *nothing* 'that interferes with the words, or with the utmost possible clarity of impact of words on audience'. Hence no 'chord-harmony', no orchestration of several instruments to build up and blur a note with their '*very* different overtones', and no developed '*instrumental* counterpoint'. He meant to constrain his singers to sing the music *in* the words, and to use the instruments of his orchestra very sparingly just to support and enforce that music. His problem would be to get his performers to understand that he was not 'setting words to music | BUT | setting music to words', and that 'the music is simply an emphasis on the meaning and shape of Villon's words'. Another thing, though he called *Le Testament* an opera he did not want it sung by voices developed to sing nineteenth-century Grand Opera; he wanted 'tough, open-air singing', or that of a music hall or cabaret singer such as Yvette Guilbert, singing that would concentrate not so much on the notes as on the sound and rhythm of the words. Getting across the 'emotive contents', he would call that, or, alternatively, 'Inducing emotional correlations'.

In July, on the 10th, Dorothy who was with her parents in London, asked, 'What the devil does this mean "Op. I revision is at p. 67" in your letter?' Pound replied on the 14th that it was 'a musical work now at p. 119'. Then Agnes Bedford was over in Paris 'for a few days', and on the 23rd Pound was wondering whether she would 'have time to work on the opera'. (In his next letter he mentioned that he had 'succeeded in dancing the tango on the sabath' for the first time in his life, 'at Bullier—with that Herald reporteress whom I met at Miss Beaches'.) Bedford probably had no choice in the matter of the opera, and a few days later they were 'Chewing into op. mostly 4–6 hours per day', with 'orchestral climax and final 6 part song to tackle'. 'Ezra sang and beat out the rhythm', Bedford later recalled, 'and also picked out the tunes on [Natalie Barney's] piano while he sang them.' She particularly remembered how he 'sang each of the parts of the concluding canon separately, and it all fitted together'—'A miracle,' she thought. On 6 August they were still at work, now 'up to as much as 8 and 9 hrs per diem', and Pound was hoping that 'A.B. may hang on for another week'. By the 10th, though, he was able to tell Natalie Barney that he had 'got through worst of my struggle' and was 'eternally grateful for the piano'. The same day he wrote to Dorothy that he had devised 'nice contrapuntal hurdy gurdy of trombone, cello, bassoon, for "Pere Noé" [the drunkards' song], running against jazz'. Finally, on 2 November 1921, he wrote to Bedford that the opera was finished.

In fact it was only the first, Pound–Bedford version, that had been completed. A second, Pound–Antheil version, was to follow in 1923.[2] Pound met Antheil, then a very young musical prodigy, in mid-1923 and was delighted to secure his approval of his orchestration of the opera. 'I naturally think him a genius,' he wrote to his parents between jest and earnest, 'Nobody but a genius COULD approve of my orchestration.'[3] That autumn, in two months up to '11 o'clock Dec. 31', he had Antheil go over the work, under his direction, re-noting 'it all with highly fractional nota-tion == bars all sorts of lengths from $\frac{1}{8}$ to $\frac{17}{32}$—$\frac{7}{16}$ etc.' Antheil 'made no attempt to understand the words', Pound later told Bedford, 'Simply took down the stuff as [I] hummed it.'

Robert Hughes observed that 'The most salient feature' of the Pound–Antheil version was 'its use of micro-rhythms' and 'fractional metrics'—these were even more elaborate and more irregular than in Stravinsky's *Sacre du printemps* (1913) and *L'Histoire du soldat* (1918). For example, these are the measures in bars 74–86 of the *ballade* of the old woman regretting the time when she was young and beautiful:

---

[2] This is the one that has been performed a number of times since Robert Hughes edited the score for performance and directed the world première of the complete work in Berkeley, California, in November 1971. See appendices for an outline of the opera and of the successive states of the score.

[3] George Antheil (1900–59): American pianist, composer, and iconoclast in the musical avant-garde in Paris in the 1920s—his *Ballet mécanique* (1926) provoked a famous riot. Admiring his demanding 'short hard bits of rhythm hammered down, worn down so that they were indestructible and unbend-able' (*GK* 94–5)—Antheil's *Mechanisms* (1923) would be one instance—EP promoted him as a Vorticist in music, and wrote *Antheil and The Treatise on Harmony* (1924) to present his thinking about Antheil's and his own music. They drifted apart after 1933 when A. went to Hollywood to compose and direct background music for films. Published his autobiography, *Bad Boy of Music*, in 1945.

$^{7}/_{16}$ | | $^{7}/_{16}$ | | | $^{1}/_{2}$ | | $^{1}/_{4}$ | $^{3}/_{4}$ | | | $^{9}/_{8}$ | | | $^{1}/_{2}$ | | $^{1}/_{4}$ |

Pour l'a|mour d'ung| garson ru|sé, /| Auquel j'en| feiz grande| largess|e. /|

All for the love of a tricky lad / To whom I yielded all I had /

$^{1}/_{4}$|$^{13}/_{32}$ | | $^{7}/_{16}$ | | $^{3}/_{8}$ | -

A |qui que je| feisse fi|ness|e

Though I did finesse him too

Pound's orchestration was similarly fractional, calling for the vocal line to be supported ('generally at the interval of the unison or octave') after this fashion: in bars 74 and 75 by flute, oboe, bassoon, and horn; in 76 by bassoon and tambour (each a single note); by cello and contrabasse in 77; in 78 ('Auquel') by oboe, bassoon, and drum; at 79 it is oboe, drum, cello, and contrabasse; at 80 and 81 just cello and contrabasse; 82–5 ('A qui') have solo flute accompaniment; in 86 the cello plays a single note. Hughes found that this fragmenting of the vocal line among a group of instruments, 'a *klang-farbenmelodie* technique similar in concept to Webern's'—though evidently arrived at quite independently by Pound—is 'the dominant instrumental concept' of the opera as a whole.

Pound was deploying his varied musical resources[4] to give emphasis to the specific shape, tone, time, and resonance of each scrupulously assayed phrase and word and syllable. In bars 74–86 past feelings are revived one upon another: a yielding to the memory of having once really loved, a simple statement of how much she had loved, a softening regret (or is it remorse?) that she also did for her man. Through the following forty bars (eleven lines of the verse) all the distinct feelings making up the complex of a helpless love for a heartless pimp are rendered with immediacy and intensity: a core of inner calm from knowing she would have done anything for him, even though he cared only for what she brought him; the pain of having abased herself to his abuse; and the self-disgust, the sense of profound self-betrayal, at having made love not with but for him with lecherous gluttons. All this is in the words, but it is there as music is in the written score. It is only in the performance of the music, in the singer's interpretation of it, that we hear the tender and sardonic and self-lacerating overtones and undertones of the withered whore's memories and are moved to responsive insight.

---

[4] The 1923/71 score calls for ten solo voices, chorus, and seventeen instrumentalists who among them play an unusually diverse lot of instruments: 'nose-flute, flute and piccolo (one player), oboe, saxaphone, bassoon, trumpet (for two bars only!), horn, two trombones, mandolin, violin, cello, three contrabassi, a variety of drums (including six tympani), bells, "bass bells" (sic)…gongs, sandpaper, dried bones and a percussionist whistling' (Robert Hughes).

There is no sunlight in this work, and no glimpse of a sunlit world timeless in its time. There is not a single image to give confidence in the life-force. Time here is irresistibly destructive, nothing but a passing away of life's energies and loves and a bringing on of physical decay and death. A song celebrating the vine associates it not with Dionysos but with Noah, acclaiming him as the first to plant a vineyard. The revelling singers would have known that in Genesis 9 he next drinks of the wine and falls into a drunken stupor, as they are doing. They then invoke Lot who in his drunkenness mated with his own daughters. Before their counter-rhythmic, dissonant clamour, which dies away into mere incoherence, there has been much articulate rage and regret, grief and cynical realism, disillusion and horror, the full gamut of lacerating emotions from bleak disappointment with life through memory's torments to the turning in despair to the vanities of church, brothel, and tavern. The only resolution, if that is what it is, comes in the final concord of the several voices singing in harmony of their dissolution on the gibbet.

This final chorale is at once ruthlessly realistic and out of this world. The hung corpses ask for pity from their fellow beings and mercy from God; but the burden of their singing is of how their flesh has rotted and been pecked away by magpies and crows, of how the rain has scoured and cleansed them and the sun dried out and blackened them, and now they are simply bones swinging in the wind. 'Pray God absolve us all' is their refrain, meaning 'forgive us our sins'. But this is not the terrified crying of Villon's mother imagining the pains of hell. These voices are beyond fear and terror, almost beyond expectation of either heaven or hell, though their voices rise to that plea for absolution. The most profound conviction in their harmonies is of the solemn reality of physical dissolution, which they accept as their state with simple humility, and in that is their purgation and their peace. The effect is of a poignantly compassionate and humane catharsis.

Pound's Villon, like his Rihaku, his Propertius, and his Mauberley, is a register of the mental and moral condition of his time. His specific *virtù*, to Pound's mind, was that, along with having 'neither optimism nor breadth of vision', he had no illusions and was 'able to realize his condition, to see it objectively'. This is the Villon who somehow distilled into his occasional *ballades* an impersonal and universal vision of his life 'in this bordello of a world where we belong' (*En ce bordeau ou tenons nostre estat*), while otherwise filling out his long last will and testament with a very personal and mordant settling of old scores and with complaints of his poverty and many misfortunes. Pound was not interested in his personal life and character, but only in bringing out the specific vibrations and resonances of his *virtù*.

What further characterized Villon for Pound was that, unlike Dante, he 'lacked energy to clamber out' of his hell on earth, his *inferno terrestre*. This was represented, in the dramatic frame which Pound sketched in 1959 for the second BBC radio production, by Villon's not moving as his friends urge him to flee the scene to escape imminent arrest. In the opera itself the lack of energy or will to rise above the condition of the gutter is all pervasive, and emerges as the dominant and unifying concept.

Immobility and depersonalization are the main features of Pound's notes for a minimalist staging, one that anticipates late Beckett. The scene, according to his notes, is 'Church—St Julien les Pauvres | bordello built in between buttresses | right, The Prison | left, tavern with two very poor tables'. The principal soloists were to have the upper half of their faces masked, apart from La Beauté (Rose in the 1971 score), or else to have make-up 'stylized to the utmost'. The notes insist on 'The general immobility of most of the play', and especially of Villon who, stage centre, should be 'completely immobile from start to finish' with 'eye fixed on window of La Beauté, in bordello'. Beauté should have 'no change of expression save in eyes. Maximum of non-attention and observation'. La Heaulmière, she who was once the beautiful armouress or helm-maker, 'has a nervous swinging of the arms—from left to right, right to left', but only while she sings. Villon's mother, while she sings, has 'a certain jerkiness'. The brothel-keeper—'Pornoboskos' in Pound's notes—'oscillates but does not move, save for jerking thumb over shoulder', as he sings his drunken aria about his whore, Fat Margot, at the end of which he passes out. Only two minor soloists have some moves: the Priest crosses from church to brothel as he sings a snatch of a *carpe diem*; the Gallant 'enters bordello, Beauté closes the window...[he] staggers out stabbed, sings Je renaye amours, crashes left, back of stage'. In the 'Père Noé' drunken chorus, however, there is, in absolute contrast with the rest of the work, a 'general hurley burley... maximum confusion'. In the silence following that, 'back drop is raised showing Les Pendus'—whose sextet, 'Frères Humains', then comes from the (presumably now unlighted) soloists, male and female, who have not moved. Thus the staging, with the notable exception of the drunken chorus, at once dramatizes the fixed state of Villon and his world, and does nothing to distract from the action of the words being sung into the minds of the audience. The drama is all in the mind's ear.

Greek drama has been proposed as a model for Pound's *Le Testament*, also the Japanese Noh, the latter especially because it is essentially music-drama. A nearer model, and one more appropriate to Villon's fifteenth century, would be the medieval morality play such as *Everyman*. But then Pound's is a morality without the wicked tempters and the guardian angels.

It presents simply the doomed life of a world without the grace of enlight-
enment, and with no way out except through the absolution of death.
'Villon', Pound wrote in 1934, 'the first voice of a man broken by bad
economics',

represents also the end of a tradition, the end of the mediaeval dream, the end of a
whole body of knowledge, fine, subtle, that had run from Arnaut to Guido
Cavalcanti

This 'very complicated structure of knowledge and perception, the paradise
of the human mind under enlightenment', had been 'hammered out' of
Villon, Pound implied, not by his sins, but by the decadence of the Church
and by the 'bad economics' which placed no value on his genius and so
drove him to a life of poverty and crime and dissoluteness. He was 'The
hardest, the most authentic, the most absolute poet of [his] France', of a
France which had 'lost the increment of intelligence'. *Le Testament* pre-
sents, as does Dante's *Inferno*, the hell of those who have lost 'the paradise
of the human mind'.

A new theory of harmony

Composing his *Testament* was one thing, and getting a hearing for it quite
another. 'It will be twenty years before they will stand it', Antheil said to
Pound, but, as it turned out, it would be nearly fifty years before there was a
performance in which the music sounded as they had written it. The forever
changing, unpredictable, micro-rhythms presented difficulties exceeding
even Stravinsky's measures, and performers in the 1920s and 1930s found
them simply unplayable. Besides, Pound had no standing among profes-
sional musicians and their patrons in Paris, and had to make do with small
resources and scarce opportunities.

Two of the lesser songs, Ythier's 'Mort, j'appelle' and the Gallant's 'Je
renye amours', were sung by the tenor Yves Tinayre to Olga Rudge's solo
violin in the course of an Antheil–Rudge concert at the Salle Pleyel on 8
July 1924. Those two songs were engraved and printed for 'private circu-
lation only' in 1926, with a note that 'The violin accompaniment was
written for the concert and makes no attempt to condense or to represent
the orchestration intended for use in the opera'. The measures were indeed
greatly simplified.

Pound's next move was to plan a 'by invitation' concert performance. He
mentioned to Agnes Bedford at the end of November 1925 that he was
'thinking of cutting up Villon for concert', with Tinayre as Heaulmière, one
other male voice, and violin and harpsichord accompaniment. Around the

turn of the year he was 'having another fit of work (bordering on insanity)' on *Le Testament*, and was excitedly reporting his discovery that a ⅝ bar 'seems to be MY nacherl measure'. He thought that that was what he must have been hunting for through Antheil's 'indubitably earnest endeavour to ascertain the duration of the notes', and now that he had found it Antheil's fractional notation seemed to him excessive, a 'hypercalculus' which would drive a singer to take 'refuge in the comparative simplicity of Einstein's hexagonal theorem of the indivisibility of abstract space by french mutton'. The ⅝ bar seemed 'to fit a good deal of the Heaulmière', and to throw the emphasis where he wanted it, on the front of the bar; and 'for the earlier numbers' it was 'the GREAT LIGHT'.[5] By March 1926 the seven or eight numbers selected for 'the June show'—among them Heaulmière, Bozo, 'Père Noé', and 'Frères humains'—had been 'tentatively at least, laid out largely in ⅝'. And that was how it was performed, for an audience of three hundred or so guests in the Salle Pleyel at 9.15 in the evening of 29 June 1926. 'Paroles de Villon', read the invitation from 'M. et Mme. Ezra Pound', 'Arias and fragments from an opera . . . Musique par Ezra Pound'. Yves Tinayre, who sang most of the arias, wore a shawl over his head and assumed a cracked old woman's voice for La Heaulmière. Robert Maitland, a 'REAL BASS barrel tone', sang Bozo. Olga Rudge's violin provided the main accompaniment, except for 'Père Noé' where a harpsichord and trombones contributed to the row and Pound himself played a kettle-drum. For Bozo there were the two drunken trombones (or 'bumbones'). 'Frères humains' was sung as a duet in two-part harmony accompanied by the ensemble. It was all very very far from the opera as Pound had conceived and composed it in 1923, but 'At any rate', he told Agnes Bedford, 'have now got a notation that is practicable & that seems right'.

Many years later, in 1951 or thereabouts, Pound told Peter Russell that the Antheil score was 'a curiosity, due to inexperience and Antheil's total ignorance of language and articulation of same'. Possibly he should have added that he himself had been carrying to its extreme his idea of reproducing the *virtù*, the very vibrations of Villon's voice. After all he did not have, could not have had, an absolute knowledge of how Villon's language of fifteenth-century Paris had been pronounced. In spite of that, and in spite also of his readiness to simplify the notation in order to make the opera playable, it is the 1923 version that is now being performed and recognized as a wholly original and significant invention in twentieth-century music. R. Murray Schafer, the Canadian composer and

---

[5] 'Heaulmière' in the 1926 version for voice and violin, in 'simple though mixed meters' (*CPMEP* 148 n. 10), is printed photographically from a score in Olga Rudge's hand in *GK* 361–5.

musicologist, called it 'an unduplicated little masterpiece of musical com-
position'; and in 2003 Richard Taruskin the Stravinsky scholar wrote in the
New York Times that it 'constitutes Ezra Pound's slim sound claim to
musical immortality'.

Antheil celebrated Pound's music in 1924 as 'a grand liberation' from
'the developments of music during the last three or four hundred years'. An
article in the *Paris Times* of 29 June 1924, evidently inspired if not actually
written by one or the other of them, was more specific, proclaiming Pound's
'renovation of XVth century music', and declaring boldly that his opera 'has
abolished harmony'. The laws of harmony in modern Western music lay
down which notes may follow, or not follow, a given other note. Pound
abolished those laws by declaring that as a matter of fact *any* note could
follow any other note provided that the correct time-interval between them
was observed. In *The Treatise on Harmony* (1924) he remarked that 'the
element grossly omitted from all treatises on *harmony*', until that moment,
was 'the element of time ... of the time-interval that must elapse between
one sound and another if the two sounds are to produce a pleasing
consonance or an *interesting* relation'. He then laid down his new, liberating
axiom:

A SOUND OF ANY PITCH, or ANY COMBINATION OF SUCH SOUNDS, MAY BE FOLLOWED
BY A SOUND OF ANY OTHER PITCH, OR ANY OTHER COMBINATION OF SUCH SOUNDS,
providing the time interval between them is properly gauged; and this is true for
ANY SERIES OF SOUNDS, CHORDS OR ARPEGGIOS.

Because of this insight and what lies behind it Pound's slight and informal
treatise is, in the judgement of R. Murray Schafer, one of 'the three
contributions to the science of harmony' in the first half of the twentieth
century, the other two being Schoenberg's *Harmonielehre* and Schenker's
Harmonielehre. Like Schenker, Schafer observed, Pound was 'retrieving an
ancient conception of musical composition' in emphasizing the horizontal
progression as against the vertical and relatively static, post-Bach concep-
tion of harmony which, in Pound's uncompromising phrase, made music
'like steam ascending from a morass'. 'No modern book', Schafer wrote, 'so
cogently forces us to see harmony as a study in movement.' At the same
time, as Margaret Fisher notes, unlike Schoenberg whose '12-tone system'
imposed 'rigid rules of intervallic patterning for atonal construction',
Pound, 'by allowing for any sequence of pitches', was creating 'an open
system that could and did accommodate older music techniques as well as
newer methods'.

The openness and freedom of Pound's system depended upon the proper
gauging of 'time intervals'; and that in turn depended upon the ear's ability

to hear a note's time or duration as well as its pitch. A sounded note is measurable as so many vibrations per second, bass notes being of lower and slower frequencies, treble of higher and faster frequencies; moreover, what is heard as pitch actually arises from the vibrations of the note. As the vibrations are rhythmic and the basis of rhythm, and as the specific timing or rhythm of the note determines its pitch, it can be said that pitch is primarily rhythm. Back in 1910 Pound had asserted that 'music is...pure rhythm; rhythm and nothing else, for the variation of pitch is the variation in rhythms of the individual notes, and harmony the blending of these varied rhythms'. In 1933 he would advise Mary Barnard that 'the difficulty in WRITING music...is in the RHYTHM NOT in pitch...[in] the DURATION of the note'. That of course was why he had had Antheil re-notate *Le Testament*, to register as precisely as possible the durations and rhythms of Villon's words.

Pound's theory and practice become still more innovative and challenging when the overtones of notes are brought into play, and the physics and mathematics of the science of acoustics have to be invoked to explain the development which he termed 'Great Bass'. This, according to Robert Hughes, was 'a *logical* idea whose time had come', and which Pound came to by following through the implications of his first axiom. Along with abolishing the established sense of harmony he abolished the well-established custom of composing within the range of a particular key, as in Mozart's *Sonata in C major* (K545) or Stravinsky's *Symphony in C* (1940). In its place he proposed a new form of composition based on taking a fundamental bass note and observing the range of frequencies or 'overtones' generated from it. 'In its simplest operation', Hughes and Fisher explain,

Great Bass posits a lowest common denominator (below the hearing range of sixteen cycles per second) which in its multiplication determines and governs the principal elements of musical composition—rhythm, harmony, and structure, and to some extent, melody.

The theory is founded upon 'the natural divisions of sound waves into tones and their overtones', and upon the organic ratios or proportions in the relations of tone and overtones. It assumes that all the elements of a composition have a natural relation to each other within their 'relationship to a fundamental rhythmic base'. If then a composer 'employs a chord that does not belong to the family of ratios of the work's "great bass", the music will "brace and strain" against an anticipation of...a chord that *is* within the multiplication of Great Bass'—and which of course may be deliberately withheld, as in 'Dame du ciel'.

'Let us say that music is a composition of frequencies', wrote Pound in his *Treatise*, getting down to the simplest, most basic and universal truth of music, and implying thereby some far-reaching and not at all simple consequences. The frequencies are the given, just *there* in the sounds things naturally make when struck or stroked or otherwise sounded. For them to be composed into some kind of harmony takes an ear which can distinguish one sound very precisely from another and a mind which can combine distinct sounds according to their natural relations. Pound would go on to speculate that it should be possible to bring into harmony all the noises thrown up in a factory or machine-shop, if only their diverse frequencies were accurately measured and the appropriate time-intervals observed; and this, he suggested, would make a positive difference to the physical and mental health of the workers. A harmonious composition of frequencies, after all, is made up of measured energies organized and given direction in accord with their natural rhythms, moving energies which are at once in and of the natural world and in and of the mind. It is that which would make music, as Pound thought, 'perhaps the bridge between consciousness and the unthinking sentient or even insentient universe'. So he could write of the 'order-giving vibrations' of the mind that 'is close on the vital universe'; and say that 'The magic of music is in its effect on volition'. He would have found support for these ideas in the 'treatise on music' in *Li Ki*, the ancient Chinese book of rites and ceremonies, which stated that music is both the expression and the cause of harmonies within the individual, and in all relations from those between individuals up to those between the state and heaven. In line with that, as Michael Ingham has observed, Pound's theory of Great Bass with its 'prescription for just organic proportion is...resonant with the Confucian idea that the central tone from which all others are measured, if ill chosen, will foment chaos in society, and, if correctly chosen, stimulate order and harmony'.

Perhaps it needs to be re-emphasized following those ideal conceptions that Pound's idea of harmony is concerned with moving energies, not with static states. So far as harmony implies coherence with wholeness or completeness these qualities are to be looked for, as in the ongoing process of the Cosmos, in the actual ordering and composing of the music, and of the individual being, and of the state. In the light of his new theory we have to learn to think of the composing as a process and not as aspiring to a perfected final state. Its wholeness will be in its inclusiveness, in how much of the totality of a given world can be brought into harmony; and harmony here is another term for the coherence of moving energies (vibrations) in their just relations. Its end, to which there is no end, is to bring the mind and the mind's little world into accord with the Cosmos in its process.

Back in 1917 Pound had written of the importance of 'main form' or 'major form' in musical composition, and that idea has proved helpful in grasping how in his cantos the disparate details are generated by a 'main concept' and are held together by their relations and interactions. The theory of Great Bass may be seen as a more technical, more purely musical development of the idea, with a fundamental tone in the place of 'a central main concept', and with the overtones in their just interrelations and interactions in place of the disparate but interrelating 'details' or 'materials'. Does this more developed theory apply equally to the cantos? It would be a possibility, given that pure music and the music of words are alike compositions of vibrant energies in process. But is there in a canto that basis, that fundamental word or verbal rhythm, from which all else flows? It is at the least a possibility worth looking out for.

Year 1 of a new era: kaleidoscope

'Honoured Progenitor', Pound began a letter to his father in February 1921, while in his relaxed mood at Saint-Raphaël, 'The proof that I know something about economics lies in the fact that I lead considerably more of a life than Rockefeller and Morgan ... & do extremely little that I wdnt do if I had a ballance equal to theirs.'

In Paris he rejoiced in the sense that 'nobody seems to feel responsible for anyone else's taste'. 'Even I', he wrote in his 'Paris Letter' dated 'September, 1921', with a nod to how differently he had felt and behaved in London, 'Even I have not tried to improve any one's mind since I got here.'

His sense of his liberties extended to not feeling at all responsible for Joyce and Lewis and Eliot. In May 1921 he wrote in a letter to John Quinn, 'I can't go on valeting for Lewis as I was ready to do while he was under stress of Military necessity.' Nor could he be expected 'to support him in a bid for the British picture market', any more than he could be expected 'to enthuse over Eliot's becoming a Times reviewer'. And Joyce was altogether 'off my hands', being now very well looked after by Miss Weaver and other patrons and helpers.

Pound would not have been himself though if he had not continued to care about others and about the state of the world. He exercised his freedom to please himself quite dutifully.

He had not given up on saving Eliot from his bank. He went on doing what he could to get Lewis into the revived *Little Review* and to set up contacts which might lead to exhibitions of his work. Lewis thanked him by asking to be left alone. Joyce expected him to be as busy as ever about getting his, Joyce's, work published, as Pound reported to Dorothy in

August 1921. At this moment it was the French translation of *Portrait of the Artist*. Joyce was 'again fairly well, very so from his humour', and 'longly conversational last evening, re greeks, Newman, eyes, french and german languages etc.' In the following summer, however, he was suffering from painful iritis and Pound arranged for Dr Louis Berman, the endocrinologist, who was just then in Paris, to examine him. Berman had 'Joyce's head X-rayed [and] found three dental abcesses under the diseased eye', and warned that he could go blind if they weren't fixed at once. Joyce, though, put off having his teeth attended to, saying 'he wanted "two months complete rest first"'. Pound gave up, reflecting, as a Confucian, that it 'is J.J.'s head, and . . . his own affair'.

In the same letter to Dorothy in August 1921, in the midst of asking her to thank the now sadly neglected Allen Upward for sending a copy of his just published autobiography, and the mentions of how his opera was coming on and what this person and that had said about it, and the report of his conversation with Joyce, etc., Pound took time out to give a thought to Miss Weaver's 'solitary life' and his fear that she might be 'giving out under the strain' of it. Do have her to tea, he urged Dorothy, and introduce her to Agnes Bedford when she returned to London, and 'O.S. also might assist'. Just the exchange of a few words occasionally might do her good— 'No use in having her go melancholy mad, after all her nobilities and utilities'.

Pound went over to London early in October, about the 8th or 9th, and stayed for eight days with Olivia Shakespear in Brunswick Gardens. On Monday the 10th he wrote back to Dorothy in Paris, 'Pried up the edge of the tragic veil yesterday and felt justified in coming over. | Hope you aren't worrying.' Whose the 'tragic veil', and why Dorothy might worry, I do not know. He may have gone over to see what he could do for Mrs Bride Gould-Adams (née Scratton), with whom he had shared the wish 'to build a dream over the world' in his early years in London, and who was trapped in a bad marriage. She would be with him in Paris and Verona in 1922, and in 1923 he would agree to be cited as co-respondent to enable her to obtain a divorce. During his week in London Pound invited Ford and Stella to lunch on the Friday; went up to Oxford to see Yeats, whom he found 'somnolent', on the Thursday; and on the Wednesday evening saw Eliot, who had been 'at last ordered away for three months' of complete rest and appeared 'rejuvinated at prospect'. On the Tuesday he had attempted, in a hotel infested by British undercover police, to persuade Sinn Fein's Arthur Griffith to found the new Irish Free State upon Douglas's Social Credit, and had been told, 'can't move 'em with a cold thing like economics'.

Eliot's nerves were bad, or so 'a nerve specialist' had told him when consulted about his 'feeling very nervous and shaky' and having 'very little self-control'—apparently he had 'greatly overdrawn [his] nervous energy'. 'Tom has had a rather serious breakdown', was how Vivien put it to Scofield Thayer, adding that she had 'not nearly finished [her] own nervous breakdown yet'. About the end of Pound's week in London Eliot went down with Vivien to Margate, the seaside resort on the north Kent coast, and stayed there for a month at the Albemarle Hotel, Cliftonville. Though advised to write nothing, he did do 'a rough draft of part of part III' of the long poem he was struggling to finish. Then he went on to Lausanne, on the way spending a few days in Paris where he saw Pound on 18 November, and leaving Vivien there at the Hôtel du Pas-de-Calais. In Lausanne Dr Roger Vittoz, the 'best mental specialist in Europe', confirmed that his 'nerves' were 'a very mild affair, due, not to overwork, but to an *aboulie* and emotional derangement which has been a lifelong affliction'. Eliot particularly marked the 'paragraph concerning "Aboulie", want of will', in his copy of Dr Vittoz's book, *Traitement des psychonévroses par la rééducation du contrôle cérébral* (1911; 3rd edn., Paris, 1921). The diagnosis relieved his anxiety that there might be something wrong with his mind, and the re-educative exercises left him feeling well enough to work on his long poem. When he left Lausanne on 2 January 1922 he had drafts for the whole work ready to show to Pound in Paris. There he rejoined Vivien, who was in quite a bad way on her own account, and stayed on for a fortnight, this time in Hôtel Bon Lafontaine in the same street as Hôtel du Pas-de-Calais.

The Pounds had moved out of the latter hotel about the end of November, and were now renting for £75 a year what seemed to Vivien Eliot 'a most exquisite Studio' at 70*bis* rue Notre Dame des Champs, up from the Luxembourg Gardens and near the intersection of Boulevard Saint-Michel and Boulevard du Montparnasse. The studio was one of several reached down a passage beside no. 70, on the ground floor, with a 'serre' or glass-walled conservatory fronting a courtyard in which there were a few trees and 'a mouldering plaster statue' of Diana with a hunting hound. Inside, behind the conservatory, there was the Studio, the one habitable room; behind that was a 'dressing room', and a small 'ex-kitchen' which they used as a box-room; and, up some stairs, there was a small 'lounge room' or bedroom. Pound cooked over an alcohol lamp in the main room, and cooked even better than he had in London, according to Lewis.

December and January were busy months for Pound. He told Thayer that he was 'in the midst of plumbers, gasistes, fumistes, stovistes, building furniture, and trying to clean the walls of this atelier, untouched since anterior decade'. The *'cheminée'* was being 'rebuilt at landlord's expense' and a new 'poêle Godin' put in to heat the main room. He nailed undressed boards together to construct tables and chairs, and made them firm by the simple efficiency of a design that had been known in ancient China, each immoveable joint three sides of a cube formed by three boards fixed at right angles to each other. A low tea-table was painted scarlet; the chairs had slung canvas seats, and one was large enough for bulky Ford to feel stranded in. Dorothy was out of action with a whitlow on her left forefinger and was in hospital for a few days in December.

Eliot probably presented his 'new poem in semi-existence' to Pound on 3 January. That evening Pound, Joyce, Eliot, and Horace Liveright, the young New York publisher, met over dinner. It was Liveright who had commissioned Pound's translation of Gourmont's *Physique de l'amour*, and who had just published his *Poems 1918–1921*. He was in Paris for six days and he and Pound were seeing each other every day, Liveright looking to Pound to introduce him to new talent, and Pound seeking a publisher for his modern movement. Both were eager to work together. Liveright offered to publish in the USA *Ulysses* and Eliot's as yet inchoate poem, as well as Pound's next collection of poems; and he made a contract with Pound which would 'take care of his rent... for the next two years'. In return for a non-repayable advance of $500 a year Pound was to translate French books of Liveright's choosing, but would not be expected 'to undertake more than one thousand dollars worth of translating in any one year', and would not be asked to put his name to his translation of any work he considered 'a disgrace to humanity or too imbecile to be borne'.[6]

By 16 January, when Eliot returned to London, Pound had twice gone over his drafts and had, as Eliot later put it, turned them 'from a jumble of good and bad passages into a poem'. The drafts had been accumulating over some years and Eliot, in his exhausted state, was unable to distinguish the good from the bad, while Pound, virtually at a glance, saw what needed to be cut away in order to bring forth *The Waste Land*, the archetypal modern poem. He was able to do that by virtue of his own 'technical mastery and critical ability', as Eliot would say, and because he was 'a marvellous critic [who] didn't try to turn you into an imitation of himself [but] tried to see what you were trying to do'. Exactly how he delivered Eliot's poem to him is on display in Valerie Eliot's facsimile edition of 'the original drafts including the annotations of Ezra Pound'. Where the writing lacked fresh

---

[6] It appears that under this contract Pound received $500 in all. His translation of Édouard Estaunié's *L'Appel de la route* as *The Call of the Road* was published by Boni & Liveright in November 1923, with the translator named as 'Hiram Janus'. 'Estaunié is a bad writer' he told his mother in 1924, 'couldn't escape the translation but... got my year's leisure to do the Malatesta'.

invention in perception and rhythm he struck it out ruthlessly, as with the whole of the seventy lines of satirical couplets in the manner of Rochester or Pope at the start of the draft of 'The Fire Sermon'; and where it became 'O.K.', as at 'A rat crept softly through the vegetation', he wrote 'STET' or 'Echt', the real thing, and moved on. He cut the episode of the typiste and 'young man carbuncular' from seventy lines of over-stuffed rhyming quatrains to just forty lines, removing the stuffing with no regard for the conventions of the form, and thus transformed it into a passage of concentrated realism. When he read the final part, which had come seemingly spontaneously to Eliot in Lausanne, he wrote on the manuscript 'OK from here on I think'; and when he saw the typed version a little later he left it alone apart from noting half a dozen small corrections. Altogether Pound's was a unique feat of releasing what had new life in it from the mess of materials in which it might otherwise have been stillborn.

What Pound did for *The Waste Land* was all the more remarkable given that he had very mixed feelings about it. He celebrated it, in a private letter to Felix Schelling, as 'the justification of the "movement", of our modern experiment, since 1900'; and he wrote to Thayer that 'it is as good in its way as *Ulysses* in its way—and there is so DAMN little genius, so DAMN little work that one can take hold of and say "this at any rate stands, and makes a definite part of literature"'. He also felt challenged by it, and felt that it exposed his own shortcomings, especially by its realism and its registration of the modern world. In a self-deprecating verse 'squib' sent to Eliot in January he put down his own poems for omitting 'realities'; and that judgement appears to lie behind this remark to John Quinn,

About enough, Eliot's poem, to make the rest of us shut up shop. I haven't done so; have in fact knocked out another Canto (not in the least *à la Eliot*, or connected with 'modern life').

His new canto would have been the 'Eighth Canto' which became canto II, and which might well stand as the antithesis to *The Waste Land*.

Beyond the sense of being challenged there appears to have been a profound dismay at what Eliot had done, a sense that his 'justification' of the modern movement had actually set it back. The only public evidence of this is in the first line of his next set of cantos, 'These fragments you have shelved (shored)', a critical allusion to one of the closing lines of *The Waste Land*, 'These fragments I have shored against my ruins'. It is in the drafts of these 'Malatesta cantos' that we will discover, when we come to them, exactly what Eliot's poem meant to Pound at the time, and how his own genius responded to it. It will become apparent that he saw it as an all too powerful statement of Eliot's *aboulie* in the face of the prevailing realities, and as tending to paralyse the constructive, civilizing will which he himself wanted to mobilize, and which he thought it the main function of poetry to mobilize. Pound never said anything directly critical of *The Waste Land*, but then his nearly absolute public silence about the poem, once it is registered, must declare some profound reservation or inhibition. It was his way to proclaim just as widely and forcefully as he could the virtues of the literature and the art he believed necessary to the advance of civilization. He was about to boost *Ulysses* in both French and English. But on *The Waste Land*, the justification of *our* modern effort, I can find almost nothing in his published prose; apart, that is, from one sentence in a *New Age* article in 1922 and a letter in a little magazine in 1924, and in both cases his endorsement of the poem amounts to shelving it.[7] He did virtually place it on the library shelf among the old volumes when he told Quinn privately that he considered Eliot 'as good as Keats, Shelley or Browning'. More interesting than that judgement, though, is Pound's having become pre-occupied for quite some time after January 1922 with the paradox that while *The Waste Land* was a work of genius, it was yet one which threatened to negate what he held to be the essential work of genius. He would resolve the contradiction by attacking it from both sides, that is, by attempting to release Eliot from the bank so that he might write in spite of his *aboulie*, and by finding the way to affirm constructive will in his own poem.

In mid-January 1922 Yeats was in Paris to help bring the Irish diaspora together in support of the new provisional government of the Free State at their International Irish Race Congress. Pound, who attended on Yeats while he was in Paris, thought his effort at political propaganda, in a speech on the Abbey theatre and John Synge, was 'affable, but no impact'. But he had a 'pleasant dinner' with Desmond Fitzgerald 'and some of the other Provisional lights'. Those he met would all shortly be caught up in civil war in Ireland.

Joyce's *Ulysses*, which Pound had assisted into print in instalments in the *Little Review* and the *Egoist*, appeared at last in full on 2 February 1922, published in Paris by Sylvia Beach under the imprint of Shakespeare & Co. *Ulysses* was '"out" triumphantly', he wrote to Alice Henderson in March, 'Record sale for one day was 136 last Tuesday'. By mid-February Pound

---

[7] The single sentence came in the context of Pound's *Bel Esprit* initiative: 'During his recent three months' absence [from the bank] due to complete physical breakdown he produced a very important sequence of poems: one of the few things in contemporary literature to which one can ascribe permanent value' ('Credit and the Fine Arts', *NA* 30.22 (30 March 1922) 284). The 1924 letter made a point about the notes—that the poem should be read without them. Of the poem itself it said only that it 'seems to me an emotional unit', and that its unity was from 'intensity or poignancy of expression' ('A Communication', *1924: A Magazine of the Arts* 3 (1924) 97–8).

had read through all of its '732 double sized pages', and he immediately set about proclaiming it a great work. 'All men should "Unite to give praise to Ulysses"', he trumpeted at the start of his next 'Paris Letter' for the *Dial*. He wanted it to be read as 'an epoch-making report on the state of the human mind in the twentieth century', and one which exposed to the withering light of unblinking intelligence all its mind-numbing banalities and clichés, all its paralysing fixed ideas, all its inertias and gangrenes of spirit. As such it was the culmination of the tradition that ran from Rabelais through Cervantes to Flaubert; and it was the answer to the prayer, in one of his *Little Review* 'pavannes', for hell to 'spew up some Rabelais'

> to define today
> In fitting fashion, and her monument
> Heap up to her in fadeless excrement.

That was the 'public utility' of prose realism, in Pound's scheme of things, to analyse and flush away all that negated the constructive, desire-driven work of genius; and Joyce had produced '*le roman réaliste par excellence*', a new Inferno and 'a great work of Katharsis'. It was a purge for the period in which 'the whole occident [was] under the domination of capital', and surely meant the end of the 'age of usury'. And it had, as Pound recalled in 1938, a special significance for him:

The katharis of *Ulysses*, the joyous satisfaction as the first chapters rolled into Holland Place, was to feel that here was the JOB DONE and finished, the diagnosis and cure was here. The sticky, molasses-covered filth of current print, all the fuggs, all the foetors, the whole boil of the European mind, had been lanced.

Pound must have felt that with the modern inferno done once and for all he could go on from it to build in poetry a possible paradise.

He certainly saw Joyce's bringing the old era to its end as opening the way for him to begin upon the new. Pound could name the exact moment at which the old era, the Christian era as he was calling it then, had definitely ended—it was 'midnight of the 29–30 of October (1921) old style'. That was when Joyce finished writing *Ulysses*; and the 30th happened also to be Pound's own birthday. In the calendar which he drew up for the new era that day was declared the Feast of Zagreus, or of Dionysos in his manifestation as lord of life in the world of the dead. 'Year 1 p.s.U.'—that is, post scriptum *Ulysses*—began from there. *Ulysses* belonged to the past which it monumentalized, not to the age in prospect. The era 'p.s. U.' was to be the era of *The Cantos of Ezra Pound*; and it is, in these mythopoetic terms, as Zagreus more than as Odysseus that we should look for him in them.

'I am afraid Eliot has merely gone to pieces again', Pound told Thayer on 10 March 1922, 'Abuleia...'. By the 12th he was busy orchestrating a campaign to get him out of the bank. In one of several letters he hammered out on his typewriter on that day he outlined his strategy to Alice Corbin Henderson:

Eliot works in a bank, but the poems do not get written and the world is thereby the poorer.

He broke down completely this winter. HAD to have three months off, in which he did very possibly the most interesting 19 page poem in the language. . . .

He then went back to his bank, and has since got steadily worse. *It is the greatest WASTE in contemporary letters.*

Joyce has now a permanent subsidy . . . Eliot ought to have the same.

. . .

Pas de blague. Something has got to be done. I pro<po>se turning Eliot into a limited liability company. With his poor health and wife, the minimum necessary is £300 per year (1500 bones). I propose to divide this into 30 guarantees of 50 dollars.

Aldington and I start the show with one share each, the pledge is annual for life, or for as long as Eliot needs it.

I can see about 20 shares. God knows where the remaining ten are to come from.

'I don't want him to write anything but poetry', he explained in a letter to Aldington sent the same day. A few days later he told him that Natalie Barney had given the scheme a name, *Bel Esprit*, and was giving it her support. In fact her residence at 20 rue Jacob was the 'official seat, birth place and address' of the scheme, and Miss Barney had become a full partner in it. There would be a prospectus in French, headed by an engraving of a pillared temple, and the aim would include helping Paul Valéry as well as Eliot. Pound, possibly at Quinn's instigation, had an appeal slip in English, with the heading *BEL ESPRIT*, printed by John Rodker in London 'for private circulation only'. 'In order that T. S. ELIOT may leave his work in Lloyd's Bank and devote his whole time to literature, we are raising a fund...', was how it began. But to Agnes Bedford he declared, 'We are saving civilization'; and to Aldington, 'We are restarting civilization.'

Eliot's particular case had become the occasion for Pound to campaign for a general cause. In a letter to Williams on 18 March he named others who might be released once Eliot had been freed; and stated the motive behind *Bel Esprit* as '"Release of energy for invention and design" acc [ording to] best economic theories', by which he meant Douglas's Social Credit. He developed that idea in an article in the *New Age* at the end of March, 'Credit and the Fine Arts: A Practical Application', and returned to it in his *Dial* 'Paris Letter' dated as 'October, 1922'.

The best economist, to Pound's mind, would be one who started from the principle that a society's primary resource is its intelligence, that is, its best informed and most creative individuals. Such an economist would recognize that the arts are of public utility, and should be kept up. And that can be done at small cost, Pound would insist, given a cheap attic and cheap daily salt bread, since there were only a 'few dozen artists and writers now capable of producing anything of interest', and since all they really needed was their independence and leisure in which to work as they pleased and without interruption. Modern democracy, however, he would then say, 'has signally failed to provide for its best writers'; and its market-based economy 'as applied to the arts has NOT worked', 'the worst work usually bring[ing] the greatest financial reward'. In short, 'there is no functioning co-ordinated civilization in Europe' capable of selecting and supporting the best new work. There was a time 'when the individual city (Italian mostly) tried to outdo its neighbour in the degree and intensity of its civilization, to be the vortex for the most living individuals'. Once, in the fifteenth century, there was 'a man in a small town who had Pisanello, Pier Francesco, and Mino da Fiesole all working for him at one time and another'. Now, though, 'The individual patron is nearly extinct'; 'The rich are, with the rarest exceptions, useless'; and 'One cannot wait until the masses are "educated up" to a fine demand', there being 'no sign whatever that they are tending in that direction'. Quality in the arts, Pound concluded, had become a luxury which only a few had the taste for. It was up to those few then, he argued, to get together to pay for it, and so 'to establish some spot of civilization', some vortex of intelligence. But will they do that, he demanded, or would they 'continue to sponge on the artist'?

In a long letter to John Quinn in July, much of it about *Bel Esprit*, he wrote 'we have now 21 out of the thirty subscriptions', though some were 'rather shaky'. His list included, as well as Aldington, Miss Barney, and himself: Romaine Brooks, Miss Barney's friend; May Sinclair; Richmond, editor of the *Times Literary Supplement*, and his wife; Eliot's wealthy friend Sidney Schiff; Robert McAlmon, the American writer who had married H.D.'s lover Winifred Ellerman, known as Bryher; and Quinn, who was down for 6 shares '(or 7 on condition Liveright be excluded)'. Williams, who in his reply to Pound's letter had exclaimed 'What the hell do I care about Elliot', had nevertheless sent in $30, possibly as a first payment towards a $50 share; and Dorothy was 'ready to pay up to £10/ in any year' for any member who defaulted.

'For me my £10 a year on Eliot is an investment,' Pound explained to Quinn, 'I put this money into him, as I wd. put it into a shoe factory if I wanted shoes,' or, 'Better simile, into a shipping company, of say small pearl-fishing ships, some scheme where there was a great deal of risk but a chance of infinite profit.' 'What wouldn't one give if one could have kept Keats alive a year or two more;...he was just getting his technique.'

Eliot had schemes of his own in hand. On 12 March, the day Pound began spreading word of *Bel Esprit*, Eliot wrote to him about two of them. There was the matter of his negotiations with Liveright and the *Dial* to find how much they would pay for *The Waste Land*. And there was the matter of the new quarterly review he was going to bring out, 'to raise the standard of thought and writing in this country'. It would have Lady Rothermere's money behind it; but the venture would be impossible, he told Pound, 'without your collaboration'.

'Willing to do anything for you personally', was Pound's immediate reply, but, as for England, he couldn't see it having anything to do with any future civilization. Only if an English review absolutely guaranteed to provide Eliot with enough to get him out of the bank and let him devote his entire time to literature could he be interested in it. 'Rather odd your writing just at this time,' he added, alluding to his own scheme which he had not been going to mention until it was working. (Yet his article about *Bel Esprit* in the *New Age* at the end of the month, about which he was altogether coy in this letter, was going to name Eliot as the first beneficiary.)

Towards the end of May Eliot, still complaining of his own ill health and exhaustion and of Vivien's persistent ailments, went to Lugano for a fortnight's holiday, and from there he travelled down to Verona to meet up with Pound. By his account they talked of the endocrine glands and Pound suggested that Vivien might be helped by Berman. They talked of *Bel Esprit*, and Eliot came away feeling that the scheme was in too 'nebulous' a state for him to commit himself to it. He felt indeed that the whole thing was 'unsatisfactory', lacking 'a dignified committee', lacking definite assurances concerning 'income, tenure and security', and all too likely to embarrass him personally.

By Pound's account they drew up '*in manuscript*', in Verona's Café Dante, 'a literary program' for Eliot's review—now to be called *The Criterion*, a title suggested by both Vivien and Pound independently—but the programme, he would later complain, 'was neither published nor followed'. In the absence of the manuscript there is no knowing what he thought they had agreed on.

In July Dorothy passed on to Eliot in London the equivalent of $200 raised by the Authors Club of New York in response to Pound's appeal. Pound told Harriet Monroe that 'with two lump gifts, the £300 for the first year is either in hand or promised'. Eliot, however, told Pound that £300 a year was not enough for him to live on. (In a letter to Sydney Schiff he would say in effect that salt bread and a cheap attic might suffice for those—such as Pound?—'who are accustomed to small and precarious incomes', but in his circumstances he needed 'more money and more security'.) He would not discourage Pound's finding out how much he could raise—£600 would not be 'a penny too much'—but nor would he pledge himself to accept the terms of *Bel Esprit*. As for *The Criterion*, he had decided, he informed Pound—possibly referring here to the Verona programme—'not to put any manifestoe in the first number, but adopt a protective colour for a time until suspicion is lulled'. He would play possum.

At the end of July Eliot put Pound's name down in his *Criterion* circular as a future contributor; and asked that the name of Lloyd's Bank should be deleted from Pound's *Bel Esprit* circular. 'I *cannot* jeopardise my position at the Bank before I know what is best,' he wrote. Nor did he like having his private circumstances publicized. In fact, 'If this business has any more publicity I shall be forced to make a public repudiation of it and refuse to have anything more to do with it.' In November, however, he asked Pound if he could get him the *Bel Esprit* money without the condition that he leave the bank immediately. He wanted to get free of Lady Rothermere, and needed money to buy the *Criterion* from her. 'If you and I could get the *Criterion* into our own hands', he wrote, 'it would be the thing of our lives.'

Pound replied at once that 'NO periodical could be the "thing of our lives"', and advised, 'You jess set and hev a quiet draw at youh cawn-kob'. He thought Eliot must be mad to be proposing to pay money for a loss-making review of which he was the only asset. Eliot protested that he was '*not* thinking of buying the *Criterion*'; that he had not yet received the 10,000 francs Lady Rothermere had got an American in Paris to pledge; and that he would 'leave the Bank as soon as I have such guarantees—for my life *or for Vivien's life*—as would satisfy a solicitor'.

On the 16th a short article appeared in the *Liverpool Post*, ostensibly about *The Waste Land* which had just appeared in the first number of *The Criterion*, but mainly about *Bel Esprit*—which it considered an excellent scheme if that poem was its product. The account of *Bel Esprit* followed Pound's circular fairly accurately, except in implying that it had enabled Eliot to write *The Waste Land*; and, more offensively, in relating 'an amusing tale' that two years before Eliot's friends had raised £800 so that he might devote himself solely to literature, and the joke was that he had taken the money but stayed on at the bank. Eliot was not amused, consulted his solicitors and a King's Counsel about this 'libellous falsehood', and on 30 November the *Liverpool Post* published his letter denying everything in the tale of £800, and adding that he had not 'received any sum from *Bel Esprit*', and that the scheme had neither his consent nor his approval.

That was the public repudiation he had threatened, and it was the end of *Bel Esprit*, publicly at least. Eliot, however, did accept such sums as were contributed to it, the last recorded being in July 1923. When he left Lloyds Bank, in 1925, it was to become a Director in the firm of Faber & Gwyer, publishers, later Faber & Faber. He edited *The Criterion*, and was *The Criterion*, until he brought it to an end in 1939, Pound contributing irregularly throughout its existence. There would be no break, but they were set on diverging paths.

In 'The Hollow Men', the poem that followed on from *The Waste Land*, Eliot would contemplate the shadow that falls between an ideal and the real world. Pound, however, was not haunted by the failure of *Bel Esprit* to impact upon Eliot's hard-headed sense of realities. In the *Dial* in November he reaffirmed with some passion his radical ideal of restarting civilization by releasing artistic energies from the routines of capitalist society. This time he did not associate the scheme with Eliot, only saying that he had been 'entoiled in three months of private controversy' on account of it. He did not reveal that the intended beneficiary had inconveniently insisted on having a life beyond the production of poetry, and had proved unwilling to be released from the bank if that meant giving up the style of life the bank enabled him to afford. The fact was that at its first trial the scheme had been nullified by Eliot's cautious adherence to the very system it was designed to counter. Pound did not address that directly, but nor did he surrender his will to change the world.

A renaissance man

On Good Friday, 14 April 1922, a postcard signed 'D. Pound', but apparently in John Rodker's hand, was posted in Siena to Margaret Anderson of the *Little Review*, announcing Pound's death and informing her that two photos of his death-mask were on their way to her. Pound himself had just written to Homer,

Dear Dad, If you hear a rumour of my demise | please DO NOT | contradict it...I want a little repose...I shall rise again at a suitable time. Possibly in six weeks.

He wrote to John Quinn to much the same effect, 'I shall be dead to the world.' The *Little Review*, however, although at that moment enthralled by Dada, declined to play along, and Jane Heap inserted into the spring issue, instead of the death-mask—in fact a life-mask taken by Nancy Cox McCormack—a dour note refusing to be hoaxed by 'some phoney death masks'. Pound, in a letter dated by his new pagan calendar, '13th Athene,

Annus Primus', drew their attention to the date on the postcard and chided them for having 'no respect for precedent'.

Ezra and Dorothy had left Paris at the end of March to spend three months travelling in Italy. They reached Genoa, after a 'not exactly restful' trip, on the 29th; on the 31st went on to Carrara, where there are the great marble quarries; were in Siena for at least the ten days of 4–14 April, and may have gone by bus to Florence. They moved on to Perugia—they were there on the 23rd—and Pound visited Assisi, Cortona, and Spoleto, partly in search of a good place for his parents to retire to. His mother had mentioned that they were thinking of retiring to California, and Pound, afraid that if they did he would never see them again, was intent on persuading them to retire instead to Italy. He also visited Ancona, Rimini, and Ravenna on the Adriatic coast with that in mind, and with a new canto in mind. He was in Venice on 4 May—apparently back in Perugia on the 6th—and in Venice again on the 22nd and the 28th. In early June he met Eliot in Verona, and for the rest of that month he and Dorothy were at Sirmione on Lake Garda. They returned to Paris via Milan, and were back at 70*bis* rue Notre Dame des Champs on 2 July.

From Sirmione he had written to Quinn on 20 June that he had 'had busy spring' and had 'blocked in four cantos—(Including the "Honest Sailor", which I hope I haven't spoiled)'. The 'Tale of the Honest Sailor', which he had from Quinn, features in canto 12, along with the financial adventures of Frank Bacon—'cuban pennies Bacon'—an old New York friend who would turn up in Paris as if on cue on 13 July. He was also 'At work on the "Hell" canto, chiefly devoted to the English'. By the 29th he had '4, probably 5, cantos blocked out', two of them—most likely the 'Honest Sailor' and 'Hell' cantos—'unprintable—dealing with modern life'. Once back in Paris he wrote that he had 'five cantos blocked out', and was 'about ready for the vacation I did not take in Italy'.

A busy summer followed, with Dorothy away in England from 13 July until 7 September. He had to finish off translations, for a London publisher, of Paul Morand's *Ouvert la nuit* and *Tendres Stocks*, short fictions which he had praised for looking with a clear eye at the wreckage of Europe. (The publisher would reject his translations in August, their reader having objected among other things to Pound's 'vulgar American' style, though Morand himself, whose English was good, had approved his work. Still Pound was paid the £25 due to him.) On Tuesday 11 July 'Mr Ezra Pound, Mr Tami Koumé and Capt. J. Brinkley' invited a select company 'to tea at Mr Pound's Studio . . . To see some paintings by Tami Koumé'. As well as Frank Bacon, Berman 'the gt. gland sleuth' was in Paris in July; and Wyndham Lewis, who found Pound receiving a boxing lesson in his studio from the nonchalant tough guy Ernest Hemingway. Pound was blue-pencilling Hemingway's adjectives in return. Sibley Watson of the *Dial*, who was passing through on his way to Vienna to see 'the surgeon who does Steinach's operation', thought Pound looked 'pretty unhealthy', though Pound himself said he was 'feeling damn fit', and was playing tennis with Hemingway to prove it. He had urged Watson to publish 'Obsequies', a story by Bride Scratton, telling him that she 'will never write again unless now encouraged'. (Her story evidently appealed to Eliot, who published it in *The Criterion* in April 1923.) Throughout the summer months people came flooding through his studio, Rodker, Etchells of the Vorticists, Hilda Aldington with her mother, 'Kitty Heyman with two flappers in tow', the Dean of Hamilton College with family—fifty-six visitors in one week in August. At the start of that month he set about commissioning a number of fifty-page booklets which would be published by Bill Bird's Three Mountains Press on the Île Saint-Louis and would indicate 'the state of prose after *Ulysses*, or the possibility of a return to normal writing'. He approached Ford, Williams, and Hemingway as writers who would 'tell the truth about *moeurs contemporaines*'. (He would also include Bride Scratton's stories under the title *England*.) In September he began some sort of *affaire* with Nancy Cunard, Lady Cunard's now grown up and very liberated daughter, and for a time was one of her occasional and more passionately desired lovers. There was the ongoing ado about *Bel Esprit*. And above all there were the 'blocked out' cantos to be worked up.

'I don't at present see that I shall get around to any music this summer', he told Dorothy in July, 'There is a lot of Sig. to do'. 'Sig.' was Sigismondo Pandolfo Malatesta (1417–68), once lord of Rimini, now the subject of the first of the five new cantos Pound had brought back from Italy 'in rough draft'. He had thought that canto might 'swell out into two', but in fact it would grow through a year of intensive reading in Paris and research in Italian archives into a suite of four. They would be published in the fourth number of the *Criterion* in July 1923 as 'Malatesta Cantos. (Cantos IX to XII of a Long Poem)', and would subsequently become cantos VIII–XI.

The first draft, handwritten at Sirmione, begins with the bold declaration, 'I have sat here for 44,000 years | yes precisely', thus asserting a commanding overview of human culture from its notional beginnings, and outdoing Eliot's Tiresias who could claim only to have seen and foresuffered the sad vanity of sexual desire since his Theban times. The following lines place the speaker in present-day Verona, at the very moment, as will appear in a later draft, of Pound's recent meeting there with Eliot. Then comes a proclamation of Pound's new era: '& the world began again | last

October'; and that is rhymed, as it were, with Sigismondo's reviving the old pagan gods in Rimini, '& the Tempio—in October'. The rest of this draft sketches in the vicissitudes of Sigismondo's career as a *condottiere*, a soldier of fortune, who sold his outstanding military skills to one city state after another and had lost most of his own minor state by the end, with the Popes after his lands and the Medici bank against him; and who yet, in spite of his warring, his shifting allegiances, his powerlessness when dealing with the major powers of Venice and Milan and the Papacy, in spite of his defeats and disgraces, did succeed in having a Gothic church transformed by some of the best artists of his age into a Renaissance temple adorned with inspired 'pagan' bas-reliefs to the greater glory of himself and his adored Isotta. He thus, as historians have remarked, 'embodied the renaissance'—that is the key statement of this draft—'having some sense of life | no morals, infinite heroism | & a respect for tradition'. Later, in *Guide to Kulchur*, Pound would stress his combination of individualism and representativeness, writing that 'Malatesta managed *against* the current of power' 'all that a single man could', and that his 'Tempio Malatestiano is...a cultural "high"' and 'perhaps the apex of what one man has embodied in the last 1000 years of the occident'.

In an early typescript draft, probably done in July soon after Pound's return to Paris, Sigismondo's achievement is attributed to 'the urge to refound the world'; and that urge is connected with a 'gai saber', a cult of love, such as existed in the troubadours' Provence, with the implication that it was his love of Isotta, his lifelong mistress and third wife, that moved him 'to refound the world'. Evidently what interested Pound in Sigismondo was that he was a 'bhloomin historic character'—that is, not a fantasy but someone who had actually lived, loved, and acted in a particular world and time—someone who could 'be used as illustration of intelligent constructivity', and whose life also afforded 'a certain boisterousness and disorder to contrast with his constructive work'. He represented on a heroic scale the qualities Pound was finding admirable, in October 1922, in the poet and playwright Gabriele D'Annunzio after he had seized Fiume in a grand *coup de théâtre* which heralded Mussolini's March on Rome, 'some sort of vigour, some sort of assertion, some sort of courage, or at least of ebullience that throws a certain amount of remembered beauty into an unconquered consciousness'. 'The Malatesta cantos', he would declare in *Guide to Kulchur*, 'are openly volitionist, establishing...the effect of the factive personality, Sigismundo, an entire man'.

In the typescript draft of July 1922, however, the affirmation of Sigismondo's 'urge to refound the world' only goes to show up both Eliot and Pound as helpless and hopeless to do anything about their own

42

disintegrating world. 'These fragments you < *T.S.E.* > have "shelved"', is the first line of this draft; and the next line points to Sigismondo's contrasting action in stealing marble slabs from a church in Ravenna and having them carved with pagan gods for his temple, to stand 'Against his ruin and [his] house's ruin... Fragments against his ruin'. Eliot and Pound sit by the Roman arena in Verona as they had sat 'on the Roman mound' at Excideuil three years before, and Eliot, perhaps both then and now, identifies with Dante's image of Arnaut Daniel purging himself of earthly desire in the fire of Purgatory; while Pound identifies rather with Dante's image of Bertrans de Born in Hell, a stirrer-up of strife with head divided from heart. Pound thinks of them as in another age, Eliot with 'soild lace cuff', and himself 'lifting sedan chairs, preparing the revolution | ... & never learning'. The sense of futility and decay is generalized: 'Things run, and run to the worse'—'Byzance, the empires gone, slide[s] to nothing here in the marsh drift, | Caesarea, gone, roof deep in the marsh.' Against that, Pound recalls the enduring splendour of the tomb of the Byzantine empress Galla Placidia at Ravenna, which he had visited in May, and where he had seen in the gold mosaic of its walls 'the souls, | gonads in organdy, rose-flakes in the arid darkness'; and had seen how the gold gathered to itself 'against the gloom' the yellow sunlight penetrating the alabaster panes. He recalls also the magnificent tomb Sigismondo had raised to his divine Isotta at the heart of the Tempio which he had visited in Rimini. But as for the live woman who is with him in Verona, 'Ti', later identified as the divorcing Bride Scratton but for the moment 'Galla's hypostasis', she will have no such setting. Yet the mood of despondency is not absolute. Even the circus in the arena, and 'Ti', and Eliot with his bitter drink, can be seen as 'sprouts in the loam'; and the draft ends upon living things, 'a wing exists for a moment and goes out, | ~~flame intermittent,~~ | an emerald lizard peers through the border grass'. Those images may promise a basis for renewals, not of course from the flying grasshopper and the lizard in themselves, but from the power of the mind to so perceive them. But the contradiction remains, between Sigismondo's magnificent monument, and Galla Placidia's, and the apparent failure in Pound and Eliot, in the modern movement, of the urge to refound the world.

Perhaps the mood behind that July draft is summed up in another typescript fragment:

> Chien de metier,
>> hopelessness of writing an epic
>
> Chien de metier
>> hopelessness of building a temple

Chien de métier, a lousy line of work to be in, or something to that effect. Still, the hopelessness of writing an epic must be tempered by the knowledge that Sigismondo did 'build his temple'. Even though it was unfinished and roofless when he had to abandon the reconstruction in 1461, at least, Pound would assert in *Guide to Kulchur*, he did register his concept, and 'There is no other single man's effort equally registered'. Eliot might cynically regard human history as simply an 'immense panorama of futility and anarchy'; but for Pound it had the positive use of showing what was humanly possible, and so of encouraging, inciting to, constructive effort.

That fragment points up something else which is fundamental to the final version of the Malatesta cantos, something which critics tend to miss. The *virtù* of Pound's Sigismondo is not to be found in his often violent and morally dubious career as a *condottiere*—indeed as a man of action he is merely typical of his often violent and morally dubious times, and is shown to have achieved by his deeds nothing of lasting significance. His *virtù*, in Pound's rendering, his 'intelligent constructivity', is all in his 'building a temple'. It is by that alone that he 'cut his notch . . . registered a state of mind, of sensibility, of all-roundness and awareness'. That is the aspect of Sigismondo with which Pound equated his own will to write an epic, with the implication that it is by a temple, or an epic, that civilization will be begun again.

Yeats wrote to Pound from Ireland in August 1922 about being 'shut in by battles', though he was nevertheless 'contented and busy' in his tower. He would have been working on his 'Meditations in Time of Civil War', brooding on how the grace and beauty of an ancestral house might come from 'Some violent bitter man, some powerful man'. In October, after months of sometimes violent civil disorder in Italy, Mussolini marched his forces on Rome and was appointed by the King to resolve the crisis of government by initiating the Fascist new order. Pound did not register the event—'Life was interesting in Paris . . . nobody bothered much about Italy.' Besides, a friend in Milan had assured him, when asked 'What is this fascio?', that 'there was nothing to it'. In October Lincoln Steffens was in Paris talking of how the Russian Revolution had been prepared by propaganda, by getting the word 'revolution' into the minds of the people, and by Lenin's short speeches at the critical moment, and Pound listened to him with intense interest and put the essential facts of that history into canto 16, setting it against testimonies to the crass and savage absurdities of the late wasteful war.

Pound did not desire a revolution—'JE NE VEUX PAS, non je ne veux pas de révolution', he had insisted in 1921. He knew, in his 'measured moments', or so he told Felix Schelling in July 1922, 'that all violence is useless (even the violence of language...)'. But how to decide where the border lay 'between strong language and violent language'? There were, after all, certain 'excrements' it was imperative to destroy, for instance '*all* British journalism'. Hence, one may conclude, the strong language of the 'Hell' cantos. Then there was Christianity to be overthrown:

Christianisme: malgré qu'il ne soit plus la croyance de l'homme pensant européen, il n'y a pas une seule coutume, loi, convention ni de l'Europe, ni de l'Amérique qui ne soit pourrie à cause de cette base—totem de tribu SHEENY, Yid, taboo, pourriture... *monotheos*.

MONOtheism, l'idée la plus crûment et immaturément idéologue, intellectuelle, maladivement cérébraliste, idée la moins fondée, la moins prouvée qui ait jamais été avalée par ⅜ de la race humaine.

[*Christianity*: in spite of its being no longer the belief of thinking Europeans, there is not one custom, law, convention of Europe or America which is not rotten from this root—this tribal totem of SHEENY, Yid, taboo, corruption... *monotheos*.

MONOtheism, the crudest and immaturest ideological intellectual idea, morbidly cerebralist, the least well-founded, least proven idea ever to have been swallowed by ⅜ of the human race.]

Even allowing for the fact that this appeared only in a supplement to Picabia's small Dada magazine *381*, and allowing too for what was then current on the streets of New York, 'SHEENY, Yid' must strike us now as transgressing into violence. And why drag in race at all when it is religion that is in question, if not to charge up the attack on monotheism with the emotion of race prejudice. With hindsight one can read there an early warning of what would become a disastrous habit in his later propaganda. At the same time Pound was quite able to express his strong views in straight terms, as in the letter to Harriet Monroe in which he protested against 'Damn remnants in you of Jew religion' because of her trying to keep her readers in ignorance of the fact that he did 'NOT accept... the dregs of the Xtn superstition', 'refuse[d] to accept ANY monotheistic taboos whatsoever', and considered 'the Hebrew scriptures the record of a barbarian tribe, full of evil'. He wanted her to let it be known that he considered 'the Writings of Confucius, and Ovid's *Metamorphoses* the only safe guides in religion'. Hence canto 13, beginning 'Kung [or Confucius] walked | by the dynastic temple'. Hence his approval of Sigismondo's Tempio with its many pagan divinities, and its honouring Isotta's divinity. In his combining a will to construct a *paradiso* in words with occasional violent verbal transgressions Pound was not unlike his Sigismondo.

In early August 1922 Pound was 'reading up historic background for Canto IX', and he kept at that all the way through to December, by which time he had 'got three of the Malatesta cantos into some sort of shape'. He called up books in the Bibliothèque Nationale—his seat was 58ter when he called up a volume in Latin of Sigismondo's court poet Basinio published in Paris in 1538. He looked out particularly for references to documents and primary sources, and noted in which archives they were to be found. There were in Milan, for example, letters from Sigismondo to Francesco Sforza, Duke of Milan; and in Rimini there was an unpublished chronicle of Sigismondo's campaigns written by one Broglio who had been with him in the wars. He wrote to antiquarian book dealers in Milan, Florence, and Rimini in search of materials, and was invoiced by Ulrico Hoepli of Milan for five volumes, one of them Giovanni Soranzo's *Pio II e la politica italiana nella Lotta contro i Malatesti (1457–1463)*. From that work he drew a number of details in the Malatesta cantos, among them the exact intemperate insults to which Sigismondo and Count Federigo d'Urbino descended at a meeting intended to make peace, *'"Te cavero la budella del corpo!"'*—equivalent to (in a different vernacular) *I'll have your guts for garters*—and the response from the Count, *'"Io te cavero la corata a te"'*, *And I'll pluck out your giblets!*

On 30 December 1922 Pound was issued a new United States passport valid for 'Literary work and travel' in all countries. His occupation was given as 'Correspondent'. His personal description was: age 37 years; height 5 feet 10½ inches; forehead: broad; eyes: gray green; nose: straight; mouth: moustached; chin: bearded; hair: light; complexion: fair; face: oval. He used his new passport at once to go into Italy, and was there from early January to mid-April 1923.

For the first four or five weeks Ezra and Dorothy were in Rapallo, at the Hotel Mignon, Pound 'chewing along on Malatesta' and playing tennis with a young American called Strater, and Dorothy doing some drawing. For a week or so in February they were joined by Hemingway and his wife Hadley, and the four of them toured Sigismondo's old battlefields in Tuscany, such as Rocca Sorano near Siena. 'Geographical verification', Pound called that, 'cross country in wake of S. M. to see how the land lay'. The Pounds went on down to Rome, where Ezra wanted to verify details in 'documents preserved in the Vatican concerning Rimini and other towns of central Italy', and they were there from 17 February to 1 March. On the 2nd he was in the archives in Florence consulting *La Guerra dei Senesi col conte di Pitigliano*, which he would cite with shelf mark in canto 10. At that point Dorothy asked Stella Bowen, who was with Ford and their daughter at Saint-Jean-Cap-Ferrat on the Riviera, to spend a fortnight travelling with her in Italy while Pound was visiting libraries and archives, and then began a complicated sort of dance with postcards from

Pound to Dorothy in Perugia or Assisi or Siena crossing postcards from Dorothy to Pound in Cesena or Rimini or Fano, etc. Dorothy was settled back in the Hotel Mignon in Rapallo from the 18th, while Ezra kept on the move until they met up again in Milan in early April.

He had thought the Malatesta cantos as good as done, yet March 1923 was his most intense and concentrated spell of research for them in all the towns with Malatesta archives or associations. On the 7th he was in Bologna, where, on the 8th, he had a 'Somewhat full day. Three libraries—all voluble—and amiable'. On the 9th he went on to the State Archive in Modena; and on the 10th he was in Cesena, in the splendid library founded by Malatesta Novello in 1452. There he was assisted by the very amiable young librarian Manlio Dazzi who took him that evening to a concert 'of the highest quality'. (Dorothy was in Assisi on the 10th, where there was to be a 'Big fascist meeting tomorrow'.) On the 13th Pound was in Rimini, and cursing because the library was 'closed *at least* until the 20th as the damn *custode* has flu', and he was forced to go on, with a sense of laboriously filling in time, to San Marino, Pennabilli—where he stayed at the Albergo Ristorante Malatesta—then Pesaro, Fano, Urbino on successive days, and at last back to Rimini on the 20th where he appreciated the comfort of the Palace Hotel for a full week.

He did get into the library this time because his hotel-keeper, who happened also to be a founding member of the local *Fascio*, and a Commandante della Piazza charged with keeping order in the town, had taken it upon himself to see to it that Il Poeta was able to do what he had come for. Just before going to the library on the 21st Pound scribbled to Dorothy, 'Hotel-keeper ready to sack the place and have up the mayor if it isn't open; he is a noble fascist'. Evidently the mayor did have to be called in, since at the end of the week Pound told Dorothy that the *Reggio Commissario*, the mayor, had 'descended on the librarian (who may die of the shock). *Very* sympatique the *Gran Cordone.*' Pound was not only very grateful, as what researcher wouldn't be, but also deeply impressed by this evidence of a new energy and civic sense in Italy. He was ready to believe his hotel-keeper's insistence that it was out of devotion to Mussolini that he had had the old library unlocked.

After Rimini Pound was in Ravenna on the 28th and 29th, then in Venice on the 30th and 31st. Everywhere he was making notes; checking details he already had from printed books against the original documents; struggling with his untrained eye to decipher the Renaissance manuscripts, getting some words wrong; and constantly shaping the materials (far more than he would use) with a view to fitting them into a canto. By the time he finished off the four Malatesta cantos, back in Paris in the latter half of April, his 1922 drafts had undergone a radical transformation.

Pound did have other things to think about while travelling around Romagna. Nancy Cunard was also on the move in Italy, on a separate trajectory, but hoping they might arrange to coincide. When he was in Rimini she wrote from Positano in the south that she was reserving April for him, and could they not meet, with or without Dorothy, in the north somewhere? Pound's reply has not survived, but there is reason to suppose he was not tempted. Then there was Bride Scratton's impending divorce. Dorothy wrote that she had not heard from her mother 'since ever', and was there any 'divorce news' she might have seen? In his letter to her of 21 March Pound said he knew of nothing new since Bride had told him 'it wd. be some time in April', and he expected 'the matter will be attended to with whatever decorum is possible'. Pound's being named as co-respondent may have been the reason for Dorothy's staying on in Italy when he returned to Paris. On 27 April 1923 she was issued in Rapallo with an authorization to be a sojourning foreigner.

Pound sent off the Malatesta suite to the *Dial* on 24 April, but when he learnt that publication there was subject to Thayer's veto he withdrew the manuscript. (A formal rejection letter on Thayer's behalf was sent to him all the same.) Eliot had accepted the four cantos sight unseen for simultaneous publication in the *Criterion*, and they did appear there in July 1923. They appeared, however, without the opening allusion to *The Waste Land*, 'These fragments you have shelved (shored)', Eliot having objected to it 'strongly on tactical grounds'. His reason was that people were already too 'inclined to think that we write our verses in collaboration', though it is much more likely that the allusion would have been read as a calculated riposte to Eliot's poem.

One remarkable thing about the finished suite is that all reference to the meeting in Verona has disappeared, and so too has the peculiarly personal and discouraged mood associated with it. Moreover, all that remains of the splendour of 'Galla's rest' is one isolated and now cryptic line, 'In the gloom, the gold gathers the light against it'. The self-regarding material, and the reflection of the helpless alienation from modern decadence of the beauty-seeking individual, these have been altogether squeezed out. At the same time the account of Sigismondo's life and works has been greatly extended and built up from the objective documents and the contemporary records and eye-witness reports so that he is viewed, Cubist fashion, from a variety of angles and points of view. And here the rhetorical assertions of Sigismondo's embodying the Renaissance and being driven by the 'urge to refound the world' have been squeezed out. There is no direct statement at all of those grand claims which Pound makes in his prose for Sigismondo and for his Tempio. Thanks to his having gone over the ground and sweated in the archives he had no need now to imagine or to invent anything, and no need to assert anything on his own account. He had recovered the objective poetic self, so painstakingly developed through the experiments of 'Near Perigord' and the early trial cantos, which he had lapsed out of in the first, post-Verona, draft; that is, he had become again simply the active intelligence of his materials, simply the maker of his poem, and neither a propagandist nor a hapless revolutionary.

His Sigismondo is now primarily the *condottiere*, the magnificent mercenary, a fighting man with no clear aim in his going to war to serve others' strategies, an action man putting himself at the mercy of those others and of the fortunes of war. There is just one letter, in canto 8, showing him as the enlightened patron participating—that is how Pound had encouraged John Quinn to view a patron's role—in a master painter's creation; and that letter, written from the field of war while he was besieging Cremona in the Venetian interest, is interleaved as it were between an ingratiating letter to his Florentine master of the moment and the cold record of Florence's terms for taking him on. Similarly interleaved in the latter half of the canto is brief mention of Gemistus Plethon, the Byzantine Platonist whose advocacy of a return to classical polytheism lay behind Sigismondo's incorporating the classical gods into his Tempio. At the exact centre of the canto is a single verse from a love song Sigismondo wrote for Isotta, and this is given in Pound's translation a most musical measure which sets it utterly apart from the documentary style it briefly interrupts. In its invocation of the pagan 'spirits who of old were in this land', and its directing them to 'awaken | The summer within her mind', it represents what moved him to build the Tempio. But there will be only one other recognition of that prime cause in the entire suite. Though it is structurally at the heart of the canto, and evidently at the heart of Sigismondo's private life, it appears to have not the least effect on his life as a *condottiere* nor on the ways of his world. He must report immediately to Florence that Venice has taken him on 'At 7,000 a month' etc. Then follows an elaborate description of the festival he staged in Rimini for the newly married Francesco Sforza, with whom Sigismondo was just then allied; and that amounted to nothing more than the usual grand parade and fashion show, with the ironic additions that Francesco's great pleasure on that occasion was fishing, and that he was on his way to a war in which he would receive 'an excellent hiding'. War, not love, is what keeps Sigismondo and his world in a perpetual whirl.

49

From the last lines of canto 8 until half way through canto 9 Broglio the chronicler takes up the story, in the style of 'one damned thing after another':

> And 'Florence our natural ally', as they said in the meeting
>   for whatever that was worth afterward
> And he began building the TEMPIO,
>   And Polixena, his second wife, died.
> And the Venetians sent down an ambassador...

In the tally of what Sigismondo did and what others did to him one episode stands out, his night-raid 'with more than an hundred | two wheeled ox carts' to carry away 'marble, porphyry, serpentine' from the ancient basilica in Ravenna. Otherwise the upshot is, 'And the jobs getting smaller and smaller'. The second half of canto 9 consists of extracts from eight of the fifty letters found when the Sienese seized his postbag in 1454. All of the extracts concern affairs back home in Rimini, and while they mostly report how the building of the Tempio is progressing, their main effect is to give an impression of how Sigismondo is regarded in his own court, of how things are ordered there, and of how his absence is felt. The canto ends with a coda, 'The ideograph', as Pound called it in one typescript, giving the essence of Sigismondo's life and works: 'that "he lived and ruled"', and loved to distraction Ixotta degli Atti, who was worthy of his love, '"and built a temple so full of pagan works"'. This carries the more weight for coming not from Pound, nor the sympathetic Broglio, but from the papal denunciation of Sigismondo.

Cantos 10 and 11 continue the chronicle of Sigismondo's failing career. Much of canto 10 is given over to the papal condemnation and excommunication, some of it in Latin capitals, as if graven in marble, and all of it throwing at him every sin and crime in the book. It was, as historians now recognize, an exercise in character assassination, most of the charges being trumped up and the whole thing being politically motivated; but the dirt stuck for centuries, and the great Burckhardt accepted as 'the verdict of history' that Sigismondo embodied a 'disinterested love of evil' and was indeed guilty of 'murder, rape, adultery, incest, sacrilege, perjury and treason', and so forth and so forth. Pound for his part treats the speech for the prosecution as overblown 'bunkum', and moves on to Sigismondo's surviving being burnt in effigy as 'God's enemy and man's enemy', and surviving more direct attempts on his life. In one battle, the first episode in canto 11, he even defeats the papal forces which outnumber his ten to one in cavalry and have twice as many footsoldiers. He won that battle, Pound implies, by putting into the minds of his men the potent image of the eagle that 'lit on his tent pole' and telling them, 'The Romans would have called that an augury'. But the rest of the canto shows him steadily losing the war, forced to sign away most of his towns, and with his luck and his strength deserting him. He sits in the unfinished church—referred to thus as what it had been, 'the chiexa', not as the 'Tempio'—'noting what was done wrong'. Anecdotes illustrative of his humanity and intelligence, and of his popularity with his people, fill up the vacuum of his wasted last years. The final image of the once fearsome *condottiere* is of his entering into a solemn contract about some practical joking. In these two cantos Isotta is never mentioned.

The Malatesta suite ends upon the note of humane comedy, with Sigismondo neither a tragic figure, nor an idealized one. He is certainly not, as some have taken him to be, a simple celebration of 'the factive personality', if that means, as some have taken it to mean, the man who gets things done with all necessary violence. The fact is that his making, in Pound's portrayal, is all in his effort to build a fitting monument to his love; and that effort, shown more as a struggle than as an achievement, is pretty well eclipsed throughout the latter two cantos. Pound's Sigismondo has much in common with his Bertrans de Born, the *persona* bafflingly but apparently completely split between his love of a woman and his love of war. These cantos have much in common also with the *Cathay* and *Propertius* and *Mauberley* portraits, in that each of them exhibits a maker, an individual of genius, registering a concept of constructive love while being ultimately subdued to the antithetical ethos of his time. Some would see Sigismondo as a prototype of Mussolini, not without reason; but then he would be also a forefiguring of what was to be Mussolini's fate when his vision of a new society was compromised and undone by violent political and military action. Again, one could read in him a forefiguring of Pound's own fate, when he lost his centre 'fighting the world'.

Pound wanted to bring about a renaissance, to recover such a vision of the universe alive as would move men of good will to make a paradise on earth. Sigismondo Malatesta afforded a case study of what a man possessed of the vision which brought about a renaissance in Italy in the fifteenth century had actually achieved under the conditions then prevailing. The historical records, when Pound took them fully into account, spoke overwhelmingly of his failure, and the Malatesta cantos faithfully reflect that. In Pound's own terms too Sigismondo was a failure, in that his active life was not on the whole directed by his enlightened vision. And yet Pound could write, under the frontispiece to *Guide to Kulchur*, that he was 'a failure worth all the successes of his age'. He could discount the record of his life because Sigismondo had realized his vision in an enduring creation. Even the seal reproduced as frontispiece, a mere 'wafer of wax . . . between two surfaces of paper in a letter from the young Salustio Malatesta', could still, in 1938, convey 'the thoroughness of Rimini's civilization in 1460'.

That is a profound indication of the orientation of Pound's mind. Committed as he was, as an artist, to working in and making the best of his actual world, to realizing a 'paradiso *terrestre*' in spite of the shambles of war and the hells of *aboulie* and obstruction, it was nevertheless in enduring works of art that he placed his ultimate faith. That the vision would not often, and never lastingly, direct human affairs—the universal lesson of history—is a truth he appears to have accepted without question. He concentrated, as an artist, on the forms in which the vision could be kept alive in the mind. But then he was not only and not always the artist.

Life and times: 1923–1924

In early May 1923 Their Imperial Britannic Majesties King George V and Queen Mary made an official five-day state visit to Italy, during which the King bestowed the Order of the Bath upon Signor Mussolini and thus, in the press and the popular mind, set the British seal of approval upon his Fascist regime.

Pound, in Paris in May, would *not* visit Gurdjieff at his Institute out at Fontainebleau, even though Gurdjieff's Persian soup was of peerless delicacy, and nor would he visit Orage while he was there, holding as he did to the view that 'Confucius [is] about as good a guide as one can want in this vale of imbecilities'.

William Bird[8] was proposing a 'de looks edtn. of Malatesta' from his Three Mountains Press, and Henry Strater was already 'at work on special capitals' for it. Very soon it was to be

a dee looks edtn of my Cantos (about 16 of 'em, I think) of UNRIVALLED magnificence. Price 25 dollars per copy, and 50 and 100 bones for Vellum and illuminateds.

It is to be one of the real bits of printing; modern book to be jacked up to somewhere near level of mediaeval mss. No Kelmscott mess of illegibility. Large clear type, but also large pages, and specially made capitals.

Not for the Vulgus. There'll be only about 60 copies for sale; and about 15 more for the producers.

---

[8] William Bird (1888–1963): in 1922, while European Manager of Consolidated Press Association of Washington, DC, acquired a seventeenth-century Mathieu printing press in order to pursue an interest in typography and hand-printing, and set up his Three Mountains Press at 29 Quai d'Anjou on the Île Saint-Louis in Paris; entered into an association with Robert McAlmon and his Contact Editions, and gave Ford space from which to run his *transatlantic review*; published the 'Inquest' series of six small books edited by Pound, and Pound's *Antheil and The Treatise on Harmony* (1924) and *A Draft of XVI Cantos* (1925). Printed nothing after 1925, and sold his press and Caslon Old Face type to Nancy Cunard who used it for her Hours Press.

Several of those sixteen cantos had yet to reach their final state.

In June Pound was 'doing a canto on Kung', using 'Pauthier's french translation of the Four Books; and a latin translation of the Odes'. Confucius' 'idea of beginning in the middle, i.e. on oneself is excellent', he told Homer, thinking of what 'Kung said, and wrote on the bo leaves':

> If a man have not order within him
> He can not spread order about him;
> And if a man have not order within him
> His family will not act with due order;
>   And if the prince have not order within him
> He can not put order in his dominions.
> And Kung gave the words 'order'
> and 'brotherly deference'
> And said nothing of 'the life after death'.

All that, Pound wrote to Homer, was 'The exact reverse of Christianchurchism'. The contrasting 'Hell' cantos which came next were his 'portrait of contemporary England, or at least Eng. as she wuz when I left her'—that was how he described them to Lewis; and to Ford he said they were, 'THE STATE of ENGLISH MIND in . . . the post war epotch'. He wanted to show why the British Empire was in a state of disorder and 'DECOMPOSITION', and wrote of politicians as arseholes who talk through their arseholes, and of preachers as 'vice-crusaders, fahrting through silk, | waving the Christian symbols'. Those terms, he would maintain to Ford, were 'the nearest thing to the exact word attainable'.

Dorothy's solicitor father, Henry Hope Shakespear, was gravely ill in June and died in early July. Dorothy was with her mother in England until about the middle of August. She told Ezra on black-bordered notepaper not to come for the funeral, expressing no particular feeling—it was Olivia who wrote that 'it has all been fearfully painful'—but being concerned about papers to be signed and having to wait three months 'to know for certain about money matters'. She hoped 'to be able to settle some' money on Ezra, 'and perhaps extract a lump for B. Esprit (incognito)'.

On 27 June Ezra mentioned to Dorothy that he had 'had O. Rudge play over [his] opera arias on violin; and am dining with her tonight'; on 17 July, 'The Rudge has taken "permanence" at cinema, instead of substituting for other violin'; and on 7 August, 'Olga played over some of the Villon'.[9]

---

[9] Olga Rudge (1895–1996), b. Youngstown, Ohio; educated in Europe from the age of 9, at first in England, then from 1910 at the Paris Conservatoire; her mother, a noted singer, made her home in London, then in Paris, at 2 rue Chamfort in the XVIth *arrondissement*, and took Olga into the musical and literary *salons* of Parisian society. By 1914 Olga was giving concert recitals in Paris, London, and

Those signs of growing familiarity masked a rapidly developing intimacy. On 6 June 'O.R.' had sent Pound a *petit bleu* by the *Pneumatique*—Paris's system of sending messages written on blue paper by pneumatic tube between local post offices to be then delivered by messengers on bicycle— 'Mi rencusi tanto—ma impossibile per oggi'. They generally wrote to each other in Italian, and that was to say, 'So very sorry—not possible today'. On 6 July she sent another, 'Caro, Aspetto te . . . O.', 'Dear one, expecting you'. In August Olga and Ezra went walking together in the Dordogne, '25 kilometers a day with a rucksack', and visited Ventadour, Ussel, and villages pictured but not identified in Olga's 1923 photograph album.

Dorothy was with her mother at Lewiston Manor on 21 July, 'trying not to panic': 'I wonder how much of my life I ought to devote to her', she mused to Pound, 'I thought I was just evolving a little freedom.' By 9 August she knew that 'Father left everything to Olivia', who had said she would increase Dorothy's allowance. Shortly after that she was in Paris again. 'Our combined intake is now probably more than yours,' Pound told his mother at the end of August.

In mid-July he was 'rewriting the first three cantos; trying to weed out and clarify' for the 'edtn. de LOOKS'. 'I have now a sense of form that I hadn't in 1914,' he told Dorothy, and 'WITH sense of form, very difficult to get it all in'. He had a draft of the first three done by 1 August. He then wanted, in order to revise canto VI, a small booklet of historical documents about Henry Plantagenet and Louis VII of France which he had left with Agnes Bedford. Around 18–24 August he was working 'on 16th, i.e. 5th after Malatesta'—though he would be still working on that in October.

Nancy Cox McCormack who had been sculpting a portrait of Mussolini in Rome was in Paris again this summer and eager to pass on her impression that Il Duce was 'a creative force evolving and directing the beginnings of a renaissance'. Pound's interest was aroused. 'To clear up what I said the other day', he began a letter to her dated 15 August 1923,

---

other European cities and receiving excellent reviews. Antheil, when he first heard her play in 1923, considered her 'a consummate violinist . . . with [a] superb lower register of the D and G strings'. In the 1930s she had a small house in Venice; an apartment in a house at Sant' Ambrogio above Rapallo; and spent much time in Siena as Secretary of the Accademia Chigiana. She was a principal performer in the concerts Pound organized in Rapallo between 1933 and 1939; catalogued in 1936, at Pound's instigation, the 309 unedited instrumental pieces by Vivaldi in manuscript in Turin; co-founded the Centro di Studi Vivaldiani in Siena, and became a central figure in the Vivaldi revival. She was the mother of Pound's daughter, and their intimate relationship endured for nearly sixty years, though it was lived out in discreet privacy until his last decade. In her own last years she was cared for by their daughter at Schloss Brunnenburg in the Italian Tyrol.

it would be quite easy to make Italy the intellectual centre of Europe; and that by gathering ten or fifteen of the best writers and artists. . . . I shouldn't trust anyone's selection save my own. There is no use going into details until one knows if there is or could be any serious interest in the idea; that is to say, if the dictator *wants a corte letteraria*; if he is interested in the procedure of Sigismundo Malatesta in getting the best artists of his time into Rimini, a small city with no great resources. I know, in a general way, the fascio includes literature and the arts in its programme; that is very different from being ready to take specific action.

You have to avoid official personages, the deadwood of academies, purely pedagogical figures. The life of the arts is always concentrated in a very few individuals; they invent, and the rest follow, or adapt, or exploit.

Italy has an opportunity *now* . . . Germany is busted, England is too stupid, France is too tired to offer serious opposition; America is too far from civilization . . .

Pound had speculated, back in January 1915, that the Quattrocento renaissance had come about 'because the vortices of power coincided with the vortices of creative intelligence'. Now he was beginning to dream that the twentieth-century renaissance he had been looking for might flow from a coming together of Mussolini and himself. His efforts to arrange a meeting with Il Duce came to nothing, however. He would meet the man of power only once, and that not until January 1933, and then to no evident effect.

Young George Antheil came onto the Paris scene in June 1923, with a reputation from his recent German tour of causing 'uproars, fiascos, and hostile demonstrations', a reputation to recommend him to the Dada element, to Satie, and to Pound. He had come for the première of Stravinsky's *Les Noces*. Pound at once wanted to hear his music, and took him to Natalie Barney's to play hours of it for him on her piano. He was impressed by the 'demoniac temperament' apparent in the playing, and—prompted by Olga Rudge—asked him to compose a violin sonata or two for her. A brief notice in the *Chicago Tribune* of a concert on 11 December suggests his manner of playing: 'Hitting the piano keys with his wrist and palm as well as with his fingers, Mr George Antheil . . . drew from the instrument strange barbaric sounds and created a sensation'. He had set off 'a riot of enormous dimensions' in October when he performed three of his compositions— *Sonata sauvage*, *Airplane sonata*, and *Mechanisms*—as a curtain-raiser for the opening night of the Ballets Suédois at the Théâtre des Champs-Élysées. Pound would recall how the theatre 'turned into bedlam five minutes after Antheil was at the piano', and would hint that in the bedlam his own voice 'could be heard above all others [comparing] the intelligence of the French public to that of sucklings', while Satie sat next to him applauding. He would present Antheil as 'The Cagney of music', and write that he 'rose from an atmosphere of "gangsters", the "tough guy", the police hoodlum, perhaps the only composer today who has been able to become an "honorary member of the Paris police"…because of the warm sympathy he inspired, during a night of cheerful company with some characters out of a thriller, in the chief of the metropolitan police'.

More or less amusing, more or less boisterous riotousness following deliberate hard drinking was a feature of Paris in the 1920s, more especially on the part of the expatriate Americans and British. It is in the atmosphere, and is sometimes the main matter, of the Left Bank memoirs of the survivors; and it is a significant element in Hemingway's *Fiesta* (1927), in Scott Fitzgerald's *Tender is the Night* (1934), and in the early novels and stories of Jean Rhys. There were always dancing and drinking parties. Ford Madox Ford, while he was in Paris with Stella Bowen from September 1923, threw regular parties, and theirs are refracted in Jean Rhys's writings along with her ungrateful relationship with Ford. Then too there were always the cafés and bars. Writers and artists living in cheap hotels or cramped flats naturally did as Parisians do and met up there. Pound is occasionally noticed, in the Left Bank memoirs, in a group in a café; though more usually he is seen passing swiftly in the street by someone seated at a table. Jimmy the Barman of The Dingo, one of the centres of expatriate existence in *Fiesta,* had him down as a careful drinker, a 'white winer' who didn't touch the hard stuff.

Basil Bunting turned up in Paris that summer, young, broke, an original poet in the making, and sustained in that effort by the example of Pound's *Homage to Sextus Propertius.* He first saw Pound 'playing a swashbuckling kind of chess' in a café. Some time later he got himself 'locked up for a colossal drunk' during which he had mistaken his hotel, tried to break down the door to a room not his own, jumped into bed with the concierge, and rebelliously and with violence to a gendarme resisted arrest. Pound got to hear of this and found him next morning reading Villon amongst the night's catch 'of petty thieves, pickpockets, prostitutes, pimps' in the *grande salle* of the Paris court, where, as he was quite aware, Villon had awaited his trial. Having heard his story Pound rushed away to get him an *avocat.* A day or two later Bunting sent Pound a note, from 'Prison de la Santé, Don[jon] 9, Cellule 16', asking that it be said in his defence that the violence he admitted to; but as to the charge of 'Carrying arms', his knife was simply 'to sharpen my pencils & to cut bread & cheese when I eat my lunch in the Luxembourg or the Tuilleries'. He got two weeks, then worked as a barman at the Jockey Club until Pound introduced him to Ford and had him taken on as assistant editor and dogsbody for Ford's *transatlantic review.* Bunting would identify with Villon in the first of his poems to be preserved, 'Villon'

(1925), a 'sonata' upon his own imprisonments, primarily his imprisonment for refusing to bear arms in the late Great War.

Ford's new review, a monthly, had as its 'Administrateurs', Messieurs Ford, Pound, Quinn, and Bunting. It would run only from January to December of 1924, but would publish a good deal that would outlast its moment: Ford's own *Some Do Not*, the first part of *Parade's End*; versions of Pound's 'Kung' and 'Baldy Bacon' cantos; an extract from *Finnegans Wake*, Joyce's 'Work in Progress'; Gertrude Stein's *The Making of Americans*; stories by Hemingway—who succeeded Bunting as assistant editor in January, and did what he could to subvert Ford's internationalism by giving preference to Americans. The review was largely financed by John Quinn, who was photographed with Ford and Joyce (and the Diana) in the courtyard of 70*bis* in October of 1923. It was his only meeting with Joyce for whom he had done so much for so little thanks, and with Ford, and his last with Pound. He was already in pain from the undiagnosed cirrhosis which would kill him next July.

The combination of Antheil, a piano, and Pound tended not to make for harmony. It appears that Pound had a piano installed in his studio so that Antheil and Rudge could rehearse for their 11 December concert in the Salle du Conservatoire. They were to perform two pieces for unaccompanied violin by Pound, one his transcription of the twelfth-century melody of Faidit's 'Plainte pour la Mort du roi Richard Cœur de Lion', the other his own 'Sujet pour violin (resineux)'; and they were to première Antheil's first and second sonatas for violin and piano. A Bach gavotte would be played between Pound's pieces, and Mozart's 'Concerto en la majeur' between Antheil's—presumably in the spirit of 'compare and contrast'. Antheil's sonatas, according to Irving Schwerke writing in the *Chicago Tribune*, required 'strenuous exertions' on the part of both performers and 'imposed a severe strain on the naked tympanum', the 'copious draught of sound' being, for some, '"music" pure and absolute', for others 'degenerate noise and crash'. In the rehearsals in Pound's studio the 'noise and crash' dimension so disturbed the Swedish neighbours overhead that they complained to the police. To his father, Pound frankly admitted that 'George *was* making hell's own merry noise'. But when summoned before the Commissaire de Police, as he gleefully reported to William Bird,

> He discussed the sins of Scandinavians at length,
> also their propensities to dance above his head at three
> a.m.
>   he pointed out that the Scandinavians also had a
> piano, ils ne sont pas des musiciens mais ils

jouent au piano.
After some discussing M. le Commissaire wrote:
Monsieur répond qu'il est compositeur de musique
et qu'il est nécessaire qu'il fasse du bruit.
That he makes no more noise than habitually.

From which it would appear that Pound took upon himself Antheil's disturbing of the peace. There were no further proceedings.

That Pound, in his usual way, was engaged on several fronts that autumn is evident in his letters, particularly those to Dorothy. She was in England from 7 October until the end of November 1923, sorting out her parents' house with her mother, flat hunting with her, and accompanying her to stay with friends. On 20 October Pound reported: that he and Antheil were well on with their re-notation of *Le Testament*; that he had got his 'violin stunt into some sort of shape'; that O. had played through *Les Noces* for him; that Léger had approved the section of canto XVI dealing with his account of Verdun, and Steffens had filled in some troublesome details about Petrograd. He might have mentioned also his involvement in the editing of a 'vorticist film-experiment' to be called *Ballet mécanique* with Léger, Man Ray, Antheil, and Dudley Murphy. In November, from the 22nd to the 29th, specimen pages of the *de luxe* edition of the first sixteen cantos were on show at Shakespeare & Company. And 'Eliot turned up at 11 this a.m. on his way to 12 o'clock train'—this was on the 25th—'There is a chance of [his] leaving the bank in Feb. if Bel Esprit can be revived'. On 10 December Homer wrote, 'My Dear Son, . . . We would like to know who Olga is? . . . Now do tell us about OLGA??' But about Olga Pound was not forthcoming—he would say only that she had an aunt or an uncle living in Wyncote.

Ezra and Dorothy intended to leave Paris for Italy at the start of January 1924, but were delayed by Pound's suffering an attack of appendicitis and being rushed into the American hospital at Neuilly. He did not have to be operated on, however, and was out again on 6 January. 'Must stay on diet for a while', he wrote to Homer, 'Booked sleeper for Rapallo, tuesday a.m.', i.e. the 8th. The printer's setting copy for cantos I–VII and XII–XVI of *A Draft of XVI Cantos* is dated '6 Jan. 1924', indicating that he gave Bird the final version of those cantos either on the day he left hospital, or on the Monday, his last full day in Paris that winter.

They stayed in Rapallo, at the Hotel Mignon, or in the *albergo* at Monte Allegro 2,000 feet above the town, until about the middle of March, with Ezra feeling in need of a period of recuperation. There would be an important article on Antheil in the *Criterion* in April; and other material for *Antheil and the Treatise on Harmony* would be appearing in the *trans-atlantic review* over the coming months—though the 'Notes for Performers, by William Atheling, with Marginalia Emitted by George Antheil', were actually Agnes Bedford's selections from Atheling's *New Age* reviews. Pound appears to have been mainly resting, apart from composing a little music for violin.

Ezra and Olga were exchanging love notes. 'Darling...amor mio', 'mi spiace che non sei qui', that from Pound, 'I am sorry you aren't by me'. And from Olga, 'Caro—Inamoratissima', 'ti voglio vigliacco—e come!', 'I want you awfully, and how!' Towards the end of February Pound invited Olga to come to Rapallo, ostensibly for further work on *Le Testament*, and, there being no room next door at the Splendide, booked her into the Mignon 'for a few days'. Olga arrived, took in the situation, and immediately removed herself to the Monte Allegro *albergo*. After three days Pound sent up a message that he 'had the miseries' and wanted her, but was still too weak to climb the mountain; if she would walk down one day 'for tea and toast' after his game of tennis, he would walk part way back with her. She did not descend, so he had to climb up to her. After a week Dorothy followed; and Olga then left for Florence. Ezra and Dorothy remained up the mountain for a week or two before going back to the Mignon '& thence to interior'. Around 20 March Dorothy was writing from Rome to Ezra in Florence; and Pound was writing from Florence to his parents, 'Am here—in palazzo. with huge rooms & bath—Musicians treated better than poets'. He had just finished a 'new violin suite...for Olga's London concert', and had other music he wanted to do, but 'Am not yet well enough to work at long stretch'. He was still in Florence on 10 April when he told his parents he had lunched with Berenson. By 24 April Olga was in London for her concert, another Rudge–Antheil affair, on 10 May. After the concert Olivia Shakespear wrote to Dorothy that 'Ezra's things...were liked by those I spoke to'. (The critics, it has to be said, were not impressed by what they heard of his *Fiddle Music: First Suite*.) Olivia had taken Olga to lunch at her Club, and thought her 'a charming girl, and so pretty'.

Once Olga was out of the way Dorothy rejoined Pound in Florence, and they spent some time together in Perugia and Assisi, though at the end of May Dorothy was in Rome again, and Pound was in Rapallo on his way to Paris.

From Florence he wrote to Bird demanding the elimination of 'super-fluous rubbish' from Strater's designs, especially the 'love knot in lower right hand corner' of the initial page of 'The Fourth Canto', and the long tail on its capital P, and the extra scene across the top of the page. He had wanted Strater to be confined to the capitals, 'Restricted space to intensify

1. Rudge/Antheil Concert poster, Aeolian Hall, London, 10 May 1924.

output'. As to the extra work he was asking of Bird, 'As anybody who has ever made a good job of anything knows the last 2% of excellence takes more time than the other 98%. That's why art and commerce never savvy one another.'

While in Perugia he copied a number of secular songs from a fifteenth-century manuscript collection. In Assisi Dorothy was 'doing sketches of frescos in church here. & of mountains', while Pound was 'reading large work on the Este' of Ferrara. He would draw on that in cantos 20 and 24. By mid-May he was blocking out 'a few more cantos' and 'beginning to want typewriter again = sign of awakening energy'. He was asking Homer for the low-down on US presidents, anything he might have picked up in Washington or from his Congressman father, Thaddeus C. Pound, 'facts indicative of personality', such as 'Jefferson trying to get a gardener who cd. play the french horn in quartette after dinner'. That detail would go into canto 21, and some material Homer sent over would appear in canto 22. In June, when he was back in Paris, he mentioned that he 'had just summarized Marco Polo's note on Kublai Khan's issue of paper currency'—that would start off canto 18. By the end of August he would have 'another large wad of mss. for cantos, to go on with after Bill has got through printing the 16'.

When Pound got back to Paris on 1 June Williams was there, winding up a six-month sampling of the seductions of Europe—'Pagany' as he called it in his wonderfully self-affirming fantasy account of the trip. Pound introduced him to his Paris—to Léger and his art, to Brancusi in his studio, to Natalie Barney's salon, to Cocteau—and Williams, like one of Henry James's American pilgrims, steadfastly saw that there was nothing there for the autochthonous American genius. Pound wanted to talk about music, 'renaissance music, theory of notation, static "hearing", melody, *time*', and Williams as usual found it all suspect. He could credit Pound with an extraordinary sense of time, accruing from his fine ear for the musical phrase in verse, but remained convinced that he did not know one tone from another and had no natural musical ability or capability whatsoever. He wouldn't have believed that in his compositions for Olga's violin it was precisely the tones that could be got from the instrument that Pound was investigating.

Olga performed some of Pound's music at a private concert of 'Musique Américaine: (Declaration of Independence)' arranged by 'M. et Mme. Ezra Pound' in the Salle Pleyel on 7 July. On the programme were two of his renovations of fifteenth-century music from the Perugia manuscript, his *Fiddle Music: First Suite*, and a 'Fanfare' for violin and tambourine to provide an entrance for Antheil. Antheil's *Second Sonata for Violin and*

Piano was performed, and then the première of his *String Quartet*. Pound's pieces interested and pleased at least one critic, as specimens of 'horizontal' music. Antheil's, to another critic, provided 'a gargantuan feast of cacophonies'. Williams was not in the audience, having elected to go champagne-tasting that weekend with William Bird who was a connoisseur of fine wine as of fine printing. But Joyce and Sylvia Beach and the two editors of the *Little Review* and Hemingway were there. Many in the audience, it was reported, went on immediately to the Dôme, their nerves in a shaken condition from 'Mr Antheil's hammer-blows on the piano'.

Shortly after the concert Dorothy was in London with her mother, now at 34 Abingdon Court W8, to the south of Kensington High Street. Pound took himself off for a walking tour in the region of the Puy-de-Dôme, based on Ussel and visiting Châtelguyon for its 'intestinal waters'. Back in Paris on 31 July he wrote to Dorothy that he was much better for the walk, 'First day I was sickish, next day better, and then began to eat two large meals daily.' A few days later he was hoping it was 'not a bad sign' that he was 'taking pleasure in digestion'. On 15 August he reported that a 'general survey at hospital' had revealed that his appendix had gone down to nothing and he was perfectly well, but still too high-strung. His 'general malaise' was due to other causes. Dorothy responded with sympathy, and observed that he need not do any heavy work, only his cantos. Towards the end of August he did another walking trip, this time for six days in the Vienne around Poitiers. On this one at least Olga was with him. After it he told his parents, 'My health seems OK at last.' Dorothy wrote that she had been thinking of Italy for September, but 'I shall keep my plans as fluid as possible ... until I can definitely settle ... I imagine it makes no difference to you?' At the beginning of September she wrote that she was about to return to Paris, if that would not put him out; and Pound replied in his customary third person and with their ritual cat greeting, 'Mao | He will be glad to see her. Will be at [Gare du] Nord at 4.5.'

They had decided to give up the studio at 70*bis* and move permanently to Italy, departing early October. Pound had had 'a special book case trunk constructed' in July with a view to that move, and in August he had been disposing of unwanted books and periodicals. Olivia joined them in Paris on the 8th, and would be with them in Rapallo for the first month or so.

In their final fortnight there was a distraction. The 'melancholy man' who lived across their courtyard and played better chess than Pound, an American poet and opium addict by the name of Ralph Cheever Dunning, fell ill and had no one to look after him, so Pound was kept busy taking the delirious poet to hospitals and finding doctors and dealers. His last act was to buy a cold-cream jar of raw opium from a Cherokee chief on the avenue de l'Opéra and leave it with Hemingway to give to Dunning if there was another emergency. Hemingway tells the story in *A Moveable Feast* as an instance of the great kindness Pound was capable of. (He also says that when the emergency did arise a deranged Dunning threw the jar back at him, and followed it up with several accurately aimed milk-bottles.) Pound's reward was to discover that Dunning, though 'not in the movement', had written 'a very fine book of poems during the last year' which he recommended to Liveright before leaving Paris.

He had gone to Paris in 1921, he said in an interview in 1956, because the life of the mind was there then, and the life of the literary mind in particular. But after 1924 the life of the mind was no longer in literature, 'It was in thinking about civic order'—'and nobody in Paris was doing any of that'. Italy had become the interesting place to be.

2 : FROM RAPALLO, 1924–1932

Human complications

Olga Rudge wanted to conceive Ezra's child; the more so, she would record in her later years, because Dorothy would not have a child. In mid-November 1924 she wrote in her diary, 'piantato un figlio', a son planted, though it would be a daughter she would give birth to the following July. Then, fifteen months after that, in September 1926, Dorothy did have a child, a son, but not by Ezra. He observed these 'awkward human complications', and refused to let them disturb his concentration on composing cantos. What he wanted was to conceive a vital form of mind and to impregnate at least America with it.

For the next twenty years he would be working at that from Italy. He had been 'rejuvinated by 15 years in going to Paris', he told Lewis, and had now 'added another ten of life, by quitting same'. He told his father that 'the north side of the alps is an error, useful only to make one glad to get to this side'. Rapallo in mid-October was 'empty and tranquil'; the sun was warm; he played tennis, having bought a new racquet; he loafed, and 'D. bathed in the gulf yesterday'. Someone at the tennis club offered to build them a house, but he did not 'want to settle just yet'. They had taken an extra room at the Mignon; and just about everything they needed, 'save the clavicord and a few woiks of Aht', was contained in their trunks and suitcases and the travelling book case. 'Racquet, typewriter, bassoon' were the 'necessaries' he thought worth mentioning. More cantos were on the way, with 18 and 19 in draft in November.

In mid-December they went down to Sicily and toured around over the next two months with a view to settling there. It had its interest, they decided, but wasn't a place for them to live. Dorothy found plenty to paint, including an apparently passive Etna from Taormina, but the fleas made it hard to find somewhere to paint from. Yeats and his wife joined them for a couple of weeks in January. He and Pound tried out the acoustic of 'the old out-of-door Greek theatre in Siracusa', and Pound annoyed him by bellowing Sappho's Greek and refusing 'to spout English poesy', because the

64

'English verse wasn't CUT'. In Palermo Pound borrowed Yeats's typewriter and 'typed to the end of XX'. He mentioned having got so far in a letter to Dr Saunders at Hamilton College. Saunders had wondered if he might return to America to lecture or as a visiting professor, and Pound was telling him there would not be enough money in that to warrant the loss of time. He thought he 'ought to stick at' his long poem, having for the moment 'a certain amount of leisure & uninterruptedness to go on with' it.

In mid-February Pound was in Rome, and so too was Olga. Between her concert engagements they visited the zoo and looked at the lions until Olga expected their child would turn out to be a *leoncino*, a lion cub. Pound apparently 'had a phobia' against getting her a wedding ring, though when he was back in Rapallo he changed his mind about that, for appearance's sake. He was at once supporting Olga in having the child, and maintaining the distance respectability demanded. She, accepting that, was seeking somewhere discreetly to lie up or to die in, as she put it, and wondering under what law it might be best to have the child, French, Swiss, or Italian. Pound advised against Monte Carlo because the US immigration quota for persons born in France could make it difficult to get into America in the case of war; but then, he added, there might not be another war 'for forty years'. While in Rome he wrote to his mother that he was doing 'a little general reading for the Florentine canto'; and he told his father that he was acting for the inventor of a new type of locomotive and wanted Homer to see if 'Baldwins' could be interested in buying it—it would depend on whether they could 'buck the coal interest by a better type of non coal burning engine'. 'Study the two last cantos I sent you', he urged, referring to the anecdotes of the ways of big business in XVIII and XIX.

He wrote to Olga from the Mignon on 4 March to ask her to find out the make of the electric heater in the friends' apartment she had been lent in Rome. He and Dorothy were 'In act of taking apartment, plumb on roof on sea front'. The address on the notepaper he had printed was 'Via Marsala 12, int. 5'—their flat was on the fifth floor, at the top. There were a hundred steps or more to climb—it was in the contract that the lift did not work—but the small apartment's narrow rooms gave on to a broad rooftop terrace looking south over the hill-enclosed bay to the open sea. At first they went on taking their meals at the Mignon, for 'about 8 or 9 [dollars] a week, each'; but they soon settled into the routine of eating in the sociable café-restaurant of the Albergo Rapallo on the ground floor of the building. 'Via Marsala 12, int. 5', the flat on the roof above the Albergo, was to be the Pounds' 'permanent locale' until they were evicted along with the other sea-front residents by the German military in 1943.

The cantos continued. By 25 March Pound had 'typed out most of seven cantos, taking it up to XXIII'. April was 'mostly borasco'—the blustering cold wind from the north—'very annoying as nothing to do but tennis'. About this time a new magazine called *This Quarter* and published in Paris dedicated its first number to '*EZRA POUND* who by his creative work, his editorship of several magazines, his helpful friendship for young and unknown artists, his many and untiring efforts to win better appreciation of what is first-rate in art, comes first to our mind as meriting the gratitude of this generation'. However, Pound failed to praise the young editors in return and the dedication was withdrawn in the third number. At the beginning of June he told Agnes Bedford that he had just been on a 'two weeks chase' through Rimini, Cesena, San Leo, and Bologna. He didn't say what he had been after, but that would have been when he had the handsomely bound *A Draft of XVI Cantos* celebrated as 'a CAPOLAVORO magnifico', a majestic masterpiece, by the Fascist Commandante dalla Piazza in Rimini, and when he personally presented a copy to the Malatestine library in Cesena.

Olga Rudge, meanwhile, had been waiting out her time in Sirmione, trying to avoid acquaintances and gossip. 'She hasn't been so bored', she wrote to Pound in their usual impersonal style, 'since she was in her teens and nothing ever seemed to happen.' 'Where OFFICIALLY is she', Pound asked, 'I feel the reports shd. coincide.' They needed to devise a cover story, in particular for Antheil who was organizing lucrative and prestigious concerts in America and could not understand why she would not commit herself. In early June Olga moved to Bressanone-Brixen in the Alto Adige and arranged to give birth in the hospital there. Then there was the problem of the name to go on the birth certificate for the father. It could not be 'Ezra Pound' since he was married to someone not the mother, and 'N. N.' for no name would brand the child for life. So Olga made up a marriage to one Arthur, the name of her brother killed in the war, and when Maria Rudge was born on 9 July 1925 she was declared for official purposes to be 'figlia di Arturo'.

Olga informed Pound that she had given birth to a '[leon]cin*a*', and he received the news with enthusiasm. It appears though that she had no clear idea of what to do with the child she had so much wanted. She was determined to resume her career as a violinist and could not, would not, look after the baby and bring it up herself, 'having no talent that way'. Leaving it in a local orphanage seemed a way out, that was if the child survived. After ten days she wrote to Pound that she had not expected him to come, only 'if you would like to see the child you had perhaps better come as it will probably not live—there is very little left of it . . . it just doesn't catch on'. It would have been different, she was told, if she had consented to nurse. Then came the turn of fortune. 'There is a contadina here whose child has died—who can nurse it a few weeks at least . . . I think it will go if it only gets a start—it looks very grim and determined.' Maria was given into the care of the farming woman, Frau Johanna Marcher, and did begin to thrive. Pound arrived; the child, Frau Marcher, and her farm at Gais near Bruneck were approved; and it was settled that Maria would be fostered and brought up by the Marchers in the Pustertal mountain valley. Her parents would visit from time to time, descending like gods from their mysterious heaven with gifts and ordinances; but throughout her childhood it was, according to her own matchless account, her peasant Mamme and Tatte who nourished, loved, and formed her with generative humanity and wisdom.

In September Olga was in Florence, doing serious exercises and dancing to recover her figure, and practising to resume playing at concert standard. On the 14th Pound mentioned to his parents that it was 'D's birthday . . . 9 new plants fer the roof; funny lookin articles; not my province, herbage'. They had visitors through from Paris, Natalie Barney and Romaine Brookes, and Nancy Cunard. In October Dorothy and Olivia Shakespear went off to Perugia and Florence; while Pound went to Milan, to Modena for the Este library, and then on to Venice. From Venice he wrote to Dorothy that there were letters for her there, sent on no doubt with his from Rapallo, including 'one from Egypt'. Olga sent him some Edelweis from the mountains and reported that 'la mia leoncinina' was doing well. She was in Paris through November and her concert on the 30th, as Pound heard from Natalie Barney, was 'crowded and successful'.

'Canti XXII to XXIII are about finished', Pound told his mother at the end of October, 'Am going on to XXIV etc.' At the end of November he was thinking of cutting up his *Villon* for a concert performance—he would become caught up over the next two or three months in thoroughly revising the score. He was also preparing for Liveright a definitive edition 'of all Ezra Pound's poems except the unfinished "Cantos"', but 'throwing out . . . the "soft" stuff, and the metrical exercises'. The latter, he confessed, were 'what I once bluffed myself into believing were something more than exercises but which no longer convince me that I had anything to say when I wrote 'em; or anything but a general feeling that it wuz time I wrote a pome'. *Personae: The Collected Poems of Ezra Pound* would appear, handsomely printed on good paper, in December 1926, with a second printing in February 1927, a third in January 1930, and a fourth in May 1932. The poet was becoming known and appreciated for what he had put behind him.

Dorothy Pound sailed from Genoa for Cairo on the *Esperia* about 10 December, and was met there by 'R'. Ezra was expecting Olga in Rapallo on the 11th—she would be with him for Christmas—and Eliot came for four days, having 'at last escaped from Lloyds' Bank'. To divert him Olga 'played him the Bach Chaconne before breakfast', and Pound took him to tea with Max Beerbohm. Dorothy, writing to Ezra from the ship, affected a footloose and fancy free gaiety; but in a letter from Cairo on the 20th she wrote, 'At the heart of all this, I have had a couple of quarts d'heures of tragedy—which I knew I should find.' 'I hope you are all right', she ended, 'warm and not in too much confusion?'

Pound had workmen in to decorate their flat in February, apparently because Olga had told him he *ought* to have it done up. He told her that he had 'at last thought out a decorative scheme that he trusts will satisfy her fastidious taste'. In his letters to his father he mentioned more than once, as if not knowing what else to say about her being in Cairo, that Dorothy 'seems to be enjoying pyramids'. He had received from her 'one oriental drapery...emitting THE most enormous and foul stench of mice', and had hung the shawl out on the terrazzo hoping 'it will have disinfected itself by the time D. gets back'. It was still stinking though when Dorothy returned on 1 March, 'somewhat worn by trip; or at least dessicated with Egypt'. She was 'half ill' for some weeks after getting back, and for that reason, Pound explained to Olga, he was unable to get to Milan to see her. 'Troppo incommodo. Sorry.', he had wired, to which she replied, 'She is not pleased'. It might be his idea that a '*maîtresse convenable*' should be 'a convenient mistress', but it was not hers. She confessed to 'a coup de désespoir' when he wouldn't come; but then passed that off as perhaps an effect from 'noting Muss's acquisitions' in an exhibition in Milan. She 'thoroughly understands', she wrote in fierce submission, 'that <u>nothing</u> <u>ever</u> must be done to compromise him in the eyes of the U. T. C.', the Rapallo tennis club. In the midst of that exchange Pound wrote in a notebook: '24/3/1926 // There exist paradisal states | not death their portal | nor death in them...'.

Their letters resumed their usual topics: his music, her concerts; private jokes—as about the lioness who escaped from a circus and walked through Alessandria; news of Ford who had been in Rapallo, and had there received information he needed to complete 'crucial part of the final spasm of Tietjens', that is, exactly what it was that drove Tietjens mad in *A Man Could Stand Up—*. In April he wrote that he had nine cantos more or less finished—they would have been 17 to 25—'but they don't make a vollum'. He went on, 'She suggest a nice simple and continuous subjeck of UNIVERSAL INTEREST, to run from 26 to 33,' which would imply that he had it in mind to match the first major division of Dante's one hundred cantos.

In mid-May he mentioned to his mother that he had 'just been down to Rome for four days, heard a lot of modern moozik'. In fact he had gone down for a concert in which Olga Rudge and the pianist Alfredo Casella played music by Satie and Ravel, and Pound's own 'Homage Froissart', a piece for violin and piano he had completed in February at Livorno. By the end of May Olga and the Pounds were all three in Paris, Olga in the apartment her father still leased for her at 2 rue Chamfort on the Right Bank, and Dorothy and Ezra on the Left Bank in the Hôtel-Restaurant Foyot, rue de Tournon, just down from the Palais du Luxembourg. In June there was the riot of Antheil's *Ballet mécanique* on the 19th; then on the 29th the concert performance of *Le Testament*, with Olga Rudge violin, before an audience invited by M. et Mme. Ezra Pound.

The Pounds stayed on in Paris through August and September. On 11 September Pound wrote, 'Dear Dad | next generation (male) arrived. | Both D. and it appear to be doing well.' That was the first his parents knew of any 'next generation'. It was Hemingway who had gone with Dorothy to the American hospital at Neuilly; but the next day Pound went to the Mairie there to register, 'sur déclaration du père', the birth of Pound, Omar, on 10 September 1926, to Ezra Pound, man of letters, and his wife Dorothy Shakespear. Omar would also be registered as a US citizen. On the 27th Pound himself was in the hospital, and sent Olga a note: 'Have had small operation—My fambly leave hospital today about 2.30. He would be pleased to see her.' He remained in the hospital for a week, having 'all the possible taps, tests, analyses etc.', and being told there was nothing wrong with him. He was just 'completely exhausted' and worn out, and was still in that state when he was back in Rapallo in October and 'Damn glad' to be there.

It had been arranged that Omar would be looked after for the time being in Paris by Raymonde Collignon whom Pound had known as a young singer in London, and that Olivia would informally 'adopt' her grandchild in England. The following June Dorothy, with a nurse to accompany her, fetched him from Paris and placed him in the Norland Institute and Nurseries, 11 Pembridge Square, near Kensington Gardens. 'Omar's *eyes* give the show away *badly*', she told Pound, 'heaven help us'. Later the boy would live with a retired Norland nurse in the village of Felpham near Bognor Regis on the Sussex coast. Dorothy would spend time with him on her summer visits to England, but otherwise would be a rather absent parent. Young Omar would see his legal father only once, or possibly twice, until after 1945.

Pound had sufficiently recovered from his 'exhaustion' in November to be thinking of bringing out a magazine of his own, to be known as *The Exile*.

'Do you favour excluding all women writers?', he asked Olga. His letters to her were all about her concert engagements and how she should be promoting her career, about the state of the sea and the weather in Rapallo, and about where he had got to with his cantos. He was with her in Rome in December, and again in February when she performed for Mussolini in private. In time the arrangement was that they would be together, usually in Venice, while Dorothy was away in England. Dorothy made it clear that she didn't 'see much fun in being alone in Rap. for long', and especially did not fancy being stuck there while Ezra was away with Olga. Otherwise she seemed complaisant about their continuing relationship. The Rapallo apartment was adorned now with the Gaudier sculptures— 'Cat and Water Carrier contemplating the marble Embracers'—and with their Lewis and Gaudier drawings. Later there was the clavichord too, and eventually the Gaudier 'Hieratic Head of E.P.' would be mounted on the terrace, its stone eyes fixed upon the ever-varying sea.

In these years at the end of the 1920s Pound was trying to persuade Olga to accept him as a 'somewhat functional' being, that is, as concerned only with the WORK in hand, and as NOT interested in personal feelings, neither his own nor those of others. When she was depressed about her playing or about never knowing when she might see him he would tell her, 'I do not think life is possible if you stop to consider peoples' personal feelings'; and besides, if he had the energy to reply to her desperate letters 'he wd. putt it into his job'. 'You have a set of values I don't care a damn for', he wrote to her at a critical moment in their relations, 'I do not care a damn about private affairs, private life, personal interests'. He simply had no use and could see no use for the personal and the subjective at this time.

That dismissal or denial of 'personal feelings' would go some way to explaining the personal predicament he had got himself into. In time it would prove to be the tragic flaw by which he would be undone in his private life. He had held to the conviction—it had appeared fundamental to his constitution—that the individual should be untrammelled by social conventions or by narrow-minded laws. Yet he was now bound by law to recognize as his own the child that was not his; while in law he could not be recognized as the father of his own child. The consequent inner conflict, and his inability to acknowledge let alone resolve it, precisely because it was profoundly personal and subjective, could well account for the state of exhaustion he was in around the time of Omar's birth.

To keep up appearances, for Dorothy's sake probably, his passionate relationship with Olga had to be hidden—though only the indifferent would have been unaware of it. That he had a daughter he was proud of had to be kept secret—it was some years before his own father found out, years more before his mother was told. Nothing could be allowed to disturb the bland conventional perception of the devotedly married Mr and Mrs Ezra Pound. Charles Norman was told by Mrs Willard Trask how she was struck by them at a dinner given by Ford in Paris in 1930. Pound was 'very American, talking like an American, somewhat pompous', while Dorothy was 'absolutely beautiful, beautiful with authentic beauty', and 'such a lady'. The Pounds had sat 'side by side on the sofa', and 'looked devoted'. That devotion, however, would have depended upon their leaving personal feelings aside. 'The only reason people can live near each other is because they let each other ALONE,' Pound had asserted to Olga.

Ford had said to the Trasks 'that Pound had told him once that Dorothy was the only woman he had ever met who could say *anything*, and it "would be all right, she was such a lady"'. Evidently Dorothy could *do* anything too and it would be all right, because she could do it with perfect manners and without showing any disturbing emotion. She could cuckold her husband, apparently with premeditation and cool determination, and in a manner which rather violently contravened the principles and the prejudices of her class. ('A touch of the tarbrush', people would signal to each other when Omar's eyes gave the show away.) Pound may have been confused, confused even to the point of inner exhaustion, by her doing it without any apparent alteration of affection. But it had to be all right by his principle of not taking personal feelings into account, and of allowing others to do whatever they had to do provided they made no emotional demands upon him.

Even so, it was perhaps an error on his part to pay no attention to what might have driven Dorothy to act as she had. Given her previous determination not to have a child, and given the conventions by which she lived, it might have occurred to him that she had acted out of furious hurt and outrage, and that this child, conceived, to all appearances, in reaction to Olga's having his child, was intended to cancel out that other child. There were the makings here of a Greek tragedy, only it would prove to be a tragedy in which the Fury wore the mask of the perfect lady, and in which the flawed hero would accept his fate without protest or self-pity, as if in a state of godlike detachment.

Saving the world by pure form

In the autumn of 1927 Pound was busy about many things. In September he sent off the twenty-seventh canto to John Rodker for his de luxe *A Draft of the Cantos 17–27*, and was already blocking in 28–30. He was making a 'new American version' of the 'testament' of Confucius, the *Ta Hio*—that went off in November to be published by the University of Washington Book Store in Seattle. He was trying to get together his thinking on Great Bass, or 'how to RHYTHM', and his thinking about the aesthetics of engineering machines; and he was studying the philosophy behind Guido Cavalcanti's poems. He was writing 'How to Read', a new *Poetics*, 'the summa of all I have learned about literchoor'. He was editing his own little magazine, *The Exile*. And he had time to converse with Joseph Bard about the meaning of the word *paideuma* in the work of Leo Frobenius, the German anthropologist; to play daily tennis, sometimes up to six sets in a session; and to go to the cinema—Rapallo by then had three, and Pound could 'carry dissipation to THE howling limit, i.e. leaving bad one and finish the serrata at the other'.

Running through that seeming miscellany of activities was a constant preoccupation with the inner, shaping forms of things. This was not a new preoccupation, of course. The *Imagiste* complex and the dynamic forms of Vorticism were directed to the shaping of the mind and its world. But now Pound was concerning himself more explicitly with the forms of social and political life, as with the organization of work in a machine-shop, and of individuals in the state. He had always had the conviction, even in his idealizing youth, that the forms of art had, or should have, a social function, even a biological function. 'Art for life's sake', was his cry, never 'art for art's sake'. Now he was seeking to engage his art with the public life of his time.

At the end of 1926 he had written to the editors of *New Masses*, an American Communist-affiliated magazine, saying that he had read five numbers 'with a good deal of care', and was prepared to be further educated by them, specifically on such matters as labour struggles, the Russian Revolution, and US dollar diplomacy. The editors headed his letter, over-hopefully, 'POUND JOINS THE REVOLUTION!' He did then contribute an article on how the workers on the factory floor might so orchestrate the noise of their machines as to give rhythm to their day and thus free themselves from the condition of robots. But he also sent a letter in which he protested against Hugo Gellert's mistaking Brancusi for an 'art for art's sake' aesthete just because his work was detached from wars and politics. Brancusi, he declared, 'is trying to save the world by pure form'. To which Gellert replied in mockery, '"to save the world by pure form..." Tra la.' He didn't want to know, and Pound didn't stop to explain, just how art which 'has no political opinion' could 'save the world'.

Pound's most revealing remark on that occasion was probably the extraordinary statement that 'Art is part of biology'. That would have been intended to set art apart from political arguments and abstract ideas, and to set it with the genetic processes which sustain, conserve, and evolve individual and social organisms. In thus identifying art with the formative processes by which we live Pound might well have had in mind what de Gourmont had written about instinct in *Physique de l'amour*. Taking as an example the sphex, an insect which instinctively paralyses 'with three perfectly placed stabs the cricket which is to feed its larvae', de Gourmont argued that the 'genius' which enables the insect to do this must be 'the sum of intellectual acquisitions slowly crystallised in the species'; or, as Pound later paraphrased it, 'After the intellect has worked on a thing long enough the knowledge becomes faculty—There is one immediate perception or capacity to act instead of a mass of ratiocination.' That was what Pound now wanted art to be doing, to be crystallizing useful intelligence into instinct, habit, custom, and tradition.

He found support for his thinking in the work of Leo Frobenius, particularly in Frobenius' concept of the *paideuma* of a people or a culture. Pound understood that term to mean 'the mental formation, the inherited habits of thought, the conditionings, aptitudes of a given race or time'; and these as 'the active element in the era, the complex of ideas which is in a given time germinal, reaching into the next epoch, but conditioning actively all the thought and action of its own time'. A particular instance, in the case of America at the time of its revolution, would be the conviction that 'All men are born free and equal'. The accumulated intelligence of enough people, crystallized in that formulation, had come to command instinctive assent and so had become an active principle in the conduct of the nation's affairs.

For his own time, Pound declared in one of his editorial notes in *The Exile*, 'the organizing thought is concerned with the emergence or the resurgence of the idea of a cooperative state', that is, one constituted of consenting and cooperating individuals. The '18th century', by which he evidently meant what came to be called the French Enlightenment, had found 'the formula for the right amount of individual liberty compatible with civilized institutions: The right to do anything "*que ne nuit pas aux autres*"', anything that does no harm to others. Now, in 1928, 'We need possibly another fifty years of hard thought (and a lot of people busy at it) to find the true equation for the extent of state power compatible with civilization'. He noted that there was the 'soviet *idea*', as expressed in making banking a state monopoly; and the 'Fascist idea' as expressed in holding individuals in government responsible. Those, he said, were 'interesting phenomena'; but his preferred idea, the one he was promoting in *The Exile*, was that 'The republic, the res publica means, or ought to mean "the public convenience".' He would put that on his letterhead, '*Res publica: the public convenience*'. It was a variant of the idea of 'government *for* the people', and projected a government which both safeguarded the rights of the individual by its social justice, and served the common good through its public works—well-constructed buildings, roads, intelligent afforestation—and through fostering useful scientific discoveries and enduring works of art. Judged by these measures, however, the modern 'capitalist imperialist state'—and it was clearly the American state that was foremost in Pound's mind—'will not bear comparison with the feudal order; with the small city states both republican and despotic'. Instead of being a convenience, therefore, it is 'an infernal nuisance'.

For a model of the cooperative state Pound looked away to Confucian China, and to its governing idea as formulated in the *Ta Hio*, a work which he had translated, he said in 1927, in order to remedy 'the present state of national and international imbecility'. He introduced his 1945 version with this note:

Starting at the bottom as market inspector, having risen to be Prime Minister, Confucius is more concerned with the necessities of government, and of govern-mental administration than any other philosopher. He had two thousand years of documented history behind him which he condensed so as to render it useful to men in high official position . . .

His analysis of why the earlier great emperors had been able to govern greatly was so sound that every durable dynasty, since his time, has risen on a Confucian design and been initiated by a group of Confucians. China was tranquil when her rulers under-stood these few pages. When the principles here defined were neglected, dynasties waned and chaos ensued. The proponents of a world order will neglect at their peril the study of the only process that has repeatedly proved its efficiency as social coordinate.

That is a remarkable recommendation given that, generally speaking, a *paideuma* would be culture-specific—it would be 'the aptitudes of a given race or time'; yet Pound evidently considered the Confucian *paideuma* to be of universal utility, unlike the American Constitution or the Christian Ten Commandments.

Even more remarkable, when we come to consider the first chapter of the *Ta Hio* which is thought to preserve Confucius' own words, is how few pages he needed to hold the crystallized intelligence of those two thousand years of documented history. It all comes down to seven brief paragraphs which set out, not the abstract principles of good government, but rather the method or process necessary to bring about good government. The development of a certain kind of intelligence is the key, specifically the intelligence which 'increases through the process of looking straight into one's own heart and acting on the results', and which is at the same time 'rooted in watching with affection the way people grow'. In its more advanced formulation the process is a continuous loop with constant feedback:

The men of old wanting to clarify and diffuse throughout the empire that light which comes from looking straight into the heart and then acting, first set up good government in their own states; wanting good government in their states, they first established order in their own families; wanting order in the home, they first disciplined themselves; desiring self-discipline they rectified their own hearts; and wanting to rectify their hearts, they sought precise verbal definitions of their inarticulate thoughts [the tones given off by the heart]; wishing to attain precise verbal definitions, they set to extend their knowledge to the utmost. This completion of knowledge is rooted in sorting things into organic categories.

When things had been classified in organic categories, knowledge moved toward fulfilment; given the extreme knowable points, the inarticulate thoughts were defined with precision [the sun's lance coming to rest on the precise spot verbally]. Having attained this precise verbal definition [aliter, this sincerity], they then stabilized their hearts, they disciplined themselves; having attained self-discipline, they set their own houses in order; having order in their own homes, they brought good government to their own states; and when their states were well governed, the empire was brought into equilibrium.

From the Emperor, Son of Heaven, down to the common man, singly and all together, this self-discipline is the root.

That is the Confucian *paideuma* in its pure form, stripped of all particulars. There are no commands to do this and not do that; no indications of specific rights and wrongs; no moral teachings or required rites; no guidance at all on the practicalities of living and governing.

The only definite value is that there should be order throughout the empire. But then that would be not just any order, certainly not an order imposed from above or by force. It would be one which comes about when all the things of which the empire is constituted are in order; and that would be when all things are attuned to the individual heart's tones. However, to translate that into the Christian principle of individual conscience would be misleading; and to associate it with Western individualism would be quite wrong. There is no suggestion of a Holy Spirit prompting the Confucian heart; nor is there any suggestion that the individual should be fulfilling his or her personal desires. No value is being accorded to the private life or to personal feelings and interests. The orientation of the Confucian *paideuma* is altogether away from the individual and towards the common good. The heart that is rectified in the process of intelligence grows to know and to be at one with others and with its world; and it thus comes to desire not its own private ends but the good of all. 'Know and act thyself' grows into 'know and act according to the truth of all that you can know'.

It could be that in commending this Confucian ethic to the American and European 'proponents of a world order' Pound intended that it should act as a corrective to the contradictions and excesses of their individual-centred, Christian-sanctioned, and notionally democratic culture; a corrective, that is, to its making the individual everything, and nothing; to its putting private profit before public benefit, and putting corporate and national self-interest above considerations of natural justice and natural law. The challenge was even more radical than that, however, a challenge not merely to the democracies' failures to live up to their idea but to the very foundations of that idea. The Confucian ethic has no place for any divine authority or revelation; nor does it vest authority in the state. And while it looks to the individual heart as the source of order, the desired order is not of or by or for the individual person, but of and by and for the whole people in harmony with the Cosmos. In canto 52 Pound will express that as 'the abundance of nature | with the whole folk behind it'. Its order would be, if it were ever to be realized, one form of totalitarianism.

It would not be the same as the totalitarian regimes of the twentieth century, Soviet Communism, Italian Fascism, and German National Socialism; ideally, indeed, it would be their opposite, since power would genuinely be with the whole people. But it probably would be anathema to the European and American democracies, because it did not value the individual person for his or her own sake. Yet Pound, who would define himself as a Jeffersonian democrat, would also practise that Confucian discipline. In Western terms, he would cultivate a mind attuned not to the human personality but to the Cosmos, to the ordered totality of the vital universe. He would be of a mind with Osiris, or Dionysos.

To be of such a mind means to see the world and to articulate one's vision of it in ways that are strange to European thought. It means of course de-centring the 'I', the subjective, self-regarding self. Then it means, as Fenollosa observed in his essay on *The Chinese Written Character as a Medium for Poetry*, concentrating the attention upon particular, concrete things, and seeing them as acting themselves, or acting the forces that pulse through them; and then as acting upon and interacting with other things. It means seeing the natural processes going on in and through everything we take in, and going on too within ourselves. An adequate articulation of that vision must involve preserving the specific qualities of things while presenting them in their multilateral relations and interactions—in a total vision such as canto II is working towards.

That way of thinking which respects and seeks to follow the processes of nature both within and around us is quite contrary to the method which has made European thought so efficient in its determination to master nature. This was Darwin at work:

When we see leaf-eating insects green, and bark-feeders mottled grey; the alpine ptarmigan white in winter, the red grouse the colour of heather, we must believe that these tints are of service to these birds in preserving them from danger.

So he proceeded by logic and reason from the particulars towards the general law of the survival of the fittest, and in the process refined out everything his eye had observed. The abstraction he was left with proved immensely powerful, but at the cost of removing the mind from the rich complexity of his birds and insects.

Pound deprecated such 'talk of science as if it were a desiccation not an enrichment', but then he was looking to science to provide 'ways of thinking and thought instruments' that would be adequate to the rich complexities of things. In the fourth and last number of *The Exile* he wrote:

We continue with thought forms and with language structures used by monolinear mediaeval logic, when the aptitudes of the human mind developed in course of bio-chemical studies have long since outrun such simple devices. By which I mean that the biologist can often know and think clearly a number of things he can not put in a simple sentence; he can dissociate things for which there is as yet no dissociated language structure.

And writing, he went on, should no longer pretend 'that it cannot think (or express) perfectly comprehensible things that don't happen to fit the syllogism'. In a related note he insisted that 'Familiarity with the perceived complex of visual or sensuous data...must inevitably beget something more apt for its conveyance than is the simple monolinear sentence'. The challenge was to devise a 'sentence' that would hold together in the mind several things at once, or several aspects of a thing, without reasoning them into some single idea or line of argument. By 1930 he had become confident that 'We are as capable or almost as capable as the biologist of thinking thoughts that join like spokes in a wheel-hub and that fuse in hyper-geometric amalgams.' That was the form of sentence he was then constructing in his cantos, a sentence that was in the Confucian mode, and definitely not Aristotelian or Scholastic.

It was a mode of writing and a form of art designed to accord with the Confucian *paideuma*, that is, a mode and a form which would be true, not to an abstract idea, a theory, or an ideology, but to 'human consciousness and the nature of man', and to 'the motions of "the human heart"'; and which would thus feed the mind, biologically, 'as *nutrition of impulse*'.

A sextant for 'A Draft of XXX Cantos'

A Draft of XXX Cantos, with initials in her Vorticist style by D[orothy] S[hakespear] P[ound], was published by Nancy Cunard at her Hours Press in Paris in August 1930, in an edition of 212 copies. It brought together and superseded John Rodker's *A Draft of the Cantos 17–27* 'with Initials in red and black ink by Gladys Hynes', published in London in September 1928 in an edition of 101 copies, and William Bird's *A Draft of XVI Cantos of Ezra Pound for the Beginning of a Poem of some Length now first made into a Book* 'with Initials by Henry Strater', published in Paris at his Three Mountains Press on the Île Saint-Louis in January 1925 in an edition of 90 copies.

All but six of the cantos had appeared in magazines—the exceptions being 14, 15, 16, 21, 25, and 26. Pound had wanted the hell cantos, 14 and 15, to be read with other cantos in order to bring them into proportion, and he may have felt the same about 16. The other three, dealing with Medici and Venetian matters, were completed by early September of 1927, up against Rodker's deadline but still with time for magazine publication if Pound had wanted that. Apparently he did not, and again he may not have cared to have them read in isolation.

A Draft of XVI Cantos was Bird's project, largely carried through while Pound was away from Paris, and Pound had very little say over the format and Strater's designs. He saw the latter only after the blocks had been cut, and objected to Strater's straying from the capitals down the margins. He called for more concentration and less ornamentation, but for reasons of expense the changes he wanted could not be made. Rodker's *A Draft of the Cantos 17–27* had exactly matched Bird's format and even his paper, but this time the designs were done by Gladys Hynes (1888–1958) under Pound's direction. Dorothy's initials for *A Draft of XXX Cantos*, the plainest and cleanest cut of all, were no doubt done in even closer collaboration with Pound.

Pound delighted in having his cantos so magnificently printed. He was even more pleased that the *de luxe* editions enabled him to bypass commercial publishers and printers. It was inflation, he wrote later, which, 'at the price of enormous human suffering', had made it possible for a few years to escape their 'stifling censorship' and to print 'books which AS BOOKS tried to equal those of Soncino and Bodoni as issued in the 1500's and 1700's'. That, and getting into print 'difficult' work for which the audience didn't yet exist and which therefore would not interest a commercial publisher, were the positive gains. None of those concerned looked to make money from the ventures. In the case of Bird's *XVI Cantos*, even if every one had been sold (which was far from being the case) of the five autographed copies on Imperial Japan paper at $100, and the fifteen on Whatman paper at $50, and the seventy on Roma paper specially watermarked at $25, then Bird and Pound would have received about $250 each after all expenses were met. That would have paid the rent on Pound's Paris flat for several months, but not for all the years it had taken him to produce those cantos. There was too the serious loss of another kind, in the fact that the cost of these luxury editions put them out of reach of most of the few who would appreciate this launch of a new epic.

In its beginnings an epic was the foundation myth, the once and future story, of a tribe, a nation, a people. Ancient Greece had its *Iliad* and *Odyssey* and its classic tragedies; Rome had its *Aeneid*; mediaeval England had the Arthurian romances and the Mystery plays; Elizabeth's England had Shakespeare's histories; and England after the Civil War had *Paradise Lost*. Then the story changed, with *Pilgrim's Progress*, and became concerned rather with the life of the individual than the fate of a people. England's epic in the eighteenth century was Richardson's *Clarissa*; and after that came Byron's *Don Juan* and Wordsworth's *The Prelude, or The Growth of the Poet's Mind*, and next Browning's *Sordello*. In the mid-nineteenth century, in a United States still inventing itself, Whitman felt the need to reconnect the individual poet with his people, and asserted that his experience must be the common, democratic experience of everyone in America. Pound went on from that to create an epic in which an individual poet would again tell the tale of the tribe, only his tribe would be all of humanity that one man could comprehend; and his tale would be not of himself but would be a universal story, and it would shape a future not for any one nation but for all. *The Cantos of Ezra Pound* would be the foundation myth of a universal civilization. The global order capitalism has been busily creating is quite possibly the antithesis of what he had in mind.

One way of finding one's bearings in Pound's epic is to use the 'sextant' which he added to *Guide to Kulchur* in 1952. This sextant consists of a list of books with brief indications of what he thought them good for. At the head were 'the Four Books' of Confucius and Mencius, these providing an all-sufficient guide, for 'a man who really understands them', 'to all problems of conduct that can arise'. As ancillary to these he then named the *Odyssey*, for 'intelligence set above brute force'; Greek tragedy for 'rise of sense of civic responsibility'; and the *Divina Commedia* for 'life of the spirit'. He also named Brooks Adams's *Law of Civilization and Decay* as the 'most recent summary of "where in a manner of speaking" we had got to half a century ago'. Those indications, taken together, provide an abstract of the major themes or preoccupations of the *Cantos* in general, and of *A Draft of XXX Cantos* in particular:

- above all and through everything a preoccupation with 'problems of conduct', as in the *Ta Hio* (digested in Canto 13);
- specifically, a concern for the ascendancy of intelligence over brute force;
- then that the intelligent should develop the sense of civic responsibility;
- and beyond that, the life of the spirit, or the divine states of mind which move men to benevolent and constructive action;
- with a concern always with 'where have we got to now?'

There are also of course the counter-themes: that there are muddy states of mind, irresponsible rulers, brutal wars; and that unenlightenment is the norm. The drama of this epic is the struggle of a few individuals throughout history to establish an enlightened order amidst and against blank apathy, malignant stupidity, rapacious greed, and jealous possessiveness, while (in Yeats's words) 'The best lack all conviction, while the worst | Are full of passionate intensity'.

The war at Troy lies behind the *Cantos* from the start as the archetypal instance of possessiveness leading to catastrophe. That was a war fought for possession of Helen, daughter of Zeus, and it ended with the total destruction of Troy. The spirits of those killed crowd about Odysseus in canto 1, 'Souls stained with recent tears, girls tender. | Men many, mauled with bronze lance heads'. In canto 2 the old men of Troy foresee the doom being brought upon their city by its holding on to Helen, and an association is set up with the doom the sailors bring on themselves in blindly trying to seize Dionysos. The fate of Troy is evoked again at the start of canto 4, as striking the key-note of jealousy and possessiveness for that canto. Cantos 5 and 23 note the re-enactment of Troy in the Auvergne, when Pieire de Maensac 'took off the girl ... that was just married to Bernart [De Tierci]'. Eleanor of Aquitaine is perceived as another Helen in cantos 6 (and 7). To attempt to take possession of the life in others or in things is seen to be the prime cause of wars and the destruction of civilizations.

The intelligence to rise above possessiveness comes from being mindful of the divinity in things, as Acoetes and Tiresias are mindful of Dionysos. Then there is the Chinese king saying '"No wind is the king's"' in canto 4;

and, in canto 6, there are Bernart de Ventadour absenting himself so that his lady may be set free, and Cunizza freeing her slaves. In the cantos dealing with more recent times, however, the gods exist only in the poet's private phantasmagoria, as in 'Gods float in the azure air, | Bright gods and Tuscan, back before dew was shed'. That passage in canto 3 is literary pastiche, wistfully expressing what the young poet would like to have seen in Venice or Sirmione in order to have a vision of the vital universe to set against the drear waste left behind by 'heroic' violence. Again, in canto 7, his 'Passion to breed a form in shimmer of rain-blur' projects an image of naked beauty, of 'Nicea' moving before him in deathly post-war London. In his Renaissance Italy recognitions of the whole and the flowing are just as unlikely, and the consequence there too is a dearth of enlightened conduct.

Canto 12 brings in the world of the poet's day—'"where in a manner of speaking" we [have] got to'—with Baldy Bacon as a small-time Odysseus and 'miraculous Hermes' who knows the ways of the world and how to work them. 'Baldy's interest | Was in money business, | "No interest in any other kind uv bisnis," | Said Baldy.' He is a bustling comic hero in a canto which becomes a thoroughly Chaucerian account of money business. Baldy's is a tale of making killings and going bust. In contrast, the tale of Dos Santos is a success story, the man who saw the chance that others missed and grew to be 'a great landlord of Portugal' by putting his all into fattening pigs. A third tale, the 'Tale of the Honest Sailor' told by John Quinn to a boardroom of bankers, turns on a comic inversion of the medieval connection of usury with sodomy. Persuaded that he has given birth to a son the formerly drunken sailor reforms and saves all his pay, buys a share in a ship then a ship of his own and eventually has 'a whole line of steamers', all to leave to his son. This story of honest virtue prospering by devoted saving and investing is aimed to show up the respectable bankers,

> the ranked presbyterians,
> Directors, dealers through holding companies,
> Deacons in churches, owning slum properties,
> *Alias* usurers in excelsis

Here the tone is not comic. The bankers, 'whining over their 20 p.c. and the hard times', represent the complacent greed which would enslave Dionysos: or, in modern terms, the greed which changes producers into debt-slaves, and which restricts the distribution of 'the abundance of nature', by charging excessive rates of interest and generally pursuing private profit without regard for the common good. In canto 14, the first of the 'hell cantos', they are mentioned as 'the perverts, who have set money-lust | Before the pleasures of the senses'.

'Mr Pound's Hell', Mr Eliot objected in his notorious and yet very curious put-down in *After Strange Gods*, 'is a Hell for the *other people* ... not for oneself and one's friends'. One must allow that Pound did not share his friend's taste for damnation. More to the point, Eliot's remark is a doubtless deliberate attempt to place Pound's hell within his own Christian frame of reference, which Pound had very deliberately excised. The guide here is not Dante but Plotinus, and the sinners are those who offend against the light of intelligence, against the *Nous*. The first line of canto 14 is from the *Inferno*, 'Io venni in luogo d'ogni luce muto', *I came into a place where the light had died out*; but Pound does not go on with Dante to note 'the carnal sinners'. Instead he follows Plotinus' idea that evil is whatever is not animated and formed by the universal light and so falls away 'in gloom and mud', into endless dissolution and darkness. That makes hell in Pound's vision the 'last cess-pool of the universe', an 'ooze full of morsels, | lost contours, erosions', 'The slough of unamiable liars, | bog of stupidities'. In the ooze are the unenlightened, 'politicians', 'Profiteers drinking blood', 'financiers', 'the press gang | And those who had lied for hire', 'slum owners, | usurers ... pandars to authority', 'pets-de-loup ... obscuring the text with philology', 'monopolists, obstructors of knowledge, | obstructors of distribution'. When the poet feels himself being sucked into that bog Plotinus, in the guise of Perseus, warns him to keep his eyes on the mirror-shield of Minerva, the shield in which the mind sees these things as they are reflected in the divine Mind. What saves him and can save the reader is the intelligence which sees through all the disgusting deliquescence to a clear and definite *idea* 'of mental ROT'.

In canto 16 the poet gets out of that hell into a kind of Elysium where there are 'the heroes, | Sigismundo, and Malatesta Novello, | and founders, gazing at the mounts of their cities'. There in 'the quiet air' he falls asleep in the grass by a pool and hears voices telling anecdotes of modern wars and revolution. In effect these voices give us the contemporary purgatory. Just as Pound's hell represents the prevailing state of unenlightenment, so his purgatory represents the conditions of the relatively enlightened caught up in the absurdities and horrors of wars started and kept going by the unenlightened. He sees neither punishment nor purgation in this purgatory of war, simply an evil state of affairs that must be endured. And his heroes are not the conventional war-heroes. They are writers and artists, his friends Aldington, Gaudier, Hulme, and Lewis, and Fernand Léger, men of clear-sighted intelligence who fought as they had to without letting the passions of war cloud their minds. Their heroism is akin to that of Sigismundo, whose achievement was his Tempio in spite of all his warring, and that of his brother Novello who endowed Cesena with a library, a hospital, and a school.

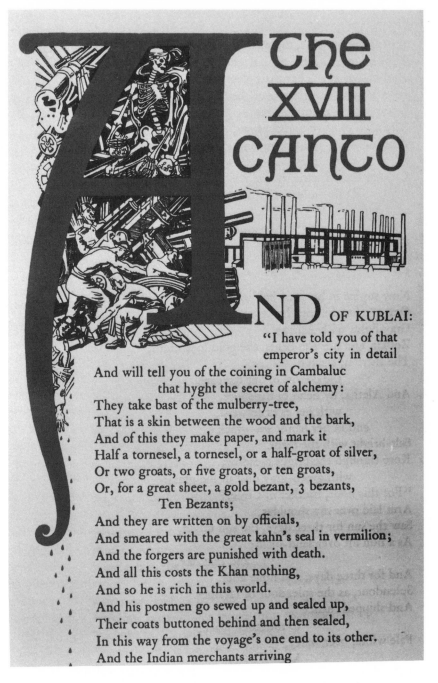

THE XVIII CANTO

AND OF KUBLAI:
                "I have told you of that
                    emperor's city in detail
And will tell you of the coining in Cambaluc
            that hyght the secret of alchemy:
They take bast of the mulberry-tree,
That is a skin between the wood and the bark,
And of this they make paper, and mark it
Half a tornesel, a tornesel, or a half-groat of silver,
Or two groats, or five groats, or ten groats,
Or, for a great sheet, a gold bezant, 3 bezants,
                Ten Bezants;
And they are written on by officials,
And smeared with the great kahn's seal in vermilion;
And the forgers are punished with death.
And all this costs the Khan nothing,
And so he is rich in this world.
And his postmen go sewed up and sealed up,
Their coats buttoned behind and then sealed,
In this way from the voyage's one end to its other.
And the Indian merchants arriving

2. 'The XVIII Canto', initial by Gladys Hynes, in *A Draft of the Cantos 17–27* (1928).

Cantos 18 and 19 go on with 'where we have got to', largely in the style of muck-raking journalism. The underlying issues here are civic responsibility, or rather, in 18, the civic irresponsibility of a one-man financial–industrial–military complex; and, in 19, the mysteries of who does control the economy and in whose interest. The point, for Pound, of Marco Polo's account of Kublai Khan's paper money, with which he opens canto 18, is that it gave the tyrant control of credit throughout his empire and that he used it to accumulate wealth for himself. That prefigures the contemporary monopolist 'Zenos Metevsky' who, having grown from selling arms to presiding over their manufacture, 'was consulted before the offensives'; became '"the well-known financier, better known," | As the press said, "as a philanthropist"'—the latter on account of his endowing 'a chair of ballistics'; and, now 'Sir Zenos Metevsky', was 'elected President | Of the Gethsemane Trebizond Petrol', thus tying up in the modern way oil, the arms industry, big money, and political influence.

Canto 19 goes into the ways in which new inventions and other natural resources are controlled by vested interests, incidentally observing that an inventor doesn't have to sell out to the corporation that means *not* to develop his patent. The suspect notion of a genuinely democratic and humane economic system is glanced at—Tómaš Masaryk of CzechoSlovakia, 'the old kindly professor' in the corner, believed in that, as did Douglas—and 'the stubby fellow' upstairs, Arthur Griffiths of Sinn Fein, agreed, but could not get his people to see it. '"Can't move 'em with a cold thing like economics"', he said. In the background the Communist revolution is getting a mass of disillusioned soldiers moving. (Later, in canto 27, there is a song to put down 'tovarisch'—'the unit submerged in the mass'— who rose up 'and wrecked the house of the tyrants', then 'talked folly' and built nothing, 'Laid never stone upon stone'. The trouble with the Russian Revolution, Pound would say, was that it could not be run from below— 'Things get done from the TOP'.)

It is a common mistake to assume that Pound looked back to the Renaissance as a golden age when constructive intelligence prevailed.[1] That is evidently not the case in the Malatesta cantos, where Sigismundo's temple for Isotta and the pagan gods is achieved against the general current of his life and times. It is even more clearly not the case in canto 5, where 'The

---

[1] The fifteenth-century Renaissance rulers whose conduct is scrutinized in *XXX Cantos* are, besides Sigismundo Malatesta (1417–68): Niccolò III d'Este (1384–1441), and his son Borso (1413–71); and Cosimo de' Medici of Florence (1389–1464), his son Piero (1416–69), and Piero's son Lorenzo or Lauro (1449–92).

light of the Renaissance shines in Varchi', the objective historian 'wanting the facts', and not in the two Medici, the one, Lorenzo, murdering the other with terrible deliberation, and the victim, his cousin Duke Alessandro, holding 'his death for a doom. | In abuleia'. It is worth bearing in mind that for Pound 'the finest force' of the Renaissance was 'the revival', in the writings of Lorenzo Valla and of Machiavelli, of 'the sense of realism'.

Canto 24 (with part of canto 20) deals with Niccolò d'Este who owned and ruled Ferrara. The first page consists of entries in Ferrara's 'book of the mandates' or state orders recording his young wife Parisina's orders for payments to her jockey and for her shopping, and in particular 25 ducats for a green tunic embroidered with silver for her lord's natural son, Ugo. We know from canto 20 that Niccolò, in his rage, will have both their heads cut off for their adultery and then become delirious with jealousy and grief. Yet he would give Ugo a state funeral; marry again and beget legitimate children; be praised as 'Affable, bullnecked, that brought seduction in place of | Rape into government', and for having on three occasions made peace in Italy. He knew how to keep his territory intact. Nevertheless he appears as a man dominated by his passions, and as intellectually and spiritually unawakened. In his youth he had made a sort of Renaissance grand tour, 'in the wake of Odysseus', 'To Cithera (a.d. 1413) "dove fu Elena rapta da Paris"', and to Jerusalem, everywhere having a good time as a tourist visiting a past that was dead, simply dead for him. In his mind there was no renaissance, no awakening to what had been and might be. And he left no enduring legacy. His statue and Borso's were melted down in Napoleon's time for 'cannon, bells, door-knobs'; and Ferrara, it was said, had turned into a paradise for tailors and dressmakers.

The Medici are noticed, rather cursorily and very pointedly, in canto 21. They too believed in peace-making in Italy, for the reason that peace served their business interests better than war. Their business was banking, accumulating money, and extending credit to the rich and powerful not only in Italy but throughout all of Europe. In fact they were the inventors of modern loan capitalism, and their contribution to the development of high finance, though masked by their patronage of high culture, was of deeper and more lasting consequence for European civilization. They gave the example in the fifteenth century of how control of credit could bring with it effective control of public affairs, and it is this aspect of the Medici that the canto highlights. Far from being associated with the re-awakening evident, for instance, in Botticelli's *Birth of Venus*, they are shown bringing in the new rule of money. '"Keep on with the business"', Cosimo's father urged him, '"That's made me, | And the res publica didn't."' And young Lorenzo, when he inherited the business and effective control of the 'res publica', remarked that it was tough being the rich man of Florence if you did not at the same time own the state.

The latter part of this canto belongs to a completely different mental world from that of the Medici. It is made up of a rather hectic sequence of apparently random images, mostly natural images, and most of them charged with suggestions of 'the discontinuous gods', of Dionysos, Artemis, and Pallas Athene, an 'Owl-eye amid pine boughs'. 'Confusion' is the apt comment, but with the emphasis 'Confusion, source of renewals'. The passage is like a welling up of what has no place in the banking business, a return of the repressed in a confused dream. And as can happen in a dream one statement stands out, '"Damned to you Midas, Midas lacking a Pan!"' King Midas, according to Ovid, being an initiate in the Orphic orgies, recognized old Silenus as a fellow member when he was brought to him in a drunken state, and entertained him well before conducting him to Dionysos, his foster-son. To reward Midas the god said he might have whatever he wished, and, out of his mind with greed, the king asked that everything he touched should turn to gold. When he discovered his mistake and confessed it the god removed the unnatural power, and Midas, now hating riches, spent his days with Pan in his groves and mountains. That tie with nature, the dream warns, is what the money-making Medici had lost.

Pound's treatment of Renaissance Venice in cantos 25 and 26 is closely related to his treatment of the Medici and Nic d'Este. The great 'BOOK OF THE COUNCIL MAJOR' records petty regulations—'1255 be it enacted; | That they musn't shoot crap in the hall | of the council'—and another book records for posterity as if it were the wonder of all wonders that the Doge's lioness gave birth to three cubs. Otherwise, what the Council mainly enacted through the fourteenth century appear to have been a series of improvements to the Doge's palace, including building a grand new council hall for themselves 'out over the arches' by the Grand Canal. Ruskin, in *The Stones of Venice* which Pound would surely have known, says that the Doge's palace was the focal building of Venetian culture as the Parthenon was of Athens, and that what it expressed was, first, that Venice was no longer governed by its best individual but by an oligarchy, and second that its public policy was determined only by commercial self-interest with religion playing no part. For those reasons Renaissance Venice, in Ruskin's view, lost its creative energy around 1423 when the new council hall was first used, and thereafter fell into luxury and decadence. Pound's vision of the palace with the new hall appearing to hang 'baseless' in the dawn mist could accord with that, if one reads the image as not just a fine aesthetic effect after Turner, but as declaring that the culture and government of Venice had no ground under it, no *virtù*, no individual genius, and no enlightened vision.

86

The central passage of canto 25 weaves together several themes, some new and some repeated from previous cantos, to make explicit what Venice lacked. 'Sulpicia', a minor Roman poet who sang out her love in clear direct speech, is introduced as a still living natural phenomenon, 'green shoot now, and the wood | white under new cortex'. Then the art of a Gaudier is evoked, '"sculptor sees the form in the air | before he sets hand to mallet"'. Sulpicia again, now 'As ivory uncorrupted', sings to the man she loves '"Pone metum Cerinthe"', *put away fear Cerinthus—*

> Lay there, the long soft grass,
>> and the flute lay there by her thigh,
> Sulpicia, the fauns, twig-strong,
>> gathered about her;
> The fluid, over the grass
> Zephyrus, passing through her,
>> 'deus nec laedit amantes'.

—the god does no harm to lovers. Against that is heard 'from the stone pits', as from those who made over the Doge's palace, 'heavy voices' saying,

> 'Nothing we made, we set nothing in order,
> 'Neither house nor the carving,
> 'And what we thought had been thought for too long ...'

Sulpicia's song breaks in, now from the chorus of young fauns moving to the notes of a Pan pipe. The heavy theme resumes, 'the dead words keeping form | ... The dead concepts, never the solid, the blood rite'. At the end of the passage Sulpicia's song of life leads back to the sculptor's vision,

> And thought then, the deathless,
> Form, forms and renewal, gods held in the air,
> Forms seen, and then clearness ...

—as Aphrodite might be seen taking form in the sea, with the fluid waves holding that form, 'as crystal'. But what Venice asked of its greatest painter Titian—so the canto continues—was to paint in the 'fourth frame from the door on | the right of the hall of the greater council ... The picture of the land battle'; and when he hadn't fulfilled the commission after twenty years the Council asked for their money back. Canto 26 mainly documents the decline of Venice into sumptuous *luxuria*, dead concepts, cautious intrigues, and prosperous commerce, with the epitaph 'And they are dead and have left a few pictures'.

The Venetian oligarchy are not made to appear evil, any more than are the Medici or the Este. All of them are credited with a preference for peace over war and for intelligence over brute force, even if for self-interested motives; also with having had some sense of civic responsibility, though again only so far as it served their own interests. But that self-servingness is their radical defect: they were not moved to serve the larger life of the spirit. Their famed Renaissance, therefore, was no renaissance at all from Pound's point of view.

Where then in these cantos is the life of the spirit in evidence as the main motive of conduct? One thinks again of Acoetes in the mythopoesis of canto 2, attempting to open Pentheus' eyes to energies beyond his comprehension; and of Bernart de Ventadorn's song to free his lady of Eblis; and of Cunizza who lived in love, and who set free her slaves. But after Cunizza, that is, after the time of Cavalcanti and Dante, there is only Sigismundo's odd and wonderful monument to his love for Isotta and to the gods. Otherwise, down to the present day, one finds only the poet's own attempts to recreate the lost vision and motive.

In canto 29 some fun is had at the expense of this poet as a young and innocent student all at sea in his American milieu, a 'Lusty Juventus' sublimating his desire in 'a burning fire of phantasy', and not yet aware that actually it seeks fulfilment in the seemingly alien 'biological process'. The young poet and his world are that far removed from the culture of Cunizza and Sordello, and from the fulfilment of his desire. But then the distance, the tension between the desire by which he lives and its possible paradise intensifies the desire and makes it the driving force of his poem. The poem must give form and substance to what he seeks but can find in his actual world only in hints and vestiges and fragments. He knows of a world that seems responsibly ordered, in Confucius' China as caught in the mirror of Canto 13, but that is a world elsewhere governed by a different if complementary vision. His own world, that of the hell and the other contemporary cantos, has lost all coherence and is in the dark of ignorant passion. To remake it he must somehow grow into the role of Zagreus, lord of life in the world of the dead.

That is what canto 17 is about—or it is about the difference between the mind that is ever at the interpretation of the vital universe and the mind (such as that of Venice) in which the universe is not alive. This is the formal structure of the canto:

ll. 1–6 1st subject: 'So that the vines burst from my fingers . . . IO ZAGREUS!'

ll. 7–12 response: Diana moving in the dawn woods with her hounds;

ll. 13–18 counter-subject: stone Venice, 'marble trunks out of stillness';

88

ll. 19–42 response: Cave of Nerea, seeing the principle of life even in stone by a 'light not of the sun' (meaning the light of the mind?);

ll. 43–55 development of 1st subject: Zagreus & Co. in full light;

ll. 56–7 the keynote image as central pivot: 'the great alley of Memnons' where the stone sings when the first light strikes it;

ll. 58–84 development of counter-subject: an alley of cypress, then stone Venice and its crafts by torch-light;

ll. 85–103 variation on the main theme: envisioning gods in their splendour;

ll. 104–12 repeat of counter-subject: the stone place, unliving and deadly;

l. 113 resolving chord: 'Sunset like the grasshopper flying'—the live creature flares crimson for its moment in the air.

The whole canto is a musical composition of images and their tensile associations, formulated in firm rhythmic phrases, and organized into a complex which calls for contemplation, not monolinear explication. The ear, the inner eye, and the intelligence are all engaged here, and the contemplation needs to be just as active as the composition in envisioning and critically discriminating one image against another, the oak woods on the green slope against the forest of marble, the sea cave shaped and coloured by waves against the still waters reflecting 'Dye-pots in the torch-light'. From this process a definite structure will emerge, amounting overall to a setting of natural energies against artefacts—against even beautiful artefacts. The canto itself asks to be taken not as an aesthetic object but as an act of mind, an act, that is, of the hearer's and reader's mind as much as of the poet's. Further, this act is necessarily critical, judgemental, though not according to any code. The discriminations are based upon the simpler and fundamental preference for energies in action as against stasis, for 'Zagreus' against 'arbours of stone'.

The final canto of the first thirty applies something of a reality check to that feeling for energies in action. It has Artemis/Diana damning things foul and 'growne awry', and complaining that because Pity preserves them 'Nothing is now clean slayne | But rotteth away'. She would have only healthily growing trees in her forests, and would cut away all rotting and dead wood. In that spirit Venus (the canto implies) should not keep old Vulcan's embers warm, but play with young Mars instead; and there is something terribly wrong in young King Pedro's enthroning beside him his murdered and long dead bride.

Though she may seem opposed to life-giving Zagreus/Dionysos, ruthless Artemis would also serve the life-principle, as surgery, and antibiotics, do. Or, as in the hell and Metevsky cantos, satire and realist writing would. Pound found the idea expressed in a Confucian ideogram, *hsin*[1], which brought together 'the growing tree ... the orderly arrangement above it, and the axe for cutting away encumbrance', and which meant 'to cut down wood, to renew, to renovate'. Pound read the ideogram as MAKE IT NEW and adopted it as his emblem.

Set with and/or against Venus and Pedro—how to discriminate here?— is the wicked Lucrezia Borgia, who was at least a force of nature in her time, manifesting (like Lorenzaccio de' Medici in canto 5) a fearsome resolution. 'Madame "YΛH' she is called in the canto, that being the Greek, according to Pound, for 'uncut forest, the stuff of which a thing is made, matter as a principle of being'. Defective as she was in intellectual and spiritual virtue, a real *mafiosa*, Lucrezia had yet the virtue of crude energy. And that, even as it subsists in a jungle wilderness, was affirmed as the 'Basis of renewal' in canto 20 following Nic d'Este's breakdown into delirium. This would suggest that the renewing energies of a renaissance are not primarily spiritual or intellectual but are from the raw basis of life.

Still, beyond the raw material of a Lucrezia there is the carving of it into intelligible forms, as in the cutting of letters for the printing of books—and as in the making out of such matters 'something to think about | objects worth contemplation'.

Literary relations old and new

In January 1928 *The Dial*, in giving its annual Award to Pound, declared him 'one of the most valuable forces in contemporary letters'. However Eliot, his old friend in letters, when invited to endorse the award was rather equivocal about Pound's poetry and seemed intent on playing down its relevance. Under the heading 'Isolated Superiority', with his emphasis falling on the first of the two words, he granted that Pound was immensely influential, on account of his superior mastery of verse forms; and yet he had made no disciples, he claimed, because 'one makes disciples only among those who sympathise with the content', and with the 'content' of Pound's poetry he himself was wholly out of sympathy, and so too, he appeared to assume, would be all the world. 'I am seldom interested in what he is saying', he wrote in his best putting down manner, 'but only in the way he says it.' Eliot knew perfectly well that this form/content dichotomy was untenable, that form, to be at all interesting, had to be the form of something of interest; but he was now attempting to criticize literature from the point of view of his Anglo-Catholic faith—in other words he was heresy-hunting—and what he was really after was 'what does Mr Pound believe?' Pound's short answer to his inquisitor was, 'read Confucius and Ovid'. In due course Eliot would declare him a heretic, a follower of alien gods, an outsider; and Pound would riposte that to return to the bosom of the one God of Judaeo-Christianity was to give up the struggle for enlightenment. Their differences now set such a distance between them intellectually.

Yet they were not personally estranged. Pound could tell the American agent for *The Exile* that he was 'on the best possible personal terms with Eliot, though our literary camps do not coincide'. He even tried to persuade Williams to send Eliot 'a nice little note of welcome' upon his appointment as Norton Professor of Poetry at Harvard, hoping that opposition to what Eliot stood for 'might be cordial and amiable'. 'A difference of belief CAN among decent human beings be conducted' with decency, he suggested. While he would have nothing to do with Eliot's royalism and his Anglo-Catholicism, he could still recognize his *literary* discernment, 'discriminating retroactive academicism' though it might be, as solid enough to be worth rebelling against.

Wyndham Lewis also cast off Pound intellectually in these years and did all he could to denigrate him as a poet. In 1927, in his short-lived magazine *The Enemy*, and then in his book *Time and Western Man*, he put Pound down as a kind-hearted, well-meaning 'revolutionary simpleton'. His poems, he declared, were parasitic upon a romanticized past with which Pound was too much in love; and Pound simply did not have the intelligence and the originality to be the revolutionary modernist he set up to be. Lewis registered that he had been always generous and graceful to him personally, and had helped him out financially. He might have made more of Pound's unflagging support for and promotion of his work, as in recommending him in the strongest terms to the new Guggenheim Foundation in 1925, but then he no longer wanted to be associated with him as an artist or writer. Pound was to him now 'an intellectual eunuch'. The charge that he was altogether bound up with the past and incapable of understanding the present, let alone of grasping the enduring forms of things, would have touched Pound where he was most ambitious as a poet. Yet he took no offence. When his father showed concern Pound advised him, 'Don't worry about Lewis—all large fauna shd. be preserved.' And he could say to Williams in 1929 that 'ole Wyndham getting out and kussing everyone (me included)' showed a 'healthy tendency'. His devotion to what he thought Lewis's best interests was unaffected, and he continued to count him as one of the 'large and vivid mental animals' of his generation who had saved him from feeling that he lived in an intellectual desert.

There remained Joyce from his wartime vortex, and here it was Pound who became disaffected. He declined to sign a protest against the pirating of *Ulysses* in America on the ground that the protest should be directed, not against the unscrupulous publisher, but against the copyright and decency laws which gave him his opportunity. He may have been right in principle, but Joyce felt it as a personal disloyalty. More serious was Pound's making nothing whatever of a fragment of *Work in Progress* Joyce had asked him to read. 'Nothing short of divine vision or a new cure for the clapp can possibly be worth all the circumambient peripherization', was the verdict he promptly returned. And that remained his judgment upon what became *Finnegans Wake*. In 1933 he pronounced it deficient in awareness of what was going on in the contemporary world—in the operations, for example, of 'the network of french banks and international munition sellers'—and to be therefore not the work of a great writer. 'I never had any respect for his common sense or for his intelligence', he wrote in a review published in Paris in 1931, 'I mean general intelligence, apart from his gifts as a writer'. Joyce, so far as Pound was concerned, was now history.

Pound's relations with Yeats were at once closer and more antagonistic than with the men of his own generation. In 1928 Yeats and his wife, Dorothy's close friend George, decided to spend much of each year in Rapallo and took an apartment there. 'I shall not lack conversation', Yeats reflected after an hour on Pound's rooftop listening to his efforts to lay out the system of his 'immense poem'. He seems to have felt a need to make up his mind about Pound, 'whose art is the opposite of mine, whose criticism commends what I most condemn, a man with whom I would quarrel more than with anyone else if we were not united by affection'. The affection shows in his account of going out with Pound into the seafront garden at night where Pound would call the cats of Rapallo and feed them bones and pieces of meat and relate each one's history. Yeats's narrative, however, turns to reflection upon the scene, and he thinks that really Pound has no fondness for cats but feeds them out of some general pity for the outcast and oppressed; and that same pity, or 'hysteria', he suggests, may be what inclines him in his criticism to become violent against injustice. In the same way there is a sceptical undercurrent subverting his account of Pound's explanations of how he was structuring the cantos. The whole poem when complete, he reports, will 'display a structure like that of a Bach Fugue'; but then he puts in a series of negatives, 'There will be no plot, no chronicle of events, no logic of discourse', no 'conventions of the intellect' at all. A footnote draws in Lewis's attack on Pound's art in *Time and Western Man*, saying that it 'sounds true to a man of my generation' that 'If we reject, [as Lewis] argues, the forms and categories of the intellect there is nothing left but sensation, "eternal flux"'. The footnote is qualified by the recognition that 'all such rejections stop at the conscious mind'; but Yeats does not follow through to the corollary that there may be orders other than the conscious mind's logic. By 1936 these reflections in Rapallo had hardened into unqualified judgements. 'Ezra Pound has made flux his theme', Yeats stated flatly in the Introduction to his *Oxford Book of Modern Verse: 1892–1935*, 'plot, characterization, logical discourse, seem to him abstractions unsuitable to a man of his generation'. And in consequence, 'Like other readers I discover at present merely exquisite or grotesque fragments.' As for his work as a whole, Yeats now found 'more style than form' in it; and then that its sometimes noble style

is constantly interrupted, broken, twisted into nothing by its direct opposite, nervous obsession, nightmare, stammering confusion; he is an economist, poet, politician, raging at malignants with inexplicable characters and motives, grotesque figures out of a child's book of beasts. This loss of self-control, common among uneducated revolutionists, is rare—Shelley had it in some degree—among men of Ezra Pound's culture and erudition.

Yeats's baffled account of the cantos shows how very far beyond his comprehension they were; but his views on both the cantos and Pound in general were becoming commonplace.

Pound was irritated by Yeats's negativity towards his work to the extent of saying that Yeats would not know 'a fugue from a frog'. He may also have been reassured by it. The true revolutionary finds confirmation of his project in the resistance it provokes. At the least he must accept that it is in the nature of things that those who stand by the established order will put down any nascent new order as disorderly; and that a liberation from convention will be felt by the conventional as a loss of control. Any genuine intellectual revolution will be, according to the received forms of reason and logic, irrational, illogical, and a menace to society. Only those who have a vital interest in changing the existing social and intellectual order are likely to respond positively to a radically new way of thinking.

Ford could accept in his breezy way that '*Melopoeia, Phanopoeia* and the rest of the screw-wrenches and claw-hammers of Mr Pound's engineering bench are merely his formidable tools for monkeying with the screw-nuts of human consciousness'. That, after all, was what good writing did— monkeyed with human consciousness! It was Williams, though, almost alone of Pound's friends and contemporaries, who really took up the radical challenge of the cantos fearlessly and without prejudice. He perceived that in them the intelligence was seeking to penetrate 'a closed mind which clings to its power', and that in order to do this it had to 'move . . . away from the word as symbol toward the word as reality'. 'The word as symbol' would have been aimed at Yeats and at Eliot, and at one tendency of English poetry; and it would have been aimed through them at those habits of 'logical discourse' which serve to maintain the hold of the closed mind on language. Among those habits would be such preconceived 'forms and categories of the intellect' as Eliot's 'belief', and Yeats's 'plot and character'. There would also be the poets' habit of glancing off things in themselves into subjective associations, of thinking 'what is it *like*' and thus avoiding the challenge to observe exactly what it *is* and *does*; and there would be the related habit of thinking 'what does it *stand for*' and thus thrusting off into abstraction and generality. The opposing term, 'the word as reality', would have had behind it 'the principal move in imaginative writing today'— Williams might as well have said in *American* writing—for which his own favoured formulation was 'no ideas but in things'; and for which there was also Wallace Stevens's 'not ideas about the thing, but the thing itself'— Stevens's 'thing' being invariably and overtly the thing in the mind; and of course there was Pound's own 'direct treatment of the "thing", whether subjective or objective'. This was a move to reform the language in poetry in order to free the mind from mediating preconceptions and conventions and to open it to a more direct apprehension of the facts of its world. Of necessity the process of forming a new intelligence of things involved breaking up the existing frame of mind.

Pound was far from being alone or 'isolated' in this intellectual revolution. Williams and Wallace Stevens and Marianne Moore, each in their own way, were committed to it. And a new generation of poets was going on from them in pursuit of 'the revolution of the word', some of them even as, loosely speaking, disciples of Pound. The most advanced of these was Louis Zukofsky.[2] Zukofsky submitted his deeply unconventional 'Poem Beginning "The"' for publication in *The Exile* in August 1927, and Pound accepted it immediately as 'First cheering mss. I have recd. in weeks, or months'. That was the beginning of a warm and sustained literary relationship, in which Pound encouraged and gave confidence to Zukofsky as he went beyond Pound on his own line of invention, while Zukofsky was ready to acknowledge Pound as his father in poetry, as Browning had been Pound's, without ever turning Oedipal on him. The basis of their

[2] Louis Zukofsky (1904–78), poet and prose writer, born and mostly based in New York; EP published his 'Poem Beginning "The"' in *The Exile* no. 3 (Spring 1928), and put him in touch with WCW; in that year he began his long poem *A*; in 1931 formed the Objectivist group with George Oppen, Carl Rakosi and Charles Reznikoff; was involved with them in TO, publishers and Objectivist Press; edited *An 'Objectivists' Anthology* (1932); completed *A*, a work of major significance, in 1975. Collected works: *Bottom: On Shakespeare* (1963, 1987), a critical study in parallel with *A* 1–24; *All: the collected shorter poems 1923–1958* (1965, 1991); *Prepositions: The collected critical essays* (1967, 1981); *A* (1978); *Collected Fiction* (1990). A selection of his extensive correspondence with EP was published in 1987.

relationship was a common understanding of what poets could and should be doing in their particular world and time.

In a review of cantos 1–27 published in 1929 Zukofsky took in his stride a number of things which other readers were balking at. There was the 'problem' of Pound's mixing up times and places and persons without regard to where historians had shelved them, as in his shifting straight from Odysseus to Sordello, from Proteus to the Dogana's steps in Venice, and from Sigismondo Malatesta in Rimini to Baldy Bacon in New York. How was a reader supposed to know where he was! But to Zukofsky Pound could do this quite safely 'because all new subject matter is ineluctably simultaneous with "what has gone before"'—that is, it is so in the mind thinking these things. In the mind, 'the living them at once . . . is as much a fact as those facts which historians have labelled and disassociated'. The poet's business, Zukofsky implied, was with the particular facts actually present to the mind, lived facts bound up with their historical and human contingencies yet still free from the arbitrary constructions of historians or of any other authorities. In the perspective of the poetic mind Dionysos might be nearer than Odysseus, and Confucius might be a contemporary. On a deeper level, an inferno, a purgatorio, and a paradiso could be realized as states of the intensely observing mind and be manifest 'as hate, comprehension and worship rather than as religious geometry'; and these states, moreover, could be 'continually intersecting'. It was evident to Zukofsky as to few others that it was those states of mind and those emotions—hate, comprehension, and worship—which were the driving force of the cantos, and the organizer of form in them. Certainly, he did not find them formless or incoherent. In the preface to his *'Objectivists' Anthology* he judged them 'the greatest poem of our time'. And he dedicated the anthology to Pound as 'still for the poets of our time | the | most important'.

Pound did not want to 'make disciples'. He wanted the new generation to 'make it new' in their own way, and as his influence grew he used it to urge the young to organize themselves and make their own revolution. In December 1931 he told Zukofsky to pay no attention to his doubts about whether *A* could be sustained as a long poem. 'Every generation has to do something its granpap can't quite make out', he wrote, 'If you think you are right, go ahead, and don't listen to me or any of yr/ other damnd ancestors.' He could see that Zukofsky was 'working out a new musical structure', 'an abstracter kind of poesy than my generation went in for', and that he needed to concentrate on his 'own aesthetic'. 'There is no REASON', he wrote. 'why I shd. be able to be any more use to you (as critic) 1930 to 1950 than yeats to me 1910 to 1930.'

At the same time he placed remarkable faith in Zukofsky as an editor of the new generation—remarkable because until then he had never trusted anyone's judgement but his own. In the fall of 1930 he persuaded Harriet Monroe to have Zukofsky edit an 'Objectivists' number of *Poetry*. (After the event she noted how in 'the arrogance of youth' he had swept away all the poets she had celebrated in *Poetry*; yet she still bravely offered 'the glad hand to the iconoclasts' who had 'resisted and overthrown' numerous tyrannies, among them 'the tyranny of the comma, the capital, the verb, the sentence, of syntax, so long sacrosanct'.) Pound 'gave over to younger poets the space offered him'. He also lavished advice in a series of long letters—four in as many days in October—on what should and should not be included, all the while protesting that he did not want to 'insert my point of view'. Zukofsky was urged to 'produce something that ... will stand against Des Imagistes' and emphasize 'progress made since 1912'; he should 'give your decade', 'make it a murkn number', and aim for 'the DRIVE | or driving force or xpression of same'. 'AND the verse used MUST be good. | preferably by men under 30.'

Pound was constantly telling young editors and writers to organize themselves into groups. 'A group is very useful, for gathering information, etc., both enlightenment, and stimulus to action,' he advised Zukofsky in August 1928. He was urging him to 'form some sort of gang' around the idea of getting interesting books printed and distributed 'without too damnd much bother' from commercial considerations; and, secondly, of mounting 'simultaneous attacks in as many papers as poss. on abuses definitely damaging la vie intellectuelle'. 'Find some cheap restaurant and dine together once a week', he wrote; 'make a NEW grouping'; 'avoid tired and worn out personalities', also 'definite party men (like Mike Gold)'; 'NOT too many women, and if possible no wives'; 'got to have a busy man'; 'must have some access to journals'—and so on, at length. 'Always 60% of group duds', he acknowledged, 'but it don't matter'. Zukoksky dutifully contacted some of Pound's nominations, but no group materialized as a result. He, and the other Objectivists, were not group minded.

In these years Pound was in touch with any number of little and mostly fugitive magazines, with *New Review* (Americans in Paris), *Blues* (Mississippi), *Contempo* (North Carolina), *Morada* (New Mexico), *New Masses* (New York), *Front* (The Hague), *Bifur* (Paris), *Variétés* (Brussels), *Stream* (Melbourne), *Midland* (Iowa), *Frontier* (Montana); and with the 'most solid' of the small magazines, *Hound and Horn* (Cambridge, Mass.), which saw itself as a successor to *The Dial*. 'Every generation or group must write its own literary program', he told Charles Henri Ford, editor of *Blues*—and then asked him to print Pound's own 'Program' as enclosed.

However, he was not expecting the editor to agree with it. 'My son', he wrote to another editor, Lincoln Kirstein of *Hound and Horn*, 'elucidate thine own bloody damn point of view by its contrast to others, not by trying to make the others conform.' What he wanted was some definite point of view with the drive to make its impact. It was always time for some new 'group move' to be made, 'to stir up the animals and in general put some life into the "corpse"', i.e. into the US body politic and its culture.

Pound had his reasons for investing so much energy in advising, encouraging, and hectoring the editors of little magazines for very little measurable return. There was the 'need for intellectual communication unconditioned by considerations as to whether a given idea or a given trend in art will "git ads" from the leading corset companies'. And there was the fact, as he had observed over twenty years, that

The work of writers who have emerged in or via [the impractical or fugitive] magazines outweighs in permanent value the work of the writers who have not emerged in this manner. The history of contemporary letters has, to a very manifest extent, been written in such magazines.

Big magazines with their heavier 'overheads' could not 'afford to deal in experiment'. There had to be little magazines if there was to be uncommercial new writing. The revolution depended on them.

Towards the end of 1926 Pound was considering starting up an independent little magazine of his own. He had a publicity card printed on which he declared,

EXILE will appear three times per annum until I get bored with producing it. It will contain matter of interest to me personally, and is unlikely to appeal to any save those disgusted with the present state of letters in England...

To Aldington he added that its existence would be justified by 'mss.... which cdn't appear elsewhere'. To John Price, who was helping to launch the magazine in America, he was more ambitious, telling him that his 'new show ought to bring force to a focus'. He was thinking back to the 'push that was in the ideogram: Joyce–Lewis–Eliot–E.P. in 1917'; but he had to admit that any force equivalent to that '"vortex" doth NOT at the present date *yet* appear'. That was on 12 January 1927. Just a week later he was persuaded 'to go ahead AT ONCE' by John Rodker's 'novel or "nouvelle"', *Adolphe 1920*: 'The Rodker is a definite contribution to literature, and it is the quality of that and nothing else that has decided me,' he told Price.

Adolphe 1920 took up two-thirds of *Exile* no. 1 ('primavera | 1927'), was continued in no. 2 (Autumn 1927), and concluded in no. 3 (Spring 1928).

97

It gave one answer to Pound's wondering what could be done in prose after *Ulysses*. Along with it Pound published in the four numbers of *Exile* quite a miscellany of other prose, most of it realism by Americans about Americans, with Robert McAlmon's 'Truer Than Most Accounts' the longest and most impressive. No. 3 contained mainly verse: two of Yeats's new poems, 'Sailing to Byzantium' and 'Blood and the Moon'; Zukofsky's long and strikingly innovative 'Poem Beginning "The"'; a substantial part of Pound's own 'Canto XXIII'; and then, after these most advanced poems of the day, twenty-five pages featured R. C. Dunning's finely crafted and charmingly old-fashioned prose and poems. William Carlos Williams's *The Descent of Winter*, a notebook sequence in verse and prose, took up forty pages of no. 4. There was more prose and verse from Zukofsky, poems by Carl Rakosi, and a piece by McAlmon on (and against) Gertrude Stein. The remaining forty-odd pages contained various editorial comments and short articles by Pound which he had had to hold over from the other numbers.

There had been no contributions from Joyce, Lewis, Eliot, or Ford; but then their work was appearing elsewhere. The justification of the short-lived magazine, on Pound's own terms, would have been its publishing Rodker's *Adolphe 1920*, Williams's *The Descent of Winter*, and above all its introducing Zukofsky's new poetic. Beyond that the remarkable thing is that Pound for once had no defining programme or principle in mind, and no idea of organizing a literary movement. His editorial choices do seem to have been governed simply by what interested him personally, namely realism both objective and subjective, experiment and innovation, and the condition of America. And his prose blasts, which one would expect to have been directed towards bringing his chosen forces into some particular focus or vortex, were directed instead towards other preoccupations and a distinctly non-literary agenda.

In the sphere of action

When he accepted the *Dial Award* in 1928 Pound said that it would have to be for his verse, since his prose was 'mostly stop-gap; attempts to deal with transient states of murkn imbecility or ignorance'. 'Occasionally one has to kick a traffic cop. (verbally)', he had told John Price, 'My verbal boot has cleared a few spaces. The "prose" if you want to call it that belongs to the sphere of action, not to "art and letters".' He had of course written no end of 'critical prose' in the sphere of 'art and letters' but that was intended simply 'to make people think'. Now his 'social or political prose' was meant 'to make people act', like Lenin's short and effective speeches which helped get the Russian Revolution going in 1917. Its function was to get across some basic, 'root' idea that would stir people into action, 'preferably after they have been booted into thinking', against the unenlightenment and oppression of the moment.

He was not unaware that such prose was a deflection, for the artist, into agitation and propaganda—a deflection, for him, from poetry into agitprop. In 'Dr Williams' Position' (1928) he explicitly contrasted himself with Williams in this respect. Whereas he could not 'observe the nation befouled by Volsteads and Bryans without anger', or 'see liberties that have lasted for a century thrown away for nothing...without indignation', Williams could contemplate such things without feeling driven to immediate action. 'Where I want to kill at once', Pound wrote, Williams would meditate on his dissatisfactions and not be goaded into 'ultra-artistic or non- artistic activity'.

Pound really did believe in the efficacy of indignation and disgust. 'Improvements in human conditions are mainly due to disgust,' he told a 'lady from Omaha' who appeared to be calling for a more tolerant disposition towards 'public imbecility'. 'America lacks it', i.e. disgust, he lamented, 'oh, abysmally lacks it!' 'Personally', he declared, 'I experience strong desire to annihilate certain states of mind *and* their protagonists.' What that often meant in practice, however, was merely a rhetoric of cussing and calling out, as in this 'lyric' response to a request for his autograph from Judge Beals of the Supreme Court in the state of Washington:

> *Damnation to bureaucrats*
> *Damn the betrayers of the national*
> *constitution. Hell take the*
> *souls of Wilson & the flea-headed*
> *Coolidge.*
> *God DAMN those responsible*
> *for copyright evils, passport*
> *idiocy, red tape,*
> *article 211 of penal code made*
> *by gorillas for the further stultification*
> *of imbeciles   God DAMN all*
> *those who take no active*
> *part in eliminating these*
> *evils. Damn those who*
> *invade the private domain of*
> *the individual directly or by*
> *making of suffocating iniquitous laws.*
> *against all these*
> > *maledictions &*
> > > *major anathema*
> *Ezra Pound | 7 May 1930*

99

That is at least a handy summary of Pound's pet hates in those years. Whether it had any effect on Judge Beals's judgements is not, so far as I know, a matter of record. Nor is it recorded that the lady from Omaha was moved by Pound's prose to a more active disgust at what he thought wrong with America.

'A good state', as Pound defined it in 1925, 'is one which impinges least upon the peripheries of its citizens'; and its function 'is to facilitate the traffic, i.e. the circulation of goods, air, water, heat, coal (black or white), power, and even thought; | and to prevent the citizens from impinging on each other'. At the same time, perhaps paradoxically, he declared civilization to be impossible without an aristocracy; and 'the duty of an aristocracy is to educate [the nation's] plebs'. But this, he observed, aristocracies had regularly failed to do, thus bringing on their 'own bloody destruction', and leaving 'the whole of woodenheaded humanity... to concentrate its efforts on production of another lot, equally piffling and light headed'. By 1930, still more paradoxically, he was looking for an individual leader to manage the state and maintain civilization:

THE SANE METHOD OF STUDYING HISTORY consists (or wd. if it were ever practised, consist) in learning what certain great protagonists intended, and to what degree they failed in forcing their program on the mass.

For example:...J. Q. Adams' intention of conserving national wealth for purposes of national education and civilization...

Jefferson's continual struggle to import civilization from Europe (getting measurements of la Maison Carrée...)

Apparently Pound considered the forcing of an enlightened programme on the mass of the people to be not tyrannous or oppressive. He may even have been implying that the failure to enforce enlightenment would have been due to allowing too much representation to the ignorant mass. 'The democratic idea', he had pointed out, 'was not that legislative bodies shd. represent the momentary idiocy of the multitude.' Yet that extreme way of stating the case might provoke one to reflect that 'the democratic idea' would not necessarily lead to the idea of 'the great protagonist' either; and further, that 'the great protagonists' in the 1930s would be, not a Jefferson or an Adams, but Mussolini, Stalin, and Hitler.

In Pound's mind, however, Mussolini was beginning to stand with Jefferson as a force for enlightened government. In November 1926 he remarked to John Price that 'The more one knows of Mussolini the more one inclines to think Italy very fortunate, and the less credence one gives to hostile reports.' That was a widely held view of Il Duce at that time. But then Pound's previous remark has an odd inflection. 'I don't think the Fascio will object', he wrote—object, that is, to his forthcoming magazine *The Exile* which he was discussing with Price. It is as if the shadow of Fascist censorship had crossed his mind, only without arousing his usual negative reaction to any form of censorship. The odd, uncalled for remark—uncalled for since the magazine was to be published in Paris, then Chicago, and was unlikely to be of any concern to the Fascio—is an indication of Pound's disposition to think well of Mussolini and Fascism, and to be passive about things which, if he were to suspect them of America, would drive him to act out of anger and indignation.

He found plenty of reasons for taking the hopeful, positive view of Mussolini. He was impressed when Olga Rudge, after giving a private performance for Mussolini in 1927, reported that he played the violin himself, preferred the classic composers, and could talk intelligently about music. He was impressed too by Mussolini's saying, 'We are tired of government in which there is no responsible person having a hind-name, a front name and an address.' That, 'the raison d'être of Fascism' for Pound, could be seen as at once an attack on faceless bureaucrats and their obstructive imbecilities, and an encouragement to individuals to act responsibly on their own authority, as the Rimini Commandante della Piazza had done in the matter of the library there. Mussolini's style of leadership seemed to follow from that. In contrast with America's 'passport imbecility', he had simply given 'a comprehensive order re/ frontiers, to the effect that travellers were not to be subjected to needless annoyance'. More generally, Pound was moved to say in an interview with an Italian journalist that Mussolini's 'effective program, which includes land reclamation, the "battle for grain", and the mobilization of the nation's internal credit', put him in mind of Thomas Jefferson; and that 'Italy is the only country in the world . . . that can't be governed better than it already is'. Altogether Pound was working towards the conclusion that Mussolini was, like Lenin and like Jefferson, a leader of the most effective type, 'an opportunist *with convictions*'; or, as he would phrase it in 1933 in *Jefferson and/or Mussolini*, 'an OPPORTUNIST who is RIGHT, that is who has certain convictions and who drives them through circumstance, or batters and forms circumstance with them'. By that date he would be convinced that Mussolini was contemporary Italy's 'great protagonist'.

It was the phenomenon of Il Duce, the effective leader of his people, that really engaged his increasingly enthusiastic support. But on occasion he would credit the Fascist Party with fulfilling the role of an aristocracy. In 1931, in 'Fungus, Twilight or Dry Rot', a contribution to Samuel Putnam's *New Review*, he equated aristocracy with a sense of responsibility.

Capitalist democracy, he began, 'does not, apparently favour the sense of responsibility or even ask for it in public servants'. In the most important matter of 'the nation's credit', those who control it should, ideally, be 'responsible to the nation'; but 'the real complaint against "capitalism" is that an unjust proportion of this credit is diverted to the private use of usurpers and scoundrels'. That meant that power, in capitalist democracy, was with the Plutocracy; and the Plutocracy does not encourage 'a greater degree of amenity or a higher critical selectivity in life and the arts'. Disgust with the failed state of democracy brought Pound to look favourably upon Communist Russia and Fascist Italy. 'Possibly no other aristocracy in 1931 has so great a sense of responsibility as the new Russian "party"', he wrote without irony, and although aware of 'horrors reported'. (Those would have been the horrors of Stalin's first Five Year Plan in which the Party's Commissars ruthlessly forced through the collectivization of agriculture and the development of heavy industry at a terrible cost to both peasants and workers.) Elsewhere, he suspected, 'the sense of responsibility... is confined to a few Italian Fascists and a few "god damned cranks"'. In his conclusion he effectively accepted, as the alternative to failed or corrupt democracy, a dictatorship of such aristocracies, as he had already in effect accepted the dictatorship of the great protagonist:

An aristocracy often dictates, it rules as long as it is composed of the strongest elements i.e. as long as it maintains its sense of the present. One might almost say as long as it maintains its news sense.

Both the communist party in Russia and the Fascist party in Italy are examples of aristocracy, active. They are the best, the pragmatical, the aware, the most thoughtful, the most wilful elements in their nations.

Hindsight probes those terms and finds them dangerously empty of particular, defining instances. In *Jefferson and/or Mussolini* Pound would go some way to providing the needed particulars in the case of Italy, and to developing the implications of 'the strongest' and 'the most wilful' beyond a crude 'might is right'. But did he know enough, and was he exercising his critical intelligence enough, to warrant his readiness to accept the dictatorship of those 'aristocracies' and of their leaders? He did know, when being critical of others, that 'Thought, dogblast you, thought is made up of particulars, and when those particulars cease to be vividly present to the consciousness in the general statement, thought ceases and blah begins.'

A striking feature of that 'Fungus' article is the evident loss of faith in the power of creative intelligence to influence the government of the state. There is no invocation now of the aristocracy of artistic genius. Instead we are told simply that 'Plutocracy does not favour the arts', and that 'The exploiter hates the intelligenzia (with reason)', as if there was nothing more to be said about the function of intelligence under democracy. As for Fascism, there it would appear that the artist had been displaced by the activist. That impression is confirmed by the terms in which Pound approved of Marinetti in 1932. In a letter to Zukofsky he mentioned that he had 'Had amiable jaw with Marinetti in Rome and have come back loaded with futurist and Fascist licherchoor.' Marinetti had dedicated Futurism to the service of Mussolini's Fascist regime, 'the glorious advent' of which, in Mussolini's own words, 'Futurism had prepared with twenty years of incessant artistic warfare consecrated in blood'. Pound recalled, in one of his notes in the Rapallo paper *Il Mare*, Marinetti's standing up in the public gallery during a session of the Italian deputies in 1919 to denounce Francesco Nitti, the prime minister, 'A nome dei Fasci di Combattimento, dei Futuristi e degli intelletuali', and to accuse him in unparliamentary language of sabotaging the victory. Gabriele D'Annunzio had congratulated him on that action; and Pound, in 1932, while conceding that Marinetti was not an especially good writer, saluted him as 'Marinetti activist' and suggested that he was to be honoured for having gone beyond writing into the further dimension of action. That achievement connected him, in Pound's thinking, with Lenin and Mussolini, 'the two who in our day know how to "move" in the highest degree, who are masters of speech that goes into action'.

That was the condition Pound's own prose aspired to in Italy—'speech that goes into action'. He began relatively mildly with a series of 'Appunti'—meaning 'notes to the point' or 'precisions'—in *L'Indice*, a fortnightly literary paper published in Genoa; but by the time of his wartime 'Radio Speeches' broadcast on Rome Radio from January 1941 to July 1943 he would frequently be playing the violent demagogue.

The score or so 'Appunti' contributed to *L'Indice* in 1930 and 1931 were not on the whole political. Pound's commission from the editor, Gino Saviotti, was to inform Italian readers about foreign literature and culture, and he did that by repeating his usual literary propaganda—on Lewis, Cocteau, Hemingway, Joyce; on the little magazines he was in touch with; and on such themes as the importance of realism and the need for international standards. Going on from that, he took it upon himself to tell Italian writers that they must learn to match the economy of English by cutting out all their unnecessary words, and that they should bring their work up to date by digesting the best in modern American and French writing. He was trying to do for Italian literature what he had tried to do for America in his London years. There was the difference though that rather than writing with the exasperation of an alienated exile he was establishing sympathetic relations with Fascist Italy. He told his interviewer in 1931 that he expected the surge of energy Fascism had unleashed to bring forth a new renaissance. He told his readers in *L'Indice* that 'every reinvigoration of Italian' must come from its origins in Latin; and he acknowledged his own debts to their Dante and Cavalcanti. He went so far as to say that had he been living in Italy in 1912 to 1924 he would have made common cause with the Futurists, at least on the need, in Italy, to clean out the dead past and to have a live contemporary perception precedent to the work of art. When his association with *L'Indice* ended in December 1931—the paper apparently 'went bust'—he intensified his effort to play an active part in the literary and cultural life of Italy by getting a local vortex going in Rapallo.

With Gino Saviotti and half a dozen other collaborators, notably Basil Bunting, Pound organised a 'Supplemento Letterario' which appeared every other week as an insert in Rapallo's weekly paper, *Il Mare*. For eight months, from August 1932 to March 1933, it was a two-page supplement, and then, from April to July 1933, was reduced to a single 'Pagina Letteraria'. The promise that it would reappear in October 1933, after taking a summer holiday, 'with, as always, the collaboration of the best Italian and foreign writers', was not kept. In its first phase the 'Supplemento' was determinedly international, with contributions from and about Italian, French, Spanish, German, and American writers and writing, and could claim to be giving a local focus to the most innovative and avant-garde work of its time. Pound contributed occasional 'Appunti', and recycled his *Little Review* 'Study of French Poets' and his notes on Vorticism. In one of his 'Appunti' he asserted that Futurism, the best of which satisfied the demands of Vorticism, had to be the dominant art of 'l'Italia Nuova'.

Pound had not given up his kicking against 'murkn imbecility and ignorance'. Towards the end of 1930 he initiated a correspondence with US Senator Bronson M. Cutting (1888–1935) of New Mexico, a Progressive Republican who had 'advocated the liberalization of federal laws governing censorship and copyright'. In fact in the debate in 1929–30 on censorship by the customs authorities Cutting had won 'the reputation of being the most literate and cultured man in the Senate'. In the course of his argument he had observed that censorship was 'a tool of tyranny', and that it was 'characteristic of the Fascist government of Italy, and equally characteristic of the Bolshevist government of Russia'. Pound made no comment on those points, but heartily agreed with him that it had no place in a free democracy. He wrote to Cutting to encourage him to move next against the censorship still exercised by the Post Office under 'Article 211 of the Penal code', the then current version of the 1873 Comstock Act which he described again as 'made by gorillas for the further stultification of imbeciles'. Cutting needed no convincing that 'the Baboon law...ought to be out of the criminal code altogether'. But he was a practical legislator in the real world of the democratic process, and had to accept that there was not 'the slightest chance of eliminating it'. However, he saw 'a tactical advantage in leaving the criminal feature, because in that shape it would go to the semi-liberal Judiciary Committee instead of to the hopeless Post Office Committee'. Even so, his amendment died on that occasion in the Judiciary Committee. 'Don't be too hopeful', he had advised Pound, 'It is hard running up against the organizations of canned virtue.' He kept on patiently trying to build support for an amendment in the following years, though still without success.

Pound, impatient with the Senate's complicated workings and with Cutting's pragmatic step-by-step activism, was inclined to hold democracy itself responsible, on account of its electing illiterates to represent it. He had asked Cutting for 'a list of the literate members of the senate', and been given the names of just ten Senators, '& I suppose Dwight Morrow'. That confirmed his conviction, expressed in a letter written to Langston Hughes in June 1932, that while 'the American govt. as INTENDED and as a system is as good a form of govt. as any, save possibly that outlined in the new Spanish [Republican] constitution', it allowed, as it was currently practised, 'the worst men in it to govern and...[lent] itself repeatedly to flagrant injustice'. In time that conviction would reduce itself to the outraged and absolute simplification which irrupts in canto 91, '*Democracies electing their sewage.*'

The pursuit of 'theoretical perfection in a government impels it ineluctably toward tyranny'. Pound could see that in the petty tyranny of customs inspectors burning with the righteous moral fervour of the crusade to preserve the nation from foreign obscenities such as Joyce's *Ulysses*. Yet he did not see it writ large in Bolshevist Russia and Fascist Italy. And he did not see that his own drive for a perfect system of government, with his absolute intolerance of the compromises and imperfections endemic in the democratic system, was impelling him ineluctably toward the embrace of tyranny. He had recorded in canto 8 how Plato the Idealist 'went to Dionysius of Syracuse | Because he had observed that tyrants | Were most efficient in all that they set their hands to'; but had he taken the point of the story, that Plato found 'he was unable to persuade Dionysius to any amelioration'?

The ameliorations Pound desired were on the whole enlightened. The trouble was not with his ideas in themselves but with his lack of realism as to how they might be put into effect. There was nothing undemocratic about his campaign for the abolition of censorship, of restrictive copyright laws, of passports and visas, and of anything else which acted as a barrier to the free passage of new invention. He supported the workers' demand for a universal forty-hour week—something proposed by Italy in a meeting of the International Labour Organization in September 1932, and opposed (then as now) by the government and employers' organizations of Great Britain. He was even more enthusiastically with those who called for a shortened working day of four or at most six hours, with no reduction in workers' pay. This he regarded as the workers' just dividend from advances in industrial productivity; and also, in the Depression, as a better remedy for unemployment than the dole. Again, observing that 'We live in a pluto-cratic era, i.e. *de facto* governed by money, with a thin wash of democratic pretense', he wanted to see the Federal Reserve Board 'democratized', so that the nation's credit should serve public need rather than private profit. All of these ideas were in the spirit of Jeffersonian democracy.

He campaigned above all, occasionally in violent terms, for the study of the causes of war, 'to prevent another slaughter by millions for the benefit of a few'. He identified the 'two causes of war' as 'the fight for markets', and 'the specific interest of the ineffable lice who want to make money by selling guns and munitions'; and he demanded detective work to expose the men and the forces making for war. These things should be *news*, he insisted, and wrote his own findings into his *Cantos* as 'news that STAYS news'.

The *Cantos*, of course, were not designed to have immediate effect in 'the sphere of action'. They belong to that other sphere of art in which Pound was a master of his medium. But he was not a master of the medium of political action. He was a more or less isolated individual, without a power base, without an organization, with no place in nor any leverage upon any political institution, with no political or diplomatic standing, without even an effective platform from which to hold forth. His prose 'Poundings' were scattered ineffectually among small magazines and the letters columns of newspapers, or were addressed as private instigations to senators, editors, authors, to anyone who caught his attention.

The prose itself, his only instrument in the sphere of action, was often such as to antagonize rather than persuade. It was characteristically charged with anger, contempt, and the will to kill (verbally). 'Certain kinds of mental slop, certain kinds of drivveling imbecility, do not survive . . . acquaintance with my better productions,' he boasted in the *New York Sun*'s 'The Bear Garden' section under his own, possibly self-mocking heading, 'That Messianic Urge'. At least one 'public enemy' did survive that attack, however, and counter-attacked the following week with a scornful dismant-ling of Pound's person, works, and reputation. It was all in the spirit of a bear garden, full of 'strife and tumult', and signifying very little. Moreover, the more aggressive Pound became in his prose, the more applicable to himself was the distinction he made in a private letter to Mike Gold, the editor of *New Masses*. As against effective writing 'where you are talking facts about what you know', there was the quite distinct 'mere blow off of egotism & irritation & impatience with everyone who don't kowtow to your particular . . . set of ideas'. That was the sort of writing Pound could lapse into, and it was not the likeliest way to change or to improve anyone else's mind, let alone to change the ways of governments.

The merely egotistical sounding off in Pound's more impatient activist prose, and its tendency to use language as a blunt instrument, must have been due to his feeling disempowered, to his inability to get an objective grip upon such complex actualities as the democratic process under capitalism and to act effectively upon them. It sounds like the protest of the individual who feels he must speak out but cannot make himself heard in the crowd. And here perhaps we come upon the solution to the nagging paradox of Pound being a passionate advocate of individuality and of the freedom of the individual, and yet being at the same time disposed to think better of dictatorship than of democracy. The powerless individual may look to an all-powerful individual to do what he would if only he could, and to manage the intractable masses who don't want to know what's best for them. It is individuality itself, when driven to desperation or carried to excess, that is the fraught bond between the free individual and the dictator.

There is another paradox to be teased out, if it is not an irreducible contradiction. How could Pound be such a master of words in his art and yet so ill-use them in his activist prose? He was fully aware that 'propagandist literature' was not 'serious literature', and that it was only the latter which had the power to renovate minds and thence governments. He had defended Brancusi's detachment from political action and insisted on the possibility of his saving the world 'by pure form'. He insisted on that again in 1929 when he was translating Boris de Schloezer's *Igor Stravinsky* for *The Dial* and was provoked into appending a striking note to the statement that 'the classic work [of art] does not come back into life, its action remains purely aesthetic'. 'So far as I can see', he wrote,

the setting up of such an [art-made] order comes back upon life very violently. The assertion or presentation of such an order in itself being the strongest possible attack on human imbecility, and the most effective means of disgusting the auditor with the idiocy that the millions of ape-men accept.—E.P.

Now what is striking about this is the assertion of the power of pure art in the language of the crude propagandist. Even more striking is the attempt to conscript that power into the agitprop attack, as if the contemplative artist might after all be serving the murderous activist's 'ultra-artistic or non-artistic' desires. Is it possible for the artist's 'rage for order' to be at one with the activist's rage to destroy whatever gets in the way of that order? They may have this in common, that both desire a right ordering of things. Yet their methods are so opposed that surely the negative must cancel out the positive, unless it be subordinated to the creative impulse. In the *Cantos* there is that subordination. But when one takes Pound's writings as a whole, prose and poetry together, one is confronted by the unresolved coexistence in him of the will to create and the will to destroy. This has been seen as evidence of self-contradiction, even of a schizophrenic or split personality. We are accustomed to thinking in binary terms, *either* this *or* that, and have difficulty allowing for *both* at the same time. It is possible nevertheless to conceive of creation and destruction, or of the contemplative and the warring, as phases of the one life. I rather think that the evidence will increasingly require us to think of Pound as (like Krishna in the *Bhagavad Gita*) willing *both* destruction and creation, as being both a destroyer and a maker. It is a problematic combination, and often a tragic one.

Cavalcanti: the intelligence of love

In the autumn of 1927, along with his other activities, Pound was deepening his understanding of the poetry of Guido Cavalcanti (1250–1300), and especially of the difficult 'Donna mi prega', a philosophical *canzone* defining the intelligence that is born of love. In mid-September Pound was in Venice and mentioned in a letter to Dorothy in London that he was working on 'Guido'. In October he mentioned in a letter to Olga in Paris that he was working on 'Guido's philosophy', and had been finding out, mostly from Étienne Gilson's book on medieval philosophy, about 'natural dimostramento'. That was a phrase in 'Donna mi prega', which Pound would make much of. If it meant, as he took it to mean, 'proof by natural reason' or even 'proof by experiment', or still further 'biological proof', then it would show that Guido's mind was not subject to the authority of medieval theology and to the syllogisms of Aquinas, as his young friend Dante's was. His thinking about love would have instead the authority of knowing it truly 'from nature's source'.

Pound was in Florence in November, studying early commentaries on Cavalcanti's poetry in the libraries there, and 'by miracle found and bought' from Orioli for just 300 francs a copy of the 1527 (Di Giunta) first printed edition of his works. Shortly after he formed the intention of putting together a new edition 'with full text in reproduction of original mss. etc.'

He submitted a proposal to T. S. Eliot at Faber & Gwyer for a book to have this title page:

Guido Cavalcanti | Le Rime | His Poems | Critical Text, with Translation and Commentary and Notes by | Ezra Pound | with a Partial Translation of the Poems by D. G. Rossetti | and with 48 Reproductions of the More Important Codices | Giving a Full Text of the Works in Facsimile...

'Specimen pages were prepared', Gallup notes in his *Ezra Pound: A Bibliography*, 'but it soon became evident that Pound's stipulations as to type-size and the inclusion of additional material would make the book much too expensive for Faber and Gwyer to undertake.' The small Aquila Press in London then agreed to take it over and in spring 1929 announced 'a monumental and definitive edition of the works of Guido Cavalcanti'.

Through 1928 and 1929 Pound worked away at his edition. In the libraries which held the early manuscripts—the Ambrosiana in Milan, the Capitolare in Verona, the Quirini Stampalia and the Marciana in Venice, the Riccardiana and Laurenziana in Florence, the Communale in Siena, the Vatican in Rome—he noted the variant readings and the explications of the various commentators. He marked up for the printer the translations of Cavalcanti in a 1908 Temple Classics edition of Rossetti's *Early Italian Poets*—these were to go on the right-hand pages facing the originals. He translated 'Donna mi prega' for the first time, and devoted his commentary and notes to elucidating it. This new work, the translation and commentary, appeared in sections in the *Dial* in March and July 1928, and, with the addition of 'Guido's Relations' (from the *Dial* of July 1929), became the 'Cavalcanti' essay in *Make It New* and *Literary Essays*. The photographic reproductions of the most important manuscripts were commissioned, and the printing of what was now to be called 'The Complete Works of Guido Cavalcanti' was begun. Fifty-six pages were type-set by hand in a truly 'monumental' format and printed off, and then, in the summer of 1930, the Aquila Press failed.

Pound recovered the five hundred or so sets of completed sheets, had the forty plates of reproductions printed off in Germany at his own expense, and paid Edizioni Marsano of Genoa to print the Italian text of Cavalcanti's poems with the variant readings given as marginal glosses, and also to print the very detailed apparatus concerning the manuscripts. The new pages containing the Italian text were numbered 1 to 56, as were the fifty-six pages salvaged from the Aquila Press. Both sets of pages were bound with the apparatus (pages numbered I–XVI) and the plates (numbered 1 to 40) in stiff paper covers, clear red in colour, to make up the book published in January 1932 as *Guido Cavalcanti Rime/Edizione rappezzata fra le rovine*, that is, an edition patched together from the ruins.[3]

David Anderson records that *Rime* received good reviews in England and the United States, while 'Italian scholarly journals failed to show any interest'. In Italy, apparently, only Mario Praz wrote on it at any length, 'and he ridiculed its disorderly appearance and suggested that Pound was not a good philologist'. Pound's meticulous work on the manuscripts seems not to have been taken into account by later editors. Étienne Gilson, reviewing the work in Eliot's *Criterion*, welcomed it warmly as a critical edition in his first paragraph, and then disagreed at length and fundamentally with 'the general interpretation of *Cavalcanti* which is everywhere implied' in it. He agreed that the 'Canzone d'amore' was very obscure; but he also thought certain parts more intelligible and simpler in the original than in Pound's version, and that the translation sometimes bore 'no relation whatever to the text'. As for Guido's philosophy, he feigned ignorance of it while asserting that it must have been simply what 'was commonly known and accepted by any man who had attended schools in his time'. In short, writing as an orthodox authority on Scholastic philosophy, he could not see and was not even interested by what Pound wanted to make of the 'Canzone d'amore'.

Pound was attempting to recover that 'very complicated structure of knowledge and perception, the paradise of the human mind under enlightenment', which he believed 'had run from Arnaut [Daniel] to Guido Cavalcanti' but had been 'hammered out of' François Villon. The word 'paradise' in that sentence, it should be noted, is delimited by 'knowledge and perception' and by 'the human mind': it would be a paradise of the mind, not of an immortal soul.

At the time of his first immersion in Cavalcanti, in 1910–12, Pound had celebrated him as a supreme 'psychologist of the emotions'. He particularly valued Guido's keen understanding and precise expression

---

[3] The patching showed in more than the numbering of the pages. The first part, a scholarly edition of the original texts of the *sonetti* and *ballate*, was in Italian, without facing English versions, except that Pound did insert new translations for five of the sonnets. In the second part a number of the remarks in the 'Indice dei manoscritti' and in the captions to the plates were in English because the printer had been given the manuscript prepared for the English edition. The third part, described on the contents page as 'Frammenti dell'edizione bilingue', presented first, in English, all but the final section of the 'Cavalcanti' essay of 1928–9, these thirty-six pages amounting to a scholarly edition of the *canzone* 'Donna mi prega' with translation and commentary. Then followed twenty pages of what was to have been the bilingual edition of the *Sonnets & Ballate*. Pound's introduction to his 1910–12 translations was given here, followed by the first pages of the *Sonnets*, with his newly edited Italian text facing his early versions— even though he could admit that 'my early versions of Guido are bogged in Dante Gabriel [Rossetti] and in Algernon [Swinburne]' (*LE* 194). *Rime* ended with the Italian text of sonnet 6 facing a blank page.

of pain itself, or of the apathy that comes when the emotions and possibilities of emotion are exhausted, or of that stranger state when the feeling by its intensity surpasses our powers of bearing and we seem to stand aside and watch it surging across some thing or being with whom we are no longer identified.

None of that is what the word 'emotions' would ordinarily bring to mind, especially not in the context of love poetry. Well, yes, the pain of love is a commonplace. 'Apathy', however, and even more 'that stranger state' point away from the commonplace to what Pound noted in Cavalcanti's 'psychological' 'Ballata XII', that Guido, 'Exhausted by a love born of fate and of the emotions', turns away to an intellectual love born out of that first love, and in this intellectual love 'he is remade', becoming another person.

He is changed, as one might say after Eliot, from a man who suffers into a mind which contemplates. But without the initial and initiating emotions there would be no change. 'It is only when the emotions illumine the perceptive powers that we see the reality', Pound declared, and then added this further emphasis, 'It is in the light of this double current that we look upon the face of the mystery unveiled.' That it is a 'double current', with the emotions lighting up the perceptive powers and the clarified perceptions intensifying the emotions, means that the 'new person' formed of and by desire is the same lover only in a different state of being. It is not the orthodox case of the intellectual soul rising above the physical body. It is rather that the mind has come to know and to understand what the lover's emotions have to tell of the nature of things. One might say that his emotions are what have made him intelligent. Pound, in Cavalcantian mode, would go further and say (with all that the words imply) that the intelligence that is born of love is the intelligence of creation itself.

What Pound had made of Cavalcanti in 1910–12 was most fully worked out at that time in the part of his own *Canzoni* which followed a mystic cult of love from its origins in the rites of Persephone at Eleusis, through the *fin amor* of Provence, to its culmination in the poetry of Dante and Cavalcanti. 'The Flame' in that volume was a celebration of what he then understood to be the rite by which a follower of that cult, rapt in the ecstasy of sunlit nature, might find a new identity in the light that is the life of the world, and so pass beyond the love of mortals. When he returned to Cavalcanti fifteen years later he came at him rather through his philosophy. It is important to note, however, that he was coming at the philosophy 'not as platonic formulation... but as psychology'. He was pursuing still a paradisal state of consciousness to be attained through the refinement of love. But he could speak of it now as a 'super-in-human refinement of the intellect', thus implying that it was a state of mind to be entered into through philosophy;

and yet at the same time he maintained that this Cavalcantian paradise had been lost in the philosophical speculations of Cavalcanti's time. The only way to resolve the apparent contradiction is to conclude that for Pound the philosophy does not matter, as Eliot could say at the heart of *East Coker*, 'The poetry does not matter.' That is, the philosophy is a means to an end beyond itself, not what the mind should remain caught up in. It is the attainment of the paradisal state of mind that matters, not the mere thinking about it, instrumental as that may be.

In 'Mediaevalism' (1928), the first section of his 'Cavalcanti' essay, Pound set out to isolate the specific new quality or *virtù* which distinguished the medieval Tuscan poets from 'the Greek aesthetic' and also from the troubadours of Provence. The 'Greek' or 'classic aesthetic' he characterized as 'moving toward coitus' and 'immediate satisfaction'. The troubadours had broken with that world by valuing 'the fine thing held in the mind' above 'the inferior thing ready for instant consumption'. The Tuscan aesthetic went on from that to demand something more than the heartening image in the mind's eye of the absent beloved. It cultivated 'the residue of perception, perception of something which requires a human being to produce it—which may even require a certain individual to produce it.' That involved 'an interactive force', and in that 'interactive force' was the Tuscan *virtù*.

But what exactly is this 'interactive force'? One gathers that it has to do with the 'Effect of a decent climate where a man leaves his nerve-set open, or allows it to tune in to its ambience', as Pound had tuned in (one reflects) to his ambience at Sirmione. Then there is 'The conception of the body as perfected instrument of the increasing intelligence', that is, as a receptive instrument. And what is to be received is 'the radiant world . . . of moving energies', of 'magnetisms that take form'; a world in which things are perceived as radiant energies, in which light moves *from* the eye, and in which 'one thought cuts through another with clean edge'. At the back of this there is the idea of light as informing every living thing. Pound cites Gilson's summary of the thinking of Robert Grosseteste (*c.*1170–1253) to the effect that light is an extremely rarefied physical substance which gives off of itself perpetually in every direction; and that it is the stuff of which all things are made, and their primal form. Pound read Cavalcanti's *'risplende in sè perpetuale effecto'*, which he translated in canto 36 as 'shineth out | Himself his own effect unendingly', as identifying Love's action with that of light; and thought it 'quite possible that the whole of ["Donna mi prega"] is a sort of metaphor on the generation of light'. Love then, in the *Canzone*, is Light; and Light is Love, that which animates and moves desire and thence illuminates 'the increasing intelligence'. The *Canzone* in Pound's reading is altogether concerned with the formative action of light upon the mind in love, and with the mind's interaction with it as it comprehends the light and reflects its shaping forms upon its world. At one point he questions the meaning of '*intenzion*', asking does it mean 'intention (a matter of will)? does it mean intuition, intuitive perception?' He leaves the question open, but might well have answered it by referring to Dante's line addressed to the spirits filled with love in his *Paradiso*, '*Voi che intendendo il terzo ciel movete*'—'*You who by understanding move the third heaven*'. Those spirits are not only illuminated by the light of divine love but understand it, and understanding it they will its action upon their sphere.

Pound quite deliberately stops short of any suggestion of Dante's paradise of beatified souls, as does Cavalcanti's *Canzone*. Its light is wholly natural, and works to perfect nature, and particularly to perfect natural intelligence. There is no hint of an immortal soul or of an eternal heaven, nor indeed of a Deity; and with those foundations removed Dante's whole system, and the entire Catholic system, would fall apart. One is in another mind-set; one is in, roughly speaking, the modern mind—which is, presumably, what Pound meant when he observed that Cavalcanti was 'much more "modern" than his young friend Dante Alighieri, *qui était diablement dans les idées reçues*'. As if to emphasize that difference Pound looked not to Aquinas but to Arab philosophers to help explicate the more difficult technical terms of the *Canzone*. In his copy of Ernest Renan's *Averroës et l'Averroïsme* (Paris, 1925) he particularly noted passages concerning the *active intellect* and the *passive intellect* and their relations. One might roughly transpose that into what Coleridge, defining Imagination in his very different world and time, called 'the eternal act of creation in the infinite I AM'—that would be the *active intellect*—and the *passive intellect* would be its 'repetition in the finite mind' where it is 'the living Power and prime Agent of all human Perception'. The Arab philosophers, in Renan's account, sought the union of their receiving intelligence with the informing and shaping intelligence of the universe. One wrote, 'the perfection of the rational soul is to reflect the universe', meaning to reflect it by actively knowing its process. All agreed that this felicity was to be attained only in this life: there was no question for them of a paradise out of this world or anywhere save in the mind.

The mystical philosophy becomes very technical and specialized in Pound's wrestling with the possible meaning of certain words in 'Donna mi prega', though what he was after was perhaps not so very far from his *Imagiste* mind 'ever at the interpretation of this vital universe', 'the universe of fluid force ... the germinal universe of wood alive, of stone alive'. By the time his *Guido Cavalcanti Rime* finally appeared he had had enough of 'the active and passive intellect (*possibile intelleto*, etc.)', and of trying to appre-hend the *Canzone* by way of the vocabulary of medieval philosophy. That had entangled him in confusions and obscurities, and brought him to the conclusion that the mystery was not to be explained in words, or at any rate that 'Verbal manifestation is of very limited use'. The trouble, he declared, is that one knows more than one ever puts into words, and that once one's immediate knowledge gets into 'the vain locus of verbal exchanges, it is damnably and insuperably difficult to get it thence into the consciousness' where it can be contemplated and assimilated. The mind of Europe had lost in that way what Paganism knew, or at least 'the ancient wisdom seems to have disappeared when the mysteries entered the vain space of Christian theological discussion'.

In 1931 Pound was recommending in his prose 'that students trying to understand the poesy of southern Europe from 1050 to 1400 should try to open it' using as the key, not the philosophy of the time, but instead the cult of Eleusis. That would explain, he suggested, 'not only general phenomena but particular beauties in Arnaut Daniel or in Guido Cavalcanti'. As to what he meant by 'the cult of Eleusis', he gave the hint that at the root of the mystery was 'consciousness of the unity with nature', while pointing out that those words would be an empty formulation without the immediate intuition of the interaction. He also went so far as to translate a rather wordy sentence from an Italian brochure to the effect that 'Paganism...not only did not disdain the erotic factor in its religious institutions but celebrated and exalted it, precisely because it encountered in it the marvellous vital principle infused by invisible Divinity into manifest nature'. Again he remarked that the idea was at once '"too well known"' and 'not in the least well *known*'. In an unpublished note he wrote, 'Coition the sacrament...The door to knowledge of nature...shd/ be moment of highest maximum consciousness...enlightenment.'

Partly in despair of expressing through translation and explanation all that Cavalcanti meant to him Pound turned to setting a selection of his poems to be sung in the original. 'The meaning can be explained', he wrote, 'but the emotion and the beauty can not be explained.' They could, however, be brought 'to the ear of the people, even when they can not understand it, or can not understand all of it at once'.

The idea of his composing another opera, this time with radio in mind from the start, seems to have come up when he was in Paris in May 1931 working with A. E. F. Harding of the BBC to adapt *Le Testament* for its radio production. That involved changing the 'visual libretto into an audible one'. In Venice that summer the air was 'full of radio . . . opry etc.'—he had heard a 'very good Rigoletto', he mentioned in one of his letters to Dorothy. When his *Villon* was broadcast on two successive evenings in October he listened to it on shortwave on both occasions in a Rapallo electrician's kitchen, and learnt something of the limitations of the still relatively undeveloped medium. His next opera, he told Dorothy, 'will be much clearer', by which he meant much simpler musically, and better adapted to the frequencies that could be transmitted without excessive distortion or loss.

He had started sketching out music based on some of Cavalcanti's *ballate* in September, and these sketches led to his composing in the latter half of October a set of four short *Sonate 'Ghuidonis'* for solo violin. That work was premiered by Olga Rudge in Paris in December. The melodies from the *Sonate* then went into the opera which was mainly composed between July and October 1932, with some final tidying up in June 1933. By then, however, Harding had been moved to another section of the BBC and the idea of a radio production lapsed. The score was put away, some in a suitcase under a bed and some among other manuscripts, and it was as good as lost until 1983, a full decade after Pound's death and half a century after it was completed, when it was recovered, edited, and produced in a concert version by Robert Hughes.

The opera is not so interesting musically as the earlier *Le Testament*, and does not bring out, to my ear at least, much in the way of 'the emotion and the beauty [that] can not be explained'. I find the interest to be rather in Guido's psychology and in the way he lives out his ideas. The selection of his *ballate*, and the *Canzone d'amore*, present his developing states of mind; and these are so arranged as to trace out the course of his life. The attention is thus shifted from the philosophy to what it would mean to live by it.

The first love of youth is already behind Guido in the opera, his songs of commonplace desire left for others to sing in the streets. Love draws him now to serve the idea of Love, and drives him to seek to know and to understand what it is by analysing and meditating upon his own experience. So his love grows intellectual, and the opera builds to the 'Donna me prega' in which the lady must be Sophia, the intellect's beloved. For her he defines the action of love as the process of universal light illuminating the mind. There was the light in a woman's eyes which first roused his desire, and which then, treasured in the mind, has so lit up his understanding that it has brought him 'into the clear light of philosophy' where he sees into the mystery of being. In the final act, as he dies having committed himself to the Lady he has served, a Lady characterized by her 'sweet intelligence', it appears that his desire is entirely absorbed and satisfied in that intellectual vision. The audience is made aware, however, that his philosophical para-dise is in his own mind only, and that it ceases with him. The light from Eleusis and from the troubadours of Provence has at once reached an extreme expression and has failed in him. His enlightenment has been without effect upon his world; and now, the opera concludes, the world will be given over to the vagaries of Fortune.[4]

Pound's Cavalcanti it would appear, is another of his isolated individuals of genius, another who sees the light others are impervious to but is unable to make it prevail. His new mind, his new *forma mentis*, did not set a renaissance going. All the same, being registered in his canzoni, it would outlast his and the time's failings.

In 1932 and 1933 while he was finishing his *Cavalcanti* Pound was also sketching out two other compositions on related themes. The one he completed was a transformation into wordless music for solo violin of Dante's 'Al poco giorno', a sestina expressing the condition of being locked in frustrated desire for a young woman who seems the figure of joyful Spring but towards the poet is unyielding stone. Pound at first draws contrasting melodies from the words but progressively takes off into a purely musical development of them to produce, in Robert Hughes's judgement, his 'most ambitious and advanced work for solo violin'. One may take the music to be a sympathetic yet critical response to Dante's poem, treating it as the negative aspect of his sublimation of desire (as in *La vita nuova*); but the music remains beyond words, and mysterious.

The other work was a planned but never completed third opera, 'Collis O Heliconii'. This was to feature, first, Catullus' epithalamium, 'Collis o Heliconii' (Carmen LXI), with its repeated invocation 'o Hymenaee Hymen, | o Hymen Hymenaee' as the bride is brought to her man and the Roman marriage bed; and then Sappho's ode (the one that begins 'Poikilothron') calling upon Aphrodite to light in the one Sappho loves a passion as ecstatic as her own. In Margaret Fisher's apt formulation, the opera was to have been 'a celebration of the sacrament' following upon 'the intellectualization of the sacrament' in *Cavalcanti* and 'the degradation of the sacrament' in *Le Testament*. Pound's not completing it will have had some-thing to do with its presenting 'no small technical problem'; but was probably due more to his being drawn out of music by his increasing activism. Some time in 1932 he told the poet and translator Robert Fitzgerald, 'I live in music for days at a time.' After 1933 those days were over.

---

[4] See Appendix C for a more detailed account of the opera.

Threads, tesserae

Olga Rudge told a story about Wanda Landowska, the renowned harpsichordist. Landowska had been interrupted in mid-sentence by the arrival of friends and a fuss about tickets, and had come back after a quarter of an hour and continued her sentence from where she left off. 'Is it the working with different voices in the fugues etc. makes her able to keep all the threads in her hand separate and distinct?', Olga wondered, 'like in a way the cantos?'

Rapallo, in 1928, set Yeats thinking of 'The little town described in the Ode on a Grecian Urn'. Keats as a matter of fact gave no description of his 'little town by river or sea shore'; but he did place it, 'emptied of [its] folk' and silent and desolate as it is, in the deathless condition of the wellwrought urn. Yeats, who was feeling his mortality upon him, was in search of a quiet haven away from the strenuous life he had been leading as an Irish senator, 'away from forbidden Dublin winters and all excited crowded places', and he must have been hoping that in Rapallo he might be able to write his rage against old age into the stillness and silence of art. For him the mountains which surround the town appeared to 'shelter the bay from all but the south wind', and its houses were 'mirrored in an almost motionless sea'. On his walk along the sea front he remarked 'peasants or working people' of the town, 'a famous German dramatist', and only 'a few tourists seeking tranquillity'. He was glad to find 'no great harbour full of yachts, no great yellow strand, no great ballroom, no great casino', and relieved that 'the rich carry elsewhere their strenuous lives'.

Pound appreciated other advantages of Rapallo, notably its being on the main railway line from Rome to Genoa and all places east, north, and west. It was easy to get away to Verona and Venice, to Austria, Germany, Switzerland, to Paris and London, or to go south to Siena and Florence or to Rome. It was convenient too for friends, fellow writers and artists, to stop off on their travels; and from time to time interesting new people would turn up on the sea front and in its cafés bringing news of what was being done in one metropolis or another. In 1927 Adrian Stokes was there 'with large trunk full of highbrow books (Spengler etc.)', and Pound read *The Decline of the West* 'in return for tips on XV century'. He told his father that 'As S. seems to mean by "The West" a lot of things I dislike, I shd. like to accept his infantine belief that they are "declining"'; but he was more taken by the Hungarian novelist Joseph Bard's talk of Leo Frobenius and the concept of *paideuma* or culture-formation. Relying on such communications, and of course on international mails, Pound used Rapallo as a base from which to mount his energetic campaigns to reform the world. Rapallo, he told his mother, was 'rapidly becoming the intellexshull centre of yourup'.

The small town seems not to have gone in for the manifestations of enthusiasm for Mussolini that were common elsewhere. McAlmon wrote in Pound's *Exile* that 'Italy then was maddening with rowdy, Fascistic, Italy-saving arrogance' on the part of 'her Mussolini-hypnotized town-toughs'. Mary and George Oppen saw something of that in Venice in 1932. As Mary Oppen recalled the incident, the Piazza San Marco suddenly filled with Black Shirts crying out, because Mussolini's life had been threatened, 'Il Duce—pericolo del morte', and on the faces of the press of young men they could see 'only a blind fanaticism, in ecstasy and worship of Il Duce'. So far as one can tell from Pound's correspondence that did not happen in Rapallo. One does find other refractions of Fascism in his letters, as his mentioning to Dorothy in October 1931 that 'evidently Vinciguerra and Lauro were sentenced to 15 years each…L. was drowned.' Lauro de Bosis, a gifted young writer they had known in Paris, upon being sentenced to *confino* or internal exile flew over Rome dropping thousands of anti-Fascist leaflets then flew on out to sea and was not seen again.

Both Ezra and Dorothy were often on the move away from Rapallo and from each other. At the end of April 1928 Dorothy was in London and Ezra was on his way to Vienna. He stopped off to visit Mary in Gais and to give her a tiny violin from her mother. (Mary, not yet three, 'banged it hard on the chicken coop, creating great fracas among the fluttering hens'.) George Antheil was in Vienna, giving well-received concerts and having his music published; Olga Rudge was there to play Mozart; and Pound was there encouraging her in her career and doing what he could to promote it and to get Antheil to promote it. An Antheil–Rudge American tour was in prospect. Also in prospect was a new Antheil production of Pound's *Le Testament*, in Germany or possibly in Dublin. Neither that nor the American tour materialized.

One thing that did come out of the weeks Pound spent in Vienna was 'the Mensdorff letter', as Pound would call it. Count Albert von Mensdorff was European agent for the Carnegie Endowment for Peace, and Pound persuaded him to write to his chairman in New York, Professor Nicholas Murray Butler, calling for an investigation of the causes of war. The 'active forces toward war' included, according to the letter, first, 'the whole trade in munitions and armaments'; and secondly, 'Overproduction and dumping, leading to trade rivalries'. The letter went on to ask for clarification of 'The principles of international law as recognised by the decisions of the permanent international Court of Justice', and then to ask the meaning of the unwillingness of the USA to adhere to that Court. The letter, with its very pertinent concerns, was politely acknowledged and ignored, to Pound's lasting disillusionment with the Carnegie Endowment and its chairman.

Dorothy wrote from London that Kitty Heyman, who had been playing Scriabin there, had spoken 'so warmly of Olga'. She wondered how Kitty could 'play so well with all that mystic mist?!' In Neumayer's bookshop she had found a set of Morrison's seven-volume *Dictionary of the Chinese Language* and 'would almost certainly get it'. Little Omar was a 'very cheerful soul—not very demonstrative'; yet, given a photo of Ezra by Olivia, he had 'kissed it passionately twice, so I suppose he has adopted you'. He 'Can lay the lunch table!'—this at eighteen months—and was 'very quick to learn with his hands: very preoccupied with my bag or box'. At the beginning of June Dorothy enquired of Pound, 'Is Vienna now the centre of the world?', and would he be returning to Rapallo?

Pound was in Rome at the end of September and through October of 1928 researching the Cavalcanti manuscripts in the Vatican library. Nancy Cunard was in Rome too, and sent a note to his hotel signed 'Avril', 'Longing to see you...Do we dine early?' Next morning there was another note from 'Avril': 'No but really I never saw anyone get electrically drunk (you) and as for what I (head mouth stomach) this 9 a.m. feel no-one need discuss'. 'Oh Ezra', the note went on, 'I'm not yet grounded enough in my new love life [with Henry Crowder] to be without certain whispers of need-company such day after-drunk days as this...when, where, where you?'

In October Olga Rudge seized a chance offered her to buy a small house in Venice. Calle Querini 252, San Gregorio, was in a quiet cul-de-sac not far from the Dogana and the church of Santa Maria della Salute. 'Three matchboxes on top of each other' was how it impressed one visitor. She raised the money by asking a good friend to pay a promised legacy in advance and asking her father for the rest. It was to be a place of her own, a private place for Pound to come to when he would. Only Pound just then was concentrating on his edition of Cavalcanti, and on his next cantos, and showed no enthusiasm for her project. Through the winter of 1928–9 Olga fell into an anxious depression and told him in one fierce letter after another how lonely and unhappy she was and unable to work at her violin through never knowing when she would see him if at all and feeling that he was casting her off for his legitimate wife. 'Five minutes of lucidity', Pound assured her, 'ought to show you that when I have been with you I was by no means magnetized TOWARD anyone else, or wanting to get BACK to anyone.' Then he added, 'It is only when you are doing your own job that there can be any magnetism'. There he was not choosing 'perfection of the work' against 'perfection of the life'; he was making the one the condition of the other. And it was in this moment of crisis, when Olga had written, 'Caro, I beg you, if you can explain or help, to be quick—I am just about finished', that he declared that his life would be impossible if he stopped to consider people's personal feelings. Perhaps she should take a younger man as her lover, he considerately advised. In time the little house would become their 'hidden nest', but just then Olga's heart was no longer in it.

In late March 1929 Pound left Rapallo and headed for Venice with the intention, he told Olga, of doing the beams, arches, and furniture of her *casa*. He did not tell her about his *amour de voyage* with a certain Miss Pamela Lovibond, though he did say something cryptic about having 'calf on the brain'. Miss Lovibond, one gathers from his letters to her, was a young English woman who knew Greek as well as Italian, had an interest in art, and was travelling in Italy with her family. From Verona, where he was trying to get into the library to check Cavalcanti's 'l'aere tremare', he wrote to Miss Lovibond at the Hotel Verdi in Rapallo, 'Darling...If I don't think you may arrive in Venezia on Wednesday—I am incapable of thinking anything, anyhow—except along complicated Machiavellian reasons that wouldn't take in a mouse.' His address in Venice would be 'Seguso, | 779 Zattere'. That was a Pensione half a mile or so from Calle Querini—it was where Olga was staying while her house was made habitable. His next letter, to 'Dearest Pam', was forwarded from Rapallo to Brioni, a small island off the Istrian coast across the Adriatic, the Lovibonds having gone there without stopping in Venice. 'Divine radiance lacking an address', Pound wrote, 'light of my life', and signed off 'il tuo intendido. | E.' A few days later—it was now Thursday 4 April and he had evidently heard from the goddess—he had to tell her 'can't use telephone in open hall', and nor could he disguise himself as a golfer in order to join her on Brioni. Golf, he believed, was what one did on Brioni. After that his ardour cooled rather rapidly. In a week it was 'Darling: Adrian [Stokes] says he will show you Venice', giving her Stokes's Venice address; and a week later, 'Dearest Pam', his own next address would be the Hotel Foyot in Paris. Miss Lovibond wrote to him there from Venice, a letter which eventually reached him in London at the end of May, by which time she was back home in Surrey. They met for lunch 'at Pagani's up stairs', and the glamour evidently had quite gone. The rest was a dozen friendly letters over the next three years, ending upon the note of a shared reminiscence of 'the venerable William sitting on the front' in Rapallo.

On 27 June that summer in London Mr and Mrs Ezra Pound invited a select audience 'to an evening of Mozart at 26 New Cavendish St. W.1 (by kindness of Mrs P. G. Konody)'. Three sonatas for violin and piano were to be performed by Olga Rudge and Vladimir Cernikoff. On 8 July Pound consulted Edgar Obermer at 14 Gower St. WC 1 and was advised to take: an endocrine preparation for the parathyroid gland; daily injections of Pituitrin; courses of Atophon; also powders supplied by Obermer. As to diet, 'cut down animal protein to a minimum—no reason to restrict sweets and starchy foods of all kinds—fluids, plenty of water; wine and all alcohol to be very occasional, a well-diluted whisky not objectionable'. Some at least of this regime Pound seems to have followed. The following May, finding it prohibited in Paris, he asked Dorothy to get him a repeat prescription of Pituitrin, two boxes of six ampoules, also Parathyroid pills, 'and the anti-cold serum'. Dorothy, consulting Obermer on her own account, was diagnosed as having 'poor circulation and a vile rheumaticy heredity'. In July she asked if there was any 'Obermer medicine' she could bring from London for Olga. 'Thyro-manganese cachets', Pound replied, to be mailed to Olga in Paris.

Earlier in the summer of 1929 when Pound was in Paris he had been with H.D. and Nancy Cunard's Henry in a taxi, and according to H.D. who told Aldington who then told Brigit Patmore, Henry Crowder—a native Indian and Negro jazz musician—'said "Pray Ezra", and Ezra invented a long prayer about Jordan, and Henry kept shouting "Halleluiah"'. H.D. had had 'a lovely time', apparently, though she then wrote to her lover Bryher, who couldn't stand Pound, that Pound was 'so terribly ridiculous and grown fat'.

Homer Pound retired from the Mint in June 1928 at the age of 70. Ford, visiting 'Ezra's people' the previous November, had found them 'delightful—particularly the father: it was really like visiting Philemon and Baucis'. Ezra was looking forward to their retiring to Rapallo and had been looking at empty apartments for them and sending detailed advice on what household goods to bring and how to transport books and pictures. He had also offered Homer advice on investing in bonds: 'If you are investing say 5000, put it in five different places . . . leaves one less disturbable by winds of political hogwash, wars pestilences etc.' The elder Pounds sailed for England on 1 June 1929, and would have been greeted there by Pound and introduced to little Omar about whom they had heard so much in Dorothy's letters. They went on to Rapallo to see what they thought of it and by September had decided they would take up permanent residence there and sell the Wyncote home. Isabel, Ford's 'Baucis', wrote to a friend,

Wyncote is very lovely, but does not equal Rapallo (Italy). We now have a blue cottage amid the gray green olive trees where the birds sing, the sea chants, waves roam and splash and the mountains remain quiet, waiting for Mohammed to come to them. Flowers are in bloom in all the gardens, Narcissus, Japonica, Jonquils, Heliotrope etc. Oranges hang on their trees, we have lots of fruit, walnuts and almonds, and life goes very pleasantly.

When, in July 1930, Yeats and his wife decided to return to Dublin the Homer Pounds took over for a time their fine, modern apartment on the fourth floor of via Americhe 12.

In the last week of October 1929 the bottom fell out of the US stock market. For two years there had been feverish speculation in 'securities' and, when the boom turned to panic, investments and investors, banks and borrowers, were wiped out. The Wall Street Crash spread economic depression like a tsunami wave all round the globe. Banks foreclosed on mortgages and called in credits, primary producers and industries went bankrupt, demand for goods slumped, and mass unemployment spread. Bankers, economists, and politicians were all held responsible; and, by the more thoughtful, the self-regulating capitalist financial system was called in question. Thus the stage was set for the rise of national socialist political movements committed to state regulation of capitalist enterprise, and for the rise of another charismatic political leader.

Olga Rudge was fortunate to have bought her Venetian house just before the Crash since that was to leave her father hard up and unable to go on supporting her financially. She moved into the Calle Querini *casa* in August or early September 1929, and Pound was with her for the last two weeks of September. He then went to meet up with Dorothy at Brescia for a few days on Lago d'Iseo, and on his way confessed to Olga from Verona, rather in a tone of surprise and self-congratulation, that he had experienced a brief but 'mos' noble feeling of desolation'. He could assure her that, 'filled with most noble sorrow for 45 minutes... [h]e was ready to take the next train to Zattere'. However, his librarian friend Dazzi had taken him to the Dodici Apostoli restaurant and his next experience was of the remarkable effect of 'bird and booze' on such sorrow.

In November Olga remarked, 'it is a year and a half since anyone has seen the child, and as I have been in Italy most of that time it looks bad... I only want to be sure in most selfish manner that duty to offspring not going to lose mi amante.' It was agreed that the Leoncina should be brought to Venice by Frau Marcher for a week or so in December, and that Pound should be there too. It was a great event for Frau Marcher, while the child remembered the kindness of 'the Herr', and how he 'looked at me approvingly and hugged me'. Her clearest memory was of 'leaning out of a gondola, splashing with my hands'. From Rapallo Pound wrote to Olga that he had told his father that he had a granddaughter, and that Homer was 'duly and properly pleased'. It is likely though that Homer had known for some time. Father and son apparently agreed that Isabel would be too deeply shocked and should not be told of young Mary's existence.

In January 1930 Olga, in freezing Paris, relapsed into despair and mentioned suicide. Pound wrote express that it was not the moment: 'That she shd do this just as she reaches the quality of amore that she had wanted—no—ça serait trop bête', it would be just too stupid. He followed that up with long daily letters remarkable for his attending to her situation and needs rather than to his own, and for his not insisting they each do their own independent thing without impinging upon the other. 'She dont seem to understand when she gets inside him', he wrote in one letter, adding 'Which she did not at first'; then a few days and letters later, 'she get it into her head that he dont want to go on without her either', with the postscript, 'e ti voglio bene, con amore; and not with any plain benevolenza'. Olga meanwhile was trying to tell him that what she loved was the god she discerned in him, and that she wanted her god incarnate—which was not to say that she thought him a god. He accepted that in his own terms, replying that if he was to be the centre of her universe, still his work remained the centre of him, and she should come to him 'when she was feeling that she wanted to see him ed anche [and also] wanting to help him work'. He had already taken part of a 'casa sulla montagna' for her to come to. And from February 1930 Olga did make her own whenever she was in Rapallo the upper floor of *casa* 60 Sant' Ambrogio, a peasant family's house forty-five minutes' walk above the town and overlooking the bay. They had come through the crisis of their relationship by breaking through to its core, and upon that it would now be durably established.

It was still though a relationship that could not speak its name, respectability dictating that they must not be seen together in the town, or at any rate that there should be no appearance of intimacy. Even, or perhaps especially, Homer and Isabel were kept in the dark about that. When Olga was in her *casa* Pound would walk up the hill of an afternoon. When Dorothy was away Olga might come down to Pound, but her meals would have to be sent up from the restaurant to the rooftop apartment, and if anyone called she would have to hide herself away.

In April Ezra and Olga were together in Paris, Pound correcting proofs of *A Draft of XXX Cantos*. From there he reported to Dorothy: 'Uproarious evening with Joyces. Norah insisting on my swallowing 25 frs. worth of caviar—no expense to be spared.'

Dorothy had written, 'Omar comes to tea today, Saturday'. Also that she and Olivia were thinking of going to Frankfort in May for Antheil's

Transatlantic. The readers of the Jenkintown *Times-Chronicle* were informed about the same time that Homer Pound and his son would be in Frankfort for the première of the opera. Homer's main motive may have been to see his granddaughter en route. A photograph taken at the time shows a trinity of benevolently brooding grandfather, the poet as father reaching out to his daughter, and a sturdy small girl with a self-possessed but doubtful expression. On their way back from Frankfort, in Verona, Homer had Pound send Dorothy a postcard of the statue of Can Grande on his horse, for her to show Can Grande's grin to Omar.

Antheil presented a copy of the vocal score of *Transatlantic (The People's Choice)* to Pound with the inscription, '*For Ezra, truest of all friends I dedicate this first of my really printed works... March 23, 1930*'. The leading persons of the opera were Helen, Hector, Ajax, Jason, Leo, Gladys; the place was NY City; and the time 'modern'. Bootleggers, gangsters, politicians, and crooks strutted and sang against a background of skyscrapers, transatlantic liners, jingling telephones, and newspaper bulletins. Act 3— twenty-seven scenes played on four simultaneous stages and a movie screen—opened with a street scene outside Hector's HQ in a US Presidency campaign. Critics applauded, but it was noticed that Antheil's music had become relatively conventional, and that the scoring was simpler 'than, say, the followers of Wagner and Richard Strauss'.

Pound's relations with America were as ever a mixup of love and hatred. A fundraising letter sent to him as an alumnus of Hamilton College provoked an outburst against its professors as pampered parasites upon ill-rewarded writers, and as never considering 'the relation of literature to the state, to society or to the individual'. Yet he was pleased to recommend Zukofsky for an assistant professorship at the University of Wisconsin (Madison). However, it was the America of the Founding Fathers that he was most in sympathy with. For the next decad of cantos he was casting about for biographies and letters and diaries of Jefferson and the Adamses. Did Zukofsky 'know anything of the whereabouts of J. *Quincy* Adams' diary'? and Martin Van Buren's autobiography, 'or maybe it's a diary'? In April 1931 he was 'swatting at' John Adams in the Bibliothèque Nationale in Paris, 'but the "woiks" wd take 50 days at 100 pages per diem. // must invent some skimmier method', he wrote to Dorothy. (He would acquire his own set of the *Works* and find his 'skimmier method' for digesting Adams into a decad of cantos in 1938.) As for contemporary America, it was getting on for twenty years since he was last there, and he knew of its Jazz Age and Prohibition Era only by report and through its repercussions in Paris. The young Oppens, in France and Italy to see how America looked from a distance, paid a visit to Pound in Rapallo before going home. In her autobiography Mary Oppen recalled Pound's impressing upon them, 'Read, study the languages, read the poets in their own tongues.' Their message to him would have been, 'You are too far away from your own roots... Go home.' But he knew too well what to expect if he were to do that. The US authorities had recently seized a copy of *A Draft of XVI Cantos* and attempted to prosecute under the Comstock Act the bookseller who had imported it.

Yvor Winters, the American poet, critic, and academic who had arrived at a dogged belief in rhyme and set forms of verse and who had deplored Pound's 'abandonment of logic in the *Cantos*', wrote to Pound from Palo Alto, 'fifty years hence my name will be in better repute than yours'. Pound retorted that there were more forms of logic than Winters could imagine.

In mid-August 1931 Ford had run out of money and asked Pound if he could lend him a hundred dollars. Pound sent the hundred dollars at once. Neither mentioned the developing sterling crisis. Dorothy wrote from Sidmouth at the beginning of September, 'The Child is a queer object: it's very pretty: and chatterbox.... He has bought a little present for you.' Later in the month she wrote that she was arranging the sale of some of her mother's shares, the proceeds to be made over to Pound. It seems that Olivia Shakespear had been giving him £300 a year, and was now making over the capital which should bring in that amount. She would be leaving her estate to Omar, she had told Pound, but Dorothy was to have a life-interest.

Dorothy and Olivia became extremely concerned as to how the sterling crisis would affect the investments on which their incomes depended. The value of the pound was at that time fixed by its being notionally redeemable in gold. In fact it was propped up by foreign investments, and when foreign investors withdrew their money en masse in August and September the gold standard had to be abandoned and the value of sterling allowed to fall. Pound reported from Rapallo that hotels in France were giving only 85 or 90 francs to the pound instead of 123. In New York it was down from around $5 to $4.15. If it could be held at $4, he advised, there would be nothing for Olivia to worry about; and it was a blessing that Dorothy had money invested in America. But of course the English money which she transferred into *lire* for use in Italy would yield much less than before. 'I dare say I could start doing the cooking again,' Pound reflected.

He was less worried though than stimulated by the crisis, which he was finding 'more exciting intellectually than Aug. 1914'. It showed that Douglas had been right about the nation's credit, and that the value of the currency should be related not to gold but to productive work. Perhaps now people would take notice of Douglas, though it might need 'a complete collapse [to] civilize the country'. In October he advised that it would be as well for Olivia to get 5 per cent of her capital out of England 'as an insurance policy', and to invest it in industrials in New York, such as 'Detroit Edison' and 'Am/ Smelting and refining'. And if Parkyn, the family solicitor, could extract a thousand pounds out of Dorothy's £8,000 capital she might 'plug that into Italian electric'. Olivia let him know that it was all very well for him, a 'man without a country', to be advising her to get her money out of *her* country before it sank completely. Parkyn evidently shared her patriotic feelings. And Pound wrote to Dorothy, 'I spent 12 years trying to save her dithering and dodgering hempire. I rubbed Keynes nose into Douglas etc. etc; AT A TIME WHEN it might have been some use'. In any case, 'A completely crashed England etc// might get round to knowing what it needs/'.

Late one afternoon in early October 1931 Dorothy 'ran into a terrific crowd of unemployed' around Marble Arch at the top of Park Lane. The area was swarming with police and traffic was held up for miles. Then she 'met 'em all marching along Wigmore [Street]: 1000s with police mounted and on foot'. 'Rather awful', was her reaction. Pound's *Villon* was to be broadcast by the BBC later in the month. He would be paid just £50 for the two broadcasts, less tax at five shillings in the pound, less probably a further 25 per cent due to the devaluation of the pound. However, he did get his bust by Gaudier out of England that November, and eventually had it set up on his rooftop terrace in Rapallo.

'When I can git on wif my pome, I ain't so restless.' Pound had explained himself thus to Aldington in 1927, and it was no doubt how he felt. Yet he was able to combine the still intensity of composition with a busily active life. In the years 1930, 1931, and 1932 he was much occupied with his Cavalcanti edition and opera; with the BBC production of *Le Testament*; with a host of little magazines; with correspondents ranging from Zukofsky to Senator Cutting; with putting together *Profile*, an anthology 'of poems which have stuck in my memory', and *Active Anthology*; and with preparing a comprehensive collected edition of his prose. There was also his hardly tranquil private life. With all that he made steady progress from canto 31, which he began drafting in the autumn of 1930, through to canto 41 completed some time in 1933. Cantos 31–3 were ready for publication in *Pagany* in the summer of 1931. That autumn he mentioned to Dorothy, almost as an aside in the course of advising and commenting upon the sterling crisis, 'have now material for three more canti/ . . . toward vol. 3 of folio'. He was evidently hoping then for a third *de luxe* edition to go on from *17–27*, and suggested that Dorothy could be thinking at her leisure about doing the capitals for it. A year later he was 'proceeding toward Canto XXXX', and 'dead with work'. Now, thanks to the intervention of Archibald MacLeish, he had a contract with an American firm, Farrar and Rinehart, for the publication of *A Draft of XXX Cantos*, to be followed by publication in England by Faber & Faber; and the same publishers would bring out *Cantos XXXI–XLI* in 1934 in England and 1935 in the United States. He was conscious, as he told Ford, that the growing poem was not *yet* a 'shining example' of 'major form' or 'Form of the whole'.

Pound had been working at a collected edition of his prose writings from at least 1929, when the Aquila Press was going to bring it out after doing his Cavalcanti *Rime*. When Aquila failed, Caresse Crosby's Black Sun Press thought about taking it on. In 1931 the newly formed firm of Hamish Hamilton asked for first refusal. Then young George and Mary Oppen, with Louis Zukofsky as their editorial adviser, set up as publishers from their rented farmhouse in the middle of a vineyard near Le Beausset, inland from Toulon on the road to Marseille. Calling themselves To, Publishers— 'To', Zukofsky explained, 'as we might say, a health to'—and using French printers with a scant knowledge of English, they published Zukofsky's major *'Objectivists' Anthology*, William Carlos Williams's *A Novelette and Other Prose*, and then brought out the first of a projected twelve volumes of Pound's prose. Paperbound, it was to sell relatively cheaply at $1 a copy, only there was no sales organization, and the Oppens' capital ran out. In August 1932 George Oppen wrote to Pound, 'There is no possibility of continuing To "under present conditions"....I'll have Darantière return your Ms. Registered.' That was the end of the collected edition. In its place Faber & Faber published in September 1934 *Make It New*, a fined down selection of Pound's major literary essays.

The collected edition could well have been a monumental mess. Pound's idea, as he explained it to his mother in November 1927, was that the whole of his prose to date should be recast in such a way that 'the until-now apparently random and scattered work all falls into shape, and one sees, or shd. see wot is related to wot, and why the stuff is not merely inconsequent notes'. *How to Read* had to come first as 'a sort of pivot' giving the central idea around which everything would fall into order. In accord with that the To Publishers volume, titled *Prolegomena I*, contained *How to Read* followed by 'Part 1' of *The Spirit of Romance*, i.e. chapters I–IV with the new chapter V, 'Psychology and Troubadours'. After that, according to Pound's outline for the twelve 'Books' of his 'Collected Prose', books III–V were to give his 'Manifestos on reform of poetry and contemporary movements' of 1912–18, drawn from *The Egoist, New Age, Poetry, Little Review*, etc.; and books VII–X would give the later prose of 1920–8. *Instigations* would be

preserved as book VI, *Indiscretions* as book XI, and *Ta Hio* as the conclud-
ing book XII. In recasting the materials from periodicals Pound selected,
revised, and corrected extensively, and also added a linking narrative and
commentary. Altogether he assembled more than 1,653 pages. As the
researcher leafs through them the words 'megalomania' and 'doomed' flit
through the mind. Why fight past battles over again? And whatever
happened to his principles of selection and condensation, to the economy
of the luminous detail? Was it that his hates, his 'instinct of negation', knew
no bounds? His readers in the 1930s had reason to be grateful that in *Make
It New* and *ABC of Reading* (1934) he found a better way of getting across
his provoking and instructive critical effort.[5]

The two anthologies Pound put together at the start of the 1930s
practised a different order of criticism, one that was affirmative and cura-
torial, and which did its work by presenting selected exhibits with a
minimum of commentary. *Profile: An Anthology Collected in MCMXXXI*
and published by Giovanni Schweiller in Milan in 1932 was, according to
Pound's note in *Active Anthology*, 'a critical narrative' attempting 'to show
by excerpt what had occurred during the past quarter of a century'. That
was, in effect, to go back to his own arrival in London in 1908, and then to
come forward to where he was now. He placed first Symons's 'Modern
Beauty' from the 1890s, then represented Ford, Hulme and Williams as
preceding the Imagists, followed by 'Imagist and post imagist additions'
(H.D., Aldington, and his own 'Coming of War: Actaeon'); Eliot's
'Hippopotamus' and 'Burbank', Marianne Moore and Mina Loy, a war
poem by Donald Evans, and an extract from *Mauberley*, carried the narra-
tive from '1915 to 1925'; and '1925 and after' was represented by a rather
mixed lot of individualities, including Cummings, Zukofsky, Dunning, Eliot
('Fragment of an Agon' from *Sweeney Agonistes*), and Bunting ('Villon').
Rather tellingly, Zukofsky is the only one of the American Objectivists to
feature in *Profile*. Pound would endorse Zukofsky's *'Objectivists' Anthology*
as 'the first effort to "clear up the mess" since my effort in or about 1913'.

---

[5] *Make It New* was published in September 1934 by Faber & Faber in a format matching that of
Eliot's *Selected Essays* (2nd edn., revised and enlarged, October 1934). It contained 'Troubadours: Their
Sorts and Conditions' (1912) and 'Arnaut Daniel' (1920)—these classified as examinations of 'speech in
relation to music'; 'Notes on Elizabethan Clasicists' (1917), 'Translators of Greek' (1918), and 'French
Poets' (1918)—these classified as examinations of speech; 'Henry James and Remy de Gourmont'
(1918, 1919)—examinations of 'General state of human consciousness in decades immediately before
my own'; 'A Stray Document', reprinting the principles of *Imagisme*; and finally 'Cavalcanti' (1910/
1931), 'as bringing together all these strands, the consciousness, depth of same almost untouched in
writing between his time and that of Ibsen and James' (*MIN* 15). All of these studies, with the exception
only of 'French Poets', were included in *LE* in 1954.

But at the same time he was dissociating himself from this new effort on account of its tendency to 'a sort of neo-Gongorism, that is a disproportionate attention to detail at the expense of main drive', or a tendency to be so attentive to language as to destroy 'the feel of actual speech'. To balance or counter that failing Pound included in *Profile* a dozen pages of 'proletarian' verse from *New Masses*, among them several 'Negro Songs of Protest'. It was as if he wanted to point up the direct voice of political consciousness as the missing element in Objectivism.

There is the same emphasis on the world in the word, on the signified rather than the signifier, throughout *Active Anthology* (1933). Reopening the volume after an interval Pound was pleased to find 'something solid' in Bunting's poetry and Zukofsky's, to which he had devoted respectively fifty pages (nearly a quarter of the whole) and forty-three pages; and to find that, after theirs, Marianne Moore's twenty-one pages were 'the solidest stuff in the Anthology', and that Williams's realism, to which he had given twenty-five pages, though 'not so thoughtful', had a 'solid solidity' comparable to Flaubert's. Poetic realism then was what he had put on show, to the end, as he intimated in his preface, that a moribund Britain might see what it was missing. He did not mention Eliot among the solid contributors, although he had included 'Fragment of a Prologue' (from *Sweeney Agonistes*). Instead he spent most of his preface quarrelling with Eliot's recently published *Selected Essays 1917–1932* for conceding too much to a British literary bureaucracy which did not want live poetry and an active culture. 'If I was in any sense the revolution', he declared, then 'I have been followed by the counter-revolution'. Louis Zukofsky saw it differently when he looked into the anthology in the much altered world of post-war America. 'I must say I have never felt so inclined to admire Ezra's perceptions', he wrote to Williams in 1949, it having struck him that Pound had seen in his own work, and in Bunting's and Williams's, 'a necessity' that had not been apparent even to themselves at the time. 'As a piece of criticism', he wrote, 'his anthology of 1933 emerges as a work of genius.'

In her letter from London on 11 September 1932 Dorothy mentioned that 'We had Omar's birthday yesterday—Cake and candles'. Parkyn, the family solicitor, had been in attendance, also Marquesita, a contralto famous as Lucy Lockit in *The Beggars Opera*, and there had been 'presents all round'. In Rapallo Homer had reminded Pound that it was Omar's sixth birthday.

In December 1932 Pound heard from Caresse Crosby that 'Max Ernst is being sold at auction on Thursday; furniture, shoes, tableaux'. He immediately sent her 500 francs, all he had available, either to give to Ernst in cash so that his creditors could not get at it, or to buy up his pictures in the auction and let Ernst know that he could have them back whenever he wanted them for whatever Pound had paid.

The 'Decennio', the first decade of Fascist rule in Italy, was being celebrated in 1932–3, and F. Ferruccio Cerio, one of the editors of the 'Supplemento Letterario' of Rapallo's *Il Mare*, drafted a scenario for a film treatment of the story of Italian Fascism, with the title 'Le *Fiamme Nere*', 'The *Black Flames*'. Pound was called in to adapt the scenario to make it suitable for foreign distribution, and the scenario with his notes was privately printed in Rapallo in December 1932. Pound immediately went down to Rome and sent a copy in to Mussolini's private secretary with a request for an audience with the Duce. He had sought one before in vain, but this time he was told that Mussolini would see him on 30 January of *anno XI*.

PART TWO : 1933–1939

Think of your own work. Nothing else matters,
we have been mad with crusading.

—EP to Alice Corbin Henderson, 5 May 1916

3 : A Democrat in Italy, 1933

Il Poeta meets Il Duce

Signor Benito Mussolini was now in his own person, by law, the supreme law-maker of Italy, and as such was known as *Capo del Governo*; more, he was by both law and popular assent *capo* of the nation, its head and leader, *Il Duce*. Though formally subject to the King, and only to the King, he ruled much as kings had ruled before there were republican revolutions. He went so far as to claim to embody mystically the State and the People as kings were once held to do; and the Italian people for the most part, rather than holding him answerable to themselves, put their faith in him and loved and followed him as if he were indeed the incarnation of the nation's spirit.

Yet it was by a republican, even a socialist, revolution that Mussolini had come to such singular power. His position was altogether a cornucopia of contradictions. And it was by virtue of those contradictions that this son of a village blacksmith had managed to unite in himself an Italy which just ten years before had been breaking down into anarchy as the old ruling class proved powerless to contain the rising but still weak forces of Communism and socialism. It had been a dogfight lacking a top dog until Mussolini seized absolute power by a combination of calculated violence, inspired opportunism, ruthless suppression of opponents and dissenters, and acute political insight amounting to genius. The cartoon versions of him as a puffed up buffoon or thick thug are good for anti-Fascist propaganda, but are otherwise simply ridiculous. He was a man to be taken very seriously. In the ten years since the King had appointed him to form a government in October 1922 he had seen off the opposing parliamentary parties by parliamentary process, so that his Fascist party, having full control of the state, in effect became the state; and he had purged his party of its violent and criminal elements once they had served their turn, and then subordinated its at-first independent regional leaders to his will, so that he now stood over and above his party and personally ran the state. At the same time he had replaced trade unions, employers' organizations, and professional bodies with Fascist organizations, effectively incorporating all classes and kinds of workers into the Fascist project; along with that he had required of all teachers, university professors, and public servants an oath of loyalty to the state; and he had set up Fascist institutions to organize and direct all intellectual, cultural, sporting, and leisure activities. He had thus brought into being not only the idea but a partial realization of a totalitarian state, one in which all its consenting members and all its activities should be bound together as in a single entity with one mind, one purpose, one will, and that mind, purpose, and will his own. That was the idea of the Fascist emblem taken over from ancient Rome and emblazoned everywhere in Mussolini's new Italy: thin rods each weak in itself but of great strength when cut and shaped by the axe of lawful authority and bound tightly together.

Mussolini was still generally perceived, in 1933, as a benevolent dictator, that is as one exercising his all-encompassing authority to promote a better order in Italy. The great Decennale Exhibition in Rome had some major reforms to celebrate, beyond getting the trains to run on time. The Fascist social and welfare provision for workers was ahead of even that of New Zealand: there were already in force an eight-hour day, a minimum wage, guaranteed work and continuity of employment, regulation of the work of women and children, compulsory TB and sickness and accident insurance, provision for old age, and workers' representation alongside employers in the new Fascist corporations. Then there was a vast programme of public works, 'whose crowning glory was the draining of the malaria-infested, largely uninhabited Pontine Marshes to the south of Rome which emperors, popes, kings and the odd prime minister had all tried and failed to make habitable'. Millions of hectares of once waste land were brought into cultivation. There was new housing; new towns were built and old ones, especially Rome itself, were renovated. New roads were constructed, including Europe's first motorway, and new bridges and aqueducts. 'The great Public Utilities of the State', Mussolini could claim, 'railroads, mail, telegraph, telephone' had been made to function efficiently, and even 'the Italian Bureaucracy, proverbially slow, has become eager and agile'. Not only did the trains run on time but they ran faster, thanks to the electrification of the railway network. And still there were people, Mussolini observed, who 'whine because there is efficiency and order in the world'.

His new 'efficiency and order' did involve a good deal of regimentation. 'The citizen in the Fascist State', Mussolini had declared, 'is no longer a selfish individual to whom is given the anti-social right of rebelling against any law of the Collectivity.' Put another way, the Fascist individual would find his fulfilment in transcending his personal desires and living within and for the state. Fascism was austerely, religiously, anti-individualistic and anti-democratic, and indeed rather despised capitalist democracy as having failed—perhaps terminally in the 1929 Crash—through allowing excessive freedom to the selfish individual. At the same time Fascism was not against private property or private wealth, the former being accepted as making for social stability; and capital being welcomed as 'an increasingly important actor in the drama of production', on condition that it be deployed not for private profit but in the collective interest as determined by the Fascist state.

It was held to be in the collective interest that Italy should become strong among the industrially advanced, capitalist nations; but it was also held to be in its collective interest to solve the problem of the unequal distribution of wealth and 'to end the cruel fact of poverty in the midst of abundance', a socialist aspiration. This synthesis of capitalism and socialism was Mussolini's 'Third Way'. Fascism was to supersede the economic liberalism of capitalism, by regulating and directing the economy in the national interest; and it was to supersede the Marxist Leninist form of socialism by not abolishing private property and not nationalizing the means of production. That said, it was on good terms with capitalists and capitalism; and at enmity with Communism—its own Communists were regarded as enemies of the state and were the most liable of its dissenters to be sent into exile or imprisoned. Hence the bitterness of Communist critiques of Fascism; and hence the early friendliness of the capitalist democracies to Mussolini's Fascist Italy.

Winston Churchill, speaking in February 1933 as a Conservative member of parliament to the British Anti-Socialist and Anti-Communist League, declared that 'The Roman genius impersonated in Mussolini, the greatest law-giver among living men, has shown to many nations how they can resist the pressures of Socialism.' America's *Fortune* magazine, the glossy display window of US capitalism, praised him for showing 'the virtue of force and centralized government acting without conflict for the whole nation at once'. And Franklin Delano Roosevelt, newly inaugurated as President of the United States, let Mussolini know that he regarded Italy as 'the only real friend of America in Europe'.[1]

---

[1] I have been asked why there is no mention here of anti-Semitism, and the answer is simply that Mussolini's Fascism, unlike Hitler's National Socialism, was not racist nor anti-Semitic. Jews along with all other Italians were incorporated into the Fascist state, and criticized or attacked, like any other Italian, only insofar as they resisted or gave their allegiance elsewhere (see Meir Michaelis, *Mussolini and the Jews* (1978), ch. II). In 1933 American Jewish publishers selected Mussolini as one of the world's twelve 'greatest Christian champions' of the Jews (John P. Diggins, *Mussolini and Fascism: The View from America* (1973), p. 40). However, anti-Semitic laws were introduced in 1938 following the alliance of Italy with Nazi Germany.

Pound's frequently expressed admiration for Mussolini and his works thus placed him in good—if for him rather odd—company. The democratic consensus, especially in the United States and most especially among its business leaders, was that Fascism was not only good for socially chaotic and economically backward Italy but a reproach to both the anarchy of capitalism and the tyranny of Communism. But it was not the anarchy of capitalism that Pound objected to so much as its injustice and its anti-social conduct; and his objection to state tyranny was muted when the state made itself responsible for the needs of the whole society. He was caught up in the contradictions of a time when a Fascist dictator cared more for the welfare of his people than the governments of the capitalist democracies did for theirs.

When Pound visited the Decennale Exhibition he particularly remarked the reconstruction of the Milan office in which Mussolini had edited his socialist newspaper, *Il Popolo*, and from which he had organized the rise of Fascism to power. Pound associated the exhibit with the *New Age* office in which at about the same time he had got hold of the gist of Major Douglas's Social Credit. 'Ours was like that', he would note in a canto, 'minus the Mills bomb'—that was the hand grenade Mussolini kept on his desk. It was as if he was seeking common ground between his own and Mussolini's efforts to change the existing economic order, while recognizing that Mussolini's had had more force behind it. The nature of that force, as he explained it to the readers of *Il Mare* back in Rapallo, was 'VOLONTÀ'. It had struck him for the first time, he told them, that the power behind the constructive action of the Fascist revolution was emotion, the WILL to get things done. It was that which made all the difference between merely having a good idea and carrying it through into practice. He instanced Mussolini's having cleared away in central Rome a mess of squalid building accumulated over the centuries to reveal again the glory that had been Rome and to create a new imperial avenue, 'la Via dell'Impero è la VOLONTÀ', leading from the Coliseum to the Piazza Venezia where he had his office.

The Palazzo di Venezia overlooked the Piazza, and from its balcony Il Duce would address the great crowds who gathered to hear him. His office was in its Sala del Mappamondo on the first floor, a vast room forty feet high, sixty feet in length, and as wide as it was high. The space was quite empty from one end to the other except for the desk at which Mussolini worked at the far end, with just one or two tables nearby and a few chairs. He insisted on absolute silence, no sound being allowed in from the piazza outside, and if a fly buzzed he called for it to be swatted. It was into this room that Pound was brought for his audience with Mussolini at 17.30 on Monday, 30 January 1933.

Pound presented to Mussolini a copy of the Hours Press *A Draft of XXX Cantos* and opened it to show him the Malatesta cantos. But, as Pound later told Mary de Rachewiltz, he 'went poking around till he got to Trotsk and the zhamefull beace' in canto 16, and said—he was learning English at the time—'But this is not English', and Pound said, 'No, it's my idea of the way a continental Jew would speak English', and that led Mussolini to say, 'How entertaining!', 'Ma qvesto è divertente'. Pound would put that remark into canto 41, and tell a correspondent that 'One of [my] most valued readers seemed to find the Cantos entertaining; at least that's what he said after 20 minutes, with accent of relieved surprise, having been brought up to Italian idea of poetry: something oppressive and to be revered.' Mussolini asked what was his aim in writing *The Cantos*, and Pound replied, 'to put my ideas in order'; and Mussolini said, 'What do you want to do that for?', 'Perché vuol mettere le sue idee in ordine?', and to that Pound had no better answer than 'Pel mio poema'.

'Then', as Pound told it, 'we turned to economics, and I showed him a list of things that I thought ought to be done', a handwritten list eighteen items long apparently. Mussolini 'started to read it, and said, "Ugh, these aren't things to answer straight off the bat. No, this one about taxes"—it would have been the third or fourth item, that in the Fascist state taxes were no longer necessary—"Ungh!", he said, "Have to think about THAT".' And that was the end of the interview.

Pound wrote to Dorothy that evening that he had 'had a long hour' and was 'feelin a bit weak after the event'. The Capo del Governo had been 'vurry charmin', but vurry'. He had told Pound to get his questions 're/ economica' typed out and to stay on in Rome in case he wanted to see him again about them. One of the things Pound did while waiting for another appointment was to see Greta Garbo in *Grand Hotel*—the early 'talkie' in which she vamped 'I want to be alone'—and he marvelled at 'the perfect clarity in every word' of the film. By the end of the week it was apparent that there was not going to be a second meeting, although the private secretary was being 'very cordial & said C.G. wd. like to see me'. There were new affairs of state to be attended to, among them Hitler's coming to power in Germany. Hitler had in fact been appointed Reichschancellor about noon on the day of Pound's audience with Mussolini.

The big news back in Rapallo was that their American poet had met Il Duce, and when Pound returned in early February the town band was at the station to greet him in communal celebration.

He immediately went to work on a book in which he would attempt to define the genius of Mussolini. He had other commitments on his mind—his fortnightly articles for Orage's *New English Weekly*, a series of lectures on 'volitionist economics' he was to give in Milan in March, the cantos dealing with the early American law-givers and their war with private banks for control of the nation's credit—and nevertheless he completed *Jefferson and/or Mussolini* and sent it off to his agent before the end of the month.

The ground of his argument, as he put it in a letter dated 18 February, was the confident faith that Mussolini 'would end with Sigismondo and the men of order'. 'I believe', he affirmed, 'that anything human will and understanding of contemporary Italy cd. accomplish, he has done and will continue to do.' He believed in Mussolini, he said, because of his own direct experience of Fascism in Italy—'Fascism as I have seen it' stands as the subtitle to *Jefferson and/or Mussolini*. In the course of the book, however, it becomes apparent that the things he has seen interest him only as outward evidences of Mussolini's genius, and that he is more deeply engaged in comprehending the genius than in analysing the Fascism. Further, as he develops his understanding of the genius, he perceives Mussolini more and more in his own terms rather than those of Fascist practice. And his own terms, as he declares under his name on the title page, are those of his 'Volitionist Economics'. His Mussolini is the leader he could believe in, one who is like himself an artist, a maker, only an artist able not only to conceive an enlightened social order but actually to will it into existence. He is in effect, though Pound does not so designate him, what Pound himself had aspired to be, an avatar of Zagreus, or, to go further back in his mythology, of Isis–Osiris, the bringer of grain and laws and civilized ways into a failing world.

Among the things Pound had noticed in Italy was '"Dio ti benedica" scrawled on a shed where some swamps were', and he read that as a prayer for Mussolini in gratitude for his persuading 'the Italians to grow better wheat, and to produce Italian colonial bananas'. Then there was his hotel-keeper in Rimini, the Fascist Commandante della Piazza, who got the local library opened up for him out of what Pound took to be a sense of responsibility fired by devotion to Mussolini. ('This kind of devotion...doesn't come to a man like myself,' he reflected.) There was the time in Modena when the regional Fascist leader, Farinacci, had his *squadristi* beating up all the working men in the district as his way of honouring 'the Fascist martyrs', and after a few days notices signed 'Mussolini' had appeared on the walls indicating Farinacci's summons to Rome and an end to that violence. There was another occasion early on, before Pound knew anything at all about Fascism, before the March on Rome, when he had been sitting in Florian's in the Piazza San Marco in Venice and the 'cavalieri della morte' in their black shirts and 'with drawn faces' passed through 'and everyone stood to attention and took off their hats', but 'damned if he would stand up or show respect until he knew what they meant', and 'Nobody hit me with a club', he recorded, 'and I didn't see any oil bottles'. He may not have seen any, but by the time he wrote that he evidently knew how clubs and purges of castor oil had been weapons of choice in the Fascist takeover of local powers throughout Italy, and still it did not concern him. That was because he would see through such details to what they meant to him, to what much of his experience of Italy now pointed to, and that was Mussolini's superhuman ability both to move his fellow Italians to action and to control and direct their action according to his will.

WILL, a complex word implying a will to *do* something or to have something *done*, is the key word in *Jefferson and/or Mussolini*, which Pound once said was his *De Monarchia* or blueprint for efficient government. 'Will-*power*' adds an emphasis, meaning the power to effect what is desired; but the will-*to*-power is excluded from Pound's lexicon, at least so far as it signifies the desire for power for its own sake. Moreover, before concerning himself with the power to govern, Pound nearly identifies the *will* to govern with the *intelligence* to do so, so that the intelligence, knowing the desired end, shall direct the will's power to that end. *Directio voluntatis*, he insisted, taking the Latin tag from Dante's *De Monarchia*: what matters is that the will-power be rightly directed. At the same time, as he insisted with equal force, intelligence counts for nothing 'until it comes into action'. What might be a good idea is no good until there's the will to do it.

Pound's key word, *will* or *volition*, thus comes to signify, beyond mere force of will, *efficient intelligence*, or intelligence in action. And here Pound shifts the emphasis once again by proposing an analogy between the most efficient kind of human intelligence and the instinctive intelligence of insects. He refers the reader to the 'chapters on insects' in Remy de Gourmont's *Physique de l'amour*, and there we read (in Pound's translation) that instinct is 'a partial crystallisation of intelligence', in that only 'Useful acts habitually repeated . . . intellectual acts . . . useful for the preservation of the species' become instinctive. 'When a human being', Pound wrote, 'has an analogous completeness of knowledge, or intelligence carried into a third or fourth dimension, capable of dealing with NEW circumstances, we call it genius.' And—here shifting his analogy and taking a further step in his argument—'The ideas of genius, or of "men of intelligence" are organic and germinal', they are *seed* ideas which both conserve patterns of behaviour and come up differently under different conditions—witness the effectiveness of the conviction that *All men are born free and equal*, and the variety of its flowerings in France and the United States and elsewhere.

It follows in this line of thought that the 'germinal ideas' of Pound's two men of genius, his Jefferson and his Mussolini, must be nearly related to what he understood Frobenius to mean by *paideuma*, that is, as noted in Chapter 2, 'the active element in the era, the complex of ideas which is in a given time germinal... conditioning actively all the thought and action'. In effect, Pound is now locating the *paideuma*, the cultural matrix, in the individual genius. That would be the meaning of his observation that Italy had had 'a *risorgimento*, a shaking from lethargy, then a forty-year sleep, from which the next heave has been the work of one man, pre-eminently'. But the deeper and more challenging meaning there is that the will of this one man, this dictator, represented in an unusually profound sense the will of the people.

Lincoln Steffens, the hardboiled, muckraking, American journalist with unimpeachable democratic credentials, wrote in his own terms that he had witnessed just that: 'I was there. When Mussolini said that they, the people, might stop governing and go to work—he would do it all—it was almost as if all Italy sighed and said, "Amen". And the people did go back to work, and they worked as they had not worked before', and Steffens found himself questioning whether Fascism might be a more effective way to achieve the government of the people and for the people than democracy as practised in the United States or in England or France. A later historian, A. James Gregor, found reason to conclude that Mussolini's Fascism was a genuine expression of the experience and the aspirations of Italy following the 1914–18 war, and that his undoubted political genius consisted in leading its people in the direction they needed and wanted to go in the conditions then actually prevailing. It would appear that Pound's perception of Mussolini, in 1933, as 'driven by a vast and deep "concern" or will for the welfare of Italy... for Italy organic, composed of the last ploughman and the last girl in the olive-yards', that this perception, though frankly a construct of faith and hope, and though invoking the unfashionable idea of society as an organism organized by its men of genius, did indeed have its truth. It may be an uncomfortable truth, as Steffens found, but then, as he also remarked, it does us no harm to have our settled notions shaken up.

Steffens was able to come to terms with Mussolini's abolishing individual liberties by reminding himself that all governments and peoples abolish liberty and submit themselves to dictatorial leadership in the emergency of war. Pound did it by concentrating on 'his passion for construction' and treating him as an artist—'Treat him as *artifex* and all the details fall into place'. First among the 'details' was the principle that 'Who wills the end wills the means'; and then that 'any means', i.e. any legal or administrative forms, 'are the right means' if only they will 'remagnetize the will' to put into effect 'the best that is known and thought'. So authoritarian dictatorship could be the right means to the end of reconstructing Italy, and the very sign indeed of Mussolini's 'intelligence'. Instead of sighing worthily for social justice he had been 'presumably right in putting the first emphasis on having a government strong enough to get the said justice'. And to achieve that it had been necessary, given the critical condition Italy was in, for him to take the power and the responsibility of the state upon himself alone.

Steffens wrote of how in a financial crisis Mussolini had told parliament they were incapable of decisive action and had sent them out to cuss him in their cafés while he, within a week or so, 'did, somehow, stabilize the lira'. Steffens and Pound both made much of his breaking free from the preconceptions and precedents, the established axioms and theories, the obfuscating rhetoric and social snobberies, which got in the way of the facts and prevented effective action. That had always been a main task of the artist for Pound. 'It takes a genius', he now wrote, 'a genius charged with some form of dynamite, mental or material, to blast [humanity, Italian and every other segment of it] out of [its] preconceptions'. Mussolini invented new laws and altered existing ones to suit the circumstances of the moment, to the distress of distinguished lawyers who could not know from one day to the next what the law would be. He put an embargo on emigration, as to America, a restriction which Pound, who loathed passports and all such restrictions, nevertheless approved of since Italian workers were needed at home; and 'the material and immediate effect [were] *grano, bonifica, restauri,* grain, swamp-drainage, restorations, new buildings'. He did something about 'birds friendly to agriculture'—presumably banning the snaring or shooting them in spite of ingrained tradition—and already there were 'more birds in the olive-yards', as Pound must have seen for himself as he walked up the footpath from Rapallo to Sant' Ambrogio. Such were the dictator's original works of art.

Along with its celebration of what Il Duce was achieving, *Jefferson and/or Mussolini* outlined what Pound thought Mussolini ought to be doing in the way of economic reform. Basically, he wanted the problem 'of poverty in the midst of abundance' to be seen as not just a problem of the distribution of goods but as, fundamentally, a problem arising from the unequal and inadequate distribution of credit or purchasing power. 'We have had the century of the "benefits of concentration of capital" (and the malefits)', he wrote, and 'We have come to the point where money must be got into people's pockets if goods are to move and modern life to continue "the good life".' And the only way to achieve that, he argued, instancing America's 'bank wars' in the time of Jefferson and Van Buren, was by taking over control of credit and finance from private interests so that they should be used not for the profit of the few but for the benefit of the whole nation. In 1920 he had seen 'nothing in Europe save unscrupulous bankers, a few gangs of munitions vendors, and their implements (human)'. In 1933 he could see 'no other clot of energy in Europe' save Mussolini 'capable of opposing ANY FORCE WHATEVER to the infinite evil of the profiteers and the sellers of men's blood for money'. By 1934 he was convinced that Mussolini was in fact 'damning and breaking up the bankers' stranglehold on humanity', and that the dividends were being 'distributed as better wheat, and better drainage and cheaper railway transport'. The following year he informed anti-Fascists in England that while Italy had not nationalized its banks they were subject to national orders, and that 'the use of the public credit for the ultimate public weal of Italy has been in process and is being accelerated'. A 'GREED system' had been replaced by a 'WILL system'.

Pound was seeing Mussolini as a dynamic, even a daemonic force for a new order in Italy, one directed by the human will toward social justice and equity. On the last page of *Jefferson and/or Mussolini* he reasserted his 'firm belief that the Duce will stand not with despots and the lovers of power but with the lovers of | ORDER'; to which he added, as if to define 'ORDER', 'τὸ καλόν', signifying the thing—it would be the public thing or republic— that is beautiful because rightly and harmoniously ordered. Behind that he would have had the Confucian vision of the Chinese empire as a well-ordered totality. Also, he was dreaming again as he had dreamed in London in 1915 of a renaissance born when 'the very apex of power coincided with the apex of culture'. 'I dream for Italy an epoch', he wrote in December 1933, that 'will resemble somewhat the [*quattrocento*], an epoch in which the highest culture and modern science functions at maximum'. That is what Pound expected, or hoped for, from Mussolini's dictatorship of Italy.

He did not advocate Fascism in and for America, and thought 'the American system *de jure* . . . probably quite good enough [for America], if there were only 500 men with the guts and the sense to USE it'. At the same time he considered that Mussolini's Fascism, with its 'greater care for national welfare', did put 'our democratic system' on trial with the challenge, '*Do the driving ideas of Jefferson, Quincy Adams, Van Buren, or whoever else there is in the creditable pages of our history, FUNCTION actually in the America of this decade to the extent that they function in Italy under the DUCE?*' Pound's opinion was 'that they DON'T', and that America needed 'an orientation of will' under the stimulus of Mussolini. It did not need to import the 'accidental' features of Fascism, the parades and the methods peculiar to the culture and condition of Italy at that time, but only 'the permanent

"Università Commerciale Luigi Bocconi,,

La S. V. è invitata ad assistere al corso di conferenze sul tema
AN HISTORIC BACKGROUND FOR ECONOMICS che il Poeta
EZRA POUND terrà in questa Università sotto gli auspici della
"Serena Foundation,, nei giorni sottoindicati del mese corrente:

Martedì 21 ore 17¹/₂ — Introduction. Forms of thought in two different systems.
Why or how a poet came to be drawn into economic discussion·

Mercoledì 22 ore 17¹/₂ — Problems that have been there. Economics for
Mohamed, Kublai Khan, the middle ages.

Giovedì 23 ore 17¹/₂ — The transition.

Venerdì 24 ore 17¹/₂ — Economic ideas of the early and constructive
American presidents: Jefferson.

Sabato 25 ore 10 — John Quincy Adams.

Lunedì 27 ore 17¹/₂ — Martin Van Buren.

Martedì 28 ore 17¹/₂ — The " new ,, economics in England.

Mercoledì 29 e Giovedì 30 ore 17¹/₂ — Conclusions

Venerdì 31 ore 17¹/₂ — What literature has to do with it - The function
of good writing in the State.

Milano, 15 Marzo 1933 - XI

IL RETTORE
ULISSE GOBBI

3. Invitation to Pound's series of lectures, 'An Historic Background for Economics',
Università Commerciale Luigi Bocconi, Milan, March 1933.

elements of sane and responsible government'. It would appear, since
Pound was calling for the Constitution to be not altered but followed
more faithfully, that dictatorship and totalitarian ways were to be classed
as 'accidentals' and not as necessary means to a more enlightened American
order. Indeed, when Franklin Delano Roosevelt, inaugurated as President
of the United States in March of 1933, began talking about a New Deal for
America, Pound paid attention in hope that he would be the one to effect
the needed re-orientation of will in what he subscribed to as 'our democratic
system'. When Roosevelt proposed his Civil Works Administration Pound
wrote to Dorothy, 'At last I have a country.'

Revolutionary economics

It was not only with Mussolini that Pound wanted to talk economics. He
would talk and write economics at anyone and everyone through the rest of
the 1930s, very often as if it were the only bee in his bonnet. The capitalist

143

democracies, America, Britain, France, and the rest, were in deep crisis, with their millions workless, their industries shut down, their markets stagnant, their farmers foreclosed upon by mortgagors, and with their governments paralysed by the contradiction between the needs and interests of their impoverished citizens and the needs and interests of the gravely threatened system of self-regulating capitalism in which they put their trust. Pound could see with blinding clarity what needed to be done, quite simply, that capital, the nation's wealth, should be made to serve the needs and interests of the whole nation. He thought this should be self-evident to anyone of good will; and that it was the duty of everyone with a sense of social responsibility, from writers up to president or prime minister, to proclaim that solution and to make it happen.

For the moment, for the decade, the struggle to make other people see what was needed to bring about a just economic order was his dominant preoccupation. 'Contemporary economics goes over my desk NOW,' he told Morton Dauwen Zabel, the new editor of *Poetry* in 1934, 'just as the Joyce, Lewis, Eliot etc/ went over it in 1917'. And to Ibbotson, his old Hamilton mentor who had become the college librarian, he wrote, 'the vitality of thought NOW (1935) is in econ/ that is where the live thought is concentrated | for a few years'. To the young American writers associated with *Contempo* he was more insistent: 'Without an understanding of economics no one can have any grip on the modern world or any understanding of what goes on, or what anything means. No one can understand the "news" in the daily papers.' 'Your generation has got to BOTHER about economics, and even politics, as mine bothered about philology', he advised them in another little magazine, since 'no man can write anything valid unless he has brains enough to SEE the social order about him and to know cause and effect in that order.' Moreover, as he cordially informed W. E. Woodward, a historian and Roosevelt adviser, 'god dam it to understand | history you GOT to understand ECON.'

In 1934 he was chiding Eliot for showing no awareness, when writing about 'the modern mind', of the economic realities confronting that mind. It was not that 'economics constitute "the ONLY vital problem"', he allowed, but, given that 'poverty and the syphilis of the mind called the Finance-Capitalist system kill more men annually than typhoid or tuberculosis', it seemed to him that to engage in purely aesthetic discussion just then was like stopping to discuss 'blue china in the midst of a cholera epidemic if I possessed the means to combat the epidemic'. Pound was even more impatient with Joyce's indifference to economic realities—Joyce who had once been his model realist. And he berated 'son' Zukofsky as 'worse than blind Joyce', and warned him, 'The next anthology will be econ/ conscious and L/Z won't be in it'. He even wrote to McAlmon, a rather tough-minded observer of his world, 'I think both you *and* Hem have limited yr. work'—which he still held in high regard—'by not recognizing the economic factor'. Williams, another he would not accuse of being out of touch with reality, he attempted to stir up to spread the word about Social Credit and stamp scrip—'if you agree, GIT AXSHUN'—but Williams wrote back, 'Aw what's the use, you wouldn't understand. . . . But as fer action as action. Taint in me. No use gettin mad.'

Pound did get mad, not at Williams and not at individuals he knew personally, but at the whole uncomprehending and apathetic world in general, and at young writers in particular who didn't want to know about economics. He declared himself fed up, in January 1935,

fed *u p* (up) with young idiots who can't see that history does not exist without economics; who do not know that Bithinian mortgages at 12% are a matter of history; who think that . . . 'l'histoire morale' can get on without economics any more than any other department of history, or that literature keeps its head in a bag.

It was left to him, he raged, to do all the work of instruction on his own, and to write out the ABCs of economics, 'because the circumjacent literati are weaklings, they are piffling idiots that can't get on with the job, they can not even write text books . . . and I can type for eight hours a day'.

It is necessary for me to dig the ore, melt it, smelt it, to cut the wood and the stone, because I am surrounded by ten thousand nincompoops and nothing fit to call an American civilisation or a British civilisation . . .

He saw himself as the lone hero desperately embattled, or as the scorned prophet seeing the truth none dared face. In a prefatory note drafted for a proposed collection of his essays, possibly late in the 1930s, he refracted the alien image his opponents had of him, 'a stray crank', into a drama of doomed heroism, then found consolation and a kind of triumph in the certainty that anyway his vision was superior to their ignorance:

Against [the] phalanx of academic writing the stray crank hurls himself vainly. He has seen the light, he has seen the landscape illuminated during tempest by one flash of lightning. His adversary has never seen it at all.

And they were afraid of him, he boasted—this was as early as November 1933—'The college presidents of America dare not read either *How to Read* or my *ABC of Economics*'; and the professors of economics, and all the 'clercs' in the beaneries, dared not face his facts. 'The cretinism of their era has left them no shred of decency,' he fulminated. Then, having boiled over with rage—and observed himself doing so with detached interest and approval—he would temper it by saying to someone not an imbecile, 'all my cursing and blasting is against ONLY those who refuse to look facts in the eye'.

Deeper than his rage there was his hatred, a murderous hatred, as he himself declared, for a murdering capitalism. 'What causes the ferocity and bad manners of revolutionaries?', he asked rhetorically in an essay in Eliot's *Criterion* in July 1933, 'Why should a peace-loving writer of Quaker descent be quite ready to shoot certain persons whom he never laid eyes on? . . . What has capital done that I should hate Andy Mellon as a symbol or as a reality?' The direct answer was this, 'I have blood lust because of what I have seen done to, and attempted against, the arts in my time.' He was thinking back to what he had seen in London, the lack of support for and the suppression of the radically new writing and sculpture and painting of the time, and the best musicians 'gradually driven off the platform'. He had 'no personal grievance', he said, 'They tried to break me and didn't or couldn't.' But 'hatred can be bred in the mind', and 'head-born hatred is possibly the most virulent'. He had come to understand that the source of the harm done to the arts was the unjust distribution of credit at the heart of the capitalist economic system. And that, evidently, was why he nursed his virulent hatred of the bankers and plutocrats and politicians whom he held responsible for obstructing the flow of creative intelligence in England and France and America.

The evil, he now saw, afflicted not only the arts but infected the whole society, and the cure therefore must be a radical reform of the entire socio-economic system. There had been a time when he had imagined that the problem of the unemployment of the best artists might be settled by one millionaire patron, and 'without regard to the common man, humanity in general, the man in the street, the average citizen'. That idea he now retracted and apologized for. The unemployment of artists was only a special case of the general unemployment of the millions. The miserliness towards the arts went with the 'miserliness in regard to sanitation, healthy houses, medical and dental services'; the waste of talent went with the waste of lives— in England 'three million lives in peace time for every million lives spent in the war'. And what was needed 'to release more energy for invention and design' was the same as was needed to overcome the social evil, nothing less than a new economic system that would deliver social justice to all.

Pound conducted his own campaign for economic enlightenment on two fronts, in his cantos containing history where he was inventing objects for contemplation, and in his prose where he was trying at once to make people see the light and to blast the forces of darkness. *Cantos XXXI–XLI* are largely concerned with banking and economics from Jefferson to Mussolini, with the focus mainly on the American Revolution and its betrayal; *The*

Fifth Decad of Cantos is concerned with banking and economics mainly in Europe, with much attention paid to the founding of a bank in Siena and the very different founding of the Bank of England. More or less at the same time as he was composing those cantos Pound was hammering out on his typewriter letters to editors, articles for whatever newspaper or periodical would publish him, and letters to senators and anyone else whom he thought might be moved to use their influence in the cause of economic reform. Of the 375 items he contributed to newspapers and periodicals in the years 1933, 1934, and 1935, about four in every five were on economic matters, with the frequency of those rising year on year from 80 to 100 to 130. On top of that there was his very extensive and no less furious private correspondence.

Pound particularly targeted a few US senators whom he hoped would steer Roosevelt in the desired direction, and also some of the officers of the President's think-tank, the Committee for the Nation to Rebuild Prices and Purchasing Power. He wrote as 'A Jeffersonian or very left wing Fascist', though one who didn't 'care a damn about the theory' or 'the political system' of Fascism—'Call me a Jeffersonian. brought up to date', he told W. E. Woodward who was serving on two government advisory councils. Whomever he was writing to, whether it was Woodward, or Senator Cutting of New Mexico, or Senator William Borah of Idaho—or indeed to whatever newspaper or periodical or fellow writer—it was always the same few fundamental ideas out of Douglas's Social Credit and Gesell's stamp scrip that he was trying to get across.

The immediate and pressing problem was the mass unemployment of the Depression and the damage being done by that to both the unemployed and the economy. In the United States in 1932 around four hundred in every thousand of the farming population were out of work; in 1934 about 17 million workers altogether were reckoned to be unemployed, and there were forty million living below the poverty line. The Secretary of Agriculture was ordering the destruction of crops and livestock because so many hadn't the money to buy the food. Pound urged that the available work be shared among those willing and able to work, with a reduction in the hours each worked, but with no reduction of wages. A government subsidy would be needed to keep up wages, but that would be a better use of the state's money than leaving men workless and doling the money out to them. He was all in favour of creating useful new jobs through Public Works schemes such as the Tennessee Valley Authority, provided they were financed from government credit and not by borrowing from private banks. But the main thing was to tackle the root cause of the Depression, which was not excess production, as orthodox economists maintained, but the lack of purchasing power where it was most needed, among the mass of the people. 'There is NO real overproduction as long as there are people who WANT the stuff/ god damn it there is plenty of stuff still WANTED | the clog is in the money <u>system</u>. | (overproduction begins when the stuff is not WANTED, not when people merely can't buy it.)'

The banks having control of the nation's credit was one side of the problem, as Pound had learnt from Major Douglas, and as quite a number of economists and politicians now perceived. (The other side was how to get the purchasing power to the people.) The banks were called upon to create new money to meet the nation's demand for credit, but they held it as their money not the nation's, and lent it out and called it in to their own profit without regard to the common interest. And the worst of it was that the nation's government, in order to finance its projects, went to the private banks for the money, which the banks created out of nothing, and on which the government then paid them interest. This was 'an infamy', Pound protested, 'It is an infamy that the STATE in, and by reason of, the very act of creating material wealth should run into debt to individuals.' It was infamous because it was directly contrary to the Constitution, which vested the power to issue money in the government of the Union; and behind that was the idea of natural justice, that the nation's credit was its common wealth and belonged to the whole people. The Constitution and its democratic principle had been overridden after the Civil War as the power to issue money and control credit had passed from the government to private banks. Senator Cutting was one who wanted to put the government back in control. 'What does the government do', he asked in anger in a speech in May 1934,

when it goes to the rescue of its needy and starving citizens? It floats loans through the banks. It pays interest to private organizations for the use of its own credit. The thing becomes more preposterous when we realize that an enormous proportion of the relief expended by the government has gone to the aid of great banking institutions. So that actually the government is getting itself into debt to the banks for the privilege of helping them to regain their stranglehold on the economic life of the country.

Cutting proposed in the Senate that the banks should be nationalized in order to 'monopolize the credit system of the country for the benefit of the public not for the benefit of the bankers'. Pound, while maintaining that it was not necessary to nationalize the banks Bolshevik fashion in order to control them—Mussolini had demonstrated that—thought Cutting might have made it clear that in any case the profits on the nation's credit should accrue to the nation. That was underlining the radical principle, which Cutting was asserting, 'that the nation owns its own credit, and that the whole people should benefit by this fact'.

The basis of credit, in this view, is the nation's common wealth, that is, its natural resources, or 'the abundance of nature', plus the labour to make useful products of those resources; and then the accumulation of skills and knowledge which increases the productivity of labour in both quantity and quality. Marx, in his nineteenth century, had made labour the measure of value, but 'that's OLD stuff | no longer fits facts', Pound insisted to Woodward; 'Values now from a <u>little</u> (ever decreasing) amount of work: | AND a huge complex of mechanical inventions | which are "the cultural heritage" | and have got to be used for THE WHOLE PEOPLE, | nobody really <u>owns</u> 'em ANYHOW.' More largely, the cultural heritage consists of 'the whole aggregate of human inventions', 'improvements of seed and of farming methods', 'and the customs and habits of civilization'. Douglas had brought forward this perception of the cultural heritage as the main source of economic and social value, with the correlative that it belonged to no one man and to no group; and he had thus expanded the proposition that all men are born free and equal into the claim that all therefore have a right in common with others to the earth's resources and to the benefits of human progress.

Douglas's idea was that the surplus value or credit accruing from the cultural heritage should be distributed to all citizens as a national dividend, and that this would be a fair mechanism for providing the needed increase of purchasing power in the economy. Pound took up the main idea but wanted it modified. Douglas did not mind whether people worked for their dividend or not. In Pound's view, however, everyone had both a right to work and a need to work, though only for so many hours a day as would get the nation's work done and allow everyone to share in it, and he therefore would have wanted the social dividend to go into subsidizing work-sharing and keeping up wages. At the same time he allowed that the dividend might take various forms, such as the control of rents and prices to keep them in line with wages, as was being done in Italy; or it might go into the improvement of public utilities and infrastructure, and the provision of better education, health care, and welfare. All such public benefits could be, and should be, financed out of the public credit, without recourse to 'the buggering banks'.

These were revolutionary ideas threatening the freedoms of the capitalist order in its moment of crisis, a moment when the contradiction between the interests and workings of capitalism and the interests and needs of society as a whole was painfully exposed by the Great Depression. Of course the ideas were dismissed as unworkable, as 'crank economics', by those who opposed or simply feared the changes that would follow from them. And because they were not effectively carried into action in any capitalist democracy their power to bring about a more truly democratic order remained unproven.

Yet the principles behind those ideas, Pound and others maintained, were fundamental to democracy, especially to one which honoured Jefferson as a founder. In the United States they were upheld by many responsible legislators addressing the disastrous breakdown of their social economy. In 1933 Senator Hugo Black of Alabama proposed a six-hour working day and a five-day week to spread the existing jobs among 25 per cent more workers, and a majority in the Senate approved. In 1934 and 1935, according to Walkiewicz and Witemeyer, 'There was a growing consensus that the causes of the Depression had more to do with poor distribution and underconsumption' than with problems of production, and in March 1934 President Roosevelt called for 'an increase in the purchasing power of the people'. His Administration's large-scale public works schemes were one way of bringing that about, though, as Senator Cutting pointed out, his financing those schemes by borrowing from private banks was counter-productive. Cutting's own proposal to nationalize the banks had considerable support in the Senate and in the country, though it died in committee, the great objection to it being, as he noted, that it was too radical.

There were other, less temperate, voices spreading these ideas over the radio, the mass medium of the time, and getting a responsive hearing for them from millions of listeners. There was Father Coughlin, the radio evangelist of his day, who, as Pound observed, was preaching social justice in simple terms the populace could understand. Pound, enthusiastic about the texts of his broadcasts and deeply impressed by his speaking to and for so vast an audience, bombarded him with suggestions and instigations, and received only form letters in return.

Another powerful voice attracting Pound's particular interest was that of the Governor of the State of Louisiana and US Senator Huey P. Long (1893–1935), known as the 'Kingfish', and much followed and much castigated as 'a populist demagogue'. Woodward told Pound that Long had 'a splendid education—brilliant mind ... with the manners and speech of a ward politician or a street corner orator'. 'Better a wild man that wants justice than a tame one who just don't care for the people and who won't look at the nature of money,' such was Pound's attitude. On that basis he urged American Social Creditors to work with Long, though they might disagree, as he did himself, with some of his ideas. The essential thing was that 'Long WANTS a new economic system. The root is in VOLITION; in the direction of the WILL.' As evidence of direction he cited Long's 'radio speech of March 7th [1935]', in which he had spoken against the situation in which too few controlled the nation's money and wealth, while too many

- Capital is a claim on others, property is not: it is possible therefore to attack the 'rights and privileges' of capital without attacking property. (13–14)
- The problem of production is solved, i.e. the problem of meeting all the world needs.
- As mechanical efficiency increases production requires progressively less human time and effort.
- Sane economy demands that this effort be shared. (15)
- Men should have some sense of responsibility to the human congeries. (16)
- The only economic problem needing emergency solution is distribution. (17)
- Why should anyone starve? (18)
- Purchasing power to be correlated with work via work-sharing—say, an equitable wage for 5 hours per day. (20)
- Everyone has the right to useful and needed work. (27)
- State control of the nation's finances never known in England. (28)
- Pound's Volitionist economics based on Will, not intellect (33)—'*The science of economics will not get very far until it grants the existence of will as a component; i.e. will toward order, will toward "justice" or fairness, desire for civilization, amenities included. The intensity of that will is definitely a component in any solution.*' (38)
- That capital should be considered everlasting or indestructible probably an error. (72)
- The overwhelming question: the problem of money, or the creation and distribution of purchasing power. (75)
- What should be produced? 'Everything useful or desirable'. How much? 'All that is wanted'.
- The amount wanted will govern the length of the working day, i.e. paid work, beyond which should be leisure to do as one pleases. (87)
- 'A small amount of "money" changing hands rapidly will do the work of a lot moving slowly.' (91)
- 'After all, this is a very rudimentary treatise.' (92)
- 'The state conceived as the public convenience. Money conceived as a public convenience. Neither as private bonanza.' (93)
- 'The earth belongs to the living' (Jefferson)—i.e. don't mortgage the future. (98)
- 'An economic system in which it is more profitable to make guns to blow men to pieces than to grow grain or make useful machinery, is an outrage, and its supporters are enemies of the race.'
- Taxes are an anomaly. (125)
- When enough exists, means should be found to distribute it to the people who need it.

ABC of Economics (1933) in gists.

Although I shall be termed a clerical dabbler in economics and politics, nevertheless I shall rest undisturbed, fortified by that pronouncement of . . . Pius XI that this present social question with its concentration of wealth in the hands of a few, its unbridled mass production, its gold-worshipping, its poverty in the midst of plenty, its usurious bonds, is a question not so much related to economics as to morals and to religion.

—Revd Charles E Coughlin, *The New Deal in Money. As broadcast over a national network October, November, December* 1933 (Royal Oak, Mich.: Published by the Radio League of the Little Flower, 1933)

Under the Vinson plan the United States Government, possessing 12 billion in idle gold and silver shall run to banks possessing less than 700 million and pretend to borrow more than 2 billion. If the banks pretend to loan this money, those same banks will still have the identical 700 million the day after the loan will have been made.

—Revd Charles E. Coughlin, radio broadcast of 5 January 1936, *A Series of Lectures on Social Justice* (Royal Oak, Mich.: Published by the Radio League of the Little Flower, 1936), as cited by EP, 'For a Decent Europe' (14 Mar. 1936)

Will we now have our generation and the generations which are to come, cheated of [their heritage] because of the greed and control of wealth and opportunity by 600 families?

In 1929 too much was produced for people to consume—too much cotton, wool, food: so much of it was thrown away, dumped, destroyed. Yet Department of Agriculture statistics show that there was not enough food, particularly milk, eggs, butter and dried fruits, for everyone to have a healthy diet. The problem was not overproduction, but that people did not have the money to buy what they needed. So what they needed to sustain life was plowed under and burned and thrown in the river.

God's law and the Pilgrim Fathers and our great statesmen like Jefferson, Webster, Lincoln, Theodore Roosevelt and Waldo Emerson—all teach that all the people should share in the land's abundance . . . a just and equal distribution of wealth . . . for every child a fair chance for life, liberty and happiness.

If any man or one hundred men own the wealth produced by all the people it is not because they produced it but because they stole it . . . In this land of abundance they have no right to impose starvation, misery and pestilence.

—*Senator Huey P. Long's Letter: The Share Our Wealth Principles* (broadside, n.d.), 'To enforce the principles on which this country was founded'. (Long's Share-Our-Wealth clubs spread across the entire country, reaching seven million people.)

Exhibits from Father Coughlin and Senator Huey Long.

were without the money 'to buy the things they needed for life and comfort'; along with that he cited Long's broadside, 'The Share Our Wealth Principles', which affirmed as a founding American idea 'that all the people should share in the land's abundance'. 'Huey for president', Pound fantasized,[2] wanting to see him where he would be most able to put 'his WILL into practice'. Long, however, was assassinated in the Louisiana State Capitol in September 1935.

'The root is in VOLITION; in the direction of the WILL'—that emphasis, with the implication that the means to the desired end of social justice are negotiable, is the key to understanding Pound's economic propaganda. The means and methods by which the fruits of abundance might be distributed were not of fundamental importance to him. 'With sane economics', he told Woodward, 'the political system can be pretty much ad lib/.' So Mussolini's totalitarian regime could be 'utterly necessary in Italy' given that country's history and present conditions, but 'inconceivable' in England with its parliamentary tradition, or in America with its own democratic principles that it ought to be following. The system of distribution could be equally 'ad lib', whether by a 'national dividend' or a 'material dividend' or whatever else, just so long as everyone received enough to ensure life, liberty, and happiness. Pound cared about the end, but not so much about the means.

Moreover, the instrumental ideas which he promoted so persistently were in no sense his own, being derived from Douglas and Gesell and other reformers, and being very widely known and debated in that time of economic crisis. Indeed in respect of having ideas about how best to manage the nation's credit Pound was rather like Churchill in the anecdote in canto 41: '"Never", said Winston...waste time having ideas",' '"Be a GUN, and shoot others' munitions".' That is very much how Pound behaved in the field of economics, shooting off the gists and piths of a few of the more explosive ideas that were then current with the aim of driving them into 'the mind of the people', and more especially into 'the few powerful public leaders who really desire the good of the people'. His purpose was to generate a passion for social justice, and to move leading politicians to enact it.

'Can't move 'em with a cold thing like economics', so Griffith, the Sinn Fein leader, had informed him back in 1921, and now Pound seemed determined to do something about that. The people and their politicians

---

[2] For the full text of this important statement of Pound's thinking about economic reform in America see Appendix D.

had to be motivated, their will to act had to be roused. The rationale of his *ABC of Economics*, he declared, was 'to base a system on will, not on intellect', on 'will toward order, will toward "justice" or fairness, desire for civilization', and on 'the intensity of that will'. He was consciously echoing Dante's definition of rectitude as direction of the will towards justice, and conscious also of being probably 'the first writer to formulate an economic system...from that point'. *Volitionist economics*, 'an heretical movement', was to be his original contribution to the science of economics, the heresy being in his seeking to make the economics answer to the desire and the will for social justice. In doing that he was very deliberately shifting its ground from cold science to ethics and morality.

Dante also wrote, in his *De Monarchia*, that it is the love of justice which animates and directs the will towards right action, and from that it would follow that to 'move 'em' Pound should be rousing a love of the desired order of things. Pound's agitprop prose, however, as he frankly admitted in 1928 when comparing himself to Williams, was given rather to murderous hate than to love. A typical letter would go like this one in the *New English Weekly* in May 1934:

Sir,—Without claiming that stamp scrip distributes purchasing power as effectively as the Douglas dividend would do, there are the following reasons for mentioning it (stamp scrip) LOUDLY and on *every* possible occasion.

I. It terrifies the unspeakable filth that made the last War and is trying its best to make the next one.

II. It is definitely a form of currency (auxiliary) that cannot be hoarded.

III. The tax falls on the currency itself and cannot therefore ever fall on anyone who is not in a condition to pay it, and to pay it without hardship.

IV. It has produced the greatest hush-hush in the ranks of filth that has occurred since Douglas's first volumes 14 years ago. This ought to prove that the enemies of mankind are afraid of it. And all honest men therefore ought to examine it, and to spread the news of it all day and every day.

V. The liars, scoundrels and paid pimps who wouldn't discuss Douglas in 1919 and who will not discuss him NOW are equally averse from discussing Unterguggenberger, Woergl, Gessel. Anything that can make their lives unlivable is an infinite gain to humanity.

That was to charge the idea of stamp scrip with vehemence and invective, and the effect was unlikely to be a better understanding of it or a deeper desire to have it put into practice. A reader not already in the know might be some time discovering that 'Unterguggenberger' was the mayor of the small town of Wörgl in the Austrian Tyrol who had been responsible for issuing, in the autumn of 1931, a local currency or stamp scrip of the sort advocated by the economist Silvio Gesell (1862–1930). The scrip was good for payment for goods and services within Wörgl, but to remain valid it had to have a stamp worth 1 per cent of its face value stuck on to it every month, and that was both a tax and an incentive to keep spending. The town had been on the verge of bankruptcy because of the Depression, and suddenly, within little more than a year, it was prospering thanks to the speedy circulation of just 12,000 or 30,000 schillings (accounts differ) of this local money. The more often it was used the more value was got out of it. The town's books were balanced and, so the story goes, it had been able to spend up to the value of 100,000 schillings on public works including a new bridge and a ski jump. There are appropriately arcane explanations of how the miracle was worked, but Pound hardly went into them. He would make more of how the story ended. In November 1933 the National Bank took the mayor to court and had him found guilty of violating its sole right to issue banknotes. The bank was terrified, Pound concluded, by the demonstration that 'the state need not borrow', and 'all the slobs in Europe were terrified'. So the Wörgl experiment came to represent in Pound's repeated references to it not so much the virtue of Gesell's stamp scrip, as how enlightenment might come to a small town only to be snuffed out by 'the enemies of mankind' determined to maintain their 'strangle hold on the unfortunate townsmen'.

Even when he was writing for the first time to a US senator Pound could be instantly on the attack as if assuming the worst. Senator William A. Borah of Idaho held views similar to Pound's on a number of issues, among them the need to restore purchasing power instead of reducing acreage and destroying food. In 1933, when the Bankhead–Pettengill bill was before the Senate calling for an issue of $1b in stamp scrip to get the currency circulating, Pound wrote to Borah,

Sir: As an Idahoan, it wd. interest me to know whether your ignorance of the Bankhead bill is real or pretended, and whether the American press boycotts mention of it from decent or indecent motives.

Is there a political game on, which requires that Stamp Scrip remain unmentioned, or are all of you crooks and ALL OF YOU afraid to touch the dangerous subject of a real and PROVED remedy for a lot of trouble?

Borah replied mildly but pointedly, '"As an Idahoan" I suggest that you come back to Idaho and to the United States. It isn't fair to give us so much "hell" at so great a distance.' Pound continued to write to Borah from Italy, in fragmentary, exclamatory, hectoring letters, putting him straight on stamp scrip and related matters and laying out for him the basic platform on which he should run for president. His influence on the senator, not surprisingly, was negligible. After a couple of years Borah wrote back a brief note, 'Thank you for your several letters.... We have had a perfectly marvelous autumn...' Later, in 1937, he would be saying in his speeches that any American citizen who advocated or believed in Fascism must be a traitor to America.

In one of his more extreme bids for influence with the powerful Pound nominated himself to be Secretary of the Treasury under Huey Long as president, in a letter which affected the lingo and persona of a gangster's enforcer, or of the redneck rough-houser he may have imagined Long to be:

> KINGFISH; You iz' goin' ter
> need a CABINET
> DIFFERENT
> from the present one. You iz goin to need a sekkertary of
> the treasury whose name is NOT Morgenthau/stein, or
> Richberg/ovitch
> or Mordecai Ezekiel OR Perkins.
> You is going to need a Sekkertary of the Treasury,
> THAT'S ME.
> I'm a tellin you 'cause no one else will.
> LET THE NATION USE ITS OWN CREDIT
> instead of paying tax FOR IT
> to a gang of sonsofbitches that DON'T own it.

The senator's response, if any, is not recorded. The letter might have amused him, if he ever saw it; it is unlikely he or anyone around him would have given it a moment's serious consideration. As a way of getting his attention it was surely self-defeating.

Pound's economic propaganda is often rubbished as 'crank economics', as ill informed, wrong-headed, even wicked. In fact, so far as it was advocating his chosen ethically based economic prescriptions, it was none of those things. But there was crankiness, there was self-defeating error, in the manner of his advocacy. One fundamentally disabling defect, given the nature of his project, was that the predominance of rage and hate meant that there was too little evident love of the justice he was after. Even when there is a glimpse of the shining city set on a hill, or a radiant image of the just society to move the will to act, it is attributed to Fascism—there seem to be none in the capitalist democracies—and Fascism, after 1935, ceased outside Italy to be a recommendation for any line of action.

A further and not unrelated disability was that generally there was more vehemence and invective than specifying detail in his attacks. It was as if he were impatiently assuming that the reader ought already to be in possession of the facts; though it could also seem that he did not himself have immediate and intimate knowledge of what he was going on about. Why, for example, did he hate Andrew Mellon?[3] As he well knew, it needs 'a sufficient phalanx of particulars' to enforce a general truth; and yet in his prose propaganda his tendency was to assert the general truth as if it were self-evident fact—'It is definitely a form of currency (auxiliary) that cannot be hoarded'—and then to enforce it with a charge of emotion, usually negative emotion—'the enemies of mankind are afraid of it'. The emotion, the invective, stands in for the demonstrative detail; and that leaves the desired constructive action as a relatively abstract idea, while any will towards it is directed by a hatred of evil rather than by a positive attraction toward the good to be done.

Worse, the evil itself tends to be defined by the fear and hatred directed against it rather than by a demonstration of its effects. All we are told about 'the enemies of mankind' in that letter is that they are terrified of stamp scrip and will not discuss it; and instead of their names, places, actual words, we read 'ranks of filth', 'liars, scoundrels and paid pimps'. Sometimes the hatred is given a more definite focus by naming names, as in 'Morgenthau/stein, or Richberg/ovitch'; and the names more often than not are Jewish or are given a Jewish twist, so that the stereotyped and prejudicial association of Jews with money is stirred up and anti-Semitism is drawn on to reinforce the hatred of the evil banks do. 'The people are damn well FED UP with slimy and ambiguous crooks', Pound wrote in a letter to Borah in May 1935, 'also with Morgenthaus, Baruchs, Mordecai Ezekiels, Lehman's etc.' Those names, generalized and altogether detached from anything in particular the individual persons might have done or said, but potentially charged with the endemic

---

[3] Andrew Mellon as US Secretary of the Treasury (1921–32) had advised President Hoover after the 1929 Stock Market Crash, for which he bore heavy responsibility, 'Liquidate labour, liquidate stocks, liquidate the farmers, liquidate real estate. Purge the rottenness out of the system.' EP probably knew that, but neglected to mention such telling details. Mellon is mentioned in canto 38/188.

fear and hatred of Jews, are made to stand in for the entire private banking system and its 'stranglehold' on America. In that way Pound's 'will to order' would be more and more subverted in his fighting prose by the will to destroy, with Jewish names and the Jewish race standing in for what was to be destroyed. Anti-Semitism would become the dark force in his propaganda for revolutionary justice in America, to the tragic undoing of his enlightened intention.

And yet—and this is hard to take in—Pound's anti-Semitism was, like his stamp scrip or National Dividend, instrumental, a means to the end of financial revolution, not an end in itself. He did not hate Jews, he hated what they could be made to stand for; and when writing to those who were simply anti-Semitic he became concerned lest their prejudice distract them from the real enemy. When he became disillusioned with Roosevelt for continuing in the old way of financing public works by borrowing from the private banks, he called him 'Roose(n)velt', said he was under the thumb of 'the Lehmanns, Barachs, Morgentsteins, etc.', and was 'fundamentally the usurers' champion'. That was using anti-Semitism to attack the President's economic policy. But to the Silver Shirts, who were modelling themselves on Nazism and were as anti-Semitic as Hitler could wish, Pound wrote that the 'S/S/ should attack financial tyranny BY WHOMEVER exercised, i.e. whether by international jew or local aryan'. And to an English writer in sympathy with Nazism and its anti-Semitism he wrote, 'The anti-semitic fury blunts perception', that is, it distracts attention from all the usurers who are not Jewish, and 'EVERY IRRELE-VANCY weakens your attack'. His real enemy was always the banking system which he held responsible for a great deal of human misery. He could see that anti-Semitism would distract and deflect the attack from that enemy; and still he would persist in using it as a weapon in his economic war. He was able to do that because his objection to it was superficial, merely instrumental. And his indifference to its inhumanity would negate his humane intention.

There can be no doubt though that he was genuinely struggling to bring about a just society. And he really did believe that the principles of Jefferson's Declaration of Independence were made new in Mussolini's speech in the Piazza before Milan Cathedral 'on the 6th of October anno XII (1934)', when the Duce promised to resolve 'the problem of the distribution of wealth, so that we will no longer experience the illogical, paradoxical and cruel fact of poverty in the midst of abundance'. Pound understood that to mean 'No more an economy putting the accent on individual profit, but an economy concerned for the interest of the whole people (*interesse colletivo*)'. That made the Fascist dictator, in Pound's view, the proponent of a higher social justice, and a shining example to the United States.

Making music of history: 'Cantos 31–41'

Here is another paradox. In his cantos, even when dealing with those same matters of economics and banking in the United States and in Italy, Pound was able to write in a manner totally opposed to that of his agitprop prose. In the cantos there are no urgings to instant action, no raging animosities, no generalizations and abstractions. Instead there are great heapings up of demonstrative detail, whole phalanxes of particulars; and readers are not told what to think but—often to their dismay—are required to discover their own reactions and to draw their own conclusions from the data laid out before them. They find themselves in an absolutely different mental world, though of course it is objectively the same world, only the mind perceiving it has altered in its way of operating. Now it is intent on what is to be known and understood rather than on what is to be done, and the aggressive mentality of the activist wielding a range of fixed ideas against the enemies of society gives way completely to its opposite, the open intelligence of the poet about its proper work.

'An epic is history set to music', Pound noted about 1936, meaning, presumably, that the poet would be studying the facts of history with a mind sensitive to their harmonies and discords, and intent on discriminating their values, their moral or ethical overtones, and on composing them into a pattern to appease the humane rage for order.

'Never has been a LONG hortatory poem', Pound advised John Hargrave, the leader of the Green Shirts, a militant wing of Social Credit: 'Epic...is not incitement to IMMEDIATE act/ you tell the tale to direct the auditor toward admiration of certain nobilities, courage etc.' Or, putting it another way, this time to Basil Bunting as a fellow poet, 'The poet's job is to *define* and yet again define till the detail of surface is in accord with the root in justice.' Behind that lies the principle of *le mot juste*; but for the poet there is more to it than the accurate word; there must be justice also in the arrangement of the words and in their tones and rhythms. That sort of justice, the natural justice of language, does not come naturally. It was as much as he could do, it was like forging pokers, Pound told another young poet, Mary Barnard, 'to get economic good and evil into verbal manifestation, not abstract, but so that the monetary system is as concrete as fate and *not* an abstraction'.

It is demanding work for the poet, and even more so for the reader. This is what the readers of the New York little magazine called *Pagany* had to contend with in the summer of 1931:

> Tempus loquendi,
> Tempus tacendi.
> Said Mr Jefferson: 'It wd. have given us
> time.'
> 'modern dress for your statue . . .
> 'I remember having written you while Congress sat at Annapolis,
> 'on water communication between ours and the western country,
> 'particularly the information . . . of the plain between
> 'Big Beaver and Cuyahoga, which made me hope that a canal
> '. . . navigation of Lake Erie and the Ohio. You must have had
> 'occasion of getting better information on this subject
> 'and if you wd. oblige me
> 'by a communication of it. I consider this canal,
> 'if practicable, as a very important work.
> T. J. to General Washington, 1787
> . . . no slaves north of Maryland district . . .
> . . . flower found in Connecticut that vegetates when suspended in air . . . .
> . . . screw more effectual if placed below surface of water.

Those details at the opening of canto 31 are all, apart from the Latin lines, from the historical record, mostly from the 'ten fat volumes' of *The Writings of Thomas Jefferson* which Eliot had been given by his father and had passed on to Pound. The whole canto in fact is made up of snippets of the known history of the American Revolution and its times, and so too are the following three cantos. They are composed of what Jefferson actually said and wrote, and of what his friends and fellow founders of the United States of North America, Madison and John Adams and John Quincy Adams and the rest, actually said and wrote. Pound invented nothing, put no words into their mouths. What he did was to select passages, or, more often, phrases, from their correspondence with each other and from their journals or state records, and set them down item by item. Sometimes the source and context is indicated, but often not; and how one item might relate to another is left to the reader to fathom.

Many readers, if not most, give up and write off the poem as a ragbag stuffed at random with odd scraps out of unfamiliar books. An early reviewer of *Cantos XXXI–XLI* in the New York *Nation* amused himself with the conceit of Mr Pound taking correspondence courses in such subjects as 'History of the U.S. Treasury from the Revolution to the Civil War (from the Original Documents)' and making notes diligently on small pieces of paper which a gust of wind scattered over the hills about Rapallo, and which he then picked up and sent to the printer as he found them. Seventy years on and J. M. Coetzee, the distinguished novelist, critic, and then member of the Committee on Social Thought at the University of Chicago, still felt able to assure the seriously cultured readers of the *New York Review of Books* that *The Cantos* is 'a great ruin ... built out of fragments' and best 'quietly dropped', apart from 'a handful of anthology pieces'. The only alternative, according to one determined scholar, William M. Chace, would be an immense labour of dogged source-hunting and explication. The sources must be known before any sense can be made of a canto, he insisted, while recognizing the very real risk of thus burying the poem beneath a mountain of prosing exposition. That way one might well be turning a ragbag into a dustheap.

Pound firmly dismissed the ragbag reaction in an interview with Pier Paolo Pasolini in 1968, and at the same time he raised the possibility of an unprosaic approach. 'They say they are chosen at random, but that's not the way it is', he said, 'It's music. Musical themes that find each other out.' He had evidently attempted to explain this to Yeats, but without much success. 'Can impressions that are in part visual, in part metrical, be related like the notes of a symphony,' Yeats had queried sceptically in the introduction to his *Oxford Book of Modern Verse* (1936), or 'has the author been carried beyond reason by a theoretical conception?'

One would have to allow that a music made of words will have quite different possibilities and conditions as compared to a music of sound only. Its resonances and its accords and discords will arise as much from the meanings and associations of the words and images as from their melody and rhythm. It would be a music of the whole mind at work. Thus there is an intellectual chord in the first two lines of canto 31, *A time of speaking, | A time of silence*. The resonant phrases are from Ecclesiastes, and they go with the Preacher's exhortation, 'Whatsoever thy hand findeth to do, do it with thy might; for there is no work, nor device, nor knowledge, nor wisdom, in the grave, whither thou goest.' Speak, act, while you have time in this world of vanities, is the Preacher's message. Jefferson's saying 'It wd. have given us time' rhymes with that, and with both *time* and *speaking*, not to the ear but to the understanding. A feeling for the time is there again in '"modern dress for your [i.e. Washington's] statue"'. Speaking and acting in time modulates in the following lines through 'remember having written you ... water communication ... information ... a canal | navigation ... better information ... a communication of it ... T. J. to General Washington, 1787'. Those lines compose an 'intellectual complex' or vortex and generate a general idea of constructive communications at a particular moment in time. The reader makes out their idea precisely by attending to 'musical' relations over and above the straight sense of Jefferson's prose. The last two lines of the extract are another instance of themes finding each other out. Jefferson's insight, that the newly invented ship's screw will be 'more effectual if placed below surface of water', first accords (as a matter of scientific interest) with the curious flower 'that vegetates when suspended in air'; and then plays off against it, visually, and also intellectually since the screw is a product not of vegetable nature but of human invention and insight. All that is an effect quickly passed over, and yet the pair of lines encapsulates an enlightened culture out of which came the discovery that would prove to be a major contribution to navigation. Things not syntactically connected can link up thematically.

When they do so link up they are likely to yield more than their surface meaning. Two lines can specify a culture at a certain moment; a dozen and a half lines can define the *virtù* of Thomas Jefferson. In Pound's view, as he expressed it in *Jefferson and/or Mussolini*, Jefferson was the shaping force in the American Revolution, guiding and governing it 'by what he wrote and said more or less privately', especially in 'conversation with his more intelligent friends', and with his influence lasting through to Van Buren's presidency. 'He canalized American thought by means of his verbal manifestations'—and that is what Pound has him doing in cantos 31 to 33. His Jefferson exhibits, in the detail of his private correspondence as much as in drafting the Declaration of Independence, a highly developed 'civic sense', characterized by a rational direction of will towards what will be useful and beneficial to the new Union, and by unwavering contempt for ignorance and error, especially in unelected heads of state and aristocrats. He stands, in effect, as the inventor of the new American *paideuma*.

A major theme running through canto 31 is that the basis of Jefferson's revolution is intelligence in all its senses: first the gathering of accurate intelligence about whatever needs to be known; then the intelligence that carries sound knowledge into practice; and beyond these, enlightenment about the ends of government. The counter-theme, in Jefferson's and John Adams's observations, is a general lack of intelligence in the way Europe's kings and governments manage their affairs. The theme is taken up and developed in canto 32, beginning with this statement of it, '"The revolution," said Mr Adams, | "Took place in the minds of the people".' In the next canto he will add, 'and this was effected from 1760 to 1775 in the course of the fifteen years...before Lexington'. That is a quite radical revision of the usual perception of how the American states freed themselves from British rule. The War of Independence, 1776 and its battles, all of that is eclipsed by '"Took place in the minds of the people"', where the overthrow of monarchical government is registered in the democratic '"minds [plural] of the people [collective singular]"'. At the heart of canto 32 is a setting off against each other of the new mind of America and the old European mind. Jefferson would civilize the Indians, but not in 'the ancient ineffectual' way of religious conversion—

> The following has been successful. First, to raise cattle
> whereby to acquire a sense of the value of property...
> arithmetic to compute that value, thirdly writing, to
> keep accounts, and here they begin to labour;
> enclose farms, and the women to weave and spin...
> fourth to read Aesop's Fables, which are their first delight
> along with Robinson Crusoe. Creeks, Cherokees, the latter
> now instituting a government.

That is of course a purely eighteenth-century, patriarchal, and un-Native American model of civilization. One might even call it European, if it were not that the monarchical European way, in Jefferson's view, was 'to keep [the people] down'

>   by hard labour, poverty, ignorance,
> and to take from them, as from bees, so much of their earnings
> as that unremitting labour shall be necessary to obtain a sufficient surplus
> barely to sustain a scant life. And these earnings
> they apply to maintain their privileged orders in splendour and idleness
> to fascinate the eyes of the people...as to an order of superior beings

In fact these 'superior beings' behaved as 'cannibals' eating their own people. Worse, having always their own way meant they never had to think about anything, 'and thus are become as mere animals'—

> The successor to Frederic of Prussia, a mere hog
> in body and mind, Gustavus and Joseph of Austria
> were as you know really crazy, and George 3d was in
> a straight waistcoat.

'A couple | of shepherd dogs, true-bred' would be more worth importing from Europe, as being likely to prove more intelligent and more useful for any rational purpose.

Canto 33 states its general theme in its opening lines, with John Adams writing to Jefferson in November 1815—a few months after the defeat of Napoleon at Waterloo—that all despotisms, whether monarchical, aristo-cratical, oligarchical, or of 'a majority of a popular assembly', are 'equally arbitrary, bloody, | and in every respect diabolical'. Jefferson had observed this in his own fashion in 1779, in the case of a quartermaster who failed in his duty to distribute to the troops the resources plentifully available in the country. Whether the possessor of wealth and power be 'baron, bojar or rich man matters very little', Adams remarked, implying that private interest would always win out over public service. The canto moves through various instances of that to come to Marx's account, in *Das Kapital*, of how the diabolical factory-owners of England ruthlessly exploited child labour while denouncing the ineffectual factory inspectors 'as a species of revolutionary commissar pitilessly sacrificing the unfortunate labourers to their humanitarian fantasies'. The final self-serving despotism is that of the American Federal Reserve banks—this is in Senator Brookhart's time, in 1931, the year in which the canto was written—and the bankers' manipulation of the public credit for private gain and their insider dealing marks the extent of the betrayal from within America of Jefferson's democratic revolution.

Canto 34 goes back in time to the beginnings of that betrayal. Pound condensed into seven printed pages Allan Nevins's 575-page *Diary of John Quincy Adams* (1928), a selection from the twelve large volumes of *The Memoirs of John Quincy Adams, Comprising Portions of his Diary from 1795 to 1848*, published by Charles Francis Adams between 1874 and 1877. John Quincy Adams (1767–1848), son of John Adams, spent his entire life in the public service, as a diplomat in Europe (1794–1816), and at home as senator, Secretary of State to President Monroe (1817–25), President (1825–9), and representative in Congress (1829–48). Throughout his last twenty years in the House he worked tirelessly, and of course unsuccessfully, for the abolition of slavery in the Southern states. Pound thought that 'the new or then renascent CIVIC sense' of John Adams and Jefferson 'reached its highest point in John Quincy Adams'. The canto demonstrates that, and demonstrates also that both as President and in Congress he failed to win consent to his enlightened policies.

This is a large and ambitious canto and its composition is worth pausing over. Pound began by working through, possibly 'skim-reading', the Nevins abridgement of the *Diary*, and copying fragments onto a 'Blocco Rapallo' notepad. He then typed up from the notepad a first draft, occasionally altering the wording or phrasing, but keeping to the order of the excerpts and including nearly all of them. The whole canto was almost there in the earliest notes. Some further revising of the first typescript and then of a second typescript, apart from adding some telling details (such as '"The fifth element: mud." said Napoleon'), was simply intent on clarifying the sense and refining the music of sound and rhythm. The canto can be divided into three main sections or movements, the first covering Adams's time as a diplomat in Russia and Paris (1809–16); the second his return to

America and service as Secretary of State and President; and the third his twenty years as representative for Massachusetts.

Analysis of the first movement reveals how Pound was composing his fragments into a form of music. (Underlinings and other markings, bold type for key words, have all been added; also the dividing spaces, apart from the space after '*Journal de l'Empire*'.)

And a black manservant, to embark on a voyage to Russia.... [4]

Consistent with **their peace** and their separation from Europe....
English **pretentions, exclusive**, auf dem Wasser.... (a.d. 1809)   *5*
'En fait de **commerce** ce BONAPARTE est un étourdi,' said Romanzoff...
Freedom of admission, for ships, **freedom** of departure, **freedom**
         of purchase and sale... [5]

Are the only members of the corps diplomatique who have any
         interest in literature, conversation..   *10*
we talked of Shakespeare, Milton, Virgil and of the Abbé Delille....
'Monsieur Adams' said the Emperor, 'il y a cent ans que je ne vous ai vu.'[6]

June 4th 1811:
         The idea occurred to me of a treaty of **commerce**.
Told him his government wd. probably make **our peace**.   *15*
'How?' said the ambassador (french).
                 'By not keeping her word.'[7]

And he, BONAPARTE, said to Romanzoff:
         'After the **peace** of Tilsit, where cd. I go but Spain?'
For he must always be *going*.[8]   *20*
It is reported that the two empresses will return to the city
As is said to be customary
At least in **wars** *un peu interessants*, which **war** Alexander

[4] JQA Minister Plenipotentiary to the Russian Court, 1809.

[5] JQA speaks ll. 4 and 7, introducing main subject; Romanzoff, Tzar Alaxander's Minister of Foreign Affairs, speaks ll. 5 and 6, the counter-subject (or antithesis). 'Un étourdi'= 'a scatterbrain', even 'a dolt'.

[6] These four lines introduce a contrasting (or second) subject, which is given some development in the second movement. (See also ll. 30 and 44.)

[7] Main subject and counter-subject developed—'our peace' would be with England, and would be made by France opening its ports to US trade and so breaking its agreements with other European states.

[8] 'peace of Tilsit', agreed between Napoleon and Alexander 1807. Napoleon's forces were finally driven out of Spain by the Duke of Wellington in 1814. In June 1812, breaking the Tilsit treaty, Napoleon invaded Russia—this ten-line passage develops the Bonaparte component of the counter-subject into a first episode.

Has done all he can **to prevent**.
French army 500 thousand, the Russian 300 thousand,   *25*
But counting on space and time.
'The fifth element: mud,' said Napoleon.

—

<u>A black, Claud Gabriel, in the emperor's service</u>
<u>Was very ill used <u>in America</u>.</u>[9]

—

Aug. 14th to Oranienbaum.
Where was Lord Cathcart (that is at Madame de Stael's)   *30*
And she wanted to know how she cd.
Receive her interest from United States funds
While in England, and a war on between them.[10]

Here the nobility have given one man to the army
From every ten of their peasants.   *35*
      Qu'il fit la sottise de Moscou
and he BONAPARTE had to borrow six shirts from
his minister, and four thousand louis....[11]

Mr Gallatin,
Mr Bayard...answer from Romanzoff...Mr Gallatin
did not think that 'They cd.' (Did not   *40*
think that our actions against Florida could be justified).
Against rights on the Mississippi...our
Rights to fish, dry fish and cure...off Newfoundland.[12]

At the opera: <u>Tamerlan</u>, and the ballet of Télémaque.
1815, March 18th was expected <u>BONAPARTE</u>   *45*
      last night at Auxerre,
Ney to be here (Paris) tomorrow, because it is the
King of Rome's birthday...
March twentieth: The King, Bourbon, left the Tuilleries,
To take, they say, the road going toward Beauvais...   *50*
At the Seance Royale last Thursday he had talked of
His death in defence of the country.

---

[9] The off-rhyme with l. 3 marks a close to the first half of the movement. The second half will repeat the structure while developing the thematic material.

[10] Re-statement of the England component of the counter-subject.

[11] Further development of Bonaparte component, concluding the 1812 episode; and contrasting with the following five lines. 'La sottise'= 'senseless folly' or 'stupid mistake'.

[12] Resolution of main subject and the England component of its counter-subject: US delegation negotiating a treaty of commerce with Russia, and a peace with England based on respecting the commercial interests (or rights) of both parties. (Americans keeping their word.)

And when they wish to make the troops cheer, the
Soldiers say: Ah, voui, Vive le Roi.
Newspaper this morning headed *Journal de l'Empire*.   *55*

... arrived last evening with the troops that had been sent out
        against him....
which is due to Bourbon misconduct.[13]

Evidently it is necessary to possess or to be willing to acquire a little historical knowledge. Beyond that, reading the canto involves distinguishing one item from another, discriminating the bearing of each one, then making out their relations and interactions as the organization of the particular details builds the dramatic contrast between Adams's will to civilized order and Napoleon's barbaric—the mention of Tamburlaine is not accidental—will to power.

The common reader is entitled to say, 'I can't read it, that's not my way of reading.' The critic, if willing and able to read it musically, will quite properly question the utility and the validity of this way of thinking. But one thing that cannot justly be said is that the writing lacks form and makes no sense. Far from being a random ragbag those pages are thoroughly organized by an intensely active intelligence, only that intelligence is making out the meaning of things in an original and still unfamiliar mode. We are accustomed to the re-orderings of our ways of perceiving the world in the visual arts and in music, but we do find it more difficult when it comes to words to venture beyond the reliable disciplines of hard-learned grammar, syntax, and logic. But there it is, whoever would read *The Cantos* must risk a new way of ordering things in the mind, one which might lead to an unconventional understanding of the world.

At the least this ideogrammic method, as Pound called it, has the virtue of forcing the mind to attend to the detail and to the various possible relations of the things that concern it; and thus of keeping the mind free from powerful and dangerously simplifying generalizations and abstractions. For Pound himself it was the antidote to the one-eyed or closed mind, and it made all the difference, in his own case, between the tendency in his propaganda to narrow down into murderous prejudice and the open and growing vision of his poetry.

---

[13] This fifteen-line passage is the second Bonaparte episode, and the conclusion of the first movement (apart from a five-line bridge passage.) Napoleon, having escaped from Elba, becomes Emperor once more in Paris, thanks to the Bourbon King's 'misconduct'. (He will be finally defeated at Waterloo in June.) The movement has been built upon the contrast between the constructive will of JQA in working to establish American independence in peaceful commerce with other nations, and the destructive will-to-power of Napoleon, Europe's representative man of the moment.

In the second and third movements of canto 34 John Quincy Adams is back in America. He reflects upon the prevailing manners and morals there and finds little to praise. 'Banks breaking all over the country', he observes, most of them fraudulently, and 'prostrate every principle of economy'. In the minds of statesmen, 'moral considerations seldom | appear to have much weight . . . | unless connected with popular feelings'. Henry Clay, bidding to be Vice-President, is 'Defective in elementary knowledge and with a very | undigested system of ethics'. In fact, 'almost all eminent men in this country' are 'half educated'. When he was President, 'They (congress) wd. do nothing for | the education of boys but to make soldiers, they | wd. not endow a university (in 1826)'. Later, from the House of Representatives, he tried unsuccessfully to prevent the states from sacrificing 'all their rights to the public lands'. (He might have saved some of the nation's land 'for the nation', Pound remarked in *Jefferson and/or Mussolini*, if he had not been 'deficient in capacity for human contacts'.) Everywhere he observed greed subverting the principles of Jeffersonian democracy, principles which he still steadfastly defended—

> The world, the flesh, the devils in hell are
> Against any man who now in the North American Union
> shall dare to join the standard of Almighty God to
> put down the African slave trade . . .

The canto closes with a Latin inscription, 'Constans proposito. . . . | Justum et Tenacem', words which, as Adams recorded, were applied to him in recognition of his constancy of purpose and his tenacity in the abolitionist cause. Alongside them Pound set the Chinese character for true sincerity, which he read as an upright man standing by his word.

With that character Pound seals Adams's self-portrait in his diaries as a faithful upholder of the revolutionary values of Jefferson and his father. Indeed he appears to stand, in his own account, as the solitary upholder of those values among a mob of venal, corrupt, and hostile mediocrities. However, the canto, as a dramatic monologue will do, brings out other less flattering features. The other side of his self-righteous isolation might be that 'deficient . . . capacity for human contacts', a considerable handicap in a politician, and he does indeed declare himself at one point in the canto 'a misanthropist, an unsocial savage'. Moreover, whereas Jefferson and John Adams established the revolution 'in the minds of the people' through networks of correspondence, John Quincy, as we read him, is talking only to himself. He may be dramatizing what has happened to the democratic revolution, that it now depends on the mind of one man. At the same time, though, he is revealing his own unfitness to govern efficiently in a democracy. He suffered from 'puritanitis', Pound wrote in *Jefferson and/or Mussolini*, implying an inability to take humanity as it comes and to be committed to the politically possible. He was too absolute in his demands for justice and for social justice, perhaps because too concerned to be justified. He saved his own honour, Rhadamanthus might judge, but the state he could not save. A less severe judge could say, he stood for what was right, but could not bring it into effect. In canto 37 it will appear that Martin Van Buren, whom Adams rather looks down on as 'L'ami de tout le monde' and as a protector of the scandalous Mrs Eaton against 'the moral party', will be more successful in defending the public currency against the greed of private interests.

The banking and financial system will be the dominant concern of a sequence of cantos starting with 37. First though, the story of the American Revolution is interrupted by two very different cantos.

Canto 35 is concerned, in its first half, with the condition of 'Mitteleuropa' in the aftermath of the 1914–18 war and the break-up of the Austro-Hungarian empire. A series of anecdotes in the sardonic manner of 'Moeurs contemporains' suggests that with the passing of the imperial order the prevailing values are now those of the cultivated Viennese Jewish family, personal, aesthetic, most warmly familial. One comment is, 'sensitivity | without direction'; but another goes, 'and the fine thing was that the family did not | wire about papa's death for fear of disturbing the concert | which might seem to contradict the general indefinite wobble'. The general impression, especially after the four cantos concerned with the values of good government, is that there is now little or no civic sense in Austria and Hungary. The second half cuts to Mantua in 1401 and Venice in 1423, to observe two varieties of civic sense in that earlier age of Europe. In Mantua a loan bank is decreed, 'to lend money on cloth so that they cease not to | labour for lack of money'; and with that arrangements are made to give Mantuan cloth a competitive edge over the surrounding cities, 'to the augment of industry' and increase in the wealth of the city. Also, it is sardonically remarked, to the luxurious clothing of 'Madame ὕλη, Madame la Porte Parure', alias Lucrezia Borgia who came, in canto 30, clothed 'with the price of the [altar] candles'. Venice also is wholly materialistic in its dealings, regulating all trading in and out of Venice 'for the upkeep of "The Dominant"'. Both cases, the Mantuan and the Venetian, exemplify a civic sense directed by a rational but rather limited self-interest.

Canto 36, placed in the middle and as the pivot of the 1934 *Eleven New Cantos XXXI–XLI*, consists of a translation of Cavalcanti's 'Donna mi prega'—a radically different translation from the one printed in *Rime* and the 'Cavalcanti' essay—and to that is attached, as if in response, a passage drawing in the Carolingian philosopher Scotus Erigena (?800–?877) and the Mantuan troubadour Sordello (?1189–?1255). Suddenly we are in another realm from that of the surrounding cantos, in the realm of 'the intelligence of love', apparently at the furthest remove from the events and concerns of the capitalist era. That distance suggests the readiest relation of this canto to the other ten, that it is presenting a reach of intelligence lost to the modern mind. Certainly Pound's American observers see nothing of it in the courts of Europe, nor in Napoleon, nor in the owners of banks and factories, nor indeed among the majority of their fellow Americans; and that could be because that concept of love does not enter into their conversation and is simply not part of their culture. Nonetheless it may prove pertinent to our understanding of Pound's representation of them, and to his dominant concern with economic order.

He gave a hint in 1933, when, in responding to the question 'what has been the most important meeting of your life?', he wrote that it was with Guido Cavalcanti, and that the meeting of minds was important for its bearing on 'le problème des surréalistes: état de conscience et (ou) force morale'. The problem would be in the 'and (or)'—to cultivate hyper-real (or 'super-in-human') states of consciousness *with* a moral or ethical direction, or to go for the one *or* the other. The remarkable thing, given that Cavalcanti is likely to be thought of as a love poet, is that there is no mention of romantic love. His significance for Pound is now in the sphere of the intellect and the will to order.

The argument of the *Canzone d'amore*, very simply put, is that the Light which is the life of all we know illuminates the receptive mind, takes form there, and thus informs and directs it to enlightened action. When Pound wrote that Jefferson 'informed' the American Revolution, 'both in the sense of shaping it from the inside and of educating it', he is likely to have had that idea in mind. The form of the beloved in that case was of course not figured as a *donna ideale*, but as the Declaration of Independence and the Constitution of the United States; and its shaping power was constantly manifest in Jefferson's 'verbal manifestations', in John Adams's care for justice (the subject of the later 'Adams Cantos'), and also in John Quincy Adams's clear sense of the principles of the democratic revolution. One might say that the essential form of democratic justice so profoundly possessed their minds that it directed their every political word and action. The effect of thinking back to their cantos in the light of the *Canzone d'amore* is to have the focus shift from their words and deeds to that 'forméd trace in [the] mind', a telling shift from what passes in time to what is 'in the mind indestructible'. In the Pisan prison camp Pound will be encouraged by the conviction that the precisely defined Constitution, though 'in jeopardy | and that state of things not very new either', is among the resurgent icons 'formed in the mind | to remain there | *formato locho* | . . . to forge Achaia'.

Following the paradisal canto 36 we descend again into the purgatory of political action, and then, in canto 38, into the inferno of those who profit from arms sales.

Canto 37 contains the major episode in Pound's treatment of the American Revolution in this suite of cantos: the critical war for supremacy between the effectively private Bank of the United States and President Jackson representing the people of the United States. The war was carried on in the Senate, in the financial economy, and in the press from 1829 to 1835. Pound took as his principal source for that part of the canto *The Autobiography of Martin Van Buren* (published in 1918). Van Buren (1788–1862) was Secretary of State and then Vice-President (1833–7) to Andrew Jackson, and succeeded him as President (1837–41). Pound credited him with having been the brains behind Jackson's saving the nation by freeing the Treasury from the despotism of the Bank, and the canto could lead the reader to see him as the main protagonist in that war, and to assume that his is the epitaph 'HIC | JACET | FISCI LIBERATOR', 'here lies the Treasury's Liberator'. However, in Senator Thomas Hart Benton's fully documented account of the Bank war, in his *Thirty Years' View, or A History of the Working of the American Government* (1854), the hero is unquestionably President Jackson, and Van Buren is not seen to play a leading role, in part because while Vice-President he chaired the Senate Debates and could have no voice in them. (That difference raises the question of historical accuracy to which I will return.)

The first third of canto 37 weaves together thirty or more items, most of them things said by Van Buren or taken up by him over the many years from 1813 when he was a New York state senator to 1840 when he was President. The passage is a prime instance of Pound's method of adding one detail to another without providing the conventional syntactical and logical connections, in order to allow a more complex web of relations to develop. Banks fraudulently failing, wealthy landowners and factory owners, high judges and the Chief Justice himself, senators, financial speculators, all are implicated in defrauding immigrants of the value of their banknotes, in driving settlers off the land they would cultivate, in denying workers the vote, in preventing local government of local affairs, and in '"decrying government credit. | . . . in order to feed on the spoils"'. Van Buren exposes and opposes this systematic injustice of the wealthy and powerful towards both the people and the state. He reaffirms the basic cause of 'our revolution', *No taxation without representation*; he insists that government revenue 'be kept under public control' and not be given over to the banks to speculate with; and he endorses President Jackson's saying 'No where so well deposited as in the pants of the people, | Wealth ain't'. All the details add up to an account of Van Buren's 'life-long fight for economic and social rightness in the U.S.'; and at the same time they indicate a national state of affairs in which the Bank war was a major and symptomatic event.

A condensed account of that war, from Van Buren's point of view, is given in the rest of the canto, interspersed with his views of certain of his contemporaries, mostly unflattering, and with some of his political opponents' unflattering views of him. John Quincy Adams had remarked 'servility' in him, others that he was 'a profligate'; he remarks in return that Adams 'deplored that representatives be paralyzed | by the will of constituents'. In short, he observes the imperfections of others and they observe his in the usual way of politics. But in the serious business of putting an end to the despotic power of the Bank he is impersonal and coolly forensic. He gives figures for how much the Bank increased the amount it had out on loan, from forty to seventy million dollars within two years, when its charter was coming up for renewal; he mocks Daniel Webster's then complaining that if the charter were not immediately renewed that thirty million dollars of loans would have to be called in; he gives figures again to show that while the Bank controls '6 millions of government money | (and a majority in the Senate)', the President has control of only '15 to 20 thousand'; he charges the Bank with deliberately creating panic to obtain 'control over the public mind', and to keep control over the public credit; and he charges Nicholas Biddle, the president of the Bank, with 'controlling government's funds | to the betrayal of the nation' and never hesitating, on the precedent of Alexander Hamilton the Bank's first founder, 'to jeopard the general | for advance of particular interests'. In the event President Jackson vetoed the Senate's bill which would have renewed the charter, gradually withdrew the government's funds from the Bank of the United States, and so 'saved the nation and freed the American treasury'.

Those are Pound's words, in *Jefferson and/or Mussolini*, only he was applying them there to Van Buren, as he does at the end of the canto. For that he could be open to the charge of misrepresenting the historical facts. But then it could be said in his defence that he was presenting an interpretation of the facts, as historians generally do. In crediting Van Buren with freeing the public treasury from private control he was in effect declaring that while Jackson wielded the presidential veto it was Van Buren's brains and will that were the efficient force directing him in that act. There is more going on here than an alternative version of who did what. Pound was privileging the moral force over the mere fact, in order to create another Jeffersonian hero, an ethical hero, consistently committed to a just ordering of society.

'Canto XXXVIII. where is FACTS', Pound wrote to Ford in 1934, 'where facts is what there aint nothing else BUT.' He had been telling him how to read the earlier Hell cantos, and mentioned canto 38 in that connection, with the implication that it was a more 'lyric' hell and of 'greater force'. Its hell is not that of England just after the war, but rather that of contemporary Europe at large; and its facts are mainly drawn from Pound's current reading and recent conversations. It would have been thoroughly topical to the readers of Orage's Douglasite *New English Weekly* in which it first appeared in September 1933.[14]

Its central and blindingly illuminating fact—a light from paradise, the canto declares it—is Douglas's diagnosis of the canker at the core of capitalism, the fact that 'the power to purchase can never | (under the present system) catch up with | prices at large'. That, Pound would have readers of his prose understand, is 'THE evil of the capitalist system', by which he meant 'the basic evil causing all the particular evils'. The prevalent Depression would have been the most immediate particular evil, but this canto does not go into that.

Instead its final part brings into focus the anomalous fact that, while all else in the economy was sinking, the arms industry remained buoyant. Governments that could not or would not subsidize the consumption and thus the production of the necessities of life nevertheless could and did invest in the production and purchase of the means of mass killing. That meant that manufacturing and trading in armaments was more profitable, as Pound observed in one of his prose articles, 'than the production of foodstuffs, the improvement of housing or any other act conducive to causing men to live like human beings'. In the canto he has 'Herr Schneider of Creusot' say, "More money from guns than from tractiles"'. Monsieur Schneider had said words to that effect in 1932, at a meeting of the *Société Anonyme Schneider et cie* at which a dividend was declared 'of 100 francs on every 400 franc share'. '"While our departments of railway and marine…

---

[14] Orage returned to England and started up his *New English Weekly* in April 1932 to promote Douglas's new economics. 'He was completely convinced of the general truth of the Douglas analysis … that the cause of the economic frustration of our civilization, ever since the Great War, was essentially financial', and 'that the accepted principles of finance were a tangle of illusions, obscuring all true values and tending to disintegrate all genuine human relations' (Philip Mairet, *A. R. Orage: A Memoir* (London: Dent, 1936), pp. 112–13). Orage died in October 1934. Pound continued to contribute to the *NEW* articles, letters, and light verse (his Social Credit 'Poems of Alfred Venison') until June 1940.

are suffering considerably from the general crisis"', he reported, '"the departments preparing the defence of our country have...been more than moderately satisfactory."' Another French manufacturer of both agricultural machinery and artillery reported likewise that the 'works engaged on war material are going nicely' thanks to important government orders, while 'the others work with great irregularity' because 'orders from private concerns have greatly diminished'. The arms industry was becoming the dominant force in the French economy. It was able to draw on unlimited bank credit since profits were guaranteed by government investment and a sellers' market of both 'friends and enemies of tomorrow'; it was able to control the press through its shareholdings; and it had its representatives in parliament. In effect the *Comité des Forges*, the union of arms manufacturers, now held the position in France that the Bank of the United States had held in America a century before, that of a virtual state within the state, and one able and willing to put its own business interests before the interests of the nation—'"faire passer ses affaires | avant ceux de la nation"'. The war now, as Pound saw it, was 'between humanity at large and one of the most ignoble oligarchies the world has yet suffered'. And that oligarchy, that military–industrial complex, was the creation, as the private Bank of the United States had been, of the evil financial system.

The canto carries a pertinent epigraph from Dante's *Paradiso*, in which the Just Rulers speak of the woe brought upon Paris by Philip the Fair's debasing the currency to finance a war. Its first line then names 'Metevsky' who figured in canto 18 as the type of the arms dealer who created his own military–industrial complex. What happens then, however, is disconcerting. A recapitulation of Metevsky's way of selling arms to both sides is intercut with several unrelated items—the Pope's curiosity about Marconi's wire-less radio, Lucrezia wanting a rabbit's foot, '(three children, five abortions and died of the last)', and Dexter Kimball's account of cigar-makers being read to 'for the purpose of providing mental entertainment' as they worked 'almost automatically'. The canto goes on like that for the first one hundred lines, in the most extreme instance so far of Pound's 'not proceeding according to Aristotelian logic but according to the ideogrammic method of first heaping together the necessary components of thought'.

The 'thought' in this case turns out to be an ideogram composed of what was in the news in the mind of Europe in the 1920s and early 1930s, and signifying the lack of vital intelligence in that news. The immediate effect of the passage is rather like glancing through a newspaper and registering one miscellaneous item after another—the day's news, gossip, titbits of interest, information both relevant and useless, opinions informed and misinformed, sheer silliness—all are indiscriminately thrown together.

The news that the Italian marshes have been drained at last is buried in a brief item, with no thought given to how it was done or what it might signify. Ghandi's revolutionary thought, 'if we don't buy any cotton | And at the same time don't buy any guns', receives no more attention than 'the soap and bones dealer's' precisely wrong assurance, in May 1914, that there would be no war, '"On account of bizschniz relations"'. There are disconnected indications of the drift towards another war—Metevsky's dealings, two Afghans at the Geneva Disarmament Conference looking to pick up 'some guns cheap', money in Persian oil-wells, 'So-and-So' with shares in Japan's Mitsui corporation—but no conclusions are drawn as to what is happening and why. The culminating item concerns a modern Juliet being prepared for burial and knowing that her Romeo was suiciding outside her door, a stark image of failed communications amidst warring factions.

In all that heap of news one looks in vain for a European *paideuma* to set alongside Jefferson's American *paideuma*, for a sense of values held in common, for some basis for constructive action beyond the business of making money from guns. And one looks in vain for what Pound clearly considered the most vital news, first, Douglas's potentially life-saving and civilization-saving revelation of the economic cause of depressions and wars, and then intelligence of the war against humanity being carried on by the military–industrial complex. There is the ironic suggestion that the Africans who 'spell words with a drum beat' may be more efficient at getting their message through, and the further suggestion that there may be more intelligence in primitive 'languages full of detail | Words that half mimic action; but | generalization is beyond them'. After a tailor's wonderful assertion, at the close of the first movement, that '"Sewing machines will never come into general use"', the poet breaks away to spell out the real news from Douglas and about the cannibals of Europe being at it again.

He then turns, in canto 39, from the contemporary shambles and goes right back to his starting point, Odysseus' epic wandering after the shambles of Troy, and his being shown his way home by Circe, the bewitching goddess. Circe (like Aphrodite), born of Sun and the Sea, is a force of divine nature, seductively beautiful and wise in her ways, fatal to some men and to others life-enhancing.

Odysseus' men, war-weary and hungry, thoughtlessly take what she offers and instantly she makes swine of them. That happens in the first movement of the canto, where Circe is the young witch, her 'Song sharp at the edge, her crotch like a young sapling'; she is surrounded as if in a Titania's brothel by 'fucked girls and fat leopards', 'All heavy with sleep'; and she feeds the sailors 'honey at the start and then acorns'. The rhythm of this movement is heavy, as if with her drug. Its first line is 'Desolate is the roof where the cat sat'; and its last, 'illa dolore obmutuit, pariter vocem', tells how Hecuba, wife of King Priam of Troy and now an item in Odysseus' spoils from that war, is struck speechless by the grief of coming upon the corpse of the one child she thought had survived. In Ovid's account the line marks the ultimate desolation of that war fought for possession of a Circean woman. The first movement thus enforces the alienated view—an essentially male view—and the bestial experience of Circe's powers.

The second movement is framed by Circe's directions to Odysseus, given here in the original Greek—they will be given in translation in canto 47—and, at its close, by Odysseus' awed response to being told he must go by way of Persephone's bower, this in Divus' Latin with a colloquial rendering, 'Been to hell in a boat yet?' This movement is relatively light and quick, and associates Circe with a series of light-bringing mother-figures. Egyptian Hathor, 'bound in that box | afloat on the sea wave', is a divinity of many benign aspects, mother of the sun, goddess of love and joy, of dance and music, and protector of the dead on their arrival in their other world. After Hathor come two lines from Dante's *Paradiso*. In the first Dante declares that the delight of the circle of illuminated spirits surrounding the mother of Christ and singing '*Regina coeli*', '*O Queen of Heaven*', will never leave him; in the second, Beatrice, herself a resplendent light, empowers him to perceive as a fiery river of light, 'fulvida di folgore', the perfected forms of all that divine Love generates. And Circe, taking Odysseus into her bed, will initiate him into her mystery. He is prepared for the initiation by Hermes who gives him a herb to keep his mind and senses clear of Circe's charm, yet bids him not refuse the pleasures of her bed. 'Coition, the sacrament', Pound had noted, 'The door to knowledge of nature'; and in canto 36 he had followed Cavalcanti's philosophical canzone with the statement, 'Sacrum, sacrum, inluminatio coitu'. The illumination of mind is the saving grace, the becoming conscious of 'the unity with nature' and actually seeing nature alive.

The vision of Circe's mystery comes in the song and dance of the third movement, a rite of Spring out of Catullus and the *Pervigilium Veneris*. Instead of 'fucked girls' there is '"Fac deum!"', and the bride's song, '"His rod hath made god in my belly"'. These girls are not 'leery with Circe's tisane', rather they are 'Beaten from flesh into light'. The flame and the lightning that is in them is implicitly the god Dionysos, but this is the women's rite under Circe. The vision of Dionysos was in canto 2, and that was all male. Here in both the initiation and the vision the manifest powers are all female, and all, including Circe when approached intelligently, would initiate the male protagonist into the realm and the process of generative love.

Against the chorus of girls making the spring, and against the bride's 'Beaten from flesh into light', the opening lines of canto 40 sound harshly ironic:

> Esprit de corps in permanent bodies
> 'Of the same trade,' Smith, Adam, 'men
> 'never gather together
> 'without a conspiracy against the general public.'

Those lines state the main theme of the canto. There follows the counter-theme, that the nation's money should be held by the nation's own bank, a notion advanced in medieval Venice but only carried into practice two centuries later. The rest of the canto down to 'Out of which things seeking an exit', pivots on the isolated line restating the counter-theme, '*"If a nation will master its money"*'. Both the passage preceding that line and the one following—each of thirty-four lines—develop the main theme through variations upon 'conspiracy against the general public'. J. P. Morgan figures prominently, for selling the government its own arms (condemned arms) in the Civil War at extortionate profit; business in general took advantage of that war and prospered by its failures; the banks (with the Rothschild bank leading) got control of treasury bonds to their own profit, and made a killing by buying up depreciated Civil War bonds then having them redeemed in gold, the price of which Morgan had forced up; then there were the cheating manipulations of bonds for railway construction. And all this was for private luxury, 'Toward producing that wide expanse of clean lawn | Toward that deer park', 'With our eyes on the new gothic residence, with our | eyes on Palladio, with a desire for seignieurial splendours'. The statement and the restatement of this third theme enclose the passages developing the main theme, and expose the vanity of anti-social greed. Its monument might be a list of the accumulated objects to be auctioned when the failed seignieur's residence is sold up, 'haberdashery, clocks, ormoulu, brocatelli, | tapestries, unreadable volumes bound in tree-calf, | . . . flaps, farthingales, fichus, cuties, shorties, pinkies | et cetera'.

That is a view of what became of America during and after the Civil War. 'We were diddled out of the heritage Jackson and Van Buren left us', Pound had complained in *Jefferson and/or Mussolini*, 'The *de facto* government became secret, nobody cared a damn about the *de jure*.' That had led him on to propose that the governing ideas of Jeffersonian and Jacksonian democracy were now to be found in Mussolini's Fascism, and that is the starting point of canto 41. Taking an overview of the cantos from 31 up to this point one might say that the thesis of the sequence is the democratic heritage of Jefferson, Jackson, and Van Buren; that the antithesis is the rule of private greed in Europe and the falling off from Jeffersonian democracy into private greed in the United States; and that now Mussolini is to be put forward as the synthesis, that is, as a European proponent of democratic values with an active and exemplary sense of civic responsibility. (Cantos 36 and 39, representing the life of the spirit, appear to stand rather apart from the rest, while having a significant bearing upon them.)

Formally canto 41 is a fugue, that is, its thematic materials are organized as they might be in a musical fugue. Fugue is not a set form—as Yeats may have thought, and so failed to understand what Pound was trying to tell him in 1928—but is rather a set of procedures for developing two or more melodic lines in interaction with each other. Thus one episode of the canto is in strict counterpoint; and there is, as is common practice in musical fugues, an accelerated *stretto* passage preceding the final cadence. The first theme (or subject, in musical terms) is good government as exemplified by Mussolini at the start of the canto and Jefferson at its close. The second theme, which grows out of the first, is good intelligence or news concerning the management of the economy. Then there is the inversion of each theme, misgovernment, and misinformation or ignorance. Those have been the leading preoccupations of the preceding ten cantos, and this fugue is the way of drawing them together into a concluding statement.

Each canto has been a new experiment in form, a new invention, and this one, while following a classic musical form, is at the extreme of innovation in English poetry. It is difficult, as it needs to be given its ambition, but probably no more difficult than a Bach fugue once one has made out the themes and the process of their development.

A.[1] *1st subject*	Mussolini, 'the Boss', is introduced as the man of quick intelligence and efficient action in the common interest—draining the marshes, causing grain to grow there, providing water supply and housing;
B.[1] *response*	a story of the Boss's dealing with 'the potbellies' who want their cut from the public works by sending them into internal exile;
C.[1] *counter-subject*	the commandante della piazza's 'we'd let ourselves be scragged for Mussolini', demonstrating popular devotion to the Boss.

(25 lines, 1–25)

D.[1] *2nd subject*	The ignorance of the people (out of the mouth of a babe);
E.[1] *response*	Messire Uzzano's advice, in 1442, on how to manage the money supply, thus overcoming ignorance and its ill-effects;
F.[1] *counter-subject*	'and you must work...	to keep up your letters'.

(20 lines, 26–45)

1st episode	*(related to 1st and 2nd subjects: the Boss, and formation of the young)*

Details of the Boss's youth and training—his being exploited and underpaid as a mason in Switzerland, then trained for mountain warfare (in the 1914–18 war), and deliberately bombed (so it was said) while wounded in hospital—these details counterpointed against the formation of 'the young Uhlan officer' (i.e. a German cavalry lancer), 'never out of uniform from his | eighth year until the end of the war', and trained up in a militarism characterized by a book depicting the 'Renewal of higher life | in the struggle for German freedom', a book presented to him by the empress in 1908 'with a tender and motherly dedication'.

(31 lines, 46–76)

2nd episode   *(inversion of 1st episode: military commanders lacking intelligence)*
'Feldmarschall Hindenburg' (the young Uhlan's General in command), characterized by his ignorance of music—'Mozart... all this god damned cultural nonsense'—and his concern for his pension; the (presumably French) high command being on vacation in the summer of 1914, a minor bureaucrat files 'the Hun ultimatum'; and Winston Churchill (being in 1914 First Lord of the Admiralty) at least 'had the fleet out', according to his 'mama' (cp. the 'motherly dedication' of the German empress), though he would not 'waste time having ideas'.

(23 lines, 77–99)

D.^{2} *2nd subject*   *(a natural modulation from the 2nd episode into)*
'That llovely unconscious world' of European decadence;

E.^{2} *response*   what it has for news is '"Pig and Piffle"', (highly profitable); *The Times*, which it 'Pays to control... for its effect on the markets'; and a press free from state censorship, but with 'a great deal of manipulation'—
(this is an inversion of E.^{1});

F.^{2} *counter-subject (a return to E.^{1})*
a proper 'news sense' notes 'Cosimo First's' banking (see canto 21); the self-regulation of the bank of Siena, Monte dei Paschi (see cantos 42–4 in the following decad); also Douglas; and 'Woergl in our time'.

(22 lines, 100–21)

B.^{2} *1st response* As Mussolini dealt with the profiteers, Jefferson exposed the tobacco tax racket in France (see canto 31);

A.^{2} *1st subject*   as Mussolini's good government is manifest in his public works, Jefferson governed by his 'verbal manifestations', represented in a *stretto* passage climaxing in 'Independent use of our money... toward holding our bank'.

(26 lines, 122–47)

Cadence   A sequence of closely related news items concerning the arms trade and its indiscriminate arming of belligerents—'120 million german fuses used by the allies to kill Germans' etc. (cf. canto 38 and the two war episodes above)—this being the consequence of not mastering the nations' money for the benefit of the whole people.

(5 lines, 148–52)

At the end of the canto is a dateline, 'ad interim 1933', equivalent to 'up to now' or 'this is the state of affairs in 1933'. It is a reminder both of the time in which *Cantos XXXI–XLI* were being written, and of the fact that their historical leads always come out at what is going on in the present. The American story from its revolution to the post-Civil War robber barons and bankers runs in counterpoint with the European story over the same period and on through its Great War up to the present moment, a moment at which it appears that America's revolutionary will to secure life, liberty, and happiness to all the people is now to be found at work in Europe in the person of the Boss, Il Duce. The root of good government is shown firmly planted in the American Revolution, and these cantos are unequivocally committed to the American idea of democracy. But then that idea of democracy evidently transcends America, since the United States can lapse from it into the reign of private greed, while it can be seen to be more effectively practised by the Italian dictator.

It has to be recognized, if we are to get on, that Mussolini is as much an invented or mythical figure in these cantos as Jefferson, or Van Buren, or indeed as Odysseus. He is just as much transfigured out of history into the poem Pound is making up, and he plays his part there in an ethical drama which may be not at all an accurate fit with the political drama of the era. Pound is not writing Mussolini's story, nor Jefferson's nor Van Buren's. He is writing, as it will turn out, the epic of the capitalist era, in which the will to social justice, as embodied in some few heroic individuals, must contend against the greed of the wealthy and powerful and the abuleia of the many. It is a story based on real persons and real practices, and its credibility does depend in some degree on its truth to what is commonly known of those persons and practices. Beyond that believability, though, there is another order of reality, that of meanings and values; it is with these that the epic poet is most engaged, and in creating images of what is to be admired or hated he will bend history to his ends. But then the nearer a reader is to the history in question, the more problematic this can be. There is a problem, and there will be so long as the actual Mussolini is remembered, in accepting the Mussolini of the *Cantos* as a hero of the struggle for universal social justice. It is a problem that anyone who wants to read the work must just learn to live with.

History may instruct us that the myth has grievously simplified the facts; and the myth may reveal things facts alone can never tell. We need both history and myth, but should take care not to confuse either with the other.

Note: A historian, the Bank Wars, and the New Deal

Our accounts of the past 'are far from stable', Arthur Schlesinger Jr wrote in the *New York Review of Books* in April 2006, 'They are perennially revised by the urgencies of the present.' So he had written *The Age of Jackson* (Boston: Little Brown, 1946) in the light of Roosevelt's 'struggles to democratize American capitalism', wanting to show that 'FDR was acting in a robust American spirit and tradition': 'Jackson's war against Nicholas Biddle and the Second Bank of the United States . . . provided a thoroughly American precedent for the battles that FDR waged against the "economic royalists" of his (and my) day.' Roosevelt himself had seen the precedent as early as November 1933. Schlesinger cites a letter of that month to Colonel Edward M. House in which Roosevelt wrote,

The real truth of the matter is, as you and I know, that a financial element in the larger centers has owned the Government ever since the days of Andrew Jackson . . . The country is going through a repetition of Jackson's fight with the Bank of the United States—only on a far bigger and broader basis.

Schlesinger continues,

Jackson and Roosevelt, it appeared, had much the same coalition of supporters— farmers, workingmen, intellectuals, the poor—and much the same coalition of adversaries—bankers, merchants, manufacturers, and the rich. There was conse- quently a striking parallel between the 1830s and the 1930s in politics, and there was a striking parallel in the basic issue of power—the struggle for control of the state between organized money and the rest of society.

That striking parallel was what Pound was pointing out to America in 1933 and 1934, in *Jefferson and/or Mussolini* and the *Eleven New Cantos*, and quite directly in canto 37. Only he could not see Roosevelt defeating 'organized money'.

4 : THINGS FALL APART, 1933–1937

To spread order about him

> *And Kung said, and wrote on the bo leaves:*
> *If a man have not order within him*
> *He can not spread order about him*

Joseph Bard, the Hungarian novelist who had told Pound about Frobenius' concept of *paideuma*, spoke in a lecture in 1961 of the Pound who had been his friend in Rapallo in the later 1920s and early 1930s. He recalled how alive and irreverent he was, and how his vehemence 'radiated from a deep and serious intention'—

I could see a unique dedication, a rare sense of responsibility for the clarity and proper functioning of the mind, but nothing either obscure or wild...Never did I observe anything excessive in him, in fact, the order he was cultivating in himself to be adequate to the experiences he may have to undergo forced a certain sense of order on his friends.

Theirs was a tragic time, Bard said, 'in which dormant forces have woken up, hidden but unfolding to the sensitive eye, forces which human reason in its present potential cannot control'. He was thinking of the ungraspable forces behind the Great Depression and the approaching world war, and celebrating Pound as a source of order in a disintegrating world.

Bard recalled in particular how for Pound 'the stress of earning a living by good literature against the deviating pressure of commercial literary nabobs was a necessary discipline and a participation in the life of the struggling mind'. He recalled also how Pound 'was always on the alert to save his friends' mental energies from being drained by trivialities, by small pleasures within the range of every idiot'. He cared that their minds should be nourished and recreated by the better human achievements.

Bard's Pound is not the single-minded revolutionary out 'to GET ACTION', as in his work for Orage's *New English Weekly*; nor the frequently raging

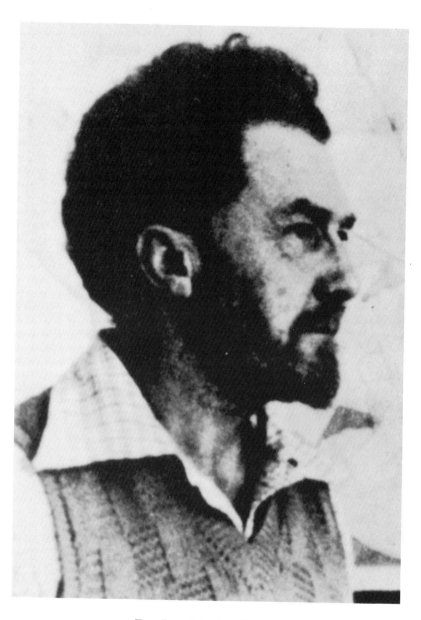

1. Ezra Pound in Rapallo, 1920s.

2. Ezra Pound at his desk in his Paris studio, 1922.

3. James Joyce, Ezra Pound, Ford Madox Ford, John Quinn, in Pound's studio, 1923. Ford and Quinn are on chairs made by Pound.

4. Olga Rudge, violinist, *c*.1923.

5. George Antheil and Olga Rudge, Paris, 1923.

6. Olga Rudge, c.1923.

7. Ezra Pound, 1920s.

8. Dorothy Pound, *c.*1930.

9. Ezra Pound in Vienna, 1930 (*Photo: Bill Brandt*)

10. Pound on the tennis court, Rapallo, 1926.

11. Ezra Pound on the rooftop terrace of his apartment, Rapallo, 1930s (*Photo: Arnold Genthe*)

Direbbesi un caprone
che il monte un dì discese
è invece un artistone
dell'almo snolo inglese.

12 (*left*). Basil Bunting in caricature
by Gubi, *Il Mare* 13 August 1931.

13 (*below*). Louis Zukofsky, 1933.

14 (*right*). W. B. Yeats and
T. S. Eliot, Harvard, 1932.

15 (*below*). James Laughlin,
1930s.

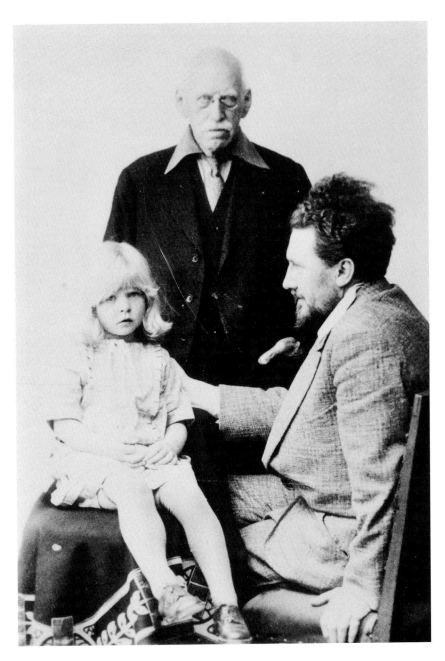

16. Maria Rudge, Homer Pound, Ezra Pound, Gais, 1930.

17 (*right*). Maria Rudge and her father, Venice, 1935.

18 (*below*). Maria Rudge and her mother, Venice, 1935.

19 (*left*). Dorothy Pound, 1930s.

20 (*below*). Ezra Pound, 1930s.

21. Pound in his Rapallo apartment, *c*.1938, with Gaudier Brzeska sculptures (*Cat* and *Embracers*), and with Wyndham Lewis's *Red Duet* (1914) on wall (*Photo: Arnold Genthe*)

22 (*left*). Olga Rudge, 1930s.

23 (*below*). Pound arriving New York, April 1939.

Pound of the crusading journalism flung in the face of those who could not and would not see the saving truth; and not the overreaching megalomaniac single-handedly taking on the evil economic system of the capitalist democracies and their empires. He is the man Bard knew among his friends in Rapallo, an individual in a small town, spreading about him in that little world such order as he could 'build in his own ambience'. It was good for the energetic American with his characteristic desire to get hold of the best and to be the best in the world—so Pound himself admonished small-town America—it was good for him to learn from the older countries such as Italy that civilization is local. His friend Manlio Dazzi had shown him in 1923 in Cesena, where he was then librarian of the Malatestine Library, how it was possible 'to have first rate music in a small town'. 'There is all the difference in the world', Pound wrote, between the man who builds well with what he has to hand, 'and the lunatic who thinks he is Napoleon'.

* * *

By the end of March 1933, within two months of being appointed Chancellor, Herr Hitler had seized total control of the German state. The burning down of the Reichstag on 27 February had given him cause to suspend civil liberties, to set his Brown Shirt thugs upon his Communist and Social Democrat opponents, to create concentration camps at Sachsenhausen and Dachau as instruments of terror—27,000 had been imprisoned by the end of the year—and to spread anxiety and fear among the people at large. On 1 April a one-day boycott of Jewish shops was decreed as a statement of intent; then laws were issued excluding Jews from the public services, the professions, and the universities; and the robbing, beating up, and murdering of Jews began. On 10 May a torchlight parade of thousands of students ended opposite the University of Berlin and there the students burned twenty thousand 'subversive' books, thus inaugurating the new Nazi era of German culture. And still too few of those whom it concerned elsewhere in Europe and in the United States took notice of the Nazi agenda openly laid out by Hitler in **Mein Kampf**—*an agenda driven by the will to lead an Aryan Master Race destined for world conquest.*

* * *

Through May 1933 Pound was in Paris at the Hotel Foyot; Dorothy was in London. Ezra reported to her his catching up with old friends—Joyce, Léger, Bill Bird; 'Miss Weaver present for 5 mins.'; Caresse Crosby, Duchamp the surrealist, Tibor Serly the Hungarian-American composer who was often in Rapallo, Walter Rummel, Natalie Barney. Brancusi had been ill and was a bit low. Cocteau had done a new play. Harding of the BBC was over to discuss the proposed production of *Cavalcanti*. Cummings, whose new book about

Russia, *Eimi*, Pound was impressed by, was in Paris; also George and Mary Oppen. In his last letter to Dorothy before returning to Rapallo he mentioned that Max Ernst had presented him with a 'beeyewteeful blue seascape worth much more than emergency chq. I sent up'. Ernst had said, '"entre nous—such questions—i.e. re value—can't arise"'.

Back in Rapallo he wrote to Dorothy, 'O is livin up at St Ambrog/ but I trust will be able to combine something with Muench & thereby have a status. Also hopes for Siena job, which wd start before long.' 'Muench' was Gerhart Münch, a gifted young pianist and composer from Dresden with a scholarly interest in early music, and Pound at once seized on the chance of his presence in Rapallo to organize a 'Settimana Mozartiana'. The Teatro Reale cinema was hired for the evenings of 26, 27, and 28 June, and twelve of Mozart's sonatas for violin and piano were performed by Olga Rudge and Münch, four each evening, 'under the auspices of the Fascist Institute of Culture'. The rest of Mozart's thirty-four violin sonatas were 'done privately so that a few of us heard the whole set'. Then 'the aristocracy of the Gulf of Tigullio', as Pound expressed it in a note in *Il Mare*, 'decided to organize a private subscription concert', at which Münch would play Scriabin, in order to encourage him to remain permanently in Rapallo as the pivot of the 'effort to achieve a higher degree of musicality in the Gulf'. The Musical Section of the 'Amici del Tigullio', Pound declared, were determined to put on in the future more concerts like the Mozart series. After the Scriabin concert on 12 July Pound left for Siena to join Olga, who had just been confirmed as administrative secretary to Count Guido Chigi Saracini's very distinguished Academy of music. Dorothy wrote that she was not telling Olivia that Pound was with Olga in Siena, it was 'too complicated'.

Dorothy was finding England 'deader than mutton'; but 'Omar was fairly lively: knows his twelve times table'. He was too old now to stay with the Norland Nurseries, and she was at her wits' end to know what to do about him. That problem was solved at the end of June when a Miss Dickie, who was retiring from the Nurseries to a cottage near Bognor, offered to have him with her and to send him to school nearby. This arrangement would cost Dorothy about the same as with the Norland. Earlier in June she mentioned a 'Very lucid and well-spoken street-corner meeting of British Fascists on Sunday 12.30 in High Street [Kensington]'. In July she noted that Wyndham Lewis was very positively interested in Social Credit. She would return to Rapallo about 10 August, and wanted Ezra to be back from Siena for her then. 'All right', she wrote as that date approached, 'We will try cooking upstairs if you think so.' To which Ezra replied, 'Don't purrpose to cook more'n one meel a day anyhow.'

In August there was a stellar conjunction in Rapallo of Pound, 'the pride of the town', Basil Bunting (who observed him in that role), Louis

Zukofsky the Objectivist, and, in brief transit, an 18-year-old Harvard undergrad who signed himself 'James Laughlin IV'. Bunting, because Pound was there, had been drifting in and out of Rapallo since 1924, when he was not being a music critic in London—1925–8 on *The Outlook*—or getting married in America, in 1930. Yeats had seen him as one of Pound's 'more savage disciples', though he was at the same time rather fiercely independent. Bunting was named as a contributing editor on the stationery Pound got up for the *Il Mare Supplemento Letterario* in August 1932, and was a member of the committee for the concerts inaugurated with the Mozart Week in June 1933. In November a lack of money would force him to move with his wife and child to the Canary Islands. Zukofsky, having been frequently urged by Pound to see Paris, i.e. to encounter the writers and artists Pound thought worth knowing there, had dutifully sailed from New York and done a fortnight in Paris, assisted by 500 francs from Pound. But he had his own reason for the trip, 'to see you', as he wrote to Pound, '& discuss what can be done for 'Murka'. To an interviewer in Budapest he said he had come 'chiefly to meet the master of American poetry and in a sense its father'. In Rapallo he was put up in a large room with its own bathroom in Homer and Isabel's apartment, formerly the Yeatses', and was impressed by their gallery of photographs of Ezra and of Omar. He had his meals with the Buntings, for which Pound paid, went out with Basil in his boat, and observed Ezra swimming far out on his own. The main event of each day was leisurely tea with Ezra and Dorothy, Ezra talking with 'wit and brilliance', and Dorothy 'silent most of the time'. Zukofsky asked Pound to read a canto, then read it back to him 'very quietly and clearly'. With Bunting he tried to persuade Pound to read in a more natural voice—they both thought their own very different ways of reading the cantos better than his Yeatsian chaunt. At the same time Pound and Bunting were telling Zukofsky that he should cultivate a more natural language, to no effect. He returned to New York in September confirmed in his devotion to Pound and also—like Bunting, his fellow leading light in Pound's *Active Anthology*—confirmed in his determination to go on working out his own independent poetics.

Young Laughlin had yet to grow into his independence. Introducing himself to Pound he declared a readiness to become his most devoted servant, if Pound would advise him 'about bombarding shits like Canby & Co', and elucidate for him 'certain basic phases of the CANTOS' so that he could 'preach them intelligently'. Though he was from a Pittsburgh steel dynasty, he was, he assured Pound, 'full of "noble caring" for something as inconceivable as the future of decent letters in the US'; and, being an editor on both the *Harvard Advocate* and Yale's *Harkness Hoot*, he was in a position 'to reach the few men in the two universities who are worth bothering about, and could do a better job of it with your help'. He clearly knew how to appeal to Pound as a well-instructed neophyte, and was hospitably received in Rapallo. After his two or three days there he thanked Pound 'cordially for . . . the most vital experience of the summer', and returned to Harvard fired up to do 'A complete exposure of Jeffers and Robinson', something on the arms merchants, 'an estimate of WCWms: proper praise of ACTIVE ANTH. when it comes', and did Pound think 'Zukofsky or Doc Williams could be enlisted in the cause?' Soon Pound was sending him prose blasts for the university magazines, and for *New Democracy*, Gorham Munson's Social Credit magazine in which Laughlin, at Pound's instigation, had been given a column under the rubric 'New Directions'.

That summer of 1933 Pound was issued with a journalist's pass entitling him to a 70 per cent reduction on the Italian State Railways. He used it, according to the record on the pass, not for journalism but to travel from Siena to Rapallo on 9 August; to go from Genoa to Brunico in early September—that would have been to see Maria—and on the 8th to return from Bolzano to Genoa; to go from Genoa to Venice on 15 October, and to return on 25 October.

A series of concerts to make 'music in winter' was announced by the 'Amici del Tigullio', one in each month from October to March. The Mayor of Rapallo was showing his support by putting at their disposal the 'Gran Sala del Municipio', the newly panelled and decorated grand chamber of the Town Hall. The concerts would be under the auspices of the Instituto Fascista di Cultura Commune, and would be sponsored by the Amici. Among the named supporting Friends were two marchesas, a contessa, and a conte, Mrs Ephra Townley, Reverendissimo Desmond Chute, Miss Natalie Barney, Dottoressa Bacigalupo, Signor H. L. Pound, and Mrs D. Pound. The Friends had opened a subscription to pay for a Steinway which they would present to the town, to be 'used only for concerts of distinction'.

Pound wrote a series of articles for *Il Mare*, starting with three in September setting out the idea of the concerts. Later articles would introduce the music and the performers, and review some of the performances. The emphasis was to be on early music up to Bach and Mozart, with a few examples of later music for purposes of comparison. Münch, with funding from the Amici, would be preparing for the concerts transcriptions from the rich collection of unpublished early music built up by the musicologist Oscar Chilesotti, and would thus be making 'a real addition to the whole body of existing music'. One of his first transcriptions was Francesco da Milano's sixteenth-century setting for lute of Clement Jannequin's *Le*

Chant des Oiseaux, a chorus for several voices imitating the songs of many birds. In Münch's 'metamorphosis' of the song for Olga Rudge's solo violin this featured frequently in the Rapallo concerts, and Pound would reproduce Münch's score dated '28.9.33' in canto 75. Along with Münch and Rudge the regular performers would be 'prof. Marco Ottone, 'cellist from Chiavari' just down the coast from Rapallo; and 'Maestro Sansoni, whose merits are sometimes forgotten by those who see him conducting the municipal orchestra in the open air or playing jazz in the Kursaal'. 'Our aim', Pound wrote, 'is to develop a group of local performers sufficient for our needs and desires, and not to spoil our musical life as in so many countries by trusting and encouraging only the so-called "stars".' First-rate musicians who happened to be 'passing through the town' would also be invited to perform—and would feature, indeed, more and more in the later series. But Pound was aiming at the creation of a local culture of musical excellence, founded on the well-ordered harmonies of pre-romantic composers, and in this he largely succeeded until the coming of war in 1939 put an end to all that.

* * *

The long-running League of Nations Disarmament Conference was getting nowhere and Mussolini proposed in the summer of 1933 that Britain, the old enemies France and Germany, and Italy should make a pact to guarantee the peace of Europe for a decade. Lloyd George, who had been British Prime Minister when the League was set up, said to the Italian Foreign Minister, 'Either the world follows Mussolini, or the world is doomed.' The Pact of Four was signed in the Palazzo Venezia on 15 July. In October, however, Germany walked out of the Disarmament Conference, and a few days later withdrew from the League of Nations, thus, said Mussolini, scuppering all at once the Pact, the Conference, and the League. Hitler was determined to re-arm Germany and to prepare for all-out war. In November over 90 per cent of registered voters in Germany endorsed the withdrawal from Geneva and elected a single-party Nazi slate to the Reichstag.

* * *

In the autumn of 1933 Mary Barnard, a young woman living in small-town Vancouver across the river from Portland, Oregon, desiring to learn how to write poems and considering that Pound 'knew more about the technique of writing poetry than any other living poet', sought out his address in *Who's Who* and mailed a sample of her poems to him in far-away Rapallo. 'How hard and for how long are you willing to work at it?', came back his challenging response on a postcard. He advised her to study Greek metres since she knew Greek; and, more generally, to study 'the MEDIUM, i.e.

language and everything it consists of. consonants, vowels, AND the relative duration of the different sounds'—'Get a metronome and learn HOW long the different syllables, and groups of them take'. 'There aren't any RULES', was the only rule he laid down, but also, 'work to a metric scheme/—when you can do it strictly, on yr/ head, dead, drunk or asleep, then you can begin loopin the loop and taking liberties with it'. When she showed that she was willing to work at writing in sapphics Pound put her in touch with Marianne Moore and with Williams, and sent her poems to Eliot for his *Criterion*, to the *New English Weekly*, and to some young poets in America and England whom he was encouraging to put together an anthology of new talent. A quarter of a century later Mary Barnard, by then an established poet and writer, would publish a musically sculpted translation of Sappho.

'Do understand that at yr/ tender age'—this was Pound writing to Mary Barnard in January 1934—'too much criticism is possibly worse than none.' However, his *ABC of Reading*, then about to be published in England, 'contains part of the lessons', he told her. This *ABC* was written to develop and to simplify 'How to Read', his 1929 essay written for the *New York Herald Tribune Books* supplement. There he had begun by attacking both the American university system as he had experienced it at the University of Pennsylvania, and the general state of literary culture in England as he had found it in 1908–12 when he was young and eager to learn. What had been borne in on him, one gathers, is that the young must find out for themselves what they most need to know. 'The teacher or lecturer is a danger', he instructs his young readers in the *ABC*, because liable to be enforcing his own opinion. Criticism, his own especially, 'shd. consume itself and disappear', leaving its readers seeing the thing in question for themselves.

The *ABC of Reading* is a wonderfully liberating, anti-academic, textbook. 'Gloom and solemnity', Pound declares on the first page, 'are entirely out of place in even the most rigorous study of an art originally intended to make glad the heart of man.' The joyful students in his book will be the ones who as they work through it grow in confidence in their own power to read and to write well. You do not need to know everything, Pound tells them, lifting one burden of scholarship; you need only to discriminate the best, the exemplary. And you do that by first-hand examination, by direct analysis and comparison, by actually listening to the sounds of words, and seeing the images they create, and thus apprehending their meanings. *Melopoeia*, the making of music in words, *phanopoeia*, the making of images in the mind, and *logopoeia*, 'the dance of the intellect among words', these are the means by which the common language is condensed and intensified into poetry. Pound presents as exhibits his selection of poems in which one or more of those qualities are at a peak of attainment, having previously warned 'YOU WILL NEVER KNOW either why I chose them, or why they were worth choosing, or why you approve or disapprove of my choice, until you go to the TEXTS, the originals'. Enjoy the excitement of working it out for yourselves, he urges the students, and you won't need to listen 'to me or to any other long-winded critic'.

As an incitement to study literature the book appeals mostly to the idealism of youth, and then a little also to its nihilism. 'Literature is news that STAYS news', Pound declares, meaning that the best of it carries news of what is perennially true of human nature and desire and fate. Its use for the individual is that it both eases the mind of the strain of our endemic uncertainty and ignorance about things, and positively feeds it as incitement to live more fully. Its usefulness to the state is in maintaining the energies and the efficient working of language upon which depend good government and civilization. After that, nearly at the end of the book, comes the bait for 'The natural destructivity of the young', a hint of the excitement and the fun of detecting and exposing 'counterfeit work' and 'The hoax, the sham, the falsification'. The young can be instructed in this, Pound writes, while implying that they will go to it very readily. One thinks of young James Laughlin IV and his 'complete exposure of Jeffers and Robinson', and his gleeful 'we debunk Stein (Toklas) in the current issue'.

The winter series of Rapallo concerts are mentioned in *ABC of Reading* as an example of its method of examining musical compositions under laboratory conditions in order to discriminate the first-rate from the second-rate, with Debussy played after Corelli and J. S. Bach, or Ravel after Bach. 'The point of this experiment is that everyone present at the two concerts now knows a great deal more about the...relative weight, etc., of Debussy and Ravel than they could possibly have found out by reading ALL the criticisms that have ever been written of both.' Pound was also eager to introduce newly recovered early music. In March 1934 the Rapallo musicians premiered six of the sonatas by William Young (d. 1672) from the edition just published by W. Gillies Whittaker, and were looking forward to receiving freshly edited scores of Purcell and Dowland.

'Nevuh hav bin so aktiv as in last 2 or 3 years', Pound wrote in a letter to Agnes Bedford in April 1934, 'probably incipient paranoia...vast economic correspondence'. He would tell Langston Hughes, 'I spend about 95% of my energy at this typewriter trying to CREATE a REAL revolution'. To his old friend Viola Baxter Jordan he did also mention 'wackin a tennis ball to keep me belly from bulgin', and going 'to the movies average of twice or more per week', that being, after a hard day's work, 'Only way to STOP'.

Along with the certainly rather paranoid economic outpourings—the paranoia not altogether unwarranted in the light of current events—Pound was being active as ever on his other fronts, as in shepherding the young who showed promise, and in attempting to keep his peers and his elders in order. To John Drummond, a student at Cambridge in England, he wrote that it was time for 'a new heave by the young', and that 'If you people at Cam. can do anything in the way of a nucleus, I'll do what I can to bring in the scattered and incongruous units of my acquaintance'. He told his respected elder Laurence Binyon that he had gone through his new verse translation of Dante's *Inferno* 'syllable by syllable', and offered some very detailed notes on particular words and rhymes as collaborative criticism and encouragement. He was doubtful about 'syntactical inversions' in Binyon's English, having a preference for the natural word order; and he noted that Dante was 'definitely putting money-power at the root of Evil'. In June Yeats, on his last visit to Rapallo, asked Pound what he thought of the lyrics in something he had just written, *The King of the Great Clock Tower*, a brief play rehearsing an old romantic theme of his, and Pound, according to Yeats, 'would talk of nothing but politics', then returned his manuscript next day saying the lyrics were 'putrid', and written in 'Nobody language' which was no good for drama. Pound told Bunting that he was finding it increasingly difficult to read 'the buzzard'.

A young Jewish Lutheran sculptor turned up broke in Rapallo in April 1934. This was Heinz Clusmann (1906–75), who renamed himself Heinz Henghes. He wanted to see Pound's Gaudiers, and Pound took him in, fed him, put him up in what Laughlin described as 'a large dog kennel' on his roof-top terrace, found him some stone and tools from the cemetery stone-cutter, and let him get to work. 'New sculptor loose on roof, and marble dust dappertutto', everywhere, Pound wrote by way of explaining the seal on the envelope of his letter to an American college student. (He was telling her what her generation should be up to.) Henghes had offered the seal, a little animal carving, to show what he could do; and had shown a drawing of a seated centaur which later became the New Directions' very Gaudier-like book colophon. According to Laughlin, Pound persuaded Signora Agnelli, wife of the head of Fiat, to acquire some of his first works at a good price; and Henghes went on to become a successful sculptor and to win, after the war, prestigious commissions in London and New York.

In the summer of 1934 Dorothy was as usual in England. Throughout August all her time was devoted to Omar, leaving her 'unable to do or think anything but Omar'. 'P.S. This family life seems curiously unreal—like an uneasy sleep,' she wrote to Ezra. At the end of August he went up to Gais to collect Maria and take her down to Venice for ten days. 'Child very good,' he told Dorothy. He would write in the mornings, then take the Leoncina with him while he shopped with care for the best coffee, fruit, pastries, and cheese. Sometimes they would swim at the Lido. He bought her a violin so that her mother might teach her, but Olga insisted she must first learn solfège. The child remembered time hanging heavily that year in the enforced siesta in the small house where the intense music and talk were foreign to her and where it seemed that everything was to be done according to some unforgiving etiquette. She could not feel at home in its demanding order.

* * *

Germany's President and Head of State, Field Marshal von Hindenburg, died on 2 August 1934. The previous day Hitler's cabinet had decreed Hitler his successor though it had no legal power to do so. Then it was announced that Hitler would combine in himself the offices of head of government and head of state and be known as Führer and Reichschancellor. In this usurpation he had the enthusiastic support of the heads of the armed forces, having assured them that their secret re-arming would be accelerated and that the Nazi private army, the SA or Brown-shirts whose violence had brought him to power, would be disarmed. To back up that assurance his SS and Gestapo had massacred all the leading members of the SA in a bloody June purge. All members of the German armed forces now swore an oath of allegiance not to the German state but to its Führer, Adolf Hitler. On 19 August over 90 per cent of Germany's registered voters endorsed his seizure of supreme power. At the Nuremberg Nazi Party Congress in early September he was acclaimed with frenzied adulation. William Shirer the American corres-pondent was there and could see that 'whatever his crimes against humanity, Hitler had unleashed a dynamic force of incalculable proportions'.

* * *

'Education by provocation, Spartan maieutics', that was Samuel Beckett's summary characterization of the essays in *Make It New*, and it would apply equally well to *How to Read, ABC of Reading*, and even to *Cantos 31–41*. There were reviewers who received Pound's provocations as educative, and there were others who were goaded into reaction. The Scots poet Hugh MacDiarmid made *How to Read* his book of the year; while F. R. Leavis, the fiercely serious academic critic, responded with *How to Teach Reading* (1932), giving it the acid subtitle 'A Primer for Ezra Pound'. Although *ABC of Reading* was generally well received, the London *Spectator* dismissed it as a 'bundle of prejudices', 'not very convincing as criticism and quite useless in the classroom'. Eda Lou Walton in the *New York Times Book Review* even found its tone 'insulting'. The *Times Literary Supplement* praised the excellence of Pound's criticism, but deprecated his 'atrocious style', his 'affectations', and his 'arrogance'. As for the really Spartan challenge of *Cantos 31–41*, there was a tendency to discover that it was the poetry and not the reader that was failing to come to a clear consciousness. Pound 'seems to have been stumped by the problem of combining poetry and economics', reported Philip Rice Blair in the New York *Nation*; and Babette Deutsch, in the *New York Herald Tribune Books*, wrote that 'The design is wanting' for 'these fragments Pound has shored against his ruins'. Then the English poet Rayner Heppenstall, writing in the *New English Weekly*, warned that Pound's cantos in general were 'a serious menace', because of their influence on other poets. But that was as much as to admit that Pound was now, whether one was receptive to him or not, an important and influential presence as a poet and a literary critic. Still Pound would complain that editors refused to print his views on economics, and that publishers kept asking him instead for his autobiography, when he had no wish to look back and there was so much more to be done here and now.

When young Laughlin, now 'Jas' to Pound, proposed that he spend some time in Rapallo—he had taken a long leave from Harvard—Pound wrote, 'I have more bloody work than I can do | I damn well need assistance', and then 'unless you are DOING somfink in Paris, you might just possibly LEARN as much, get just as much eddikashun (without emission of bank paper) here as anywhere else'. A couple of days earlier he had been suggesting in a letter to Zukofsky 'that some brat educate himself by PUTTING himself at the disposal of New Democracy/ to run my errands', and 'cat shit for the young if they can't at least provide ONE active animal fit for training'. Laughlin would testify that in the two or three weeks he spent at his 'Ezuversity' in December of 1934 he 'learned more that was useful about what mattered in literature than I did in four years at Harvard'. He also found how to make himself useful. He had been writing short stories, with some success, and was 'trying very hard to write poetry'. Pound wasn't interested in prose fiction, and was not impressed by his poetry. He advised Jas just before he left Rapallo to give up the writing and try something useful. 'Go back and be a publisher,' he said, so Laughlin went back and created New Directions and became the publisher of Pound and Williams and many other independents, and 'never regretted obeying his edict'.

Laughlin fondly recalled that the daily class usually met before lunch at Pound's table at the Albergo Rapallo, and 'began with Ezra going through his mail and commenting on the subjects raised in the day's letters'—

He had a huge correspondence from all over the world—he told me that postage was his largest expense. Economics were already his major concern in 1934, but there were letters from writers, from translators, from professors, from scholars of Chinese and the Renaissance, from monetary theorists, from artists, from Eliot, from Cocteau, from Hemingway—insulting letters, sycophantic letters . . . In every case there would be perceptive and witty comments from Ezra with anecdotes to fill in the background.

Then 'Pound would turn to more serious subjects—literature, history as he wished to revise it, poetics, the interpretation of aspects of many cultures'. All the time he would be speaking 'in the colloquial', with mimicry, and in a variety of accents and personae. The instruction would continue on their walks, and Laughlin remembered Pound explaining to him about the Eleusinian mysteries on one of the steep stone paths behind Rapallo.

He observed how organized Pound was for his work: 'So that he could easily find them, he hung his glasses and his extra glasses, his pencils, his pens, his scissors, and his stapler on strings from the ceiling over his desk'. He also observed how, 'in the fury of composition', 'He would assault his typewriter with an incredible vigor...he couldn't always take time to go all the way back to the left margin; he would slap the carriage and wherever it stopped that determined the indent.'

Among the items Pound was beating out on his typewriter were those many letters to editors and hurried pithy articles campaigning for the economic revolution needed to save the United States from its financial system, and seeking to persuade Americans that there was much to admire in Mussolini's Fascism. It was quite natural then that when the Italian Ministry of Press and Propaganda established a short-wave radio service beamed at the United States in the autumn of 1934 it should occur to Pound's journalist friend Francesco Monotti to propose that he be invited to do a broadcast. Pound was excited by the possibility of an invitation. 'I spose the keynote will be to giv me opinyum of Italy', he wrote to Monotti, and then gave the references to a dozen recent letters and articles in which he had been insisting on the constructive element in Mussolini's Fascism. He knew that at least one article had been seen by Count Ciano, Mussolini's son-in-law and head of the Ministry, 'as we mentioned it over the telephone' at the time. He hoped he would be able to go through the relevant pieces with Ciano 'and pick the most useful 8 minutes'—it would have to be 'condensed | gotter to be oratory or nuffink'. On 23 November he was sent the formal letter signed by Count Ciano inviting him 'to make a short speech (8 minutes)', and to record it in Rome on 10 December. 'They pay *nothing*', Monotti warned. Pound replied at once to Ciano, 'greatly honoured by the invitation to speak to America, and will be in Rome... unless I drop dead on the railway platform running'. His first radio talk, and his only one until 1940, was transmitted on Friday, 11 January at midnight in Rome, 6 p.m. in New York, and was announced as 'Conversazione di Ezra Pound su "Come il Duce risolve il problema della distribuzione"'. The talk was heard by William Bird who took it to be about 'the economic triumph of Fascism'. But Pound received a note from the Ministry a few days after the broadcast, 'don't understand what you are driving at. Be specific.'

One of Pound's correspondents in 1935 was W. H. D. Rouse, a former classics teacher and an editor of the Loeb Classical Library, who had published the beginning of his 'translation of Homer's *Odyssey* into plain English' in the *New English Weekly*. Pound was encouraging him to keep to plain, direct speech and to avoid literary turns of phrase; and when the completed translation was published in 1937 Rouse credited him with being 'the onlie begetter of this book', for having 'suggested it' and for having offered 'trenchant comments' which gave him the courage of his own convictions. Pound wanted Rouse to say something in the *New English Weekly* 'about the campaign for live teaching of Greek and Latin', and for 'some means of communicating the classics to the great mass of people...who weren't taught Greek in infancy' and whose lives were impoverished by the modern world's loss of 'contact with and love for the classics'. But that wasn't all, there were 'more questions in my head than I can set down with any apparent coherence'. For instance, 'Along with direct teaching of the language, is there any attempt to teach real history? Roman mortgages 6%, in Bithinya 12%'. And what was the 'explanation for the obsolescence and decline of Gk. and Lat. studies after, let us say, the Napoleonic wars?' Wasn't it because the classics were taught without facing the economic facts? And wasn't that because 'Wherever one looks— printing, publishing, schooling—the black hand of the banker blots out the sun.' 'My generation was brought up in black ignorance', Pound insisted; and could Rouse not 'see in Brit. education during your time a reason why the country tolerates a governing class that can't see that: Work is not a commodity. Money is not a commodity. The state has credit. The increment of association is not usury?' Altogether, 'I have been for two years in a boil of fury with the dominant usury that impedes every human act, that keeps good books out of print, that pejorates everything.' Rouse was simply hoping to produce 'a readable story, that is, a story which can be read aloud and heard without boredom'; but for Pound that laudable if modest undertaking was ineluctably linked through the education of the young to the state of the world.

The Rapallo concerts of course had their economic aspect. 'What we have done', Pound claimed in July 1935, 'we have done by liberating the ability of performers from the noose of international finance.' More, 'What Dougla-sism can do for music in one town (having almost no population) it can do for any and every human activity in any town on this planet.' Douglasism as practised in Rapallo meant '*a local demonstration of credit*'. The municipality provided the hall and put in steam heating; the interested public provided the piano; the music was largely cultural heritage; and thus *all* the proceeds went to the performers 'save *ten* lire to the janitor and doorkeeper and the small printing expenses', i.e. the cost of reprinting the programme which the collaborating town paper first printed as news. Concerts in William Atheling's London had been 'a racket whereof the main proceeds did *not* reach the producer', that is the musician who performed the music in the concert hall. Even well-known performers had to pay expenses in advance to the impresario in order to obtain a booking. And the musicians dared not innovate or depart from the established repertoire.

That was where Rapallo differed most interestingly for Pound. In escaping 'the black rot of usury' it had freed its musicians to experiment, to discover lost masterpieces, and, increasingly, to introduce new works. In the 1934–5 season, along with Scarlatti and Pergolesi and Bach and Mozart, there were compositions by Tibor Serly; Bartok's 4th String Quartet (1928) played after his 1st Quartet (1908); also Stravinsky's *Petroushka* (in his reduction for piano), *Pulcinella* (in his reduction for violin and piano), and the *Sonata for piano* (1924). Pound wrote that 'Serly sees the birth of the new music in the use not merely of polytonality, but in correlation (with due opposition) of two scales, major and minor, of the same key', and Bartok and Stravinsky were of that movement or phase. He also wrote, after mentioning having heard his *Capriccio for piano and orchestra* directed by the composer himself in Venice, that 'Stravinsky is the only living musician from whom I can learn my own job'.

In July 1935 Pound wrote from Venice to Dorothy in London, 'am at Dead End & doing NOWT…feeling extremely well // only dead stop in head—which izza blessin.' He was aware though that something was up over Abyssinia. It was 'no use arguing', he wrote, 'no theory but political and econ. necessity'.

In the first week of August Pound and Olga went up into Austria for the opera at Salzburg. They travelled part of the way, possibly from Innsbruck, with Jas. Laughlin in his hired Ford tourer, and stopped off at Wörgl, about halfway between Innsbruck and Salzburg, to call on Herr Unterguggenberger and hear all about his blighted stamp scrip. The ex-mayor as it happened was out on the mountain, but they had a 'long tale from Mrs U.—very clear—and human', and came away with some used, partly stamped, scrip. In Salzburg they heard *Don Giovanni, Falstaff, Cosi fan tutte,* and *Fidelio*—which last, according to Laughlin, Pound walked out of in disgust. Laughlin then drove Olga and Pound back to Venice. There is no record of their noticing the troops Mussolini had ordered to the Brenner and other borders to put a stop to the Nazi takeover of Austria and the Alto Adige which Hitler had intended should follow the assassination of Austria's Chancellor Dollfuss on 25 July. They went by Gais to pick up Maria, who 'proudly showed them [her] beehives and the goldenrod in full bloom'. After she had been three weeks in Venice Pound wrote to Dorothy,

'Marieka very satisfactory, great progress since last year'. His pride in her shone in his telling Laughlin, 'That amazin kid has just sent a communique which went straight on the PAGE of the noo econ. book at the exact place I was typing'. She had written, in the Italian he had told her she needed to learn, 'Where we live people are sad because store goods cost so much and their sheep, hogs, cows, horses sell for nothing.'

He had somehow instilled in her the gist of some LAWS FOR MARIA:

3. That if she suffers, it is her own fault for not understanding the universe. | That so far as her father knows suffering exists in order to make people think. That they do not usually think until they suffer.

Then three more advanced laws:

I. First thing to learn is: NOT to be a nuisance./I think you have learned this.
II. Autarchia personale. To be able to do everything you need for yourself: cook, sew, keep house./(otherwise unfit to marry. Marriage: a partnership, mutual help.)
III. Autarchia. The ideal is that everyone should be Bauernfähig./The moment a family is separated from the land everyone must be able not only to DO something, or MAKE something, but to sell it....

There was also a 'Curriculum': typewriting, 'Lingua Italiana without which you will not be able to sell what you write in Italy', translation, and, query, 'Inventive writing? first simple articles, then the novel'. In short, 'I can only teach you the profession I know.'

The turning point: 1935–1936

On 16 March 1935 Hitler publicly decreed a massive re-armament of Germany and instituted universal military service, in direct violation of the Treaty of Versailles. The British, the French, and the Italians met at Stresa and condemned his action, but did nothing about it. In May Hitler made a great speech in the Reichstag on the theme of Germany's need and desire for peace in Europe, telling the governments of Britain and France what they wanted to hear. The Times of London welcomed it as 'the basis of a complete settlement with Germany'.

On 15 September 1935 Germany enacted the first of its 'Nuremberg Laws', by which German Jews were stripped of their citizenship and forbidden to marry or have sexual relations with Aryans. By the summer of 1936 Jews had been excluded either by law or by Nazi terror—the latter often preceded the former—from public and private employment to such an extent that at least one half of them were without means of livelihood'. This persecution of German Jews appears not to have become a factor in international affairs.

On 2 October 1935 Mussolini announced to an enormous crowd in the Piazza Venezia that Italy was invading Abyssinia, Haile Selassie's Empire of Ethiopia. Mussolini's intentions had been no secret to Britain and France, and he had been given reason to think neither would interfere. However, Abyssinia had been admitted to the League of Nations, and the British Government on this occasion decided to uphold the League's principle of protecting member states against foreign aggression, even though it wanted even more to have Italy's continued support in containing Hitler's Germany. The League declared Italy in breach of its Covenant and called for sanctions, that is, for an embargo on supplying arms, a trade embargo, and financial sanctions. There was no embargo on supplying oil; nor did Britain and France, who owned the Suez Canal, interfere with Italy's shipping its troops and supplies through it, being anxious to do nothing that might lead them into war with Italy. In search of a resolution they offered to cede to Italy territory from their own colonies neighbouring Ethiopia, and to cede even a substantial portion of Ethiopia itself. Mussolini, caught up now in the pride and glory of conquest, refused their offers, and by May 1936 his vastly superior forces had conquered Ethiopia, and Haile Selassie had fled from its capital Addis Ababa into exile. In July the League lifted its sanctions. Although they had not been applied with much conviction nor to any great effect, they were profoundly resented in Italy, and Britain, being held primarily responsible for them, became an object of anger and hatred. Their main effect was to destroy the loose Stresa alliance of great powers intending some resistance to Nazi Germany, and to drive Mussolini towards an unwilling alliance with Hitler whom he regarded as a mad and very dangerous megalomaniac.

Mussolini apparently foresaw quite clearly what would be the outcome. Already in June 1936 he told a French Socialist that if he were forced by British and French attitudes to reach an agreement with Hitler, 'First of all there will be the Anschluss [i.e the absorption of Austria into Hitler's 'Greater Germany'] within a short time. Then, with the Anschluss, it will be Czechoslovakia, Poland, the German colonies etc. To sum up, it is war inevitably.'

On 7 March 1936 Hitler had sent troops in to garrison the demilitarized part of Germany west of the Rhine, again in deliberate violation of the terms of the Treaty of Versailles. He then offered a twenty-five-year non-aggression pact on his western front: 'Germany will never break the peace', he declared in another impassioned speech in the Reichstag, having first whipped up a frenzy of militarism. France, which had demanded the demilitarization of the Rhineland as a buffer against another German invasion, was in a condition of political paralysis; and Great Britain led the way in neither resisting the re-militarization nor imposing sanctions.

One explanation of the British Government's inclination to appease rather than to oppose Hitler had been formulated by Claud Cockburn, an independent Irish journalist, in 1933. In October of that year, following Germany's withdrawal from the Disarmament Conference and the League of Nations, he had written in his mimeographed newsletter The Week, *that 'A large and influential body of opinion in the City and in British business circles is more or less vaguely sympathetic to the Nazi regime as a "bulwark" against Communism.' For finance and industry the enemy then was Communism; and Hitler, who had been helped into power by German industrial interests, was seen as an ally of capitalism and not a threat to it. His Brown Shirts were seen as good for destroying the trade unions and revolutionary organizations. In November Cockburn had reported, 'The main line of Hitler propaganda in the upper reaches of London society are (1) Hitler is saving the world from Communism, (2) there is a Jewish conspiracy against Hitler, (3) Hitler is providing the German people, especially German youth, with an ideal.' In February 1934 Cockburn had observed that the British Government, in spite of its denials, was consistently supporting the Nazi regime in Germany as urged by financial interests in the City and by the Bank of England; and that in particular it was letting it be known that in its view it would be acceptable if the Nazis within Austria were to take over the country and choose to unite with Germany, since that would not be the same as the absorption of Austria by Germany. (It was mainly due to Mussolini's concern to hold on to the Tyrol and Alto Adige that Hitler was prevented from engineering the Anschluss in just that way until 1938.)*

In Spain in July 1936 General Francisco Franco led a revolt of military commanders against the Popular Front Republican Government, and appealed for aid from Hitler and Mussolini. The latter sent arms, planes, and 60,000 or more troops; Hitler sent tanks, arms, and planes—the pilots of his Condor Legion perfected dive-bombing techniques which would be used throughout Europe after 1939. German and Italian planes operating together destroyed the town of Guernica on 26 April 1937. The Republicans had appealed for aid from Communist Russia, and received it until the end of 1938 when there was a change of Russian policy, leading to a collapse of the Republican forces early in 1939. Great Britain and France, which had throughout maintained a policy of non-intervention, were quick to recognize the victorious General Franco's forces as the legitimate government of Spain, and his long reign as dictator followed.

The Spanish Civil War gave Hitler an opening to draw Italy into agreeing a common policy on foreign affairs, one based on the differences between their interests and those of France and Britain. On 1 November 1936 Mussolini referred to this as an 'axis' around which other European powers 'may work together', and thus gave its name to the Nazi–Fascist Axis. 'German and Italian rearmament is proceeding much more rapidly than rearmament can in England', Hitler remarked to Ciano, now Mussolini's Foreign Minister, 'In three years Germany will be ready...'

'The boss knows his business'

In the English, French and Italian newspapers which Pound was keeping up with in August and September 1935 there was a storm over the likely invasion of Abyssinia, and over the League of Nations' threat of sanctions against Italy if it did invade. Homer Pound became alarmed, and Ezra dashed off a reassuring postcard to him from Venice: 'Keep KAAAAAAM. The boss knows his business.... Continue yr/ banking habits as usual.' 'Ever hear of the Seminoles?', he prompted, as if to account for what Mussolini was up to.

That was a startling analogy. 'The long Seminole war of 1835–42, the hardest fought of all the Indian wars', according to the old *Encyclopædia Britannica*, 'was due to the tribe's refusal to cede their lands'—i.e. the greater part of Florida—'and remove to Arkansas'. At the war's end the Seminoles were removed, and then were 'recognized as one of the "Five Civilized Tribes"'.

In October, with the invasion now well under way, Pound wrote to Senator Borah, 'you can have perfectly clear conscience that 7 million of subjected population in Abyssinia will be benefitted by conquest'. Still, he was sorry that Italy had started a war. Though it was 'necessary', he told Williams, it was 'regrettable, in some ways'. By November, however, he was telling Borah it was 'wrong' to see 'Italy's activity in Abyssinia as war'. Apparently it was 'road building etc.', and freeing 'victim tribes' from slavery. His faith in Mussolini was such that he was sure he would be bringing an 'enormous advance in living conditions' to the uncivilized Abyssinians, just as he had done for 'the people in backward parts of Italy during the past five years'. In a note with the date line '6 Dec. anno XIV' included in *Polite Essays*, he took the statement 'We have had no battles but we have all joined in and made roads', 'from a letter of Captain Goldoni's', to indicate the new Fascist 'forma mentis' in action in Abyssinia. Later though, in April 1936, he would frankly declare (here partly echoing what Mussolini had said in March), 'Italy needs Abyssinia to attain ECONOMIC INDEPENDENCE, by which... I mean the MATERIAL WEALTH, the raw materials necessary to feed and clothe the people of Italy.' To that he added, 'And

I hope Italy gets every inch of it.' When Italy had conquered Abyssinia, which it was able to do in a matter of months thanks to its great superiority in weapons, to its being able to bomb and strafe unopposed from the air, and to its use of poison gas, Pound at least once referred simply to 'the Abyssinian acquisition', and another time to the new 'Italian empire'.

He was sensitive to the charge that he was representing the Italian point of view, that he was writing Italian propaganda. No, he insisted in the *British-Italian Bulletin*, which had been set up to put the Italian point of view in London during the Abyssinian crisis, 'I am, if you like, writing European propaganda for the sake of a decent Europe wherein the best people will not be murdered for the monetary profit of the lowest and rottenest, and wherein the divergent national components might collaborate for a sane unstarved civilization'. Or again, he was representing an 'international' point of view; and, beyond that—this was in that note in *Polite Essays*—'I am writing for humanity in a world eaten by usury.'

Those disclaimers don't altogether carry conviction. Pound, who had been at Aquila in the Abruzzi with Dorothy, went immediately to Rome when the invasion was announced, put up at the Albergo Italia, and (as he would write in the *British-Italian Bulletin*) remained there 'during the two months of greatest tension, and did not leave the Capital until, to my mind, the time of that particular danger was past'. His idea appears to have been to rally to the Italian cause. On 15 October he submitted for Mussolini's consideration a project for an international organization to replace the damned League of Nations. He wanted to talk with Il Duce, but was rebuffed. He called on the Minister of Agriculture, and met Olivia Rossetti Agresti, an enthusiastic supporter of Mussolini's economic policies. His most important contact appears to have been Odon Por,[1] who described himself as 'an old New Age–Orage man... trying to propagate Social Credit here', and who had influential contacts within the Fascist government. Pound seems to have worked on some pro-Italian journalism with Por; and it may have been Por who introduced him to the *British-Italian Bulletin*. Pound began contributing to this supplement to *L'Italia Nostra*, a newspaper for Italian-speaking residents of Great Britain, in December

---

[1] Odon Por (b. 1883): Hungarian-Italian journalist and economist; in London around 1912 had contributed to Orage's *New Age*, and served as correspondent for Mussolini's *Avanti*; took up Social Credit; wrote an early account of Fascism, *Fascism* (1923), and other books on the Corporate State; became director of the Rome office of the Institute for the study of International Politics; in May 1935 wrote on Pound's economic thought in one of his 'Cronaca della "Nuova Economia"' in *Civiltà Fascista*, an important monthly review published by the Fascist National Institute of Culture and edited by the philosopher Giovanni Gentile. Described himself as 'Syndicalist. Guild Socialist. NOT fascist. Free lance'. (Redman, 156, 160; Witemeyer in *EP/WCW* 333.)

1935, and sent in nearly thirty articles over the following ten months. He told Por, 'British Ital Bulletin offered to pay me and of course I can NOT accept money for writing Ital propaganda.' That could mean that he knew he was writing propaganda, and felt there was something not straight about his doing it. On the other hand, it could mean that he would not be hired to write propaganda, and thought that it if he were to accept money it would appear that he was.

There is evidence that Pound did have his own agenda and would not be dictated to. In January 1936 Por arranged for him to discuss doing some radio broadcasts for the Ministry of Press and Propaganda. He warned him, 'do not talk about money & so on. It confounds them...they think you are crank and try to avoid you.' (The previous June Por had persuaded the editor of *Civiltà Fascista* to let him ask Pound for an article, and been told 'anything except economics'. Pound did not write for *Civiltà Fascista*.) Pound's response on this occasion was to the point: 'what do I want to talk about on the RADIO? unless it IS money??' He was not tempted, as Redman comments, by the possibility of the regular position Por hoped he would be given, 'without the understanding that he would be free to speak about what he wanted'. And what he wanted, he told Por, was '1. Stave off pan European war...2. get sane economics started SOMEWHERE'; and he did not 'care a fried hoot about talking over the radio UNLESS it conduces to one or all of the above activities'.

If we look again, in the light of that, at Pound's correspondence with US senators, and at his contributions to the *British-Italian Bulletin*, it is apparent that for the most part he was pushing his own line of political and economic propaganda, and that his attempts to justify Italy's invasion of Abyssinia are infrequent asides or interjections. When he was writing in an organ of Fascist propaganda, it was not on the whole Fascist propaganda that he was writing, and the Ministry of Press and Propaganda was wary of him on that account. Por was told, 'can't put [him] on the wireless—because [he] said strange things before'. 'The Foreign Office is afraid of you', he wrote to Pound in May, 'so is the Ministero Stampa'. The fact was that the Italy Pound was promoting was not so much their Italy as the exemplary and ideal Italy he believed in, one that, whether it existed or not, he was bent on projecting. Moreover, his war was not theirs.

In his mind, as he wrote in his first article for the *British-Italian Bulletin*, 'A strong Italy is the key-stone of Europe for peace, for the good life, for civilization'. In fact, as he saw things, Italy alone was standing out against the pressure towards war in Europe. (As for Italy's small war in Africa, that, he suggested in a letter to Borah, was a price worth paying to keep war out of Europe.) 'The pressure towards wars is economic', he wrote, 'usury is the root of ruin'. Europe had 'lost the distinction between **usura** and **partaggio**, [between] usury and fair sharing', and had lost with it the sense of '**civic** responsibility' which Italy still maintained. It followed, for Pound, that in imposing sanctions on Italy, England and France, themselves in a depression brought on by a usurious financial system, and in the grip of financiers with vested interests in arms sales and wars, were attacking the preserver of peace, of the good life, of civilization in Europe.

The evil of the moment, then, was not Italy's invasion of Abyssinia, but the League of Nations' attack on Italy. The real war, for Pound, was between usury and a good society, with the League as the arm of *usura*. To Senator Borah he declared that 'the attempt to starve Italy, for the sake of crushing the Duce over a technical quibble is larger scale crime than any implied in colonial settlement'. And behind that attempt was the English Government whose 'main purpose . . . is to hide the MONSTROUS fake and evil of the usury system'. 'The question of Abyssinia', he had written to both Borah and Senator Tinkham when the invasion was about to be launched, is 'whether ANY nation that doesn't crawl on its belly and take orders from London (from the most treacherous nation of earth) is to have the league used against it; is to suffer unlimited and unscrupulous blackmail, wangled by England'. He had in his files, he assured the readers of the *British-Italian Bulletin* in February 1936, 'signed statements and first-hand information to the effect that the U.S. regards Geneva as a bureaucracy hired largely by London, as a shop front, a camouflage covering financial iniquity, as a tool of Britain'. The clinching detail for Pound was his discovery that Anthony Eden, who represented Great Britain on the committee of the League which decided on sanctions, had 'married into the powerful banking family of Beckett—Sir Gervase idem. director of Westminster bank', had entered parliament in the same year, and 'Nacherly hiz rize wuz rapid'. The plot thickened when he learnt that Lord Cranbourne, who had joined that same Westminster Bank as a director in 1933, had just resigned to become Under Secretary for League of Nations Affairs. To Pound it seemed obvious that 'the men now crying out for the starving and, as they call it, "sanctioning" of Italy represent the same errors, the same weaknesses of mind that have caused the "sanctioning" of great masses of the English and French and American population'. What Italy was doing in Abyssinia— (which in any case would be better off, he thought, under the Duce's rule)—appeared to Pound insignificant beside the economic war he could see being waged against, not just Italy, but against humanity.

Mussolini's secretariat at the Palazzo Venezia thought Pound deluded and out of touch with reality. His project for a new league to take the place of the existing League and thus break British tyranny was dismissed as the weirdly conceived project of a befogged mind which, having seen a small glimmer of truth, imagined it had discovered a brilliant solution. Pound proposed that Italy call a conference at once, within 24 hours, before England could become suspicious, a conference in which the world's peoples could come to know each other's genuine will and aspirations, without interfering in each other's internal affairs and commerce, and without any coercive power, without sanctions. Japan, Germany, Brazil, Hungary, Austria, would be glad to join such a league. Germany could join without being humiliated; and the United States—which had kept out of the League of Nations—could join this purely moral league without breaking its principle of isolation from European politics. Why not call in the foreign ambassadors at once and issue invitations with Roman ceremony, with Latin grace, in Bodoni typeface. Act now, Pound urged at one point, dropping for the moment from moral idealism into realpolitik, create a tactical diversion, and Abyssinia will be forgotten. An official in the secretariat coolly advised that, given Pound's enthusiasm and goodwill towards Italy, it would be enough to point out that, however ingenious the proposal, such a conference could not be put together in 24 hours; that, as things stood, Italy, Austria, and Hungary were members of the League of Nations and would not be free to set up an alternative to it for at least two years; and that his proposal would be held over for detailed consideration of its legal implications at some future date. This was to treat Pound diplomatically as a fantasizing friend of Italy who should be brought gently down to earth.

In the end it is difficult to know quite what to make of Pound's behaviour in relation to Italy's conquest of Abyssinia. Certainly he went on pursuing his own quixotic agenda. In his last words in the *British-Italian Bulletin*, in October 1936, he was insisting that 'The total purchasing power of the community must equal the total needs, and stretch thence upward toward the total desires of the whole people, before prosperity reigns in any nation.' He would write about money, and for a peaceful society.

But then his war on usury became mixed up in an attack on the League of Nations for imposing sanctions on Italy. And his defence of Italy as a just society became contaminated with justifications of its aggression against Abyssinia. Some of those justifications, moreover, such as the assertion of Italy's need to attain economic independence, and the apparently damning exposure of Eden's links with banking, are close to what he would have been reading in the Fascist press. Then there is his writing almost weekly for an organ of Fascist propaganda. He was on the whole speaking his own mind there, and the Italian authorities certainly did not read him as speaking for them. Yet it is not to be wondered at if others in England and America thought he was writing propaganda on Italy's behalf.

One thing at least is clear, that through these complications and confusions Pound was trying not to be distracted from what seemed to him most real and urgent, the great economic war. Basil Bunting, who kept a more open mind, was moved to tell him mildly, 'You turn a blind eye to a good many things, Ezra.' Bunting had decided, even before the conquest of Abyssinia, that while Mussolini was a great man he had done all the good he was likely to do for Italy or for Europe, and that it was high time he was got rid of. But Pound maintained his faith in Mussolini, and saw only what he believed or hoped was the case. When Mussolini celebrated the military virtues Pound somehow saw his militarism as leading, not to war, but to Italy's having the courage to resist the forces of international usury. And when the Bank of Italy was nationalized in March 1936 he saw that as a victory over the usurers, and was confirmed in his belief that Italy was driving towards what Jefferson had called for, and what Social Credit called for, that the nation should have control of its own credit and should use it for the good of the whole people. In December 1936 he would be urging Mussolini to go further. 'DUCE! DUCE!', this letter begins, 'Molti nemici molto onore'. But the enemies of Italy he had in mind were the usurers, and he was telling Mussolini again, as he had when he spoke to him in person in 1933, that his next step should be to abolish taxes. The letter was filed by the secretariat, probably unseen by Mussolini, and probably not understood by anyone who did see it.

Music, money, cantos

In the spring of 1936 Pound announced in Rapallo's *Il Mare* that in place of the usual concert season there would be a series of 'Studi Tigulliani', or musical seminars. Gerhard Münch had gone back to Dresden the previous summer, fearful of 'being interned in event of war', and hoping to get on as a pianist and composer in the new Germany. Attendance at the concerts had become disappointing. And there was the distraction of the war, then at its height. To maintain Rapallo's standing as a musical centre, and so that the League of Nations sanctions should not altogether break them up, as Pound put it, the Amici had resolved themselves 'into a study circle with the immediate intention of hearing as many of the... concerti of Vivaldi as were available in printed editions and executable by one or two violinists and a piano'.

Vivaldi's music was at that time of interest only to a few 'eccentric musicologists'. Pound was able to list as in print just twenty-nine sonatas and concerti; and *Grove's Dictionary of Music* said Vivaldi had composed no more than seventy. Olga Rudge, however, would shortly find 309 hidden away in the National Library in Turin, and there were 90 more lying neglected in the State Library in Dresden—Pound would have Münch send him photocopies of those. The great Vivaldi revival had yet to get under way, and Pound and Olga Rudge were among the first to appreciate his rich musical heritage and to set about getting it performed and published.[2]

Accounts of Pound's lectures for the first two 'Studi Tigulliani' appeared in *Il Mare* in April; and a summary by Olga Rudge of the third session appeared there in May. 'The problem of the relationship between Vivaldi and Bach' had been discussed, and whether Italy could claim in Vivaldi a composer equal to Bach; but there could be no answer to that, it was concluded, until Vivaldi's manuscripts had been edited and published. The third meeting seems to have been the last, but through the following years Olga Rudge's work, and Pound's, to bring the lost music to performance and to add it to the cultural heritage would go on.

Music makes order, or at least it presents 'an example of order', so Pound would write in his *Guide to Kulchur*. More, 'its magic . . . is in its effect on volition', on the will to order. And its contrary, subverting every good work, is usury or money-greed. At this time, in 1936, Pound's thinking about economics was tending to fix upon that evil. What would become canto 45, 'With Usura', appeared in J. P. Angold's little magazine called *Prosperity* in London in February; and what would become canto 46, attacking the 'hyper-usura' of the modern banking system, would appear in Laughlin's *New Directions in Prose and Poetry* with a dateline '30 Jan XIV'. The major preoccupation of the entire block of cantos he had been working on through the months of the Abyssinian crisis and war, and which he would deliver to Faber & Faber in November 1936 as *The Fifth Decad of Cantos [XLII–LI]*, was 'usura, sin against nature'.

Henry Swabey's recollections of Pound in 1935 and 1936 bring out how dominant this preoccupation was at that time, not only in his writings but even in his daily conversation. Swabey (1916–96), then a very young Englishman studying at Durham University and preparing to take orders

---

[2] Olga Rudge was probably the prime mover. In January 1936 she was in Cambridge and seized the chance 'to look up the Vivaldi mss. in the Fitzwilliam [Museum]'. Among her finds was the oratorio *Juditha Triumphans* which would be given its first modern performance by Count Chigi's Accademia Musicale in Siena in 1939. More important was her bringing to light the vast collection in Turin. She had stopped off there for a day in December 1935 to look into the Vivaldi manuscripts, and had been permitted to see just two of the many volumes. When she went back the following October with the intention of making a thematic catalogue she was told she could not see the manuscripts because a Milan publisher was contracted to publish the music. However, she did contrive to see at least 131 unpublished concerti and to begin copying them. Her *Antonio Vivaldi: Note e documenti sulla vita e sulla opere* was published in Siena in 1939. She was called on in that year to rewrite the entry on Vivaldi in *Grove's Dictionary of Music and Musicians*.

in the Church of England, had found *Make It New* 'more stimulating than Thucidides' and had written to Pound as 'the most approachable of the sages of my youth'. Pound had suggested that since the bishops of Durham had once minted money he might 'make a study of ecclesiastical money in England', and find out 'When, if ever, did usury cease to be a mortal sin?' Swabey duly wrote his thesis on 'The Church of England and Usury'. He visited the sage in Rapallo in the early summer of 1936, and Pound met him at the station wearing 'an orange blazer' and appearing 'larger and tawnier' than Swabey had expected. (The orange blazer, a surprising sartorial detail, may have been down to his membership of the Rapallo tennis club. Pound was rather proud of having been defeated by the champion of Italy, no less, in the doubles in the town's recent International Tournament.) At tea in the Pounds' flat Swabey noticed the Gaudier Hieratic Head, 'but EP steered me away from his book on Gaudier and lent me a book on the Governors of the Bank of England'. They went out once or twice into the bay on a raft fitted with a seat, EP paddling skilfully; evenings they 'wandered round the town, pausing for glasses of water at various cafes', EP leaving 'an appropriate consideration at each stop'; and all the time, Swabey remembered, 'He talked mostly about economic subjects.'

To George Antheil, who didn't particularly enjoy talking about credit and taxes, Pound was off-putting. Antheil was looking for concert openings, but Pound wrote, 'I don't see you functioning publicly in Italian picture.' There was no American colony of the kind they had known in Paris. And Italy was 'more interested in getting a good life for the peasants than in spending money on ballets'. It was 'a damn good country for a bloke interested in ECONomics', only that was not Antheil's line. 'If you were a specialist in manure or drainage...', Pound offered, rubbing it in that he now saw Antheil as just another unawakened aesthete.

His treatment of young Swabey was so different. 'Now that I had reached Italy he opined that I should see as much of the country and its works of art as possible,' Swabey recalled, 'So, he wrote out a full itinerary', and 'spared no trouble on my behalf, even sending a telegram to a Rome hotel'. Swabey was advised to spend one day in Pisa, and sleep that night at 'Hotel Corallo, Livorno (20 minutes further by train)'. Then 2 days in Rome; 1 day in Siena—'(hotel Canone d'Oro)', 'can walk round Siena in half hours'; 2 or 3 days for Perugia and Assisi; Firenze—'Hotel Berchielli, on the Arno'; 2 days in Venice—'Pensione Seguso, sulle Zattere... Bar Americano, Piazza San Marco. for sandwiches... Santa Maria Miracoli, hard to find. But best renaissance... San Giorgio Schiavoni, back of S. Marco (Carpaccio)'; Verona could be seen 'Between trains', i.e. 'San Zeno (inside)', the central piazzas, 'get into any d. church you see', and 'Also an arena'; and finally

Milan, '2 nights' to take in galleries and churches. Swabey gives the impression that he followed Pound's 'guide to Italy' both dutifully and gratefully.

Towards the end of July Pound joined Olga in Siena in her apartment with a painted ceiling in the Palazzo Capoquadri. Dorothy wrote from England, 'Depressing country and rotted and decayed top & bottom—more especially top.' Pound wrote back that he had been in the Biblioteca Communale looking into a big history of Siena's Monte dei Paschi bank, and was glad to find 'Main points Monte P. OK== abundance of natr & will of the whole people as basis of credit // nacherly the 10-vol bloke don't stress that'.

He was finding confirmation of what he had written about the Monte dei Paschi in his *Social Credit: An Impact*, a pamphlet published in London in 1935. He had invoked it there as an example of 'banks built for beneficence, for reconstruction', as against 'banks created to prey on the people'. Around 1620, after being conquered by Florence, 'Siena was flat on her back, without money.' Ferdinando II, Grand Duke of Tuscany, 'underwrote a capital of 200,000 ducats', taking as his main security the grazing rights of the Maremma pastures worth 10,000 ducats annually. The bank lent out at 5½ per cent, paid 5 per cent to its investors, kept its expenses to a minimum, and made over any profit 'to hospitals and works for the benefit of the people of Siena'. It thus stood for Pound as an example of moral banking, contrived 'not for the conqueror's immediate short-sighted profit, but to restart the life and productivity of Siena'. And it pointed the lesson of solid banking, that 'Credit rests in ultimate on the abundance of nature', in that case 'on the growing grass that can nourish the living sheep'. Evidently the interest charged had to be a reasonable proportion or share of the added value. 'That bank is open today', Pound wrote, 'It outlasted Napoleon. You can open an account there tomorrow.' And in July 1936 he did just that, opening an interest-bearing current account.

Through the heat of August—'hot here. but air moving & not suffocating'—Pound spent much of his time 'on damn HARD Liberry seat' and in the archives, filling five notebooks with the raw materials and rough drafts for cantos 42–4, drawing them directly from the original documents as well as from 'the 10-vol bloke' and from other historians. Those cantos, which tell the story of how the Monte dei Paschi bank was created and how it endured, would be finished off in Venice in September.

He was hearing good music in Siena; and in mid-August there was the excitement of the horse race around the central Campo in which the seventeen contrada or city wards compete against each other to win a banner, the Palio. From his window Pound watched four white oxen being cleaned up and decorated to draw the triumphal chariot in the spectacular parade which would precede the race. 'Time | consumed 1 hour and 17 minutes', he noted when recording that operation in canto 43. He sent Omar a postcard of the Palio, and Dorothy returned Omar's 'thanks & love', with (in brackets) 'he has bought you a little present—all on his own'.

All the while he was looking for signs of the spread of Social Credit. He mentioned to Dorothy that there had been a 'new raise in pay', in Italy, and he took that to be Social Credit in practice, because it was centrally controlled and went with price control. In the United States there was a Social Credit Conference at the University of Virginia's Institute of Public Affairs, with Gorham Munson and Jas. Laughlin of *New Democracy* among the speakers, and also William Carlos Williams. In England the Green Shirts, the militant wing of Social Credit, were being active. Pound had dedicated his *Social Credit: An Impact* to them, and was in correspondence with their leader, John Hargrave, though he contributed only once to Hargrave's journal *Attack!*, and that was a piece of ranting and bantering street-corner oratory about 'money money money' and who makes it. He had told Hargrave that he was all for getting Social Credit 'OUT of Bloomsbury and into the East End', and had suggested using music hall routines to put its message across.[3] Then there was the British Union of Fascists. Pound didn't think much of its leader, Sir Oswald Mosley, at this time, but he was encouraged by a private letter saying that the BUF 'Accept Social Credit analysis'. That, he told Homer, was 'Big nooz IF they stick to it'. Perhaps it was in the hope of keeping them to it that he would contribute an article on economics to nearly every issue of Mosley's *British Union Quarterly* from its first in January 1937 up to its tenth in April 1939. He was charged with a sense of AGENDA, of what needed to be done. As he

---

[3] Into the *Attack!* rant Pound introduced a verse from his music hall 'Song of the six-hundred-odd M.P.s' by 'Alfred Venison', his Social Credit persona.

'We are 'ere met together
In this momentous hower   . . . .
Ter lick the' bankers' dirty boots
an' keep the Bank in power.

We are 'ere met together   'O Britain, muvver of parliaments.
  Ter grind the same old axes   'Ave you seen yer larst sweet litter?
And keep the people in its place   Could yeh swap th' brains of orl this lot
  a'payin' us the taxes.   fer 'arft a pint o' bitter?'

We are six hundred beefy men   'I couldn't', she sez, 'an' I aint tried,
  (but mostly gas and suet)   They're me own', she sez to me,
An' every year we meet to let   'As footlin' a lot as ever was spawned
  some other feller do it.'   to defend democracy.'

told Dorothy towards the end of that summer in Siena, 'I am not merely pickin' daiseyes'.

Dorothy in London was noticing the 'word "fascism" getting more and more hopelessly vulgarized—Spain now'. Evidently it had become a convenient term for lumping together the forces allied against the fissile Communist, Socialist, and Anarchist Popular Front in Spain, even though Mussolini's Fascism, Hitler's National Socialism, and Franco's nationalistic anti-communism were essentially different from each other. What they had in common at that moment was their hostility to international Communism. Pound's response to Dorothy, 'Stalinists acc/ Telegraph are calling the executed Trotskists fascists', underlined the way 'fascist' was being redefined in the negative, as signifying anti-communist, anti-socialist, anti-democratic. The British Union of Fascists may have contributed to this shift of meaning as Mosley moved his affiliation from Mussolini's Fascism to Hitler's National Socialism. And shortly the Fascist–Nazi Axis would be declared. Significant distinctions were being lost in the clash and confusion of ideologies. And it was not only the perception of Fascism that was affected. To many at the time 'socialism' and 'democracy' appeared to be embodied in Stalin and the dictatorship of his Comintern, if only because he was lending some support to the Popular Front.

On a postcard to Homer at the end of August Pound wrote, 'have got to end of Analects again'—that was the second or third time he had worked his way through the ideograms. One of the sayings of Confucius that he kept coming back to was the answer to a disciple's question, if he were to form a government what would he do first? And Confucius said, Call people and things by their correct names, otherwise there will be confusion and corruption in the state.

Pound left Siena on 2 September, took the train to Bolzano, a journey of eleven hours, then went on to Gais 'to fetch Marieka' and take her with him to Venice and Olga. 'Waal, the place is hottern Siena', he told Homer from Venice, 'but it has not the hellish NOISE of that latter city.' As soon as he had recovered his typewriter 'out of O's attic', he went to work. 'Waal this machine sticks but I knocked out 2 articles yester. and a canto collected from notes and a nuther canto this a.m.'—that was on the 3rd or 4th. He had also 'bathed yester at Lido'.

On the 5th he was telling Dorothy that he would shortly send her 'imperfect copy 3rd of new cantos'—that would have been canto 44. 'I think technically the best I have done', he wrote, '& AT last a block to balance the Malatesta | 3 all of a piece with sestina <under work> & seguito'—that is, with continuity. 'Even if it don't run to 4', he went on, remembering how many there were in the

Malatesta suite, 'the USURA wd fit it & cd. count as symmetrizing.' That in fact is how it worked out, 'the USURA' being placed as canto 45. On the 7th he wrote, 'did frame for a fourth this a.m. but must let that one set/don't want it thinner than the other 3'—this 'fourth' actually found its place as canto 50. He was so sure of the first three, though, that by the 10th he had sent them off to be printed, and they would appear in Eliot's *Criterion* the following April.

On the 10th also he told Dorothy, 'By vast heave the Dunning mss in order & shd go to post oggi'. Ralph Cheever Dunning was the old-fashioned poet he had befriended in Paris, and there was an 'amateur publisher wanting to print the "whole of D's poetry"'. (The amateur publisher would change his mind when he saw how bad much of it was.)

There was new music at the Venice Biennale of Music that year, and Pound was greatly stimulated by Honegger's second string quartet, performed by the Gertler Quartet; by Hindemith's viola concerto, *Schwanen-dreher*, with the composer himself playing the viola; and by Bartók's fifth string quartet, performed by the New Hungarian Quartet. This last meant most to him, because he felt it to be, like his own *Cantos*, the record of a struggle and revolt against the entanglements of a civilization in decay. He immediately determined that he must get the New Hungarian Quartet, one of the best in Europe, to play that work in Rapallo, and that he must get Hindemith too, 'which is some WANT on no assets', as he admitted to Dorothy. Would the New Hungarians come, he asked Tibor Serly, a mutual friend, 'for 500 lire and a night's lodging?' Not that he was able even to '*offer* the 500 lire yet', having no assets save what he could earn, and having yet to sell the stuff he 'proposed to shove into 'em'. Somehow by December he could write to Münch, 'I think the New Hungarian Quartet is fixed to come,' and they did indeed perform Bartok's 5th, together with his 2nd and with a Haydn quartet 'sandwiched between' as 'engine-cooler or whatever', in the Town Hall of Rapallo the following March, although to a 'shamefully small audience'. He had hoped that Münch might know Hindemith well enough to sound him out about 'the minimum he wd. take to give an all Hindemith program' in Rapallo, 'with you and Olga if there is a trio', but nothing came of any approach Münch may have made.

Hearing this new music was probably Pound's most intense experience that summer in Venice. It was a kind of revelation to him to find contemporary composers doing deep and difficult and beautiful things, and he rejoiced that 'the richness and abundance of music in 1936 is infinitely greater than it was in the 1920's, when most of us could deeply admire no one save Igor Stravinsky'. He spread the good news in enthusiastic articles in the BBC's *Listener* in October, then in *Music and Letters* and *Delphian*

Quarterly in January; and in his accounts of the 1937 Rapallo concerts for *Il Mare* he often referred back to the 1936 Biennale.

An important experience of a different order was spending a few days with US Congressman George Holden Tinkham. Tinkham, with whom Pound had been corresponding since February 1933, was an isolationist and an obdurate opponent of America's getting involved in the League of Nations, so that was one bond. Moreover, in Tinkham's view Mussolini was a great man who had had a great triumph—meaning, apparently, in Abyssinia. 'Any man who can successfully defy England and the League of Nations', he had told Pound in June 1936, 'is a man of strength and he has my admiration.' The congressman arrived in Venice 19 September and flew out on the 25th, and Pound spent much if not most of the intervening days in his company to the exclusion of all else. On the 20th, the Monday, they drove, taking Maria with them, up to the Piave to see the place where, on 11 December 1917, Tinkham had fired the first American big gun against the invading Austrians, and then to the top of Monte Grappa where his staff car had been blown up by the Austrian artillery. Mary recalled how 'Uncle George' and 'her papa talked relentlessly in the back of the car'. 'Eleven hours solid conversation yester', Pound wrote to Dorothy on the 21st. 'And of course much more concentrated than any printed history', he added on the 22nd, '30 years public office, 22 in Congress'. To Homer he wrote that day, 'Sorry you can't meet brother TINKHAM. eight hours CONversation yesterday. which you wd have NNNjoyed.' He wrote again on the 25th, 'We putt in nine hour day yesterday, an I learned more amurikun history than you cd. in a month of museums.' 'Don't compromise G.T. with the electors by mentioning this incident,' he warned. And to Dorothy he showed the same impulse to dramatize the significance of their talks, 'Better not say to anyone how much we have seen of each other.' Tinkham, writing from Paris on his way home in mid-October, simply thanked Pound 'for all your courtesies and attention while I was at Venice'. 'Had I not had you, I should have been deprived of a great deal of pleasure,' he wrote, 'All of the places you took me to were little "gems" which I never should have seen.'

Dorothy let Pound know that she would be back in Rapallo about 22 October, and Pound asked, 'whereafter what does SHE think she wants to do?... Rome in December?' On 16 October she was in Paris, and Pound wrote to her there, 'I seem to be pushing out articl/ a day for somewhere or something. Hope it will Rome/ us in affluence'. In mid-November, however, he had to take Dorothy into hospital in Genoa, for haemorrhoids. 'Worst supposed to be over. operation yesterday', he wrote to Homer on the 20th, 'now resting. better reserve strength than I had expected.' He thought of joining Olga in Turin, where she was working on the Vivaldi manu-scripts, but 'cdn't figure a way to do it wif decorum an elegance, wot she has so impressed on him'. At the end of December he went down to Rome on his own for a few days. About that time Homer and Isabel entertained Olga in Rapallo with 'turkey and chocolates'.

'The Fifth Decad': against Usura

> *...you who think you will*
> *get through hell in a hurry...* (46/231)

In the 'Siena cantos', that is cantos 42–5, the poet is first of all a reader in the archives. He is an exemplarily active reader, extracting the telling details and arranging them to bring alive in the mind the drama and the meaning of what had been buried away in the old volumes of documents 'most faithfully copied' in 1623 and 1622 by 'Livio Pasquini, notary, citizen of Siena'. The poet notes Pasquini's cross in the margin against the place where a document was to be signed and sealed. He has fun with the copyist's abbreviations of titles, 'YYHH' = 'YYour HHighnessess', plural— ('the left front ox' being prepared for the procession will voice that as 'Mn-YAWWH!!!'). He is generally unimpressed by the pomp and circumstance reflected in the documents, as in 'present...the | illustrious Marquis Antony Mary of Malaspina | and the most renowned Johnny something or other de Binis | Florentine Senator'. He is thoroughly serious though about the action that does interest him, how they created a new bank in Siena. For this he renders the Italian and the Latin of the records into his own current language, keeping a sense always that he is working through and translating from those originals, but striving for a direct understanding of what was achieved and how it was done.

There was the initial germ or seed, the idea of a new kind of bank, 'FIXED in the soul, nell'anima, of the Illustrious College'—that was the college of Magistrates, the ruling council of Siena. Actually, the scholar-sleuths point out, the document has 'nell'anim*o*', 'in the mind', and Pound appears to have misread it; unless, they concede, he was deliberately altering the sense, to fix the idea of the bank not in the mind only but in the spirit. Since that would make all the difference between simply having a good idea, and having the will to carry it into effect, we may take it that Pound's 'anima' was no slip. He was not copying the record, he was interpreting it, in this case to build in his conviction that the new bank of Siena must have been not merely conceived but actively willed into existence. This will be a Volitionist episode.

The idea had been around for ten years when, in 1623, the Magistrates sought the views of the Senate on the details—

> and 6thly that the Magistrate
> give his chief care that the specie
> be lent to whomso can best USE IT
> (*id est, più utilmente*)
> to the good of their houses, to benefit of their business
> as of weaving, the wool trade, the silk trade

Before this there had been, in 1622, a petition to 'YY. HHighnesses' the regents of the young Grand Duke of Tuscany, this with a rather different emphasis upon the benefits of such a bank to its investors and shareholders. That is, 'companies and persons both public and private' might put money into it in exchange for shares and have their 5 per cent guaranteed by the Sienese upon the security of the city's assets, and even upon 'the persons and goods of the laity'. Upon that security

> TTheir HHighnesses gratified
> the city of this demand to
> erect a New Monte
> for good public and private

And they agreed 'to lend the fund', that is, to invest in it,

> 200,000 scudi
> capital for fruit at 5% annual
> which is 10,000 a year
> assigned on the office of grazing

In other words, the Grand Duke's 10,000 a year was the assured income from the town's pastures, and for that reason the new bank, or Monte, would be known as the Monte dei Paschi, the Bank of the Pastures. In Pound's reading the true basis of the bank's credit becomes then the grass nourishing the sheep, not the Grand Duke's 200,000 scudi investment; and his interest too, his 5 per cent 'frutto', was first 'the fruit of nature'. As Pound had written, 'Credit [and, implicitly, a just interest] rests *in ultimate* on the abundance of nature.'

The other great feature of the bank is that it was brought into being by the will of the people and had the whole of Siena behind it, 'Senatus Populusque Senensis'. The formal Act, for our enthusiastic reader, shows democracy in action:

> there was the whole will of the people
> serene M. Dux and His tutrices

and lords deputies of the Bailey, in name of Omnipotent God
    best mode etcetera, and the Glorious Virgin
convoked and gathered together 1622
general council there were 117 councillors
in the hall of the World Map, with bells and with
    voice of the Cryer

At the start of canto 52 Pound will recapitulate, 'And I have told you... |
the true base of credit, that is, the abundance of nature | with the whole folk
behind it'.

Cantos 42 and 43 repeat that main theme several times with variations
according to the various (and quite repetitive) records of the steps taken to
get the bank set up. (It may have been those recurrences that for Pound gave
an under-sense of sestina.) These cantos also weave in some indications of
the state of things in Siena before they had their bank, especially the fact
that there was a shortage of money, and that what money there was was
taken in taxes or tied up in usuries, so that production and 'licit consump-
tion [were] impeded', and 'few come to buy in the market | fewer still work
in the fields'. Against that there are indications of the benefits flowing from
the bank down to Pound's time, among them the great Palio and its
procession—the Monte dei Paschi supported that. In general, by meeting
the need for money it brought 'WORK for the populace', and brought back
prosperity to Siena's 'business | as of weaving, the wool trade, the silk trade'.
Over a century later, in 1749, the bank was able to give '1000 scudi | for
draining the low land | 2000 to fix the Roman Road'. The contrast with
the great Medici bank which ran Florence and made loans to the great
and powerful throughout Europe is noted with curt irony. Its lending
was neither based on the abundance of nature nor invested in useful
production and distribution, and in 1743 when its rule ended Florence
was left with public debt amounting to 'scudi 14 million | or 80 million lira
pre-war'.

Canto 44 carries the story on through the times of the Grand Dukes
Pietro Leopoldo (reigned 1765–90), and his son Ferdinando III (reigned
1790–9, 1814–24)—the interruption in the latter's reign being due to
Napoleon's conquest of Italy. The Monte dei Paschi is in the background
now, and the attention is on the exemplary rule of the Grand Dukes in
Tuscany, with Napoleon figuring as the anti-hero. The good deeds of
Pietro Leopoldo frame the canto. At the beginning there is his shutting
down grain imports in a year when the Grand Duchy had a 'Heavy grain
crop unsold', and his setting a legal maximum on interest, 4 per cent in
1783. The closing passage is a retrospective celebration of a duke 'that

wished state debt brought to an end', and 'lightened mortmain that princes and church be under tax | as were others'—

> that ended the gaolings for debt;
> that said thou shalt not sell public offices;
> that suppressed so many *gabelle* [taxes];
> that freed the printers of surveillance
> and wiped out the crime of lèse majesty;
> that abolished death as a penalty and all tortures in prisons...

He also 'split common property among tillers', and his actions extended to 'roads, trees, and the wool trade, | the silk trade, and a set price, lower, for salt'. He was altogether a ruler who cared for the public good above private profit and glory. And his son Ferdinando III was of the same mould. The main episode in the first half of the canto is a great day of celebration in Siena in 1792 to mark Ferdinando's relaxing a law imposed by Florence to restrict the sale of grain and to keep down its price at the expense of the growers. When he was driven out of Tuscany by the French armies in 1799 his people called him 'il piu galantuomo del paese', their best, their most honourable man.

Things were very different under Napoleon—

> the citizen priest Fr Lenzini mounted the tribune
> to join the citizen Abrâm
> and in admiring calm sat there with them the citizen
> the Archbishop
> > from 7,50 a bushel to 12
> by the 26th April

This was a revolution that overthrew the established order in Tuscany, corrupted the clergy, unleashed violence against Jews—the ghetto sacked and 'hebrews...burned with the liberty tree in the piazza'—and which undid the very meanings of words. In the name of 'fraternité' the 'citoyen' Monte dei Paschi was invited to 'turn over all sums in your cash box'. Citizen Tuscany was absorbed into a new kingdom of Etruria, with a 'King of Etruria, Primus, absolute, without constitution', and this Louis levied new taxes, 'so heavy they are thought to be more than | paid by subjects of Britain'. Citizen Napoleon—who had already crowned himself Emperor of France in 1804—had himself crowned King of Italy in 1805. He then deposed and dismissed 'Madame ma sœur et cousine', the widow of the first king of Etruria and Queen Regent to her infant son his successor, and installed his own sister, nicknamed 'Semiramis of Lucca', as Grande Duchesse of Tuscany. Napoleon is represented by a letter to the Queen Regent in which he shows no care at all for the will or the welfare of the people, and is concerned only for rank and majesty, especially his own, and for the extension of his empire. 'I have given orders', he writes, 'that she'— the dismissed Queen Regent—'be | received in my kingdom of Italy | and in my French States with honours that are due her'. Mention of Lisbon prompts the thought, 'My troops shd have by now entered that capital | and taken possession of Portugal.' He had made himself 'Primus, absolute'; 'I' and 'my' rule in his sentences; and, as we know, he would fall. The line, 'And "Semiramis" 1814 departed from Lucca', marks his first fall, along with these other lines from the record, 'and this day came Madame Letizia, | the ex-emperor's mother, and on the 13th departed'—both sister and mother were sailing to join him in his exile on Elba.

In this revisioning of history Napoleon figures as of less significance than the usually forgotten Grand Dukes of Tuscany. Yet the canto does briefly note the recognitions in the multi-volume history of the Monte dei Paschi that his 'law code remains. | monumento di civile sapienza'; and that, moreover, his administration 'dried swamps, grew cotton, brought in meri-nos', improved the mortgage system. '"Thank god such men be but few"', is the ambivalent conclusion. The canto turns back with relief to the good times under Pietro Leopoldo, and then to the restoration of Ferdinando III and his enlightened rule. It concludes with this summary affirmation of the Monte dei Paschi, 'The foundation, Siena, has been to keep a bridle on usury', a line to bind the first three cantos together, and to lead into canto 45.

Thus far Pound has been rendering the fairly heavy prose of his sources into clearly phrased and measured verse for a flexible speaking voice, a voice inflected with humour or irony or enthusiasm, alert to the moral nuances and complexities of the story, but staying always close to the recorded facts and the implicit viewpoints of the time. He is not writing timeless lyric, but working at recovering what was done in that place at that time, and with a keen awareness that one must act in time. There is this single moment of lyric reflection,

> wave falls and the hand falls
> Thou shalt not always walk in the sun
> or see weed sprout over cornice
> Thy work in set space of years, not over an hundred.

That might be the notary's hand, or his own, and his reader's. That 'Thou' is the all-inclusive singular which is addressing equally one's own self and other selves, speaking to all individually and inwardly. Pound himself walked in the sun in Siena and saw 'weed sprout over cornice'; and in his sense of the moment there is a timeless, impersonal, insight. It is a moment, a mood, which will be caught up into canto 47.

Canto 45 distils a very different mood from the action of the preceding Siena cantos. This is, on the face of it, an Old Testament preacher's or prophet's passionate denunciation of usury. The word occurs twenty times in the fifty lines, and is linked throughout to insistent negatives, as in

> with usura
> seeth no man Gonzaga his heirs and his concubines
> no picture is made to endure nor to live with
> but is made to sell and sell quickly

'Usura' blurs 'clear demarcation', keeps the stone cutter from his stone, 'blunteth the needle in the maid's hand | and stoppeth the spinner's cunning'. The remarkable thing about this canto though, more especially when one thinks of the wholly negative rage of Pound's attacks on usury in his prose, is that here the fury of denunciation is accompanied by a strong opposite sense of the good things usury destroys. Devastation may be the dominant theme, yet the things that are loved, the productions of nature and craft and art, stand out very clearly as the counter-theme—

> With usura hath no man a house of good stone
> each block cut smooth and well fitting
> that design might cover their face

What usury prevents is nevertheless made present to the mind there, and it is the same throughout the canto. The positive feelings for good bread made of mountain wheat stand against 'with usura, sin against nature, | is thy bread . . . stale as paper'. A whole way of life, Siena's as it might be, is evoked in the painted paradise on the church wall; in the wool that should come to market, and in the spinner's cunning and the weaver's loom; in the stone-cutter and his chisel; and in the artists, Duccio and others, who 'came not by usura'. As the denunciation builds to its powerful climax so the images of what usury undoes grow more urgent and compelling—

> Usura rusteth the chisel
> It rusteth the craft and the craftsman
> It gnaweth the thread in the loom
> None learneth to weave gold in her pattern ;
> Azure hath a canker by usura; cramoisi is unbroidered
> Emerald findeth no Memling
> Usura slayeth the child in the womb
> It stayeth the young man's courting
> It hath brought palsey to bed, lyeth
> between the young bride and her bridegroom
>   CONTRA NATURAM

That is so very different from Pound's prose, and so much more effective. There is no incitement to immediate action, no association of usury with the Jewish race, and no flailing language. Rather there is precise definition and justice in the measured words—the canto practises what the poet is in love with—and thus while it allows the ill-effects of usury to appear dominant in time, it maintains in the mind a strong vision of a better, a properly natural order.[4]

There is an abrupt time-shift in canto 46 from 'how it was under Duke Leopold' to how it is now, in the present moment. Moreover the poet shifts his identity. He is no longer a searcher of archives, nor the preacher against usury. Now he is a contemporary investigator and prosecutor of crime. He has been on the case for seventeen years and longer, ever since he grasped what Douglas was going on about in the *New Age* office in 1918, that is, that the government can create credit and distribute purchasing power to its people. He can see the crime, has the evidence and a confession, but can he get a conviction?

The criminal he wants to put away is the banking system which has usurped the power to create credit and which exercises it for private profit and against the public interest. The confession was made by William Paterson, one of the speculators who set up the Bank of England in 1694, in its prospectus or charter. The Bank, he wrote, 'Hath benefit of interest on all the moneys which it, the bank, creates out of nothing'.[5] That is placed, underlined for emphasis, as the centre and pivot of the canto. It is followed by an observation said to have been made by Senator John Sherman of Ohio to Rothschilds in London during the American Civil War, and repeated by them in a letter to a New York firm. Sherman was at that time a member of the Senate Committee on Finance and an active proponent of the National Banking Act of 1863, the act which opened the way for US banks to gain control of the nation's credit and to use it for private gain:

> Said Mr RothSchild, hell knows which Roth-schild
> 1861, '64 or there sometime, 'Very few people
> 'will understand this. Those who do will be occupied
> 'getting profits. The general public will probably not
> 'see it's against their interest.'

---

[4] In 1970 this note (which Pound first published in 1957) was added to canto 45: 'N.B. Usury: A charge for the use of purchasing power, levied without regard to production; often without regard to the possibilities of production. (Hence the failure of the Medici bank.)'

[5] For details see Appendix E.

And because people don't understand the banking system, and don't see how it works against the public interest, the prosecutor despairs of getting a conviction. Three times he asks, 'Will any jury convict?', and implicitly answers, not while they can't or won't see the evidence that is all around them.

The first half of the canto has been working up a general sense of the lack of clear-sighted discriminations and firm convictions in London as Pound knew it around the time of Orage's *New Age*. Max Beerbohm's un-genteel and politically pointed cartoons were suppressed. According to Orage other opinion shapers, Shaw and Chesterton and Wells, would not declare an opinion; while as for Pound, 'trouble iz that you mean it, you will never be a journalist'. Then there was the amusing suburban garden party, at which he observed religious conviction dissolving into a polite drawing back from conversion or communion; and only the camel driver in the would-be Uniter's story practises a faith not split off from his way of life. There too Mr Marmaduke remarked on the English government's habit of not meaning what it said—he might have been talking about T. E. Lawrence's Arabia—

> 'They are mendacious, but if the tribe gets together
> 'the tribal word will be kept, hence perpetual misunderstanding.
> 'Englishman goes there, lives honest, word is reliable,
> 'ten years, they believe him, then he signs terms for his government,
>   'and, naturally, the treaty is broken. Mohammedans,
> 'Nomads, will never understand how we do this.'

All that, from genteel obfuscation of facts, through belief with no ground under it, up to governments not meaning their word, is what the prosecutor is up against in making his case.

The latter part of the canto glances hastily, even despairingly, over manifestations of usuries and evasions through the ages, as if hurriedly turning over file upon file of a mountain of evidence. There is too much here to make a clear case—'London houses, ground rents, foetid brick work'—Regius Professors appointed to spread lies—the Manchester slums—'Bank creates it ex nihil'—'Jefferson . . . Van Buren'—Antoninus, 'usura and sea insurance', Athens—'TAXES to build St Peters', that is, the Church selling its sacraments and disregarding Luther's protest, and 'Thereafter design went to hell, | Thereafter barocco, thereafter stone-cutting desisted'. At that point the poet himself breaks out, speaking as 'narrator' in the Church's own Latin as if taking up its neglected duty to denounce usury, 'Aurum est commune sepulchrum', gold, the common grave, 'Usura, commune sepulchrum'; then, with the epithets Aeschylus coined for Helen as cause of the Trojan war, he names it destroyer of men, of cities, and of governments, 'helandros kai heleptolis kai helarxe'. He is heaping up denunciations from across the ages, building up to Geryon, the classical monster which Dante placed in the pit of hell as the figure of Fraud, of usury upon usury. That outburst of controlled rage having cleared his mind, there is at last a passage of simple direct evidence—

> FIVE million youths without jobs
> FOUR million adult illiterates
> 15 million 'vocational misfits', that is with small chance for jobs
> NINE million persons annual, injured in preventable industrial accidents
> One hundred thousand violent crimes

There, in the condition of the United States in 1935, was a 'CASE for the prosecution'—only the Attorney General of the moment was wanting out, wanting the Postmaster's job instead, according to 'headline in current paper'. 'England a worse case', the canto concludes, 'France under a foetor of regents', meaning the Regents of the Bank of France. Altogether, the canto has been not so much about the iniquity of usury as about the difficulty, the apparent impossibility, of getting people to open their minds to the evil of it, and to stop tolerating it. The key word might be 'conviction', that is, the lack of conviction, and the consequent failure to convict.

In his prose Pound would often be driven to baffled fury by that want of conviction. Here, though, in the following canto, instead of the further fulminations against the tolerance of usury that we might expect, he celebrates the profound, primal, vision that is needed to see clearly how usury goes against nature. Canto 47 enacts a rite to open the mind to the generative force of nature, and to dispose it to understand its world and to live in it with the conviction of that illumination.

This rite affirming and renewing humanity's unity with nature is conducted in the language of natural process and of the alert experience of nature; and it makes a powerful and rich music of its words to concentrate the mind and to bring it into accord with what is revealed in the experience. The vowels are 'cut', sharply defined, by the consonants; their tones are composed into quite complex harmonies and a natural melody; and the measure is controlled throughout by a steady though variable double-beat, like the heart-beat;—

> And the small stars now fall from the olive branch,
> Forked shadow falls dark on the terrace
> More black than the floating martin
>   that has no care for your presence,

His wing-print is black on the roof tiles
And the print is gone with his cry.
So light is thy weight on Tellus
Thy notch no deeper indented
Thy weight less than the shadow

That particular passage is in the same mood as the lines noticed above in canto 42, 'wave falls and the hand falls', a mood in which one lapses out of one's active self into an impersonal awareness of being simply in and of the living world. That is, strictly speaking, a religious awareness, religion being the binding together of the many that are also one.

The canto is divided into two parts by a line-break (after l. 78), and, reading it as a rite, I take the first part to be the preparation of the candidate for the sacramental act of the second. The preparation consists of three statements or challenges followed by the candidate's responses. The composition, as Pearlman noticed, is in the manner of a fugue.

The opening statement is Circe's guidance to Odysseus, that he must sail after knowledge to blind Tiresias who, though in hell, sees the mystery of being that the living are too often blind to. The passage was given in the original Greek in canto 39, in which Odysseus was initiated into Circe's mystery before being sent on his way. At the outset of the *Cantos* his voyage had led to his '"Facing the sunless dead and this joyless region"', but to no revelation of Proserpine, the light of Tiresias' seeing. Now the underworld is represented very differently, as 'the bower of Ceres' daughter Proserpine'; and it is Tiresias' vision of and from Proserpine that he must seek.

The response is indirect, not out of the *Odyssey* but out of the rites of Babylonian Tamuz and Greek Adonis, rites that were still observed in Pound's Rapallo. One night at midsummer lights in small jars are set in the water to float seaward, so that 'The sea is streaked red with Adonis.' In the ancient rite of Adonis women called upon the god lamenting his death, as his lover Venus-Dione had wailed and wept for him. Yet by his dying 'Wheat shoots rise new by the altar, | flower from the swift seed'. (Venus, according to Ovid, changed the dead god into a flower.) Adonis dies annually and is deathless, like the other divinities figuring the seasonal dying and self-renewing of nature. He is akin to Proserpine, who, in another version of his myth noted by Lemprière, 'restored him to life, on condition he spend six months with her, and the rest of the year with Venus'. The response then is the way available to Pound in the 1930s of participating in Tiresias' knowledge of the undying, perpetually self-renewing life-force.

It is not clear who speaks the second statement. Pearlman suggests Tiresias; I incline to Circe as the speaker, the Circe to whom the witless sailors were creatures of blind instinct. In any case there is no doubt about what is being said, that the life-force in woman, in the shoot of a plant, in moth, bull, and man, is blind, unconscious, driving irresistibly to its end. 'To the cave art thou called, Odysseus', she declares; yet she recognizes that he does not go blindly, 'By Molü art thou freed from the one bed | that thou may'st return to another.' The response is again indirect, in part out of Hesiod's *Works and Days*, and in part out of what Pound could see in the hills and olive groves around Rapallo. 'Begin thy plowing | When the Pleiades go down to their rest', that is in November; and 'When the cranes fly high', in October, 'think of plowing'. That came from acquired knowledge of the seasons and birds, and shows both intelligence beyond blind subjection to nature, and an established tradition of working in harmony with nature. The persistence of that tradition is noted in Pound's own observations, which are very like Hesiod's, 'Two oxen are yoked for plowing | Or six in the hill field | White bulk under olives, a score for drawing down stone'—that might be stone for 'a good house'. The response thus modifies the statement by adding the specifically human component, the conscious determination of what must be done. It does this without setting man apart from or above nature. 'By this gate art thou measured', it insists, repeating that line from the first response, 'Thy day is between a door and a door'—as between birth and death, and between the plowing for sowing and the harvest. 'Thus was it in time', this passage concludes, implicitly endorsing the natural scope of human life and work.

The third statement was cited above—'And the small stars now fall.' This goes on from 'Thus was it in time,' only shifting from rural activities into recognitions of our transience and insignificance. The voice here I take to be humanity's own inner voice informed by traditional wisdom. The response also is out of experience, but now the inner voice counters the humbling or elegiac intimations of mortality by asserting an active part in the process. First there is the turn upon 'Yet'—'Yet hast thou gnawed through the mountain'—as it might be in the tunnelling for the railway and for roads all along the mountainous Ligurian coast. There is a further turn then, back to Circe and her ingle, and back also to Adonis—

> Hast thou found a nest softer than cunnus
> Or hast thou found better rest
> Hast'ou a deeper planting, doth thy death year
> Bring swifter shoot?
> Hast thou entered more deeply the mountain?

Those are affirmative questions, leading into the sacrament and mystery of coitus—and here, at the climax of the canto, the initiate speaks in his own person, finding his identity in the act:

> By prong have I entered these hills:
> That the grass grow from my body,
> That I hear the roots speaking together,
> The air is new on my leaf...

—the almond bough will put forth its flame, and 'Fruit cometh after'. This rite is a celebration not so much of the union of persons as of an intense awareness of being caught up in the process of nature and of existing at the very quick of it, a celebration enacting the life-principle itself in full consciousness of being for the moment what Adonis represents. That knowledge, that illumination, if it outlasts the act and is constant and deep enough, can become a power to perceive and to live in accord with our constructive and creative part in the universe. And it would confer 'the power over wild beasts', making us see at once that usury comes not from love of what we can know and do but from rapacious greed.

Critics tend to pass over canto 48 and to move directly from canto 47 to canto 49, which also closes upon 'the power over wild beasts'. The serene 'stillness' of the idyll of ancient China in 49 appears to accord well with the 'healing' rite of Eleusis, and 48 can seem an unnecessary and unwelcome breaking of the celebratory mood. For George Kearns, one of the most perceptive of Pound's readers, it comes as an 'annoying interruption' and seems simply 'a miscellany into which the poet has crammed scraps of anecdotes, documents and historical bits—a modern babel among which we discern familiar themes'. The change of mood is certainly abrupt and harsh, as jarring as dropping out of rapt contemplation into a brainstorming session. Yet what is in question is still knowledge and the transmission of intelligence, only now we are no longer in the lyrical ideal but in the problematic real world, and here the poet is thrown back upon his method of gathering together and heaping up all sorts of scraps of information and anecdotes bearing upon his central preoccupations: how is vital intelligence to be passed on so that it goes into action? and what obstructs and prevents the communication of it?

The first part of the canto, lines 1–35—already beyond the first stage of tackling its problem, that of simply writing down more at less at random whatever comes to mind—has arrived at a pattern of discriminations. The passage is in fact ring-composed into a sort of vortex around its central anecdote:

a Jefferson's neglected rhetorical question, who should pay rent on money, 'Some fellow who has it on rent day, | or some bloke who has not?'

b the death of the last Ottoman sultan, the end of his line and its ways

c the deployment of '80 loudspeakers' to broadcast a Vatican beatification

d a spy whose information helped save Vienna from the Turks, opened the first Viennese coffee-house where people meet and talk

e Herr Von Unruh miming the sergeant at Verdun who 'jammed down the cadavers . . . with his boots | to get the place smooth for the Kaiser'

d² Charles Francis Adams reported that he had found no good conversation in London

c² the non-publication of Van Buren's autobiography in which he had written of the U.S. bank war

b² Marx's observation that the children whose health was ruined in England's mills would 'become fathers of the next generation' and so pass on their tuberculosis

a² a Rothschild's remark that 'nations were fools to pay rent for their credit'.

Herr Von Unruh had been a German officer in the late war, and was, when Pound knew him in Rapallo, an Expressionist writer in exile from Nazi Germany. His account of 'the sergeant tramping down the corpses to get the place tidy for William' appealed to Pound as effectively communicating an insight into 'The meaning of capitalism' or 'what capitalist mentality leads to'. The same might be said of the several items following the anecdote. Indeed the more one considers the whole passage the further from random it becomes.

The middle passage of the canto is also ring-composed, only this time the main elements—a letter addressed apparently to Queen Victoria, and another from Pound's own Maria—enclose the lesser items. These latter concern mainly the acquisition and proving of navigational skills by voyagers, and the passing on of those skills—

> They say, that is the Norse engineer told me, that out past Hawaii
> they spread threads from gun'ale to gun'ale
> in a certain fashion
> and plot a course of 3000 sea miles
> lying under the web, watching the stars

The letter to 'Your Highness' is reassuring about the good pedigree and breeding of 'yr cairn puppy'. (Details of how a US Secretary of State was appointed without his pedigree being looked into are inserted in counterpoint.) There is a subdued sense of high nonsense about that episode. The other letter is distinguished rather by the simplicity and directness of its description of a 'bella festa' in Maria's mountain village, and by an intelligence that shows her to be her father's daughter—an intelligence that is in the genes, as one might say. Altogether, this letter off-rhymes quite richly and humourously with the one concerning the Queen's 'little dog [that] is doing...very well at Mr McLocherty's'.

The final third of the canto observes two or three instances of the genetically transmitted intelligence of insects, which Pound had read about in Remy de Gourmont's *Physique de l'amour* and had referred to in his discussion of volition in *Jefferson and/or Mussolini*. The instinctive martial behaviour which ensures the survival of their species is set against the broken Cathar fortress of Mt Segur, where the light from Eleusis was put out, and against the buried Roman city six feet down near San Bertrand de Comminges in the same region of southern France. The insect intelligence outlasts civilizations. Yet there is still the wheat field, and 'an ox in smith's sling hoisted for shoeing'; and still an eye for the way 'sun cuts light against evening...shaves grass into emerald'.

After that demanding and unsettling re-encounter with the modern situation canto 49, known as 'the Seven Lakes' canto, seems to offer relief and rest in a natural paradise created and recreated over the centuries in paintings and poems by generations of Chinese artists, and made new again in Pound's limpid verse. That is, many readers find here 'The still centre of the *Cantos* [where] the images speak with quiet power, expressing the repose and harmony with the universe of Pound's Confucianism'. One could be tempted to fall in with that sentiment.

There was in Pound's family a Japanese 'screen book', consisting of eight ink paintings, each accompanied by a poem in Chinese and another in Japanese, representing eight classic views about the shores of the Xiao and Xiang rivers in central South China. In 1928 Pound met in Rapallo a scholar and teacher from that region, a Miss Tseng, and had her translate at sight the eight Chinese poems. His version, in lines 1–30, is not a translation, however, but a free composition of images suggested by both poems and paintings. Zhaoming Qian, in his expert account of this background, notes that the 'Seven Lakes' tradition goes back to the time of 'The eighth Song emperor, Huizong (reigned 1101–25)', who

turned government over to his ministers in order to spend more time on artistic activities. His neglect of state affairs eventually led to his capture by the invading troops of the Jin, and the loss of half China.

It was an era, in Qian's words, of artistic vigour and political impotence. The Confucian historians, seeking always models of good government, put

Huizong down as a Taoist and a bad example. Pound, following them, will say of him in canto 55, 'HOEÏ went *taozer*, an' I suppose | Tsaï ran to state usury'; his dynasty 'died of taxes and gimcracks'.

Pound's version of 'the Seven Lakes' is unmistakeably Taoist, not Confucian—the Confucian riposte will come in the final third of the canto. The scene is contemplated in a mood of quietist detachment, autumnal, in twilight, or in the evening at sunset. While there is an attentive sympathy with natural phenomena, and some finely observed images, the human presence is distanced and rendered inert. There are few strong verbs; none at all for human action until, 'on the north sky line', 'the young boys prod stones for shrimps'. A passive, mildly melancholy, peacefulness reigns.

> Autumn moon; hills rise about lakes
> against sunset
> Evening is like a curtain of cloud,
> a blurr above ripples; and through it
> sharp long spikes of the cinnamon,
> a cold tune amid reeds.
> Behind hill the monk's bell
> borne on the wind.
> Sail passed here in April; may return in October
> Boat fades in silver; slowly;
> Sun blaze alone on the river.

The vowel music is pleasing, the rhythm slow-paced, reflective; and the images have a restful clarity. This is the poetry of withdrawal from the troubling world into rural retreats. It refines a state of mind that has its place, its function, in the human economy; but it should not be confused with the Confucian ethos of communal responsibility, nor with Pound's volitionist ethic. The will to order, to civilize, to act in harmony with others and with the universe, is precisely what it does not express. Further, its way of communing with nature is so very far from the rites celebrated in cantos 39 and 47. To seek repose in nature, harmonizing as that may be for the solitary mind, is not at all the same as responsibly enacting our part in the universe, or in society.

The turn when it comes breaks the quietist mood, asserting, as if in protest, the preoccupation that mood would soothe away—

> State by creating riches shd. thereby get into debt?
> This is infamy; this is Geryon.

> This canal still goes to TenShi
> though the old king built it for pleasure

That return to the realm of constructive action, and to what would undo it, is followed by a block of four lines of four syllables which can be pronounced but which few will understand. This, we are told, is a verse composed by the legendary emperor Shun and regarded as the hymn of an ideal society, a hymn, apparently, for the imperial transmission of the mandate of heaven throughout the empire. In 1958 Pound translated it thus:

> Gate, gate of gleaming,   [clouds]
> knotting, dispersing,
> flower of sun, flower of moon   [rays]
> day's dawn after day's dawn   new fire

Here, however, Pound presents it in a (not altogether accurate) representation of how it would sound in the Japanese pronunciation of the Chinese characters, that being closer than modern Mandarin (so Fenollosa had suggested) to the archaic Chinese pronunciation. In that form, according to Achilles Fang, it would not be especially meaningful to Japanese readers, and would be unrecognizable to Chinese readers. Indeed, for most readers of canto 49 the block of syllables can only represent something not immediately available to us. Their portentous sounds communicate not Shun's vision so much as its inoperancy. Already in the twilight scenes of the Taoists of the Seven Lakes that ancient tradition of all-energizing light was quite lost.

The imperial hymn is followed by an even earlier folk song, said to express the contentment of the peasants under the rule of the legendary good emperor Yao. In Pound's version their simple life is bound up with nature and is all strong verbs—

> Sun up; work
> sundown; to rest
> dig well and drink of the water
> dig field; eat of the grain
> Imperial power is? and to us what is it?

The naive questions are read as showing that the people are not oppressed by imperial taxes and exactions; and the simple order of their lives shows that the state is well ordered. The folk are behind the abundance of nature; and the emperor, it is to be understood, is making new the total light process of sun and moon day after day. There, rather than in the Seven Lakes verses, was the Confucian idea of the good life.

The canto closes upon a chord: 'The fourth; the dimension of stillness. | And the power over wild beasts.' That last line takes us back to canto 47, then to canto 39, and still further back to Dionysos in canto 2. It doesn't so much arise out of canto 49 as add to it a reminder of what is not there. 'Kung and Eleusis', Pound will write later, meaning that each needs the other. 'The fourth: the dimension of stillness', is more teasing. One is tempted to connect it with the passive repose the Taoist contemplative is after; but that would make a discord with 'the power over wild beasts', and with the active order of imperial power. It connects rather with the stillness of the all-creating Light of Cavalcanti's philosophy in canto 36—'He himself moveth not, drawing all to his stillness'. This is the paradoxical stillness of the unmoved mover of everything that moves, the stillness of light. Its action is implicit, though hidden, in the emperor's hymn; and shines through in the peasants' song. That light, properly understood, is one with the light of Eleusis, so that the two lines are a natural chord. The active intelligence of love, the illumination in coitus, and the properly functioning state, all grow from the one root, 'consciousness of the unity with nature'.

The last two cantos of the decad resume the matter of usury. Canto 50 deals, in a manner close to Pound's prose polemic, with the defeat by the forces of usury of the attempts at reform and revolution in Tuscany. Most of the canto is drawn from Antonio Zobi's five-volume history of the Tuscan state up to the failed revolution of 1848, *Storia civile della Toscana* (1850–2). Zobi saluted the American Revolution as a precedent for Italy's efforts to free itself from foreign domination, especially from that of Austria. And because Napoleon wrested Italy from Austria and brought in something of the spirit and laws of the French republican revolution he is named here as 'First Consul' rather than as emperor, and figures as a righteous opponent of the usurious monarchies of Austria and England.

There is first a keynote 'rhyme' of the American Revolution and Pietro Leopoldo's reforms in Tuscany, both having occurred about the same time. A telling difference, however, is that the one, as John Adams said, 'took place in the minds of the people', whereas the other doesn't appear to involve the people in the same way at all. It is the Grand Duke who sets about clearing the state debt left by the Medici—'its interest ate up all the best income'—and it is he who cuts down the taxes. These were enlightened reforms, but not a popular revolution, and they left Tuscany still under the Austrian empire.

Vienna, the capital of that empire, is presented in images out of the early 'hell cantos', as 'hell's bog', 'the midden of Europe... the black hole of all | mental vileness... the privy that stank Franz Josef', all this because 'In their soul was usura and in their minds darkness'. Given that vision of Austria, Napoleon did well to defeat its army at Marengo in 1800 –

> Mars meaning, in that case, order
> That day was Right with the victor
> mass weight against wrong

Carlyle, in his *Heroes, Hero-Worship, and the Heroic in History*, had seen Napoleon's 'brilliant Italian campaigns' in that light, as inspired by 'a faith in Democracy' and as an assertion of the enlightened spirit of the French Revolution against the 'Austrian Simulacra'. Yet Italy had then come under Napoleon's empire, and the best Zobi had to say about that was that when Napoleon was forced out in 1814 at least Ferdinando Habsburg 'got back a state free of debt | coffers empty | but the state without debt'.

And still Tuscany and Italy were not free. With Napoleon exiled to Elba the Congress of Vienna was called to put Europe back together again, and the four great powers, Austria and England, with Prussia and Russia, met to carve it up between them and to restore it to its pre-revolutionary state.

> England and Austria were for despots with commerce
> considered
>   Put back the Pope but
> reset no republics: Venice, Genova, Lucca
> and split up Poland in their soul was usura
> and in their hand bloody oppression

While they were still negotiating Napoleon escaped from Elba, gathered an army again, and 'for a hundred days [hope spat] against hell belch', that is, until his final defeat at Waterloo. 'The force which he challenged', so the argument runs in Christopher Hollis's *The Two Nations*, a work which Pound read with approval, 'was the force of usury'; and the victory of that force 'laid finally in the dust the great hope of the world's freedom from the empire of usury'.

The restored monarchies of Europe, Hollis explains, were now 'weighed down by a burden of debt which made their creditors the effectual masters of policy'. In this analysis, the Napoleonic wars which culminated in the battle of Waterloo had given the bankers who financed them—Hollis names the Rothschilds—the opportunity to become the dominant power in Europe, and to put down the power of the people.

This interpretation, which differs radically from the generally received story, is the key not only to this canto's treatment of Napoleon, but also to Pound's understanding of most of the world's wars from 1815 through the American Civil War to 1939–45. The conflict for him is always between the true values of democracy and the interests of finance, with the latter too often triumphant. He saw the nineteenth century as 'the century of usury', the century in which 'the revolution born of the Leopoldine reforms in Tuscany, and quite manifest in the Jeffersonian process' in America, was betrayed by men so 'steeped from the cradle in usurious preconceptions' that they knew not what they did in following the dictates of finance. So Wellington, when he drove Napoleon's army out of Spain, 'was a jew's pimp | and lacked mind to know what he effected'. And at Waterloo, implicitly, he carried the day for *usura*, for Geryon.

'Mind' is a major motif of the canto: the revolution 'took place in the minds of the people'; it was betrayed and defeated by minds in 'darkness and blankness', and by minds in which 'was stink and corruption' of usura. Then there is what Zobi wrote in 1850 as if to account for the failure of the 1848 revolution, 'Italy ever doomed with abstractions...By following brilliant abstractions'. Pound endorses that with an example—

> Not, certainly, for what most embellishes il sesso femminile
> and causes us to admire it, they wrote of Marie de Parma
> [Napoleon's] widow.

But isn't 'a jew's pimp' an abstraction, and a far from brilliant one? And that nasty little charge of prejudice, doesn't it make for 'darkness and blankness'? That is street-corner rant, not the poet's way to make a revolution in the mind. The lapse goes with the rapid shifting of the mind, in the attack on England and Austria, away from the few really telling facts, such as 'split up Poland', to the rhetorical abstraction, 'in their soul was usura'. Further, there is nothing in particular to make the mind see Napoleon standing for Hope 'against hell belch'. That is another cryptic abstraction, a possibly illuminating one this time, but for want of some defining detail the mind is likely to be left blank and in the dark. After all, Napoleon in 1815 was not an obvious representative of the spirit of the French Revolution.

As Pound said often enough, intelligence is particular, it needs the impress, the direct knowing of things both subjective and objective. There is a deep, Dantescan kind of knowing in 'hell belch', if only the intelligence is engaged at that point. It would help engage it if there were more fact to inform the impassioned rhetoric. The new republics in northern Italy were handed back to the Austrian empire. The splitting up of Poland, as Jerome J. McGann has recalled, meant bloody oppression for the

Polish patriots whom England had promised to support in their struggle to get free from Russian and Austrian control. McGann also helpfully informs us that 'Wellington was the key English figure' in bringing back the old European order at the Congress of Vienna; and that he had not only driven the French out of Spain, but had agreed, at the Congress of Verona in 1822, to the suppression of 'the newly fledged Spanish patriotic revolution' and the betrayal of the Spanish nationalists to the restored French Bourbons. If these betrayals of revolutions and reforms are not brought to mind effectively the hellish language will lack warrant and sound as empty rant.

The canto closes on a suddenly personal note. 'Lalage's shadow moves in the fresco's knees', and she, Lalage, 'is blotted with Dirce's shadow'. In classical literature 'Lalage' would imply a courtesan or mistress; and Dirce was a woman who imprisoned and tormented her husband's former wife Antiope when she became pregnant, not knowing that Zeus was the father and thinking her husband unfaithful. Her trying to blot out Antiope and her child would rhyme with the canto's concern with peoples oppressed and denied justice and independence. The final lines cut from the troubling shadows to the calm light casting them: 'dawn stands there fixed and unmoving | only we two have moved'.

The opening of canto 51 takes off from that into a snatch of song from the Tuscan poet and precursor of Cavalcanti and Dante, Guinicelli:

> Shines
> in the mind of heaven God
> who made it
> more than the sun
> in our eye.

Guinicelli's canzone, like Cavalcanti's *Canzone d'amore*, is concerned with the working of the light of the divine intelligence in the human heart and mind in the form of love—a preoccupation unlikely to have been brought to the reader's mind for some time. The next line returns us to where we were, 'Fifth element; mud; said Napoleon'—a line repeated from canto 34, where it was connected with 'la sottise de Moscou', his thoroughly unintelligent invasion of Russia.

There follows a reprise of canto 45, 'With usury has no man a good house', only condensed to half the number of lines, now in simple current English, and in a quieter, reflective tone. The devastations caused by usury are not so much preached against as stated as plain fact. There is passion still in the words, but the rhythm has lost its assurance, its power, and the sense of the good things in nature and art is much subdued. This is canto 45 with its counter theme muted.

New matter is introduced in lines 33–50, from *The Art of Angling* by Charles Bowlker, a very popular work first published in 1758, revised and reprinted many times through the next hundred years, and regarded by fly fishermen as a classic of their craft. Pound has abbreviated Bowlker's description of two artificial trout flies, one of them the 'Blue Dun':

> A starling's wing will give you the colour
> or duck widgeon, if you take feather from under the wing
> Let the body be of blue fox fur, or a water rat's
> or grey squirrel's. Take this with a portion of mohair
> and a cock's hackle for legs.

The other fly, the 'Granham', requires 'Hen pheasant's feather', 'Dark fur from a hare's ear', 'a green shaded partridge feather', 'grizzled yellow cock's hackle', 'harl from a peacock's tail', and it 'can be fished from seven a.m. | till eleven; at which time the brown marsh fly comes on' and 'no fish will take Granham'. To one very persuasive critic, Robert Demott, these artificial flies are 'examples of traditional craftsmanship and artistry which have withstood usury for centuries and continue to do so'. They require precise observation and accurate imitation of nature, for their creator must copy exactly the tiny insects which are the staples of the trout's diet in order to lure it into mistaking the artificial fly for the live insect. Demott invites us to see the skilled fly tyer and fly fisherman as a hero of the cantos, in harmony with nature, and the antithesis of the usurer. The *Companion to the Cantos* goes along with that, asserting that 'since fly-fishing is an art that depends on nature's increase ... it has none of the destructive effects of usury, which is CONTRA NATURAM'.

The canto itself declares, 'That hath the light of the doer, as it were | a form cleaving to it'; and adds in Latin, from the same source in Albertus Magnus, words to the effect that the adept intellect in apprehending the works of God takes in with them the creative light, that is, the form cleaving to them, and day by day recreates that form. The idea is cognate with the philosophy in Guinicelli's canzone, and in Cavalcanti's. It would seem just here to make the creating of artificial flies a repetition as it were of God's creating the living swarm. It would regard 'the doer' as truly like the Prime Doer, and truly in union with the being and becoming of nature.

Is this then what they have come to, those moments of 'consciousness of unity with nature' in the rites of Dionysos and Circe-Aphrodite and Adonis, to the craft of 'factitious bait'? Well, when Eva Hesse questioned Pound about the passage in 1959 he told her,

trout rise to artificial fly | no nutriment
  vide description, cocks hackle, great art in
devising fish-bait by non-aesthetes,
                      very high degree of craftiness
      METAPHOR (cf/ AriStotl) on apt use of
        for USURA

That is, for Pound himself in 1959 the passage exemplified not craft but craftiness, craft turned against nature. And indeed, at the simplest level, doesn't the passage represent a *nature morte,* and quite lack any apprehension of the life in things? Imagine the bench heaped with all those dead birds and beasts the fly tyer needs to have by him, and his having an eye only for the bits and pieces of them he can use. Then there is his luring the trout with a fraudulent imitation of its food. If this crafty art is to be thought of as an imitation of the action of all-creating love it can only be as a bold parody, or an outright fraud. It can only be Geryon, 'twin with usura', who would claim that for it. Geryon is named as the speaker later in this final passage, but the whole passage from 'That hath the light of the doer' must be in his voice.

If the passage is not taken that way the reader will be in even greater difficulty with the other item which is said to have 'the light of the doer' about it—

                      Thus speaking in Königsberg
  Zwischen die Volkern erzielt wird
  a modus vivendi.

—'between the peoples may be achieved a modus vivendi'. It was Rudolf Hess, Hitler's deputy and close associate, who spoke those words in a radio broadcast on 8 July 1934. Pound, in a note made some years later, took his meaning to be that a 'system of living together should not be beyond the capacity of... the four main racial groups in Europe', i.e. German, Italian, French, and English. It was of course not apparent at the time that Nazi Germany was talking peace while secretly preparing for war, nor that it was at that very moment plotting the murder of Austrian Chancellor Dollfuss and the annexation of his country. (Dollfuss was killed, on 25 July, but the Nazi takeover was prevented that year.) Only later did it become clear that Hess's talking peace was a fraud. He was not spreading divine light, but doing the work of Geryon who sings in the following lines, 'I pay men to talk peace.'

Dante's Geryon, the figure of Fraud, is 'the savage beast with the sting in its tail that breaks through walls and weapons and pollutes the whole world'; and 'His face is the face of a just man'. He is associated with the usurers who are being punished among the fraudulent in the lower region of the *Inferno* for doing violence to both nature and art. Virgil has previously explained to Dante that as 'Nature takes her course from the Divine Intellect, and from its art', and as human art follows nature and 'is, as it were, the grandchild of the Deity', then the usurer, in disdaining the way of Nature and her bounty, sins against God, nature, and art. Pound's Geryon is clearly from the *Inferno*, and when the allusion is tracked back to Dante's cantos 11 and 17 it becomes evident that Pound's canto is following Dante's lead, that it is in a sense 'written over' that part of the *Inferno*. It is his pit of hell, and the lowest point in his epic.

The utmost fraud of Geryon-Usura would be to put over the unproductive counterfeit as a godlike product of nature and art. The true meaning of 'The light of the DOER, as it were a form cleaving to it', is 'an ACTIVE pattern, a pattern that sets things in motion', constructively—something not to be found in this canto. This Geryon is 'merchant of chalcedony', and that means, if we catch the echo of Revelation 21: 19, that he is in the business of selling off the foundations of the temple of the new Jerusalem.

On the title page of *The Fifth Decad of Cantos*, and again on the last page after this canto, Pound set the Chinese characters *chêng⁴ ming²*. According to Karlgren's *Analytic Dictionary, ming²* is what is called out in the dark, and in combination with *chêng⁴*, meaning 'upright, correct, just', it signifies speaking one's own identity honestly—not cloaking oneself in darkness—and also correctly identifying what is in darkness. It is close to the *Ta Hio's* Confucian ideal that the precise verbal definition of nature and of human nature is the basis of good government. One could think of it as a variation upon the Flaubertian and Fordian ideal of *le mot juste*, the word that does justice. Pound maintained that a truly enlightened perception and articulation of the things that concern us is the only sure defence against usurious fraud and injustice.

The form and pressure of the time

The idea becomes real only in action, Pound held to that. But did he allow for all that might get in the way of the idea in practice? Did he allow enough for the complexities and contradictions of the time, for proper uncertainties and necessary compromises, and for his own susceptibility to certain of its pressures? To call things by their right names, to discriminate honestly and accurately, that is an excellent idea; but when the things in question are as instant and as opaque as current events tend to be, the judgement is likely to be partial, and right action difficult to determine. Faced with a decision to go to war, or to change the terms of trade or of the social contract, who can see at once all that is involved? We fall back on prepared positions, on our principles and fixed convictions; or we accept what we are told by those who ought to know the facts.

Pound distrusted general principles and established convictions as unlikely to do justice to the particular case. He maintained the awkwardly humane view that the individual should not be oppressed by the majority, and further, that the truth is in the particular rather than in the general case. He advocated his ideogrammic method of piecing together the significant, the luminous details into 'a sufficient phalanx of particulars', that image implying an organization of the mind that would go into right action. It was 'a new mode of thought', he wrote, which 'would eliminate certain types of imbecility, in particular the inaccessibility to FACT glaringly lit up in 1935 by the peril of world conflagration caused by the type of mind which festered in the ideologues' who hold with fanaticism 'an abstract received "idea" or "generality"' and 'who NEVER take in concrete detail'. By mustering the facts he would save the world from destruction by the ideologues, and by those who more or less blindly went along with them. Yet in that darkening time, in haste to keep up with menacing events and to counter the blatant contradictions of high principles by low conduct, he too could rush to judgement upon a conviction of what must be the case rather than upon a sufficient grasp of the details. And then mere opinion, or propaganda, or banal prejudice, could stand in for accurate perception and make an ideologue of him also.

In December 1936 Edward VIII, just a few months after being crowned King of England and Defender of the Faith, was compelled to abdicate the throne. He wanted to marry an American divorcée and the British Establishment would not allow it. According to its strict conventions, being a commoner without wealth or title, a foreigner, and, most damning of all, a divorced woman, made Mrs Simpson simply unacceptable as the consort of the titular head of the nation and defender of its faith. The King, told that he must choose between marrying Mrs Simpson and his duty to the nation's morals, chose Mrs Simpson and a life of luxury abroad as Duke of Windsor. Before his coronation, as Prince of Wales, Edward had visited South Wales and expressed sympathy with the unemployed miners and their hungry families, and the people at large had liked him for that. Now the Communists and the Fascists and the Social Creditors and others who resented the dominance of the conservative establishment argued that the real reason for the enforced abdication was Edward's sympathizing with the poor and the unemployed, and that at bottom it was part of the general conspiracy of the ruling class against their people. Basil Bunting, who was back in England at the time, told Pound—even though he was (according to Zukofsky) 'a British-conservative-antifascist-imperialist'—that he was convinced that it was on account of Edward's speech in South Wales that Prime Minister Baldwin had made him abdicate. And Pound built that 'fact' into an article about the absolute evil being worked against the starving millions in England by Baldwin and the all-powerful bankers, and about Edward Windsor's being now in a better position to oppose that evil 'than he ever could have done on a throne surrounded with flummydiddles and gold braid and flunkies'—

I mean if the man has it in him to want his ex-subjects nourished, to want the fruits of the Empire delivered and eaten, and the spun cloth of his ex-realm worn, and the fuel used to heat poor men's houses, he can now say so.

The ex-king, however, showed no disposition to express those humane sentiments. It was a case—a minor instance—of Pound's following wishful thinking beyond any real knowledge.

Pound's efforts to come to terms with the Hitler phenomenon present a more complex case. When Hitler came to power in 1933 Pound dismissed his incipient Nazi state with its 'pseudo-Fascist rage' as 'a parody, a sickly and unpleasant parody of Fascism'. To spread the *interesting* element of Fascism, he wrote in the conclusion to *Jefferson and/or Mussolini*, there was no need for 'parades, nor hysterical Hitlerian yawping'. A year later he was objecting in the *New English Weekly* to the confusion of 'Italian Fascism with the Hun's travesty'. 'Adolphe is an, almost, pathetic hysteric', he wrote, and, 'so far as I can make out, a tool of *almost* the worst Huns'. In whose interest was it, he demanded to know, 'to create confusion re the Thyssen-owned Hitler, and the founder of the Italian Corporate State'. A further year on, in 1935, he wrote to Gorham Munson of *New Democracy*, 'Do CAN those asses who talk of Fascism as if the Corporate State/ Hitler and stinky Mosley were all one'. And to Claude Cockburn he wrote, 'I am not a HITLERITE/ thass another kettle of MOlasses'.

One fundamental distinction between Fascist Italy and Nazi Germany was that, as he told Cockburn, there was 'certainly no anti-semitism in Italy'. 'There has never been any anti-Semitism HERE', he told Arnold Gingrich of *Esquire* in August 1934, so 'it might be time to dissociate Germany and Italy'. The leading characteristic of Nazism for Pound at that time was its anti-Semitism, and while that, as he wrote in the *New English Weekly* in April 1935, was one of the two 'main trends or drifts of Europe', Italy's Corporate State stood for the other and very different trend, meaning economic enlightenment. Behind that was an implicit objection to Nazism on economic grounds, Pound believing in 1935 that since Nazism was partly financed from London Hitler must be the puppet of international finance.

So far Pound's negative view of Nazism was fairly much in line with Mussolini's determination to keep his distance from Hitler. Later though, in 1936 and 1937, when relations between the two dictators were becoming closer, he began to find signs of economic sense in the Führer. In a letter to Congressman Tinkham in March 1936 he noted that 'EVEN Hitler in one clause of his last outbreak [had seen] certain FACTS' about money. He had said something about 'Germany being forced to "accept credits"' which put it in debt to international finance, and that was in accord with Henry Ford's observation, '"Debt business, only business that hasn't suffered from the depression"', and with the fact that happy bankers were enjoying 'largest dividends in years', and all this somehow went to show that 'Hitler is "ON"' the Social Credit programme. Better, Germany was imitating and learning from the new Italy, though 'under very unfavourable conditions'. It was at least showing a disposition, in Pound's view, to follow the Fascist state's 'principle of LIFE, of continuous renewal and renovation', and so to go against the destructive injustice and inhumanity of the 'usury State'. In April 1937 he told Tinkham that 'both Germany and Italy seem to begin to see that nations money shd/ be based on national productivity', not on usurious lending, and that Hitler, according to Por, 'was out for National Dividend—The Führer [had] said "jeder Kontrahenten" ought to have his part'. Evidently he was, along with India, Alberta, and Italy, 'getting wiser to London (Jew and nonjew) Bank racket'. About that time Pound was congratulating Wyndham Lewis in *Guide to Kulchur* for having sensed on a visit to Berlin in 1931 that Hitler was a force for 'the resurrection' of Germany. 'I hand it to him as a superior perception', he wrote, 'Superior in relation to my own "discovery" of Mussolini'. Lewis had associated Hitler's with Social Credit's hostility to *Leihkapital*, the loan capital of international finance, thus reinforcing the hopeful notion that Hitler was 'ON'.

By April 1938 Pound's perception of Nazism had become altogether positive. When Gerhart Münch, still desperately poor and unable to get work as a musician in Munich, wrote that while he had previously preferred not to work with the Party circumstances were now forcing him to do so, Pound wrote back at once, 'Do for God's sake work WITH THE PARTY the party is right and is the future.' He may have been thinking simply of Münch's career prospects, but his urging him to work with the Party in those terms does imply an endorsement of Nazism as the future for German culture and society. He could do that because he had become convinced that its economic programme was now fully in accord with his own principles. In May 1938, following the successful invasion and takeover of Austria, Hitler made a state visit to Italy, accompanied among others of his ministers by Schacht, head of the Reichsbank and responsible for Germany's economic miracle. On 26 May Pound sent Tinkham a 'Note // in case it has missed you'—

SCHACHT during the Roman love feats has come out VERY clear for monetary ideas that I was pestering you with in Venice.

Ribbentrop apparently started letting parts of the cat out last year at Leipzig fair/ Hitler this spring/ and now Hjalmar H. Greely Schacht to all intents using my definitions (naturally in blissful ignorance of the honour)

He was quite right about Schacht's monetary ideas being largely in accord with his own. What he did not see was that Schacht had successfully implemented those ideas and proved their effectiveness in order to enable Hitler to mobilize Germany for total war.

* * *

Dr Schacht had been charged even before September 1934 with the economic preparation of Germany for war, and in a secret law of 21 May 1935 he was appointed Plenipotentiary-General for War Economy. Everything in the economy was to be subordinated to the build-up towards war, and it was that policy which brought about the reconstruction of Germany. In January 1933 there were 6 million unemployed—by 1937 there was full employment. The transformation was effected by the state taking total control of credit and doing away with private banks and Leihkapital; by strict regulation of wages, prices, and dividends; by state-financed public works—such as the new autobahnen, designed for the rapid deployment of armoured troops; and by the stimulation, regulation, and direction of both private enterprise and the labour-force. Schacht's creation of credit in a country that had been effectively bankrupt by printing money at need within a tightly controlled economy demonstrated that the Social Credit theory did work in practice. That it was directed by a totalitarian dictator towards bringing on the hell of war, and not at all towards the more just and more humane democracy Pound and the Social Creditors dreamed of, was another of the terrible contradictions of the time.

* * *

That Nazi Germany showed signs of being on what he believed to be the right lines economically was enough to persuade Pound that Nazism was altogether right. He either didn't notice or didn't really give his mind to everything else that was going on there. He signally failed to connect the economic miracle with the militarization of Germany and Hitler's mounting belligerence. And though he did know about it, he appears to have been untroubled by the ever-intensifying Nazi persecution of Jews.

But then his attitude to anti-Semitism in general had become thoroughly mixed up and conflicted. There was a lot of it about. It was licensed and commonplace and also objected to in much of Europe and America, though only in Nazi Germany was it state policy and turning murderous in a way that would shortly lead on to genocide. I have noted in previous chapters how Pound would resort to the racist stereotypes of anti-Semitism in his war on usury. What emerges now is his struggle with the endemic prejudice, as with a tar-baby. He 'Never expected to go anti-Semite', he told a correspondent, and there is evidence that he wanted not to; and yet, though he could be critical of anti-Semitism, he seems to have regarded it strategically, and never to have seen it clearly as an offence against funda-mental human rights and values. In time he became simply unable to keep clear of it whenever the issue of usury came up.

By his own standards he began to go wrong when he fell into the way of speaking of Jews in the abstract, as a race instead of as individuals. In a letter to his father in 1926 he mentioned that he had recently read some selections from the Talmud and commented, 'Never disliked jews before; but as it now seems they were responsible for Christianity, I dare say they deserve all the kicks they get.' The next day he added, perhaps after reflecting that his father was after all a Christian, that Christ had 'tried to kill judaism, [but] the racial force was too strong...and all the worst features cropped up again'. 'Racial curse too strong for the individual', he wrote the same day to Richard Aldington. The particular curse he had in mind was 'the monotheistic idea', which he might have had reason to judge 'the root of evil', but not to attribute to Jewish genes. At other times he did think of Jews as individuals, as when some friend of his father suggested in 1927 that Pound hated Jews—

oooo sez I 'ates the jews? Ask him why he thinks I 'ate the jews. I hate SOME JEWS, but I have greater contempt for Christians. Look wot they dun to america: Bryan, Wilson, Volstead, all goyim. horrible goyim...Of course some jews are unpleas-ant, ask any Jew if they aint.

'Personally I like jews (I mean some jews)', he wrote in a letter to Olga that year, 'but it is not necessary to embrace the Torah or wot ever they call it.'

Louis Zukofsky was one Jew he related to very positively, and precisely as a Jew. In their correspondence which was sustained right through the racially problematic 1930s both were always conscious of his racial and religious situation, even when Zukofsky would declare himself an anti-Semitic Jew, or write, 'The only good Jew I know is my father: a coinci-dence.' In 1929, when Zukofsky followed up his own submissions to *Exile* with a selection of Charles Reznikoff's writings, Pound was excited by the thought that the dynamic 'next wave' of literature might be Jewish. At the same time he accepted as simply a fact of American and European life the prejudice and the exclusions Zukofsky would be subject to. In February 1929 he wrote to his father, 'Zukofsky is coming to Phila. re/ a new quarterly mag. I shd be glad if you cd. put him up for a night or two . . . you might invite him at once, unless N/Y/ race prejudice intervenes.' (It did not, as he would have known it would not.) In April 1933, when Hitler had just come to power in Germany and Pound was encouraging Zukofsky to make a trip to Europe, he warned him of what to expect:

Mittle and Nord Europa less seasonable for Semites than they wuz/ last year. HAVE just seen THE most perfect specimen here on the sea front. But HE got out in a box car.

Nooz is that H.D. is consortin with Siggy Freud. Have axed her to axe F. to hexplain it, (I mean the outburst toward pogrom in boscheland)

That reads as the expression of a detached curiosity about some natural phenomenon.

By 1934 Pound was suggesting that 'the Jews' were themselves to blame for what was being done to them. Zukofsky had sent him an issue of William Dudley Pelley's Silver Shirt journal *Liberation*, thinking that it should alert him to the fact that Pelley's Silver Shirts were followers of Hitler's Nazism and anti-Semitism. Pound's response, however, was to write at once to the Silver Shirts in the hope of persuading them to adopt his Social Credit ideas and to heed 'Mussolini's great work for the benefit of the ITALIAN PEOPLE'; also to urge them (as noted in the previous chapter) to 'attack financial tyranny BY WHOMEVER exercised, i.e. whether by international jew or local aryan'. They should expose and foil the plots and conspiracies of 'jews AND others' in order to keep the attack focused on usury rather than on Jews. (All the same he fell for Pelley's story that, 'According to Bismarck, the awful Civil War in America was fomented by a Jewish Conspiracy', and he repeated that in two lines in canto 48.) To Zukofsky he wrote that Pelley was a stout fellow who understood 'the murkn mind', and that he, Zukofsky, should take his anti-Semitism to heart. 'Waal I sez, sez EZ/ serve yeh god damn well right IF YOU don't wake up and start/ a anti=bankshit movement right inside the buggarin sanhedrim. . . . If you don't want to be confused with yr/ancestral race and pogromd.' He may not have been wholly serious—the tone of the letter is somewhere between jokiness and earnest—but he was nonetheless intimating that Jews were persecuted and killed because they were responsible for usury, and that even if they were not themselves usurers they would still be held responsible, unless they actively mobilized against it. He was finding a rationale for anti-Semitism, even an implicit justification, in the old prejudice that identified Jews as usurers and usurers as 'Jews'; and still he protested to Zukofsky, in all sincerity, that he was not speaking to him 'aza anti-semite' but simply trying to prod him into right action 'with two pronged fork of terror and cajolery'.

Pound would insist that race was not the issue, that it was 'utterly irrelevant', that 'Race prejudice is red herring—The tool of the man defeated intellectually, and of the cheap politician'; and that, moreover, it was a distraction which served the conspiracy of bankers and usurers. 'Usurers have no race', he would write, one is as another and 'Hell makes no distinction'. He could bring forward Shakespeare's Shylock as the archetype of the usurer without mentioning his race. In demanding a pound of Antonio's fair flesh he is out to castrate Antonio, and that makes him 'an allegory not only of the usurer, but of concentration of sabotage, the fundamental opposer of natural increase...The root sin in person.' That is a penetrating insight into one side of the play, and into the nature of usury, and it has nothing to do with race. But then in a later article, in November 1935, Pound returned to the play and asked, 'Are we never to see that Shylock betrays his race, by hiding behind it? Charged as a usurer in attempt toward mayhem, he cries "I am a jew."' The argument was carried further in another article published about the same time. 'The Jew usurer...runs against his own people' because 'No orthodox Jew can take usury without sin, as defined in his own scriptures.' Worse, when the outlaw hides behind his race he makes his own people the scapegoat for usury, and sets up 'the plain man Jew to take the bullets and beatings'. He named Rothschild the great Jewish banker as the contemporary 'great chief usurer', the prime sinner against natural abundance; and he wanted to write on the first page of canto 52 that his sin was 'drawing vengeance' on 'poor yitts'. The Jews are supposed to be clever', Pound wrote, but there was a lack of cleverness in their not finding a way to stop 'the whole Jewish people' being made the 'sacrificial goat for the usurer'.

He was not advocating genocide, which in any case was not then in anyone's mind, unless it was hidden in Hitler's. He was rather wanting, as in his letter to Zukofsky, to terrorize and cajole clear-headed Jews and their leaders into at least enforcing observance of their own law, and beyond that into forming a principled opposition to the practice of usury. In March 1936, having read in the New English Weekly mention of a book by Mordecai J. B. Ezekiel, an American government economist, he wrote to him that 'If the book is honest social credit it shd/ be very useful in checking antisemitism', and that there was 'No doubt that semitophobia has been encouraged by the lack of jews in MONETARY reform movements'. In March

1937 he told James Taylor Dunn, editor of *The Globe*, that 'there wd. be no need of any anti-semitic stuff at all' if only 'the Jews wd. take any sort of part in econ/ reform', and that 'The fight ought NOT to have been fought on the lines of race prejudice'. The 'Only way to avoid that', he insisted, 'is by spread and acceleration of economic light'. But as things were, 'Even in Engl/ and Italy people are being forced into anti-semitism by Jewish folly— I mean people who never thought of it before and who ON PRINCIPLE are opposed to race prejudice and race discrimination.' The Jews themselves were making it 'hard as hell to do justice'.

But was it the case that anti-Semitism in the 1930s was directed against usury? Hitler's anti-Semitism, being the product of racial hatred allied to a mad fantasy of 'Aryan' racial purity and supremacy, had little or nothing to do with that. And the endemic anti-Semitism of Europe and America, for all that it drew on historical resentments of Jewish money-lending, was hardly the expression of a burning concern for bank reform. The fact is that Pound was using racial anti-Semitism to enforce his own economic agenda. That made his a rather special variant, and all the more extraordinary insofar as it was deployed not to incite race hatred but to motivate Jews to save themselves from persecution.

At the same time it was remarkably disingenuous of him to be surprised, when his 1934 letter to Pelley's Silver Shirts was printed in *New Masses* in 1936, to receive letters 'warning ME against antisemitism in the face of the fact that I was answering an antisemitic manifesto, and capitalizing "AND Aryan" almost every time I wrote jew'. Zukofsky was one of those warning him that 'Even decent Jews will miss yr "And" "or Aryan"', and that 'the cry of anti-semitism [will] be raised all over the country against you'. Rather than protesting that he had no anti-Semitic intent, he might have asked himself why, since race was irrelevant, he kept bringing it up, and why was he constantly reinforcing the prejudicial association of Jews with usury? Why speak at all in terms of Jew and non-Jew if it was not the historical origins but the contemporary practice of usury that was in his sights? Given the militant anti-Semitism of the Nazis, of Mosley's British Union, of Action Française, why was he not more careful to keep clear of what could only confuse the issue?

An exchange of private letters in March 1937 shows how his monomania about usury was skewing his intelligence and preventing him from facing the facts of anti-Semitism in the Europe of his time. Lina Caico, an Italian writer, critic, translator, and literary friend of Pound, wrote asking if he would do something to help a gifted German Jewish pianist who was 'eating her heart out in despair' in Berlin because the Nazi race laws made it impossible for her to pursue her career or even to earn enough to live on. Would Pound use his musical contacts to seek help? Pound, usually so generous, especially towards artists, would not. 'You hit a nice sore spot', he replied, and proceeded to sound off about Jews as a race. 'Let her try Rothschild and some of the bastards who are murdering 10 million anglo saxons in England,' he began; and then, 'I am not having any more' until the Jews accept their responsibilities as a race, and in particular until 'they at least participate in study of and attack on usury system'. That system had crushed out almost all the musicians he had known over twenty-five years, and 'the Jews NEVER attack' it. Besides, he went on, the Jews themselves 'are the GREAT destroyers of value... the shifters of boundary stones'. So to his conclusion: 'Occasionally a good one has to suffer for the sins of the race.' He did add, 'Hubermann [in Tel Aviv] is your friend's one hope', thus not wholly ignoring the individual victim of Nazi anti-Semitism. But she had become an occasion for Pound to attack, first, his great figure of usury, 'Rothschild', and then the Jewish race as a whole.

He was shifting the issue from a specific instance of the Nazi persecution of Jews on racial grounds to his own concern with the economic war, and shifting from the individual case to an unrelated abstraction. It was a shift which enabled him to view the Jewish race not as the victims but as the destroyers; and thus to see them as deserving persecution—not on racial grounds, he would insist, but because of the economic harm they could be held responsible for. Thus he could be against anti-Semitism as a race-prejudice, while endorsing it on economic grounds—a distinction which would make little or no practical difference. Lina Caico wrote back very gently on a postcard, 'Dear Ez, really you're getting economics on the brain! I don't deal with races but with individuals.'

In June 1937 Nancy Cunard printed in Paris SPAIN: THE QUESTION, a single sheet inviting writers and poets to declare themselves 'for, or against, the legal Government and the People of Republican Spain | ... for, or against, Franco and Fascism | For it is impossible any longer to take no side'. The paragraphs leading up to the question left no doubt of the right answer:

We have seen murder and destruction by Fascism in Italy, in Germany—the organisation there of social injustice and cultural death—and how revived, imperial Rome, abetted by international treachery, has conquered her place in the Abyssinian sun. The dark millions in the colonies are unavenged.

Today, the struggle is in Spain....

But there are some who, despite the martyrdom of Durango and Guernica, the enduring agony of Madrid, of Bilbao, and Germany's shelling of Almeria, are still in doubt, or who aver that it is possible that Fascism may be what it proclaims it is: 'the saviour of civilisation'.

Nancy Cunard sent a copy to Pound and appended this note: 'Dear Ezra, I have no idea what you feel about these things embodied in this. Please answer it. Love, N.'

'Dearest N', Pound typed back, 'I am very happy indeed to see that you aint leff yr/ blood an bones in Barrcerloner.' But then, 'As to the questionaire, I think your gang are all diarohea ... IF they wont look at WHY men are oppressed. If they will talk about ISMS.' Her 'gang' were mainly Communist or Communist-sympathizing anti-fascists, and Pound was clearly not with them. At the same time, surprisingly, no more was he with Franco's Falange. 'Spain is one barbarism and Russia another,' he wrote. His formal answer, as published in *Authors Take Sides on the Spanish War*, was simply this:

Questionnaire an escape mechanism for young fools who are too cowardly to think; too lazy to investigate the nature of money, its mode of issue, the control of such issue by the Banque de France and the stank of England. You are all had. Spain is an emotional luxury to a gang of sap-headed dilettantes.

Evidently the real question, for him, and the only one that mattered, was one that was not being asked: are you for, or against, a people controlling its own credit for its own benefit? His response was classed as 'Neutral?' along with 15 others—there were 126 for the Republicans, just 5 for Franco—but in fact he was not being neutral as between the opposing Communist and Falangist-Fascist-Nazi sides, he was saying 'neither of these'. He would not choose between them because both sides, in his judgement, were serving the interests of their military–industrial–financial supporters. Instead he was taking his stand on his own singular perception of the fundamental struggle of the time, and that meant, in the eyes of the majority of his fellow writers and poets, that he was not 'on side', indeed that he was putting himself offensively 'off-side'.

Zukofsky told Pound in March 1935, 'you're not being read in the U.S.A. for reasons you ought to be able to find out for yrself'. 'You seem to think you are the Messiah', he complained in another letter. And in March 1936, when Pound's letter to Pelley's Silver Shirts was published, he told him it was 'purblind' of him to have written it, but 'If you're dead set on completely losing whatever readers you still have in America, keep it up.' Zukofsky seems to have been right about Pound losing readers: the American edition of *Eleven New Cantos: XXXI–XLI* (1934) sold about 1,000 copies up to the summer of 1940, whereas *The Fifth Decad of Cantos*, published in November 1937, had sold only about 300 copies by then.

Bunting wrote from London in September 1936 to warn Pound that he appeared to be in danger of finding himself 'on the wrong side all round'. 'You are suspect to the [Social Credit] brethren, or else I very much misread the signs, because of your pro-Italian propaganda.' 'And if your activities have really led you to Hargrave, I'm convinced there's something wrong with your activities'—Hargrave of the Green Shirts being a 'footling Fool'. Again, 'Angold accuses you of connections with the British Union of Fascists: which I refuse to believe.... They spell Finance with three letters, J E W, and that's all you'll get out of them.' Bunting went on—

You are too valuable a pearl to go and cast yourself before swine of that sort, and I think, too acute to imagine that an identity of name necessarily indicates any further correspondence whatever with Italian Fascism. If that lot takes up Social Credit, it will complete the discredit which is patently threatening the whole movement.

Altogether, Bunting was trying to save Pound from being, in Zukofsky's words, 'too damn gullible'.

Hargrave had his own view of Pound. His propaganda for Social Credit was 'worthless'—'It was like a series of explosions in a rock quarry,' he told Gorham Munson, one of the founders of the American Social Credit Movement. And Munson told Charles Norman that Pound had become a liability, because of his anti-Semitism—both his Movement and Hargrave's Social Credit Party of Great Britain said that they did not accept anti-Semites as members—and because 'Pound was trying to combine social credit economic democracy with Fascist political totalitarianism'.

Munson was quite right about what Pound was trying to do, and, being anti-fascist, he would not even try to understand how Pound could see more promise of economic democracy in Fascist Italy than in the American or British democracies. In trying to combine what American democracy, according to his understanding of its founding principles, ought to be, with what Italian Fascism, to his mind, promised to be, Pound was projecting promises and possibilities upon a world riven by contradictions and by competing ideologies. Zukofsky, writing to Pound as a Marxist Communist, chided him for lauding 'the Boss's reclamation of the marshes' yet saying 'nothing about the Soviets doing the same'. (Did Zukofsky not know that Soviet farm collectivization had involved the imprisonment and exile of millions of peasants, and that it had caused such a famine that 4–5 million peasants died of malnutrition and hunger-related diseases in the winter of 1932–3?) Bunting was more conscious of contradictions. He reported himself grateful that Britain had not gone to war with Italy over Abyssinia, or with Germany over the Rhineland; but found it unsettling that 'the manoeuvres by which the peace was kept...were engaged in patently at the behest of the bankers, who have a lot invested in both Hitler and Mussolini'.

The simple black and white view of the political situation of the 1930s would set up the free democracies against the totalitarian dictatorships. But then how to account for the way Mussolini and Hitler were enthusiastically received as saviours of their countries by vast majorities of their peoples? And what to make of the way the freely elected governments of the democracies were floundering and failing a great mass of their people? To explain how those contradictions could come about the economic story needs to be told. Once the political situation is understood in terms of laissez-faire economies on the one side, and state-controlled economies on the other, it becomes clear that in the one freedom to vote went with having a very limited claim upon the state in respect of one's basic human needs; whereas in the other the state, while denying the individual a voice, did provide for the basic needs of all who served it. The individual was likely to be better off materially, therefore, under the Italian or the German dictatorship which suppressed his individuality, than under the democracies which left individuals free to provide for themselves or go under. The dictatorships were frankly undemocratic, even anti-democratic, and allowed no appeal to individual liberty. The free democracies though had a worm of contradiction at their core—the contradiction between the spirit of democracy and the spirit of capitalism. From the founding principle of universal equality should flow equal rights for all to a fulfilling life, and for that there must be government of, by, and essentially *for* the good of the whole people. But capitalism does not favour the ideal of the common wealth; and it rejoices in its freedom to use its accumulations of financial power to shape societies to serve private ends.

Pound passionately believed that the aim of democratic government should be 'to distribute the purchasing power of the nation so that both social and economic justice shd/ be attainable in degree not heretofore known, to give every human being...his share in the inheritance of humanity'. When he looked into the capitalist democracies he saw not true democracy serving the needs of all; he saw the capitalist financial system serving the greed of the few, and taking over democracy, cynically and perversely, in the name of individual liberty. Concerned by this crisis in democracy, and very much in the contradiction-ridden spirit of the time, he held up Italian totalitarianism as a model of how democracy might be saved from capitalism. Totalitarian democracy was of course a contradiction in terms, but not more so than that other oxymoron, capitalist democracy. Pound was not against democratic equality and social justice; he was against the subversion of democracy by the injustices and inequalities of the capitalist system. But even his friends in America and Britain had little patience with his claim that this was why he endorsed Mussolini's Fascism. He was isolating himself and alienating a good many people by his singular idea of how the disorders of the time might be put right.

5 : Ideas of Order, 1937–1939

'Immediate need of Confucius'

'Am sending you a spot of Confucius,' Pound wrote to Congressman Tinkham in July 1937. What he sent under separate cover could have been any one of a number of items he had then on his desk. There was 'Immediate Need of Confucius', an article he had just written for a Bombay magazine, *Aryan Path*. Or it might have been his 1928 version of the *Ta Hio*, recently republished by Stanley Nott in London. He had described that in the *Aryan Path* article as 'the most valuable work I have done in three decades', valuable, that is, as a remedy for the desperate condition of the Occidental world. Most likely, though, it was his *Confucius/Digest of The Analects*, a small pamphlet published the previous month by Giovanni Schweiller in Milan and consisting of the first chapter of *Guide to Kulchur*. That chapter digests the *Analects* into the *Ta Hio*'s fundamental principle of good government, '*To call people and things by their correct names . . . to see that the terminology [is] exact*'—so that, for instance, 'a man should not be called controller of the currency unless he really controls it'. Precise verbal definition, or complete integrity, as defined in the first chapter of the *Ta Hio*, was now Pound's urgent prescription for the ills of his time.

Guide to Kulchur can be read as an extended doctor's note diagnosing the cause of the disease and recommending the appropriate treatment. It was written rapidly and off the top of his head in just three months, between February and the beginning of May 1937. On the original dust-jacket it was said to be 'a digest of all the wisdom [Pound] has acquired about art and life during the course of fifty years', and to be 'emphatically a book of *wisdom*—a concentration of the "new paideuma"'. At the core of his 'new paideuma', as the first chapter would make clear, was the wisdom of Confucius. Even before he received the contract from Faber & Faber Pound was 'a-sailing into what the Greek flyozzerfers *ain't* by comparison with Kung-fucius'; and at the head of the final chapter he affirmed, 'I believe that the *Ta Hio* is veritably the Great Learning, to be taken with the Odes . . . and the rest of Confucius' teaching.'

What the Greek philosophers lacked was the sense of social responsibility, 'a feeling for the whole people'; and Christian thought was just as bad. 'Plato's *Republic* notwithstanding, the greek philosophers did not feel communal responsibilities ... The sense of coordination, of the individual in a milieu is not in them. Any more than there is a sense of social order in the teachings of the irresponsible protagonist of the New Testament.... The concentration or emphasis on eternity is not social.' Over time an excessive emphasis upon the life and fate of the self-fulfilling individual had led to private greed being valued above public need, to the point where 'Rapacity is the main force in our time in the occident', and the 'hoggers of harvest' have become dominant. In the *Analects*, in absolute contrast, 'you have the main character filled with a sense of responsibility. He and his interlocutors live in a responsible world, they think for the whole social order.' That was the foremost reason for Pound's prescribing for the modern world the Confucian 'way of life' and its 'disposition toward nature and man'.

This thinking for the whole social order was necessarily 'totalitarian', Pound insisted. That is, it involved understanding all 'the processes biological, social, economic now going on, enveloping you as an individual in a social order'. It meant seeing those processes not in isolation but as interactive. And it required the discrimination of the relative value of things, and a perception of their right order. Thomas Jefferson 'had the totalitarian view' in this sense. And Confucius, Pound would say, was 'superior to Aristotle by totalitarian instinct. His thought is ... root volition branching out, the ethical weight is present in every phrase.'

It was precisely within the ancient and traditional written language of Chinese poetry and thought that Pound was seeking the Confucian way of perceiving the world. James Laughlin, while he was with Pound in Rapallo, had noticed that 'Most days after lunch he would go up to his bedroom', lie down with a volume of Morrison's big dictionary propped on a pillow on his stomach, and study ideograms with the help of Morrison's analyses of their components. He was teaching himself to read the characters in the light of Fenollosa's essay on *The Chinese Written Character as a Medium for Poetry*—he had managed to get that 'ars poetica' republished by Nott in 1936. Then in the summer of 1937 when he was in Siena with Olga Rudge he tried the experiment of spending several hours each day studying without the aid of a dictionary Legge's editions of the three classic Confucian texts and of the works of Mencius. Legge did provide both a translation and an exegetical commentary under the Chinese texts, but 'When I disagreed with the crib or was puzzled by it', Pound recorded, 'I had only the look of the characters ... to go on from.' On 4 August he wrote to

Dorothy, who was as usual in England, that he was learning to read in the original, putting in four hours per day with 'one hour on and one [hour] rest'. He told his Japanese correspondent Katue Kitasono that he could 'read a good deal of ideogram (say as much as five year old infant in Japan or China)'. By the 15th he had got through Mencius, 'and started Kung again'; a fortnight later he had 'got to end of Analects on 3rd round'; and a week after that he was beginning on Mencius again. The result of going 'three times through the whole text and having perforce to look at the ideograms and try to work out the unfamiliar ones from their bases' was that he gained 'a better idea of the whole and the unity of the doctrine', and, most valuably, that he had 'the constants', the recurrent characters or components, 'impressed on my eye'.

He wrote up the experiment in an essay published in the *Criterion* the following year. Among the 'constants' impressed on his eye there was the 'sign recurring and again recurring, of the man who stands by his word'; and also the character which combines the human being with the number two, signifying a life lived in relation to others and to the linked pair of earth and heaven, or humanity in its full scope. He saw 'Man, man, man, humanity all over the page'; and 'land and trees'; the 'constant pageant of the sun, of process'; verbs 'meaning CHANGE or MOVE' and 'RENEWAL'; and everywhere a doctrine of action. Mencius was asked, 'What is the scholar's business', and answered in two characters which Legge translated as 'To exalt his aim'. Pound saw in the second character 'the scholar-officer sign, and its base the heart', and read that as *will*, 'definitely Dante's *directio voluntatis*'. 'No one with any visual sense can fail to be affected by the way the strokes move in these characters', he wrote, 'the twisted as evil, the stunted', and 'the radiant' as in 'the bright ideogram for the highest music' or 'the sign of metamorphosis'.

The characters read in this way, as visible signs rather than as sounds, would serve, or so Pound believed, as 'a door into a different modality of thought', into a different way of perceiving and being in the world from that of Western capitalism. It avoided the Western way of thinking in abstractions and indefinite generalizations, and of speaking in words disconnected from anything in particular and so conveying and effecting nothing in particular. The Chinese written character 'abstracts or generalizes in the known concrete', it gives the universal in the particular, so *spring* is 'the sun under the bursting forth of plants', and *male* is 'rice field plus struggle'. Moreover, as in those instances, it represents a world of active relations, 'of things in action and action in things', as Fenollosa put it. Written and read as a poetic language it preserves a direct experience of things and persons as they are, not just in themselves but in their interactions, and that, in Pound's view, is the basis of Confucian wisdom in government.

It meant that 'at no point does the Confucio-Mencian ethic or philosophy splinter and split away from organic nature', as European thought has tended to do. Because its intelligence was rooted in the total process of nature, it honoured all that is alive and growing, and 'was for an economy of abundance'. In government it accepted responsibility for improving the whole social order—in Mencius' words,

an intelligent ruler will regulate the livelihood of the people, so as to make sure that they shall have sufficient to serve their parents, and sufficient wherewith to support their wives and children: that in good years they shall be abundantly satisfied, and in bad years shall escape danger of perishing.

Pound notes that 'Mencius distinguishes a tax from a share', and perceives that 'a fixed tax on grain is in bad years a tyranny, a tithe proper, no tyranny'; also that 'To treat the needy as criminals is not governing decently, it is merely trapping them.'

But these ethical conclusions, Pound hastened to say, were simply what honest men everywhere would come to, if only they saw straight—

The 'Christian virtues' are THERE in the emperors who had responsibility in their hearts and willed the good of the people; who saw that starvation can gnaw through more than the body and eat into the spirit; who saw, above all, that in so far as governing the people went, it begins with a livelihood, and that all talk of morals before that livelihood is attained, is sheer bunkum and rotten hypocrisy.

Implicit there is Pound's judgement that in his world the Christian virtues were not active in government. 'The level of civilisation recorded in these ideograms', he wrote, 'is higher than anything in the near eastern tradition.' He would describe himself indeed as 'the citizen of a chaos which has long lacked a certain code of ideas and perceptions'. And since China's civilization, proceeding always from a Confucian centre, had persisted for over five thousand or so years, and through all 'the alternating periods of order and confusion' of its historic process, it could well be, so Pound hoped, that the West, in studying the illuminating ideograms of Confucius and Mencius, might absorb what it needed to restore its own civilization to sanity.

In a letter to Congressman Tinkham towards the end of November 1937 Pound mentioned that he had been 'spending my spare time on Confusius and Mencius and can read more chinese than I cd/'. Tinkham wrote back, 'I think you are intellectually wise to divert your mind from the present state of affairs by turning to Confucius and Mencius.' Pound showed how little diverted he was by replying, 'Am only doing Mencius because he is more explicit statement of where the Confucian ROOT (Ta Hio) sprouts in economics/ against usury, against tax ramp.' Then in February 1938, wanting to do something useful, he suggested that Tinkham get him over to Harvard or Yale 'to give a few lectures on Confucius and Mencius'. 'With the light of two thousand years of Chinese history', he reassured Tinkham, 'there wd be NO NEED to allude to the present administration.'

Tinkham had referred to 'Great historical events...occurring in the Far east', meaning the Japanese invasion of China—Shanghai had already been captured in November and Nanking fell in December—but Pound showed little or no concern for what was going on in contemporary China. He was more engaged at that moment by the classic anthology of poetry selected by Confucius which he had just received from Katue Kitasono—he had asked for 'a cheap edition' of the Odes in the original, meaning one that was 'good, and clear but not fancy'. Pound's China was a China of the mind, to be discovered only in the ancient writings attributed to Confucius and his followers. Shortly he would condense the Confucian history of China from its legendary first emperors up to about 1776 to make up his next decad of cantos. His translation of the Odes from the original ideograms would come much later, after the looming world war.

Signor Mussolini speaks

The London Morning Post *of 21 August 1937 carried a report of a speech delivered by Signor Mussolini in Palermo the previous day at the conclusion of the naval manoeuvres. Half a million people were massed before him in the Humberto Forum with the Italian fleet in the Bay of Palermo beyond them, and the Duce's words were carried over the water by wireless. Throughout the length and breadth of Italy all activity ceased, buses came to a standstill, shops were closed, and the people crowded around the loudspeakers. The broadcast was transmitted to twelve nations in Europe, to South and Central America, and was translated into eighteen languages. And what Il Duce had to say was that there had been a great misunderstanding over the previous two years in the relations between Britain and Italy, that it was time for more cordial relations with France, and that Italy had no need to heed the League of Nations in Geneva. There was now a new reality to be taken into account, and that was the Berlin–Rome axis.*

To educate

Dorothy wrote from London in September 1937, 'So much prosperity here owing to munitions that Social Credit has sunk to a minimum of members.'

Earlier in the summer, from Nutcombe Heights Hotel in leafy Hindhead, Surrey, she had written, 'The Child has about 700 stamps and knows a lot... Could you write his initials or summat on a small scrap of paper that we could paste into his yellow Kung?' The 'yellow Kung' may have been the Stanley Nott edition of *Ta Hio: The Great Learning*, which was bound in yellow paper boards with a yellow-dust jacket—though Scheiwiller's little book *Confucius/Digest of the Analects* was also in yellow paper wrappers. If it were the *Ta Hio* Omar, now 10, might have wondered about the meaning of certain remarks concerning the relations of sons and fathers, particularly in chapter IX where it is said that 'To govern a state one must first bring order into one's family', and that 'the man who, being incapable of educating his own family, is able to educate other men just doesn't exist'.

Pound was attending to his 12-year-old daughter's education. Towards the end of September he brought her down by train from Bolzano to Venice, with a stopover in Verona, and she would recall him on the steps of the Romanesque church of San Zeno there, 'looking at the bronze doors, and explaining, explaining, focusing his attention on some detail, wondering out loud'. Her own attention, she confessed, had been more on the presents he had bought her, 'a tiny wristwatch and a pair of new shoes'—'bring something beautiful for the signorina', he had told them in the shoe shop.

That autumn she was to enrol as a boarder at a convent school near Florence, the Istituto della Signora Montalve at La Quiete, but in Venice her father 'seemed very eager to educate me himself'. He gave her Heine's *Buch der Lieder* and would have her read to him from it, then take over and read the poems himself, so powerfully that the images became alive and the rhythm unforgettable. To broaden her mind, as she understood at the time, he took her about with him, to the Quirini Stampalia Library, to friends who were painters, musicians, poets, or into 'a long, narrow second-hand book-shop at the end of the Calle Larga'. Some evenings friends came to hear Pound reading his cantos, and while he read there would be an intense stillness, a tableau of the poet and his listeners with only the sound of his voice, but the questions and long arguments that followed bored her. Some afternoons there were concerts, at which her mother played Vivaldi, or she would be practising for an evening concert. There were few idle moments. Even at the Lido there was 'No loafing around on the beach; we were there to swim and to row and it was done with zest and speed.' And on the *vaporetto* to and from the Lido, 'If Babbo and I were alone, he would engage in conversation.' He set her to writing in Italian—which she was still struggling to learn, German being the language of the Pustertal—an account of all she knew about life in Gais. 'It was the content that mattered', he told her, and where she could not find the words in Italian 'he remedied by translating the

"Storie di Gais" into English'. Indeed the proud father typed out his translation and sewed the pages to make a little book, which he sent to T. S. Eliot at Faber & Faber, and to Kitasono who translated 'the charming stories about Tyrol' into Japanese and had them printed in December 1938 in 'the most refined girl's monthly in Japan'. Pound then hoped 'that she wont get a swelled head', and that making her debut in Japan 'will have a civilizing effect on her'. 'School hasn't quite quenched her intelligence,' he told Kitasono, 'But of course impossible to tell whether she will ever be able to write anything again after having been taught Grammar etc/.'

'Then a huge fuss broke out over a missal.' That is, the girls were required to have a Latin–Italian missal, but Mary asked could she have a Latin–German one—she was 'Mary' now—and the nuns ordered one for her, and when it came it turned out to cost 'almost three times as much as the Italian ones'. When Pound, who was paying Mary's fees, received the bill, he wrote to the Mother Superior, 'I take a very grave view of encouraging a child to spend money out of proportion to its probable expectations.' There had been talk of only 30 lire for a missal but this one cost 87 lire—and 'a book at this price is a luxury'—and 'the lack of precise statement will do more to destroy any morality'—and 'You will destroy any respect the child has for religion, if religion or the religious object is associated in the child's mind with an action not scrupulously honest'—and so on. However, after explanations from the Mother Superior and contrition from Mary the Confucian parent was appeased. All was forgiven, but Mary was to pay off the 57 lire in instalments, 'simply to get it into her head that one cannot be careless about 57 lire UNLESS one is much richer than she is'. Two things she should learn, that 'I must always make myself *clear*', and that 'I must not spend money that is not there': 'Education is worth nothing unless one has these two habits.'

In Venice on 29 October 1937, under the title 'Omaggio ad Antonio Vivaldi', Olga Rudge, with Giorgio Levi and David Nixon, performed a programme composed entirely of music from *L'estro armonico*, something that had probably not happened, Pound remarked, 'since the days when Vivaldi himself conducted'. A Vivaldi Society was formed in Venice soon after, and Pound, noting this in *Il Mare*, pointed out that his Rapallo study group had been 'the first to seek a revival of Vivaldi's music'. And now, Olga Rudge reported, David Nixon was agitating to start an international Vivaldi society, with headquarters in Paris and herself as honorary secretary.

The 'Tigullian Musical Season' for 1938 was opened by the New Hungarian Quartet on 21 January, with Honegger's Quartet on the programme, along with Mozart, 'Quartet to be decided', Stravinsky's 'Concertino', and a quartet by the unfamiliar Hungarian composer Sandor Veress. Then,

'Starting [Tuesday] February 1 and continuing all week', according to Pound's announcement in *Il Mare*, 'there will be a concert every evening, presenting twelve sonatas by Purcell contrasted and compared with music by Debussy and Hindemith, and with references to the important forms of the concerto as conceived by Vivaldi, and of the sonata as envisioned by Mozart'. The aim was 'to present "the concept of the sonata for strings and keyboard" as it developed in the mind of Henry Purcell (1659–1695), who was among the finest English composers, a great unknown for us, equalled perhaps only by Dowland and Jenkins'. The Purcell sonatas had just been 'brought to light' and published in Paris by W. Gillies Whittaker, and this might well have been their first modern performance. The performers would be the usual distinguished local talent, 'Olga Rudge and maestro Sansoni, violins' and 'the fine cellist Marco Ottone from Chiavari'. In the place of Gerhart Münch, however, he having decided at the last minute to remain in Germany, there would be the pianist Renata Borgatti, 'the daughter of our distinguished fellow citizen Commendatore Giuseppe', a famed Italian tenor. Pound, as William Atheling, had found her a 'wooden' accompanist to Olga Rudge back in 1920, but she had become a successful soloist performing throughout Europe, and Pound in an article in *Il Mare* had now nothing but praise for her 'consistent development in musical understanding and intelligence'. She would be the pianist and Olga Rudge's accompanist in both this season and the next and last in 1939.

Meanwhile, since Münch could not come to Rapallo, Pound gave him a 'PLAN of work' to follow in Germany. 'The first thing you do ANYWHERE shd/ be to LOOK at the catalog/ of local library... and make note of manuscripts and old edtns/ of Vivaldi in it (if any)'—'That ought to be first act after dumping luggage in hotel'. In Dresden he was to work direct on the manuscripts, going on from what he and Olga already had on film, so 'Start next on page 160.' Vera, whom Münch had just married, could do a lot if he were busy with other matters, for instance, she could 'Look up and report to me on Leica reading machines | is there a cheap portable one.' 'The day is 24 hours long//,' this letter concluded.

Pound seems to have organized the whole Rapallo show himself, securing the musicians, doing the advance publicity and the programmes, writing up the concerts afterwards, no doubt making sure the Amici remembered the dates, then welcoming them on the evening, taking the money of those who were not subscribers, and sharing the takings among the performers. He was in every sense the animator of the season. At the same time, the regular concerts relied absolutely on Olga Rudge and her violin. But we are given another image of her dedication. After each concert she would return by herself in the dark up the hill to Sant' Ambrogio, a climb that could take an hour. The cobbled mule-track was too stony for town shoes, and, doing as the peasant women did when they had been into town, she would put on the old espadrilles she had hidden at the foot of the *salita* on the way down, sling the violin-case on a strap over her shoulder, and carrying her 'high-heeled golden or satin shoes and a music case in one hand and holding up the long evening gown with the other', she would make her way by such light as came up from Rapallo or from the night sky. 'Gee, I am tired sometimes,' she said once to Mary, and 'It's awful when it rains, the violin is so sensitive.'

On the Saturday of the Purcell week a Debussy sonata for violin and piano was preceded by a study hour examining the use of microfilm in researching and making available unpublished music. Pound saw, well ahead of the professional musicologists and music publishers, that the new microphotography made possible accurate and inexpensive reproduction and diffusion of the 'enormous quantities of musical treasures still buried in libraries'. In June 1938 he told Agnes Bedford that he had 'another 600 pages of Vivaldi' on film from Germany. He persuaded the editor of *Broletto*, a monthly magazine published in Como, to publish a complete Vivaldi concerto 'in small half-tones taken from "microfoto" Leica films'. He tried to persuade Faber & Faber to become the first in the field by publishing Olga Rudge's *Vivaldi: A Preliminary Survey*, 'with five or six inedited Vivaldis in photostat', and a thematic catalogue which would do for Vivaldi what Köchel had done for Mozart. 'The new process will OF NECESSITY revolutionize music publication,' he urged, but Mr Eliot was cautious. Even the assurance that 'there is bound to be a Vivaldi BOOM' did not convince him. So Pound presented his microfilm copies of the Dresden manuscripts to Siena's Count Guido Chigi Saracini in 1938, and they provided the scores for the performance of unpublished Vivaldi in the 1939 Settimana Musicale Senesi. Then after the war, in 1949 and 1950, Olga Rudge edited for the Accademia Musicale Chigiana two neat books presenting four and two concertos in photo-facsimile of Vivaldi's manuscript. That was when microfilm was finally catching on.

In May 1938 Pound was urging Katue Kitasono to get in touch with the US Government's Science Service with a view to making available on microfilm 'the 100 best ideogramic and japanese texts IN THE ORIGINAL'; and at the same time he was himself doing what he could 'to stir up the Washington people both about music study and oriental studies by means of this new system'. 'It will encourage them to hear from Japan', he wrote, 'and of course collaboration between the two governments should follow. Here is a field where there can be no clash of interests, and where better understanding between the two peoples wd/ be automatically promoted.'

Kitasono (1902–78), an important modernist poet in Japan and the founder and editor of the avant-garde magazine *VOU*, had first written to Pound in 1936 as, 'since Imagism movement', 'a leader on new literature'. In his reply Pound, as if to make clear how far he had come since his *Imagiste* days, had remarked that 'a poet can not neglect ethics', and had wondered if Gesell was yet known in Tokyo along with Douglas. 'Two things I should do before I die', he wrote, 'and they are to contrive a better understanding between the U.S.A. and Japan, and between Italy and Japan.' He followed this up by saying that 'neither Zen nor Christianity can serve toward international understanding in practical action in the way the *Ta Hio* of Kung fu Tseu can... [T]hat gives us a basis of ethics & of national <patriotic> action, which does not produce international discord.' It must have appeared to him that since Japan had taken over the ancient Chinese written language they should also share the Confucian culture which he found in it. But Kitasono was more interested in developing a Japanese form of Dada and surrealism than in the ethics of China's Confucius, or even in Japan's own Noh.

As a practical act Pound had had Kitasono arrange for a letter of introduction to be sent on his behalf to the Japanese Ambassador in Rome, and he himself wrote to the Ambassador to say how glad he would be 'to meet any member of the Embassy... who is interested in improving the understanding of Japanese culture in Europe and America and arranging better methods for mutual cultural comprehension'. That had led to a three-hour talk when he was in Rome at the end of December 1936 with a 'Councillor of the Embassy'—'Naturally we had too many things to discuss to do anything very thoroughly,' he told Kitasono. But he would try to have published in England the 'Councillor's' book in English on Japanese poetry; and he would send him his *ABC of Reading*, 'and perhaps he will approve of it as a text book to introduce Japanese students to western literature'. Nothing came of either possibility, but in the way of cultural exchange *VOU* was publishing some of Pound's poems and essays, and Pound did manage to get a selection of poems by the *VOU* group published in translation in Ronald Duncan's *Townsman* in January 1938 and later in Laughlin's *New Directions* anthology.

Pound made that the occasion to write again to the Japanese Embassy in Rome hoping for a more significant exchange through the use of 'The new microphotographic and photostat process... [which] opens a totally new possibility for bilingual texts'. And a year later, in May 1939, in the first of a dozen articles he would contribute to the *Japan Times and Mail*, he respectfully asked that the Japanese Society for Promoting International Cultural exchange should consider commissioning 'a bilingual or trilingual edition of the hundred best books of Japanese and ideogramic literature', the latter 'taken direct from works of master calligraphers'. With micro-photography the edition could be produced commercially 'at the same price as the Loeb library of Greek and Latin texts'. Further, all the Noh plays, 'a treasure like nothing we have in the Occident', could be made available on film, 'or at any rate the best Noh music could be registered on sound-track'. In effect he was proposing a programme for the as yet uncreated UNESCO, and resolutely promoting his idea of a common Oriental culture above the ongoing war between Japan and China. When Kitasono mentioned in February 1939 that 'Two young poets from VOU have gone to the front', Pound's response was to write about the importance of filming and recording the Noh plays, and about 'my chinese Cantos/ now on desk', and that he wanted 'a translation of the ECONOMIC volume of the Chinese encyclopedia'.

Anschluss

The Anschluss, the union of Austria with Germany, was effected in March 1938. In January Rudolf Hess, Hitler's deputy, had initialled a plan for the very opposite of a modus vivendi between the two nations: Austrian Nazis were to stage an open revolt and in the ensuing disorder the German Army would be ordered into Austria to prevent 'German blood being shed by Germans'. In February and March Schussnigg, the Austrian Chancellor and head of a one-party right-wing dictatorship which had suppressed Austria's Social Democrats, was put under extreme pressure by Hitler to resign in favour of a pro-Nazi member of his government—in effect to hand over the govern-ment to its Nazi element as the price of avoiding bloodshed. When he played for time in a vain effort to preserve Austria's independence Hitler issued an instant ultimatum, upon which he resigned, the Austrian Nazis took over the Chancellery and the streets of Vienna, and Hitler ordered the invasion which met no resistance. A telegram was then forged requesting Germany's military assistance and thus cloaking the takeover in a spurious legality. On 12 March Hitler was received with enthusiasm in Linz, his home town, where he declared that he had fulfilled a solemn mission 'to restore my dear homeland to the German Reich'. On the 13th he declared himself President of Austria, and at the same time reduced it to a mere province of the Reich. 'Unreliable elements' were immediately rounded up by Himmler's Gestapo, as many as 80,000 in Vienna alone; persecution of Jews began at once, and a special office was set up by Heydrich's SS under Karl Adolf Eichmann to seize and administer their property—Baron Louis de Rothschild's palace was looted but he was allowed to leave Vienna in return for handing over his steel mills to the Hermann Goering Works; a huge concentration camp was set up at Mauthausen; Dr Schacht arrived to take over the National Bank on behalf of the Reichsbank and to make its staff swear an oath to be faithful and obedient to the Führer. Through all this Great Britain, France, and the League of Nations scarcely murmured a protest. Hitler was more anxious that Mussolini might be moved again to protect Austria's independence, but to his immense relief Il Duce let it be known that it was no longer of concern to him. A plebiscite staged by the Nazis in April returned a 99.75 per cent vote in favour of the union with Germany.

Going wrong, thinking of rightness

> 'you are NOT to concede anything to my follies prejudices and partialities'
> —EP to Montgomery Butchart, 12 December 1938

For relaxation in the summer of 1938 Pound played tennis in Rapallo, six or even eight sets on some days. In Siena, in Olga's apartment in the Palazzo Capoquadri, he transcribed Vivaldi scores, 'copying out the Dresden concerti ... note by note' from the microfilms with the aid of a magnifying glass, 'and being pleased by the quality of Vivaldi's mind therein apparent'. His idea of relaxing could include going through Binyon's translation of the *Purgatorio* 'with a microscope' and advising on fine shades of meaning and on how a thing might be said more naturally. Another kind of amusement came from Faber & Faber's deciding that a number of passages in *Guide to Kulchur* were libellous or scurrilous and must be excised or put more politely. Eliot sent him a copy of the book, which had already been printed and bound, in which he had marked the banned passages—names were not to be named, and offensive things were not to be said of *The Times* or the Church of England, or of other British institutions such as Rudyard Kipling. Nor might he call Hardy's sisters 'his stinking old sisters' and 'aged hens' on account of their saying after his death 'that they hadn't thought it quite nice for him to write novels', a remark which Pound regarded as 'savage and degraded', and an indication of why no civilized man would have wanted to immigrate into the England Hardy had had to live in. He left a considerable blank space in the middle of p. 286 to show where that passage had been cut out. In August Dorothy wrote, 'Omar says you haven't written to him for 18 months and please will you?', and he did write. Dorothy was thinking of leaving the boy, now 12, with Mrs Dickie and at his present day school for another two years, since 'he is not yet very grown up for his age'.

In their letters that summer there was a lot about a new Fascist attitude to Jews in Italy. In July Dorothy wrote, 'Daily Mirror (vile—low—) says M. has turned jew-baiter', and 'Pope reported to be versus Muss. re Jews? Sure to be only half right in Eng. Papers.' Ezra wrote back, 'A consciousness of racial difference is appearing in It. Press.'. 'Is the Pope opposing racial purity?', Dorothy insisted. Pound sent a cutting from a French newspaper with a report from Castel Gondolfo, the Pope's summer residence, that he 'again and emphatically condemns racism and extreme nationalism, and regrets that Italy should be imitating Germany'. Mussolini's response, as reported in another cutting from an Italian newspaper, was that Italian Fascism was not *imitating* anyone.

It does appear that the race laws being introduced in Italy were Fascism's own and quite distinct from those of Nazi Germany. Indeed Dorothy Pound was quite mistaken in thinking they were concerned with racial purity—that idea meant nothing either to Mussolini or to most Italians. Under the new laws if either parent were not Jewish then a person was to be deemed non-Jewish, exactly the contrary of the Nazi laws. Mussolini's concern was for the political and social purity of the Fascist state, and the laws were directed against those suspected of maintaining a separate, non-Fascist or anti-Fascist, identity. They were directed particularly against Italy's 50,000 Jews, but not so much for being Jewish as for not being Fascist, or not Fascist enough. Jews were thought liable to have international loyalties, to 'World Jewry', or to be Zionists working for a Jewish state, or to be Communists obedient to the Comintern—there were many anti-Fascist Italian Jews in the International Brigades supporting the Republican side in Spain. Again, Jews were identified as typical members of the bourgeoisie, which had been condemned by Mussolini as 'a spiritual enemy of the Fascist faith' on account of its putting individual interests before those of the corporate state. All those who set themselves apart from the Fascist project were to be subject to what Mussolini called 'a policy of segregation'. That would mean that 8,000 Jewish refugees from Nazism must leave Italy; that over 5,000 Jewish school and university students would be excluded from state education—though those already enrolled at universities might continue their studies—and that 180 of their teachers would be dismissed; that Jews would be banned from the professions of law, medicine, journalism, and from owning large businesses or more than fifty hectares of land; that 400 government employees would lose their jobs—though not their pension rights; and that 7,000 Jews would be expelled from the armed services. At the same time 'loyal' Jews, 'Jews of Italian citizenship ... who have unquestionable military or civil merits', in Mussolini's words, would 'find understanding and justice'. Italian Jews who were over 65, or who had married an Italian before 1 October 1938, or who had fought for Italy in the First World War or in Ethiopia or Spain, or who had been a Fascist of the first hour between 1919 and 1922, would be exempt from the new laws. And 'a Jew could embrace the Fascist faith, convert to Fascism', and so be exempt, though there must be no pressure upon them to recant their Jewish faith. Freedom of worship was to continue unchanged; elementary and secondary schools for Jews were to be permitted; and Jewish communities might continue their activities. Strictly speaking, then, Fascism's 'race laws' were not racist. In their application, in the alienation and persecution of Jews and in depriving them of certain fundamental rights, they were inhumane; and in being directed specifically against Jews they were certainly anti-Semitic. Yet this was not the endemic anti-Semitism based on racial and religious prejudice which Hitler was carrying to its extreme in Germany and Austria. It would be the Nazis, not the Fascists, who would send Italy's Jews to the concentration camps.

In their reactions to the new laws Pound and Dorothy were far more anti-Semitic than most Fascists and than Italians in general. Throughout August Pound was telling Dorothy about the regular flow in the Italian press 'of excellent and sober stuff about jews', about their 'living ON us, not with us'. Calm, reasonable, irrefutable analysis, he thought it, though coming out 'like it has been bottled from good manners and everybody relieved to let fly'. At the beginning of September he greeted the new laws in a spirit of simple anti-Semitism: 'Waaal all yits wot come to Italy after 1919 iss to leave in six months | and to get OUT. and all yitts is not to be in Italian schools and in scientif/ bodies etc./ ... It is looking THOROUGH.' He had just heard from Gerhart Münch, now in good standing with the Nazis in Germany, how 'DEElighted' he was by the news. Münch, just then resting at Lake Garda, had written that his daily enjoyment was reading in the Italian newspapers about the turn 'the jewish Problem' was taking in Italy, 'so much cleverer than in Germany'. Dorothy wrote from London, 'Lots today [2 September] in papers re Jews being expelled. What a day of Judgement.' Pound was to tell a Jewish friend in Venice, according to one report, 'I am sorry for you, but they have done the right thing.' In fact he sometimes thought, in line with an earlier Fascist statement, that it would be best for all Jews to be removed from western Europe and resettled somewhere out of the way—not in Arab Palestine, possibly in Poland and Roumania 'where they touch Russia'.

Lina Caico protested to Pound, 'What are Jews to do? Suicide en masse?' He should tell 'every single Italian that you meet that he is no Christian if he allows the Jews to be driven out of Italy'. Pound replied that she should wake up to the real cause of anti-Semitism, 'Get down to USURY/ the cause WHY western man vomits out the Jew periodically.' Moreover 'the JEW wont take responsibility for civic order . . . JEW parasite on principle', and it was necessary to 'Segregate/ Quarantine/' as 'defence against parasites', and in order to resist usury. In fact, in Fascist Italy, Jews were quite fully represented among those responsible for its civic order; and as banking and finance were controlled by the Fascist state there was no grand usury to be resisted. The new laws were indeed directed against those who could be perceived as parasites, but for the rest Pound was airing his own prejudices and not attending to what was actually the case in Italy. In the early months of 1939 Lina Caico told him frankly what she thought wrong with him: 'when you have seen the value of some fact clearly it keeps you from seeing the value of subsequent events. You are beclouded by your past vision. That's your way in politics. Because you saw that something was good, you see everything perfect.' And conversely, she implied, when he saw that something was wrong, he would see only evil. So, because some Jews were usurious bankers, though not in Italy, all Jews were to be banished, even from Italy.

In 'The Revolution Betrayed', an article in the *British Union Quarterly* earlier in 1938, Pound had argued that the Jeffersonian process in America, so grievously betrayed in the nineteenth century, was being betrayed now by Roosevelt's 'aryio-kike' advisers, all of them steeped in the 'semitic poison', usury. The harm done 'by Jewish finance to the English race in America', he declared, was such that 'the expulsion of the two million Jews in New York would not be an excessive punishment'. 'A race', he wrote, 'may be held responsible for its worst individuals.' Moreover, the Jews would have only themselves to blame, having brought anti-Semitism upon themselves. That was blaming the victim; worse, it was a variant form of scapegoating—not one for the sins of all, but all for the sins of a few. And worst, it was holding the Jewish race responsible for the sins of all usurers, of whatever race. The trick there was in identifying usury as a 'semitic poison', and in 'aryio-kike', a term pretending to indicate Aryan, or non-Jewish usurers, while actually conveying anti-Semitic prejudice.

Pound was now more or less overtly dealing in that prejudice and seeking to direct it. In October 1938, in a letter in *Action*, another publication of the British Union of Fascists, he wrote,

It will be a great pity if the present wave of anti-Semitism is allowed to end in the mere beating up of a few block-headed yids in the London ghetto. It will be a great pity if the indignation isn't persistent enough to REACH the damned gold-breakers whether Hebrew or Quaker or lickspittle Anglican.

Pound must have known that the Blackshirt thugs who were beating up Jews in the East End of London were not after usurers, nor after Quaker and Anglican bankers. That is twisted thinking in twisty language, with *It will be a great pity* and *the indignation* masking an endorsement of racist thuggery. This is not straight naming, it is the technique of propaganda and of rabble-rousing, and a calculated attempt to convert racist violence, Nazi-influenced anti-Semitism, into an attack on usurers.

Another contribution to *Action*, this one in June 1938, is evidence that Pound knew what he was doing. Having noted that international usury was not entirely Jewish, and that indeed there was more Calvinism than Judaism in it, and that the Calvinist was more dangerous and deadly than the Jew, he then remarked that it was more difficult to stir up mob violence against the Calvinist than against the Jew; and further, that it had been Hitler's stroke of genius in *Mein Kampf* to find the language needed and effective to rouse the German people into turning upon their enemies, that is, upon usurious financiers. Since the dynamic of *Mein Kampf* was the most rabid and paranoid anti-Semitism, it would appear that Pound was approving and seeking to follow Hitler's insight, 'that one could not get at the masses with arguments, proofs and knowledge but only with feelings and beliefs'. He was willing to deploy anti-Semitism strategically to rouse the victims of usury to action by fear and terror of 'the Jew'.

Pound had dedicated *Guide to Kulchur* 'To | LOUIS ZUKOFSKY | and | BASIL BUNTING | strugglers | in the desert', and in November Zukofsky told Pound that he was finding it hard to get past his sentence praising Wyndham Lewis's discovery of Hitler in 1931 as superior to his own discovery of Mussolini. Pound hadn't made it clear that it was Lewis's picking out a sentence on *Leihkapital* from *Mein Kampf* that had so impressed him, and for Zukofsky Hitler was simply 'the German terror'. Pound responded, 'Why curse Adolphe/ why not git down to bedrock/ NESCHEK and the buggering vendetta of the shitten Rothschild which has run for 150 years/ and is now flopping back on Jewry at large.' There was more, to the effect that because the Jews would do nothing about the Rothschilds and *neschek* generally they were digging their own graves. Bunting was in New York in December, saw the letter, and made it the occasion for breaking with Pound. In clear and direct terms he wrote that his spewing out 'anti-semite bile' to Zukofsky was unforgivable, an abomination:

You know as well as any man that a Jew has the same physique and a similar amount of grey matter as the rest of us. You know as well as any man that to hold one man guilty of the sins of another is an abomination. You know as well as any man that the non-jews have contributed their fair share, or more than their fair share, of the bankers and other millionaires of doubtful honesty. You have the relevant facts without any need of information that cannot be found in Italy. I can find no excuse, no way of considering your activities as anything else than wilful and thought-out perversion of what you know to be true.

... It makes me sick to see you covering yourself with that kind of filth. It is not an arguable question, has not been arguable for at least nineteen centuries. Either you know men to be men, and not something less, or you make yourself an enemy of mankind at large.

Pound was unaffected. 'Dear Zuk', he wrote in January 1939, 'Lot of hot steam from Bzl/ amounts to saying that I am a shit because I won't regard a SYMPTOM as a cause ... The ROOT is avarice.... The outbreaks of [anti-Semitic] violence are mere incomprehension/ like inarticulate violent language.' And he went on justifying his own deployment of verbally violent anti-Semitism along his usual lines, arguing that it was a reaction to usury, that its cause was Semitic banking practices, and that Jews, even if they were not themselves usurers, nevertheless deserved to be attacked for doing nothing to prevent usury.

Zukofsky's attitude was that there was no use arguing with Pound. His politics were a mess, he told him, so 'let's not correspond about politics'. As for his anti-Semitism, 'I believe you're no more anti- than Marx himself, tho' the cluttered mess of the rest of your economic & political thinking makes it appear so.' Zukofsky had long been in the line of fire of Pound's anti-Semitic invective and was as well placed as anyone to pass judgement. Other Jewish friends would share his conviction that Pound was not personally anti-Semitic. Carlo Izzo would resolve the apparent impossibility of Pound's being both anti-Semitic and yet not anti-Semitic by viewing Pound's anti-Semitism as not personal but 'almost ludicrously theoretical ... Aldo Camerino was a Jew and yet Pound held him in great esteem.' It was to Camerino that Pound had said, in Izzo's presence, 'they have done the right thing'. Those best placed to judge, then, would not dispute Pound's claim, in *Purpose* in 1938, 'I am not anti-semite', while they would say, as Izzo did, that they detested his politics. And Bunting was right about what Pound was doing in his journalism and correspondence—he was guilty of practising anti-Semitism there. In his one-man crusade against usury he was, while thinking of rightness, going wrong, terribly and tragically wrong.

Czechoslovakia sacrificed

With Austria annexed, Hitler was determined that Czechoslovakia should be next to fall to the Reich, and this time Britain and France, in their anxiety to appease him, acted as his enforcers. Czechoslovakia, a creation of the peace settlement following the 1914–18 war, had a mixed population of Czechs,

Slovaks, German-speaking Sudetens, Hungarians, and Ruthenians. In spite of its minorities, under its founders Tomáš Masaryk and Eduard Beneš it was, in the words of the contemporary American journalist William Shirer, 'the most democratic, progressive, enlightened and prosperous state in Central Europe'. In the 1930s, however, Nazi Germany had been covertly encouraging the German-speaking Sudetens to demand autonomy and to create violent disturbances so that Hitler could invade, as he had invaded Austria, under cover of going to the aid of oppressed and endangered fellow Germans. When in May 1938 the Czechoslovak government under President Beneš mobilized its forces to resist an invasion Hitler was infuriated and gave orders for his army and air force to be ready to invade and to destroy the Czechoslovak state on 2 October. Britain and France had treaty obligations to defend that country's independence. At the same time Neville Chamberlain, now the British Prime Minister, and Édouard Daladier, the French Premier, desperate to avoid another war in Europe, believed they could buy peace by giving in to Hitler's demands. Chamberlain, who could see no British interest at stake in the fate of Czechoslovakia, made light of the crisis, describing it in parliament as 'a quarrel in a faraway country between people of whom we know nothing'. On 29 September Chamberlain and Daladier met with Hitler and Mussolini in Munich to settle the affair— Czechoslovakia was excluded from the meeting—and they agreed that the German army should march into the Sudetenland on 1 October and complete its occupation by the 10th. Non-German Czechs were to be evacuated at once, leaving behind all their goods and property, even their cows; and all natural resources, industries, railways, public buildings, etc. would pass to Germany without compensation. What remained of Czechoslovakia, they said, they would protect against unprovoked aggression. The next morning before flying home Chamberlain secured Hitler's signature on a sheet of paper declaring that the Munich Agreement was 'symbolic of the desire of our two peoples never to go to war with one another again'. Back in London he waved the piece of paper from a window of no. 10 Downing Street and told the cheering crowd that he had secured 'peace with honour', 'peace for our time'. President Beneš was told that if he did not submit to the Munich terms Britain and France would now back Hitler in the use of armed force. About the time in the afternoon of 30 September 1938 when Chamberlain was proclaiming as a noble victory the abandonment and betrayal of Czechoslovakia, Czechoslovak radio announced the country's surrender, 'under protest to the world'. 'We have been forced into this situation', the Czechoslovak Foreign Minister told the British and French ministers who were enforcing Hitler's terms; 'today it is our turn, tomorrow it will be the turn of others'.

Comings and goings

The Times of London reported on 5 October that Anthony Eden approved of what Chamberlain had done at Munich, and also that Chamberlain himself had paid a handsome tribute to Signor Mussolini for his part in the saving of the peace. Pound noted these facts in his next article in the *New English Weekly*, and added his own approving comment that 'Chamberlain is the FIRST British statesman to inspire any respect on the continent since 1918'. He went on to write, 'War against Germany would have meant war against a clean concept of money'. That was his remarkable view of what was now at issue, not Hitler's seizure and spoliation of Czechoslovakia, not that country's loss of its freedom and independence, not the threat to other European countries from the militarization and mounting belligerence of Nazi Germany, and not the betrayals of free nations by Britain and France in the vain hope of appeasing Hitler's lust for conquest. 'If ever war is made against Germany in our time', he insisted over the editor's protest in the Chicago *Delphian Quarterly*, 'it will be a war against this conception of MONEY'—that was a concept going back, as he explained in the *British Union Quarterly*, to 'the Monte dei Paschi's "abundance of nature and responsibility of the whole people"'. That is what Hitler and his Germany meant to Pound in the autumn of 1938, simply 'a clean concept of money'.

He made a fairly clear statement of where he stood politically at this time in a contribution to *Fascist Europe/Europa Fascista*, an Anglo-Italian symposium published under the auspices of the National Institute of Fascist Culture at Pavia in October 1938. There was the Confucian basis: 'a ruler promotes the peace of the world by the good government of his own country.' Then there was the current imperative: 'unless the root economic evils are tackled and eradicated there can be neither peace between nations nor justice within them.' And the enemy was ignorance, 'ignorance of the nature of money, its source and its mode of issue'—an ignorance which allowed the cancer of usury to spread from New York and from London. Against it Pound invoked the Fascist Corporate State, with this exceptional qualification, 'My understanding of the *Corporate State* can not be made clear unless I carry the reader back into the Tuscany of Pietro Leopoldo and Ferdinando III in the period that preceded Napoleon'—in short, he implied, see his *Fifth Decad of Cantos* with its celebration of the responsible use of 'the abundance of nature' for the benefit of the whole people. That spirit he saw at work in Mussolini's battle to harvest more grain and to ensure its equitable distribution. 'And when that spirit unites with the spirit behind [Hitler's] words on *Leihkapital*'—a singular take on the Axis—then 'we approach a new Europe', and a new *paideuma*.[1]

At that point in his article Pound turned to consider a role for himself in the development of a Fascist Europe. Perhaps he could have none, since 'It is no longer up to us, a handful of highbrow propagandists'; and anyway, while 'I can make blue prints and plans as well as the next man...I have probably no talent at all for getting the mass of mankind to accept them'. But then again, if asked, he would know how to start organizing a *fascio* or *sindicato* of 'men of my own profession', artists and writers who shared the dream of the new *paideuma* and who would spread abroad its germinal ideas. One senses there not only a willingness but a yearning to be head-hunted into the Fascist project. That was followed, though, by a counter-assertion of the prerogatives of the artist. 'The "new Paideuma",' he declared, 'the new cosmos of "culture", in the sense of the best standards of writing, of sculpture, of scholarship, is now the dream of a few dozen intellects'—that would imply that the new *paideuma* was those intellects' own vision of Fascism, as distinct from what the Fascist party might say and do. 'As poet', Pound went on, 'I have a perfect right to my preconceptions, to my projects.' Those, however, he added, quickly bridging over the possible difference, 'are certainly not independent of social organization'. Exactly what that might mean was left to the reader's speculation. All in all, one might make out that Pound was uncertain about his role as a 'highbrow propagandist'; that he did want to be recognized as a poet, an artist among artists; and that he did want to have a part in creating a Fascist Europe, only as a poet and according to his own very special vision of Fascism.

He evidently believed that he could maintain his independence and integrity as a poet, and that he could maintain even his own vision of Fascism, within a political system which demanded the total subordination of the individual citizen to the state. That he was a foreigner, and that his poetry was in English, must have helped him get away with that. And then the regime did allow him to put over his own idea of Fascism in his propaganda—on condition perhaps that he was otherwise uncritical of it. But how could he take his personal stand upon the right of the individual poet to his own preconceptions and projects while remaining undisturbed by the denial of that right to the people he lived among? The explanation is

---

[1] The words Pound had in mind were apparently these from *Mein Kampf* (1924): 'Der Kampf gegen das internationale Finanz und Leihkapital ist zum wichtigsten Programmpunkt'—'War on international finance and LOAN CAPITAL becomes the most weighty etc. in the struggle towards freedom'. (Cited and translated by EP in a note, 'The Nazi Movement in Germany', one of a set of 'Communications', *Townsman* 2.6 (Apr. 1939) 13.)

perhaps in the word 'poet', in the idea of the artist as having the capacity and the need to exercise an unfettered freedom of mind while the mass of the people, lacking his creativity, need to be guided and led by the poet's vision. It seems certain that he was indulging the delusion that by his cantos he could shape the Axis towards the ideal Europe of his dream.

In the autumn of 1938 and into 1939 Pound was working on the next two blocks of exemplary history cantos, those dealing with China and with John Adams of the American Revolution. Their composition was interrupted in October 1938 by his having to go to London following the death of Olivia Shakespear. He had scarcely arrived in Venice to be with Olga and Mary when a telegram came from Dorothy to say that her mother had died on the 2nd—Dorothy herself was in bed with a temperature of 102° and quite unable to travel. Mary remembered Olga's being 'animated and indignant' at Pound's leaving them, while he 'struck his characteristic pose: hands deep in trouser pockets balancing on toes and heels, looking straight ahead of him toward the window, lips tightly closed'. He had to go to clear out Olivia's flat and dispose of her possessions, now Dorothy's, and that was that. Entries in Dorothy's diary indicate that in fact he did not go straight to London, but stopped over in Rapallo from the 5th to the 17th, presumably to look after her. In a note to Olga on the 13th Pound wrote, 'gotta start on Canto 61 or thereabahts/ i;e; wot is ter follow the chinKantos'.

Olivia had treasured Omar's childish things—his first tooth, a Teddy bear—and Dorothy, asked 'What to do with Teddy', wrote, 'Oh… Cremate.' She was also 'against letters being kept', and Ezra should tear up Omar's to his grandmother. But 'For goodness sake', she told him, 'tip the Child 5/- when he leaves you—and look at his school report'. Omar, now 12, would enrol as a boarder at Charterhouse. Pound was inviting his friends to carry off Olivia's books and furniture 'on ridiculously generous terms, if any', according to Henry Swabey. Pound gave Swabey a Gaudier charcoal drawing and an Ovid in Latin, and offered him 'a number of books' at '10/- the lot'. Wyndham Lewis was seen by a policeman carrying home a chair on his head one midnight and stopped upon suspicion of theft. Ronald Duncan and his wife went away with their 'pockets bulging with Chinese ivory and jade, fish knives and forks', and with 'an inscribed copy of Yeats's poems…and a stool ornamented with quotations from Virgil'. Dorothy asked Ezra to 'bring her back some thing of her new possessions', and he did arrange, even after being so liberal with them, to have 13 cases of Olivia's things shipped to Rapallo.

Duncan (1914–82), a young poet, playwright, and opera librettist, was the editor—with much advice and encouragement from Pound—of *Townsman*, a lively small quarterly distantly modelled on Eliot's grander

Criterion. He had visited Ghandi in India and was a member of the Peace Pledge Union, and Pound involved him, along with Swabey and J. P. Angold, in discussions of economic matters and international peace. Neville Chamberlain had 'acted as the leader of Europe', he told them. Because he knew Benjamin Britten and theatre people Duncan was able to arrange for a Noh play to be attempted one afternoon in the Mercury Theatre, with a musician playing gongs, a dancer, and Pound reading the words. In the sparse audience were Lewis and Eliot—Pound was spending time with both of them.

Lewis had recently done a portrait of Eliot—the one the Royal Academy refused to exhibit, and which the Tate Gallery declined to purchase—and now Pound sat for him. He would swagger in, Lewis recalled, 'coat-tails flying', fling himself 'at full length into my best chair', adjust his leonine mane to the cushioned chair top, close his eyes, gruffle 'Go to it Wyndham!', and remain silent and motionless 'for two hours by the clock'. Lewis reflected that it was as if he had exhausted his aggressive vitality for the moment and had just dropped; but in his painting there is no relaxation, the reclining figure is tense, and there is concentrated energy in the still head with its closed but unsleeping eyes. It took Lewis some time to decide what to put in on the left to balance the strong diagonal of the figure, and in the end it was some folded newspapers on a small table against an expanse of blue-green sea, as if to suggest the scope of his subject's mind and its immediate preoccupations. This portrait the Tate did take.

There was a last meeting with Yeats who gave a dinner for Pound at the Athenaeum. Yeats's health was failing—he would die at the end of January—but he was cheered by his old antagonist telling him that his recent poems were 'rather good' which, from Pound he felt, was 'rapturous applause'.

Pound was looking up other old friends—Violet Hunt, Agnes Bedford, Joseph Bard—and meeting political contacts. Someone who had been in the secret service told him that 'he cd/ buy any of the big politicians EXCEPT Chamberlain', and that he 'had the dope on ALL the communist leaders . . . definitely paid by Russia for military espionage'. He heard Oswald Mosley speak at a public meeting in Lewisham, and later attacked the BBC in *Action* for keeping off the air what he had said about Chamberlain, apparently that he was not 'a moral coward'. When they met, Mosley was surprised to find Pound 'a vivacious, bustling and practical person', 'exactly the opposite of what I expected from the abstruse genius of his poetry'. Pound had the idea of telling Chamberlain in person 'what he was headed for', but missed a phone call—possibly from the Prime Minister's office.

Olga Rudge meanwhile was feeling increasingly put out by his giving up to disposing of his mother-in-law's furniture the precious time he was to have spent with Mary and herself in Venice. At the end of October she calculated that 'in 13 years the L'cna has had the benefit of His company for say 3 weeks all told'; and as for herself, 'This one feels that the best years of her life have been spent in solitary confinement out of consideration for His family's feelings—and she feels it is the limit to be sacrificed now to their furniture.' A couple of days later she exploded at his 'damn unfair' treatment of her, 'that He should always have her front door key and come and go as He likes and she never has His'. Then she sent a telegram, 'IN GREAT ANXIETY BEG HIM TO REASSURE HER OF HIS AFFECTION UNALTERED CANNOT STAND MORE DISAPPOINTMENT TENEREZZE OLGA'. Pound responded, 'ASSURED DURABLE RETURNING SOON', and wrote, 'He ain't stayin in this town for no skoit an thazzat', also that 'he purrfers St Ambrogio with her in it to London or elsewhere without her'. At that Olga wrote back, 'She breathing again—literally'.

'To make up for the short stay in Venice he took us to Rome' that Christmas, so Mary remembered. Disney's *Snow White and the Seven Dwarfs* was showing, and Ezra said they must see it at once. At the end when the lights went up, he and Mary looked at each other, and they stayed to watch it through again. 'I think he enjoyed the film even more than I did', Mary wrote. Her mother developed a cold and spent much of the week in bed. Mary and her father visited the zoo; spent the evenings with Italian friends in the Caffè Greco; visited Marinetti who showed his Futurist paintings but 'seemed more interested in what I knew about sheep'. One afternoon a monsignor took them to fashionable Doney's in the Via Veneto for pastries and hot chocolate, Pound and the monsignor 'two bulky figures talk[ing] with such animation that [Mary] feared tables and chairs would be knocked over'; then he took them in a carriage to St Peter's, and later to the garden of the Knights of Malta where he told her to look through the keyhole of a door in the high wall, and there was 'the dome of Michelangelo in the pale golden mist of the setting sun— something to remember'.

At the beginning of January 1939 Pound learnt that Eliot was closing down the *Criterion*—that month's number would be the last. He was surprised that Eliot had said nothing to him about it during his recent five weeks in London, and in fact had been rather 'projecting continuance'. But then Eliot's reason, it emerged, was that he had been 'deeply shaken by the events of September 1938', which he viewed, not as a triumph of peace-making, but as the failure of a civilization to oppose a godless barbarism. He might well have felt that Pound would not have understood his state of mind, nor sympathized with his 'depression of spirits so different from any other experience of fifty years as to be a new emotion'. And indeed Pound's reaction to the end of the *Criterion* was rather jovial. 'Who killed Cock Possum? | Who bitched his blossom?', he enquired of Ronald Duncan. And to Eliot he wrote that 'Olga, scandalized at my levity thus reproves me: "I *liked The Criterion*, it was *respectable* | *none* of your other magazines are respectable | You have no feeling for the sorrows of yr/ friend Possum".'

What would prove to be the last of the Rapallo music weeks took place that year between 2 and 13 March, four of the six concerts being devoted, as in the first series in 1933, to Mozart's sonatas for violin and piano, with Olga Rudge and Renata Borgatti the musicians throughout. The assumption behind both the first and the last series of concerts, Pound explained in *Il Mare*, was that these sonatas 'constitute a source, a concentration of musical intelligence as unique in its way as Dante's *Paradiso* is in the realm of poetry', and it had been the aim to ensure 'that at least in one part of the world the public could periodically, every year, have the opportunity to hear and re-hear this series of sonatas in its entirety, sharpening its ear and training its critical judgment'.

At this time Pound was hastening to complete his 'China' and 'John Adams' cantos. He had decided that he should go to Washington in the spring to talk some sense, his sense, into President Roosevelt if only he could get to see him, and he wanted to get those cantos off to Faber & Faber before leaving. Besides, his two great source books were not portable and he could work from them only while in Rapallo. They were the thirteen thick folio volumes of an *Histoire générale de la Chine*; and the ten fat volumes of the *Works of John Adams*. The history of China he had acquired in November 1937 and he had been working intermittently since then at condensing its 6,376 pages down towards the 2,500 lines of *Cantos LII–LXI*. The John Adams *Works* he had acquired only in June 1938, and the work of condensing its 8,000 pages down to the matching 2,500 lines of *Cantos LXII–LXXI* appears to have been his main occupation in January and February of 1939. 'Chewing thru Adams', he noted to Olga Rudge on 1 February; then 'he on vol. Ten and ult. of J. Adams' on the 3rd; followed by 'he got to the end', on the 7th, with the addition, 'J. Adams, wottaman!' He had become convinced that the neglected second president was 'much more the father of Jackson and Van Buren than Jefferson was', that indeed he was the true '*pater patriae* U.S.A. more than Washington or Jefferson/ though all three essential and all betrayed by the first congress'. In mid-February he was 'havin a helluva time' with cantos 53 and 54, and with 60 and 61, and even when he had a clean typescript of them on the 19th he still felt that two needed to be 'humanised | too condensed as they set'. By 3

March, however, his clean typescript was up to canto 67, and he had all twenty new cantos polished and shined and sent off to Faber before he sailed for America on 13 April.

The end of Czechoslovakia

Hitler had not been appeased by being allowed to seize the Sudetenland. Already on 21 October 1938 he had ordered his military chiefs to be in a state of readiness to liquidate the rest of Czechoslovakia; and then, to further destabilize the now ruined and defenceless remnant, he had encouraged the Slovaks to break away, and the Hungarians to annexe Ruthenia and the Hungarian-speaking districts, and the Poles to annex territory adjacent to their border. Then, at 6. a.m. on 15 March 1939, German troops entered Moravia and Bohemia, and on the 16th occupied Slovakia, nowhere meeting resistance. Hitler made a triumphant entry into Prague, followed by the SS and the Gestapo, and Czechoslovakia ceased to exist, being now wholly incorporated into the Nazi Reich as Austria had been. 'Neither Britain nor France', Shirer wrote, 'made the slightest move to save it, though at Munich they had solemnly guaranteed Czechoslovakia against aggression.'

Britain and France did, however, begin to realize that Hitler was not to be appeased, and to acknowledge that his next move would be against Poland. On 31 March 1939, Chamberlain declared that the two countries had given assurances to the Polish Government that if it were attacked they would lend it all the support in their power.

Hitler still had September 1939 firmly pencilled in as the moment for all-out war.

Two books for governors: (1) cantos 52–61

> More than the history of a State, or even of a people, the history of China is that of a civilization, or rather that of a tradition of culture. Its chief interest...would perhaps be to show how the idea of civilization has been able, in such a lengthy history, to keep priority, almost constantly, over the idea of the State.   —Marcel Granet

As Hitler was driving his people towards a criminal war which would devastate Europe morally as much as materially, Pound was condensing into verse the epic story of how the civilization of China was founded upon, and renewed itself dynasty after dynasty upon, the Confucian conviction that good emperors brought peace and abundance for all their people, and that those who did not would rightly be overthrown. It was a simple enough ethic, this idea that the true aim of government was to secure the welfare, liberty, and contentment of its citizens, and it had served China well through all the vicissitudes of its 5,000-year history. According to its own historians the empire flourished under good rulers, those who observed the processes of nature and distributed its abundance equitably among the whole people; and under bad rulers, those who went against the natural law or who let particular interests come before the common good, the empire fell apart and the people suffered.

It was primarily the historians who kept this ethic, this *paideuma*, in force through all that vast stretch of time, the historians being Confucian scholars who wrote up, preserved, and revised the records of the successive dynasties. Theirs were moral histories, like the books of the Bible and Shakespeare's history plays, 'school books for princes' they called them, the predominant concern being to so mirror the conduct of emperors and their officers as to make of them examples of wise rule or of misrule for the instruction of their successors. *A Comprehensive Mirror for the Aid of Government* was the explicit title given to the major compilation put together by a team of scholars in the eleventh century of our era. Their aim was not so much to record events as to pass on and to perpetuate the fundamental principles of good government and to have them acted upon.

That tradition was continued down into the seventeenth and eighteenth centuries, to the time when there were Jesuit missionaries in China, learned men who were conveying to the Chinese along with their Christian doctrine the latest advances of European science and technology, and in exchange carrying back to Europe news of China's own civilization. In this way a knowledge of the Confucian principles of government became current in Europe at just the moment when some of its leading thinkers, notably Voltaire and the *Philosophes* in France, were conceiving a social order based on natural reason and natural justice rather than on royal prerogative and religious dogma. The revolutionary ideas that were gradually taking hold, that all should have a share in the common wealth, and that governments should not tyrannize over the people but rather serve their needs, such ideas were found to have been long established in China and to have been the key to its enduring civilization. It seemed, to those seeking a more enlightened Europe, that Confucian China afforded a model of their ideal society, and Confucius himself was set up as an icon of enlightenment. His idea of civil government, as transmitted in the Jesuits' versions of the works attributed to him, and by Voltaire in his *Essai sur les mœurs*, helped form the minds of those who made the American and the French revolutions.

With the betrayal of the American Revolution very much on his mind, and with Europe descending into political chaos, Pound had written in 1937 of an immediate need for Confucius, meaning specifically a need for his model of responsible government. He had done something towards meeting the need by translating the *Ta Hio* and by making a digest of the *Analects* in *Guide to Kulchur*. Then in the autumn of 1937 he bought the thirteen-volume *Histoire générale de la Chine* (Paris, 1772–85), a translation of the *Comprehensive Mirror for the Aid of Government* made at the court of the Manchu emperor K'ang Hsi by the French Jesuit Joseph-Anne-Marie de Moyriac de Mailla (1669–1749). His 'China Cantos' would be cantos 'having to do with *instruction*'—the second part of his long poem as he had first conceived it at Hamilton College in 1904 or 1905—and they would be addressed implicitly to the governments of Europe and of America, and in a few places fairly directly to Italy's Il Duce.

Canto 52 opens in the voice of instruction, 'And I have told you'; and the body of the canto, an account of the rites and customs of ancient China, will begin in the same way with 'Know then'. What we have been told in the previous 'Siena' cantos is that 'the true base of credit'—and, by implication, of order in society—'is the abundance of nature | with the whole folk behind it'. This is to be the major theme of this canto, and the underlying theme of the entire decad. Just here the counter-theme is re-stated, that anti-social *neschek*, a Hebrew term for the usurious taking of interest, goes unopposed in the contemporary world. Even 'the groggy church is gone toothless | No longer holds against *neschek*'.

The *neschek* passage does not reprise the investigation of usury in the preceding twenty cantos, but instead distils from Pound's worst prose the vicious prejudice which would blame the Jews for the universal blight of usury, and which would go on to hold the Jews themselves responsible for anti-Semitism. 'Rothschild's sin drawing vengeance', Pound wrote, 'poor yitts paying for Rothschild | paying for a few big jew's vendetta on goyim.' When Eliot at Faber & Faber saw this passage he wrote to Pound, 'if you remain keen on jew-baiting, that is your affair, but that name of Rothschild should be omitted'. Use 'Stinkschuld' instead then, was Pound's unrepentant response; but Faber blacked out the name and blacked out five lines of petulant abuse of the Rothschilds. After Pound's death, however, the blacked-out lines and 'Stinkschuld' were restored, thus fully exposing for censure the most disgracefully flawed page of the *Cantos*.

The poem recovers from this lapse into wilful prejudice on the next page when the poet is restored to his right mind by attending to the wisdom of ancient China. The rest of the canto, a hundred or so lines, is extracted from *Li Ki*, the Confucian book of rites and folk customs. *Li* signifies traditional behaviours that make for harmony in nature and in society—these, rather than government legislation, were the guiding principles of Confucian China. Pound's rendering of the *Li Ki* is deliberately selective. He chooses to emphasize just the primary relation of man to nature, and the need for the whole folk from emperor to peasant to observe its seasons and processes in order to secure the abundance:

> Know then:
>> Toward summer when the sun is in Hyades
> Sovran is Lord of the Fire
>> to this month are birds
> with bitter smell and the odour of burning
> To the hearth god, lungs of the victim
>> The green frog lifts up his voice
>>> and the white latex is in flower
> In red car with jewels incarnadine
>> to welcome the summer
> In this month no destruction
>> no tree shall be cut at this time
> Wild beasts are driven from field
>> in this month are simples gathered.
> The empress offers cocoons to the Son of Heaven

That is when the cultivation of the silk worms is done for the year. And the empress's offering to the emperor is to be followed, so *Li Ki* goes on, by all the women, rich and poor, old and young, paying a tribute of cocoons in proportion to the number of their mulberry trees; and the silk from them will go to make the robes used in the customary rites in the countryside and in the halls of the ancestors. Pound barely notices such evidences of a developed social organization. He passes over the mass of detailed directions for imperial ceremonies, and for the written characters and musical tones appropriate to each season and each ceremony; and he leaves out nearly all the directions for the proper conduct of ministers and court officials—for example, that they should advance men of talent and open to them a career with honour. Instead his China in this first canto of the sequence appears in its primitive state, or rather in what Lévi-Strauss preferred to call the *primal* state of its civilization.

De Mailla's history, Pound's source in cantos 53–61, begins with the first stirrings of that civilization. As de Mailla tells it, the condition of the inhabitants of China before the first emperors was nearer to that of the beasts than of men: they lived in the wild without house or cottage, ate their food raw, dressed in the skins of animals, knew no laws or rules of conduct, and had no thought for anything beyond a purely animal existence. They differed from the beasts only in this, that they had a soul capable of arousing an aversion to such a life. De Mailla, being a product of the French enlightenment and a Jesuit, was pleased to see in heathen China's ascent to a civilized state proof that reason, the divine spark in man, would draw him towards heaven even without the aid of the Christian revelation. His first emperors, horrified by the brute state of their people, teach them to house and clothe themselves, to burn wood and cook food, and by page four are teaching them that in order to live well and happily they should follow the guidance of that reason with which Heaven has supplied them so that they may perform Heaven's will. In short, de Mailla's China is a China for his time.

Pound's too is a China for his own time; that is, he brings to its history his own preoccupations and ignores de Mailla's. The latter's first four pages are condensed to just three lines—

> Yeou taught men to break branches
> Seu Gin set up the stage and taught barter,
> taught the knotting of cords

That places the emphasis simply on the teaching of elementary skills, and strips away all reference to 'reason' and 'Heaven'. Pound's first pages go on to notate in 'luminous details' the incremental growth of Chinese civilization over a thousand or more years, with each named emperor both honouring his ancestors' achievements and moving to a further cultural level. The legendary Chin Nong taught what grains to grow, 'and made a plough that is used five thousand years'; the Yellow Emperor Hoang Ti, around 2611 'ante Christum', 'contrived the making of bricks | and his wife started working the silk worms'; money was in use in his time, and he measured the lengths of hollow reeds 'to make tune for song'; a century later 'Ti Ko set his scholars to fitting words to their music'; his son Yao noted 'what star is at solstice | saw what star marks midsummer'; Yu, first emperor of the Hsia dynasty, controlled the waters of the Yellow River, and 'let his men pay tithes in kind'; and Chun—who reigned between Yao and Yu but is placed by Pound as the peak of this first phase of development—on assuming his responsibilities sacrificed to 'the spirit Chang Ti' that moves the sun and the stars, and gave the instruction that 'your verses should say what you mean, and the music should accord with your meaning'. Tradition acclaims these three emperors, Yao, Chun, and Yu, as the exemplary models for all later rulers, and after naming them over Pound adds the name of Yu's wise minister of public order, Kao-Yao, with the culminating word 'abundance'—that being what he would have this first 48-line section of the canto add up to.

The second section of the canto, another episode of 48 lines but in the form of an ode, is concerned with saving and renewing the abundance in a time of dearth. It opens with an empress fleeing a usurper to save her unborn son who will grow up to restore order and continue the Hsia dynasty, and with invocations of the exemplary virtues of former emperors; it will close with further invocations, and the line 'seek old men and new tools'. It pivots upon the instigation 'MAKE IT NEW', the motto of Tching Tang, who founded a new dynasty when the Hsia had fallen through neglect of the people and of the spirits. There was drought, grain was scarce, and prices were rising, and so that what grain there was should be shared equitably Tching made copper coins 'and gave these to the people | wherewith they might buy grain | where there was grain'; and he 'prayed on the mountain' to make rain after the seven years of sterility. For thus contending against scarcity and greed, and for his caring for the people and respecting the spirits, his name is added to the list of honoured emperors in the closing invocations.

The canto then cuts to the fall after 400 years of the dynasty he founded. Wasteful luxury, depraved orgies, and barbaric cruelty characterize the reign of its last emperor; order is restored by the enlightened rebel who defeats him in battle, and a new dynasty is established, that of the Chou which Confucius himself would look back to in admiration. The rest of the canto is devoted to their rise and fall, with their name in ideogram placed at the exact centre of the canto as the pivot of the whole. The founding Chou emperor, observing the *li*, 'Dated his year from the winter solstice.' The first thing he did upon entering the city was to give out grain 'till the treasuries were empty'. He demobilized the army; set up schools—'Kids 8 to 15 in the schools, then higher training.' As a good ruler must, he kept down taxes and cared for the needs of the people. His son continued the good work, 'kept lynx eye on bureaucrats | lynx eye on the currency', and regulated weights and measures. There was peace in his reign, and his last will and testament was this, 'Keep the peace, care for the people.' That will was fulfilled under the third emperor by the wise counsellor Chao Kong, who is held to have brought about a golden age—

> Honour to Chao-Kong the surveyor
> Let his name last 3000 years
> Gave each man land for his labour
> not by plough-land alone
> But for keeping of silk-worms
> Reforested the mulberry groves
> Set periodical markets
> Exchange brought abundance, the prisons were empty.

'Yao and Chun have returned'
    sang the farmers
'Peace and abundance bring virtue.' I am
    'Pro-Tcheou' said Confucius five centuries later.
With his mind on this age.

Chao-Kong died 'on a journey he made for the good of the state',

    and men never thereafter cut branches
        of the pear-trees whereunder he had sat deeming justice
        deeming the measures of lands.

'And you will hear to this day the folk singing' about that—a song to be found in the *Shih King*, the *Classic Anthology* which Confucius is supposed to have edited as a monument to the Chou.

In the 500 years from the death of Chao-Kong down to Confucius' lifetime there were good emperors and bad, good times and disasters, but overall a steady decline from peace and abundance towards a breaking down of the great empire into warring petty states. The fourth emperor 'hunted across the tilled fields' and died 'to joy of the people'. His successor meant well but 'fell into vanity', though in old age he 'wd/ have made reparation' and did reform the criminal law. The tenth Chou was 'avid of silver', and had to be reminded of a prince's obligation to see to it that 'l'argent circule | that cash move amongst people'—or else, he was told, 'The end of your house is upon us.' By the time his son became ruler Tartar barbarians were raiding into China and he fought against them, with some success so long as he performed the rites and was not 'rash in council'—two odes in *The Classic Anthology* celebrate his expeditions. He failed, however, to perform the spring rite as laid down in *Li Ki* and there were four years of famine with 'the wild goose crying sorrow'; and when he called back his people they were reduced to dwelling amid reeds and pine trees. Thereafter the Chou empire fell into disorder: the ancestral tombs were neglected; its men would not stand together; there was much lawlessness, murders and treasons, 'Wars, | wars without interest'; and there was disturbance in nature, earthquakes, eclipses, comets. That was the state of things when Confucius was made a minister, and though he had one evildoer beheaded, he could not persuade the ruler to rule responsibly and so retired from office and went off to edit the book of odes. He saved and passed on what could be saved in a time much like Pound's own, a time of 'Greed, murder, jealousies, taxes', and of 'armament racket, war propaganda'.

Canto 53, taken as a whole, has first refined de Mailla's diffuse account of about thirteen hundred years of history into the Confucian foundation myth of the ideal state; and then, in its second half, given a summary account of the actual historical conditions under which and in response to which Confucius and his followers fashioned their reforming ideal. There is an exact balance between the early myth-making and the later critical accounts of how princes were behaving in the real world, with the clear imperative to good government poised against the evidence of how rarely and with what difficulty it was actually carried out.

The following eight cantos trace the vicissitudes of the Confucian *paideuma* through twenty centuries down to about 1776. Dynasties rise and fall one after the other as they follow or fail to follow the Confucian principles. The same fallings off recur, and the same recoveries of virtue—this history does repeat itself. Beyond that truism, though, each canto unfolds a new development in the story, and yields a further insight—there is progression both in the narrative and in the understanding of what has been and what might be. The overall structure is dramatic, much like that of Shakespeare's histories and tragedies: a pattern of civilized order is achieved in spite of enemies within and without through the first three of the ten cantos—is broken down into increasing disorder by those enemies through the middle cantos—and in the final three a new force overcomes the enemies and re-establishes right order. The constant measure is respect for the Confucian books, that is, for the History Book itself and for the Book of Songs.

Canto 54 begins with the fall of the Chou dynasty after eight centuries. A new emperor united all China and 'jacked up astronomy', but then 'after 33 years burnt the books', and his dynasty fell soon after. Then came the Han and an emperor who saw the need to restore the books and the law code and the record of the rites 'as check on successors', and who 'brought calm and abundance' so that 'the men in the vaudevilles | sang of peace and of empire'. The Han enlightenment lasted over 300 years, and near their end an academy of scholars had the books 'incised in stone | 46 tablets set up at the door of the college'. But by then the emperor 'was governed by eunuchs', there were 'wars, taxes, oppressions', and Taoists and Buddhists were subverting the administrations. The palace eunuchs, and the Taoists and the Buddhists, now figure as the enemy within, enemies even more threatening than the Tartar enemy without, the eunuchs as being irresponsible and self-seeking, the Taoists as preferring quietism and private pleasures to public service, and the Buddhists as considering 'their own welfare only', that is, for seeking individual salvation or *nirvana* while cultivating indifference to the affairs of this world. It is a telling moment when Buddhists break up the 46 tablets to get stone for a temple—then the empire rotted and 'Snow alone kept out the tartars'. And when the last Han went Taoist, 'sat late and wrote verses | His mandate was ended'. The Tang dynasty then rose, and, maintaining that 'Kung is to China as is water to fishes', turned out the 'taozers' and 'the damn buddhists', and for a time there was again justice and abundance throughout the empire. But then an empress was run by Buddhists, 'who told her she was the daughter of Buddha'; and 'there came a taozer babbling of the elixir | that wd/ make men live without end', and the peasants were complaining of being squeezed by taxes on top of tithes. Thus another 1,000 and more years passed, 279 BC to AD 805.

Through the first third of canto 55 things go on in much the same way for another century and a half, as in a repeating pattern in the fabric of time, until the rise of the Sung dynasty under whom China enjoyed both a renaissance and a fatal loss of will. 'TAI TSONG brought out the true BOOKS' about AD 978; there was a revolt against the greed of the mandarins and a demand for just distribution; 'GIN TSONG cleaned out the *taoz*ers | and the tartars began using books'; then in the eleventh century came Ngan, the next great reformer after Confucius. He re-established the regulation of markets, that the right price of things be set daily, that a market tax should go to the emperor and the poor be thus relieved of charges, and that commerce be enlivened 'by making to circulate the whole realm's abundance'.

> And Ngan saw land lying barren
>   because peasants had nowt to sow there
> whence said: Lend 'em grain in the spring time
>   that they can pay back in autumn
> with a bit of increase, this wd/ augment the reserve,
> This will need a tribunal
> and the same tribunal shd/ seek
>   equity
> for all lands and all merchandise
>   according to harvest and soil

Ngan's thoroughly Confucian reforms worked for twenty years, yet they were not only complained about by the mandarins and rich merchants whose greed they were designed to constrain, but were argued against as too radical and impractical by a fellow minister, Ssé-ma Kouang, who had them rescinded. Yet Ssé-ma Kouang was the great Confucian scholar who put together the *Comprehensive Mirror for the Aid of Government*. When he died, 'merchants in Caïfong put up their shutters in mourning'; but Ngan's fate was to be driven from office, vilified by conservative Confucians as guilty of Taoist and Buddhist errors. Ngan protested, 'YAO, CHUN were thus in government', and Pound associates his reforms with 'Reason from heaven [which] | enlighteneth all things'. On this occasion, though, the Confucian enlightenment was prevented by a Confucian who knew the books but would not carry them into action. Shortly after that the Sung 'died of levying taxes' and 'state usury'; its last emperor, HOEÏ, 'went *taozer*', and surrendered to barbarian invaders.

The Mongols take over in canto 56 for an interval of 160 years. The terrible Ghengis Khan came in having heard something of 'alphabets, morals, mores', and being surprised to learn that it was more profitable to tax his new subjects than to exterminate them in his usual fashion; but Kublai Khan, who extended Mongol domination over all China, 'was a buggar for taxes' and his finance minister was 'stinking with graft'; and though Gin Tsong honoured Kung with the rites 'his son died of assassins'. Through the main part of this canto the movement is unsettled, scherzo-like, casting rapidly back and forth between occupying Mongol and weak Sung, touching on wars, taxes, and granaries, on bandits, pirates—and a treatise on the cultivation of silk worms. Under the decadent last of these Mongols there were again 'At court, eunuchs and grafters | among mongols no man trusted other', and that dynasty fell in confusion 'from losing the law of Chung Ni (Confucius)'. This time it was the son of a poor labourer, Hong Vou, who rose up to defeat the failing rulers and restore order in the empire. 'Once again war is over. Go talk to the savants,' he said, under the ideograms naming Yao, Chun, and Chou; 'To peasants he gave allotments | gave tools and yoke oxen'; and he 'declined a treatise on Immortality | offered by Taozers'. His Ming dynasty lasted from 1368 down to 1644.

'Ming' in the Occidental mind is likely to be associated with exuberantly decorated porcelain and other works of fine art. There were major literary and historical writings too—including a gigantic encyclopedia consisting of 'all major works in Confucian classics, history, philosophy and miscellaneous subjects, totalling 22,877 rolls and involving the work of 2,316 scholars'. That is noticed in canto 57—'And YANG LO commanded a "*summa*" | that is that the gist of the books be corrected.' Remarkably though, no other detail of this dynasty's cultural achievements is mentioned. Pound's concern, like that of the Confucian historians, is with the increasing corruption of government under the Ming. There is the key statement, 'HONG VOU restored Imperial order | yet now came again eunuchs, taozers and hochang.' There was famine, and wasteful expenditure on armaments—a thousand primitive tanks that 'were never brought into action'; there was 'a rebellion of eunuchs'; there were heavy taxes, and a young emperor's chief eunuch was found to have salted away 'gold bars 240 thousand... | 15 millions in money | 5 million bars silver', and so forth.

The next emperor 'was a writer of verses | in fact he said he wd/ like to resign'; and in his time another court favourite was found to have hoarded up gold and silver, 'not to count silk of the first grade, pearls | cut stones and jewels'. Private greed and luxury were at the heart of the later Ming government, and oppression and neglect of the people.

Under the last Ming emperor, with decadence at court and disorder in the state, the hordes on the northern borders were uniting under the Manchu and driving back the Ming armies—

> And the lord of MANCHU wrote to the MING lord saying:
> We took arms against oppression
> and from fear of oppression
> not that we wish to rule over you

He wanted peace, he declared, according to the Manchu history, and took laws and letters from China for his own people, 'set exams in the Chinese manner', and 'Chose learning from Yao, Shun and Kungfutseu, | from Yu the leader of waters'. As he raided toward the capital he wrote to the governor of a nearby city,

> If children are cut off from parents
> if wives cannot see their husbands
> if your houses are devast and your riches carried away
> this is not of me but of mandarins
> Not I but yr/ emperor slaughters you
> and yr/ overlords who take no care of yr/ people
> and count soldiers as nothing.

The Manchu lord might have said that he was destroying China in order to save it, and he did ruthlessly kill and purge its corrupt elements, and impose peace and sound government. So the enemy without overcame the enemy within—the emperor himself and his mandarins being now identified with the latter—and the mandate of heaven to care for the people was assumed by the former barbarian invaders.

The first line of canto 59 is in Latin, 'De libro CHI-KING sic censeo', that is, 'concerning the Book of Odes I think as follows'. The Latin is from a Jesuit's version of the preface by the third Manchu emperor to a translation of the Confucian Odes into Manchu in 1655. The emperor was affirming the fundamental importance of the Odes for good government—

> all things are here brought to precisions
> that we shd/ learn our integrity
> that we shd/ attain our integrity

Ut animum nostrum purget, Confucius ait, dirigatque
ad lumen rationis[2]
That this book keep us in the due bounds of office
   the norm
show what we shd/ take into action;
   what follow within and persistently

Thus the Manchu re-established the Confucian basis of Chinese civilization; and Lacharme, the Jesuit translator, conveyed the Odes, and that idea of their function, into Europe's language of the learned.

Now the threat to China's Confucian culture came from Europe, in the form of Jesuit missionaries seeking converts, and from Portuguese and Dutch merchants. This canto and the next are much concerned with the interactions of the Europeans and the Chinese, more especially with Jesuit–Chinese relations. At issue is how great a presence and how much influence the Europeans are to be allowed. Kang Hsi who reigned from 1662 to 1723 had the Jesuits at his court, de Mailla among them, busy translating and exchanging the science and technology and the intelligence that each had to offer the other. The Jesuits' astronomy was welcomed—'(Galileo's, an heretic's)'—and their founding of cannon, 'which have served us in civil wars', and their mathematics and science; as missionaries, however, they were not to build churches nor to convert any Chinese. This emperor was all for the advancement of learning, but was careful at the same time to safeguard China's own traditions and culture.

Both the son whom he appointed to succeed him, and that emperor's successor, were exemplary Confucian rulers, so that the *Histoire générale*, and Pound's 'China Cantos', conclude upon an affirmative note. Yong Tching honoured his forebears and the spirits of fields and of heaven, and actively 'sought good of the people'. He reformed the laws—'No death sentence save a man were thrice tried'. The Christians were put out, for 'disturbing good customs | seeking to uproot Kung's laws'. Graft was put down, and the cheating of the poor. The distribution of rice was controlled, to maintain a just price and provide against famine. The history books were updated and reverenced. The emperor ploughed his ceremonial furrow, 'as writ in LI KI in the old days'. And as the population increased new land was opened up and there were tax exemptions for bringing it under cultivation. Thus the Confucian *paideuma* once again brought peace, justice, and abundance to China. Meanwhile in Europe and in America violent revolutions were preparing against the oppressions of their rulers.

---

[2] that our minds be purged, says Confucius, and directed/to the light of reason.

The 'China Cantos' told the story, for the benefit of Pound's Europe and America, of how an enlightened idea of government persisted in China through several millennia—the idea that the government of the people should be for the good of the people, with the correlatives that those in office should not be self-serving, and that private greed should be constrained in the public interest. The moral of the story would be that while this idea of good government had been tried out and proved practicable time and time again, its being put into practice depended always upon there being governors 'who had responsibility in their hearts and willed the good of the people'.

This fairly elementary lesson in the fundamental principle of Western democracy has been well taken by some but by no means by all. For Robert Fitzgerald, the translator of Homer and Virgil, Pound's rendering of China's entire dynastic history was 'one of [the poem's] most sustained and fascinating stretches', making palpable in elaborate metre and rich imagery 'the essentials: whatever in men, deeds and policies casts light on the practice of wise government.' George Dekker wrote that for him 'this survey of the human condition and the bases of humane government' was 'more moving and more instructive than Milton's story of mankind'. But Randall Jarrell, in 1940 a brilliant young poet and critic, complained of 'the monotonous didacticism' and declared the history 'almost unreadable'. 'Unreadable' is of course a common way of saying, 'I can't read them', but Jarrell would not be alone in saying that of these cantos. Some would say worse. 'There is no alternative', declared Donald Davie, a devoted Poundian in his way, 'to writing off this whole section of Pound's poem as pathological and sterile'.

Part of Davie's problem was that he could not follow Pound's method of making music of history. Failing to make out that the detail of Hoang Ti 'contriving the making of bricks' was one note in a progression of cultural achievements, he looked for an explanation in terms of Pound's supposed disapproval of bricks as a building material, and when that didn't work concluded that Pound's selection of detail was 'wholly arbitrary'. What made Davie altogether lose patience was the way 'the non-Confucian (Buddhist and Taoist) influences on Chinese history are consistently condemned in strident language'. Others have found this problematic. Hugh Kenner, in an otherwise illuminating chapter of *The Pound Era*, was struck by the apparent contradiction between Pound's going along with the Confucian historians' wholly negative view of Taoists while endorsing the other Confucian books in which Confucian thought is infused with Taoism. The paradox is readily resolved if only one remembers, as it is essential to remember, that the 'China Cantos', like the *Comprehensive*

Mirror, are a rather specialized guide for governors, and that the defining virtue of the good governor is that his will is unswervingly directed to the welfare of his people. When it is government that is in question it is only reasonable to insist that a man who would rather be writing contemplative poems, and painting distant lakes and mountains, lacks that particular direction of the will and is therefore not fitted for the active life of government.

Two books for governors: (2) cantos 62–71

If we are a nation, we must have a national mind.—EP

John Adams, in Pound's vision of him in cantos 62–71, was an exemplary governor, but more than that, he was to America what Confucius was to China, the man who most enlightened and formed the nascent mind of his nation. He did this, as Confucius and his followers had done it, by gathering together, and digesting and refining into clear principles, the tradition of common law and of natural law available to him; and by working out how the powers inherent in English law could be made to serve the cause of American independence. In his writings he defined in exact terms the ideas that would become, in the Declaration of Independence and the Constitution, the new nation's animating and governing principles. Then, as a practising lawyer and statesman he carried those principles into action, and did this so effectively that he, more than any of the other founding fathers, is to be honoured, so these cantos would have it, as *the* progenitor of a free and democratic America—

> the clearest head in the congress
> 1774 and thereafter
> > pater patriae
> the man who at certain points
> > made us
> at certain points
> > saved us
> by fairness, honesty and straight moving (62/350)

Pound's part, as the poet of the cantos, is like that of the Confucian scholars who kept alive in their own time and passed on to future generations the shaping idea of their civilization. His 'John Adams Cantos' are all at once an *Analects* or sayings of Adams, a *Ta Hio* or digest of his wisdom, a history book for the guidance of America's governors, and a book of odes in which all this is given musical form.[3]

Pound's method of composition, it does have to be recognized, is at its most disconcerting in these cantos. His notebooks and drafts show him skim-reading the ten volumes of the *Works of John Adams*, jotting down phrases and fragments, a half-line from here and a line or two from further on, and then typing up these bits and pieces into cantos, taking the fragments just as they came with little or no revision or rearrangement and with no respect for their original contexts. The result can seem to make, as Donald Davie thought, 'a nonsensical hurly-burly of Adams's life'. It helps, indeed it is probably imperative, to have at least a moderate knowledge of the received narrative of American history. Pound's attitude would be that if his readers, especially his American readers, don't already know in some detail the story of the founding of the United States then they should be driven to go and learn it. He is not going to tell over again the historians' tale of what happened and who was who, being committed beyond that to drawing out of the historical record the active virtue of his protagonist. To that end he reads over the top of the plain sense of his source-materials, and picks out just the details, the sequence of notes as it were, that he can combine to create a new and deeper vision of Adams as a shaping force in the life of his nation.

---

[3] John Adams, born 1735 in Braintree, now Quincy, a town a dozen or so miles south of Boston where his family had farmed since 1638. Graduated from Harvard College 1755, then took to the law and was admitted to the Bar in 1758; became legal adviser to the Boston Sons of Liberty, and in 1761 assisted in legal arguments against the searching of American vessels by English customs officers under Writs of Assistance. In 1765 led protest against the Stamp Act, by drafting the Instructions to Braintree's representatives in the Massachusetts legislature, which were then taken as models by other towns; by writing powerful articles in the Boston *Gazette*; and by arguing before the Governor and Council that the Act was invalid because Massachusetts had no representation in the British parliament. In 1774 Adams was sent as a delegate from Massachusetts to the Continental Congress in Philadelphia, and was the foremost advocate of its Declaration of Independence in 1776; during the war for independence he was president of the Board of War, and was influential in many other congressional committees. In 1779 he drafted the constitution of the commonwealth of Massachusetts. In the same year he was sent as minister plenipotentiary to negotiate a treaty of peace and a treaty of commerce with Great Britain—in the Treaty of Paris, signed 1782, he particularly safeguarded US coastal fisheries; most importantly, he then secured recognition of the United States as a sovereign nation from Holland and other European powers. Served as American Minister to the court of St James 1785–8, and while in London wrote *A Defence of the Constitution of Government of the United States* (1787). Made Vice-President under Washington 1789–97; elected President 1797–1801, with Jefferson as Vice-President; while President resisted efforts of Alexander Hamilton and others to engage in war with France, preferring to secure peace by diplomacy. Defeated by Jefferson in the contest for the presidency in 1800, he retired into private life at Quincy, where he died 4 July 1826, on the same day as Thomas Jefferson with whom he had carried on a notable correspondence in their old age.

There is a five-part overall structure deriving from the arrangement of the *Works of John Adams*:

1. *an overview of Adams's life*—canto 62 with the first page of 63, drawn from the biography in volume 1 by his son John Quincy Adams and his grandson Charles Francis Adams;

2. *Adams's own view of his life and public service (up to 1796 when he became president)*—canto 63 through to the second page of 66, drawn from his diaries and autobiographical writings in volumes 2 and 3;

3. *his pivotal ideas of government as he wrote them out in his political essays*—canto 66 through to the beginning of 68, from volumes 3, 4, and 6;

4. *the official record of his public service (from 1771 to the close of his presidency in 1801)*—canto 68 through to the second page of 70, drawn from his official correspondence and papers in volumes 7–9;

5. *Adams's retrospective views of his career, as in 'the mirror of memory'*—cantos 70 and 71, drawn from his private correspondence (up to 1818) in volumes 9 and 10.

This arrangement provides a layering of different perspectives on certain episodes, and also a narrative progression from Adams's beginnings as a young lawyer in Boston through to his last years when he was out of office.

The theme of canto 62 is given in these early lines, 'for the planting | and ruling and ordering of New England', words from the charter granted by King Charles I in 1629 'TO THE GOVERNOR AND THE COMPANIE' of the Massachusetts Bay Company. That is, the work John Adams is to be committed to in his own time, 'planting and ruling and ordering', in Massachusetts primarily, then increasingly for all the colonies. He is shown first arguing in a Boston case that the law, properly understood and applied, should be subject to reason and so should take account of human nature, of our emotions and passions; and yet at the same time it must be dispassionate, 'not bent to wanton imagination and temper of individuals'. Next he is arguing for the natural rights and liberties of the colonists against the unlawful oppressions and tyrannies of the British parliament. 'Are we mere slaves of some other people?', he demands, as he makes the case against the colony's judges being in the King's pay; and Pound comments, 'These are the stones of foundation | ... | These stones we built on.' From 1774 until Lexington, the first battle in the war for independence, he guides the public mind in the formation of self-governing state constitutions, and is recognized as the 'Clearest head in the Congress' as it moves reluctantly towards its declaration of independence and prepares for the war that will follow.

'THUMON' is Pound's salute at that point, the Greek word meaning 'that which animates, the breath, the energy, the force of mind and will' which drove forward the revolution in the minds of the people and brought about the 'Birth of a Nation'. Adams completes the process in Europe by securing diplomatic recognition of the United States of North America as a sovereign nation, and by obtaining the loans and treaties of commerce necessary for it to maintain itself as an independent and prosperous nation.

Then 'a new power arose, that of fund holders'. This was the enemy within, financial interests looking to profit from the banking system set up by Alexander Hamilton while he was Washington's secretary of the treasury (1789–95), a system modelled upon the Bank of England and designed to allow the few fund-holders or private bankers to profit from the public credit while accumulating 'perpetual DEBT' to the nation. Adams had to contend throughout his presidency with the manoeuvres of Hamilton and his faction to entangle the United States in wars which would 'create a paradise for army contractors'. Pound emphatically condemns Hamilton on his own authority, '(my authority, ego scriptor cantilenae)', as 'the Prime snot in ALL American history', thus setting him up to be the anti-type of John Adams, the subverter of his 'active Virtue' and of the just order he had conceived and fought for.

The cantos which give Adams's own view of his part in winning independence for America run to twice the length of that first outline, twenty-one pages as against ten, and they give a much fuller and more complex narrative of the revolution that took place first in the mind and then in the state of the nation. The most significant new element, a theme which counterpoints Adams's legal and political activity, is his appreciation of the abundance of nature, and of the agriculture and useful arts and manufactures which improve it. In canto 63 his following 'the study | rather than the gain of the law' is balanced by his noting Franklin's care for 'propagating Rhine wine in these provinces' (63/352, 353). In the next canto he sketches an ideal scene in which the cultivation of nature and of the art of glass-blowing go together—

> Beautiful spot, am almost wholly surrounded by water
> wherein Deacon (later General) Palmer
> has surrounded himself with a colony
>   of glass-blowers from Germany
> come to undertake that work in America, 1752,
>   his lucerne grass
> whereof 4 crops a year, seed he had of Gridley of Abingdon
> about 70 bushels of 1/4th an acre of land
> his potatoes (64/355)

A little later we have Adams improving his own land,

> lopping and trimming
> walnut trees, and for felling of pines and savins
> An irregular misshapen pine will darken
> the whole scene in some places (64/357)

Those lines stand against, 'we saw five boxes of dollars | going in a horse cart to Salem for Boston | FOR England', an indication of how England's interest is in taxing, not improving America. Adams manifests a growing concern for the useful arts by which Americans can make themselves independent financially as well as politically. He remarks that 'in Connecticut every family has a little manufactury house | and make for themselves things for which they were used | to run into debt to the merchants' (64/360). (Pound rhymes that with Adams himself proving a homegrown match for the English in law.) Then he is struck by such industry on a larger scale, '6 sets of works in one building, hemp mill, oil mill, and | a mill to grind bark for tanners', also 'a fuller's | mill for both cloth and leather' (65/365); and in 1776 he actively advances on that by having one of his Congressional committees resolve

> To provide flax, hemp, wool and cotton
> in each colony a society for furtherance
> of agriculture, arts, manufactures
> and correspondence between these societies
> that natural advantages be not neglected (65/367)

—and also that the colonies may be not dependent upon foreign manufactures.

This second part of the decad closes with a diary entry made in 1796 when Adams was in waiting for the presidency. At this critical time, approaching the culmination of his political career, he presents himself as at home on his farm harvesting what he had cultivated—one is reminded of the austere Roman general Cincinnatus who was found ploughing when the call came to assume supreme command and save Rome from its enemies—

> *July 18ᵗʰ*, yesterday, mowed all the grass in Stony Hill field
> this day my new barn was raised
> their songs never more various than this morning
> Corn by two sorts of worm
> Hessian fly menaces wheat
> Where T. Has been trimming red cedars
> with team of 5 cattle brought back 22 cedars (66/381)

Breaking into this pastoral episode with its counterpoint of abundance and blight there is talk of the forthcoming election, and pressure is put upon Adams to make Hamilton his Vice-President, Hamilton whose funding scheme menaced the nation's harvest. 'I said nothing', Adams recorded, but he took Jefferson as Vice-President. He had observed in his time as minister in London what decadent 'magnificence' could come from a national debt such as Hamilton proposed to create—his account of this is in the passage immediately before that diary entry. Adams had made visits to country estates, Woburn Farm, Stowe, Blenheim, and among them 'the seat of the banker Child'—

> three houses, in fact, round a square
> blowing roses, ripe strawberries plums cherries etc
> deer sheep wood-doves guinea-hens peacocks etc (66/381)

This banker's seat, with its three houses wonderfully circling the square, its stuffing of hothouse flowers and fruits, and its decorative deer and peacocks, is in every way the inverse of the rational and useful cultivation Adams practised and promoted in America. And it is the product of a financial and social system which greedily if not corruptly appropriates the natural wealth of the land for private luxury. Pound's Adams takes his stand against all such hogging of harvest.

The third part of the decad, an abstract of Adams's arguments in his legal and political writings, has him making new the old laws of England by applying them to the unforeseen conditions of the American colonies, and then, after 1776, developing a system of law adapted to the new free and sovereign nation. He goes back to Magna Charta of 1215, and further back as far as 'memory of man runneth... | Dome Book, Ina, Offa and Aethelbert, folcright | for a thousand years' (67/387). He invokes the Bill of Rights won in the Glorious Revolution of 1688, when the English parliament deposed James II and brought in William of Orange to protect the rights of the people against the authoritarianism of the Stuarts. He discovers the neglected Act which protected American sailors from impressment into the English Navy. He fights the Stamp Act, which 'wd/ drain cash out of the country', and forces its repeal as 'UNconstitutional' (66/382). He exposes one scheme after another whereby parliament seeks to tax the colonies, and argues point by point from his law books for the rights and liberties of free men in their own country. All this he did 'in the course of fifteen years... before Lexington' to bring about the revolution 'in the minds of the people'. Then it was time to seize the unique opportunity 'to make election of government'. 'When before', Adams marvelled, 'have 3 million people had option | of the total form of their government?' He was ready with a plan, providing for a representative body which should be 'in miniature a portrait of the people at large', with separation of 'legislative, executive and judicial' powers to ensure checks and balances, and with the general 'happiness of society' as its aim (67/391–4). From those ideas came the United States Constitution with this proud 'Preamble':

We the People of the United States, in Order to form a more perfect Union, establish Justice, insure domestic Tranquillity, provide for the common defence, promote the general Welfare, and secure the Blessings of Liberty to ourselves and to our Posterity, do ordain and establish this Constitution for the United States of America.

That the representatives of the people were of one mind in this foundation document was largely John Adams's doing.

The history books tell us that the Constitution sealed America's victory in the war for independence, and laid down the laws by which it should govern itself into a glorious future. In Pound's special version of the story the victory which it sealed was the one that had been fought and won by Adams, with his law-books for weapons along with his clear head and constant will. Yet there is in these pivotal cantos of the decad little sense of the drama of Adams's legal battling, and the reason for this is that the story is told almost exclusively in his own words and from his own point of view. The essence of courtroom drama, and of legislative debates, is the clash of opposing arguments and interests with something vital at stake and with the outcome uncertain. Here, though, we have only one side of the argument, the side that won and no doubt had right on its side; but the opposing side, the 'party for wealth and power | at expense | of the liberty of their country', is allowed no voice or force in the argument and remains a silent shadow cast by Adams's brilliance. Properly instructive as this may be, it is unlikely to move the American reader to a more passionate observance and defence of the Constitution.

The record of Adams's public service in his official correspondence, as selected by Pound in the fourth part of the decad, is very largely concerned with his furthering the emerging nation's foreign relations, especially its relations with France and Holland. His duties as a minister abroad were to obtain loans to finance the war against England; to facilitate commercial trade both for the sake of the home economy and so that America's exports might back its borrowings; to secure international recognition of the United States as a separate and equal nation; and to do all that while preserving its neutrality in regard to European politics and internal wars. Cantos 68 and 69 are consequently all about public money in one aspect and another, but mostly about how the loans were raised in Holland and recognition thereby secured in spite of French interference and English opposition. There Adams's success is evidently due to his personal integrity and complete devotion to the public interest: in all his negotiations involving millions of money he keeps scrupulous accounts and never seeks to profit personally.

In counterpoint to his raising of finance abroad there is at home a severe depreciation of the paper money issued by the several states and by the Continental government; and in counterpoint to his integrity there are speculators and swindlers out to profit from the depreciation. Adams regarded the depreciation of the currency as a tax very properly paid by Americans in the cause of their liberty, and as giving them at the same time a commercial advantage in foreign trade. He did not foresee how speculators, friends of Hamilton benefiting from inside information, would buy up the depreciated money and make huge profits on it when Hamilton had the national government redeem it at face value. Pound, though, denounces Hamilton and his friends at the close of canto 69, giving their names, associating them with betrayers of the revolutionary cause, and consigning them to the lowest pit of Dante's hell where Satan devours traitors. Pound singles out the part of Hamilton's scheme which provided for the redemption of the certificates issued as pay to the soldiers of the revolutionary army and which had depreciated to a fraction of their value—

> Mr Madison proposed that the original holders
> > shd/ get face value,
> but not speculators who had bought in the paper for nothing.
> ov the 64 members ov the House ov reppyzentativs
> > 29 were security holders.
> > > lappin cream that is, and takin it
> off of the veterans.
> > an' Mr Madison's move wuz DEE–feated. (69/408)

'These the betrayers', Pound thunders, meaning betrayers of the essential spirit of the American Revolution, 'these the sifilides', the diseased spreaders of the contagion of money-lust. In his judgement Hamilton's financial schemes had planted the evil root of greed in the United States fiscal system at its foundation. Adams's way of putting that as he retired from public life was to write of his own Federal party, of which Hamilton was a leader, 'no Americans in America | our federalists no more American than were the antis' (70/410).

That sense of the betrayal of the revolution, and more generally of the failure of his fellow Americans to live up to their revolution, sets the tone of the final part of the decad. 'After 20 years of the struggle', Adams wrote in

1789, 'After generous contest for liberty, Americans forgot what it consists of' (70/412). Among other things it consisted of keeping their right to their own fisheries—that had been Adams's 'strongest motive | for twice going to Europe'—yet 'there were Americans indifferent to fisheries | and even some inclined to give them away'. There were 'westerners wd/ do anything to obtain free use of [the Mississippi] river | they wd/ have united with England or France', even though doing so 'wd/ put an end to our system of liberty' (71/415). Clearly there had been no revolution in such minds. It becomes evident that in Adams's view, and in Pound's, the real war for liberty was against amnesia, indifference, and narrow self-interest; also against widespread ignorance and misinformation. There was abysmal ignorance about the banking set-up—

> Every bank of discount is downright corruption
> taxing the public for private individual's gain.
>   and if I say this in my will
> the American people wd/ pronounce I died crazy. (71/416)

Pound put a black sideline against that for emphasis. Again, people neither understood nor attempted to understand their own Constitution. 'How small in | any nation the number who comprehend ANY | system of constitution or administration', Adams complained, and added, '[I] know not how it is but mankind have an aversion | to any study of government' (70/412, 413). Because of that wilful ignorance public opinion could be led by a mercenary press with its 'fraudulent use of words'—'newspapers govern the world' (as the French minister said to Mr Adams). Even worse, under that 'pure uncorrupted uncontaminated unadulterated etc.' state of democracy, as the newspapers themselves would have it, the documents and histories which 'cd/ give true light or clear insight' are 'annihilated or interpolated or prohibited'. Altogether Adams, in Pound's account, sees the revolution which he had brought about in the minds of the American people failing and being undone, again in their minds, in the twenty years after 1776.

In the first of the 'Adams Cantos' Pound saluted his hero as 'pater patriae', the father of the nation, and throughout the decad the nation's welfare has appeared to depend above all upon this one man. Now that he is out of office it seems that 'things fall apart, the centre cannot hold'. Looking back, Adams regrets that even as President he could not prevent the selling of rum to Indians, though 'Little Turtle petitioned me | to prohibit it "because I had lost 3000 of my children | in his tribe alone in one year".' Again,

> Funds and Banks I
> never approved I abhorred ever our whole banking system
> but an attempt to abolish all funding in the
> present state of the world wd/ be as romantic
> as any adventure in Oberon or Don Quixote.

When he reflects on the harm done by that banking system he thinks back to a primal image of abundant nature cultivated and shared with generosity, and to the loss of that paradise—

> their wigwams
> where I never failed to be treated with whortle berries
> black berries strawberries apples plums peaches etc
> for they had planted a number of fruit trees about them
> but the girls went out to service and the boys to sea
> till none were left there...(71/416)

That dying fall of nostalgic elegy is not, however, the end of the story.

On the next page two words stand out, one Greek, one Latin, 'THEMIS CONDITOR'. 'Θεμις' Pound took from a letter of Adams to Jefferson in which he was discussing the merits of the translations into several languages of Cleanthes' Hymn to Zeus—Pound closes the canto with the hymn's opening lines in the original Greek, as Adams had copied them in his previous letter. *Conditor* signifies 'a maker, a framer, a founder', such as Adams had been in the framing of the Constitution. But here it is not Adams who is the framer, but *Themis*, the very source according to the ancient Greeks of all law and order and justice. To invoke this idea that natural law and common law act together to bring about and to maintain civilized society is to recognize that the good society does not depend on any one man. It is to accept that it depends upon the physical laws of nature, the laws which regulate growth and abundance, and which also set limits; and that it depends at the same time upon the common laws and customs which regulate civilized societies. The idea of the abundance of nature with the whole folk in accord is near to that. The Greek *Themis*, however, puts more emphasis upon the laws agreed by common consent which express the collective will of the people at their most enlightened, laws which project and institute the moral conscience and desire for good order and justice of the people as a whole. That idea must be implicit in the democratic principle of government *by* the people and *for* the common good.

Following 'THEMIS CONDITOR' there is a coda resuming several of the leading themes and motifs of the decad, and then a 25-line finale consisting of an abrupt and violent passage concerning slavery, the absolute denial of liberty and equality; then a bridging line; and, to end, the opening (in the original Greek) of Cleanthes' Hymn to Zeus. Adams had 'often wondered that J's first draft has not been published'—that is, Jefferson's first draft of the Declaration of Independence—and had supposed 'the reason is the vehement philippic against negro slavery' (65/367). The draft had denounced slavery as waging 'cruel war against human nature itself, violating its most sacred rights of life and liberty', but the paragraph was struck out in the debate so as not to lose the support of the slave-holding colonies. This fatal contradiction between the fine proclamation of the equal and inalienable rights of all human beings, and the determination of some states nevertheless to maintain the inhuman institution of slavery, would not be resolved until Abraham Lincoln could say in good faith at the dedication of the Civil War cemetery at Gettysburg in November 1863, 'Fourscore and seven years ago our fathers brought forth upon this continent a new nation, conceived in liberty, and dedicated to the proposition that all men are created equal.' That was a precise and frank way of putting it, since what was proposed had been left unrealized.

In the passage concerning slavery from a letter written in 1818, forty years after the Declaration, Adams was not directly addressing the practice in America. He was quoting from the instructions of a certain 'alderman Bekford' to his overseers in the West Indies—

> 'consider what substance allow to; what labour extract from
> them (slaves) in my interest which will work out to this
> If you work 'em up in six years on an average
>   that most profits the planter'
> with comment:
>   'and is surely very humane IF we estimate
> the coalheaver's expectation: two years on an average
> and the 50,000 girls on the streets, at three years of life (71/420)

The passage expands the slaves' loss of liberty and life, and the heartless calculation of profit, into a general condition. For Adams it represented the heartless attitude of Britain to its American colonies, and the fundamental justification of their revolt—Americans would not be 'mere slaves of some other people'. And yet they themselves continued to practise and to permit slave-holding, in flagrant contravention of the great moral principle to which they were dedicated and on which their very right to exist as an independent nation was founded. Though unstated, indeed all the more because it is not stated, that must be in the reader's mind here.

The bridging line, "'Ignorance of coin, credit and circulation!'", seems to declare the cause of those crimes against humanity. Adams may have thought that, and Pound himself may have thought it in 1939. In 1972, however, he would write, 're USURY: | I was out of focus... The cause is AVARICE.' The response to ignorance and its consequences is given here in the lines from Cleanthes' hymn, which may be freely translated as—

> Zeus,
>> glorious, undying, known by many names,
>>> shaping all things
>>>> in every instant
>> giving to each thing its nature,
>>> and according to its laws
>>>> guiding the universe

In Greek mythology *Zeus*, the self-regulating life-force, and the intelligence of the life-force, begets *Themis*, the enabler and intelligence of self-regulating societies. Both are of course ideas, conceived and having their existence in the mind, and exercising their powers there. And it is as indestructible powers in the mind that they oppose whatever wars on nature and against human nature. When Pound, having noted that Cleanthes' Hymn to Zeus was 'part of Adams' *paideuma*', drew on it for the conclusion to this decad, he was executing a shift from the still unfulfilled promise of equality and liberty for all, to the undying idea and will behind the promise.

Pound made John Adams his exemplary American governor because the ideal of liberty and equality grew to its clearest and most powerful in his mind, and because, so far as he was able in the prevailing circumstances, he carried it into action as the formative idea of the new republic. It was not his idea, it did not originate with him, and that is important. It was in the air of the time as a natural desire; and it was written in the deposit of English common law going back a thousand years. Adams's contribution was to bring the urgent desire for liberty into accord with the tradition of common law, thereby giving it the weight and force of natural justice. Once embodied in the Declaration of Independence and in the Constitution the idea had its existence in the mind of the nation as its enduring foundation and guiding principle. The compelling ideal outlives the striving man of his time.

The 'Adams Cantos' are to be read as Pound's instructions for the government of America. They do not recommend Italian Fascism as a system of government for America. Their clear message is that America should be true to its own enlightenment, that it should follow Adams in obeying the will of the people as expressed in the Constitution, and that, above all, its governors should serve the common interest before individual profit. He would have the United States be true to its own founding principle, that 'governments are instituted among men' to secure to all equally their rights to 'life, liberty, & the pursuit of happiness'. He meant to save America from its anti-American Americans.

6 : ALIEN IN AMERICA

War seemed imminent in Europe in the spring of 1939. Dorothy Pound's impression of London in mid-April was that most of it was 'dug up for shelters'. And Omar was 'travelling with gas mask—Incredible!' Wyndham Lewis wrote, 'Dear Ezz. Help! Things have become like a madhouse here'—everyone was saying '"we may be at war next month".' The Tate Gallery Committee that was to ratify the purchase of his portrait of Pound was not going to meet; and 'the Bond Street Gallery, where I was to have my show, will advance no money against sales'. It was the same 'Everywhere... a complete paralysis'—shops even were 'not renewing their stocks (of needles and thread, blind cords and whistling kettles) because they have to pay cash'. 'My poor old Ezz', Lewis wound up, 'we have fallen upon an evil time.'

Pound was saying, 'There SHOULD be no war/ the only EFFECTIVE attitude is WILL against war'. More precisely, 'My position is: No war west of the Vistula', meaning no war in Europe, Europe being 'whatever civilization we've got/', and 'damn the tartars'. He reproved Eliot for the 'depression of spirits' which had caused him to give up the *Criterion*, interpreting his 'Last Words' as a lyric outcry betraying 'the last whimper of the exaggerated egoist Anschauung—The attribution of so much importance to an individual toothache, to the oblivion of the civic value.' The civic sense he missed in Eliot was the active will to 'keep England and Europe out of yet another bloody mass-murder for the profit of gun-touts and loan-sharks'.

He was directing his own 'WILL against war' to the reform of his own country and to keeping it out of any European war. With his visit there in prospect, and with John Adams's story fresh in his mind, he had become very conscious of his deep-rooted American identity. 'I don't have to *try* to be American,' he told Hubert Creekmore in March 1939, and went on to claim that he 'Could write the whole U.S. history (American hist) along lines of family migration; from the landing of *The Lion*, via Conn., N.Y., Wisconsin... to Idaho'. He implied too an association on his mother's side with the first Adamses, because 'a plantation named Weston's' had become their 'Merrymount, Braintree, Quincy', and that was tied up with 'all I believe in or by'. But, he demanded, 'is it possible to BE American in America today?', given 'the present state of the country, the utter betrayal of the American Constitution, the filth of the Universities, and the shitten system of publication whereby you can buy Lenin, Trotsky...Stalin for 10 cents and 25 cents, and it takes *seven* years to get a set of John Adams at about 30 dollars'. How was one to maintain 'any view of what our forebears intended and what we damn well OUGHT to create'? Creekmore must have queried, Was he American?, and the answer was a furious 'Yes, damn it, AMERICAN/ but the bloody country BITCHED. Shit in office/ our revolution was betrayed.'

Pound had learnt that he had been elected to the United States' National Institute of Art and Letters in January 1938, and while appreciating the 'manifestly honorific' intention, he immediately 'exercised several privileges', such as nominating 'a few of the better writers'—among them Cummings, Eliot, Williams, Santayana, Hemingway, McAlmon, and Zukofsky. He asked Congressman Tinkham to have someone on his staff find out whether the institution had 'any official standing', and was informed that 'Mr Tinkham seems to think that there is no organization in the country of its kind with a higher standing'. He was already thinking how he might mobilize the members who were writers as a potential force in the country; and he began by 'driving for decent reprint of the gist of John Adams, Jeff/ Van Buren etc.' as 'the sort of thing an Institute could and should do'. There is no evidence that his efforts had any effect on the august body, which included many of his *bêtes noires*. He thought the distinguished editor Henry Seidel Canby who had been the one to inform him of his election needed to be 'educated or drowned'; and, as he told Ford in January 1939, 'the sap-headed nominating kummytee did *not* put [WCW's] name with Walt Disney's when it came to the annual recommendations'. Canby was moved to put it to Pound that 'scurrilous attacks upon [the Institute's] members was not the best means of elevating American culture'.

Ford had been telling Pound for some time that since he was so sure he knew what was wrong with America's universities he ought to come over and do something to put them right. Since the autumn of 1937 Ford had been writer and critic in residence at Olivet College in Michigan, a liberal arts college of 300 students and 45 faculty which hired him to be a high-profile presence and to teach whatever he liked in whatever manner he felt inclined to. Through 1938 he was trying to persuade Pound to accept a similar appointment at Olivet, telling him that he would find there 'a working, model educational machine to play with'. 'Does Olivet USE my text books?', Pound wanted to know, to which Ford replied, 'I do not approve of the use of text books'. Pound also asked, 'Will he [i.e. the college president] GET a printing press ... for the DISTRIBUTION of knowledge and ideas?', and to that Ford answered, 'They have already a press ... But they probably would not print Mussolini-Douglas propaganda for you'. All Pound wanted in that regard, however, was that 'they START by reprinting the necessary parts of John Adams and Jefferson'. Olivet was keen to have Pound, while he was merely rather pleased to be in demand, even if only by 'a very small Western College' inviting him 'to profess in the wilderness'. In the end he would not take up the offer, evidently feeling that the college could not give him what he really aspired to, a position from which he could get his ideas across to the men who were running the country.

His great idea was 'a revival of American culture ... as something specifically grown from the nucleus of the American Founders'. About February 1939 he isolated this nucleus in his *Introductory Text Book (in four chapters)*, each chapter consisting of a single brief quotation from one of the Founders. First was John Adams, attributing 'All the perplexities, confusion, and distress in America' to 'downright ignorance of the nature of coin, credit, and circulation'. Next there was Jefferson's statement of the right way to issue the national currency so that 'no interest on them would be necessary or just'. Then Lincoln's, ' ... and gave to the people of this Republic THE GREATEST BLESSING THEY EVER HAD—THEIR OWN PAPER TO PAY THEIR OWN DEBTS'. And finally, what had become for Pound the foundation stone of the Republic, Article I Legislative Department, section 8 of the Constitution of the United States, 'The Congress shall have power: To coin money, [and] regulate the value thereof ...' A note declared, 'The abrogation of this last mentioned power derives from the ignorance mentioned in my first quotation.'

Pound was urging in 1939 that those four quotations, as comprising the 'Fundamentals of American politico-economic history', should be taught in all American universities as the basis of a true American culture. He wrote to his old teacher and friend at Hamilton, Joseph Darling Ibbotson, 'I consider it utter treachery to ANY student, whether specializing in U.S. History or economics to allow him to leave college ignorant of the issues raise[d] in these FOUR quotations.' And further, 'I consider it a falsification of the supposed status of the college graduate, if said graduates are supposed to serve for the general lifting of public intelligence/ to serve as a corps for educating the public at large.' That civic sense, that awareness of being a responsible individual in an organic social system, was also an essential part of the American culture Pound would have to grow again from its founding protagonists. But the fundamental necessity was that there should be a clear understanding of money, of how it is created, by whom controlled, and for whose benefit. Money is 'the PIVOT of all social action', he insisted, and 'Only a race of slaves and idiots will be inattentive' to it.

He would say that his main aim in going to America had been to find out if it were 'possible to restore American system of govt.' His reputation was such though that when he arrived there was an expectation that he had come over to preach Fascism, and it was suspected that because he had travelled first class the Italian Government must have paid his fare. That was not in fact the case. It was Carlo Rupnik, a shipping and travel agent in Genoa, who arranged the return passage. He appears to have been something of a fixer—in January he had negotiated the safe passage through customs, with the aid of an influential friend, of the thirteen cases of Olivia Shakespear's furniture and paintings. On 3 March he quoted minimum fares of $275 first class, and $155 tourist, adding that he was concerned to obtain the best available for Pound. The next day he wrote, 'Saw again Mongiardino: he is considering your suggestions.' Mongiardino was head of the Ente Provinciale per il Turismo, and Pound's suggestions appear to have been about guided tours for Americans visiting Italy and specifically the province of Liguria—an idea he had been discussing with the editor of *The Globe*, a travel magazine published in Milwaukee. Mongiardino asked if he could count on an article for the Ente Provinciale's 'Weekly News', but none is listed in Gallup's bibliography. On the 17th Rupnik reported that 'the "Ente Provinciale" is interested for you to obtain good conditions'; then on the 21st he was able to write that he had seen the traffic manager of the 'Italia' shipping line and that Pound was to have 'un'ottima cabine di prima classe', the very best, for which he was to pay as for second class. His cheque for $299, drawn on his account with the Jenkintown Bank and Trust Co. and payable to 'ITALIA Soc. An. Navagazione, Genoa', was dated 6 April 1939. One gathers that he had been upgraded thanks to a quiet word to the effect that he would give Italy a good write-up for American tourists. 'Will see you in a few days...about some work the "Ente" would like from you in the U. S.', Rupnik had added; and Pound immediately sent him suggestions for 'descriptive booklet say 8 pages' which 'COULD be got into GLOBE'. Nothing further was said about that; but in July, after his trip, Rupnik told Pound that Mongiardino and Magnini, the head of tourism in Italy, were going to be in Rapallo and wished to meet him to discuss details of what they hoped would be 'an important collaboration'. It is clear that they were hoping for articles to promote tourism, though there is no record of his having actually written any.

On the day before his departure Pound sent a note to Dorothy, by then in London, saying 'He iz feelink deep-ressed at the idear of sailink to hiz country', and then went out and played four sets of tennis. The next day, 13 April, once on board the *Rex* in Genoa, he was delighted by his 'magnificent quarters full of gadgets, ventilation etc.', though he was already finding 'ammosphere of boat disintegrative'. He had brought along his Confucius and Mencius, 'but whether can git to it I dunno'. He sent a postcard to his father, 'Aboard in surroundings of UNrivald splendour.' On the last day, the 19th, he wrote another to Homer, 'very calm trip with all comforts & a bit of conversation'.

When the ship docked in New York on the 20th the news reporters who came on board looking for a story found him and fired their questions at him. Gorham Munson had wired, 'GIVE ECONOMIC BUT NOT POLITICAL VIEWS TO THE PRESS WHEN INTERVIEWED', but Pound was eager to feed them what he regarded as good copy:

'Will there be a war, Mr Pound?'
'Nothing but devilment can start a new war west of the Vistula . . . . the bankers and the munitions interests [are] more responsible for the present talk of war than are the intentions of Mussolini.'
'Mr Pound, you have met Mussolini . . . '
'He has a mind with the quickest uptake I know of any man except Picabia.'
'Who is Picabia?'
'Picabia is the man who ties the knots in Picasso's tail.'
'Which writers do you think important now?'
'The men who are worth anything today are definitely down on money—writing about money, the problem of money, exchange, gold and silver. I have yet to find a Bolshevik who has written of it.'
'Mr Pound, who are your favourite poets in America today?'
'I can name one poet writing today. I mean Cummings.'

A reporter wrote in the *New York Sun*, 'Literature . . . is now a minor theme in the Poundish symphony . . . immediately the talk turns to economics, propaganda, and to what he calls "left-wing Fascists" in Italy.'

'Cummings' was perhaps the first name that occurred to him because he had arranged to stay for a night or two in his apartment at Patchin Place in Greenwich Village. The Cummings were fond of him as he was of them, but he showed up in an obsessive, manic, state which they found hard to take. Cummings wrote to James Sibley Watson that his 'Gargling anti-semitism from morning till morning doesn't (apparently) help a human throat to sing', and that he was ferociously uttering such 'poopyawps and screechburps' as 'if you don't know money you don't know nothing'. They wondered if he were 'a spy or merely schizo'; and felt also that he was 'incredibly lonesome'.

Two days later, on 22 April, he was in Washington and Congressman Tinkham's secretary was making appointments for him, '10. 11. 12. 3.30'. He saw Congressman Voorhis of California who had been urging the government to take control of the nation's credit on behalf of the people, and Voorhis booked him to see his senator. He saw Senator Bankhead of Alabama, the 'stamp scrip bloke'. He had lunch with the Polish Ambassador, Count Potocki, and warned him against trusting England, and against the dangerous Winston Churchill. At the Library of Congress he lunched with the Librarian and with the heads of the music and Chinese divisions, and afterwards called up some of their Vivaldi scores. He was invited to the Japanese Embassy; and he persuaded the curator of the Japanese collection of the National Archives to put on for him a film with authentic soundtrack of the Noh play *Awoi No Uye*.

Skipwith Cannell, a poet Pound had met in Paris before the First World War and had included in *Des Imagistes*, now had a government job in Washington and one day 'found Pound wandering blindly around the administration buildings'. He invited him to Sunday dinner on 30 April, and Williams, who happened to be passing through, was there too. Williams, when he learnt Pound was coming over, had written to Laughlin, 'I can hardly bear the thought of shaking hands with the guy... if he's for that murderous gang he says he's for.' Yet when they met he hugged his old friend who seemed 'very mild and depressed and fearful', and they talked about the serious state of world affairs, though Williams thought Pound 'somewhat incoherent'. The next day, 1 May, Pound dashed off a note to Homer, 'Bill Wms here in Wash. yester.', and, 'I still keep on with Congrs. library, and the office buildings. etc.'

Tinkham took him to lunch on the 3rd, and 'fed me "diamond back terrapin Maryland style"'. On the 5th he arranged for Pound, as the grandson of Thaddeus Coleman Pound, to observe a session of the House of Representatives from a section of the public gallery reserved for members' relatives, but there was nothing to interest or amuse him in that day's proceedings—'a very poor show' he thought it, quite lacking in 'fireworks'. He also had a pass issued by Senator N. C. Lodge Jr to admit him to the Senate Chamber on that day. By the 10th his 'catch', as he wrote to Dorothy, was two senators, the Secretary of Agriculture, Henry Wallace, 'and in evening 8 or 9 econ profs'. He had also put 'Payne', possibly one of the 'econ profs', 'onto serious digging with Gesell in Congrs. Library'. Pound also wrote to Homer on 10 May, saying he had seen more senators, 'Bridges, Lodge & then this A.m. Dies', and had had 'kind word from Borah in the corridor yester.' He was 'Now on way to Harvard', and 'further mail shd go co/ F. S. Bacon 80 Maiden Lane New York'—that was 'Baldy' Bacon's office address, near Wall Street in the financial district.

Henry Wallace later told Charles Norman that 'Pound seemed normal enough when he called on me but rather pessimistic as to the future of the U.S.'—he 'had some ideas as to proper economic organization but I have forgotten what they were'. They were probably the same ideas that Pound had laid out in a long article which the *Capitol Daily* ran on the 9th. In it, according to an 'Editor's Note', the 'noted American Poet-Economist' presented 'his views on a variety of subjects, but principally on the scrip money plan', meaning Gesell's stamp scrip. But Pound's first point was that Fascism was not for America, the corporate state being an 'un-American organization', and that the tyranny Americans should fear was already present in their financial system.

Pound did not go directly to Harvard but was around New York for a few days, staying at Frank Bacon's home in Greenwich, Conn., outside the city, or with John Slocum, whom he knew as a friend of Laughlin's. He phoned Marianne Moore and they met in person for the first time. He looked up Ford on the morning of the 12th—Ford was rather hurt that Pound had not been in touch sooner—and used Ford's phone to arrange to meet Gorham Munson. At lunch with Munson at the Players Club on Gramercy Park he charmed his wife with recollections of Katherine Ruth Heyman, now her friend. Munson recalled for Charles Norman how everyone in the room was noticing Pound, a big man then in spite of all his tennis—he had weighed himself on the *Rex* at 207 pounds—in a baggy tweed suit, 'a flaring white sport shirt', no tie, and in animated conversation. He 'talked about his stay in Washington', but was 'chary of names', and he said, according to Munson, that he 'did not think war was in the offing'.

Ford would be sailing for France at the end of May, and on the 25th there was a farewell party for him in the Cummings' top floor apartment. Pound was expected, along with Williams and the crowd of Ford's New York admirers and supporters, but he failed to turn up. Before June was out Ford would be dead and buried in Deauville, and Pound would long regret the 'fatigue that prevented my gittin' to top floor in '39'. He would pay generous tribute to Ford in an obituary in August, and would recall how he had been still, when he saw him last in New York, 'a very gallant combatant for those things of the mind and of letters which have been in our time too little prized', and how he had been 'still pitching the tale of unknown men who had written the *histoire morale contemporaine* truthfully and without trumpets'.

In mid-May Pound travelled up to Harvard where Jas. Laughlin was at last finishing his degree. He had told Pound shortly after his arrival from Italy that he had 'suggested to the Harvards that they ask you to read Cantos and *comment* on them...it would be a good thing for this den of diddlers and doodlers to be told that matters economic constitute a fit subject for poesy'. The English Department asked him to give a reading in the semi-circular lecture theatre in Sever Hall, and (in Charles Norman's words) 'the steep rows of seats were occupied by undergraduates, with a sprinkling of faculty'. One of the undergraduates, John Clellon Holmes, later recalled for Norman that Pound 'read sitting down', and that he 'seemed to read an extraordinarily long time on one breath, and then take a deep one...for the next few lines of poetry, and yet the voice was too soft to be heard, unless, as he did unexpectedly, he yelled'. The Department of Speech then asked Pound to make a recording for its Harvard Vocarium collection, so, as he reported the event to Olga, 'he spent 2½ hours in abserlewtly airless room bellowing his cantos into a microphone...Wiff 2 kettle drums @ his disposal'. The bellowing in fact was only in the few places it is called for, as in the 'bloody sestina', 'Altaforte'. His voice on the recording otherwise is strong, with a range from the gentle to the enraged, dominantly contemplative or meditative—especially in canto 17—but bardic, taking off from speech into chant, and producing the words as if to a notated score, keeping the time of the rhythm and observing the pitch and duration and weight of each syllable. One can hear the disciplines of musical composition in the writing. The drumming gives a backing of occasional reverberant thunder to 'The Seafarer', and of war music to 'Altaforte', and can be heard from to time in the background elsewhere, generally in connection with doom and death or denunciation—this last towards the close of canto 45—but Pound apparently sometimes became too engrossed in his text to remember the drums. Holmes, who was assisting at the recording, thought the effect of the drums 'would have been magnificent with a rehearsal'.

Pound played tennis with his host, Theodore Spencer of the English Department, and beat him; and he was startled by the scale and the contents of the new refrigerator in his home. He wanted to meet people in the Economics Department, not Spencer's colleagues. He did meet the poet Archibald MacLeish, who was about to take up his appointment as Librarian of Congress, and the philosopher Alfred North Whitehead, and he dined with the President of Harvard. He attended a music faculty concert featuring Vivaldi's *Four Seasons* and presented by Olga Rudge's friend Nadia Boulanger. Laughlin had him to dinner, and there were parties for him, at which he was not at ease. He told Dorothy, 'academic

world orful—I mean at best. Only immature vitality can endure it. |
legislators & nooz wypers so MUCH more alive | he wants to git OUT'.

Laughlin motored him from Harvard to Yale, 'across miles of Mass and
Conn.', and taking in the 'Loomis homestead'. In New Haven he met up
with a young James Jesus Angleton, no doubt then a member of the
secretive Skull and Bones, who had introduced himself to Pound in
Rapallo, and was now precociously starting a little magazine by the name
of *Furioso*. Pound's *Introductory Textbook* would be printed in its first
number.

In New York there was a note from Tinkham awaiting him in Bacon's
office, enclosing 'letters of introduction to several persons in Boston whom
you might find it interesting to see and to talk with'. There were letters
introducing Pound as 'the distinguished poet and economist' to the gov-
ernor of Massachusetts and to the editors of the *Boston Herald* and the
Boston Evening Transcript—but it was too late for Pound to make use of
them. Tinkham also promised to 'try to arrange a definite appointment for
you with Senator Borah'. Borah, as Chair of the Senate Foreign Relations
Committee, occupied a key position in American policy-making given the
fraught international situation, and that must have made Pound especially
determined to follow up the letters he had been sending him since 1933 by
speaking to him in person.

Apparently Pound had spent some hours, on two or three occasions,
waiting in the senator's outer office in the hope of getting in to see him, but
without being admitted. At least that was the recollection forty years later of
Charles E. Corker, who had been a junior assistant in Borah's office in 1939.
(Not only the inevitable distortions of time and self-serving subjectivity must
be allowed for here, but also, as with so many post-war testimonies con-
cerning Pound, the effect on people's memories of his subsequent indict-
ment.) Corker remembered Pound as 'a flamboyant character actor...
playing (or overplaying) Ezra Pound', and that while he waited he spoke
to him about economics and world politics and the important messages he
had for Senator Borah. 'I was puzzled as I still am', Corker wrote in 1980, 'to
know whether he was crazy.' He claimed that Borah too had thought him
crazy after spending 'perhaps 20 minutes' with him—this must have been
the 'definite appointment' arranged by Tinkham—and he was sure that
Borah 'did not take Pound's political and "economic" messages seriously'.
However, Corker seems not to have known that the senator and Pound
would have been in complete agreement at least about keeping the United
States out of a European war. What Pound would record of their meeting,
in January 1942 after Pearl Harbor, was simply 'I can still feel his hand on

my shoulder as just before he was getting into an elevator in the Senate building, and I can still hear him sayin': "'Well, I'm sure I don't know what a man like you would find to DO here.'"

On 22 May Pound arranged to have lunch with H. L. Mencken in the Restaurant Robert on West 55th Street, and to meet Mary Barnard there for tea. Mencken afterwards tried to have Pound appointed as a foreign columnist with the Baltimore *Sun*, but found there was no chance of that because the *Sun* strongly supported Roosevelt, while Pound's view was rather that the President should be impeached for letting the banks control the currency. Mary Barnard was in New York writing and looking for work. Pound took her along to the Museum of Modern Art and introduced her to his sometime London protégée Iris Barry, who was Curator of MOMA's Film Library, and put it to her that a job might be found for Mary in the Museum. Before they left he engaged Alfred Barr in a discussion of the merits of Gaudier-Brzeska and Wyndham Lewis and the desirability of his museum acquiring some examples of their work. Not long after Mary Barnard was invited by Iris Barry's brother-in-law to become Curator of the Poetry Collection in the University of Buffalo's Lockwood Memorial Library. 'Pound', she later wrote, had somehow brought about 'the connection between me and the one job in the country that I was best fitted to do'. His initiative changed her life, and 'something more like fate than chance seemed to be operating'.

Miss Barnard, questioned in later years about Pound's behaviour, decided the word for it was 'punctilious'. And his 'only eccentricities of dress were the wide collar and large, broad-brimmed black hat'. But he was carrying an odd brown paper parcel, and that, he explained, was his 'overnight bag'— one gathers it contained his pyjamas, and that he had no fixed base in New York. Apparently he frequented the Museum of Modern Art in the day, and would then drop in on Tibor Serly, the Hungarian composer he had known well in Rapallo, and his wife would give him tea and Hungarian pastries— she even baked for him a 'real old-fashioned home-made strawberry short-cake', which, she said, 'he enjoyed immensely'—but the Serlys are not named among those who put him up for the night.

Louis Zukofsky was at Serly's on one occasion, and there was what Zukofsky later termed, when Pound was on trial for treason, an 'exchange of frankness [which] was accepted tacitly by both of us as a dissociation of values above personal bickering'. This had nothing to do with his being a Jew—'I never felt the least trace of anti-Semitism in his presence', Zukofsky affirmed. It had to do with Pound's 'political action', by which Zukofsky must have meant his propagandist prose—he explicitly excepted his literary work and music, saying that 'His profound and intimate knowledge and practice of these things still leave that part of his mind entire.' But in the matter of politics, though he 'did not doubt his integrity', he believed 'something had gone wrong' in Pound's head. When Pound, who had been listening to the radio, asked him 'if it was possible to educate certain politicians', Zukofsky replied, 'Whatever you don't know, Ezra, you ought to know *voices*.' That was a profound, and profoundly sympathetic, act of dissociative criticism, in that it recognized Pound's *virtù*, his poetic intelligence, and at the same time implied that, so far as Zukofsky could tell, it was damagingly inoperative in his political action.

Zukofsky, like many others, was possibly unable to see past Pound's endorsements of Mussolini and Fascism to the specific, economic, reasons behind those endorsements. One evening Pound invited the Cummings to dine with him at Robert's and asked them to bring along Max Eastman and his wife. Eastman's first impression was that Pound was 'almost rolly-polly, and with lots of laughter in the corners of his eyes—nervously restless, however'. The Eastmans were hostile to Fascism, and Eastman asked, 'Don't you, as an alien, escape the regimentation which is the essence of it?' Pound answered, 'If a man knows how to do anything it's the essence of Fascism to leave him alone—Fascism only regiments those who can't do anything without it.' Eastman dismissed that as 'a sufficient measure of his intellectual acumen', though he did find Pound 'sweet and likeable withal'. But again, Eastman was seeking confirmation of what Fascism meant to him—regimentation—and not asking what Pound saw in it beyond that. With war in Europe likely, and the Axis the enemy of the political left, America's intellectuals were not in a mood to hear any good spoken of Mussolini's regime.

Even though Pound was there with the explicit aim of getting America to be true to its own Constitution, and explicitly not to import Fascism, he had become too much identified with Fascism to be listened to. He had had a tuppenny pamphlet, 'What Is Money For?', printed by the British Union of Fascists in April, and this was the propaganda he was pressing upon his contacts in America. Its aim was to give 'an absolutely clear conception of money' as the necessary foundation of 'a sane and steady administration'. Under such headings as 'Measure of Price'—'Means of Exchange'—'The Just Price'—'The Quantity of Money'—'Social Credit'—and 'Usury', Pound set out his now familiar definitions, explanations, and analyses, in clear terms and with next to no angry and abusive rhetoric. The simple message was that a democratic and humane financial system should serve the needs of the whole people, and Jefferson and Adams were invoked as having laid down the right principles. But when he came to consider the present situation in which those principles were being betrayed, usury having 'become the dominant force in the modern world', his citations were drawn from Lenin and Mussolini and Hitler, and his final sentence read, 'USURY is the cancer of the world, which only the surgeon's knife of Fascism can cut out of the life of nations'. He may have put that in because it was the BUF who were printing his pamphlet; and he may have put in for their benefit a sentence about 'Jewspapers and worse than Jewspapers' trying to obscure the clear principles. But he was obscuring his own message to America by that quite gratuitous anti-Semitic sentence, and by invoking as the exemplary leaders of the age the founders of Communism, Fascism, and Nazism. There was also his listing 'among the worse than Jewspapers', 'the hired professors who misteach new generations of young, who lie for hire and who continue to lie from sheer sloth and inertia and from dog-like contempt for the well-being of all mankind'. That was unlikely to advance his 'desperate attempt to educate the hist. & econ. depts.' of the universities he visited. He mentioned only one person who had shown real interest in his pamphlet, the Jesuit head of Fordham University in the Bronx who taught political philosophy, and who was 'keen on J. Adams [and] had read the B. U. Pamphlet 3 times before 10.30'. That made him 'one of the serious characters I saw in U.S.'—one of the very few, Pound implied.

Pound spent the night of 5 June with Williams at his home in Rutherford, New Jersey. Williams was about to publish a review of *Guide to Kulchur* in which, as other reviewers of that book had done, he would take issue with Pound's support for Fascism and with his anti-Semitism. It was an 'essential book', he would say, with more good sense for a writer packed into it 'than you will find in all the colleges of Christendom'. And yet for all its brilliance it was a failure, because 'by its tests Mussolini is a great man'; and Pound's failure and folly was to think him so. There was the same, wholly characteristic, balancing of the negative and the positive in the account he gave to Jas. Laughlin a day or two after Pound's visit, and the same coming down in the end on the negative. Pound had 'spread himself on the divan all evening and discoursed to the family in his usual indistinct syllables', he wrote, and 'at that it wasn't bad, if you believed him'. But then, when pressed for a direct answer, as perhaps about the 'the slaughter of innocent women and children' at Guernica, he would avoid the question at issue, or argue it away 'by the neo-scholasticism of a controlled economy program'. And yet 'he does see the important faces and he does have some worthwhile thoughts and projects in hand'. Indeed, Williams admitted, 'I like him immensely as always, he is inspiring and has much information to impart'. For all that, 'the man is sunk, in my opinion, unless he can shake the fog of Fascism out of his brain'.

After spending the night with Williams Pound went up to Clinton in upper New York State, to Hamilton College, his *alma mater*, where he would stay for nearly a week, till the 13th. The College had asked if he would accept an honorary doctorate, and he had decided that giving a Commencement address could be 'useful', and that seeing 'alumni etc.' could be useful too. He would use the occasion to continue his campaign to get 'Hamilton at least to try to educate a few men to participate in keeping the country from going any further down toward hell'. The college had a new president, William H. Cowley, and Pound had read a copy of his inaugural address 'with increasing irritation' because it did 'NOT arrive at saying the Hamiltn/ graduate shd/ be a whole man EFFECTIVE IN the American social order of the TIME whereinto he graduates'; nor did it manifest 'specific urge to restore American decencies and the aims of the Founders BITCHED and betrayed ever since 1866'. In March he had sent copies of his *Introductory Textbook* to Cowley and to members of the Hamilton Alumni Committee inviting their comments, while telling them that he suspected that '95% of present incumbents of American chairs either can not or dare not face the issues involved'. What he got back was the offer of an honorary doctorate, and he rather felt he was being fobbed off, at least that's how he put it to his old friend 'Stink' Saunders who had been Professor of Agricultural and of General Chemistry in Pound's time at Hamilton. Just before going up to Clinton to receive the degree he wrote to Saunders at whose home he would be spending his first night or two, 'Ez axd [the President] a couple of leading questions & Cowley offered Ez a degree INSTEAD of answering 'em'.

He arrived on Tuesday the 6th and the Commencement Exercises were to take place the following Monday. He got in quite a bit of tennis, playing some doubles matches with Saunders's daughter Olivia as his partner. That is, he took up the net position, only on the middle line, and had her stand on the baseline to take the balls that got past him, few of which did, he being 'such an agile and fiery tennis player'. When he served it was the same. Olivia Saunders remembered him, with remarkable restraint, as 'the most individualistic partner I ever played with', and that 'We won easily'. The tennis, Pound told Olga, 'has brought me down from 207 to 195 lb'.

From the Thursday he was staying with the Edward Roots—Root had been a contemporary of his, and now taught the history and appreciation of art in the college. When Pound talked about Tinkham for President in place of Roosevelt, because he would keep the United States out of a European war, they let him know they were not isolationist and 'felt that if war came we should get into it', and after that Pound said 'not a word about isolation'. They had 'Dupont (gun family) to lunch', without incident. After lunch Pound went out to take on 'econ. & hist dept.' in his 'desperate attempt to educate', but reported no success. He was, though, he told Dorothy, meeting state politicians and generating some sense of useful activity. One of these was perhaps Charles A. Miller, a trustee of Hamilton and also a guest in the house. He was head of the Utica Savings Bank, an expert on such banks, and had charge of Roosevelt's Reconstruction Finance Corporation, and Pound talked to him about Douglas at such length that Mrs Root, by her own account, 'finally had to interpose, saying: Charles must have his rest'. There was no mention in Pound's letters, or in others' recollections, of his literary, or musical, or artistic, interests, and no mention of his poetry except in the degree ceremony itself.

It seems that Pound, at the Alumni Luncheon in the hall of Commons after the ceremony, spoke not as a poet but as a reformer. According to the report in the Utica *Daily Press*, 'he advocated as required reading his own "Text Book", a four-page leaflet attributing America's ills to its currency program', and regretted that it was not possible to purchase 'the thoughts and writings of America's founders as easily and cheaply as you can those of subversive propagandists' such as Marx and Trotsky. He spoke after another of the day's honorands, H. V. Kaltenborn, a well-known news commentator and the principal speaker. There had been, apparently, a gentlemen's agreement that Kaltenborn would avoid contentious issues of international politics, but what he had to say, while innocuous enough to his audience, was to Pound highly provocative. 'It is written in history', he declared, 'that dictatorships shall die, but democracies shall live'; and he spoke of the 'doubtful' alliance between Italy and Germany. Pound interrupted, demanding to know what he meant by 'doubtful', and went on to praise Mussolini and Fascism. Kaltenborn praised God 'that in America people of varying points of view can still speak out', but was then provoked in his turn into saying 'how wrong it was to preach such anti-democratic doctrine within the confines of an American college'. Olivia Saunders, who was in the balcony, told Charles Norman that 'the situation almost got out of hand as both men were thoroughly irritated with the other's point of view', and a good deal of calming down by Professor Saunders and by President Cowley was needed before Kaltenborn was able to finish his address—which, by his own account, the alumni applauded 'with unusual vigor'.

Pound was unrepentant. He wrote to Olga that he had 'About bust the commencement by heckling a s.o.b. that was spouting twaddle'; and he wrote in a letter to President Cowley that 'Hamilton OUGHT to exist to combat that sort of [superficial twaddle] not to honour it'. Cowley had formally invited him to contribute to the Alumni Fund, and Pound was declining rather fiercely, on the grounds that 'COLLEGES hate intellectual life and work against it'; that 'To pay teachers of literature while the whole system tries to kill off the makers of fresh literature is just stupid'; and again, 'I decline to give money and do not believe any money OUGHT to be give to any body of men who don't know what money IS and who refuse (as you in conversation did) to show any curiosity as to its real nature OR to propagate teaching of that nature to at least an elite who COULD keep the nation from going to hell under usury and monetary idiocy.' In his reply Cowley wrote:

I won't attempt to defend my unawareness of monetary problems or my insistent refusal to discuss them in relationship to the College. I do want you to know, however, how badly I felt about the Kaltenborn speech. Most of the people present seemed to think that his remarks were very much in order and that a Fascist such as you should be put in your place. I feel quite the contrary, however. It seems to me that Kaltenborn delighted in making you uncomfortable. There wasn't any reason, in my judgment, for his being so vigorous and unrestrained. I'm not sure I agree that your heckling was in good taste, but on the other hand I can understand the impulse which fathered them. Throughout my sympathies were with you when they weren't with me. Since I was the chairman of the meeting obviously I didn't want a riot.

Pound wrote back, 'git over the idea that I was in any way uncomfortable. I was disgusted at the twaddle'—indeed he had felt anger 'without which nothing gets started', and it 'Wd/ have been pusillanimous to let his twaddle pass unchallenged'. He added—possibly as a retort to Cowley's having remarked, 'obviously, the experience of the alumni lunch still rankles'—'not interested in my feelings, interested in AGENDA / feelings. mere voltometers. useful if used as such.'

Cowley had closed his letter by gracefully returning to what the Kaltenborn fracas had overshadowed, the conferring of the honorary degree of Doctor of Letters upon 'a great son of the College'. That after all, at least from the College's point of view, had been the purpose of his 'visit to the Hill'. At the dignified academic ritual in the College Chapel this citation, a judicious and sympathetic summing up, had been read by the Dean:

Ezra Pound: Native of Idaho, graduate of Hamilton College in the Class of 1905, poet, critic, and prose writer of great distinction. Since completing your college career you have had a life full of significance in the arts. You have found that you could work more happily in Europe than in America and so have lived most of the past thirty years an expatriate making your home in England, France and Italy, but your writings are known wherever English is read. Your feet have trodden paths, however, where the great reading public could give you few followers—into Provençal and Italian poetry, into Anglo-Saxon and Chinese. From all these excursions you have brought back treasure. Your translations from the Chinese have, for example, led one of the most gifted of contemporary poets to call you the inventor of Chinese poetry for our time. Your Alma Mater, however, is an old lady who has not always understood where you have been going, but she has watched you with interest and pride if not always with understanding. The larger public has also been at times amazed at your political and economic as well as your artistic credo, and you have retaliated by making yourself—not unintentionally perhaps—their gadfly. Your range of interests is immense, and whether or not your theories of society survive, your name is permanently linked with the development of English poetry in the twentieth century. Your reputation is international, you have guided many poets into new paths, you have pointed new directions, and the historian of the future in tracing the development of your growing mind will inevitably, we are happy to think, be led to Hamilton and to the influence of your college teachers. You have ever been a generous champion of younger writers as well as of artists in other fields, and for this fine and rare human quality and for your own achievements in poetry and prose, we honor you.

The colours of the doctoral hood which the President then placed over Pound's head were buff and blue, in commemoration, it is said, of the colours of the uniform of the army of the American Revolution.

But the revolution had been betrayed—was being betrayed right then, it had seemed to Pound, in Washington, in New York, at Yale and Harvard and Hamilton. Even if he stood alone, perhaps all the more because he felt that he stood alone, he would not give up his fight for the revolutionary democratic idea. He would deploy such weapons as he had, words in print, words on the air, words addressed from Italy to America out of the coming war.

APPENDICES

A. Outline of Pound's Le Testament *or* Villon

The action is continuous—the fourteen numbers[1] are sung through in a single act which lasts about fifty minutes in Western Opera Theater's 1971 recording—but one can make out a clearly structured progression, an arc through the life of Villon's world to its end. (These notes, except for arias 9 and 10, are based primarily on the performance edition of the Pound/Antheil score prepared by Robert Hughes, and on the 1971 recording—see item 11 in Appendix B.)

I Meditations on death (arias 1–3 = Villon's *Le Testament*, ll. 313–56; 976–89)
  (1) Villon begins, 'meditative, almost sotto voce' (direction in score), 'Et mourut Paris' ('And Paris died, and Helen'), and goes on to think, with stark realism sung dispassionately, how death racks and tortures the body;
  (2) Villon continues, 'Dictes moy', 'Tell me…Where are the snows of yesteryear?', thinking now, in a 'voice reflective and elegiac', that death carries all away, the beautiful, the wise, the strong, and even the Sovereign Virgin could not save Jeanne d'Arc; his voice rises at the close to an emphatic, unanswerable demand, 'Mais où sont les neiges *d'an.tan*'; 'The bite is in the RHYTHM', Pound insisted, 'Not to be got by sobstuff or tears in voice' (EP to Harding, the BBC producer, 27 October 1931, *CPMEP* 54);
  (3) Ythier, his friend, sings 'Mort, j'appelle de ta rigueur', a conventional rondeau which Villon wrote at his request—the lover complains that because death has taken his love away he too must die; sobstuff to which Pound adds an ironic and yet touching echo from La Beauté at her window;

II Old age, regrets for times past (arias 4, 5 = ll. 169–84; 453–532)
  (4) Villon's regrets are not for lost love, rather for his lost youth—'Je plains le temps de ma jeunesse'—and his complaint is of his present decayed condition; sung dispassionately; effectively a prelude to
  (5) La Heaulmière's great aria, 'Ha, vieillesse felonne et fière', a first climax in the work: a powerful, passionate, and sustained raging against the

---

[1] The libretto, in the original Old French, consists of extracts, principally *ballades*, taken from Villon's *Le Testament*, composed in 1462, plus the concluding *Ballade des pendus* composed in 1463 while Villon was under sentence to be hanged and strangled for his part in a brawl. (Sentence annulled on appeal, but Villon banned from Paris for ten years as a bad character—'eu regard à la mauvaise vie dudit Villon'.) Most of the extracts were noticed in the chapter on Villon in *SR*. Inserted amongst the poems by Villon is a hymn to the Virgin by the thirteenth-century trouvère Williaume li Viniers, a setting of which had been included as 'Mère au Sauveour', with Pound's English adaptation of the words, in Walter Rummel's *Hesternae Rosae* (1912). There are fourteen numbers as Hughes and Fisher now count them: Villon's '*Item*, m'amour' (three lines) is no longer counted as a separate number. The hymn 'Vergine pucele roiauz' is now restored to its original and correct position, following 'Dame du ciel', and assigned as Pound intended to a voice within the church. It is followed by the Priest's singing just four to six bars of 'Suivez beauté'. (See *EPRO* 121 and 262 n. 116; *CPMEP* vii; *Testament II* 213–65.)

decay of the body; unsparing in its realism, ranging from wild outrage to gentle and tender moments, and wonderfully expressive of a great range of emotion—'simple, tragique, implorant, pompeux, presque parlé, douloureux, violent, scandé, déchirant, intense, snarl, aspro, dolce, doux, triste, elegiac, resigné lent' (from Pound's 1926 markings, *EPRO* 118); altogether a heartbreaking evocation of the irredeemable loss of all she has lived for—as moving as any spirit in Dante's Inferno;

III The way we live now [i] (arias 6, 7 = ll. 942–9; 533–60)

(6) The Gallant sings 'Faulse beauté', foreseeing that the false beauty he pursues will be his undoing—see (12);

(7) 'Item', a brief extract from Villon's will (in which he leaves to his love, his dear Rose, neither heart nor liver, since her taste falls somewhere below those things); leads into 'Or y pensez', 'It's time to think of yourselves', in which La Heaulmière and two younger whores wise up—take what you can get while you still can, you'll soon be past it— sung fiercely, with violin and oboe in firm support, and Villon's Mother joining in at the close, 'very cracked and sarcastic, as it were out of tune' (direction in score);

IV A future in heaven? (arias 8, 9 = 873–909, W. li Viniers)

(8) 'Dame du ciel': Villon's Mother sings a prayer he wrote for her, calling on the Virgin to receive her into heaven, and declaring her faith in the painted paradise on the church wall where angels play harps and lutes, above the painted hell where the damned are being boiled on hell's fires—'Grant me the joy of paradise, great Goddess to whom sinners must turn'; this is sung in a voice of terrified, breathless, unstoppable pleading over a continuous thunderous rumbling in 'the cellarage' from bass-bells and/or the very bottom notes of the piano; the voice is on one pitch as in medieval liturgy, but with the dissonant intervals of the tritone, the 'devil in the scale' that never comes to a resolution; (Fisher: 2003, 31–2, 34–5, notes an effect of sustained, controlled chaos; Schafer writes of the deranging difficulty of synchronizing the measures of the vocal line with those of the accompaniment ('Ezra Pound et la musique', *Les Cahiers de L'Herne: Ezra Pound/2* (Paris: Éditions de l'Herne, 1965), p. 649)); all this places the mother among the souls on the painted wall reaching up to be saved and in terror of the devils there who would drag her down;

(9) 'Mère au sauveour', in response to and at an absolute remove from the Mother's terror of hell, is a straightforward hymn to the Virgin, sung by a chorister within the church, as if by the painted angels on the wall there, offering assurance that through her 'paradise shall be opened to us'; the words and melody in William li Viniers's thirteenth-century mode, taken from Rummel's *Hesternae Rosae* (1912), but accompanied (through first ten bars) by recurrent tubular chimes suggesting the altar

bell (cf. *EPRO* 121, 262–3 n. 116); this is not a troubadour love song, rather an orthodox hymn in which the Virgin is set apart from all women on earth, and the divine light is not looked for in a living woman;

V The way we live now [ii] (arias 10–12 = 625–6; 1591–1610, 1619–22; 713–28)

  (10) A 'Very husky priest'—Pound's markings (*CPMEP* vii, *EPRO* 121)— 'Bass profundissimus', while crossing from church to brothel, and turning—and turning the opera—back from the Virgin to the whore, bawls a few bars of 'Suivez beauté', 'Chase after beauty, run to feasting, | love as you will and take your fill' (my translation); the vocal melody is the simple $^6/_4$ re-arrangement and setting of Villon's words by Gustave Ferrari, to which Pound added an accompanying cello and bass; since Pound despised Ferrari's 'liking watered down duParc, Chausson post Debussy typical modern french puke' (EP to Harding, 27 October 1931, *CPMEP* 54), he must here be savaging his watering down of Villon, as well as a church guilty of the Virgin/whore split;

  (11) Bozo the brothel-keeper, 'hiccoughing drunk', as are the trombones, sings how he loves and serves ('Se j'ayme et sers') and like a knight defends his lady, Fat Margot, 'in this bordello where we live in state'— one is reminded of the Brecht–Weill *Threepenny Opera*; here, Pound wrote, 'Villon casts out the dregs of his shame' (*SR* 176);

  (12) The Gallant emerges from the brothel, a dying man, renouncing and cursing love—'Je regnie Amours'—rather jagged, strained singing, to a sympathetic violin;

VI Chorus 'and ballyhoo' of the mob of drinkers (13 = ll. 1238–65)

  (13) A second climax: ostensibly a prayer for the soul of the notorious drunkard 'the late Master Jean Cotart', the public prosecutor who let Villon off a murder charge; 'noise and general pandemonium to increase as it goes along', with counter-rhythms Charles Ives might have ventured; at one point 'Solo instruments ad lib as in toughest possible jazz band. Timballes smacking the rhythm on tonic, dominant or wherever convenient. All against the imitation hurdy-gurdy formed by basson, cello and trombones'; in the second stanza Pound inserted 'bits of provencal indecent melodies | hu et hu et hu et hu | . . . not a chaste rhythm' (EP to D. G. Bridson, 15 September 1958, [Beinecke]); then between Villon's second and third stanzas he inserted a fast-paced thirteenth-century trouvère aubade warning of approaching danger; at last the well-orchestrated cacophony fades upon a 'dying belch'; after 'a hush' the backdrop is raised and there is a wonderfully assured change of mood, just a few bars very precisely calculated in tone and rhythm to introduce the concluding chorale;

VII 'Frères humains'

(14) The epitaph in the form of a ballade which Villon made for himself and for the comrades with whom he was expecting to be hanged, set as a chorale for six voices (unaccompanied until the final bars), after the manner of fifteenth- to sixteenth-century homophonic motets (Josquin, Gesualdo, Tallis, Palestrina—not plain chant). See p. 21.

B. *A brief history of* Le Testament *or* Villon

1. Holograph sketches and drafts, mainly establishing the melodic line, date from about the end of 1919, continuing into 1921 (mostly in Beinecke).

2. Pound/Bedford collaboration, October to December 1920, and June to August 1921: first version in the hand of Agnes Bedford (Beinecke). AB reported that EP was 'impatient & bored & disapproving' of this version (AB to Hugh Kenner, 1964, [HRC]).

3. Pound/Antheil version of 1923, i.e. Antheil's micro-fractional 're-notation' of (2) in the autumn of 1923, completed 31 December 1923—score with music in Antheil's hand and Villon's words written in by Pound. Does not include Gallant's 'Je renye amours'. Guillaume li Viniers's words and melody for 'Mère au Sauveur' were taken from Walter Rummel's *Hesternae Rosae* (1912), but the accompaniment is Pound's. The vocal melody of the Priest's two lines of Villon's 'Suivez beauté' was taken from *Collection Yvette Guilbert* in the arrangement of Gustave Ferrari. The score calls for ten solo voices, chorus, and seventeen instrumentalists who among them play an unusually diverse lot of instruments: 'nose-flute, flute and piccolo (one player), oboe, saxaphone, bassoon, trumpet (for two bars only!), horn, two trombones, mandolin, violin, cello, three contrabassi, a variety of drums (including six tympani), bells, "bass bells" (*sic*)...gongs, sandpaper, dried bones and a percussionist whistling' (Robert Hughes). (Score now in Beinecke, and known as the 'Gold score' from its binding—see 12 (2) below.)

4. 'Mort, j'appelle' (Ythier) and 'Je renye amours' scored in simplified measures for voice and solo violin, performed by Yves Tinayre and Olga Rudge in Rudge–Antheil concert, 7 July 1924; then engraved and printed 'for private circulation' in 1926 as 'Two Songs from Ezra Pound's Opera Le Testament'.

5. Further reworkings of the score by Pound in 1924 and 1925, culminating in a private performance for invited guests only in Salle Pleyel, 29 June 1926: 'Paroles de Villon | Arias and fragments from an opera | LE TESTAMENT |... Musique par Ezra Pound'. On the programme ('probablement'):

   Hommage ou ouverture, a six-note melody 'based on a fundamental tone of D$_2$ (five ledger lines below the bass clef)' (*CPMEP* 35 n. 99), to be performed on a five-foot long alpenhorn;

Et mourut Paris and *Je plains* (Villon), and *Mort, j'appelle* (Ythier), sung by Yves Tinayre, tenor, accompanied by Olga Rudge, violin;

Motif a solo riff by Pound on kettle-drum;

Faulse beauté (Gallant) and *Heaulmière* sung by Tinayre, accompanied by violin and harpsichord;

Motifs de la foule [= 'Père Noé'], sung by Tinayre and Robert Maitland, bass-baritone, with a mix-up ('mélange') of violin, harpsichord and trombones;

Si J'ayme et sers (Bozo) sung by Maitland to the accompaniment of two trombones;

Frères humains performed by the ensemble.

The scoring for all the numbers was in relatively simplified measures, mainly in ⅝. The score for Heaulmière's aria, arranged for tenor and solo violin, was printed (in facsimile of Olga Rudge's manuscript) in two periodicals in 1938, and in *GK* in 1953. Performance edition (2008) in 12 below.

6. 12 July 1926, private performance at the home of Mrs Christian Gross in Paris, by Robert Maitland accompanied by Olga Rudge, of Villon's 'Et mourut Paris', 'Je plains', and 'Dictes moi' (*EPRO* 133). Beinecke has a manuscript score in Olga Rudge's hand corresponding to this performance. Performance edition (2008) in 12 below.

7. Broadcast version by BBC radio 26 and 27 October 1931. Pound sent the producer the unique Pound/Antheil score (3 above), with his added markings in coloured crayon, and wrote a dialogue scenario to turn the opera into a radio 'melodrama'. However, the 'small & scandalized orchestra' (AB to Hugh Kenner, 1964, [HRC]), finding the 1923 score too difficult, freely departed from it, largely falling back on the 1924 and 1926 arrangements (4 and 5 above), or on the earlier Pound/Bedford score, resulting in a musically confused and unsatisfactory production. No complete score for this production has been located, and none may have existed. (See *EPRO passim*.)

8. In 1933 Pound revised *Le Testament* once more and finally, 'hopin to make it foolproof' (*EPEC* 76), scoring all the numbers in basic measures, except for the final two choral numbers ('Père Noé' and 'Frères humains'), and leaving Heaulmière's aria in the simple mixed measures of 1926. This, the third complete score, in Pound's hand, is in the Beinecke (*EPRO* 227 n. 48; *CPMEP* 148 n. 10). Performance edition (2008) in 12 below.

9. A second BBC radio production, 28 June and 31 July 1962. The 1931 scenario was used again; but the music of the Pound/Antheil score was edited by R. Murray Schafer, who, regarding it as 'a total mess', 'weeded out Antheilisms' (Schafer to Hugh Kenner, 25 August 1962 [HRC]); greatly simplified both metrics and orchestration, partly on the basis of the Pound/Bedford version; and himself added some additional music. Bridson, the BBC producer, assigned the 'Voice from the church' singing 'Mère au Saveur' to the Priest, and put it before the Mother's 'Dame du ciel' (*EPRO* 260 n. 97).

Pound had nothing to do with the production, and judged it 'a considerable MESS' (Pound to Bridson, as recorded by Bridson—cited in Carpenter 885).

10. Performance version for the 1965 Spoleto Festival arr. Lee Hoiby and Stanley Hollingsworth based on 8 above.

11. Performance edition of Pound/Antheil score prepared by Robert Hughes, premiered 13 November 1971 by Western Opera Theater conducted by Robert Hughes, in the Zellerbach Auditorium of University of California at Berkeley; recorded 18 and 19 November 1971, and issued in 1972 as Fantasy Records no. 12001. Instrumentation: flute/piccolo, oboe, alto saxophone, bassoon, French horn, trumpet, trombone (2), percussion (3), piano, violin, cello, contrabass (3), mandolin.

Hughes edited *Le Testament* from a photocopy of the 1923/1931 score supplied by the BBC in 1961; this lacked the two pages containing 'Mère au Sauveur' and 'Suivez beauté'—which had possibly become separated in 1931—and so had to follow Schafer's accompaniment (tubular bells) for the former, and provide his own for the latter. He also followed the Bridson misplacement of 'Mère au Sauveur'. The two missing pages were discovered by Margaret Fisher in 1999, and revealed the correct order and accompaniment, and also that the Priest was to sing only the opening bars of 'Suivez beauté', with a simple cello and bass accompaniment—see *EPRO* 121, 262 n. 116.

Since 1971 there have been several productions, all of them using the 1923/1931 Pound/Antheil score as edited by Robert Hughes. The most notable was the 1980 Holland Festival production performed by the ASKO ensemble, Reinbert de Leeuw music director and conductor, recorded and released as Philips Harlekijn 9500 927. A powerful rendering of Heaulmière's aria sung by Anna Myatt, contralto, in a performance by the University of York Villon Music Theatre Ensemble directed and co-produced by Charles Mundye for the 1992 York Festival, is included on Other Minds Audio CD OM 1005–2, issued with an 80-page booklet (edited and written by Margaret Fisher), as *Ego Scriptor Cantilenae: The Music of Ezra Pound* (San Francisco: Other Minds Inc., 2003). That disk also gives 'Dictes moy' (Villon) from the Holland Festival production; and 'Dame du ciel', 'Père Noé', and 'Frères humains' from the 1971 Western Opera Theater production.

12. New, definitive, performance editions of *Le Testament* by Robert Hughes and Margaret Fisher were published in 2008 and 2011 in 2 volumes: (1) in 2008 a double volume, *Ezra Pound: Le Testament, 'Paroles de Villon'*, comprising 1926 'Salle Pleyel' concert excerpts [5 and 6 above], and 1933 Final Version complete opera [8 above]; (2) in 2011 *Ezra Pound: Le Testament*, a facsimile of the 1923 Pound/Antheil score [3 above], with extensive essays and notes, and accompanied by a re-release of the Fantasy LP recording on audio CD (see 11 above).

C. *Outline of* Cavalcanti. A sung dramedy in 3 acts

Because Harding worked in the Experimental Features section of the Drama Department and not in the BBC's Music Department, *Cavalcanti* was developed as a music drama for radio. Pound called it 'a sung dramedy in 3 acts'. 'Dramedy' was a word not to be found in the *Oxford English Dictionary*, but Pound had used it in 1920 when (as 'T.J.V.') he reviewed a rubbishy play full of sentimental gush, stagey banalities 'and a parody of every cliché' of the daily newspaper serials. He took the 'tempest of applause' it received to mean 'the last fading and hesperal flicker of British intelligence', or else 'a lifelong and ineradicable devotion to Miss Eva Moore'. The play left him sympathizing, he wrote, with 'the babu who said there were three sorts of plays: Comedy, tragedy and dramedy'. That might tell us something about the 'dramedy' element in his *Cavalcanti*.

The scenario is set up at the start of each act by the Announcer, and there is also some spoken dialogue within the acts. The plot is thin, almost non-existent; 'but wother hell can you do with super-in-human refinemengts of the intellect', Pound exclaimed to Agnes Bedford when pointing out that 'the axshun' of the second act was all to do with establishing the difficulty of 'Donna mi prega'. That action consists of: Guido among his rowdy friends and deep in a game of chess; as a practical joke his page nails him by his shirt-tail to the bench; his friends with much laughter prevail on him to sing his philosophical *canzone* while they have him thus nailed down, though they then interrupt from time to time to declare they don't understand it. The only point of the larky 'action' is to set the *Canzone* off against the friends' incomprehension and their relative lack of seriousness.

There is more ado in the first act, and all to the same point. With some companions Betto, a bore, follows Guido into a cemetery where he is brooding upon his fatal love, and tries to compel him to be a guest at their dining club; Guido escapes by vaulting over a tomb and quipping that he would not fit in since Betto and his lot are in their proper element there among the dead. The incident is from Boccaccio's *Decameron*, and it is related there to illustrate Guido's isolated superiority. The build-up to the quip tells how his propensity to philosophical speculation set him apart from what his fellow Florentines regarded as the good life and made him decline membership of their clubs. Betto has to spell out to his friends that Guido meant 'that plain unlettered dunces like us are no better than dead men compared with men of learning like him'. In Pound's scenario Guido is next threatened by a gang of his enemies, and this time he escapes over the wall, kicking as he goes a huge flower pot off the wall and over their leader's head. This is slapstick stuff, having nothing to do with what Guido sings, and that must be its point. He is the only serious character here, and he is surrounded by friends and enemies who are all fixed in the bathos and nonsense of low comedy. Between his realm of love and their unenlightened world there just is no interesting connection.

The real action of the opera is in Guido's songs and in Fortuna's finale.[2] The Overture, establishing a serious mood in which a rising melody is countered by darkly reflective cadences, leads into Guido's singing of how he is pained unto death in love's pleasing flame; and yet, in his folly, thinks himself saved because a mistress passed through his heart and carried all hope away. One must adjust (as in Erasmus' *Praise of Folly*) to a riddling point of view which inverts conventional expectation and resolves the contradictions of pleasure and pain in love by renouncing, not love itself, but what was hoped for from the mistress. Betto the bore, thinking to flatter Guido, sings him one of his conventional *ballate* in which the lover pleads for his mistress' mercy. For his pains Betto is told that the song is 'DE - RI - VA - TIVE!... Showing the influence of earlier and inferior authors'. Seriousness is restored with Guido's 'Era in pensier', 'Being in thought of love', which picks up the theme of his opening song. He meets two maidens in a wood and one sings, teasingly, 'There rains in us love's play'. Guido takes them to figure refining love, and confesses his condition: his heart has slain him with a wound it took from a lady in Toulouse. The maids understand that the lady so looked in through his eyes that by Love's power she cut her image on his heart, and that Love now resides there and looks out from his eyes with a splendour their eyes cannot sustain. Since you suffer so grievously, they tell him, recommend yourself unto Love. He can only confirm their diagnosis, saying that all he can remember is Toulouse, a lady with corded bodice, slender, whom Love called Mandetta, and that he took his death wound from the sudden lightning of her eyes. This is the statement of Guido's predicament, and the opera's real starting point. The sight of Mandetta has put an end to his ordinary life: what will he do now?

He begins Act 2 with a resolution to keep faith with love though love show him no mercy, to serve though unrewarded; and in this spirit (which is Love's gift) he finds that when pleasure pains, 'There rains within my heart | such good sweet love | that I declare, "Lady, I am all yours"'. His friends then sing 'In un boschetto', 'one of his lighter songs' become popular in the streets, and they begin (according to Pound's direction) 'with a good deal of rowdyism', though the words 'gradually get the better of the horse-play'. The song celebrates another encounter in a wood, this

---

[2] The libretto consists of 13 numbers, with an overture drawn from *Sonate Ghuidonis*.

Act 1
1. *Poi che di doglia* (Ballata I) : Guido
2. *Sol per pietà* (Ballata XIII) : Betto
3. *Gianni quel Guido* (not by G. C.) : Guido's friends
4. *Guarda ben dico* (not by G.C.) : The Cobbler
5. *Era in pensier* (Ballata VII) : Guido

Act 2
1. *Se m'hai del tutto* (Ballata III) : Guido
2. *In un boschetto* (Ballata IX): Guido's friends
3. *Donna mi prega* (Canzone) : Guido
4. *Tos temps serai* (Sordello) : Cunizza's old servan

Act 3
1. *Ailas* (Sordello) : A French soldier
2. *Quando di morte* (Ballata XII) : Guido
3. *Perch'io non spero* (Ballata X) : Ricco & Guido
4. *Io son la donna* (? G.C.,? N. Machiavelli):
   Seneschal & Fortuna

time with a fair young shepherdess who is eager for a lover, and the singer thinks, "twas but the time's provision | To gather joy of this small shepherd maid' as she draws him willingly to herself and gives him 'sight of every coloured blossom', to his unbounded joy. It is a charmingly innocent fantasy of the 'classic' kind, wholly without the complications of Guido's way to 'good sweet love', and it serves to set the common or popular dream of love against his refined vision.

There follows Guido's singing 'Donna mi prega', his philosophical *Canzone*, at considerable length. Pound saw this as the 'tour de force and danger zone' musically. He reported to Agnes Bedford that Tibor Serly 'thought melody came UP to same point too often' and was 'monotonous'; Bedford herself thought it 'DULL'. Pound's defence was that the orchestration was 'meagre' because 'this bit is mainly for radio'. But there is not much beauty and emotion in the singing to delight the ear; and the song seems to be going on not a little didactically about a meaning it insists only the already expert will understand.

However, as Pound remarked in *The Spirit of Romance*, in the Tuscan *canzone* thought was predominant, not emotion. It was devoted, he wrote, to 'supernormal pleasures, enjoyable by man through the mind'; and its drama was 'mankind's struggle upward out of ignorance into the clear light of philosophy'. Guido, in Act 2, can be seen to be engaged in that struggle, as, nailed to the bench by his jesting and uncomprehending companions, he sings out his passionate apprehension of the intellectual form of all-creating Light. And he does reach, for that moment, 'into the clear light of philosophy'.

Guido's *Canzone* is immediately followed by a song of Sordello's in the Provençal mode which he had brought into Tuscany, and the contrast is telling. Pound has Guido remark that Sordello's song has a simplicity—and, one might well put in, a simple musicality—which his own *Canzone* lacked. 'Tos temps serai' expresses a sentiment close to that of Guido's first song in Act 2: I will be ever constant in love (a soprano sings) because love causes me to serve the best and fairest of women, and it is to her honour that she does not advance me: her virtue is my reward. There is the difference that Sordello is in an interactive, mutual relation with his lady—her honour is vital to him, and also her holding him in honour; whereas in Guido's song the vital relation is with an intellectualized Love. More significant than that discrimination, however, is the background to Sordello's song. The point is made by the Announcer and again in the dialogue that Cunizza used to sing it. We need to know that she was also the inspiration of the song, having 'formed [Sordello's] genius'. Beyond that, she was for Dante and for Pound an icon of free and joyous loving. In his *Cantos* Pound records how her loving nature caused her to free her family's serfs; and, in canto 36 following the 'Donna mi prega', he records how Sordello treasured her image in his mind above the five castles his king gave him. In complementary ways they exemplify love acting freely in their world, free of possessiveness, and free also of Guido's intellectualizing. In a note, 'Background—Florence at the end of the 13th century', Pound remarked that 'Sordello's felicity and clearness [in his poetry] may well have been the despair of the men who 50 years after him tried to write philosophical verse'. That must set Cavalcanti's 'Donna mi prega' in an equivocal light.

The second act ends with Guido's being served with a decree of exile, signed by his friend Dante, 'for the tranquillity of the city'; and in Act 3 he dies in exile. Cavalcanti was, as a matter of historical record, exiled, along with the leading members of both warring factions, the Bianchi and the Neri, upon the orders of Dante acting as one of the Priors at the time; and he was brought down with malaria in 'the swamp at Sarzana'. He did not die there, however, since Dante had him brought back to Florence when he learnt of his fever. Pound has him die in exile for operatic effect.

The third act opens with another song of Sordello's, sung this time (according to the Announcer) by 'one of the stragglers of the French army'. 'What use are eyes | that see not my desire' is the refrain; while the two verses sing of dying from love. Guido, as if taking his lead from that, expands on the theme in his 'death song', 'Quando di morte', the twelfth *ballata* in which, as Pound had observed, 'Guido turns to an intellectual sympathy . . . yet with some inexplicable lack—his sophistication prevents the complete enthusiasm.' Then follows, as the culmination of the serious action of the opera, 'Perch'io non spero', 'Because no hope is left me, Ballatetta, | Of return to Tuscany'. In this Guido accepts his death, and in a final and absolute commitment sends his soul, that is, his new person fashioned from desire, in care of the *Ballatetta* itself, to dwell with and adore the Lady he has served. But who is that Lady? If it were Mandetta of Toulouse then we might think that the opera was allowing him to reintegrate as he dies, if only in his own mind, what had been separated out in the middle act, the direct vision of beauty and the intellectual conception of it. However, the emphasis on the 'sweet intelligence' of the Lady would rather indicate that his desire is to dwell with Love as he had defined it in his 'Canzone d'amore'. His paradise would be that of the Arab philosophers, a state in which the individual mind, refined into a rational soul, contemplates the universal intelligence and is at one with the light which has brought it into being.

In performance this mystery is complicated by Pound's having Guido's page (a boy soprano) sing the song with innocent clarity, though helped out (and thus interrupted) here and there by Guido's mature baritone; and it is further complicated by his having Guido say that the boy must learn the song because there is a cypher hidden in the music and he won't be let back into Tuscany unless he has mastered it. Margaret Fisher, with a fine combination of musical expertise and code-breaking ingenuity, locates the cypher 'in the motif at bars 81–83', that being 'the first instance in which the opera's motif resolves to its tonic note at the cadence'. She reads it off (by transposing the notes into the conventional pitch-names) as *ut ut re mi fa sol fa mi re ut*; then, by taking those syllables as Latin (*ut*), Provençal (*re mi[r]*), and the rest Italian, she finds *so that to gaze intently gives me light, makes me king so*. Well, as Fisher writes, 'an opera director must have some toe-hold on the cipher' since 'the show must go on', and hers is the only decryption on offer, and it does yield a credible gist of Guido's poems. But it would be a mistake, I think, and a distraction, to make too much of it, as by seeking in it some secret revelation or message. The cypher is not the song, and Guido's testament and mystery is surely in the song. The cypher is simply a password to get the page and the song into Tuscany, where the boy is to sing it and so pass on the tradition. He has still failed to master it, however, when Guido dies on the final note; and since the music is not written down we gather that the tradition stemming from Eleusis will have died with Guido.

The goddess Fortuna then takes over in the opera's finale, appearing as *dea ex machina* to declare that she is the Lady who rules mankind and its affairs. Entering into Guido's jailer she declares this in his voice and (according to Pound's notes) with his heavy and relentless energy; then she sings it again as herself, 'immortal... inhuman, impersonal... so powerful as to be unconscious of opposition'. 'Destiny', Pound noted, 'not volition'. Machiavelli, whose song this may be, would consider, in the penultimate chapter of *The Prince*, 'How far human affairs are governed by fortune, and how fortune can be opposed'; and he would conclude that 'fortune shows her power where there is no force to hold her in check'. In Dante's world-view fortune was subject to the control of Providence; but Providence is excluded from Pound's *Cavalcanti* as from Machiavelli's counsels. In their modern world it is the force of human will, of volition, that should oppose Fortune's power. And where that force is lacking, as in Guido's failure to make the intelligence of love prevail in his world, things are left to unenlightened chance.

D. EP, 'Huey, God bless him', an unpublished article intended for New Democracy, *enclosed with a letter to Gorham Munson dated '13 or 14 Aug. [1935]' (HRC)*

Social Creditors are the last people who OUGHT to be obsessed by nomenclatures, and they should either be in the front rank of fighters for clearer terminology or be led out to the ducking stool.

Meaning that we must understand what other people WANT (no matter what they call it) and that we must be and STAY aware of what is going on.

What Huey Long says and MEANS today, Roosevelt says and does NOT mean in a year or two. I said in the New English Weekly that Frank D. cd. side step any third party by a feint to the left just before the next Presidential election. He has been pushed to make that feint ALREADY.

The American highbrow etc. has underestimated our friend from Louisiana.

Huey has not STRESSED the use of FLOW. He has not, I think seen the full power that lies in the CONSTITUTIONAL right of CONGRESS to issue money.

I can't condense the summary of Jefferson's economic beliefs (printed after p. 112 in My 'Jefferson and/or Mussolini', published in England, but not yet through the american barrage and sabotage.

BUT, I accuse all the Social Credit papers of not having given enough publicity to Huey Long's more vital formulations.

Huey is no more befogged than 90% of the new economists. You still read EVEN social credit essays which do NOT distinguish between property and capital.

I don't think Huey dissociates WEALTH and purchasing power. I mean in his own mind.

NEVERTHELESS when Huey demands

'homestead allowance free of debt',

he is demanding something which WE OUGHT to recognize as a NATIONAL DIVIDEND.

WHEN he demands not only free school books, but a guarantee that every child shall be assured of as much education as it wants or can stand, he is demanding a MATERIAL DIVIDEND, and it wd. be hidebound social creditism to insist that this be given in the form of 30 cents worth of paper money.

The education of the young is their best GUARANTEE for maintaining a clean economic system after they get it.

Huey's whole emphasis on the RISING generation is centuries ahead of Townsend's plea for kindness to the decrepit (humane and charitable etc. as that may be.)

Give a man health and knowledge in youth and you will SAVE very considerably on his needs for an old age pension.

Any man who means to be alive in 1936 and 1937 must pick his rulers NOT by where they are now, but by what they WANT and where they are GOING.

LONG WANTS a new economic system. The root is in VOLITION; in the direction of the WILL.

No man has lost more by Senator Cutting's death, than his friend from Louisiana. The possibility of a third party for 1936 or 1940 (never wholly alluring) went out of American politics when Cutting plunged to his death.

But Social Credit in America will make the greatest of possible mistakes if it fails to STUDY the Senator from Louisiana and if it fails to AID the Senator from Louisiana.

Share the wealth as Long sees it is still uncut marble, but from that heavy block to

SHARE THE PURCHASING POWER!

is a possible step. Share the purchasing power, the effective ORDERS against the total production of the nation, as that production works, and as orders can and of a right SHOULD be issued against it, IS the LOGICAL CONCLUSION of what LONG WANTS. And Long WANTS it as no other man now in the Senate.

Long's resurrection of the Pilgrim's covenant is the finest appeal to OUR tradition that has come from any man now in politics. He did not get that out of millionaires' newspapers.

If you get your ideas of Huey from the British or New York papers (run by mostly the same set of cooks) [stet. not crooks but cooks in this context—EP] you will not get the REAL HUEY.

His style is better than Roosevelt's. (Look up Schopenhauer on style if you want to see why I say this). His style is better than the Astor–Moley ballyhoo, and LE STYLE C'EST L'HOMME.

The neo=Concord school and the neo=transpontine Georgians might start analyzing public writings in our time./ Long's prose is, in spots, extremely clear and incisive. It is NOT filled with the Astor=Moley=Roosevelt evasiveness./ No reader is going to believe this until he or she spends a half hour with the actual TEXTS or Long's 'Share the Wealth Principles' or with the radio speech of March 7th.

Both these represent a progress from Father Coughlin's 16 or whatever points.

There are still statements in these formulations that are more HUMAN than purely (videlicet, sterilizedly and unfructably) economic. Thank God for it! The one European who gets ACTION has denied the incarnation of the HOMO ECONOMICUS.

Long's 'please let me ask you who READ this document', is a request that WE social creditors of all people ought to grant him.

We will get NOTHING from the Tugwell=Moley=Astor=Baruch melange of abuleia and dalliance.

There is no man in our public life more free of mental conceit (love of his own fixations, enamourment with FIXED IDEAS, and wounds to vanity imminent in the modification of the details of those ideas,) than is Long.

HUEY WITH an adequate cabinet would give us a FACTIVE administration. The term 'adequate cabinet' is very probably a dream floating in the clouds above American possibility. BUT there already EXISTS a nucleus, or a scattered nebula, of men IN the U.S.A. who KNOW enough about economics (NON=STATIC but LIVING and developing economic perception) to supply Senator Long with the details and carburetters requisite to putting his WILL into practice.

If we do notwork WITH Huey Long we risk a sixteen years' delay in the establishment of A CREDIT ACCOUNT for the nation.

You do not work WITH a man if you merely hang round and say 'Yasssir!'

EZRA POUND

E. The founding of the Bank of England, and the US National Banking Act (46/233)

1.

Hath benefit of interest on all

the moneys which it, the bank, creates out of nothing. (46/233)

Pound's source was Christopher Hollis, *The Two Nations: A Financial Study of English History* (George Routledge and Sons, 1935), pp. 30 and 36. Hollis's ch. 3, a useful summary account of the founding of the Bank of England, accurately reflects what was written in the early tracts mentioned below. Doubt has been cast on Hollis's accuracy, and on the authenticity and the truth of the quotation, by Meghnad Desai, formerly a professor of economics at the London School of Economics, a leading member of the British Labour Party, and a life peer in the House of Lords. In his *The Route of All Evil: The Political Economy of Ezra Pound* (Faber & Faber, 2006) he wrote that he had been unable to trace the quote, allowed that it might have been made in a prospectus soliciting support, but dismissed its substance as 'a common fallacy as to how banks operate', one feverishly imagined by 'anti-banking agitators' and put about by 'the conspiratorially minded' (68).

I have not found the quotation in question in *Bank of England: Selected Tracts 1694–1804: A Collection of Seven Rare Works... in the Goldsmiths' Library of Economic Literature, the University of London* (Gregg International Publishers Limited, n.d.), but there is indirect confirmation of it in the earliest of these tracts. William III being in need of money to finance his war with France, it was proposed that instead of borrowing at excessive rates from the goldsmiths, the government should borrow £1,200,000 from a new private Corporation to be known as the Bank of England. This Bank would raise the money by public subscription and lend it to the King at 8 per cent plus £4,000 p.a. for expenses (Hollis, 29). In *A Brief Account of the Intended Bank of England (1694)*, attributed to Michael Godfrey or William Paterson, there is this:

This *Bank* will consist in a Revenue or Income of Eight *per Cent. per Annum*, for and upon the Money subscribed; and what Profits and Improvements can be made from the Business and Credit of the *Bank*, will be also divided among the Proprietors. Thus this Company or Corporation will exceed all others of that kind known in the Commercial World. For here will be Eight *per Cent. per Annum* certain upon the Capital; and as good and great a probability of other Profits as ever any Company had. (*Selected Tracts* 10)

The further profits, note, will be profits on its credit, not on its deposited subscriptions. In the second tract, *A Short Account of the Bank of England* (1695), attributed to Michael Godfrey, its deputy governor, we find first,

The Subscriptions to **the Bank** were made by vertue of a Commission under *the great Seal* of England, grounded upon the said **Act of Parliament**... towards the raising of the said 1200000 l.... And notwithstanding *all the Endeavours of its Adversaries*, to the great Astonishment *as well of the Friends, as of the Enemies of the Bank*, the whole 1200000 *l.* was Subscribed *in 10 days time* (1).

The tract then sets out to defend the Bank against its critics, and among its many justifications, including the 8 per cent return, there is one paragraph which reveals exactly how the Bank had benefit of interest on money which it created out of nothing:

Some find fault with **the Bank**, because they have *not taken in the whole* 1200000 *l.* which was Subscribed; for they have called in but for 720000 *l.* which is more than they have now occasion for: But however, they have paid into the Exchequer *the whole* 1200000 *l. before the time appointed by the* **Act of Parliament**; and the *less Money* they have taken in to do it with, so much *the more* they have served *the Publick:* For the rest is left to circulate in Trade, to be lent on Land, or otherwise to be disposed of for the Nations Service; and its better for **the Bank**, as well as *the Publick*, to have 480000 *l. in the Subscribers hands, ready to be called for* as they want it, *than to have it lie useless by them.* (6)

Could Pope or Swift in their satires have been so bold? (Note the hidden bonus: the Bank would receive 8 per cent on the full £1.2m, i.e. £96,000; but £96,000 on £720,000 meant an effective interest rate of 13.33 per cent.)

A 1705 tract, *Remarks upon the Bank of England... Concerning the Intended Prolongation of the Bank*, attributed to John Broughton, observed that among the Bank's many privileges were that its interest from the government was 'Exempt from Taxes, to which other Money, and Stock, and Land were liable'; and that its power to extend its credit without limit, 'and upon so good a Foundation as the security of an Act of Parliament, is perhaps a more considerable Article of [its] Profit than even so great an Interest' (13). To put it simply, the private Bank of England was authorized to lend and to charge interest on money it didn't have—in other words, to print money; its liabilities were underwritten by the government; and its profits were all its own. The Bank of England continued as a private bank until its shareholders were bought out by the state after the 1939–45 war.

When Lord Desai declares Pound altogether wrong to think 'that banks [in general] create profits out of nothing', because 'Banks have to ... have collateral assets against any credit they create by lending' (68), he is being disingenuous, since banks do lend on their credit. Witness Will Hutton in the *Observer* of 4 November 2007: 'prudence demands that [banks] have up to 8 dollars or pounds of their own capital to support every 100 dollars or pounds that they lend.' That order of 'prudence' ensured that 'Between 2004 and 2007 bank lending rose 200 per cent while bank capital went up only 20 per cent' (Will Hutton, *Observer* (13 April 2008)). In 2007 Citigroup's ratio of assets to capital proved to be 1:48, though they reported 'only' 1:22 (Jeff Madrick, 'The Wall Street Leviathan', *NYR* (28 April 2011) 72). 'In the past 10-to-one leverage would have been about par for a bank. More recently ... many large financial institutions, including now-defunct investment banks such as Bear Stearns and Lehman Brothers, reached for 30-to-one leverage, sometimes even more' (Robert M. Solon, Nobel Prize in Economics 1987, *NYR* 56.8 (14 May 2009) 4). Imprudent Bear Stearns, America's fifth largest investment bank, had collapsed early in 2008 with $11.8bn of capital 'leveraged' up to $395bn of debt, thus bringing on the great global credit crisis. In short, 'Banks [do] create money by lending' (J. K. Galbraith, *Guardian* (21 September 2012) 34. In fact, 'The essence of the contemporary monetary system is creation of money, out of nothing, by private banks' (Martin Wolf, *Financial Times* (9 November 2010)). Rather than being wrong, Pound, in 1935, hadn't seen anything yet. 'The bank makes it *ex nihil*'—not the whole £1,200,000 or whatever, but 40 per cent of it in the beginning, and a greater proportion now—and Pound might well repeat, 'Denied by five thousand professors' (46/233).

2.

Semi-private inducement
Said Mr RothSchild, hell knows which Roth-schild
1861, '64 or there sometime, 'Very few people
'will understand this. Those who do will be occupied
'getting profits. The general public will probably not
'see it's against their interest.' (46/233)

The authenticity of this quotation has also been called into question, and this time for good reason. Pound's immediate source, as Leon Surette argued in his *Pound in Purgatory: From Economic Radicalism to Anti-Semitism* (Urbana: University of Illinois Press, 1999), pp. 268–9, may have been appendix 5, 'Quotations from Prominent Men', in Father Coughlin's *Money! Questions and Answers* (1936); though it should be noted that Pound himself, in *A Visiting Card* (1942), gave his source as Willis A. Overholser, *A Short Review and Analysis of the History of Money in the United States* (Libertyville, Ill.: Progress Publishing Concern, 1936), p. 46. He said there that the quoted words—a close paraphrase, not an exact quotation—were from 'a letter of Rothschild Bros. [of London], quoting John Sherman [chairman of the Senate Committee on Finance], and addressed to the Wall Street firm of Ikleheimer, Morton, and Van der Gould, dated 25 June 1863' (*S Pr* 280, 281—see also 309). This is the letter as printed by Overholser:

A Mr. John Sherman has written to us from a town in Ohio, U. S. A., as to the profits that may be made in the National Banking business under a recent act of your Congress, a copy of which accompanied his letter. Apparently this act has been drawn upon the plan formulated here last summer by the British Bankers' Association and by that Association recommended to our American friends as one that if enacted into law, would prove highly profitable to the banking fraternity throughout the world.

Mr. Sherman declares that there has never before been such an opportunity for capitalists to accumulate money, as that presented by this act and that the old plan, of State Banks is so unpopular, that the new scheme will, by mere contrast, be most favourably regarded, notwithstanding the fact that it gives the National Banks an almost absolute control of the National finances. "The few who can understand the system", he says, "will either be so interested in its profits, or so dependent on its favors, that there will be no opposition from that class, while on the other hand, *the great body of the people, mentally incapable of comprehending the tremendous advantages that capital derives from the system, will bear its burdens without complaint, and perhaps without even suspecting that the system is inimical to their interests.*"

Please advise us fully as to this matter, and also, state whether or not you will be of assistance to us, if we conclude to establish a National Bank in the City of New York. If you are acquainted with Mr. Sherman (he appears to have introduced the National Banking act) we will be glad to know something of him. If we avail ourselves of the information he furnished, we will of course make due compensation.

Awaiting your reply, we are, etc.

Overholser also printed the response of Ikleheimer, Morton, and Van der Gould, as of 5 July 1863. In this Sherman is given the character of a hero of the age, as possessing 'in a marked degree, the distinguishing characteristics of the successful modern financier', and likely to 'prove to be the best friend the monied interests of the world have ever had in America'. Enclosed with the letter was a printed circular, prepared because 'Inquiries by European capitalists, concerning this matter, have been so numerous', setting out 'the method of organizing national banks under the recent act of congress, and . . . the profits that may reasonably be expected from such an investment'. The main points of the circular were these (Overholser 47–8):

1. Any number of persons, not less than five, may organize a National Banking Corporation.

2. Except in cities having 6,000 inhabitants or less, a national bank can not have less than $1,000,000 capital.

3. They are private corporations organized for private gain...

4. They are not subject to the control of the state laws, except as Congress may from time to time provide.

7. To start a national bank on the scale of $1,000,000 will require the purchase of that amount (par value) of U.S. Government bonds.

8. U.S. Government bonds can now be purchased at 50 per cent discount, so that a bank of $1,000,000 capital can be started at this time with only $500,000.

9. These bonds must be deposited with the U.S. treasurer at Washington, as security for the national bank currency, that on the making of the deposit will be furnished by the government to the bank.

10. The U.S. Government will pay 6 per cent interest on the bonds, in gold, the interest being paid semi-annually. It will be seen that at the present price of bonds, the interest paid by the government, will of itself amount to 12 per cent in gold, on all the money invested.

11. The U.S. Government, under the provisions of the national banking act, on having the bonds aforesaid deposited with its treasurer, will on the strength of such security, furnish national currency to the bank depositing the bonds, to the amount of 90 per cent of the face of the bonds, at an annual interest of only ONE per cent per annum. Thus the deposit of $1,000,000 will secure the issue of $900,000 in currency.

13. The demand for money is so great that this currency can be readily loaned to the people across the counter of the bank at a discount at the rate of 10 per cent at 30 to 60 days' time, making about 12 per cent interest on the currency.

14. The interest on the bonds, plus the interest on the currency which the bonds secure, plus the incidentals of the business ought to make the gross earnings of the bank amount to 28 to 33⅓ per cent. The amount of dividends that may be declared will depend largely on the salaries the officers of the bank vote themselves, and the character and rental charges of the premises occupied by the bank as a place of business. In case it is thought best that the showing of profits should not appear too large, the now common plan of having the directors buy the bank building and then raising the rent and the salaries of the president and cashier may be adopted.

15. National banks are privileged to either increase or contract their circulation at will and, of course, can grant or withhold loans as they may see fit. As

the banks have a national organization, and can easily act together in withholding loans or extending time, it follows that they can by united action in refusing to make loans, cause a stringency in the money market and in a single week or even in a single day cause a decline in all the products of the country. *The tremendous possibilities of speculation involved in this control of the money in a country like the United States, will be at once understood by all bankers.*

16. National banks pay no taxes on their bonds, nor on their capital, nor on their deposits. This exemption from taxation is based on the theory that the capital of these banks is invested in U.S. securities, and is a remarkable permission of the law.

Thus far the circular—which is not, as some have assumed, the notorious 'Hazard Circular' of 1862—is quite accurate 'as to the method of organizing national banks under the recent act of congress, and as to the profits that may reasonably be expected from such an investment'. But then there is a clause 17 which mentions 'the suit of Mr Branch against the United States, reported in the 12th volume of the U.S. Court of Claims Reports, at p. 287', but that was a case originating in events dating from June 1865, and finally decided only in December 1876, long after July 1863, the supposed date of the letter enclosing the circular. The circular therefore cannot be what it purports to be.

Neither Overholser nor Coughlin gives any source for the circular and the related correspondence, and no authenticating source is known. Further, there appears to be no record to attest the existence of the Wall Street firm of Ikleheimer, Morton, and Van der Gould. One can only conclude, in the absence of any positive evidence to the contrary, that the exchange of letters and the circular were fictions, forged by a person or persons unknown at a date unknown. The fictions are true to the main facts, but they are not what they pretend to be. The remark attributed to one of the Rothschilds, therefore, while it may have its general truth, must be deemed to have been altogether falsely attributed.

ABBREVIATIONS

The Principal Writings of Ezra Pound (1885–1972)

Arranged by date of publication, thus providing an outline of Pound's writing career. Place of publication is London unless otherwise indicated. Where editions differ the date of the one referred to in the notes is given in **bold type**.

ALS	*A Lume Spento* (Venice: privately printed, 1908). Included in *A Lume Spento and Other Early Poems* (New York: New Directions, 1965; reprinted Faber & Faber, **1965**). Also in *CEP*.
QY	*A Quinzaine for this Yule* (privately printed, 1908; repr. for Elkin Mathews, 1908)
Personae	*Personae of Ezra Pound* (Elkin Mathews, 1909)
Exultations	*Exultations of Ezra Pound* (Elkin Mathews, 1909)
Provença	*Provença* (Boston: Small Maynard, 1910)
SR	*The Spirit of Romance* (London and New York: J. M. Dent & Sons, 1910; new edn., London: Peter Owen, **1952**, New York: New Directions, 1953)
Canzoni	*Canzoni of Ezra Pound* (Elkin Mathews, 1911)
Ripostes	*Ripostes of Ezra Pound* (Stephen Swift, 1912—sheets then taken over by Elkin Mathews; Boston: Small Maynard, 1913)
Cathay	*Cathay* (Elkin Mathews, 1915)
Cathol Ant	*Catholic Anthology: 1914–1915* (Elkin Mathews, 1915)
PM	*Patria Mia* [1912–13] (Chicago: Ralph Fletcher Seymour, 1950; new edn., with 'The Treatise on Harmony', Peter Owen, **1962**)
GB	*Gaudier-Brzeska: A Memoir* (London and New York: John Lane, 1916; new edn. Hessle: Marvell Press, **1960** and New York: New Directions, 1961)
Lustra (1916)	*Lustra of Ezra Pound* (privately printed, 1916; abridged edn., Elkin Mathews, **1916**)
Lustra (1917)	*Lustra of Ezra Pound with Earlier Poems* [and 'Three Cantos'] (New York: privately printed, 1917; ordinary edn. [without 'The Temperaments'], Alfred A. Knopf, **1917**)
Noh	*'Noh' or Accomplishment: A Study of the Classical Stage of Japan* by Ernest Fenollosa and Ezra Pound (Macmillan & Co. Ltd, 1916; New York: Alfred A. Knopf, 1917; included in *T* 1953; new edn., New York: New Directions, **1959**)
PD (1918)	*Pavannes and Divisions* (New York: Alfred A. Knopf, 1918) [See *PD (1958)*]

QPA	*Quia Pauper Amavi* (The Egoist Ltd, 1919). Includes *Homage to Sextus Propertius*
HSP	*Homage to Sextus Propertius*. Repr. from *QPA*, with some alterations, in *P 1918–21*, *P (1926)*, and in all later editions of the collected shorter poems; published as a book in 1934 by Faber & Faber; published with *HSM* as *Diptych Rome–London* (New York: New Directions, 1958).
Instigations	*Instigations of Ezra Pound together with An Essay on the Chinese Written Character by Ernest Fenollosa* (New York: Boni and Liveright, 1920)
HSM	*Hugh Selwyn Mauberley by E.P.* (Ovid Press, 1920)
Umbra	*Umbra: The Early Poems of Ezra Pound* (Elkin Mathews, 1920)
P 1918–21	*Poems 1918–21 Including Three Portraits and Four Cantos* (New York: Boni and Liveright, 1921)
NPL	*The Natural Philosophy of Love* by Remy de Gourmont, Translated with a Postscript by Ezra Pound (New York: Boni and Liveright, 1922; new edn., London: Casanova Society, **1926**)
Antheil	*Antheil and The Treatise on Harmony* (Paris: Three Mountains Press, 1924; new edn., Chicago: Pascal Covici, 1927)
XVI Cantos	*A Draft of XVI Cantos of Ezra Pound for the Beginning of a Poem of some Length*, with Initials by Henry Strater (Paris: Three Mountains Press, 1925)
P (1926)	*Personae: The Collected Poems of Ezra Pound* (New York: Boni and Liveright, 1926)
Ta Hio	*Ta Hio, The Great Learning* [later version in *Confucius* as 'The Great Digest'] (Seattle: University of Washington Bookstore, 1928; new edn., Stanley Nott, 1936; repr. New York: New Directions, 1939)
Cantos 17–27	*A Draft of the Cantos 17–27 of Ezra Pound*, with Initials by Gladys Hynes (John Rodker, 1928)
XXX Cantos	*A Draft of XXX Cantos* (Paris: Hours Press, 1930)
Rime	*Guido Cavalcanti Rime* (Genova: Edizione Marsano S.A., 1932)
Profile	*Profile: An Anthology Collected in MCMXXXI*, ed. EP (Milan: Giovanni Scheiwiller, 1932)
Active Anth	*Active Anthology*, ed. EP (Faber & Faber, 1933)
ABCE	*ABC of Economics* (Faber & Faber, 1933)
ABCR	*ABC of Reading* (George Routledge & Sons Ltd, 1934; New Haven: Yale University Press, 1934; new edn., Faber & Faber, 1951; repr. New Directions, 1951)
MIN	*Make It New: Essays by Ezra Pound* (Faber & Faber, 1934; repr. New Haven: Yale University Press, 1935)
XXXI–XLI	*Eleven New Cantos XXXI–XLI* (New York: Farrar & Rinehart, 1934; Faber & Faber, **1935**)

J/M	*Jefferson and/or Mussolini: L'Idea Statale—Fascism as I have seen it... Volitionist Economics* (Stanley Nott, 1935; New York: Liveright Publishing Corp., 1936)
CWC	*The Chinese Written Character as a Medium for Poetry* (Stanley Nott, 1936; new edn., San Francisco: City Lights Books, **1964**)
PE	*Polite Essays* (Faber & Faber, 1937)
XLII–LI	*The Fifth Decad of Cantos* (Faber & Faber, **1937**; New York: Farrar & Rinehart, 1937)
GK	*Guide to Kulchur* (Faber & Faber, 1938; new edn., Norfolk, Conn.: New Directions, 1952; repr. Peter Owen Ltd, **1952**)
LII–LXXI	*Cantos LII–LXXI* (Faber & Faber, **1940**; Norfolk, Conn.: New Directions, 1940)
Por	*Italy's Policy of Social Economics 1939/1940* by Odon Por, trans. Ezra Pound (Bergamo: Istituto Italiano d'Arte Graifiche, 1941)
Confucio	*Confucio, Ta S'eu, Dai Gaku. Studio Integrale*, Versione italiana di Ezra Pound e di Alberto Luchini (Rapallo: Scuola Tipografica Orfanotrofio Emiliani, 1942)
Carta	*Carta da visita* ([Roma]: Edizione di lettere d'oggi, 1942); translated with some amendments by John Drummond, and published as *A Visiting Card* (Peter Russell, 1952), repr. *S Pr*
America	*L'America, Roosevelt e le cause della guerra presente* (Venezia: Casa Editrice della Edizione Popolari, 1944); English translation by John Drummond, *America, Roosevelt, and the Causes of the Present War* (Peter Russell, 1951)
Oro	*Oro e lavoro* (Rapallo: Tipografica Moderna, 1944); English translation by John Drummond, *Gold and Work* (Peter Russell, 1951), repr. *S Pr*
Introduzione	*Introduzione alla natura economica degli S.U.A.* (Venezia: Casa Editrice della Edizione Popolari, 1944); English translation by Carmine Armore ([Peter Russell, 1950]), repr., revised by John Drummond, *S Pr*
Testamento	*Testamento di Confucio*, Versione italiana di Ezra Pound e di Alberto Luchini (Venezia: Casa Editrice della Edizione Popolari, 1944)
Orientamenti	*Orientamenti* (Venezia: Casa Editrice della Edizione Popolari, 1944)
J e M	*Jefferson e Mussolini* (Venezia: Casa Editrice della Edizione Popolari, 1944)—Pound's Italian version of *J/M*
Chiung Iung	*Chiung Iung, L'Asse che non vacilla*, Versione italiana di Ezra Pound (Venezia: Casa Editrice della Edizione Popolari, 1945)
Treason	*'If This Be Treason......'	e. e. cummings/examind	James Joyce: to his memory	A french accent	'Canto 45'	Blast* (Siena: Printed for Olga Rudge, [1948])

Pisan	*The Pisan Cantos* (New York: New Directions, 1948; Faber & Faber, **1949**)
Confucius (1949)	*Confucius: The Unwobbling Pivot & The Great Digest*, trans. Ezra Pound, with notes and commentary on the text and the ideograms (Bombay, Calcutta, Madras: Orient Longmans Ltd for Kavitabhavan, 1949)
L (1950)	*The Letters of Ezra Pound 1907–1941*, ed. D. D. Paige (New York: Harcourt Brace, 1950; reissued as *The Selected Letters of Ezra Pound 1907–1941* by Faber & Faber, 1971)
L (1951)	*The Letters of Ezra Pound 1907–1941*, ed. D. D. Paige (Faber & Faber, **1951**). This differs in both contents and pagination from *L (1950)*, but letters can be identified in either edition by date and recipient
Analects	*Confucian Analects* (New York: Square $ Series, 1951; Peter Owen, **1956**)
Confucius (1951)	*Confucius: The Great Digest & Unwobbling Pivot*, trans. E.P. (New York: New Directions, 1951; repr. Peter Owen, 1952)
T	*The Translations of Ezra Pound* (Faber & Faber, 1953; repr. New York: New Directions, 1953; enlarged edn., **1964**)
CA	*The Classic Anthology Defined by Confucius*, trans. E.P. (Cambridge, Mass.: Harvard University Press, 1954; repr. Faber & Faber, 1955)
LE	*Literary Essays of Ezra Pound*, ed. T. S. Eliot (Faber & Faber, 1954; repr. Norfolk, Conn.: New Directions, 1954)
Rock-Drill	*Section: Rock Drill, 85–95 de los cantares* (Milano: All'Insegna del Pesce d'Oro, 1955; repr. New York: New Directions, 1956; also Faber & Faber, 1957)
Trax	*Sophokles: Women of Trachis*, A version by Ezra Pound (Neville Spearman, 1956; repr. New York: New Directions, 1957)
PD (1958)	*Pavannes and Divagations* (Norfolk, Conn.: New Directions, 1958; repr. Peter Owen, 1960)
Thrones	*Thrones: 96–109 de los cantares* (Milano: All'Insegna del Pesce d'Oro, 1959; repr. New York: New Directions, 1959; also Faber & Faber, 1960)
Impact	*Impact: Essays on Ignorance and the Decline of American Civilization*, ed. Noel Stock (Chicago: Henry Regnery Company, 1960)
LPAE	*Love Poems of Ancient Egypt*, trans. Ezra Pound and Noel Stock (New York: New Directions, 1962)—previously published as 'Conversations in Courtship'
CC	*Confucius to Cummings: An Anthology of Poetry*, ed. EP and Marcella Spann (New York: New Directions, 1964)

EP/JJ	*Pound/Joyce: The Letters of Ezra Pound to James Joyce, with Pound's Essays on Joyce*, ed. Forrest Read (New York: New Directions, 1967; repr. Faber & Faber, 1967)
D&F	*Drafts & Fragments of Cantos CX–CXVII* (New York: New Directions, 1969; Faber & Faber, 1970)
Opera Scelte	*Opera Scelte*, a cura di Mary de Rachewiltz ([Milano]: Arnoldo Mondadori Editore, 1970)
Cantos	*The Cantos of Ezra Pound*. References, in the form of canto number/page number (as 20/89), are to the New Directions collected edition of 1970 as reprinted in the Faber 'Revised Collected Edition (Cantos 1–117)' published in 1975. The two volumes of *A Companion to the Cantos of Ezra Pound*, ed. Carroll F. Terrell (Berkeley: University of California Press, 1980, 1984) are keyed to this text. [For later printings of the *Cantos* add, for those which include Cantos 72 and 73, 14 to the page number from *Pisan Cantos* on; and to those which include in addition EP's English version of canto 72 add 20.]
S Pr	*Selected Prose 1909–1965*, ed. William Cookson (Faber & Faber, 1973)
S Pr (US)	*Selected Prose 1909–1965*, ed. William Cookson (New York: New Directions, 1973) [Differs from *S Pr* in pagination, and by omitting 'Statues of Gods' (1939) and 'The Treatise on Harmony' (1924), and adding 'Patria Mia' (1912)]
EP/Dk	*Dk/Some Letters of Ezra Pound*, ed. with notes by Louis Dudek (Montreal: DC Books, 1974)
CEP	*Collected Early Poems of Ezra Pound*, ed. Michael John King (New York: New Directions, 1976; repr. Faber & Faber, 1977)
EP&M	*Ezra Pound and Music: The Complete Criticism*, ed. R. Murray Schafer (New York: New Directions, 1977; repr. Faber & Faber, 1978)
Radio	*'Ezra Pound Speaking': Radio Speeches of World War II*, ed. Leonard W. Doob (Westport, Conn.: Greenwood Press, 1978)
EP&VA	*Ezra Pound and the Visual Arts*, ed. Harriet Zinnes (New York: New Directions, 1980)
EP/Ibb	*Letters to Ibbotson, 1935–1952*, ed. Vittoria I. Mondolfo and Margaret Hurley (Orono, Me.: National Poetry Foundation, 1979)
Lettere	*Lettere 1907–58* (Milano: Feltrinelli Editore, 1980)
P/F	*Pound/Ford: The Story of a Literary Friendship*, ed. Brita Lindberg-Seyersted (New York: New Directions, 1982; repr. Faber & Faber, 1982)
Cav	*Pound's Cavalcanti: An Edition of the Translations, Notes and Essays* by David Anderson (Princeton, NJ: Princeton University Press, 1983)

EP/JT	*Letters to John Theobald*, ed. Donald Pearce and Herbert Schneidau (Redding Ridge, Conn.: Black Swan Books, 1984)
EP/DS	*Ezra Pound and Dorothy Shakespear: Their Letters 1909–1914*, ed. Omar Pound and A. Walton Litz (New York: New Directions, 1984; repr. Faber & Faber 1985)
I Cantos	*I Cantos*, a cura di Mary de Rachewiltz (Milano: Arnoldo Mondadori Editore, 1985)—Italian translation with corrected English text *en face*, and substantial commentary
EP/WL	*Pound/Lewis: The Letters of Ezra Pound and Wyndham Lewis*, ed. Timothy Materer (New York: New Directions, 1985; repr. Faber & Faber 1985)
EP/LZ	*Pound/Zukofsky: Selected Letters of Ezra Pound and Louis Zukofsky*, ed. Barry Ahearn (New York: New Directions, 1987; repr. Faber & Faber 1987)
EP&J	*Ezra Pound & Japan: Letters & Essays*, ed. Sanehide Kodama (Redding Ridge, Conn.: Black Swan Books, 1987)
Plays	*Plays Modelled on the Noh (1916)*, ed. Donald C. Gallup (Toledo: Friends of the University of Toledo Libraries, 1987)
EP/scienza	*Ezra Pound e la scienza. Scritti inediti o rari*, ed. Maria Luisa Ardizzone (Milano: Libri Scheiwiller, 1987)
EP/MC	*Ezra Pound and Margaret Cravens: A Tragic Friendship 1910–1912*, ed. Omar Pound and Robert Spoo (Durham, NC: Duke University Press, 1988)
EP/LR	*Pound/The Little Review: The Letters of Ezra Pound to Margaret Anderson*—The Little Review *Correspondence*, ed. Thomas L. Scott, Melvin J. Friedman with the assistance of Jackson R. Bryer (New York: New Directions, 1988)
Elektra	*Elektra*, A play by Ezra Pound and Rudd Fleming [translated 1949], ed. Richard Reid (Princeton, NJ: Princeton University Press, 1989)
P (1990)	*Personae: The Shorter Poems of Ezra Pound*, A Revised Edition Prepared by Lea Baechler and A. Walton Litz (New York: New Directions, 1990)
P&P	*Ezra Pound's Poetry and Prose: Contributions to Periodicals*, Prefaced and Arranged by Lea Baechler, A. Walton Litz, and James Longenbach, 10 vols. [Addenda and Index in vol. xi] (New York and London: Garland Publishing, 1991). [Contains in photo-reproduction all contributions to periodicals recorded in Gallup: 1983.]
EP/JQ	*The Selected Letters of Ezra Pound to John Quinn*, ed. Timothy Materer (Durham, NC: Duke University Press, 1991)
WT	*A Walking Tour in Southern France: Ezra Pound among the Troubadours*, ed. Richard Sieburth (New York: New Directions, 1992)

Cathay/Catai	*Antiche poesie cinesi*, [a trilingual Chinese–English–Italian edition of *Cathay*], a cura di Alessandra C. Lavagnino e Maria Rita Masci (Torino: Giulio Einaudi Editore, 1993)
EP/ACH	*The Letters of Ezra Pound to Alice Corbin Henderson*, ed. Ira B. Nadel (Austin: University of Texas Press, 1993)
EP/JL	*Ezra Pound and James Laughlin: Selected Letters*, ed. David M. Gordon (New York: W. W. Norton, 1994)
EP/Dial	*Pound, Thayer, Watson and* The Dial*: A Story in Letters*, ed. Walter Sutton (Gainesville: University Press of Florida, 1994)
EP/BC	*Ezra Pound and Senator Bronson Cutting: A Political Correspondence 1930–1935*, ed. E. P. Walkiewicz and Hugh Witemeyer (Albuquerque: University of New Mexico Press, 1995)
J e M (1995)	*Jefferson e Mussolini*, Presentazione di Mary de Rachewiltz (Milano: Terziaria, 1995)—reprints EP's 1944 Italian version of *J/M*, an edition printed by Casa Editrice Edizione Popolari di Venezia but of which nearly all copies were destroyed at the press
Lavoro/Usura	*Lavoro ed usura. tre saggi*, terza edizione (Milano: All'Insegna del Pesce d'Oro di Vanni Scheiwiller, 1996)—reprints *Oro e lavoro* (1944), *L'America, Roosevelt, e le cause della guerra presente* (1944), *Introduzione alla natura economica degli S.U.A.* (1944), and adds 'L'economia ortologica' (1937)
EP/WCW	*Pound/Williams: Selected Letters of Ezra Pound and William Carlos Williams*, ed. Hugh Witemeyer (New York: New Directions, 1996)
EP/EEC	*Pound/Cummings: The Correspondence of Ezra Pound and E. E. Cummings*, ed. Barry Ahearn (Ann Arbor: University of Michigan Press, 1996)
EP/GT	*'Dear Uncle George': The Correspondence between Ezra Pound and Congressman [George] Tinkham of Massachusetts*, ed. Philip J. Burns (Orono, Me.: National Poetry Foundation, 1996)
MA	*Machine Art and Other Writings*, ed. Maria Luisa Ardizzone (Durham, NC: Duke University Press, 1996)
EP/ORA	*'I Cease Not to Yowl': Ezra Pound's Letters to Olivia Rossetti Agresti*, ed. Demetres P. Tryphonopoulos and Leon Surette (Urbana: University of Illinois Press, 1998)
EP/DP	*Ezra and Dorothy Pound: Letters in Captivity, 1945–1946*, ed. Omar Pound and Robert Spoo (New York: Oxford University Press, 1999)
EP/GV	*Ezra Pound—Giambattista Vicari. Il fare aperto. Lettere 1939–1971*, a cura di Anna Busetto Vicari e Luca Cesari (Milan: Archinto, 2000)
EP/WB	*The Correspondence of Ezra Pound and Senator William Borah*, ed. Sarah C. Holmes (Urbana: University of Illinois Press, 2001)

EP/WW	*Ezra Pound's Letters to William Watt*, [ed.] with an introduction and notes by William Watt (Marquette: Northern Michigan University Press, 2001)
Canti postumi	*Canti postumi*, a cura di Massimo Bacigalupo (Milano: Arnoldo Mondadori, 2002; II edizione 2012)
P&T	*Ezra Pound: Poems and Translations* [selected by Richard Sieburth] (New York: Library of America, 2003)
Cavalcanti	*Cavalcanti. A sung dramedy in 3 acts*, the full score ed. Robert Hughes and Margaret Fisher, in Robert Hughes and Margaret Fisher, *Cavalcanti: A Perspective on the Music of Ezra Pound* (*CPMEP*) (Emeryville, Calif.: Second Evening Art, 2003)
CVW	*Complete Violin Works of Ezra Pound*, ed. with commentary by Robert Hughes, introduction by Margaret Fisher (Emeryville, Calif.: Second Evening Art, 2004)
Moscardino	Enrico Pea, *Moscardino*, translated from the Italian by EP [1941] (New York: Archipelago Books, 2004)
Collis	Margaret Fisher, *The Recovery of Ezra Pound's Third Opera: 'Collis O Heliconii'* [includes performance edition] (Emeryville, Calif.: Second Evening Art, 2005)
Carte italiana	*Ezra Pound. Carte italiana 1930–1944, letteratura e note*, a cura di Luca Cesari (Milano: Archinto, 2005)
EWPP	*Early Writings. Poems & Prose*, ed. Ira Nadel (New York: Penguin Books, 2005)
EPEC	*Ezra Pound's Economic Correspondence, 1933–1940*, ed. and annotated by Roxana Preda (Gainesville: University Press of Florida, 2007)
Testament I	*Ezra Pound: Le Testament, 'Paroles de Villon'—1926 'Salle Pleyel' concert excerpts & 1933 Final Version complete opera*, Margaret Fisher and Robert Hughes editors, performance editions (Emeryville, Calif.: Second Evening Art, 2008)
CWC II	Ernest Fenollosa and Ezra Pound, *The Chinese Written Character as a Medium for Poetry, A Critical Edition*, ed. Haun Saussy, Jonathan Stalling, and Lucas Klein (New York: Fordham University Press, 2008)
EP/CF	*Ezra Pound's Chinese Friends. Stories in Letters*, ed. Zhaoming Qian (Oxford: Oxford University Press, 2008)
NSPT	*New Selected Poems & Translations*, ed. and annotated with an afterword by Richard Sieburth (New York: New Directions, 2010)
EP/Parents	*Ezra Pound to his Parents: Letters 1895–1929*, ed. Mary de Rachewiltz, A. David Moody, and Joanna Moody (Oxford: Oxford University Press, 2010)
D&F facsimile	Ezra Pound, *Drafts & Fragments: Facsimile Notebooks 1958–1959* (New York: Glenn Horowitz, Bookseller, Inc., 2010)

Testament II	*Ezra Pound: Le Testament: 1923 facsimile edition edited by George Antheil*, with notes for the 1931 BBC radio broadcast, ed. Margaret Fisher and Robert Hughes (Emeryville, Calif.: Second Evening Art, 2011)
EP/SN	*One Must Not Go Altogether with the Tide: The Letters of Ezra Pound and Stanley Nott*, ed. and with essays by Miranda B. Hickman (Montreal: McGill-Queen's University Press, 2011)

Writings by Others

Abbreviations are used only for books referred to frequently in the notes. For all other books and articles full details are given at the first mention, and a recognizable shortened form is used thereafter.

Barnard	Mary Barnard, *Assault on Mount Helicon: A Literary Memoir* (Berkeley: University of California Press, 1984)
Carpenter	Humphrey Carpenter, *A Serious Character: The Life of Ezra Pound* (Faber & Faber, 1988)
CPMEP	Robert Hughes and Margaret Fisher, *Cavalcanti: A Perspective on the Music of Ezra Pound* (Emeryville, Calif.: Second Evening Art, 2003)
Conover	Anne Conover, *Olga Rudge and Ezra Pound* (New Haven: Yale University Press, 2001)
Discretions	Mary de Rachewiltz, *Discretions* (Faber & Faber, 1971; Boston: Atlantic-Little Brown, 1971; New York: New Directions, 1975, 2005)
EPRO	Margaret Fisher, *Ezra Pound's Radio Operas: The BBC Experiments, 1931–1933* (Cambridge, Mass.: MIT Press, 2002)
ESC	*Ego Scriptor Cantilenae: The Music of Ezra Pound*, Robert Hughes conductor and musical director, Margaret Fisher author, containing audio CD (Other Minds OM 1005-2) and booklet (San Francisco: Other Minds Inc., 2003)
EP: Poet I	A. David Moody, *Ezra Pound: Poet. A Portrait of the Man & his Work*, i: *The Young Genius 1885–1920* (Oxford: Oxford University Press, 2007)
Farrell	Nicholas Farrell, *Mussolini: A New Life* (Weidenfeld & Nicolson, 2003)
Foster: 2003	R. F. Foster, *W. B. Yeats: A Life*, ii: *The Arch-Poet 1915–1939* (Oxford: Oxford University Press, 2003)
Gallup	Donald Gallup, *Ezra Pound: A Bibliography* (Charlottesville: University Press of Virginia, 1983)
Homberger	Eric Homberger, ed., *Ezra Pound: The Critical Heritage* (Routledge and Kegan Paul, 1972)

Makin	Peter Makin, *Pound's Cantos* (George Allen & Unwin, 1985)
Norman: 1960	Charles Norman, *Ezra Pound* (New York: Macmillan, 1960)
Redman	Tim Redman, *Ezra Pound and Italian Fascism* (Cambridge: Cambridge University Press, 1991)
Stock: 1970	Noel Stock, *The Life of Ezra Pound* (Routledge and Kegan Paul, 1970)
Terrell, *Companion*	Carroll F. Terrell, *A Companion to the Cantos of Ezra Pound*, 2 vols. (Berkeley: University of California Press, 1980, 1984)
Tytell	John Tytell, *Ezra Pound: The Solitary Volcano* (Bloomsbury, 1987)
TSEL I	*The Letters of T. S. Eliot*, i: *1898–1922*, revised edn., ed. Valerie Eliot and Hugh Haughton (Faber & Faber, 2009)
TSEL II	*The Letters of T. S. Eliot*, ii: *1923–1925*, ed. Valerie Eliot and Hugh Haughton (Faber & Faber, 2009)
WCW/JL	*William Carlos Williams and James Laughlin: Selected Letters*, ed. Hugh Witemeyer (New York: W. W. Norton, 1989)
Wilhelm: 1990	J. J. Wilhelm, *Ezra Pound in London and Paris, 1908–1925* (University Park: Pennsylvania State University Press, 1990)
Wilhelm: 1994	J. J. Wilhelm, *Ezra Pound, the Tragic Years, 1925–1972* (University Park: Pennsylvania State University Press, 1994)
Zapponi	Niccolò Zapponi, *L'Italia di Ezra Pound* (Roma: Bulzoni Editore, 1976)

Other Abbreviations

AB	Agnes Bedford
ACH	Alice Corbin Henderson
AMacL	Archibald MacLeish
AVM	Arthur Valentine Moore
BB	Basil Bunting
Beinecke	Ezra Pound Papers. Yale Collection of American Literature. Beinecke Rare Book and Manuscript Library. Yale University
Beinecke/OR	Olga Rudge Papers. Yale Collection of American Literature. Beinecke Rare Book and Manuscript Library. Yale University
Dial	*The Dial* (ed. Scofield Thayer, Sibley Watson, Marianne Moore, New York, 1920–9)
DP	Dorothy Shakespear Pound
DS	Dorothy Shakespear
EEC	E. E. Cummings
EP	Ezra Loomis [Weston] Pound
FMF	Ford Madox Ford [FMH up to 1919]
FMH	Ford Madox Hueffer
G-B	Henri Gaudier-Brzeska

Hamilton	Ezra Pound Collection, Special Collections, Burke Library, Hamilton College, Clinton, NY
HD	Hilda Doolittle
HLP	Homer Loomis Pound
HM	Harriet Monroe
HRC	Ezra Pound Collection, Harry Ransom Humanities Research Center, The University of Texas at Austin
IB	Iris Barry
IWP	Isabel Weston Pound
JJ	James Joyce
JL	James Laughlin
JQ	John Quinn
Lilly	Pound Mansucripts, The Lilly Library, Indiana University, Bloomington
LR	*The Little Review* (1914–29)
LZ	Louis Zukofsky
MB	Mary Barnard
MCA	Margaret C. Anderson
MdR	Mary de Rachewiltz
MM	Marianne Moore
NA	*The New Age* (ed. A. R. Orage, 1907–23)
NEW	*New English Weekly*
OR	Olga Rudge
OS	Olivia Shakespear
OSP	Omar Shakespear Pound
Pai	*Paideuma.* A Journal Devoted to Ezra Pound Scholarship (1972–2009)
Poetry	*Poetry: A Magazine of Verse* (Chicago, 1912–36)
TSE	Thomas Stearns Eliot
UPenn	Ezra Pound Collections, Van Pelt Library, University of Pennsylvania
VBJ	Viola Baxter Jordan
WBY	W. B. Yeats
WCW	William Carlos Williams
WL	Wyndham Lewis
WR	Walter Rummel
W&W	E. P. Walkiewicz and Hugh Witemeyer

NOTES

PART ONE: 1921–1932

1. A YEAR IN PARIS, 1921–1924

Pound's nine 'Paris Letters' contributed to the *Dial* between September 1921 and February 1923 have served as a guide to the background of the first section of this chapter. In the notes to this chapter 'Paris Letter' will be shortened to 'P.L.'

3   too 'northern': EP to Ottoline Morrell, 7 July [1922] (HRC).
    his senses open ... 'moving energies': see EP, 'Cavalcanti', *LE* 152 and 154.
    'solid year': EP to WCW, 2 Feb. 1921, *L (1951)* 229.
    in bed with flu: EP to Thayer, 10 Feb. 1921, *EP/Dial* 207.
    'for the first time': EP to FMF, '6/4/1921', *EP/FMF* 55.
    His typewriter: EP's letters from Saint-Raphaël, as to FMF and the *Dial*, were handwritten, while those from Paris or London were generally typewritten.
    'Palm leaf hut': EP to ACH, 25 Jan. 1921, *EP/ACH* [223].
    'five hours': EP to AB, Mar. 1921, cited Carpenter 383.
    'hand in sling': EP to Thayer, '21/3/21', *EP/Dial* 213.
    silver ash tray ... 'Paris next week': EP to FMF, '6/4/1921', *EP/FMF* 55.
    'not much space': EP to FMF, 22 May [1921], *EP/FMF* 58.
4   'dismissal': EP to Thayer, 19 Apr. [1921], *EP/Dial* 216.
    'no means': EP to MCA, [22? Apr. 1921], *EP/LR* 265—see also *EP/Dial* 267.
    'special summer number': EP to FMF, 11 May [1921], *EP/FMF* 56.
    'intelligent nucleus': EP to FMF, 22 May [1921], *EP/FMF* 58.
    'in his atelier': EP, 'Parisian Literature', *Literary Review* [of the New York *Evening Post*], I.49 (13 Aug. 1921) 7. Re no abstract ideas see also EP's 'Brancusi' (details below).
    'doing what Gaudier': EP to FMF, [Aug.? 1921], *EP/FMF* 61.
    'Where Gaudier' and rest of paragraph: EP, 'Brancusi', *LR* VIII.1 (Autumn 1921) 3–7.
    'infinite beauty': EP, 'P.L. January 1922', *Dial* LXXII.2 (Feb. 1922) 188.
    'who have cast off': EP, 'P.L. January 1922', *Dial* LXXII.2 (Feb. 1922) 188.
    'sort of Socratic': EP, 'Parisian Literature', *Literary Review* [of the New York *Evening Post*], I.49 (13 Aug. 1921) 7.
    nettoyage: EP, 'P.L. September 1921', *Dial* LXXI.4 (Oct. 1921) 457.
    'contemporary average': EP, 'P.L. August 1922', *Dial* LXXIII.3 (Sept. 1922) 333.
5   'civilization': EP, 'P.L. February 1923', *Dial* LXXIV.3 (Mar. 1923) 279.
    'this new Brancusi': EP to MCA, 4 May [1921], *EP/LR* 273.
    The 'average mind': EP, 'P.L. August 1922', *Dial* LXXIII.3 (Sept. 1922) 333. Note: I have substituted 'Creon' for 'Oedipus'—the reason will become apparent.
    Sophocles' Antigone, to end of paragraph: EP, 'P.L. December 1922', *Dial* LXXIV. 3 (Feb. 1923) 278–9.
    'power to do him evil' et seq.: EP, 'P.L. December 1922', *Dial* LXXIV.3 (Feb. 1923) 279.
    Upward's suicide: see A. D. Moody, 'Pound's Allen Upward', *Pai* 4.1 (1975) 62–5.
6   'function of poetry': EP, [Answers to three questions], *Chapbook* 27 (July 1922) 17–18.
    Brancusi's 'universe': EP, 'P.L. December 1921', *Dial* LXXII.1 (Jan. 1922) 77.

'cavern': EP, 'P.L. December 1921', *Dial* LXXII.1 (Jan. 1922) 77.

'junk-shops': EP, 'Brancusi', *LR* VIII.1 (Autumn 1921) 7.

'clap-trap'... 'galleries': EP, 'P.L. September 1921', *Dial* LXXI.4 (Oct. 1921) 462.

saw Braque: EP to WL, 27 Apr. 1921, *EP/WL* 128; also to JQ, 21 May 1921, *EP&VA* 246.

'met Picasso': EP to IWP, 8 Jan. 1922, *EP/Parents* 493.

Léger: see EP, 'D'Artagnan Twenty Years After' (1937), in *S Pr* 427–8.

'at Picabia's': EP, 'D'Artagnan Twenty Years After' (1937), in *S Pr* 427.

Parade: 'a ballet extravaganza commissioned by Diaghilev for his Russian ballet and written by Jean Cocteau.... Cocteau persuaded Picasso to do the stage sets, great Cubist sculptures that looked like costumes. The music was by Erik Satie... [and] incorporated the sounds of a typewriter, a ship siren, machine guns, and the cries of a circus barker.... The programme note...by Apollinaire...introduced the word "surrealism"' (John Tytell, *Ezra Pound: The Solitary Volcano* (Bloomsbury, 1987), pp. 161–2).

7 'Satie's *Socrate*': EP to AB, [April? 1921], *L (1951)* 231.

Natalie Barney: details in this paragraph drawn from 'Ezra Pound: Letters to Natalie Barney', ed. with commentary by Richard Sieburth, *Pai* 5.2 (1976) [279]–95; also from Wilhelm: 1990, 261–2. EP recalled her salon in a 1933 note, 'The Violinist Olga Rudge', *EP&M* 342–3.

'a good piss': WCW, *Autobiography* (1951) (New York: New Directions, 1967), pp. 228–9.

'got out of life': from Barney's own words, cited by EP in 'P.L. September 1921', *Dial* LXXI.4 (Oct. 1921) 458, and from EP's paraphrase in 84/539.

'velvet jacket': Sylvia Beach, *Shakespeare and Company* (Faber & Faber, 1960), pp. 38–9.

'Rooseveltian voice': MCA, *My Thirty Years War*, pp. 243–4, as cited *EP/LR* 300.

8 Gertrude Stein: see Gertrude Stein, *The Autobiography of Alice B. Toklas* (1933) (Harmondsworth: Penguin Books, 1966), p. 217.

talked him down: see Norman: 1960, 246—citing Scofield Thayer.

'mended a cigarette box': Beach, *Shakespeare and Company*, pp. 38–9.

'wonderfully entertaining': E. E. Cummings to Charles Norman, 1959, in Norman: 1960, 247.

'a good talker': Sisley Huddleston, *Bohemian Literary and Social Life in Paris: Salons, Cafés, Studios* (Geo. G. Harrap & Co.,1928), p. 97.

Nancy Cox McCormack: this recollection is from an extract from her unpublished manuscript, 'Ezra Pound in the Paris Years', reproduced with permission from The Poetry/Rare Books Collection, University Libraries, State University of New York at Buffalo, in Tytell, *Ezra Pound: The Solitary Volcano*, p. 171.

did not enjoy... Paris: see, for example, WCW, *Autobiography*, p. 226.

the way he danced: Caresse Crosby's account in her *The Passionate Years* (New York: Dial, 1953), p. 225 is taken from Wilhelm: 1990, 290–1.

9 'one of the spectacles': Sisley Huddleston, *Bohemian Literary and Social Life in Paris*, p. 144.

Nature, genius, and the state of the world

9 Isis and Osiris: see *EP: Poet I* 169.

Imagisme: see *EP: Poet I* 225–9.

Vorticism: see *EP: Poet I* 255–6.

mind and... nature... one and the same: Whitman, of course, was there in his fashion in *Song of Myself* well before EP; and, before Whitman, Emerson, guided by Carlyle and Coleridge and Wordsworth, had been on the same track. But Pound had to find his own way in the terms of his own time to identify human genius with the organic energy of the universe.

'biological basis' etc.: EP, 'Remy de Gourmont: A distinction' (1920), *LE* 343–4.

10 'rush order': EP to AB, 21 June 1921 (Lilly).
'Speak not': EP to DP, 23 July 1921 (Lilly).
'supplementary chapter': EP to HLP, 28 June 1921, *EP/Parents* 486.
'There might be': *NPL* (1926), p. 55.
he speculated: 'Translator's Postscript', *NPL* (1926), pp. 169–80.
'scientifically demonstrable': EP, 'The Wisdom of Poetry' (1912), *S Pr* 332—see *EP: Poet I* 243.

one life in all: Spinoza, wrestling with that conception in the 1670s and coming at it from the perspectives of theology and logic, determined that all individual beings are 'modes' of the one universal being. The modern physicist has no problem conceiving of everything we know or can guess at from the boson and the quark to the whole cosmos of uncountable galaxies as made up of the one lot of moving energies— though when he comes to consider just how those stellar energies translate themselves into his calculations about them he is as much in the dark as Pound was.
'various statements': EP, 'The New Therapy', *NA* XXX.20 (16 Mar. 1922) 259–60— rest of paragraph is from this article.

11 subject to the limited knowledge ... of his time: The science of genetics in 1921 was a long way from conceiving of DNA. The chromosome had been identified as the carrier of genetic characteristics; but the exact nature of the gene and how it functioned had yet to be discovered. Further, the rational hypothesis that both parents contributed to the genetic makeup of their offspring had yet to be proved and was still a matter of debate.

conventional prejudices: paragraph based on 'Translator's Postscript', *NPL* (1926), pp. 170–1, and 'The New Therapy'. Re Marianne Moore being *not* a female chaos see *EP: Poet I* 345.

Canto II: seeing the light

11 Dionysos: ref. C. Kerényi, *Dionysos: Archetypal Image of Indestructible Life* (Routledge & Kegan Paul, 1976); *Oxford Classical Dictionary*, 3rd edn. (1996); J. Lemprière, *A Classical Dictionary* (George Routledge and Sons, 1904).

12 'You rely on force': Euripides, *The Bacchae* [with other plays], trans. Philp Vellacott (Harmondsworth: Penguin Books, 1954), p. 191.
Ovid's version: in *Metamorphoses*—see Golding's version Bk. III, ll. 642–921.

13 Homeric hymn: in Loeb Classical Library, *Hesiod, The Homeric Hymns and Homerica*, with an English translation by Hugh G. Evelyn-White (Cambridge, Mass.: Harvard University Press, 1974), pp. 428–33.
Odysseus calling up Tiresias: on this see *EP: Poet I* 314–15.
'it shouts aloud': EP to W. H. D. Rouse, 23 May 1935, *L (1951)* 363.

14 'cord welter': 'cold-welter' is an unfortunately persistent misprint.
old men of Troy: Homer, *Iliad* III, 139–60.

15 'Chinese mythological figure': EP, as cited by Mary de Rachewiltz, *Discretions* (Faber & Faber, 1971), p. 156.

16 'Church tower': see *EP: Poet I* 393.
monocular monotheism: in a letter to Richard Aldington, 4 Mar. 1926, EP wrote, 'the root of evil is the monotheistic idea' (HRC).

17 'a manuscript in the Ambrosian': EP, 'Troubadours —Their Sorts and Conditions' (1913), *LE* 97.

'Le Testament' or Pound's Villon: in the dark

This section (with the one following) is almost entirely dependent upon the published work and generous private communications of Robert Hughes and Margaret Fisher. Responsibility for the use made of their work and guidance, and for the interpretation of Pound's *Le Testament*, is of course mine alone. *Testament I = Ezra Pound: Le Testament, 'Paroles de Villon'—1926 'Salle Pleyel' concert excerpts & 1933 Final Version complete opera*, Margaret Fisher and Robert Hughes editors, performance editions (Emeryville, Calif.: Second Evening Art, 2008); *Testament II = Ezra Pound: Le Testament: 1923 facsimile edition edited by George Antheil*, with notes for the 1931 BBC radio broadcast, ed. Margaret Fisher and Robert Hughes (Emeryville, Calif.: Second Evening Art, 2011); *EPRO = Margaret Fisher, Ezra Pound's Radio Operas: The BBC Experiments, 1931–1933* (Cambridge, Mass.: MIT Press, 2002); *CPMEP = Robert Hughes and Margaret Fisher, Cavalcanti: A Perspective on the Music of Ezra Pound* (Emeryville, Calif.: Second Evening Art, 2003); Fisher: 2003 = Margaret Fisher, 'Great Bass: Undertones of Continuous Influence', *Performance Research* 8.1 (Spring 2003) 23–40; *ESC = Ego Scriptor Cantilenae: The Music of Ezra Pound*, Robert Hughes conductor and musical director, Margaret Fisher author, containing audio CD (Other Minds OM 1005–2) and 80-page booklet (San Francisco: Other Minds Inc., 2003). In addition to live performances in York, Cambridge, and Brantôme, I have listened to the 1971 Western Opera Theater production, conducted by Robert Hughes, recorded and issued in 1972 as Fantasy Records no. 12001; the 1980 Holland Festival production performed by the ASKO ensemble, Reinbert de Leeuw music director and conductor, recorded and released as Philips Harlekijn 9500 927; and a tape of the performance by the University of York Villon Music Theatre Ensemble directed and co-produced by Charles Mundye for the 1992 York Festival—Heaulmière's aria sung by Anna Myatt in this production is included on *ESC*'s CD.

17   **tones of vowels**: 'we will never recover the art of *writing to be sung* until we begin to pay attention to the sequence, or scale, of vowels in the line, and of the vowels terminating the group of lines in a series' (EP, 'The Treatise on Metre', *ABCR* 206). On 'weights and durations' see EP, 'The Treatise on Metre', *ABCR* 198–9. Duration, the time (longer or shorter) of the sounds in verse is too often neglected by prosodists—on this essential aspect see the important essay by Margaret Fisher, 'Towards a Theory of Duration Rhyme', *Testament II*, 127–80. As for the vowel scale, the sceptical might try the experiment of producing the series of vowels and carefully noting their different positions within the mouth, with their different resonances. Consonants are relatively monotone, being produced by tongue, teeth, and lips.

17   **'Will probably'**: EP to AB, 5 May 1921 (Lilly)—cited Carpenter: 1988, 386.
18   **'done 116'**: EP to AB, 16 May 1921 (Lilly)—cited *CPMEP* 99 n. 261.
        'Cello is': EP to AB, 5 May 1921 (Lilly)—cited Carpenter 386–7.
        modes of Arab: When, in the summer of 1960, R. Murray Schafer asked Pound what he really wanted *Le Testament* to sound like, EP played him a tape of some Sudanese music—Schafer to Hugh Kenner, 25 Aug. 1962 (Hugh Kenner Archive, HRC); see also Schafer's 'Postscript 1942–1972', *EP&M* 465.
        'My ignorance': EP to AB, 16 May 1921 (Lilly). Cp. 'improving a system by refraining from obedience to all its present "laws"'—EP to AB, [Apr.? 1921] (Lilly)—cited *CPMEP* 19.
        nothing **'that interferes'**: EP to AB, 25 May 1921, *L (1951)* 233.
        'setting words': EP to Elizabeth Winslow, [n.d., between 1951 and 1958], *Pai* 9.2 (1980) 355.
        'tough, open-air': *GK* 368.
        not so much on the notes: 'The singer must grasp not only the purely musical proportions of his piece but the precise way vowels and consonants of language (phonemes) must be apportioned and arranged in hierarchies within the grosser,

prescribed, purely musical notes of pitch and duration'—Michael Ingham (professional singer and Chair of Music Department at University of California at Santa Barbara), in *Cambridge Companion to Ezra Pound* (Cambridge: Cambridge University Press, 1999), p. 237.

'emotive contents': *GK* 366; 'emotional correlations': *ABCR* 63.

'What the devil': DP to EP, 10 July [1921] (Lilly).

'a musical work': EP to DP, 14 July [1921] (Lilly).

'for a few days': EP to DP, 23 July 1921 (Lilly).

'tango on the sabath': EP to DP, 26 July 1921 (Lilly).

'Chewing into op.': EP to DP, 30 July 1921 (Lilly).

19 'Ezra sang': AB to Hugh Kenner, [1964], Hugh Kenner Archive (HRC)—cf. Kenner, *The Pound Era* (Faber & Faber, 1972), pp. 389–90. R. Murray Schafer, listening in 1960 to Pound singing portions of *Le Testament*, was 'amazed at how faithful his singing was to the original [score], at least in terms of rhythm' (Schafer to Kenner, 25 Aug. 1962, [Hugh Kenner Archive, HRC])—cf. Schafer, *EP&M* 465–6.

'8 and 9 hrs': EP to DP, 6 Aug. 1921 (Lilly).

'through worst': EP to Natalie Barney, 10 Aug. 1921, *Pai* 5.2 (1976) 286.

'contrapuntal hurdy gurdy': EP to DP, 10 Aug. 1921 (Lilly).

'I naturally think': EP to HLP, 8 July [1923], *EP/Parents* 516.

'11 o'clock': *CPMEP* 30.

'highly fractional notation': EP to AB, 21 Feb. 1924 (Lilly).

'no attempt': EP to AB, 30 June 1926, *CPMEP* 49 n. 129.

'most salient feature': Hughes, *CPMEP* 30.

20 *All for the love* etc.: my trans. An equivalent to 'garson rusé' would be 'artful dodger', if it were not that the phrase is forever Dickens's.

'generally at the interval': Robert Hughes, 'Ezra Pound's Opera'—a reprint of the sleeve-note to Fantasy Records no. 12001—*Pai* 2.1 (1973) 14.

'*klangfarbenmelodie*': Hughes, 'Ezra Pound's Opera', 13.

21 Pound's Villon: see *SR* chap. 8, particularly pp. 169, 176–7; also *EP: Poet I* 119–20.

vibrations . . . of his *virtù*: see Fisher: 2003, 1; and *EP: Poet I* 155–6.

22 notes for a minimalist staging: I have conflated two TSS notes, one headed 'Staging of the Villon' and concerned with visual effects—i.e. not for radio (Beinecke YCAL MSS 53 box 32/736); the other, headed 'Villon/ stage', formerly in the possession of AB, apparently used in 1959 in connection with the 1962 BBC radio production (Beinecke YCAL MSS 43 box 4).

23 'the first voice': *ABCR* 104.

A new theory of harmony

23 'will be twenty years': *GK* 365.

performers in the 1920s: see *ESC* 19.

'The violin accompaniment': from Gallup: 1983, 438 [E3h(1)].

measures . . . greatly simplified: see *CPMEP* 31.

'cutting up Villon': EP to AB, 26 Nov. 1925 (Lilly).

24 'another fit': EP to AB, 30 Dec. 1925 (Lilly).

⅝ bar: on this see EP to IWP, 2 Mar. 1926: 'That 5/8 has taken about fourteen years to discover. i.e. neither Walter, nor Agnes, nor even young Jarge, had managed . . . to find out that most of my rhythms do not fit bars of two, three or four EVEN or equal notes; or rather they had ALL found out that, but none of em hit the simple division of two longs and a short (or the various equivalents)'—*EP/Parents* 588; see also *CPMEP* 30–3.

'nacherl measure': EP to AB, 7 Jan. 1926 (Lilly).

'indubitably earnest': EP to AB, 27 Dec. 1925 (Lilly).

'the GREAT LIGHT': EP to AB, 1 Feb. 1926 (Lilly).

'tentatively at least': EP to IWP, 2 Mar. 1926, *EP/Parents* 588.

'Paroles de Villon': Stock: 1970, 263 gives the programme of the 1926 concert; further details and discussion in *CPMEP* 34–9.

'At any rate': EP to AB, 30 June 1926 (Lilly).

'a curiosity': EP to Peter Russell, n.d., [*c.*1951] (HRC).

25   'unduplicated little masterpiece': Schafer, *EP&M* x.

'musical immortality': Richard Taruskin, in 'Arts & Leisure' section, p. 24, *New York Times* 27 July 2003 (communicated by Robert Hughes).

'a grand liberation': George Antheil, 'Why a Poet Quit the Muses' (1924), reprinted *Pai* 2.1 (1973) [3].

article in the *Paris Times*: a cutting of the article is with EP's letter to AB of 8 July 1924 (Lilly).

The Treatise on Harmony: first published in 1924 as part of *Antheil and The Treatise on Harmony* (Paris: Three Mountains Press); reprinted 1927 (Chicago: Pascal Covici), and 1962 with *Patria Mia* (Peter Owen); included in *S Pr* and *EP&M*. Citations here from *EP&M* 296–306. *Note:* the chapter on Antheil (*EP&M* 253–65), an important addition to EP's account of his theory, is not included in either *PM* (1962) or *S Pr*.

one of 'the three': *EP&M* 293–4. The English composer Edmund Rubbra was much influenced by *The Treatise on Harmony* (communicated by Richard Edwards).

horizontal progression: the *Paris Times* article stressed the 'horizontal' nature of the music in *Le Testament*, saying that it 'is composed altogether of parallel and horizontal strands of music which have nothing vertical about them'.

'like steam': *EP&M* 297.

'12-tone system': Fisher: 2003, 26.

26   'pure rhythm': 'Introduction' [to Cavalcanti poems], *T* 23–4. See also *GK* 233–4.

'the difficulty': EP to Mary Barnard, 2 Dec.1933, Mary Barnard, *Assault on Mount Helicon: A Literary Memoir* (Berkeley: University of California Press, 1984), p. 55.

'a *logical* idea': *CPMEP* 131–2.

'its simplest operation': *CPMEP* 136.

'natural divisions': *CPMEP* 139; see also Fisher: 2003, 28.

'employs a chord': *CPMEP* 137; see also *GK* 73 and 233.

27   'Let us say': *EP&M* 301.

all the noises . . . machine-shop: see EP, 'Machine Art' (1927–30), in *Machine Art and Other Writings*, ed. Maria Luisa Ardizzone (Durham, NC: Duke University Press, 1996), especially pp. 72–6, 'The Acoustic of Machinery'.

'perhaps the bridge': EP, 'How to Read' (1929), *LE* 26.

'order-giving vibrations': see *EP: Poet I* 228.

'magic of music': *GK* 283 (and 255).

Li Ki: EP owned the two volumes of *Li Ki: ou Mémoires sur les bienséances et les cérémonies*, Texte Chinois avec une double traduction en Français et en Latin par S. Couvreur S.J., 2ième éd. (Ho Kien Fou: Mission Catholique, 1913). In chap. XVII, 'Traité sur la musique' (vol. II, 45–114), he marked the Chinese as well as the French text, and wrote on the front end paper 'Harmonies & Dissociations'.

'prescription for': Michael Ingham, 'Pound and Music', in *Cambridge Companion to Ezra Pound*, p. 240

Cosmos: cf. 'These concepts the human mind has attained. | To make Cosmos— | To achieve the possible' (116/795).

28   'main form': see *EP: Poet I* 368.

Year 1 of a new era: kaleidoscope

28 'Honoured Progenitor': EP to HLP, [after 21 Mar. 1921], *EP/Parents* 480.
'nobody seems': EP, 'Paris Letter. September 1921', *Dial* LXXI.4 (Oct. 1921) 458.
'can't go on valeting': EP to JQ, 21 May 1921, *EP/JQ* 207n.
Lewis: see *EP/WL* 127–35.
reported to Dorothy: EP to DP, 10 Aug. 1921 (Lilly).

29 'Joyce's head X-rayed': EP to JQ, 10 Aug. 1922, *EP/JQ* 216. See also *EP/JJ* 212.
'Pried up the edge': EP to DP, 10 Oct. 1921 (Lilly).
'to build a dream': see Stock: 1970, 83 and 243.
Yeats...'somnolent': EP to HLP, 22 Oct. [1921], *EP/Parents* 488.
Eliot...'ordered away': EP to DP, 14 Oct. 1921 (Lilly).
'can't move 'em': see *EP: Poet I* 407.

30 'a nerve specialist': TSE to Henry Eliot, 3 Oct. 1921, *TSEL I* 584.
'Tom has had': Vivien Eliot to Scofield Thayer, 13 Oct. 1921, *TSEL I* 592.
'a rough draft': TSE to Sidney Schiff, [4? Nov. 1921], *TSEL I* 601.
'best mental specialist': TSE to Richard Aldington, 6 Nov. 1921, *TSEL I* 603. See also
TSE to Henry Eliot, *TSEL I* 614.
Dr Vittoz's book: details from Valerie Eliot's note, *TSEL I* 594n.
'exquisite Studio': Vivien Eliot to Mary Hutchinson, [20? Dec. 1921], *TSEL I* 618.
Details of studio from EP to HLP, 3 Dec. [1921], *EP/Parents* 490–2.
'mouldering plaster': Stella Bowen, *Drawn from Life* (Maidstone: George Mann,
1974), p. 88. See photograph of courtyard with statue in Peter Ackroyd, *Ezra Pound
and his World* (Thames & Hudson, 1980), facing p. 66.
cooked even better: WL, 'Ezra Pound', in *Ezra Pound: A Collection of Essays*, ed. Peter
Russell (Peter Nevill Ltd, 1950), p. 261.
'in the midst of plumbers': EP to Thayer, 5 Dec. 1921, *EP/Dial* 222.
'*cheminée*': EP to HLP, 3 Dec. 1921, *EP/Parents* 490.

31 'poêle Godin': EP to JQ, 21 Feb. 1922, *EP/JQ* 207.
to construct tables and chairs: see Kenner, *Pound Era* 390, 392, and Stock: 1970, 238;
see Ackroyd, *Ezra Pound and his World*, facing p. 58, for photo of EP in chair.
Ford...stranded: see Norman: 1960, 265.
a whitlow: DP to EP, Dec. 1921 (Lilly).
'new poem in semi-existence': EP to IWP, 8 Jan. 1922, *EP/Parents* 493.
Liveright...in Paris: Liveright to JQ, 24 Mar. 1922 (copy in Lilly)—cited Lawrence
Rainey, *Institutions of Modernism* (New Haven: Yale University Press, 1998), pp. 196–7
n. 13. For further details see Rainey, *Institutions of Modernism*, pp. 81–2.
In return for: Norman: 1960, 253 copies the contract or 'memorandum of agreement',
which was dated '4 Jan. a.d.1922' and '4 Saturnus An 1'.
'a jumble': TSE, 'On a Recent Piece of Criticism', *Purpose* X.2 (Apr.–June 1938) 92–3.
'marvellous critic': TSE, 'The Art of Poetry' [Interview], *Paris Review* 21 (1959) 52–3.
facsimile: TSE, *The Waste Land: A Facsimile and Transcript of the Original Drafts
Including the Annotations of Ezra Pound*, ed. Valerie Eliot (Faber & Faber, 1971).

32 'the justification': EP to Felix E. Schelling, 8 July 1922, *L (1951)* 245.
'as good in its way': EP to Thayer, 9–10 Mar. 1922, *EP/Dial* 236.
verse 'squib': EP, 'E.P. hopeless and unhelped', *TSEL I* 627.
'About enough': EP to JQ, 21 Feb. 1922, *EP/JQ* 206.
'These fragments': 8/28—cf. *The Waste Land* l. 430.

33 'as good as Keats': EP to JQ, 4–5 July 1922, *EP/JQ* 209.
'affable': EP to JQ, 21 Feb. 1922, *EP/JQ* 207.
'"out" triumphantly': EP to ACH, 12 Mar. [1922], *EP/ACH* 224.
By mid-February: EP to AB, 17 Feb. 1922 (Lilly).

34 '732 double sized'...'All men': from EP, 'Paris Letter. May 1922', reprinted as '*Ulysses*' in *LE* 403–9—see pp. 407, 403.
'epoch-making': EP, 'Paris Letter. May 1922', *LE* 408.
answer to the prayer: see *GK* 96, and 'An Anachronism at Chinon' in *PD (1918)*, 13.
'public utility': *LE* 409—cf. *LE* 324n. ('Most good prose arises, perhaps, from an instinct of negation...').
'*le roman réaliste*': EP, 'James Joyce et Pécuchet', *Mercure de France* 156.575 (1 June 1922), as reprinted in *EP/JJ* 208.
new Inferno: EP to IWP and HLP, 20 Apr. 1921, *EP/Parents* 483. Cf. 'Joyce has set out to do an inferno, and he has done an inferno' *(LE* 407).
'Katharsis': EP, 'Le Prix Nobel', *Der Querschnitt* 4.1 (Spring 1924), as in *EP/JJ* 220.
'the whole occident': *LE* 407.
'age of usury': *GK* 96.
'The katharsis': *GK* 96.
'midnight': EP, 'The Little Review Calendar', *LR* VII.2 (Spring 1922) [2].
Zagreus: like Osiris, dismembered by his enemies, then reborn as deathless Dionysos of the realm of Hades, the self-renewing principle of life.

35 'I am afraid': EP to Thayer, 9–10 Mar. 1922, *EP/Dial* 236.
'Eliot works': EP to ACH, 12 Mar. [1922], *EP/ACH* 225–6.
'don't want him': EP to Aldington, 12 Mar. 1922 (HRC).
Natalie Barney: EP to Aldington, 16 Mar. and 22 May 1922 (HRC). See also 'Ezra Pound: Letters to Natalie Barney', ed. Sieburth, *Pai* 5.2 (1976) 286.
appeal slip: see Gallup: 1983, 429. HRC has a copy with annotations by Pound (filed with 3 letters by TSE to J. V. Healey).
'saving civilization': EP to AB, 18 Mar. 1922 (Lilly).
'restarting': EP to Aldington, 16 Mar. 1922 (HRC).
letter to Williams: EP to WCW, 18 Mar. 1922, *EP/WCW* 53–5.

36 The best economist: paragraph based on EP, 'Credit and the Fine Arts. A Practical Application', *NA* XXX.22 (30 Mar. 1922) 284–5, and 'Paris Letter. October 1922', *Dial* LXXIII.5 (Nov. 1922) [549]–554.
attic and...salt bread: EP, 'P.L. Sep.1921', *Dial* LXXI.4 (Oct. 1921) 463.
'when the individual city': EP, 'P.L. Jan. 1922', *Dial* LXXII.2 (Feb. 1922) 192.
a long letter: EP to JQ, 4–5 July 1922, *EP/JQ* 209–14.
'What the hell': WCW to EP, 29 Mar. 1922, *EP/WCW* 56.
'my £10': EP to JQ, 4–5 July 1922, *EP/JQ* 213.

37 On 12 March: TSE to EP, 12 Mar. 1922, *TSEL I* 641–3.
'raise the standard': TSE to E. R. Curtius, 21 July 1922, *TSEL I* 710.
'Willing': EP to TSE, 14 Mar. [1922], *TSEL I* 647–51.
By his account: TSE to Aldington, 30 June 1922, *TSEL I* 686–8.
Pound's account: see 'Small Magazines', *English Journal (College Edition)* XIX.9 (Nov. 1930) 703; 72/481; also EP to Stanley Nott, 24 May 1936, *EP/SN* 213–14. On the title see TSE to EP, 9 July 1922, *TSEL I* 692.
$200: TSE to EP, 19 July 1922, *TSEL I* 707–8; see also Stock: 1970, 247.
'with two lump gifts': EP to HM, *L (1951)* 250.
£300...not enough: TSE to EP, 19 July 1922, *TSEL I* 709.

38 'small and precarious': TSE to Sydney Schiff, 2 Aug. 1922, *TSEL I* 715–16.
'manifestoe': TSE to EP, 19 July 1922, *TSEL I*, 708.
'*cannot* jeopardise': TSE to EP, 28 July 1922, *TSEL I* 712–13.
'If you and I': TSE to EP, [3 Nov. 1922], *TSEL I* 771. See also Vivien Eliot to EP, 2 Nov. [1922], *TSEL I* 770–1.
'NO periodical': EP to TSE, 4 Nov. [1922], *TSEL I* 773.
'*not* thinking': TSE to EP, [15 Nov. 1922], *TSEL I* 778–9.

10,000 francs: mentioned also in EP to DP, 21 July 1922 (Lilly); and EP to JQ, 10 Aug. 1922, *EP/JQ* 215.

a short article: copied in *TSEL I* 789–90n.

'libellous falsehood': TSE to Gilbert Seldes, 1 Dec. 1922, *TSEL I* 797.

letter denying: TSE to Editor, *Liverpool Daily Post*, [30 Nov. 1922], as in *TSEL I* 794–5.

39   did accept: TSE's June 1923 stamped receipt for £20 received from EP/Bel Esprit is in the Beinecke Pound archive (with letters from TSE to EP). In this connection see TSE to EP, 14 and 20 May 1923, *TSEL II* 133–4, 139; further, on 21 July 1923 EP wrote to DP that he had 'French cheque for 1000 francs for T.S.E.' (Lilly).

'entoiled': EP, 'P.L. October 1922', *Dial* LXXIII.5 (Nov. 1922) 550.

A renaissance man

39   a postcard: see *EP/LR* 283 for both the p.c. and the *LR*'s response.

'Dear Dad': EP to HLP, 12 Apr. [1922], *EP/Parents* 497–8.

'I shall be dead': EP to JQ, 12 Apr. 1922, *EP/JQ* 208.

40   'no respect': EP to [? MCA], [13 July 1922], *EP/LR* 287.

travelling in Italy: details of dates and places from EP's letters to his parents, AB, WL, JQ, Thayer, and WCW.

[parents] retiring: EP to IWP, 8 Jan. 1922, *EP/Parents* 493.

'busy spring': EP to JQ, 20 June 1922, as extracted in Daniel D. Pearlman, *The Barb of Time* (New York: Oxford University Press, 1969), p. 302.

'cuban pennies': EP to DP, 14 July 1922 (Lilly). See also EP to HLP, [July 1922], *EP/Parents* 500; and 12/53.

'4, probably 5': EP to AB, 29 June 1922 (Lilly).

'five cantos': EP to JQ, 4, 5 July 1922, *EP/JQ* 213.

Morand's . . . fictions: see EP, 'Paris Letter. September 1921', *Dial* LXXI.4 (Oct. 1921) 462; and Gallup: 1983, 448–9. EP's translations were published as *Fancy Goods and Open All Night: Stories by Paul Morand* by New Directions in 1984.

'Tami Koumé': taken from printed invitation on verso of which are notes for Malatesta cantos, in folder of drafts of 1922–3 (Beinecke). Tami Koumé, a Japanese painter Pound had known in London, was killed in the 1924 Tokyo earthquake.

'gt. gland sleuth': EP to HLP, [July 1922], *EP/Parents* 500.

boxing lesson: see WL, 'Ezra Pound', in *Ezra Pound: A Collection of Essays*, ed. Peter Russell, p. 261; for Hemingway's account see his *A Moveable Feast* (Harmondsworth: Penguin Books, 1966), pp. 82–3.

41   'pretty unhealthy' . . . 'Obsequies': Sibley Watson to Thayer, 29 July 1922, *EP/Dial* 245.

'damn fit': EP to JQ, 4, 5 July 1922, *EP/JQ* 213.

people . . . flooding: details from EP to DP, 17 July 1923 (Lilly); and Wilhelm: 1990, 316–17.

fifty-page booklets: for details see Gallup: 1983, 34–5; and *PD* (1958), 50–1. Six books were published in this 'Inquest', among them EP's *Indiscretions*, WCW's *The Great American Novel*, FMF's *Women & Men*, and Hemingway's *In our Time* (1924). See further EP to FMF, 1 Aug. [1922], *EP/FMF* 68–9; and EP to WCW, [? 1 Aug. 1922], *EP/WCW* 63–4.

some sort of *affaire*: Nancy Cunard's letters to Pound in 1922 and 1923 are in the Lilly Pound collection. See James J. Wilhelm, 'Nancy Cunard: A Sometime Flame, a Stalwart Friend', *Pai* 19.1–2 (1990) 202–12.

'don't at present': EP to DP, 21 July 1922 (Lilly).

'swell out': EP to HLP, [July 1922], *EP/Parents* 500.

The first draft: all the drafts referred to are in Beinecke.

Eliot's Tiresias: see *The Waste Land* Part III, and note to line 218.

42 Malatesta managed: *GK* 159. The best account of Sigismondo's Tempio, with illustrations, is Adrian Stokes's *Stones of Rimini* (1934). Hugh Kenner wrote a fine account of visiting it—see 'The Hiddenmost Wonder' in his *Historical Fictions* (San Francisco: North Point Press, 1990), pp. 3–11. For a near contemporary account of the state of Italy in Sigismondo's time see Niccolo Machiavelli's *History of Florence and the Affairs of Italy*, Bk. VI.

'bhloomin historic character': EP to IWP, 1 Nov. 1924, *EP/Parents* 546.

'boisterousness': EP to JQ, 10 Aug. 1922, *EP/JQ* 217.

'some . . . vigour': EP, 'P.L. October 1922', *Dial* LXXIII.5 (Nov. 1922) 554. Re D'Annunzio's seizing Fiume etc., see Nicholas Farrell, *Mussolini: A New Life* (Weidenfeld & Nicolson, 2003), pp. 84–9.

'openly volitionist': *GK* 194.

43 at Excideuil: see *EP: Poet I* 382 and 322.

'a wing': this would be a grasshopper in flight. Cf. 17/79; also WCW in *Paterson* Bk. II.

44 'no other': *GK* frontispiece.

'immense panorama': TSE, '*Ulysses*, Order and Myth' (1923), in *Selected Prose of T. S. Eliot*, ed. Frank Kermode (Faber & Faber, 1975), p. 177.

'cut his notch': *GK* 159. In a review of Adrian Stokes's *Stones of Rimini* (*Criterion* XIII.52 (Apr. 1934) 496), EP wrote of Sigismondo's Tempio, 'As a human record, as a record of courage, nothing can touch it.'

'shut in by battles': EP to JQ, 10 Aug. 1922, *EP/JQ* 217.

'Life was interesting' . . . 'fascio?': *J/M* 49–51.

Steffens . . . talking: see 'Ezra Pound' [a letter], *Morada* 3 (1930) 90; 16/74–5; and Lincoln Steffens, *The Autobiography* (New York: Harcourt, Brace, 1931), pp. 750–1 and 760–1.

'NE VEUX: 'Kongo Roux', [*391*, 15 (10 July 1921):] *Le Pilhaou-Thibaou* [10].

'measured moments': EP to Felix Schelling, 8 July 1922, *L (1951)* 249.

45 '*Christianisme*': 'Kongo Roux', [*391*, 15 (10 July 1921):] *Le Pilhaou-Thibaou* [10].

'Damn remnants': EP to HM, 16 July 1922, *L (1951)* 250–1.

'reading up': EP to JQ, 10 Aug. 1922, *EP/JQ* 217.

46 'got three': EP to HLP, 25 Dec. [1922], *EP/Parents* 505. See also EP to Watson, 4 Jan. 1923, *EP/Dial* 255–6; and Watson to Thayer, 10 Mar. 1923, *EP/Dial* 260–1.

58ter: call slip among drafts and notes for Malatesta cantos (Beinecke). Other details in this paragraph, including correspondence with book dealers, drawn from these notes; also from Ben D. Kimpel and T. C. Duncan Eaves, 'Pound's Research for the Malatesta Cantos', *Pai* 11.3 (1982) 406–19.

'"*Te cavero*"': see 10/43.

passport: reproduced facing p. 54 of *Il viaggio di Ezra Pound*, a cura di Luca Gallesi ([Milano]: Biblioteca di via Senato Edizioni, 2002)—catalogue of a 'bio- bibliographical' exhibition in the Sala Serpota, Biblioteca di via Senato, 17 Sept.–14 Oct. 2002.

'chewing along': EP to IWP, 19 Jan. [1923], *EP/Parents* 506.

toured . . . battlefields: see Wilhelm: 1990, 322.

'Geographical verification': EP to JQ, 17 Feb. 1923, as extracted in Pearlman, *The Barb of Time*, p. 302.

'documents preserved': EP draft note to 'your eminence', 2 Feb. 1923, with drafts and notes for Malatesta cantos (Beinecke).

dance with postcards: the postcards and letters exchanged in Mar. 1923, now in Lilly, are the primary source of information about EP's movements in the following paragraphs.

47 'Somewhat full day': EP to DP, 8 Mar. 1923 (private collection).

'highest quality': EP, 'Possibilities of Civilization: What the Small Town Can Do', *Delphian Quarterly*, XIX.3 (July 1936) 16.

'Hotel-keeper': EP to DP, [21 Mar. 1923] (Lilly). On this incident see *J/M* 26–7.

'descended': EP to DP, [28 Mar. 1923] (Lilly). I am aware of the damaging construction put upon these two notes of 21 and 28 Mar. 1923 by Lawrence Rainey, who has asserted in a number of places that they prove that what drew Pound to Fascism was a love of violence. I find that an over-determined and false reading of those notes. There is no lack of evidence to establish that Pound's interest in Fascism had quite other motivations—e.g. see his letter of 15 Aug. 1923 to Nancy Cox McCormack, cited here (from one of Rainey's own articles) on pp. 54–5. For a less lurid light on Pound's friendship with the hotel-keeper Averardo Marchetti, see Luca Cesari, 'Pound e il "farsi scannar" del romagnolo Marchetti', in *Ezra Pound 1972/1992*, a cura di Luca Gallesi (Milano: Greco & Greco editori, 1992), pp. 210–23. See *Ezra Pound 1972/1992*, 445–6 for a biographical note on Marchetti.

48   Nancy Cunard: see Wilhelm, 'Nancy Cunard: A Sometime Flame', *Pai* 19.1–2 (1990) 202–12; and Wilhelm: 1900, 324.

'divorce news': DP to EP, [Mar. 1923—misfiled as 1921] (Lilly).

'wd. be some time': EP to DP, [21 Mar. 1923] (Lilly).

sojourning foreigner: the authority is among papers of J. Atherton Parker, D's solicitor (Pound MSS II, Box 12, Lilly).

sent off ... 24 April: EP's typescript note from Paris to Watson, saying he had 'sent off the Cantos, day before yesterday', is dated '26/3/1923', *EP/Dial* 264—but he must have mistaken the month since on 26 Mar. he was in Rimini without his typewriter. An April date is supported by Watson's arranging to have the revised cantos copied for Thayer about 5 May—see *EP/Dial* 274.

'on tactical grounds': TSE to EP, [27 May? 1923], *TSEL II* 141.

49   the objective poetic self: see *EP: Poet I* 306–11, 363.

Gemistus Plethon: see *GK* 45 and 224–5.

50   historians now recognize: e.g. P. J. Jones, *The Malatesta of Rimini and the Papal State* (Cambridge: Cambridge University Press, 1974), pp. 228–31.

Burckhardt: see Jacob Burckhardt, *The Civilization of the Renaissance in Italy* (1860) (Phaidon Press, 1944), p. 278.

51   'fighting the world': *Cantos* 802, among the final fragments.

52   'paradiso *terrestre*': *Cantos* 802 (emphasis added).

Life and times: 1923–1924

52   state visit: see Farrell, *Mussolini*, p. 135.

not visit ... 'Confucius': EP to HLP, 19 May [1923], *EP/Parents* 511—EP's emphasis.

Persian soup: Stock: 1970, 253.

'de looks edtn.': EP to IWP, 11 May [1923], *EP/Parents* 511.

'a dee looks edtn': EP to Kate Buss, 12 May 1923, *L (1951)* 256.

53   'canto on Kung': EP to HLP, 'about the 21st June 1923', *EP/Parents* 514.

'Kung said': 13/59.

'exact reverse': EP to HLP, 'about the 21st June 1923', *EP/Parents* 514.

'portrait of contemporary': EP to WL, 3 Dec. 1924, *EP/WL* 139.

'STATE OF' ... 'DECOMPOSITION': EP to FMF, 16 Nov. [1933], *EP/FMF* 134. See also EP to Schelling, 8 July 1922, *L (1951)* 247–8.

'vice-crusaders': 14/63.

'fearfully painful': OS to EP, 12 July [1923] (Lilly).

'to know for certain': DP to EP, 9 July 1923 (Lilly).

'had O. Rudge': EP to DP, [27 June 1923] (Lilly).

'The Rudge': EP to DP, 17 July 1923 (Lilly).

'Olga played over': EP to DP, 7 Aug. 1923 (Lilly).

54 'Mi rencusi': OR to EP, 6 June 1923 (Beinecke/OR)—Conover, 6, dates this as 21 June.

'Caro': OR to EP, 6 July 1923 (Beinecke/OR).

'25 kilometers': OR note on snapshot, cited Conover, 7. OR's 1923 album is in Beinecke.

'not to panic': DP to EP, 21 July 1923 (Lilly).

'left everything': DP to EP, 9 Aug. 1923 (Lilly).

'combined intake': EP to IWP, 30 Aug. 1923, *EP/Parents* 518.

'rewriting': EP to DP, [13 July 1923] (Lilly).

'de LOOKS'...'sense of form': EP to DP, 23 July 1923 (Lilly).

by 1 August: EP to DP, 1 Aug. 1923 (Lilly).

small booklet: EP to AB, 3 Aug. 1923 (Lilly); also EP to DP, [? 7 Aug. 1923] (Lilly).

'on 16th': EP to AB, 23 Aug. 1923 (Lilly).

still working on that: EP to DP, 14 Oct. 1923 (Lilly).

'a creative force': Nancy Cox McCormack, 'Gifted Sculptor Gives Vivid Pen Picture of Mussolini', newspaper clipping from unidentified source dated 'Oct. 1923' among Cox-McCormack Papers in the Poetry/Rare Books Collection, State University of New York at Buffalo—as cited in Lawrence S. Rainey, '"All I Want You to Do Is to Follow the Orders": History, Faith and Fascism in the Early Cantos', in Lawrence S. Rainey, ed., *A Poem Containing History: Textual Studies in The Cantos* (Ann Arbor: University of Michigan Press, 1997), p. 95.

'To clear up': EP to Nancy Cox McCormack, 15 Aug. 1923 (Buffalo)—as cited Rainey, '"All I Want"', pp. 98–9.

55 'vortices of power': see *EP: Poet I* 262–3.

'uproars, fiascos': EP, '"Inverno Musicale": La violinista Olga Rudge', *Il Mare* XXVI.1281 (30 Sept. 1933) [1], as translated in *EP&M* 344. Antheil said it was to hear Stravinsky's *Les Noces*, first performed on 13 June, that he had gone to Paris.

hours of it: from Antheil, *Bad Boy of Music* (New York, 1945), p. 117, cited *EP&M* 245.

'demoniac temperament': EP, 'La violinista Olga Rudge', *Il Mare* XXVI.1286 (4 Nov. 1933) 2, as translated in *EP&M* 345.

'Hitting the piano': 'George Antheil Plays...', Paris Edition *Chicago Tribune* (13 Dec. 1923), as in *EP&M* 246.

'a riot':'The Mailbag', *New York Herald* (Paris), 22 Dec. 1923, cited Conover, 7. According to Alex Ross, 'it turned out that the brouhaha had been staged for the benefit of the film director Marcel L'Herbier, who needed a wild crowd scene for his thriller *L'Inhumaine*' (Alex Ross, *The Rest Is Noise* (Fourth Estate, 2008), p. 138).

three of his compositions: detail from Ellmann, *James Joyce*, 568.

'turned into bedlam'...'Cagney': EP, '"Inverno Musicale": La violinista Olga Rudge', *Il Mare* XXVI.1281 (30 Sept. 1933) [1], as translated in *EP&M* 344.

56 'white winer': James Charters, *This Must Be the Place* (Michael Joseph, 1934), p. 96—cited Wilhelm: 1990, 289. EP appears briefly, not drinking, in Robert McAlmon's 'Truer than Most Accounts'—a record of life in Paris *c.*1923–4—in *The Exile* no. 2 (Autumn 1927) 40–86.

'swashbuckling...chess': BB in *Descant on Rawthey's Madrigal: Conversations with Basil Bunting*, ed. Jonathan Williams (Lexington, Ky.: Gnomon Press, 1968), [n.p.].

'locked up': BB to Lieppert, 30 Oct. 1932 (University of Chicago Library)—as cited in Victoria Forde, *The Poetry of Basil Bunting* (Newcastle-upon-Tyne: Bloodaxe Books, 1991), p. 24.

'petty thieves': from BB's more detailed account of the episode as recorded by Caroll F. Terrell in 'Basil Bunting: An Eccentric Biography', in *Basil Bunting: Man and Poet*, ed. Carroll F. Terrell (Orono, Me.: National Poetry Foundation, 1981), pp. 41–2.

note, from 'Prison': BB to EP, [6 Oct. 1923], (Lilly)—cited Peter Makin, *Bunting: The Shaping of his Verse* (Oxford: Clarendon Press, 1992), p. 26.

57 11 **December concert**: programme reproduced in *EP&M* [249].

Schwerke: *EP&M* 247–8.

'hell's own': EP to HLP, 8 Dec. 1923, *EP/Parents* 521.

'He discussed': EP to William Bird, [? Dec. 1923], *L (1951)* 256. Cf. EP to HLP, 8 Dec. 1923, *EP/Parents* 521.

58 **20 October**: EP to DP, 20 Oct. 1923 (Lilly).

'vorticist film': see *EPRO* 230 n. 66; and John Alexander, 'Parenthetical Paris, 1920–1925: Pound, Picabia, Brancusi and Léger', *Pound's Artists: Ezra Pound and the Visual Arts in London, Paris and Italy* (The Tate Gallery, 1985), pp. 109ff.

specimen pages: see Philippe Mikriammos, 'Ezra Pound in Paris (1921–1924)', *Pai* 14.2–3 (1985) 391.

'Eliot turned up': EP to DP, 25 Nov. 1923 (Lilly).

'My Dear Son': HLP to EP, 10 Dec. 1923 (Beinecke).

aunt or an uncle: EP to IWP, 10 Feb. 1924, *EP/Parents* 524; also Conover, 53.

'Must stay on diet': EP to HLP, 6 Jan. [1924], *EP/Parents* 521.

'6 Jan. 1924': the setting copy is in Beinecke. The Malatesta cantos were probably set from the *Criterion* printing.

59 'Darling': EP to OR, from Hotel Mignon, Rapallo, [Jan. 1924], (Beinecke/OR).

'Caro': OR to EP, 22 Jan. 1924 (Beinecke/OR).

'vigliacco': in the slang of a later era, that could be 'I want you something rotten'.

'a few days': EP to OR, [Feb. 1924] (Beinecke/OR).

'the miseries': EP to OR, 25 Feb. 1924 (Beinecke/OR).

'to interior': EP to HLP, 12 Mar. [1924], *EP/Parents* 525.

'in palazzo': EP to parents, 25 Mar. [1924], *EP/Parents* 526.

'Ezra's things': OS to DP, 11 May 1924—as cited in Conover, 53.

Fiddle Music: see *CPMEP* 143–4; and Conover, 52.

'superfluous rubbish': EP to William Bird, 17 Apr. 1924, *L (1951)* 259; other details from EP to Bird, 10 and 17 Apr. 1924, *L (1951)* 257–9.

61 **copied . . . songs**: see *CPMEP* 152ff.

'doing sketches': EP to HLP, 12 May 1924, *EP/Parents* 529.

'a few more cantos': EP to HLP, 16 May 1924, *EP/Parents* 530.

'Jefferson': EP to HLP, 28 May [1924], *EP/Parents* 531.

'Marco Polo's note': EP to HLP, 21 June [1924], *EP/Parents* 534.

'another large wad': EP to AB, 30 Aug. 1924 (Lilly).

'Pagany': WCW, *A Voyage to Pagany* (New York: Macaulay, 1928).

'renaissance music': WCW, *Autobiography*, 225–6. See also Paul Mariani, *William Carlos Williams: A New World Naked* (New York: McGraw-Hill, 1981), pp. 238–41.

tones . . . from the instrument: see *CPMEP* 142ff.

'Musique Américaine': details of the concert of 7 July from: the Invitation-Programme (HRC); *CPMEP* 152–8; Conover, 53–4; Wilhelm: 1990, 340; Sylvia Beach, *Shakespeare and Company* 132; Mariani, *WCW* 240.

Fiddle Music: for an expert account and edition of EP's dozen or so compositions for violin in the years 1923–32 see *Complete Violin Works of Ezra Pound*, ed. with Commentary by Robert Hughes (Emeryville, Calif.: Second Evening Art, 2004).

62 'intestinal waters': EP to DP, [17 July 1924] (Lilly).

'First day': EP to DP, 31 July 1924 (Lilly).

'not a bad sign': EP to DP, 4 Aug. 1924 (Lilly).

'general survey': EP to DP, 15 Aug. 1924 (Lilly).

in the Vienne: EP to HLP, 'end of Aug.' [1924], *EP/Parents* 539.

Olga was with him: see Wilhelm: 1900, 341.

'My health': EP to HLP, 4 Sept. [1924], *EP/Parents* 540.
'shall keep my plans': DP to EP, [July 1924] (Lilly).
'Mao': EP to DP, 2 Sept. 1924 (Lilly).
'special book case trunk': EP to HLP, 13 July 1924, *EP/Parents* 536.
'melancholy man'...'not in the movement': EP to DP, 17 July 1923 (Lilly). Details of
this episode in Sept.–Oct. 1924 from: Hemingway, *A Moveable Feast*, chap. 16; EP to
HLP, 15 Oct. 1924, *EP/Parents* 543.

63   'fine book of poems': EP to HLP, 15 Oct. 1924, *EP/Parents* 543. Referred to by EP as
'The Four Winds' (see EP to H. L. Mencken, Feb. 1925, *L (1951)* 270); due to his
efforts twelve of the poems appeared in *Poetry* XXVI.1 (Apr. 1925); others were printed
in the *Dial* and in *transatlantic review*; and EP printed a further nine in *Exile*. (For
TSE's—and JJ's—amazement at EP's enthusiasm for Dunning's poems see *TSEL II*
557.) EP also published an article on 'Mr Dunning's Poetry' in *Poetry* XXVI.6 (Sept.
1925), and another in *Exile* no. 3 (Spring 1928). The *Poetry* selection and EP's *Poetry*
article were reprinted in *Pai* 10.3 (1981) [605]–618. In 1929 Edward W. Titus published
from his Black Manikin press in Paris *Windfalls* by R. C. Dunning containing 43
poems, but not including all that had appeared in periodicals. Titus had published
Rococo: A Poem by Ralph Cheever Dunning in 1926.
'thinking about civic order': 'An Interview with Ezra Pound' by D. G. Bridson, *New
Directions 17*, ed. J. Laughlin (New York: New Directions, 1961), p. 170.

2. FROM RAPALLO, 1924–1932

Human complications

This section is based for the most part on three sets of correspondence: letters between EP
and OR (Beinecke/OR); letters between EP and DP (Lilly); letters from EP to his parents
(Beinecke). More of the EP/OR correspondence is given in Anne Conover's *Olga Rudge
and Ezra Pound* (New Haven: Yale University Press, 2001). Mary de Rachewiltz's memoir,
Discretions (Faber & Faber, 1971)—in USA *Ezra Pound: Father and Teacher* (New York:
New Directions, 1975, 2005)—tells her own story superbly.

64   would record...'piantato': from OR Personal Papers (Beinecke/OR)—see Conover
56, 55.
'complications': EP to AB, 3 June 1926 (Lilly).
'rejuvinated': EP to WL, 3 Dec. 1924, *EP/WL* 138.
'the north side': EP to HLP, 15 Oct. 1924, *EP/Parents* 543–4—rest of paragraph *EP/
Parents* 543–4.
18 and 19: from Stock: 1970, 257.
Sicily: details from EP letters to his parents reproduced in *Lettere dalla Sicilia e due
frammenti ritrovati*, a cura di Mary de Rachewiltz (Valverde, Catania: Il Girasole
Edizioni, 1997).
'Greek theatre': EP, in 'Hell' (1934), *LE* 205.

65   'ought to stick at': EP to A. P. Saunders, 25/1/25 (Hamilton).
'a phobia': EP to OR, 13 Mar. 1921, as in Conover, 58.
advised against Monte Carlo: EP to OR, 4 Mar. 1925 (Beinecke/OR).
'general reading': EP to IWP, 11 Feb. [1925], *EP/Parents* 556
'Baldwins': EP to HLP, 15 Feb. [1925], *EP/Parents* 556–7.
'taking apartment': EP to OR, 4 Mar. 1925 (Beinecke/OR). James Laughlin described
the apartment in 'Pound le professeur', his contribution to *L'Herne: Ezra Pound I*

(Paris, Éditions de L'Herne, 1965,148): 'Behind the broad terrace were four or five small rooms, furnished with the simplicity Pound loved. Most of the chairs and tables were of his own making, from pieces of wood picked up in the local carpenters' workshops. There were the beautiful Gaudier sculptures, small but quite pure, and among the paintings a striking Max Ernst, an abstract of two white sea-shells. In Dorothy Pound's small salon were coloured drawings by Wyndham Lewis, and several of her own skilful sketches. Along the walls were low bookcases made by Pound, with fewer books than one would expect —he was constantly sifting out those he considered not worth keeping' (my translation).

'about 8 or 9': EP to HLP, [April 1925], *EP/Parents* 563.

'permanent locale': EP to HLP, [24 June 1925], *EP/Parents* 570.

66 'up to XXIII': EP to HLP, 25 Mar. 1925, *EP/Parents* 561.

'mostly borasco': EP to AB, 13 Mar. 1925 (Lilly).

This Quarter: Norman: 1960, 274–8 gives the dedication and fills out the story.

'two weeks chase': EP to AB, 7 June 1925 (Lilly).

'CAPOLAVORO': EP to William Bird, 24 Aug. 1925, *L (1951)* 273.

'so bored': OR to EP, [June 1925], as in Conover, 58.

'Where OFFICIALLY': EP to OR, 18 Apr. 1925 (Beinecke/OR).

'figlia di Arturo': see MdR, *Discretions* 203.

'[leon]cin*a*': OR to EP, 11 July 1925 (Beinecke/OR).

'no talent': OR to EP, 22 July [1925] (Beinecke/OR).

'if you would like': OR to EP, 20 July 1925 (Beinecke/OR).

67 'a contadina': OR to EP, 22 July [1925] (Beinecke/OR).

humanity and wisdom: see *Discretions*, 7–15 in particular.

'D's birthday': EP to HLP, 14 Sept. 1925, *EP/Parents* 576.

'one from Egypt': EP to DP, 17 Oct. 1925 (Lilly).

'la mia leoncinina': OR to EP, 22 Oct. [1925] (Beinecke/OR).

'crowded and successful': EP to OR, 7 Dec. 1925 (Beinecke/OR).

'XXII to XXIII': EP to IWP, 24 Oct. [1925], *EP/Parents* 579.

cutting up his 'Villon': EP to AB, 26 Nov. 1925 (Lilly).

'throwing out': EP to HLP, 28 Nov. and 2 Dec. 1925, *EP/Parents* 582.

68 met there by 'R': DP to EP, '15 Dec. 1925' (Lilly). When DP removed all her possessions from the castle at Brunnenburg *c.*1966 she left behind one book, a copy of McAlmon's *Being Geniuses Together*, in which there is a bookplate which she had designed for 'E. Hassan Riffai'. Riffai was an Egyptian army officer. In Jan.1939 'Captain Rifai' sent Dorothy stamps for Omar's collection, and in Jan. 1940 she asked Omar if he had heard anything from him—see DP to Omar Pound, 18 Jan. 1939 and 7 Jan. 1940 (Omar S. Pound Archive, Hamilton).

'at last escaped'. . . tea with Beerbohm: EP to HLP, 24 Dec. [1925], *EP/Parents* 584.

'played him': OR in unpublished transcript of interview, 1981 or 1982, by New York Center for Visual History for their film *Ezra Pound: American Odyssey*, as cited in Carpenter: 1988, 450.

'At the heart': DP to EP, 20 Dec. 1925 (Lilly).

'at last thought out': EP to OR, 17 Feb. 1926 (Beinecke/OR).

'enjoying pyramids': EP to HLP, 11 and 17 Jan. [1926], *EP/Parents* 585, 586.

'oriental drapery': EP to HLP, 2 Feb. [1926], *EP/Parents* 587.

'somewhat worn': EP to HLP, 3 Mar. 1926, *EP/Parents* 589.

'half ill': EP to OR, 20 Mar. 1926 (Beinecke/OR).

'Troppo incommodo': EP telegram to OR, 19 Mar. 1926 (Beinecke/OR).

'not pleased': OR to EP, 29 Mar. 1926 (Beinecke/OR).

'a coup de désespoir': OR to EP, 19 Mar. 1926 (Beinecke/OR).

'thoroughly understands': OR to EP, [? 26 Mar. 1926] (Beinecke/OR). 'The Rapallo Tennis Club was much frequented by the *bel mondo* of Rapallo, mainly foreign residents and artists and Italian nobility' (Giuseppe Bacigalupo, *Ieri a Rapallo*, V edizione (Pasian de Prato: Campanotto Editore, 2006), p. 182).

'24/3/1926': EP, small notebook (YCAL MSS 43, box 34, folder 804, Beinecke).

'crucial part': EP to OR, May 1926 (Beinecke/OR).

'don't make a vollum': EP to OR, Apr. 1926 (Beinecke/OR).

69 'down to Rome': EP to IWP, 13 May 1926, *EP/Parents* 699.

'Homage Froissart': see *CPMEP* 159.

'Dear Dad': EP to HLP, 11 Oct. [for Sept.? 1926], *EP/Parents* 602.

'sur déclaration': details from copy of birth certificate (Lilly). In British and US law a child born in wedlock is presumed to be the husband's legitimate child, a presumption that can be set aside only by a judicial decision based upon clear evidence that the husband is not the father. In *Some Do Not* (1924), the first part of *Parade's End*, Ford Madox Ford had his hero Tietjens say about accepting his estranged wife Sylvia's child as his own: 'a child born in wedlock is by law the father's, and if a gentleman suffer the begetting of his child he must, in decency, take the consequences; the woman and the child must come before the man, be he who he may.'

'small operation': EP to OR, 27 Sept. 1926 (Beinecke/OR).

'taps, tests, analyses': EP to HLP, [Oct. 1926], *EP/Parents* 603.

by Raymonde Collignon: details from DP's letters to EP in May and June 1927 (Lilly).

'adopt': WBY to OS, 24 Sept. 1926, cited Norman: 1960, 283.

'Omar's *eyes*': DP to EP, 9 June 1927 (Lilly). In late September or October 1926 DP told HLP and IWP that Omar's eyes were 'dark blue'; however, when sending a 'little photo of Omar' in April 1927 she wrote that he had 'brown eyes after mother'. DP's own eyes, according to her passport, were blue.

70 'Do you favour': EP to OR, 1 Nov. 1926 (Beinecke/OR).

didn't 'see much fun': DP to EP, 13 Apr. 1931 (Lilly).

'Cat and Water Carrier': EP to 'Dear Progenitors' 22 Dec. [1926], *EP/Parents* 611. The clavichord was transported early in 1928; the 'Hieratic Head' in Nov. 1931.

'somewhat functional': EP to OR, 2 Apr. 1927 (Beinecke/OR).

'I do not think': EP to OR, [22 Jan. 1929] (Beinecke/OR).

'wd. putt it': EP to OR, 26 Jan. [1929] (Beinecke/OR).

'a set of values': EP to OR, [12 Dec. 1928] (Beinecke/OR).

71 'very American': see Norman: 1960, 303–4.

'the only reason': EP to OR, [12 Dec. 1928] (Beinecke/OR).

cuckold: among EP's 'legal papers' is this undated note: 'I, Ezra Pound, declare that Omar is not my son save in the legal sense. I am cuckold.' (Beinecke YCAL MSS 53, box 37, folder 859.) Another copy of the note, in EP's hand, is preserved with OR's Notebooks (Beinecke).

Greek tragedy: cf. Aeschylus' *Eumenides*, and Sophocles' *Women of Trachis* in EP's version.

Saving the world by pure form

71 blocking in 28–30: EP to HLP, 7 Sept. [1927], *EP/Parents* 636.

'new American version': EP to AB, 22 Jan. 1928 (Lilly).

72 'how to RHYTHM': EP to OR, [Nov. 1927] (Beinecke/OR). Much of the detail in this paragraph is from EP's letters to OR in Oct. and Nov. 1927.

'the summa': EP to Glenn Hughes, 11 Apr. 1928 (HRC).

'carry dissipation': EP to OR, [Feb. 1928] (Beinecke/OR).

New Masses: for EP's brief letter in *New Masses*, New York, II.2 (Dec. 1926) 3, see *P&P* IV, 373; for his article, 'Workshop Orchestration', *New Masses* II.5 (Mar. 1927) 21, see *P&P* IV, 381; and for his further letter and Gellert's reply, *New Masses* II.5 (Mar. 1927) 25, see *P&P* IV, 382. See also *EP&M* 315.

73   'three perfectly placed': *NPL* 156.

'After the intellect': EP, 'How to Write'[1930], *Machine Art* 102.

'mental formation': EP, 'The Jefferson–Adams Letters as a Shrine and a Monument' (1937), *S Pr* 118.

'active element': EP, 'For a New Paideuma' (1938), *S Pr* 254.

'All men': EP's instance in *J/M* 21.

'the organizing thought' . . . 'We need': EP, 'Simplicities', *The Exile* no. 4 (1928) 5.

'18th century': EP, 'Simplicities', *The Exile* no. 4 (1928) 4.

'interesting phenomena' . . . 'The republic': EP, [editorial notes], *The Exile* no. 1 (Spring 1927) 89–90.

74   'the present state': EP to Glenn Hughes, 2 Sept. 1927 (HRC).

'Starting at the bottom': taken from EP's later revised version of *Ta Hio*, 'The Great Digest or Adult Study', *Confucius* 19. [EP's *Ta Hio. The Great Learning of Confucius* (1928) was translated from Guillaume Pauthier's French version in *Doctrine de Confucius ou Les Quatres Livres de philosophie morale et politique de la Chine* (Paris, 1841). EP's 1945 translation is based on his own study of the Chinese text.]

'increases through': *Confucius* 27.

75   'The men of old': *Confucius* 29–33.

76   'abundance of nature': 52/257.

Fenollosa: see *CWC* 12 and 22.

77   'When we see': Charles Darwin, *The Origin of Species* (1859), chap. IV, §7.

'talk of science' . . . 'We continue': EP, 'Simplicities', *The Exile* no. 4 (1928) 3–4.

'Familiarity': EP, 'Addenda. II' [*c*.1928], *Machine Art* 111.

'We are as capable': EP, 'Epstein, Belgion, and Meaning' (1930), *EP&VA* 166.

'human consciousness': EP, 'How to Read' (1929), *LE* 22.

78   '*nutrition of impulse*': EP, 'How to Read' (1929), *LE* 20.

A sextant for 'A Draft of XXX Cantos'

78   hell . . . into proportion: EP to William Bird. 26 Dec. 1924, *L (1951)* 263.

Rodker's deadline: information from EP letters to HLP and DP, June–Sept. 1927.

the designs: see EP to William Bird, 10 and 17 Apr. 1924, *L (1951)/5*257–9. Further information from Anthony Ozturk, in a paper to 12th International EP Conference, Oxford, 1987.

de luxe editions: in a draft letter dated 31 Jan. 1932 to the editor of the Paris edition of the *Chicago Tribune* EP wrote: 'A few years ago the de luxe edition was one of the few means of publishing anything not likely to have large commercial success' (Beinecke). For a sampling of his published comments see: 'The Renaissance. III', *Poetry* VI.2 (May 1915) 91; 'On a Book of Prefaces', [Nov. 1917], *EP/LR* 157; 'Historical Survey', *LR* VIII.1 (Autumn 1921) 39–42; 'Paris Letter. Sept. 1921', *Dial* LXXI.4 (Oct. 1921) 463; 'Paris Letter. Oct. 1922', *Dial* LXXIII.5 (Nov. 1922) 550; 'Paris Letter. Dec. 1922', *Dial* LXXIV.1 (Jan. 1923) [85]; to R. P. Blackmur, 30 Nov. 1924, *L* 260–1; to John Drummond, 18 Feb. [1933], *L (1951)* 320; *ABCE* 110–11; 'Past History', *English Journal (College Edition)* XXII.5 (May 1933) 350–1.

'Soncino and Bodoni': EP, 'Deflation Benefit', *Globe* I.5 (Aug. 1937) 66. Jerome McGann's suggestion in *The Textual Condition* (Princeton, NJ: Princeton University Press, 1991) and elsewhere that these *de luxe* editions of the cantos showed Pound under the influence of William Morris's Pre-Raphaelite Kelmscott Press is contradicted by this statement, and by Pound's determined 'No Kelmscott mess of illegibility. Large clear type...' (*L(1951)* 256). Soncino is given honourable mention at the close of *XXX Cantos*. McGann appears unaware that Pound had deliberately purged his work of Pre-Raphaelite influences before 1914.

79 **money from the ventures**: Lawrence Rainey's argument—as in 'The Creation of the Avant-Garde: F. T. Marinetti and Ezra Pound', *Modernism/Modernity* I.3 (1994) 209–12—that the *de luxe* editions of the cantos turned the poem into a market commodity are not in accord with the known facts about the production (i.e. the writing) of the cantos, about the individuals involved in the material production of those editions, and about the conditions under which the cantos had to be published at that time. That some copies—it is not known how many—were bought as collector's items and traded on the rare book market could not turn the poem into a commodity, but only those copies of it. The poem lives, after all, in the mind, not on paper.
  '**sextant**': *GK* 352.

80 '**The best lack**': WBY, 'The Second Coming'.

82 '**Mr Pound's Hell**': TSE, *After Strange Gods* (Faber & Faber, 1934), p. 43.
  taste for damnation: cf. TSE, 'Baudelaire' (1930), *Selected Essays*, 3rd edn. (Faber & Faber, 1951), pp. 427–9.
  '**Io venni**': Dante, *Inferno* V, 28.
  Plotinus' idea: see *Enneads* I. 8.
  '**mental ROT**': EP to FMF, 16 Nov. [1933], *EP/FMF* 134. See also EP to John Lackay Brown, Apr. 1937, *L (1951)* 385–6.

84 **Kublai**: see EP, 'Kublai Khan and his Currency' (1920), *S Pr* 174–6. William McNaughton, for one, reads the episode very differently, as an instance of the head of state properly exercising his sovereign power and responsibility to issue money—see *Pai* 21.3 (1992) 20. It is also true that his currency served commerce. The problem is that he neglected to distribute his wealth for the common good.
  Masaryk: see vol. i, 393–7.
  '**the unit submerged**': from EP to OR, 20 Aug. 1927 (Beinecke/OR).
  '**from the TOP**': EP to Ingrid Davies, 25 Mar. 1955, with reference to the Russian Revolution and 'my Tovarisch Canto' (HRC).

85 '**light of the Renaissance**': EP, 'Remy de Gourmont' (1920), *LE* 355.
  '**the finest force**': see *EP: Poet I* 313.
  inventors of ... loan capitalism: see Giovanni Arrighi, *The Long Twentieth Century: Money, Power, and the Origins of our Times* (Verso, 1994), chap. 2 'The Rise of Capital', especially pp. 96–109 ('The Genesis of High Finance').

86 **King Midas**: see Ovid, *Metamorphoses* V. Lemprière notes that according to Plutarch Midas later suffered from bad dreams. (To remedy the omission of canto 23 from this account the exigent reader might look up Burton Hatlen's essay 'Pound and Nature: A Reading of Canto XXIII', *Pai* 25.1 and 2 (1996) 161–88.)
  Ruskin: see *Stones of Venice*, i: *The Foundations*, chap. 1, § 1–39; ii: *The Sea Stories*, chap. 8, 'The Ducal Palace', § 13–25; iii: *The Fall*, chap. 4, § 6.

87 **Sulpicia**: her poems can be found in David Roessel, '"Or perhaps Sulpicia": Pound and a Roman Poetess', *Pai* 19.1–2 (1990) 125–35.

88 '**biological process**': 29/144–5. Cf. cantos 39 and 47.
  Zagreus: see p. 34 above.
  formal structure: cf. EP in letter to John Lackay Brown, Apr. 1937: 'the cantos are in a way fugal'—'theme, response, contrasujet. *Not* that I mean to make an exact analogy of structure' (*L (1951)* 386).

89 **natural energies**: cf. *SR* 92–3.

action as against stasis: cf. EP, 'The American or Christian morality is dastardly because it is a lie; it is false. | Greek mythology and science alike show us not a strife between a good and a bad but a conflict of forces and inertias, a conflict of different necessities and modalities; each good in a certain degree' ('How to Write', *Machine Art* 112).

90 'the growing tree': *CWC* (Stanley Nott, 1936), p. 52—not in *CWC* 1964—and see 53/ 265. [*hsin*¹ is character 2737 in Mathews' *Chinese–English Dictionary*.]
'uncut forest': *S Pr* 97n.
'Basis of renewal': 20/91–2—see also 21/98–100.
'something to think about': EP, unpublished TS leaf (Y CAL MSS 43/Collected Prose [formerly Box 77, folder 2945], Beinecke).

Literary relations old and new

90 'one of the most': 'Announcement', *Dial* LXXXIV.1 (Jan. 1928) 90.
'Isolated Superiority': 'Announcement', *Dial* LXXXIV.1 (Jan. 1928) 4–7.
'read Confucius': EP, 'Credo' (1930), *S Pr* 53.
declare him a heretic: see *After Strange Gods: A Primer of Modern Heresy* (Faber & Faber, 1934), pp. 41–3.

91 Pound would riposte: see 'Credo' (1930), *S Pr* 53.
'best possible': EP to John Price, 2 Apr. 1926, as in Barry S. Alpert, 'Ezra Pound, John Price, and *The Exile*', *Pai* 2.3 (1973) 432.
'nice little note': EP to WCW, 18 Dec. [1931], *EP/WCW* 114–15.
'revolutionary simpleton'…'intellectual eunuch': WL, *Time and Western Man* (Chatto & Windus, 1927), pp. 55–7, 85–7.
Guggenheim: see EP to Henry Allen Moe [secretary to the John Simon Guggenheim Memorial Foundation], 31 Mar. 1925, *EP&VA* 294–9.
'Don't worry': EP to HLP, 1 June [1927], *EP/Parents* 631.
'ole Wyndham': EP to WCW, 5 Nov. [1929], *EP/WCW* 98.
'large and vivid': EP, 'D'Artagnan Twenty Years After' (1937), *S Pr* 429.
pirating of *Ulysses*: see *EP/JJ* 224–7.

92 'Nothing short': EP to JJ, 15 Nov. 1926, *EP/JJ* 228.
'network of french banks': EP, 'Past History' (1933), *EP/JJ* 251–2.
'never had any respect': EP, 'After Election' (1931), *EP/JJ* 239.
'not lack conversation' et seq.: WBY, *A Packet for Ezra Pound* (1929), as in *A Vision* (Macmillan & Co., 1937), pp. 3–6.

93 'flux his theme' et seq.: WBY, 'Introduction', *The Oxford Book of Modern Verse 1892–1935* (Oxford: At the Clarendon Press, 1936), pp. xxiii–xxvi.
'a fugue from a frog': EP to John Lackay Brown, Apr. [1937], *L (1951)* 385.
'*Melopoeia*': FMF, 'Pound and *How To Read*' (1932), *EP/FMF* 103.
'a closed mind'…'word as reality': WCW, 'Excerpts from a Critical Sketch: *A Draft of XXX Cantos by Ezra Pound*' (1931), *Selected Essays of WCW* (New York: New Directions, 1969), 106–7.

94 'no ideas but in things': see WCW, *Paterson: Book One*, I.
'not ideas about the thing': Wallace Stevens, 'Not Ideas about the Thing but the Thing Itself', *The Collected Poems of Wallace Stevens* (Faber & Faber, 1945), p. 534.
'First cheering': EP to LZ, 18 Aug. 1927, *EP/LZ* 3.
father in poetry: see Barry Ahearn, 'Introduction', *EP/LZ* xix–xx.

95 'all new subject matter': LZ, 'Ezra Pound', *Prepositions: The Collected Critical Essays* (Rapp & Carroll, 1967), p. 71.
'hate, comprehension': LZ, 'Ezra Pound', 69.

organizer of form: see LZ, 'Preface', *An 'Objectivists' Anthology* (Le Beausset, Var.: TO, Publishers: 1932), p. 18.

'greatest poem': LZ, 'Preface', 24.

'still for the poets': LZ, 'Preface', [27].

'Every generation' et seq.: EP to LZ, 22 Dec. [1931], *EP/LZ* 123.

96 'Objectivists' number: *Poetry* XXXVII.5 (Feb. 1931).

'arrogance of youth' et seq.: Harriet Monroe, 'Comment', *Poetry* XXXVII.6 (Mar. 1931) 328–33.

'gave over': [LZ], 'Notes', *Poetry* XXXVII.5 (Feb. 1931) 295.

'my point of view'... 'produce something': EP to LZ, 24 Oct. [1930], *EP/LZ* 45–7.

'AND the verse': EP to LZ, 28 Oct. [1930], *EP/LZ* 55.

'A group' et seq.: EP toLZ, 12 Aug. 1928, *EP/LZ* 11–15.

'most solid': EP, 'Small Magazines', *English Journal* (*College Edition*) XIX.9 (Nov. 1930) 702.

'Every generation': EP to Charles Henri Ford, 1 Feb. 1929, *L (1951)* 301.

97 'My son': EP to Lincoln Kirstein, [? May 1931], *L (1951)* 314.

'stir up the animals': EP to Samuel Putnam, 3 Feb. 1927, *P&P* IX, 477.

'intellectual communication': EP, 'Small Magazines', *English Journal* (*College Edition*) XIX.9 (Nov. 1930) 670.

'The work of writers': EP, 'Small Magazines', 702.

independent little magazine: see EP to HLP, 15 Nov. [1926], *EP/Parents* 606.

'EXILE': postcard, statement over 'yours as circumstances permit/EZRA POUND, editor', (copy in HRC).

'mss.... which cdn't': EP to Richard Aldington, 25 Jan. 1927 (HRC).

'new show': EP to John Price, 12 Jan. 1927, ed. Barry S. Alpert, 'Ezra Pound, John Price, and *The Exile*', *Pai* 2.3 (1973) 437.

'to go ahead': EP to John Price, 20 Jan. 1927, *Pai* 2.3 (1973) 440. EP told Pascal Covici the second number was to have 'three separate sorts of thing: Poetry, prose... that is the finished work, and rapportage, i.e. wholly unassuming but s'far as I know veracious accounts of things, and this last need not have any "literary" or artistic merit' (EP to Covici, 9 Feb. 1927 [HRC]).

In the sphere of action

98 'mostly stop-gap': EP to Sibley Watson, 20 Oct. 1927, *EP/Dial* 324.

'Occasionally': EP to John Price, 8 Jan. 1926, ed. Barry S. Alpert, 'Ezra Pound, John Price, and *The Exile*', *Pai* 2.3 (1973) 430.

'critical prose'... 'social or political prose'... 'booted into thinking': EP, unpublished TS leaf (Y CAL MSS 43/Collected Prose [formerly Box 77, folder 2945] (Beinecke).

Lenin's short and effective: see EP, 'Data', *Exile* 4 (1928) 115–16, and *Cantos* 16/74.

99 'root' idea: see EP, 'Simplicities', *Exile* 4 (1928) 1–5.

'observe the nation': EP, 'Dr Williams' Position' (1928), *LE* 391–2.

'Improvements': EP, 'Poundings, Continued', *Forum* LXXX.1 (July 1928) 156–7.

'*Damnation*': EP to Judge Beals, 7 May 1930, reproduced with covering letter of 8 May 1930 in *P&P* X, 88–91; 'lyric' is from EP's letter. For 'article 211' see *EP: Poet I* 354.

100 'A good state'... 'aristocracy': EP, 'Definitions etc.', *Der Querschnitt* V.1 (Jan. 1925) 54. 'White coal' = water-generated electricity.

'SANE METHOD': EP, 'Newspapers, History, Etc.', *Hound & Horn* III.4 (July/Sept. 1930) 578.

'democratic idea': EP, 'Newspapers, History, Etc.', *Hound & Horn* III.4 (July/Sept. 1930) 578.

'The more one'... 'Fascio': EP to John Price, 8 Jan.1926, ed. Alpert, *Pai* 2.3 (1973) 435.

101 private performance: see EP to William Bird, 4 Mar. 1927, *L (1951)* 282–3.

'We are tired'... 'raison d'être': see EP, 'Simplicities', *Exile* 4 (1928) 5.

Rimini Commandante: see p. 47 above.

'passport imbecility'... 'comprehensive order': EP to Bronson Cutting, 17 Feb. [1931], *EP/BC* 50.

'effective program': EP, interview with Francesco Monotti in *Belvedere* (Mar. 1931), as translated by Redman in his *Ezra Pound and Italian Fascism*, p. 76.

'an opportunist': EP, 'mike [gold] and other phenomena', *Morada* 5 (1930) 44.

'an OPPORTUNIST': EP, *J/M* 17–18.

'sense of responsibility'etc.: whole paragraph based on EP, 'Fungus, Twilight or Dry Rot', *New Review* I.3 (1931) 112–16.

102 'Thought, dogblast you': EP, 'Our Contemporaries and Others', *New Review* I.2 (1931) 150.

aristocracy of artistic genius: see *EP: Poet* I 262–3.

103 'amiable jaw': EP to LZ, May 1932 (HRC).

'glorious advent': Benito Mussolini as cited by EP, 'Appunti', *Il Mare* XXV.1235 (12 Nov. 1932) 3—my paraphrase of EP's Italian.

Pound recalled: in 'Appunti', *Il Mare* XXV.1237 (26 Nov. 1932) 4—my paraphrase.

D'Annunzio: concerning him EP wrote in 1928, 'The only living author who has ever taken a city or held up the diplomatic crapule at the point of machine guns, he is in a position to speak with more authority than a bunch of neurasthenic incompetents or of writers who never having swerved from their jobs, might be, or are, supposed by the scientists and the populace to be incapable of action' ('Cavalcanti', *LE* 192).

'Appunti'... *L'Indice*: this paragraph is indebted to Redman.78–83.

104 interviewer in 1931: i.e. Francesco Monotti, as in Redman 76.

'every reinvigoration': EP, 'Appunti. I. Lettera al traduttore', *L'Indice* I.12 (Oct. 1930) [1].

had he been living in Italy: EP, 'Appunti. XIII. Scultura', *L'Indice* II.7 (10 Apr. 1931) [1]—my paraphrase.

'went bust': to be exact, 'The Indice has gone bust', EP to Langston Hughes, 8 May 1932, ed. David Roessel, '"A Racial Act": The Letters of Langston Hughes and Ezra Pound', *Pai* 29.1–2 (2000) 216.

'Supplemento Letterario': for a complete collection of all the contributions see *Il Mare Supplemento Letterario 1932–1933*, a cura della Società Letteraria Rapallo (Rapallo: Commune di Rapallo, 1999).

asserted that Futurism: EP, 'Appunti', *Il Mare* XXV.1235 (12 Nov. 1932) 3.

'advocated'... 'reputation': Walkiewicz and Witemeyer, 'The Poet and the Senator', *EP/BC* 15. I am much indebted to the commentary and notes of W & W.

'tool of tyranny': BC, as cited from the *Congressional Record* by W & W, *EP/BC* 18.

'Article 211': EP to BC, 8 Nov. 1930, *EP/BC* 38.

105 'the Baboon law' etc.: BC to EP, 23 Jan. 1932, *EP/BC* 69.

'amendment died': W & W, *EP/BC* 27.

'list of the literate': EP to BC, 8 Nov. 1930, *EP/BC* 38.

'& I suppose': BC to EP, 9 Dec. 1930, *EP/BC* 40.

'American govt.': EP to Langston Hughes, 18 June 1932, *L (1951)*323.

'Democracies': 91/613.

'theoretical perfection': EP, 'Bureaucracy the Flail of Jehovah', *Exile* 4 (1928) 13.

'went to Dionysius': 8/31.

106   **free passage of new invention**: see EP, 'Newspapers, History, Etc.', *Hound & Horn*
III.4 (July/Sept. 1930) 574–9.

    forty-hour week…shortened working day: EP wrote to DP, 17 Sept. 1932: 'Von
Papen has come out for 40 hour week and NO reduction in pay to workers. 15 hours wd.
prob. be nearer the mark; BUT le principe and the possibility seems to be penetrating.
N. Y. SUN printed my scorcher on short day; on Aug. 20. (I.e. before either the Muss.
or the Von P. proclamations.)' (Lilly). The London *Times* of 23 Sept. 1932 reported the
Italian proposal at the ILO meeting and the British opposition to it. On EP's support
for a shorter working day see W. & W., *EP/BC* 89–90, and EP to BC, 20 Mar. 1931, 9
Oct. 1931,11 Feb. 1932, *EP/BC* 56, 58–9, 71–2.

    'a plutocratic era': EP, 'Left vs. Right', *Chicago Tribune*, Paris (16 Mar. 1930), 5.

    'democratized': EP to BC, 20 Mar. 1931, *EP/BC* 54–5.

    'to prevent'…'two causes': EP, 'By All Means Be Patriotic', *New English Weekly* I.25
(6 Oct. 1932) 589. See also 'More Bolshevik Atrocities', *Exile* 3 (1928) 97–101; 'Peace',
Exile 4 (1928) 15–19; 'A Possibly Impractical Suggestion', *Poetry* XXXIV.3 (June 1929)
178; *Impact* 281–2 [the 'Mensdorff letter']; *Cantos* 18, 19, 31–51.

    'that STAYS news': *ABCR* 29.

    'mental slop'…'public enemy': EP, 'That Messianic Urge', *New York Sun* (4 June
1932) 12. The title is on EP's TS (Beinecke).

    one…counter-attacked: '[Burton] Rascoe's Riposte', *New York Sun* (11 June 1932) 36.

    'strife and tumult': *OED* s.v. 'bear garden'.

107   **'where you are talking'**: EP to Mike Gold, 17 Aug. 1930 (HRC).

    'propagandist literature': EP, 'Open Letter to Tretyakow, kolchoznik', *Front* I.2 (Feb.
1931) 126—repr. *Impact* 227.

    'the classic work': 'A Classic Art, by Boris de Schloezer, Translated from the French
by Ezra Pound', *Dial* LXXXVI.6 (June 1929) 464–5.

108   **'rage for order'**: Wallace Stevens, 'The Idea of Order at Key West'.

    Krishna: see *Bhagavad Gita* chap. xi.

Cavalcanti: the intelligence of love

This section is indebted to David Anderson's comprehensive *Pound's Cavalcanti: An Edition of
the Translations, Notes, and Essays* (Princeton, NJ: Princeton University Press, 1983), with a good
'Editor's Introduction'. Note that, of necessity, this does not reproduce Pound's *Guido Caval-
canti Rime* (Genova: Edizioni Marsano SA, [1932]). For some further light on the preparation
and publication of *Rime* see Stefano Maria Casella, '"To adjust the spelling of Guido"', *Ezra
Pound 1972/1992*, a cura di Luca Gallesi (Milano: Greco & Greco editori, 1992), pp. 155–98.

    The philosophical dimension has been extensively discussed. See: Georg M. Gugelberger,
'The Secularization of "Love" to a Poetic Metaphor: Cavalcanti, Center of Pound's Medi-
evalism', *Pai* 2.2 (1973) 159–73; James J. Wilhelm, *Dante and Pound: The Epic of Judgement*
(Orone, Me.: University of Maine Press, 1974); Kevin Oderman, '"Cavalcanti: That the
Body is not Evil', *Pai* 11.2 (1982) 258–79; Mohammad Shaheen, 'Pound's Transmission of
Ittisal in Canto 76', *Pai* 17.1 (1988) 133–45; Matthew Little and Robert Babcock, '"Amplius in
coitu phantasia": Pound's "Cavalcanti" and Avicenna's *De Almahad*', *Pai* 20.1–2 (1991) 63–75;
Maria Luisa Ardizzone, 'The Genesis and Structure of Pound's Paradise: Looking at the
Vocabulary', *Pai* 22.3 (1993) 13–37; Jacqueline Kaye, 'Pound and Heresy', *Pai* 28.1 (1999) 89–111;
Peter Makin, 'Pound's "Provence" and the *Duecento*', *Ezra Pound and the Troubadours*, ed.
Philip Grover (24680 Gardonne, France: éditions fédérop, 1995), pp. 91–110; Line Henriksen,
'*Chiaroscuro*: Canto 36 and *Donna mi prega*', *Pai* 29.3 (2000) 33–57; Maria Luisa Ardizzone,
Guido Cavalcanti: The Other Middle Ages (Toronto: University of Toronto Press, 2002); Peter
Liebregts, *Ezra Pound and Neoplatonism* (Madison: Farleigh Dickinson University Press,
2004).

On Pound's opera *Cavalcanti* (1931–3) I am much indebted for both information and interpretation to (a) Margaret Fisher, *Ezra Pound's Radio Operas: The BBC Experiments, 1931–1933* (*EPRO*)(Cambridge, Mass.: MIT Press, 2002), pp. 146–95; (b) Robert Hughes and Margaret Fisher, *Cavalcanti: A Perspective on the Music of Ezra Pound* (Emeryville, Calif.: Second Evening Art, 2003): *CPMEP* (1) contains their 'Perspective and Analysis' of all Pound's musical compositions, with *Cavalcanti* covered on pp. 41–124; *CPMEP* (2), pages separately numbered, presents Robert Hughes's edition of the full score of Pound's opera or 'sung dramedy', *Cavalcanti*; (c) *Ego Scriptor Cantilenae: The Music of Ezra Pound* (*ESC*), Robert Hughes conductor and musical director, Margaret Fisher author, containing audio CD (Other Minds OM 1005–2) and 80-page booklet (San Francisco: Other Minds Inc., 2003)—the Other Minds CD contains selections from *Cavalcanti* and from Pound's unfinished third opera, *Collis O Heliconii* (1932). See also Margaret Fisher, 'Great Bass: Undertones of Continuous Influence', *Performance Research* 8.1 (Spring 2003) 23–40, particularly pp. 30 and 34–9. I am indebted to Mary de Rachewiltz for a recording of the performance of *Cavalcanti: A Sung Dramedy in 3 Acts* under the direction of Marcello Fera in the Nuovo Teatro Communale of Bolzano, 14 July 2000.

108   'Guido': EP to DP, 14 Sept. 1927 (Lilly).
     'Guido's philosophy': EP to OR, [Oct. 1927] (Beinecke/OR).
     'proof': EP, 'Cavalcanti', *MIN* 345, *LE* 149.
     'biological proof':EP, Poetry Notebook 13 (Beinecke).
     'nature's source': EP, trans. of 'Donna mi prega' in 'Cavalcanti', *MIN* 353, *LE* 155.
     'by miracle': EP to IWP, 11 Nov. 1927, *EP/Parents* 639. Other details from EP to OR, [early Nov. 1927] (Beinecke/OR).
     'full text': EP to HLP, 16 Nov. [1927], *EP/Parents* 640.
109   title page: from Anderson, 'Editor's Introduction', *Pound's Cavalcanti*, p. xxi.
     'Specimen pages': Gallup: 1983, 153.
     Rossetti's *Early Italian Poets*: Pound's marked copy is now in HRC.
110   David Anderson records: Anderson, 'Editor's Introduction', *Pound's Cavalcanti*, pp. xxii–xxiii. The Gilson review is reprinted in Homberger: 1972, 273–9.
     'very complicated': EP, *ABCR* 104; see p. 23 above.
     'psychologist of the emotions': EP, 'Introduction' to *Sonnets and Ballate of Guido Cavalcanti* (1912), *T* 18, Anderson 12.
111   'Exhausted': EP, 'Introduction', *T* 20, Anderson 14.
     after Eliot: Eliot's actual words, in 'Tradition and the Individual Talent' (1919), were of course 'the man who suffers and the mind which creates'.
     'It is only when the emotions': EP, 'Introduction' to *Sonnets and Ballate of Guido Cavalcanti* (1912), *T* 24, Anderson 19.
     re *Canzoni*, see *EP: Poet I* 135–49.
     'not as platonic': EP, 'Date Line', *MIN* 15.
     'super-in-human refinement': cf. 'super-in-human refinemengts', EP to AB, 24 Oct. 1933 (Lilly).
112   'Mediaevalism': this paragraph and the first sentences of the next are based on this, the first part of 'Cavalcanti', as in *MIN* 345–52 and *LE* 149–55.
     cites Gilson: in 'Partial Explanation', *MIN* 359–60, *LE* 160–1.
113   'intenzion': see *MIN* 361, *LE* 162.
     '*Voi che intendendo*': *Paradiso* VII, 37. See *GK* 315, 317.
     'much more "modern"': EP, 'Cavalcanti', *MIN* 346, *LE* 149.
     Renan's *Averroës et L'Averroïsme*: Pound's marked copy is in HRC. Cf. *MIN* 388–90, *LE* 184–6.

'the eternal act': S. T. Coleridge, *Biographia Literaria* (1817), chap. XIII.

'perfection of the rational soul': 'La perfection de l'âme rationelle est de devenir le miroir de l'univers' (attributed to Avicenna), Ernest Renan, *Averroës et L'Averroïsme* (Paris, 1925), p. 96.

no question ... of a paradise out of this world: on this aspect see Mohammad Shaheen, 'Pound's transmission of *ittisal* in Canto 76', *Pai* 17.1 (1988) 133–45.

'ever at the interpretation': see *EP: Poet I* 225 and *SR* 92–3.

114 'the active and passive': EP, 'Terra Italica' (1931), *S Pr* 59—the rest of this paragraph is based on this important essay, *S Pr* 54–60.

'Coition, the sacrament':EP TSS note (Beinecke), cited by Margaret Fisher, *EPRO* 153.

'meaning can be explained': EP, 'Preface', *CPMEP* (2) vi. Underlining as in EP's TSS, 'Pound/Cavalcanti —General directions' (Beinecke).

'visual libretto': *CPMEP* (1) 42.

115 'full of radio': EP to DP, [Aug./Sept.] 1931 (Lilly).

'will be much clearer': EP to DP, 29 Oct. 1931 (Lilly).

Sonate 'Ghuidonis': for a full description see *CPMEP* (1) 163–9.

116 *forma mentis*: in 1935 EP wrote, 'Forma to the great minds of at least one epoch meant something more than dead pattern or fixed opinion. "The light of the DOER, as it were a form cleaving to it" meant an ACTIVE pattern, a pattern that set things in motion./ (This sentence can be taken along with my comment on Guido and in particular the end of the chapter called "Mediævalism"[in "Cavalcanti", *LE* 150–5]' (*PE* 51).

'Al poco giorno': EP's score is printed in *Complete Violin Works of Ezra Pound*, ed. with commentary by Robert Hughes (Emeryville, Calif.: Second Evening Art, 2004), pp. 126–9—commentary on pp. 67–73. The recording of a performance by Nathan Rubin is track 13 on *ESC*.

'Collis O Heliconii': there is a 'performance edition' of Pound's unfinished score, together with an extensive and illuminating critical analysis and discussion of the opera, in Margaret Fisher's *The Recovery of Ezra Pound's Third Opera Collis O Heliconii: Settings of poems by Catullus and Sappho* (Emeryville, Calif.: Second Evening Art, 2005). The recording of a selection is track 22 on *ESC*.

'celebration of the sacrament': Margaret Fisher, *ESC* (booklet) 29.

'no small technical problem': EP, *GK* 368.

'I live in music': reported by Robert Fitzgerald in *Encounter* (1956), as cited by Margaret Fisher, *ESC* (booklet) 24.

Threads, tesserae

117 Olga Rudge ... Landowska: OR to EP, 30 Sept. 1929 (Beinecke/OR).

'The little town': WBY, 'Rapallo', *A Vision* (Macmillan, 1937, 1962), p. 3.

'with large trunk': EP to HLP, 8 Jan. 1927, *EP/Parents* 616.

'As S. seems to mean': EP to HLP, 11 Jan. 1927, *EP/Parents* 617.

Frobenius ... *paideuma*: see p. 73 above; also WBY to Sturge Moore, Apr. 1929, cited Norman: 1960, 301.

118 'intellexshull centre': EP to IWP, 22 Nov. [1927], *EP/Parents* 642.

'Italy then was maddening': Robert McAlmon, 'Truer Than Most Accounts', *Exile* 2 (Autumn 1927) 45.

Mary Oppen recalled: in her *Meaning A Life: An Autobiography* (Santa Barbara, Calif.: Black Sparrow Press, 1978), p. 138.

'Vinciguerra and Lauro': EP to DP, 18 Oct. 1931 (Lilly). On Lauro de Bosis see Stock: 1970, 299; also Nancy Cox McCormack, 'Ezra Pound in the Paris Years', ed.

Lawrence S. Rainey, *Sewanee Review* CII (1994) 103 n. 16. De Bosis (1900–31), a poet and translator, author of *Icarus* (a play), flew over Rome on 3 Oct. 1931 showering anti-Fascist leaflets upon the city, then flew on towards Corsica.

'banged it hard': MdR, *Discretions*, 52; see also Conover, 78.

'Mensdorff letter': printed in *Impact* 281–3.

119   lasting disillusionment: see *Cantos* 103/737.

'so warmly of Olga': DP to EP, 7 June 1928 (Lilly).

Morrison's . . . *Dictionary*: Cf. *EP: Poet I* 287 and note. DP told Hugh Kenner in conversation in 1965 that she bought her copy of Morrison in 1914—Kenner, 'D. P. Remembered', *Pai* 2.3 (1973) 488.

a 'very cheerful soul': DP to EP, 2 May 1928 (Lilly).

'Is Vienna': DP to EP, 4 June 1928 (Lilly).

'Longing to see you': Nancy Cunard to EP, 27 [Sept. 1928] (Beinecke).

'No but really': Nancy Cunard to EP, [28 Sept. 1928] (Beinecke).

a small house in Venice: some details in this paragraph from Conover, 82–4.

'Three matchboxes': Desmond O'Grady, 'Ezra Pound: A Personal Memoir', *Agenda* 17.3–4 (1979/80) 293.

'Five minutes': EP to OR, [12 Dec. 1928] (Beinecke/OR).

'perfection': cf. WBY, 'The Choice' in *The Winding Stair* (1933).

120   'Caro, I beg you': OR to EP, 21 Jan. 1929 (Beinecke/OR).

life would be impossible: EP to OR, [22 Jan. 1929] (Beinecke/OR).

'hidden nest': 76/462.

no longer in it: cf. OR to EP, 4 Mar. 1929 (Beinecke/OR).

doing the beams: EP to OR, [? 1 Apr. 1929] (Beinecke/OR).

'calf on the brain': EP to OR, 20 Mar. [1929] (Beinecke/OR).

'Darling': EP to Pamela Lovibond [PL], [28 Mar. 1929] (Beinecke).

'Dearest Pam': EP to PL, 2 Apr. [1929] (Beinecke).

'can't use telephone': EP to PL, 5 Apr. [1929] (Beinecke).

'Darling: Adrian': EP to PL, 10 Apr. [1929] (Beinecke).

'at Pagani's': EP to PL, 11 June [1929] (Beinecke).

'the venerable William': EP to PL, 2 May 1932 (Beinecke).

'an evening of Mozart': invitation in EP Scrapbook (Brunnenburg).

121   Obermer: prescription in Pound MSS II, Box 11 (Lilly).

Pituitrin: Louis Berman, author of *The Glands Regulating Personality* (1922), wrote in his *The Personal Equation* (1925), pp. 108–9, that the pituitary gland, or more specifically its pre-pituitary lobe, was 'most important of all [in] its tonic effect upon the portions of the brain involved in the Olympian functions of reason and abstraction—in short, intellectuality'; also that it has to do with the maintenance of the sex-glands throughout life.

'the anti-cold serum': EP to DP, [May 1930] (Lilly).

'poor circulation': DP to EP, [May 1930] (Lilly).

any 'Obermer medicine': DP to EP, 11 July 1930 (Lilly).

'Thyro-manganese': EP to DP, 18 July 1930 (Lilly).

'said "Pray Ezra"': Richard Aldington to Brigit Patmore, May 1929, *Richard Aldington and Hilda Doolittle: Their Lives in Letters 1918–61*, ed. Caroline Zilboorg (Manchester: Manchester University Press, 2003), p. 207.

'so terribly ridiculous': HD to Bryher, May 1929, *Richard Aldington and Hilda Doolittle*, p. 209.

'Ezra's people': FMF, *The Correspondence of Ford Madox Ford and Stella Bowen*, ed. Sondra J. Stang and Karen Cochran (Bloomington: Indiana University Press, 1993), p. 356.

'If you are investing': EP to HLP, 1 Aug. [1928], *EP/Parents* 664.

'Wyncote is very lovely': IWP to Miss Heacock, as cited in Jenkintown *Times-Chronicle*, 6 Mar. 1930, extracted in Stock: 1976, 90. Other details in this paragraph from Stock: 1976, 89–90.

122   **via Americhe**: now Corso Cristofero Colombo.

Bankers, economists, and politicians: this sentence and the next take off from two sentences in Redman, 'Pound's Politics and Economics', *Cambridge Companion to Ezra Pound*, ed. Ira B. Nadel (Cambridge: Cambridge University Press, 1999), p. 255.

father hard up: on this see Conover, 90–1, 96–7.

Brescia . . . Lago d'Iseo: EP to DP, [Sept. 1929] (Lilly).

'mos' noble feeling': EP to OR, 30 Sept. [1929] (Beinecke/OR).

'a year and a half': OR to EP, 19 Nov. 1929 (Beinecke/OR). In *Discretions* MdR remembered it differently: 'And from now on whenever the scrupulous biographer will report a concert in Budapest, a performance in Vienna, a trip to Franfurt, Wörgl, Salzburg, it may be assumed that the journey was interrupted, for a few hours or for a few days, in Bruneck' (14–15).

the child remembered: MdR, *Discretions* 23–5.

123   **'duly and properly'**: EP to OR, 26 Dec. [1929] (Beinecke/OR). In a note to HLP dated 26 July 1927 EP wrote, 'Enclose another member of the family'. He had been photographed with Mary in Gais earlier in the month—see *Discretions* for the photo—so it would appear that Homer had a hint of Mary's existence well before 1933. In July 1928 EP sent another photograph without saying who the child was, causing Homer to ask, 'is it the same as the one you sent a year or so ago?', and to report, 'Mama wonders why she is the recipient of strange children without name, or habitation or connection' (HLP to EP, 10 July 1928 [Beinecke]). Isabel herself, in a letter of 22 Sept. 1928, asked EP, 'Why cannot the three or four of you spend the season with us?' (Beinecke).

'That she shd': EP to OR, [18 Jan. 1930] (Beinecke/OR).

'She dont seem to understand': EP to OR, 'second letter', [18 Jan. 1930] (Beinecke/OR).

'she get it into her head': EP to OR, 24 Jan. [1930] (Beinecke/OR).

the god: OR to EP, [25 or 26 Jan. 1930] (Beinecke/OR).

the centre: EP to OR, 27 Jan. [1930] (Beinecke/OR).

relationship that could not speak its name: paragraph based on OR's 'Diary–1931' (Beinecke/OR).

'Uproarious evening': EP to DP, 30 Apr. [1930] (Lilly).

'Omar comes to tea': DP to EP, 26 Apr. 1930 (Lilly).

124   **Jenkintown *Times-Chronicle***: detail from Stock: 1976, 89.

photograph: reproduced in *Discretions*—but misdated '1929' (for 1930). See also Stock: 1976, 20.

Can Grande's grin: EP p.c. to DP, [1 June 1930] (Lilly). Cf. 78/481.

'For Ezra': the inscribed copy is in HRC.

'than, say, the followers': my account of the opera and its reception is drawn from the *New York Herald*'s Paris and Berlin critics' reviews as cited by Conover, 95.

pampered parasites: EP to W. B. Johnson, 10 Aug. 1930, reproduced in facsimile in *A Selected Catalogue of the Ezra Pound Collection at Hamilton College*, compiled with notes by Cameron McWhirter and Randall L. Ericson (Clinton, NY: Hamilton College Library, 2005), pp. 18–20.

to recommend Zukofsky: cf. *EP/LZ* 37n.

casting about: e.g. see EP to DP, 30 July [1930] (Lilly), mentioning books for her to look out for in London; EP to LZ, 20 Feb. and 5 Oct. 1931 (HRC).

'swatting at' John Adams: EP to DP, 28 Apr. 1931 (Lilly).

125   **'Read, study the languages'**: Mary Oppen, *Meaning A Life*, p. 132.

seized a copy: detail from Hugh Ford, *Published in Paris* (Garnstone Press, 1975), p. 112.

'abandonment of logic': Winters's words are cited by EP in a letter to the editor, 'Mr Ezra Pound's "Cantos"', *NEW* III.4 (11 May 1933) 96.

'fifty years hence': Yvor Winters to EP, 12 June 1928 (Beinecke).

Ford . . . out of money: FMF to EP, 18 Aug. 1931; EP to FMF, 20 and 21 Aug. 1931; *EP/FMF* 92–3.

'The Child': DP to EP, 3 Sept. 1931 (Lilly).

her mother's shares: DP to EP, [? 21 Sept. 1931] (Lilly).

leaving her estate: OS to EP, 27 Oct. 1929 (Lilly). On 16 July 1927 DP had written from London to EP in Venice: 'Signed up a new Will yesterday:/Parkyn worried about my leaving you the necklace—but it's done: also all my USA money to you absolutely: and interest for life on my parents' marriage settlement money, the capital of which goes on to Omar' (Lilly).

the sterling crisis: this was the major preoccupation of the many letters exchanged between DP and EP in September and October 1931.

Pound reported: EP to DP, 23 Sept. [1931]—second part—(Lilly).

'cooking again': EP to DP, 30 Sept. [1931] (Lilly).

'more exciting': EP to DP, 23 Sept. [1931]—second part—(Lilly).

126 'insurance policy': EP to DP, [7 Oct. 1931] (Lilly).

'man without a country': in quotes in EP to DP, 13 Oct. [1931] (Lilly). On this see also EP to DP, 24 Sept. [1931] (Lilly).

'crowd of unemployed': DP to EP, 7 Oct. 1931 (Lilly).

his bust by Gaudier: see EP to DP, 1 Nov. [1931] (Lilly); and 'Peregrinations, 1960', *GB* 146.

'When I can git on': EP to Aldington, 26 Aug. 1927 (HRC).

'have now material': EP to DP, 4 Oct. [1931] (Lilly).

127 'toward Canto XXXX': EP to editors of *Contempo*, 8 Nov. [1932] (HRC).

'dead with work': EP to editors of *Contempo*, [20 Dec. 1932] (HRC).

'Form of the whole': EP to FMF, 5 Sept. [1932], *EP/FMF* III.

collected edition of his prose: see Gallup: 1983, 452 (E6h).

To, Publishers: details from Mary Oppen, *Meaning A Life*, pp. 131–2; and from Rachel Blau DuPlessis, ed., *The Selected Letters of George Oppen* (Durham, NC, and London: Duke University Press, 1990), pp. [1], 370 n. 2.

'no possibility': George Oppen to EP, [Aug.? 1932], *Selected Letters of George Oppen*, p. 3. Darantière: a printer in Dijon.

Pound's idea: EP to IWP, 22 Nov. 1927, *EP/Parents* 641.

Pound's outline: with 'Collected Prose' (Beinecke).

128 'instinct of negation': EP, 'Henry James', *LE* 324n.

'a critical narrative': EP, *Active Anth*, p. [5].

Profile: my outline follows Pound's 'Table' on p. 113.

'the first effort': EP, 'Manifesto', *Poetry* XLI.1 (Oct. 1932) 41.

129 'neo'-Gongorism': EP, *Profile* 127.

'feel of actual speech': EP, 'Notes on Particular Details', *Active Anth* 253–4.

'something solid': EP, '"Active Anthology" (Retrospect twenty months later)', *Polite Essays* 153–4.

'the revolution': EP, 'Praefatio *aut tumulus cimicium*', *Active Anth* 10; and *PE* 136.

'to admire Ezra's peceptions': LZ to WCW, 23 Feb. 1949, *The Correspondence of William Carlos Williams & Louis Zukofsky*, ed. Barry Ahearn (Middletown, Conn.: Wesleyan University Press, 2003), p. 410.

'Omar's birthday': DP to EP, 11 Sept. 1932 (Lilly).

'**Max Ernst**': Caresse Crosby to EP, 13 Dec. 1932; EP to Caresse Crosby, 15 Dec. 1932; as in Anne Conover, 'Ezra Pound and the Crosby Continental Editions', *Ezra Pound and Europe*, ed. Richard Taylor and Claus Melchior (Amsterdam: Rodopi, 1993), p. 117.

130 '**Le** *Fiamme Nere*': see Gallup:1983, 156–7 (B31); Niccolò Zapponi, *L'Italia di Ezra Pound* (Roma: Bulzoni Editore, 1976), pp. 48–9; also EP to DP, 23 Dec. [1932] (Lilly).

PART TWO: 1933–1939

3. A DEMOCRAT IN ITALY, 1933

Il Poeta meets Il Duce

Note: Mussolini's political programme is referred to throughout as Fascism (with a capital) to avoid confusion with lower-case 'fascism'—the former has a definite reference; the latter now is so ill defined and so charged with undiscriminating prejudice as to be nearly unusable. It is particularly important to observe the differences between Mussolini's Italian Fascism and Hitler's German National Socialism: the twin dynamics of Nazism were anti-Semitism and the will to be the master race destined for world conquest; while Fascism was not racist, not intent on dominating other nations, and had its own quite distinct dynamic. The current habit among critics of lowering 'Fascism' to 'fascism'—though still writing 'Nazism' and 'Communism'—does not, to put it mildly, make for accurate perception and judgement. The fact that Pound frequently omitted the capital does not establish a precedent, since he was writing before the word had become detached from Mussolini and Italy. For the sake of clarity, in quoting him, I have silently introduced the capital wherever it is apparent that he was referring to Mussolini's Fascism, as he invariably was.

In this section I have been helped by the following: John P. Diggins, *Mussolini and Fascism: The View from America* (Princeton, NJ: Princeton University Press, 1972); Nicholas Farrell, *Mussolini: A New Life* (Weidenfeld & Nicolson, 2003); Wendy Stallard Flory, *The American Ezra Pound* (New Haven: Yale University Press, 1989); Luca Gallesi, *Le origini del Fascismo di Ezra Pound* (Milano: Edizioni Ares, 2005); A. James Gregor, *Young Mussolini and the Intellectual Origins of Fascism* (Berkeley: University of California Press, 1979); Carlo Levi, *Christ Stopped at Eboli* (New York: Farrar, Straus and Company, 1947); Meir Michaelis, *Mussolini and the Jews: German–Italian Relations and the Jewish Question in Italy 1922–1945* (Oxford: Clarendon Press for the Institute of Jewish Affairs, London, 1978); Benito Mussolini, *My Autobiography* (Hutchinson & Co., [1928]); Benito Mussolini, *The Corporate State*, 2nd edn. (Florence: Vallecchi Publisher, 1938/XVI); Ernst Nolte, *Three Faces of Fascism: Action Française, Italian Fascism, National Socialism* (New York: New American Library, 1969); Odon Por, *Fascism* (Labour Publishing Co., 1923); Tim Redman, *Ezra Pound and Italian Fascism* (Cambridge: Cambridge University Press, 1991); [Lincoln Steffens], *The Autobiography of Lincoln Steffens* (New York: Harcourt, Brace & Co., 1931); Zeev Sternhell, *The Birth of Fascist Ideology* (Princeton, NJ: Princeton University Press, 1994); Zeev Sternhell, *Neither Right Nor Left: Fascist Ideology in France* (Princeton, NJ: Princeton University Press, 1986, 1996); Niccolò Zapponi, *L'Italia di Ezra Pound* (Roma: Bulzoni Editore, 1976).

133 *Capo del Governo . . . Il Duce*: see Farrell, *Mussolini*, pp. 178–9.
134 '**whose crowning glory**': Farrell, *Mussolini*, p. 190.
'**The great Public Utilities**': Mussolini, *Autobiography*, pp. 268–9. 'A lady who had long known the Duce complained about Italy's being Prussianized one day when a train started on time' (EP, *J/M* 51).
'**The citizen**': Mussolini, *Autobiography*, p. 257. The *Dottrina del fascismo* (1932) declared Fascism's idea of the state to be anti-individualistic—see Farrell, *Mussolini*, p. 222.

135 'increasingly important': Mussolini, *Autobiography*, p. 258.
'to end the cruel fact': Mussolini, 'To the Workers of Milan', 6 Oct. 1934–XII, *The Corporate State*, p. 57.
'The Roman genius': Churchill's words as cited in Farrell, *Mussolini*, p. 225. From Pound's viewpoint it appeared that Churchill could only have spoken in favour of Fascism because he did not understand it—see 'Murder by Capital', *Criterion* XII.49 (July 1933) 592.
'the virtue of force': from *Fortune* in 1932, as in Diggins, *Mussolini and Fascism*, p. 38.
'only real friend': Roosevelt's words as cited in Farrell, *Mussolini*, p. 225.

136 The democratic consensus: see Diggins, *Mussolini and Fascism*, p. 37 and generally.
'Ours was like that': 46/231.
'VOLUNTÀ': EP, 'Ave Roma', *Il Mare* XXVI.1243 (7 Jan. 1933) 3, 4.
Sala del Mappamondo: details from Farrell, *Mussolini*, pp. 228–9.

137 at 17.30: EP, note prefacing *Oro e lavoro* (1944), reprinted in *Lavoro ed usura: tre saggi* (Milano: All'Insegna del Pesce d'Oro di Vanni Scheiwiller, 1996), p. [28].
'went poking around': EP to MdR, 17 Oct. 1957 (Beinecke).
'One of [my]': EP to Sarah Perkins Cope, 15 Jan. 1934, *L(1951)* 335.
'to put my ideas in order': EP as told to McNaughton, see William McNaughton, 'Kingdoms of the Earp: Carpenter and Criticism', *Pai* 21.3 (1992) 13–14; see also 87/569 and 92/626.
as Pound told it: to McNaughton; also to John Dewey—the words attributed to Mussolini are in EP to Dewey, 13 Nov. 1934, as cited in Alec Marsh, *Money and Modernity: Pound, Williams, and the Spirit of Jefferson* (Tuscaloosa: University of Alabama Press, 1998), p. 257 n. 37. In a letter to W. E. Woodward dated 28 Nov. [1933] EP emphasized Mussolini's wanting to 'THINK before yapping' (*EPEC* 76).
eighteen items: see EP, note prefacing *Oro e lavoro* (1944), reprinted in *Lavoro ed usura* (1996), p. [28]; and 'Di un sistema economico', *Meridiano di Roma* V.48 (1 Dec. 1940) [1]–2—this gives the 18 points raised in 1933. That 'taxation is unnecessary' was a main point is confirmed by EP to Borah, 7 July 1934, *EP/WB* 29.
'had a long hour': EP to DP, 30 Jan. 1933 (Lilly).
Greta Garbo in *Grand Hotel*: EP to DP, 2 Feb. 1933 ['Giov. soir'] (Lilly).
the town band: detail recalled by Giuseppe Bacigalupo, *Ieri a Rapallo* (Pasian di Prato (UD): Campanotto Editore, nuova edizione accresciuta 2002, 2006), p. 82.

138 'end with Sigismondo': EP to John Drummond, 18 Feb. [1933], *L(1951)* 320. L's assigning this letter to 1932 is shown to be mistaken by EP's writing 'Faber is bringing out my *ABC of Economics* in a few weeks'.
Zagreus: see p. 34 above.
Isis-Osiris: see *EP: Poet I* 169.
'"Dio ti benedica"': EP, *J/M* 40.
hotel-keeper in Rimini: EP, *J/M* 26–7.
Farinacci: EP, *J/M* 53–4.

139 'cavalieri della morte': EP, *J/M* 50–1.
WILL: this and the following two paragraphs are based on *J/M* 15–21. For the sentence concerning *Physique de l'amour* see *NPL* 153–6, and p. 73 above.
his *De Monarchia*: EP to Carlo Izzo, 23 Aug. [1935], *P&P* IX, 97. Dante's *De Monarchia* is concerned with the problem of how to achieve a just society on earth, and there are indeed close parallels with *J/M*. Dante states that the well-regulated society will be achieved when love of natural perfection directs the will to act justly (*directio volontatis*); he declares the opposite of Justice to be Greed; and he maintains that only under a single ruling or guiding power, a king or an emperor, will the earthly paradise be attained.

140   'a *risorgimento*': EP, *J/M* 89.

'I was there': Steffens, *Autobiography*, 818.

Gregor . . . found reason: see Gregor, *Young Mussolini*, 233.

'driven by a vast and deep "concern"': EP, *J/M* 34.

Steffens . . . come to terms': Steffens, *Autobiography*, 818, 816.

'passion for construction': EP, *J/M* 34.

141   'any means' . . . 'the best': EP, *J/M* 95, 91.

dictatorship . . . 'intelligence': see EP, 'Dictatorship as a Sign of Intelligence', *ABCE* 119.

'presumably right': EP, *J/M* 45.

'stabilize the lira': Steffens, *Autobiography*, 824.

breaking free . . . preconceptions: Steffens, *Autobiography*, 816; EP, *J/M* 25ff., 35, 45.

'takes a genius': EP, *J/M* 26.

invented new laws: EP, *J/M* 76–7.

embargo on emigration: EP, *J/M* 72.

'birds in the olive-yards': EP, *J/M* 91.

distribution of credit: see EP, *J/M* 48, 69, 80–1, 116–17.

142   'nothing in Europe': EP, *J/M* 93.

'no other clot': EP, *J/M* 61.

'damning and breaking': EP, 'Declaration', *New Democracy* II.2/3 (30 Mar./14 Apr. 1934) 5.

'use of the public credit': EP, 'The Italian Score', *NEW* VII.6 (23 May 1935) 107.

'GREED system': EP, 'Mussolini Defines State as "Spirit of the People"', *Chicago Tribune*, Paris (9 Apr. 1934) 5.

'firm belief': EP, *J/M* 128. Cf. *ABCE* 38 re 'will toward order'.

Confucian vision: see *J/M* 112–13, and pp. 74–6 above.

dreaming again . . . a renaissance: see *EP: Poet I* 262–3.

'I dream for Italy': EP, 'Marches Civilization . . .', *Chicago Tribune*, Paris, 5, 975 ([?31 Dec. 1933]), Italian Supplement 1933, p. 21.

did not advocate . . . 'the American system': EP, *J/M* 98.

'greater care' . . . 'orientation of will': EP, *J/M* 104, 105.

'accidental': EP, *J/M* 127–8.

143   Roosevelt: EP expressed a measure of hope in his 'September [1933] Preface' added to *J/M* in the 1936 Liveright edition.

'*our* democratic system': emphasis added here.

'I have a country': EP to DP, 5 July 1933 (Lilly).

Revolutionary economics

There is a great deal of material relevant to this section in Pound's contributions to periodicals in the years 1933 to 1935 collected in *P&P* VI, 1933–5. *ABC of Economics* (1933) is included in *S Pr*, along with a substantial selection of Pound's essays on 'civilisation, money and history'. The commentary and notes by E. P. Walkiewicz and Hugh Witemeyer [W&W] in their *Ezra Pound and Senator Bronson Cutting: A Political Correspondence, 1930–1935* (1995) are outstandingly helpful. Other welcome editions of EP's politico-economic correspondence are: *The Correspondence of Ezra Pound and Senator William Borah* (2001), ed. Sarah C. Holmes; '*Dear Uncle George': The Correspondence Between Ezra Pound and Congressman Tinkham of Massachusetts* (1996), ed. Philip J. Burns; 'Ezra Pound: Letters to Woodward', [ed. James Generoso], *Pai* 15.1 (1986) 105–20—see also James Generoso, 'I reckon you pass, Mr Wuddwudd', *Pai* 22.1-2 (1993) 35–55; *Ezra Pound's Economic Correspondence, 1933–1940*, ed. and annotated by Roxana Preda (Gainesville: University Press of Florida, 2007).

Among the many studies of Pound's economics I have consulted particularly chapters in these books: Leon Surette, *A Light from Eleusis: A Study of Ezra Pound's Cantos* (Oxford: Clarendon Press, 1979); Jean-Michel Rabaté, *Language, Sexuality and Ideology in Ezra Pound's 'Cantos'* (Macmillan, 1986); Wendy Stallard Flory, *The American Ezra Pound* (New Haven: Yale University Press, 1989); Tim Redman, *Ezra Pound and Italian Fascism* (Cambridge: Cambridge University Press, 1991); Alec Marsh, *Money and Modernity: Pound, Williams and the Spirit of Modernity* (Tuscaloosa: University of Alabama Press, 1998); Leon Surette, *Pound in Purgatory: From Economic Radicalism to Anti-Semitism* (Urbana: University of Illinois Press, 1999); Luca Gallesi, ed., *Ezra Pound e l'economia* (Milano: Edizioni Ares, 2001). Extensive bibliographies can be found in the books by Marsh, Redman, and Surette: 1999.

144 'Contemporary economics': EP to Zabel, [? 1934] (Beinecke).
'The vitality of thought': EP to Ibbotson, [5 Apr. 1935], *EP/Ibb* 18.
'Without an understanding': EP, 'The New English Weekly', *Contempo* III.9 (15 May 1932) 2.
'Your generation': EP, 'To the Young, If Any', *Little Magazine* I.4 (July/Aug. 1934) 1–3.
'god dam it': EP to Woodward, 7 Feb. [1934], *Pai* 15.1 (1986) 116.
'the modern mind': EP, 'What Price the Muses Now', [a review of TSE's *The Use of Poetry and the Use of Criticism*], *NEW* V.6 (24 May 1930) 132.
not that 'economics': EP, 'Mr. T. S. Eliot's Quandaries', *NEW* V.2 (26 Apr. 1934) 48.
impatient with Joyce: see for example EP, 'Past History' (May 1933), in *EP/JJ* 251–2.
'worse than blind': EP to LZ, 28 May]1935], *EP/LZ* 169.
'The next anthology': EP to LZ, 6 Mar. 1935, *EP/LZ* 162.

145 'I think both you *and* Hem': EP to Robert McAlmon, 2 Feb. [1934], *L(1951)* 337. See also *L(1950)* 283 for EP to Hemingway, 28 Nov. 1936.
'if you agree': EP to WCW, [Oct. 1934], *EP/WCW* 146.
'Aw what's the use': WCW to EP, 23 Oct. 1934, *EP.WCW* 149.
'fed *u p* (up)': EP, 'Jean Cocteau Sociologist', *NEW* VI.13 (10 Jan. 1935) 272; repr. *S Pr* 405.
'Against [the] phalanx': EP, 'The Matter of Life or Death', unpublished TSS, n.d. (HRC).
'The college presidents': EP,'Ignite! Ignite!', *Harvard Advocate* CXX.3 (Dec. 1933) 3.
having boiled: cf. EP to Borah, 23 [May] 1935—'I observe these internal boilings, just like a man in a laboratory' (*EP/WB* 34).

146 'all my cursing': EP to John Buchan, 22 Oct. 1934, 'Letters to John Buchan, 1934–1935', ed. S. Namjoshi, *Pai* 8.3 (1979) 470.
'What causes': this paragraph and the next from EP, 'Murder by Capital', *Criterion* XII.49 (July 1933) 585–92; repr. *S Pr* 197–202.
'miserliness': EP, *ABCE* 126.

147 private correspondence: Roxana Preda in preparing her selection from EP's economic correspondence in the 1930s noted that in 1935 alone 'the poet was writing letters on economics to about seventy people—*EPEC* 43.
Committee for the Nation: see *EP/BC* 109 (under 'Vanderlip').
'A Jeffersonian': EP to Woodward, 8 Oct. [1933], *Pai* 15.1 (1986) 108, 107.
that...work be shared: see *ABCE* 20–1; also 42–5, 54–6, 74. For EP against the dole see EP to Cutting, 11 Feb. 1932, *EP/BC* 71–2.
'NO real overproduction': EP to Woodward, 7 Feb. [1934], *Pai* 15.1 (1986) 111.

148 'an infamy': EP, 'Ecclesiastical History', *NEW* V.12 (5 July 1934) 273; repr. *S Pr* 63. EP repeated this or similar formulations on innumerable occasions.

contrary to the Constitution: see Art. I, section 8, par. 5 of the US Constitution; also Jerry Voorhis, 'The Mysteries of the Federal Reserve System', *Pai* 11.3 (1982) 488–97.
'What does the government do': Bronson Cutting, 'Government Bank Urged by Cutting', *New York Times* (20 May 1934) 32, from a speech to the People's Lobby in Washington, quoted by W&W in *EP/BC* 99–100, 245 n. 41.
'monopolize the credit': BC, speaking in the Senate 27 Jan. 1934, quoted by W&W in *EP/BC* 101, 245 n. 48.
might have made it clear: EP to Cutting, 12 June [1934], *EP/BC* 136.
'nation owns its own credit': EP, 'Ez Sez', 'Cutting's Mind Was Best in the Senate', *Santa Fe New Mexican* (3 Aug. 1935) 3, repr. *EP/BC* 206.

149 **'OLD stuff'**: EP to Woodward, 7 Feb. [1934], *Pai* 15.1 (1986) 111–12.
the cultural heritage: EP, 'Individual and Statal Views: Mr Ezra Pound's Views', *Plain Dealer*, [Brighton, England], XIII n.s. 1 (July 1934); see also 'In the Wounds: (Memoriam A. R. Orage)', *Criterion* XIV.46 (Apr. 1935), *S Pr* 413–14, and 'The Individual in his Milieu: A Study of Relations and Gesell', *Criterion* XV.58 (Oct. 1935), *S Pr* 245.
Douglas's idea: for Douglas's ideas as Pound first knew them see C. H. Douglas, *Economic Democracy* (Cecil Palmer, 1920); *—Credit-Power and Democracy...With a Commentary by A. R. Orage* (Cecil Palmer, 1920); *—Social Credit* (1924) (Eyre & Spottiswoode, 3rd edn. rev. and enlarged, 1937). Since it is sometimes stated that Douglas was anti-Semitic, with the implication that his economic ideas were tainted with anti-Semitism, it should be noted that in these writings there is absolutely nothing anti-Semitic. For a brief account of Pound's initial enthusiasm for Douglas see EP: Poet I 372–4.

150 **Hugo Black...proposed**: see W&W, 'The Length of the Working Day', *EP/BC* 89–90.
a growing consensus: W&W, *EP/BC* 91. In spite of that consensus, seventy years on, eighty-five years after Douglas's analysis—see vol. i, 394–6—the problem is still 'new':

> Herein lies the conundrum. If dramatic advances in productivity can replace more and more human labour, resulting in more workers being let go from the workforce, where will the consumer demand come from to buy all the potential new products and services? We are being forced to face up to an inherent contradiction at the heart of our market economy that has been present since the very beginning, but is only now becoming irreconcilable.... This is the new structural reality that government and business leaders and so many economists are reluctant to acknowledge.
>
> —Jeremy Rifkin, president of the Foundation on Economic Trends in Washington, in *The Guardian* 48979 (2 Mar. 2004) 23.

too radical: see W&W's note, 'radical idea', *EP/BC* 138.
Father Coughlin: for expressions of EP's enthusiasm see 'American Notes. Father Coughlin', *NEW* VII.12 (4 July 1935) 225–6, and 'For a Decent Europe', British–Italian Bulletin II.11 (14 Mar. 1936) 3. Father Coughlin is invariably characterized by hostile critics as 'anti-Semitic' and 'populist', with the implicit and frequently explicit suggestion that that accounts for EP's interest in his broadcasts and writings. Such critics rarely mention Coughlin's preaching social justice, and that EP's endorsements are exclusively of his concern for social justice and monetary reform. Moreover, those endorsements were in 1935 and 1936, whereas Coughlin kept his anti-Semitism out of his broadcasts and writings until 1938.
'populist demagogue': see W&W, 'Huey Long and the "Share Our Wealth Plan"', *EP/BC* 93.
'splendid education': Woodward to EP, 7 Mar. 1935, cited by W&W, *EP/BC* 94.
'Better a wild man': EP, 'More Jazz', unpublished light verse submitted to *New Democracy*, [? 1935] (HRC).

'**Long WANTS**': EP, '**HUEY**, God bless him', unpublished TSS sent to *New Democracy* '13 or 14 Aug.' 1935 (HRC)—reproduced here as Appendix D. For EP's covering letter to Gorham Munson see *EPEC* 158–9.

153   '**With sane economics**': EP to Woodward, 8 Oct. [1933], *Pai* 15.1 (1986) 108; also *EPEC* 68.

'**utterly necessary**'...'**inconceivable**': *EPEC* 68; re England, see EP to John Buchan, [1934], 'Letters to John Buchan, 1934–1935', *Pai* 8.3 (1979) 467.

'**"Never", said Winston**': 41/204–5.

'**the mind of the people**': EP, 'Social Credit: An Impact' (1935), as in *Impact* 144.

'**the few powerful**': EP, 'American Notes', *NEW* VII.13 (11 July 1935), 245.

'**Can't move 'em**': see *ABCE* 35, *J/M* 27, Cantos 19/85, 78/481, 117/678, 113/735, and *EP: Poet I* 407

154   '**to base a system on will**': *ABCE* 33, 38.

'**the first writer**': EP, 'The Acid Test', *Biosophical Review* IV.2 (Winter 1934/5) 23.

'**an heretical movement**': EP, 'Personalia', *NEW* II.19 (23 Feb. 1933) 443.

in his *De Monarchia*: see Bk. I, chap. xi.

Pound's agitprop prose: see pp. 99, 106–7 above.

'**Sir,—Without claiming**': EP, 'Stamp Scrip', *NEW* V.7 (31 May 1934) 167. My paragraph is indebted to Flory, *The American Ezra Pound*, pp. 71–2. For Pound's review article around Gesell's *The Natural Economic Order* see 'The Individual in his Milieu: A Study of Relations and Gesell' (1935), *S Pr* 242–52. For detailed accounts of the theory and practice of stamp scrip see the relevant chapters in Flory, Redman, and Surette: 1999. For John Maynard Keynes's recognition of Gesell as 'an unduly neglected prophet' see his *The General Theory of Employment Interest and Money* (Macmillan & Co., 1936), pp. 353–8.

155   **how the miracle was worked**: in fact it can be explained very simply—

> Imagine for a moment you come across an unexpected ten pounds...you go out and spend it all at once on, say, two pairs of woolly socks. The person from the sock shop then takes your tenner and spends it on wine, and the wine merchant spends it on tickets to see *The Bitter Tears of Petra von Kant*, and the owner of the cinema spends it on chocolate, and the sweet-shop owner spends it on a bus ticket, and the owner of the bus company deposits it in the bank. That initial ten pounds has been spent six times, and has generated £60 of economic activity. In a sense no one is any better off; and yet, that movement of money makes everyone better off. To put it another way, that first tenner has contributed £60 to Britain's GDP. Seen in this way, GDP can be thought of as a measure...of velocity.
>
>   —John Lanchester, 'Let's Call it Failure', *LRB* 35.1 (3 Jan. 2013) 3.

'**the state need not borrow**', '**all the slobs**': 74/441.

'**strangle hold**': EP, 'Slim Hope', *Chicago Tribune*, Paris (3 July 1933) 4.

Borah's similar views: see *EP/WB* 7 n. 5.

'**Sir: As an Idahoan**': EP to Wm. A. Borah, 27 Nov. 1933, *EP/WB* [1].

'**"As an Idahoan"**': Borah to EP, 3 Jan. 1934, *EP/WB* 4.

156   '**Thank you**': Borah to EP, 30 Oct. 1935, *EP/WB* 45.

a traitor to America: see *EP/WB* 27 n. 2.

'**KINGFISH**': EP to Huey Long, 13 Apr. 1935 (Beinecke)—as in Redman, *Ezra Pound and Italian Fascism* 161; also in *EPEC* 148.

157   '**a sufficient phalanx of particulars**': 74/441; see also EP, 'T. S. Eliot' (1917), *LE* 420.

'**The people**': EP to Borah, 23 [May] 1935, *EP/WB* 35.

158   '**Roose(n)velt**': EP, 'American Notes', *NEW* VII.12 (4 July 1935) 225. In his 'American Notes' in *NEW* VI.13 (10 Jan. 1935), EP wrote, 'There is positively no evidence against Roosevelt's being utterly under the thumb of international finance.'

'S/S/ should attack': EP to R. C. Summerville of the Silver Shirt Legion of America, 7 May 1934, as published by *New Masses* XVIII.12 (17 Mar. 1936) 15.

'The anti-semitic fury': EP to [Graham Seton] Hutchinson, 26 May 1936, *EPEC* 190. In this connection see Miranda B. Hickman on 'Pound and Arnold Leese', *EP/SN* 289–93.

Mussolini's speech: Mussolini's words (in my translation) are from Pound's marked copy of the printed version of his speech (Brunnenburg). EP's comments are from his 'The Acid Test', *Biosophical Review* IV.2 (Winter 1934/35) 22ff. See also his letter dated 29 Oct. [1934], *New York Herald*, Paris (1 Nov. 1934) 4.

Making music of history: 'Cantos 31–41'

159 'An epic is': EP in unpublished draft preface [for *Polite Essays*], (*c.*1936) (Beinecke).

'Never has been': EP to John Hargrave, [? 1935] (Beinecke).

'The poet's job': EP to Basil Bunting, Dec. 1936, *L(1951)* 366.

'to get economic good': EP to Mary Barnard, 13 Aug. 1934, *L(1951)* 346.

160 'Tempus loquendi': EP, 'Three Cantos' [XXXI, XXXII, XXXIII], *Pagany* II.3 (July/Sept. 1931), 43.

'ten fat volumes': EP, 'The Central Problem', *Townsman* IV.13 (Mar. 1941) 15—translation from 'L'economia ortologica: Il problema centrale' (1937).

An early reviewer: Philip Blair Rice, 'The Education of Ezra Pound', *Nation* CXXXIX (21 Nov. 1934) 599–600, in Homberger: 1972, 292–3.

161 'a great ruin': J. M. Coetzee, 'The Marvels of Walter Benjamin', *New York Review of Books* XLVIII.1 (11 Jan. 2001) 33.

William M. Chace: see his 'The Canto as Cento: A Reading of Canto XXXIII', *Pai* 1.1 (1972) 89–100.

'They say they are chosen': David Anderson. 'Breaking the Silence: The Interview of Vanni Ronsisvalle and Pier Paolo Pasolini with Ezra Pound in 1968', *Pai* 10.2 (1981) 332, 338 (in part my translation).

'Can impressions': WBY, 'Introduction', *The Oxford Book of Modern Verse 1892–1935* (Oxford: At the Clarendon Press, 1936) xxiv.

A time of speaking, | *A time of silence*: see Ecclesiastes 3: 7.

'Whatsoever thy hand': Ecclesiastes 9: 10.

162 Jefferson... the shaping force: see EP, *J/M* 14–17. See also EP, 'The Jefferson–Adams Letters as a Shrine and a Monument' (1937), 'National Culture —A Manifesto 1938', and 'An Introduction to the Economic Nature of the United States' (1944), all three in *S Pr.*

164 'renascent CIVIC sense': EP, 'The "Criterion" Passes', *British Union Quarterly* III.2 (Apr./June 1939) 71.

composition [of canto 34]: the drafts are at Beinecke.

167 ideogrammic method: see pp. 76–8 above, and, *inter alia*, EP, 'Abject and Utter Farce' (1933), in *PE*.

168 'deficient in capacity': EP, *J/M* 37.

169 'puritanitis': EP, *J/M* 89.

170 'le problème des surréalistes': EP, [reply to questionnaire circulated by André Breton and Paul Éluard on 'la rencontre capitale de votre vie'], *Minotaure*, Paris, I.3/4 (15 Dec. 1933) 112.

Jefferson 'informed': EP, *J/M* 14.

'in the mind indestructible': 74/442; 'in jeopardy': 74/426; 'formed in the mind': 74/446.

171 Van Buren and Jackson: see EP, *J/M* 95; 'Nothing New', *NEW* IV.9 (14 Dec. 1933) 215; 'Woodward (W. E.) Historian', *NEW* X.17 (4 Feb. 1937) 329.

172 'life-long fight': EP, 'Woodward (W. E.) Historian', *NEW* X.17 (4 Feb. 1937) 329.
'saved the nation': EP, *J/M* 95.
misrepresenting the historical facts: on the issue of 'historicity' in this canto see Makin: 1985, 190–5. Pound may have held it against Andrew Jackson that—in John Quincy Adams's words (which were refracted in canto 34)—he had, as a general in the army, 'by the simultaneous operation of fraudulent treaties and brutal force' deprived the Cherokee nation in Georgia of their lands 'and [driven] them out of their dwellings' (Terrell, *Companion*: I, 138 n. 83). See also EP to WCW, [Jan. 1935], *EP/WCW* 156.

173 'where is FACTS': EP to FMF, 16 Nov. [1933], *EP/FMF* 134.
'THE evil': EP, 'The Master of Rapallo Speaks', *Outrider*, Cincinnati, I.1 (1 Nov. 1933) 1—in *P&P* VI, 96.
'than the production of foodstuffs': EP, 'Is it War?', *Time and Tide* XIV.39 (30 Sept. 1933) 1149—in *P&P* VI, 80.
'100 francs on every 400': both Monsieur Schneider's words and those of the other French manufacturer are as in EP, 'Orientation and News Sense', *NEW* II.12 (5 Jan. 1933) 274.

174 'between humanity': EP, 'Orientation and News Sense', 273.
'not proceeding': EP, *ABCE* 37.
The 'thought': Hugh Witemeyer reads these items very differently—see 'Pound & the Cantos: "Ply over ply"', *Pai* 8.2 (1979) 231–5.

175 a tailor's: cf. 'the tailor Blodgett', EP, *ABCR* 18–19.

176 Hathor: details from Alain Blottière, *Petit Dictionnaire des dieux égyptiens* (Paris: Zulma, 2000).
'*Regina coeli*' . . . '*fulvida di folgore*': Dante, *Paradiso* XXIII, 128, XXX, 62.
'Coition, the sacrament': see p. 114 above.

177 'We were diddled': EP, *J/M* 97.

178 civic responsibility . . . life of the spirit: see pp. 75–6 above.
Fugue: for a pioneering and still insufficiently noticed investigation see Kay Davis, *Fugue and Fresco: Structures in Pound's Cantos* (University of Maine at Orono: National Poetry Foundation, 1984).
Yeats . . . failed to understand: see WBY, *A Packet for Ezra Pound* (1929), as in *A Vision* (1937) 4–5.

Note: A historian, the Bank Wars, and the New Deal

181 The source of this note is Arthur Schlesinger Jr, 'History and National Stupidity', *New York Review of Books* LIII.7 (27 Apr. 2006) 14.

4. THINGS FALL APART, 1933–1937

To spread order about him

182 Bard . . . lecture: from TS copy of lecture in Hugh Kenner Archive (HRC).
'GET ACTION': EP to WCW, [Mar. 1935?], *EP/WCW* 169.

183 'build in his own': EP, 'Possibilities of Civilization: What the Small Town Can Do' (1936), *Impact* 81. The rest of this paragraph is from the same article—see *Impact* 75–82.
Herr Hitler: paragraph drawn from William L. Shirer, *The Rise and Fall of the Third Reich: A History of Nazi Germany* (Secker and Warburg, 1961), pp. 189–213. Sebastian Haffner wrote that there was 'a one-day—1 April 1933—boycott of Jewish shops', in his *The Meaning of Hitler* (1978) (Phoenix Press, 2000), p. 27.

'Miss Weaver present': EP to DP, [? 15 May 1933] (Lilly).

184 'beeyewteeful blue': EP to DP, 3 June [1933] (Lilly).

'"entre nous"': EP to DP, [24 July 1933] (Lilly).

'O is livin': EP to DP, 7 June 1933 (Lilly).

'Settimana Mozartiana': details of concerts in June and July 1933 from *EP&M* 331–4.

'done privately': EP to Tibor Serly, Apr. 1940, *L(1951)* 442.

'too complicated': DP to EP, 27 July 1933 (Lilly).

'deader than mutton': DP to EP, 15 May 1933 (Lilly). Further details from her letters to EP of 6 and 29 June, and 7 July 1933.

'All right': DP to EP, 30 July 1933 (Lilly).

'Don't purrpose': EP to DP, 2 Aug. 1933 (Lilly).

'pride of the town': BB to James G. Lieppert (J. Ronald Latimer), 30 Oct. 1932, as cited in Peter Makin, *Bunting: The Shaping of his Verse* (Oxford: Clarendon Press, 1992), p. 64.

185 'more savage disciples': WBY to OS, 2 Mar. 1929, as cited in Norman: 1960, 300.

'to see you': LZ to EP, 12 July 1933, *EP/LZ* 151.

'chiefly to meet': from the account in Norman: 1960, 318. Further details, Norman: 1960, 316–18. Bunting spoke of their efforts to reform Pound's way of reading his cantos at the International Pound Conference, Durham, 27–30 Mar. 1979, when reading from them in his own very fine Northumbrian voice.

'wit and brilliance': BB's phrase for EP's conversation, in interview with Jonathan Williams cited in Carroll F. Terrell, 'An Eccentric Profile', *Basil Bunting: Man and Poet* (Orono, Me.: National Poetry Foundation, 1981), p. 50.

telling Zukofsky: see EP to JL, 24 Dec. 1933, *EP/JL* 9, 10n.

'about bombarding': JL to EP, 21 Aug. 1933, *EP/JL* 3. Further details from the editor's extracts from JL's letters to EP, 29 Aug. and 8 Oct. 1933, and from his notes. See also JL's poem 'Ezra', as printed in *Pai* 26, 2–3 (1997) 231–5.

186 prose blasts: e.g. 'Abject and Utter Farce', *Harkness Hoot* IV.2 (Nov. 1933) 6–14 (included in *PE*); and 'Ignite! Ignite!', *Harvard Advocate* CXX.3 (Dec. 1933) 3–5.

at Pound's instigation: 'It was Ezra's idea and Munson seems to approve of it and want it' (JL to WCW, 20 Sept. 1935, *William Carlos Williams and James Laughlin: Selected Letters*, ed. Hugh Witemeyer (New York: W. W. Norton, 1989) p. 3).

'music in winter': details of the 'Concerti "Inverno Musicale"' from *EP&M* 336–65 and 377–83.

articles for *Il Mare*: EP wrote these in English, they were published in Italian translation, and translated (not by EP) from the Italian into English for *EP&M*.

187 *Le Chant des Oiseaux...* for solo violin: thus EP in *Il Mare*, 11 Nov. 1933, *EP&M* 346. See also *GK* 152–3.

'Maestro Sansoni': EP in *Il Mare*, 16 Sept. 1933, *EP&M* 337–8.

League of Nations Disarmament: paragraph drawn from Farrell, *Mussolini: A New Life*, 247–9; and Shirer, *Third Reich* 210–12.

Mary Barnard: 1909–2002; details from her *Assault on Mount Helicon: A Literary Memoir* (Berkeley: University of California Press, 1984), pp. 52ff.

'How hard': EP to Mary Barnard, 29 Oct. 1933, *Assault on Helicon* 53, also *L (1951)* 331.

'the MEDIUM': EP to Mary Barnard, 2 Dec. 1933, *Assault on Helicon* 55.

188 'RULES': EP to Mary Barnard, 23 Feb. 1934, *Assault on Helicon* 56, 57; cf. *L (1951)* 339.

'work to a metric scheme': EP to Mary Barnard, 28 Nov. 1934, *Assault on Helicon* 76.

translation of Sappho: *Sappho: A New Translation* (Berkeley: University of California Press, 1958).

'Do understand': EP to Mary Barnard, 22 Jan. 1934, *Assault on Helicon* 56; *L (1951)* 336. As to the lessons in *ABCR*, see particularly EP's 'Treatise on Metre', *ABCR* 197–206.

'How to Read': see *LE* 15–40.

'The teacher': *ABCR* 83.

'shd. consume itself': this formulation is from EP to Laurence Binyon, 30 Aug. 1934, *L (1951)* 347.

'dance of the intellect': EP, 'How to Read', LE 25, q.v. for EP's definitions of all three terms.

'YOU WILL NEVER KNOW': *ABCR* 45–6.

189 'Literature is news': *ABCR* 29.

eases the mind: cf. EP, 'How to Read', *LE* 20; maintaining the language: cf. *LE* 21, and *ABCR* 32–5.

'natural destructivity': *ABCR* 192–3.

'complete exposure': JL to EP, 8 Oct. 1933, *EP/JL* 4.

'point of this experiment': *ABCR* 23–4; see also *EP&M* 323–4.

William Young: see *EP&M* 356–60.

'Nevuh': EP to AB, 4 Apr. 1934 (Lilly).

'about 95%': EP to Langston Hughes, 13 May 1935, David Roessel, ed., '"A Racial Act": The Letters of Langston Hughes and Ezra Pound', *Pai* 29.1-2 (2000) 229.

'wackin a tennis ball': EP to Viola Baxter Jordan, 7 Apr. 1936 (Beinecke).

'to the movies': EP to Viola Baxter Jordan, [? 1934] (Beinecke).

190 'a new heave': EP to John Drummond, 4 May 1933, *L (1951)* 329.

'syllable by syllable': EP to Laurence Binyon, 21 Jan. 1934, *L (1951)* 336. See 'Hell', *LE* 201–13, for EP's review of Binyon's version.

'putting money-power': EP to Laurence Binyon, 6 Mar.1934, *L (1951)* 340.

'would talk of nothing': WBY, *The King of the Great Clock Tower, Commentaries and Poems* (New York: Macmillan Company, 1935), pp. vi–vii. For 'nobody language' and 'the buzzard' see Richard Ellmann, *Eminent Domain: Yeats among Wilde, Joyce, Pound...* (New York: Oxford University Press, 1967), pp. 81–2.

'large dog kennel': JL, *Pound as Wuz: Essay and Lectures on Ezra Pound* (St Paul, Minn.: Graywolf Press, 1987), pp. 13–14. *Note*: Many of the details in JL's account appear to be more colourful than accurate. Though he wrote that he 'was in Rapallo' when Henghes, 'a bedraggled figure with his feet bleeding turned up on Ezra's doorstep', he was not in fact in Rapallo at that moment (see *EP/JL* 30–2), and it may be that it amused Henghes to tell a tall tale to his friend JL. Ian Henghes, the sculptor's son, has kindly communicated the following information. Heinz Clusmann (1906–75), who called himself Heinz Henghes after 1934, 'had a Jewish mother, a Lutheran father and a Lutheran upbringing'. He was not a refugee from the Nazis, nor did he walk from Hamburg to see Pound. He ran away from home in Hamburg in 1924 and stowed away to America where he lived until 1932. He was then in Paris, where he briefly assisted Brancusi, and went on by train to Italy where he called on Pound. (That was in April 1934.) From Rapallo he wrote to a Dr Kahn: 'Ezra Pound has given me a place to stay, food & marble to work on for 3 months to finish 3 statues.' Donna Virginia Agnelli bought three pieces by Henghes in 1934 and 1935, but not (as JL wrote) 'the striking figure of a centaur, which later became the model for the New Directions colophon'. So far as Ian Henghes knows that drawing was never made into a sculpture. One further correction: the editor of *EP/JL* writes that the 'perfect schnorrer' in 35/174 is Henghes, though this is improbable since *Cantos 31–41* were already with the US publishers by Feb. 1934 (*L(1951)* 338).

'New sculptor': EP to Sarah Perkins Cope, 22 Apr. 1934, *L (1951)* 342.

'unable to do': DP to EP, July 1934 (Lilly).

'This family life': DP to EP, 20 Aug. 1934 (Lilly).

'Child very good': EP to DP, 4 Sept. 1934 (Lilly).

He would write: rest of paragraph from MdR, *Discretions* 43–57.

191 '*whatever his crimes*': Shirer, *Third Reich* 230.

'Education by provocation': Samuel Becket, 'Ex Cathezra', *Bookman* 87 (Dec. 1934) 10, cited by JL in 'Pound the Teacher', *The Master of Those Who Know* (San Francisco: City Lights Books, 1986), p. 26.

Hugh MacDiarmid: in *Scottish Observer*, 24 Dec. 1931, writing under his proper name, C. M. Grieve.

'bundle of prejudices': 'Current Literature', *Spectator* 153 (13 July 1934) 66. This and the next five notes are drawn from Vittorio Mondolfo and Helen Shuster, 'Annotated Checklist of Criticism on Ezra Pound, 1930–1935', *Pai* 5.1 (1976) 155–87.

'insulting': Eda Lou Walton, 'Ezra Pound lops off a few more heads', *New York Times Book Review* V.7 (7 Oct. 1934) 8.

'atrocious style': 'Mr. Pound as critic', *TLS* 1709 (1 Nov. 1934) 751.

192 **'stumped'**: Philip Blair Rice, 'The Education of Ezra Pound', *Nation* 139 (21 Nov. 1934) 600.

'design is wanting': Babette Deutsch, 'With Seven League Boots', *New York Herald Tribune Book Review*, 25 Nov. 1934, 18.

'serious menace': Rayner Heppenstall, 'Poetry', *NEW* VII.18 (Apr. 1935) 10.

Pound would complain: e.g. in 'The Acid Test', *Biosophical Review* IV.2 (1934/35) 24.

'more bloody work': EP to JL, 18 Oct. 1934, *EP/JL* 34.

'some brat': EP to LZ, 16 Oct. [1934] (HRC).

two or three weeks: JL was never specific as to exactly how long he spent at what he called the 'Ezuversity' on this his most extended stay. It is usually said that he was there in Nov. and Dec. JL said in *Pound as Wuz* (p. [3]) that it was arranged for him 'to study with Pound in his famous Ezuversity for several months'. However, in the summer and autumn of 1934 JL was mostly in London and Paris, and *EP/JL* gives letters from EP to JL through Oct. and Nov., with one dated 2 Dec.: since JL was spending a good part of every day he was in Rapallo in EP's company it seems improbable that EP would also be typing full letters to him while he was there. JL's thank-you letter to EP from Lausanne is dated 21 Dec. 1934—it is cited by Emily Mitchell Wallace in her invaluably informative portrait, '"A Bridge over worlds": A Partial Portrait of James Laughlin IV'. *Pai* 31 (2002) 210. Also, EP was away from Rapallo for at least a day or two around the 10th, when he went down to Rome to record a radio talk. Evidently the magnitude of the occasion for JL was not to be measured by the amount of time but by its intensity.

'learned more': JL, as cited from his *Random Essays* by Emily Mitchell Wallace in '"A Bridge over worlds"', *Pai* 31 (2002) 210.

'trying . . . to write poetry': JL, *Pound as Wuz* 7—rest of paragraph from JL, *Pound as Wuz* 7.

the daily class: JL, 'Pound the Teacher', *The Master of Those Who Know* 2–5. Cf. the similar account in *Pound as Wuz* 4–6.

193 **'So that he could easily find'**: JL, *Pound as Wuz* 6–7.

'spose the keynote': EP to Francesco Monotti, 22 Nov. [1934] (Beinecke). Further details from letters exchanged between EP and Monotti in Nov. 1934 (Beinecke). The article seen by Ciano would have been 'Mussolini Defines State as "Spirit of the People": Fascism Analyzed by Ezra Pound, Noted American Writer', *Chicago Tribune*, Paris (9 Apr. 1934) 5.

'greatly honoured': EP to Galeazzo Ciano, 23 Nov. 1934, as cited in Redman, *Ezra Pound and Italian Fascism* 158.

'economic triumph': William Bird to EP, 2 May 1935, as cited in Redman, *Ezra Pound and Italian Fascism* 158.

'don't understand': [? Ciano] to EP, 17 Jan. 1935 (Beinecke).

194 **'onlie begetter'**: W. H. D. Rouse, 'Note', *The Story of Odysseus: A Translation of Homer's 'Odyssey' into Plain English* (Thomas Nelson and Sons, 1937), p. v.

'about the campaign': EP to W. H. D. Rouse, 30 Dec. 1934, *L (1951)* 349–51.

'a readable story': W. H. D. Rouse, 'Note', *The Story of Odysseus* v.

'**What we have done**': William Atheling (E.P.), 'Throttling Music', *NEW* VII.13 (11 July 1935) 247–8, as in *EP&M* 377.

'**save *ten* lire**': EP, 'Money versus Music', *Delphian Quarterly* XIX.1 (Jan. 1936), as in *EP&M* 382.

195 '**a racket**': EP, 'Throttling Music', *EP&M* 375.

'**black rot of usury**': EP, 'Throttling Music', *EP&M* 375.

'**Serly sees**': EP, 'Tibor Serly, Composer', *NEW* VI.24 (28 Mar. 1935) 495, in *EP&M* 372.

'**Stravinsky**': *NEW* VI.24 (28 Mar. 1935) 495, in *EP&M* 372.

'**at Dead End**': EP to DP, 1 July 1935 (Lilly).

'**no use arguing**': EP to DP, 5 July 1935 (Lilly).

into Austria . . . Wörgl: details from EP to HLP, 5 Aug. 1935 (Beinecke); EP to DP, 5 Aug. 1935, (Lilly); Wallace, '"A Bridge over worlds"', *Pai* 31 (2002) 212; 74/441; JL, *Pound as Wuz* 12; see also p. 155 above.

troops . . . to the Brenner: cf. Farrell, *Mussolini*, 250–1.

'**proudly showed**': MdR, *Discretions* 79.

196 '**Marieka**': EP to DP, 2 Sept. 1935 (Lilly).

'**amazin kid**': EP to JL, 23 Sept. 1935, *EP/JL* 44.

LAWS FOR MARIA: MdR, *Discretions* 69–70.

The turning point: 1935–1936

Sources: G. M. Gathorne-Hardy, *A Short History of International Affairs, 1920–1939* (Oxford University Press under the auspices of the Royal Institute of International Affairs, 4th edn., 1950); William L. Shirer, *The Rise and Fall of the Third Reich: A History of Nazi Germany* (Secker and Warburg, 1961); Nicholas Farrell, *Mussolini: A New Life* (Weidenfeld and Nicolson, 2003).

196 '*Jews had been excluded*': Shirer, *Third Reich* 233.

197 *Hitler . . . mad*: see Farrell, *Mussolini*, 249–50.

'*First of all*': Mussolini to Jean-Louis Malvy, June 1936, Farrell, *Mussolini*, 279, citing Renzo de Felice, *Mussolini il duce*, i. 749–50.

198 '*A large and influential*': Claud Cockburn, *The Week* (18 Oct. 1933). Further details from *The Week* (30 Aug. 1933). Cockburn's weekly newsletter was mimeographed from typewritten copy and published from 34 Victoria St., London SW1. In Pound's library (now in HRC) were forty-two issues, starting with no. [20], 9 August 1933.

'*The main line*': Cockburn, *The Week* (1 Nov. 1933).

199 '*German and Italian*': Shirer, *Third Reich* 298, citing *Ciano's Diplomatic Papers*, ed. Malcolm Muggeridge, pp. 43–8.

'The boss knows his business'

199 **a storm**: see EP to Tinkham, 2 Sept. [1935], *EP/GT* 52.

'**Keep KAAAAAAM**': EP to HLP, 13 Sept. 1935 (Beinecke).

'**Seminole war**': *Encyclopaedia Britannica* (11th edn., New York, 1910), xxiv. 616.

'**clear conscience**': EP to Borah, 10 Oct. 1935, *EP/WB* 42.

sorry: EP to Borah, [15 Nov. 1935], *EP/WB* 46.

'**necessary**': EP to WCW, [1935], cited in note, *EP/WCW* 174.

'**wrong**': EP to Borah, [15 Nov. 1935], *EP/WB* 46.

'**victim tribes**': EP to Borah, [Nov. 1935], *EP/WB* 49.

'**enormous advance**': EP to Borah, 10 Oct. 1935, *EP/WB* 42.

uncivilized: see EP to Borah, [Nov. 1935], *EP/WB* 49.

'had no battles': *PE* 49, 51.

'Italy needs Abyssinia': EP, 'The Fascist Ideal', *British–Italian Bulletin* II.16 (18 Apr. 1936) 2. Mussolini had said on 23 Mar. 1936–XIV, that Italy, under siege in an economic war decreed by Geneva on account of its glorious victories in Abyssinia, 'can and must attain the maximum level of economic independence' (Benito Mussolini, *The Corporate State*, 2nd edn. (Florence: Vallecchi Publisher, 1938/XVI)).

200   poison gas: see A. W. Palmer, *A Dictionary of Modern History, 1789–1945* (Harmondsworth: Penguin Books, 1964), p. 15.

'Abyssinian acquisition': *GK* 229.

'Italian empire': EP, 'A Good Surgeon Does Not Always Amputate', *British–Italian Bulletin* II.39 (24 Oct.1936) [1].

'I am, if you like': EP, 'For a Decent Europe', *British–Italian Bulletin* II.11 (14 Mar. 1936) 3.

'international': EP, 'Twelve Years and Twelve Years', *British–Italian Bulletin* I.8 (27 Dec. 1935) 1. According to Douglas Goldring, in a letter dated 4 Feb. 1944 to the editor of *Tribune*, Pound's 'views on Abyssinia were shared by most English Catholic converts as well as by a considerable number of English Army officers and Foreign Office high-ups. Admiration of Mussolini, as of Franco, was prevalent among our Conservative class, at least until June 1940'—a copy of Goldring's letter is in Pound MSS II, Box 20 (Lilly).

'for humanity': EP, '"We Have Had No Battles But We Have All Joined In And Made Roads"', *PE* 55.

'during the two months': EP, 'For a Measure', *British–Italian Bulletin* II.12 (21 Mar. 1936) 4.

a project: see below.

Minister of Agriculture: detail from EP to HLP, [Oct. 1935] (Beinecke).

Olivia Rossetti Agresti: details from EP to DP, [Nov. 1935] (Lilly), and 76/452.

'old New Age–Orage man': Odon Por to EP, Apr. 1934, as in Redman 156.

worked . . . with Por: see EP to DP, 31 Oct. 1935 (Lilly).

British–Italian Bulletin set up: see EP, 'Readers of the *B. I. B.* Listen!', *British–Italian Bulletin* II.32 (5 Sept.1936) 3.

201   'offered to pay': EP to Por, [*c.*21 Dec. 1935], as in Redman 167.

Por arranged: information in this para. from Redman 169–70. See also EP to Por, 4 Jan. [1936], *EPEC* 175–8.

'anything except economics': Por to EP, 14 June 1935, as in Redman 163.

'can't put [him]': Por to EP, 21 Mar. 1936, as in Redman 170.

'Foreign Office is afraid': Por to EP, 13 May 1936, as in Redman 170.

'A strong Italy' . . . 'pressure towards war': EP, 'Twelve Years and Twelve Years', *British–Italian Bulletin* I.8 (27 Dec. 1935) 1.

small war in Africa: see EP to Tinkham, 2 Sept. [1935], *EP/GT* 53; see also EP to Borah, 10 Oct. 1935, *EP/WB* 42.

202   'attempt to starve' . . . 'main purpose': EP to Borah, [1935], *EP/WB* 55. *EP/WB* gives 'large scare crime', but 'larger scale' appears to be intended.

'The question': EP to Borah, 1 Oct. 1935, *EP/WB* 40; carbon copy to Tinkham, *EP/GT* 57.

'signed statements': EP, 'Italy's Frame-up', *British–Italian Bulletin* II.5 (1 Feb. 1936) 2.

Eden . . . 'married into': EP to Tinkham, 27 Dec. [1935], *EP/GT* 60; see also EP to Borah, [Dec.] 1935, *EP/WB* 52.

Lord Cranbourne: EP to Tinkham, [Jan. or Feb. 1936], *EP/GT* 65.

'the men now crying out': EP, 'Twelve Years and Twelve Years', *British–Italian Bulletin* I.8 (27 Dec. 1935) 1.

Mussolini's secretariat... project: The project is reproduced in Zapponi, *L'Italia di Ezra Pound*, pp. 205–8; for the secretariat's comments see Zapponi, *L'Italia di Ezra Pound*, p. 51.

203 'The total': EP, 'A Good Surgeon Does Not Always Amputate', *British–Italian Bulletin* II.39 (24 Oct. 1936) [1].

in the Fascist press: see Farrell 268. EP told Cunningham Graham (in late 1935?) that the letter from Captain Goldoni was 'not press propaganda' but a 'private letter from a chap I know, sent to a friend in this village' (Beinecke).

204 'a blind eye': BB to EP, 'last of 1935' (Beinecke).

time he was got rid of: BB to EP, 21 Mar. 1934 (Beinecke).

his faith in Mussolini: see for example, EP, 'Moneta fascista', *La Vita Italiana*, Rome, XXIV.274 (Jan./June 1936) [33]–37.

military virtues: see EP, 'Confucius' Formula Up-to-date', *British–Italian Bulletin* II.3 (18 Jan. 1936) 4; 'The Treasure of a State', *British–Italian Bulletin* II.13 (28 Mar. 1936) 4.

Bank of Italy nationalized: see EP, 'Great Comfort of Latin Mind: The Italian Bank Act', *British–Italian Bulletin* II.14 (4 Apr. 1936) 4; 'Organic Democracy', *British–Italian Bulletin* II.15 (11 Apr. 1936) 2; 'A Civilising Force on the Move: The Bank Reform', *British–Italian Bulletin* II.21 (23 May 1936) 3.

'DUCE!': EP to Mussolini, 22 Dec. 1936, in Zapponi, *L'Italia di Ezra Pound*, 52.

Music, money, cantos

204 announced in *Il Mare*: [EP], 'Studi Tigulliani', *Il Mare* XXIX.1409 (14 Mar. 1936) [1]; in English translation in *EP&M* 384–7.

'being interned': EP to OR, 5 May 1935 (Beinecke/OR)—cited Conover, 122.

had resolved themselves: EP, 'A Letter from Rapallo', *Japan Times & Mail*, Tokyo (7 and 8 Jan. 1940) [8]—in *EP&M* 455, in *EP&J* 158.

'eccentric musicologists': from Stephen J. Adams, 'Pound, Olga Rudge, and the "Risveglio Vivaldiano"', *Pai* 4.1 (1975) 118. This article, and R. Murray Schafer's pp. 328–30 in *EP&M*, provide expert information on the Vivaldi revival. Further details concerning Olga Rudge's part from Conover, 125–8.

205 makes order... 'an example of order': see *GK* 255 and 281–3.

would deliver to Faber & Faber in November: information from EP to LZ, 29 Nov. 1936 (HRC); also EP to AB, 2 Dec. 1936 (Lilly),

Swabey's recollections: Henry Swabey, 'A Page Without Which...', *Pai* 5.2 (1976) 329–30.

206 Pound had suggested: EP to Swabey, 3 Mar. [1935], *L (1951)* 359. See also EP to Swabey, 26 Mar. [1936], *L (1951)* 367–8.

defeated by the champion: EP to WCW, 28 Apr. 1936, *EP/WCW* 180, 181n.

'I don't see you': EP to Antheil, 4 May 1936 (Lilly).

'Now that I had reached': Henry Swabey, 'A Page Without Which...', *Pai* 5.2 (1976) 330. Pound's 'Guide to Italy' is printed on pp. 336–7.

207 painted ceiling: cf. EP from Siena to Katue Kitasono, 12 Aug. 1936, 'This is the only town where I have ever been able to live in a palace with a painted ceiling' (*EP&J* 31).

'Depressing country': DP to EP, 27 July 1936 (Lilly).

'Main points': EP to DP, 29 July 1936 (Lilly).

what he had written: see *Social Credit: An Impact*: reprinted, revised and condensed, in *Impact* 147; also 'Banking Beneficence and...', *NA* LVI.16 (14 Feb. 1935) 184–5.

interest-bearing current account: information from EP, Personal Papers (Beinecke).

'hot here': EP to HLP, 29 July 1936 (Beinecke).

'damn HARD': EP to DP, 20 Aug. [1936] (Lilly).

five notebooks: now with Poetry Notebooks in Beinecke.

'the 10-vol bloke': *Il Monte dei Paschi di Siena e le Aziende in Esso Riunite*, ed. Narciso Mengozzi (Siena, 1891–1925). EP's principle other historian was Antonio Zobi, *Storia civile della Toscana dal MDCCXXXVII al MDCCCXLVIII*, 5 vols. (Firenze, 1850–2).

good music in Siena: EP to HLP, 7 Aug. 1936 (Beinecke).

208 'thanks & love': DP to EP, 26 Aug. 1936 (Lilly).

'new raise in pay': EP to DP, 20 Aug. 1936 (Lilly).

'money money money': EP, 'Ezra Pound Shouts the Money Money Money Chorus', *Attack!* ([after 10 July] 1935) [2]. The 'Venison' song was first printed in *NEW* V.9 (14 June 1934) 205, and was collected with the other 'Poems of Alfred Venison' in a pamphlet published by Stanley Nott in 1935—reprinted in *P&T*; the collection was included in appendix II of the new edition of *Personae* (1926) published by New Directions in 1949, and in Faber & Faber's 1952 edition of *Personae*.

'OUT of Bloomsbury': EP to Hargrave, 21 Jan. 1935, as cited (with informative commentary) by Wendy Flory in her *The American Ezra Pound*, p. 76.

didn't think much of . . . Mosley: e.g. EP to Gorham Munson, [16 June 1935], 'DO CAN those asses who talk of fascism as if the Corporate State/Hitler & stinky Mosley were all one' (HRC).

'Big nooz': EP to HLP, 12 Aug. 1936 (Beinecke). Also EP to DP, 12 Aug. 1936, 'BUF agrees to Social Credit analysis' (Lilly).

209 'pickin' daiseyes': EP to DP, 26 Aug. 1936 (Lilly).

'the word "fascism"': DP to EP, 26 Aug. 1936 (Lilly).

'Stalinists': EP to DP, 29 Aug. 1936 (Lilly).

'end of Analects again': EP to HLP, 29 Aug. 1936 (Beinecke).

One of the sayings: see EP, *Analects* 13.III, 1–2; then *S Pr* 99, 303; *GK* 16; etc.

left Siena: EP to DP, 2 Sept. 1936 (Lilly).

'hottern Siena': EP to HLP, [3 Sept. 1936] (Beinecke).

'this machine sticks': EP to HLP, [4 Sept. 1936] (Beinecke).

'imperfect copy': EP to DP, 5 Sept. 1936 (Lilly).

210 'frame for a fourth': EP to DP, 7 Sept. 1936 (Lilly).

sent them off: EP to HLP, [10 Sept. 1936] (Beinecke). 'Cantos XLII–XLIV' were in *Criterion* XVI, no. LXIV (Apr. 1937) 405–23.

'Dunning mss': EP to DP, 10 Sept. 1936 (Lilly). Concerning Dunning see pp. 62–3 above.

'amateur publisher': EP, 'Responsibility? Shucks!', *Globe* II.4 (Feb./Mar. 1938)110.

new music at the Venice Biennale: paragraph drawn from *EP&M* 399–417, including EP, 'Mostly Quartets', *Listener* XVI.405 (14 Oct. 1936) 743–4; 'Music in Ca' Rezzonico', *Delphian Quarterly* XX.1 (Jan. 1937) 2–4, 11; and 'Ligurian View of a Venetian Festival', *Music & Letters* XVIII.1 (Jan. 1937) [36]–41.

record of a struggle: see *GK* 135, and Schafer, *EP&M* 400.

'some WANT': EP to DP, 15 Sept. 1936 (Lilly).

'for 500 lire': EP to Tibor Serly, [Sept. 1936], *L (1951)* 372–3; also in *EP&M* 400–1.

'fixed to come': EP to Münch, Dec. 1936, *L (1951)* 374. Details of March concert from EP, 'The New Hungarian Quartet', *EP&M* 421–2, and 'The Return of Gerhart Münch', *EP&M* 422–3—translated from *Il Mare* of 13 Feb. 1937, and 13 Mar. 1937. 'Sandwiched between' is from *GK* 183. See EP to Tibor Serly, Apr. 1940, *L (1951)* 442–3, for his clearest account of his *laboratory* idea' in the construction of a concert programme.

'richness and abundance': EP, 'Mostly Quartets', *Listener* XVI.405 (14 Oct. 1936)—in *EP&M* 405.

211 a great man, 'Any man': Tinkham to EP, 20 June 1936, *EP/GT* 75.

The congressman arrived: details of the visit drawn from *EP/GT* 75, 80, 82, and from EP letters to HLP and DP.
'talked relentlessly': MdR, *Discretions* 82–3.
'Eleven hours': EP to DP, 21 Sept. 1936 (Lilly).
'much more concentrated': EP to DP, 22 Sept. 1936 (Lilly).
'brother TINKHAM': EP to HLP, 22 Sept. 1936 (Beinecke).
'We putt in nine hour': EP to HLP, 25 Sept. 1936 (Beinecke).
'Better not say': EP to DP, 24 Sept, 1936 (Lilly).
'for all your courtesies': Tinkham to EP, 17 Oct. 1936, *EP/GT* 87.
'whereafter': EP to DP, [*c.*25 Sept. 1936] (Lilly).
'articl/ a day': EP to DP, 16 Oct. 1936 (Lilly).
'Worst supposed': EP to HLP, 20 Nov. 1936 (Beinecke).
212   'cdn't figure': EP to OR, [Nov. 1936] (Beinecke/OR)—as cited Conover, 128.
Rome on his own: see EP to DP, 29 Dec. 1936 (Lilly).
'turkey and chocolates': OR to EP, [?Dec.1936] (Beinecke/OR)—as cited Conover, 128

'The Fifth Decad': against Usura

In this section I have found especially helpful—whether in following or in departing from—the guidance of George Kearns and Peter Makin: George Kearns, *Guide to Ezra Pound's Selected Cantos* (New Brunswick, NJ: Rutgers University Press, 1980), and *Ezra Pound: The Cantos* (Cambridge: Cambridge University Press, 1989); Peter Makin, *Pound's Cantos* (George Allen & Unwin, 1985).

212   scholar-sleuths: see the invaluable researches of Ben Kimpel and T. C. Duncan Eaves, 'Sources of Cantos XLII and XLIII', *Pai* 6.3 (1977) 333–58—the misreading or change of 'animo' is noted on p. 345; 'The Sources of the Leopoldine Cantos', *Pai* 7.1–2 (1978) 249–77; 'Pound's Use of Sienese Manuscripts for Cantos XLII and XLIII', *Pai* 8.3 (1979) 513–18.

220   Canto 47: my discussion is indebted to Daniel Pearlman's profoundly insightful chapter 'Man, Earth and Stars', in his *The Barb of Time: On the Unity of Ezra Pound's Cantos* (New York: Oxford University Press, 1969), pp. 172–92.

223   'annoying interruption': George Kearns, *Ezra Pound: The Cantos* 42.

224   Von Unruh: information from Walter Baumann, 'The German-Speaking World in *The Cantos*', *Pai* 21.3 (1992) 44–6.
'the sergeant tramping down': EP, 'Waiting', *New Democracy* IV.2 (15 Mar. 1935) 28.

225   intelligence of insects: see pp. 139–40 above.
canto 49: the spacing between the 'Seven Lakes' verses was incorrect in the first edition, and though corrected in Faber & Faber's 1954 edition, and in the bilingual *I Cantos* in 1985, the error persists in both the New Directions and the current Faber editions. The four stanzas should begin: 'For the seven lakes', 'Autumn moon', 'Where wine flag', 'Wild geese swoop'—there should not be a line-space after 'cross light'. For the fullest account of the background and sources see Zhaoming Qian, 'Painting into Poetry: Pound's Seven Lakes Canto', in *Ezra Pound & China*, ed. Zhaoming Qian (Ann Arbor: University of Michigan Press, 2003), 72–95. Qian gives reproductions of the eight scenes. See also 'Miss Tseng and the Seven Lakes Canto. "Descendant of Kung and Thseng-Tsu"', in *Ezra Pound's Chinese Friends: Stories in Letters*, ed. Zhaoming Qian (Oxford: Oxford University Press, 2008), pp. 9–17. For the original poems and further commentary see Sanehide Kodama, 'The Eight Scenes of Sho-Sho', *Pai* 6.2 (1977) 131–43.

'The still centre': William Cookson, *A Guide to the Cantos of Ezra Pound* (Croom Helm, 1985), p. 53. In a 1941 article EP explicitly stated that Confucianism is not quietist, '*meno quietista*', but rather 'a philosophy for anyone taking up state office, a party seat, to administrate or to perform some public function' ('Ta Hio', *Meridiano di Roma* VI.46 (16 Nov. 1941) 7).

'turned government over': Qian, 'Painting into Poetry', *Ezra Pound & China* 73.

Confucian historians: see John J. Nolde, *Blossoms from the East: The China Cantos of Ezra Pound* (Orono, Me.: National Poetry Foundation, 1983), pp. 237, 240.

227 re emperor Shun's hymn, and the peasants' folk song, see Hugh Kenner, 'More on the Seven Lakes Canto', *Pai* 2.1 (1973) 45–6; Sanehide Kodama, 'The Eight Scenes of Sho-Sho', *Pai* 6.2 (1977) 142–5; Achilles Fang to James Laughlin, 23 May 1950, *EP/JL* 205. These helpful commentators are not responsible for my reading.

228 'the dimension of stillness': here I have been stimulated by Demetres P. Tryphonopoulos, '"The Fourth; The Dimension of Stillness": D. P. Ouspensky and Fourth Dimensionalism in Canto 49', *Pai* 19.3 (1990) 117–22; also by Peter Makin, Makin: 1985, 208–9.

229 Napoleon's 'brilliant Italian campaigns': Thomas Carlyle, 'Lecture VI. The Hero as King. Cromwell, Napoleon, Revolutionism', *On Heroes, Hero-Worship and the Heroic in History* (1841).

'The force which he challenged': Christopher Hollis, *The Two Nations: A Financial Study of English History* (George Routledge and Sons, 1935), pp. 88, 133–4.

'weighed down': Hollis, *The Two Nations*, p. 134.

230 'the century of usury': EP, 'The Revolution Betrayed', *British Union Quarterly* II.1 (1938) 36–7.

231 'Wellington was the key': Jerome J. McGann, 'The *Cantos* of Ezra Pound, the Truth in Contradiction', *Critical Inquiry* 15.1 (1988) 18–23.

'Shines | in the mind of heaven': there is a translation of Guinicelli's canzone by Dante Gabriel Rossetti in his *Early Italian Poets* (1861).

232 *The Art of Angling*: information and opinion from Robert Demott, 'Ezra Pound and Charles Bowlker: Note on Canto LI', *Pai* 1.2 (1972) 189–98.

'since fly-fishing': Terrell: *Companion* 198 n. 7.

'That hath the light': EP gives the source in Albertus Magnus in 'Cavalcanti', *LE* 186. Among the drafts for Canto LI in Beinecke there is his translation of the passage: '"that thy mind be the receiver of images (speculativa) receiving with them the light of the doer (lumen agentis) of the doer, daily more like one to other and when this is accomplished | hath the possible the light of the agent, as it were a form cleaving to it so the god's mind may give largess to it, all thing[s] mirrored, perceived/."'

233 'trout rise': EP to Eva Hesse, 17 Apr. 1959 (Beinecke).256

'a system of living': EP TS note (Beinecke). EP's citation of Hess is problematic. My reading of the lines in the canto trusts the text and the historical context which together make Hess figure as one fraudulently speaking peace. I cannot be sure that that was Pound's *intention*. A draft of canto 45 begins with Hesse's words and appears to endorse them wholeheartedly as having 'the light of the doer' about them (Za Pound/2612, Beinecke).

Dante's Geryon: *Inferno* XVII. Virgil's explanation is in XI, 91–111.

234 'The light of the DOER': EP, 'We Have Had No Battles But We Have All Joined In And Made Roads', *PE* 51.

$chêng^4$ $ming^2$: information from Paul Wellen, 'Analytic Dictionary of Ezra Pound's Chinese Characters', *Pai* 25.3 (1996) 65, 85. See also 66/382; and, again, 'We Have Had No Battles But We Have All Joined In And Made Roads', *PE* 50–5.

Ta Hio's Confucian ideal: see pp. 74–6 above; also *GK* 247–8, 281.

The form and pressure of the time

235 'a sufficient phalanx': 74/441.

'a new mode of thought': EP, 'We Have Had No Battles But We Have All Joined In And Made Roads', *PE* 51.

Edward VIII: information from A. J. P. Taylor, *English History 1914–1945* (Harmondsworth: Penguin Books, 1975), pp. 489–95.

236 Bunting... told Pound: BB to EP, Jan.1937 (Beinecke).

'British-conservative-antifascist-imperialist': LZ to EP, 23 July 1938, *EP/LZ* 195.

'flummydiddles': EP, 'Abdication', *Globe* I.1 (Mar. 1937) 87.

'pseudo-Fascist rage': EP to LZ, 6 Apr. 1933 (HRC).

'a parody': EP, 'Orientation and News Sense', *NEW* II.12 (5 Jan. 1933) 273.

'parades': EP, *J/M* 127.

'the Hun's travesty': EP, 'From Italy', *NEW* V.6 (24 May 1934) 143–4.

'DO CAN': EP to Gorham Munson, [16 June 1935] (HRC).

'not a HITLERITE': EP to Claude Cockburn, [1935] (Beinecke).

'certainly no anti-semitism': EP to Claude Cockburn, 18 Jan. [1935] (Beinecke).

'never been any anti-Semitism': EP to Arnold Gingrich, 22 Aug. [1934] (UPenn).

'main trends or drifts': EP, 'American Notes. Time Lag', *NEW* VII.1 (18 Apr. 1935) 6.

237 financed from London: see EP, 'A Thing of Beauty', *Esquire* IV.5 (Nov. 1935) 195–7.

'EVEN Hitler': EP to GT, 11 Mar. 1936, *EP/GT* 72.

'Germany being forced': EP, 'American Notes', *NEW* VIII.25 (2 Apr. 1936) 489.

'under very unfavourable': EP, 'New Italy's Challenge', *British–Italian Bulletin* II.18 (2 May 1936) 3.

'both Germany and Italy': EP to GT, 11 Apr. 1937, *EP/GT* 117.

'getting wiser': EP to GT, 12 Apr. 1937, *EP/GT* 119.

'the resurrection': EP, *GK* 134—drafted about 'March 5th, 1937' (see p. 135).

Lewis had associated: in his *Hitler* (1931)—see D. G. Bridson, *The Filibuster: A Study of the Political Ideas of Wyndham Lewis* (Cassell, 1972), pp. 109–10. EP cited in his 1939 pamphlet, 'What is Money For?', the sentence Lewis had isolated from *Mein Kampf*: 'The struggle against international finance and loan capital has become the most important point in the National Socialist programme: the struggle of the German nation for its independence and freedom' (*S Pr* 269).

'Do for God's sake': EP to Gerhart Münch, 15 Apr. [1938] (Beinecke). Münch's letter to EP, dated '14.4.38', is with EP's.

238 'SCHACHT': EP to GT, 26 May [1938], *EP/GT* 156.

Dr Schacht: information in this paragraph drawn from Shirer, *Third Reich* 258–67, and Sebastian Haffner, *The Meaning of Hitler* 27–34. See also JL, 'Notes on Ezra Pound's Cantos' (1940), in Homberger: 1972, 342.

239 noted in previous chapters: see *EP: Poet I* 392, and pp. 45 and 157–8 above.

'Never expected': EP to Fred R. Miller, 21 Dec. [1934] (Beinecke).

'Never disliked': EP to HLP, 3 Mar. 1926, *EP/Parents* 589.

'tried to kill': EP to HLP, 4 Mar. [1926], *EP/Parents* 591–2.

'Racial curse': EP to Aldington, 4 Mar. 1926 (HRC).

'oooo sez': EP to HLP, 1 Nov. 1927, *EP/Parents* 638–9.

'Personally I like': EP to OR, 29 Sept. [1927] (Beinecke/OR).

'The only good Jew': LZ to EP, 19 Dec. 1929, *EP/LZ* 27. In the same letter LZ wrote, 'it wouldn't have been the likes of an anti-semite like myself'.

240 'next wave': EP to LZ, 9 Dec. 1929, *EP/LZ* 26–7.

'Zukofsky is coming': EP to HLP, 12 Feb. [1929], *EP/Parents* 682.

'Mittle and Nord': EP to LZ, 24 Apr. 1933 (HRC).

should alert him to . . . Silver Shirts: see LZ to EP, 12 Mar. 1936, *EP/LZ* 177 and 179n.

Pound's response: EP to R. C. Summerville of the Silver Shirt Legion of America, 7 May 1934, was published by *New Masses* XVIII.12 (17 Mar. 1936) 15–16.

'According to Bismarck': see EP to LZ, 6[–7] May [1934], *EP/LZ* 157 and 159n.; also 48/240–1.

'Waal I sez': EP to LZ, 6[–7] May [1934], *EP/LZ* 157, 158.

241   *utterly* irrelevant': EP, '"VU", No. 380 and subsequent issues', *New Age* LVII.27 (31 Oct. 1935) 218.

'red herring': EP, *GK* 242.

'Usurers have no race': EP, 'American Notes', *NEW* VIII.6 (21 Nov. 1935) 105.

'Hell makes no distinction': EP, '"VU", No. 380', *New Age* LVII.27 (31 Oct. 1935) 219.

'an allegory': EP, 'Such Language', *G.K.'s Weekly* XX.517 (7 Feb. 1935) 373.

'are we never to see': EP, 'Ezra Pound Asks Questions', *Current Controversy* I.2 (Nov. 1935) 3.

'The Jew usurer': EP, 'American Notes', *NEW* VIII.6 (21 Nov. 1935) 105.

'great chief usurer': EP, 'John Buchan's "Cromwell"', *NEW* VII.8 (6 June 1935) 149.

'drawing vengeance': 52/257. When Faber & Faber refused to print 'Rothschild', Pound substituted 'Stinkschuld'—see Kenner, *Pound Era* 465.

'The Jews are supposed': EP, 'American Notes', *NEW* VIII.6 (21 Nov. 1935) 105.

genocide . . . not then in anyone's mind: on this see Albert Lindemann, *Esau's Tears: Modern Anti-Semitism and the Rise of the Jews* (Cambridge: Cambridge University Press, 1997).

'If the book is honest': EP to M. J. B. Ezekiel, 31 Mar. [1936] (Beinecke).

242   'there wd. be no need': EP to James Taylor Dunn, 18 Mar. 1937 (Beinecke)—cited in Redman, *Ezra Pound and Italian Fascism*, 178.

'warning ME': EP to M. J. B. Ezekiel, 31 Mar. [1936] (Beinecke).

'Even decent Jews': LZ to EP, 12 Mar. 1936, *EP/LZ* 177.

'eating her heart out': Lina Caico to EP, 14 Mar. 1937 (Beinecke).

243   'You hit a nice sore spot': EP to Lina Caico, [between 15 and 17 Mar. 1937] (Beinecke).

'Dear Ez': Lina Caico to EP, 18 Mar. 1937 (Beinecke).

244   'Dear Ezra': Nancy Cunard to EP, [June 1937], on copy of *SPAIN: THE QUESTION* (Beinecke).

'Dearest N': EP to Nancy Cunard, [June 1937] (Beinecke).

no more was he with Franco's Falange: Stock: 1970, 346–7, records that EP replied to a pro-Franco organization seeking his support later in 1937 in very nearly the same terms as he had to Cunard.

'Questionnaire an escape': EP's 'Answer' in *Authors Take Sides on the Spanish War* (1937), as in *Spanish Front: Writers on the Civil War*, ed. Valentine Cunningham (Oxford: Oxford University Press, 1986), p. 57.

'you're not being read': LZ to EP, 15 Mar. 1935, *EP/LZ* 164.

'You seem to think': LZ to EP, 7 June 1935, *EP/LZ* 171.

'If you're dead set': LZ to EP, 12 Mar. 1936, *EP/LZ* 177.

losing readers: information from Gallup: 1983, 53 and 60.

'You are suspect': BB to EP, 3 Sept. 1936 (Beinecke).

245   'too damn gullible': LZ to EP, 12 Mar. 1936, *EP/LZ* 178.

'worthless': John Hargrave to Gorham Munson, as reported by Charles Norman, Norman: 1960, 326.

'Pound was trying': Charles Norman's account of what Gorham Munson told him, Norman: 1960, 326.

'the Boss's reclamation': LZ to EP, 7 June 1935, *EP/LZ* 172.

Soviet farm collectivization: see Richard Overy, *The Dictators: Hitler's Germany and Stalin's Russia* (Allen Lane, The Penguin Group, 2004), pp. 42, 235.

'the manoeuvres': BB to EP, 3 Sept. 1936 (Beinecke).

246 'distribute the purchasing power': EP to James Crate Larkin, 8 Apr. 1935, *EPEC* 145—EP was laying down what he thought should be the stated aims of a proposed national credit bill.

Note: The financial crisis of 2007–8 brought many commentators to express views similar to Pound's. Robert Skidelsky, biographer of Keynes the economist who devised an answer to the Great Depression following the 1929 Crash, wrote on the *Guardian*'s online commentis-free on 15 Mar. 2008, under the heading 'Morals and markets': 'The paradox of capitalism is that it converts avarice, greed, and envy into virtues.' He also wrote of 'capitalism's lack of a principle of justice'. In the *Guardian* on 10 Apr. 2008 Ulrich Beck, Professor of Sociology in Munich and at the London School of Economics, wrote that capitalism's free market system 'has shrugged off any responsibility for democracy and society in the exclusive pursuit of short-term profit maximisation'.

5. IDEAS OF ORDER, 1937–1939

'Immediate need of Confucius'

Works consulted for this section include: James Legge, *Confucian Analects, The Great Learning* and *The Doctrine of the Mean*, translated, with Critical and Exegetical Notes, Prolegomena, Copious Indexes, and Dictionary of All Characters (New York: Dover Publications, 1971)—an unabridged republication of vol. 1 of 'The Chinese Classics' Series (Oxford: Clarendon Press, 1893); James Legge, *The Works of Mencius* (New York: Dover Publications, 1970)—an unabridged republication of vol. 2 of 'The Chinese Classics' Series (Oxford: Clarendon Press, 1895); Ernest Fenollosa, *The Chinese Written Character as a Medium for Poetry*, with a Foreword and Notes by Ezra Pound (Stanley Nott, 1936); Bernhard Karlgren, *Sound and Symbol in Chinese* (1923) (Hong Kong: Hong Kong University Press, 1971); Colin A. Ronan, *The Shorter Science and Civilisation in China: An Abridgement of Joseph Needham's Original Text*, vol. i (Cambridge: Cambridge University Press, 1978); François Cheng, *Chinese Poetic Writing* (Bloomington: Indiana University Press, 1982); Arthur Cooper, 'The Poetry of Language-making: Images and Resonances in the Chinese Script', *Temenos* 7 (1986) 241–58; David M. Gordon, 'A Rayogram M.7306...Yao⁴', *Pai* 16.3 ((1987) 93–5; Mary Paterson Cheadle, *Ezra Pound's Confucian Translations* (Ann Arbor: University of Michigan Press, 1997); Scott Eastham, 'In Pound's China —The Stone Books Speak', *Pai* 33.1 (2004) 89–117; Feng Lan, *Ezra Pound and Confucianism: Remaking Humanism in the Face of Modernity* (Toronto: University of Toronto Press, 2005); Ernest Fenollosa and Ezra Pound, *The Chinese Written Character as a Medium for Poetry: A Critical Edition*, ed. Haun Saussy, Jonathan Stalling, and Lucas Klein (New York: Fordham University Press, 2008)—note particularly pp. 118–21 and 132–8 for Fenollsa's remarks on sound in Chinese poetry, an aspect he is supposed to have not understood.

247 'Am sending': EP to Tinkham, 10 July [1937], *EP/GT* 137.
'the most valuable': EP, 'Immediate need of Confucius' (1937), *S Pr* 89.
'*To call people*': EP, *GK* 16; 'a man should not be called': *GK* 21.
as defined in...the *Ta Hio*: see pp. 74–6 and 226 above.
written rapidly and off the top of his head: at several points in *GK* EP gives that day's date thus marking the rapid progress of the writing; and there are his letters to Morley, his editor at Faber, to fix starting and finishing dates; moreover, throughout the book he makes a virtue of writing from memory and not looking things up.
'a-sailing': EP to F. V. Morley, Feb. 1937, *L (1951)* 380.
'I believe': EP, *GK* 347.
248 'Plato's *Republic*': EP, *GK* 38.
excessive emphasis: cf. 'our time has overshadowed the mysteries by an overemphasis on the individual' (EP, *GK* 299).

'Rapacity': EP, *GK* 15–16.

'hoggers of harvest': *GK* 31, 45, and elsewhere—EP's translation of St Ambrose's 'captans annonam'.

'the main character': EP, *GK* 29.

'way of life': EP, *GK* 24.

'processes biological': EP, *GK* 51–2.

'the totalitarian view': EP, 'The Jefferson–Adams Correspondence', *North American Review* CCXLIV.2 (1937/1938) 319.

'superior to Aristotle': EP, *GK* 279.

'Most days': JL, *Pound as Wuz* 263.

in the light of Fenollosa's essay: Twentieth-century sinologists, concentrating on Chinese as a *spoken* language, were generally dismissive of Fenollosa's reading the *written* language as a system of visual signs, and Pound scholars and critics have tended to accept their verdict. Fenollosa was perfectly aware that in the majority of characters there is a phonetic component related to the pronunciation, but he found it incredible that those components could be merely phonetic and contribute nothing to the play of meaning, as the lexicographers maintained. His detractors have done him the injustice of disregarding his explicit terms of reference—the *written* character as a medium of *poetry*—and of pretending that what was taken to be the case in a majority of characters was more or less true of all. Now it has been demonstrated by Arthur Cooper and by François Cheng that Fenollosa's intuition was correct and that the so-called phonetic element does often if not always have a meaningful function in the ideograms in ancient and traditional poetry.

Legge's editions: the edition Pound was using (now at Hamilton) printed only the pages giving the Chinese text of the four books with Legge's translation and exegetical notes below—it was published in Shanghai and he thought it was 'probably a Shanghai'd (pirated) edtn.' (*L (1951)* 390).

'When I disagreed': EP, 'Mang Tsze (The Ethics of Mencius)' (1938), *S Pr* 96.

249 'one hour on': EP to DP, 4 Aug. 1937 (Lilly).

'read a good deal': EP to Katue Kitasono, 14 Aug. 1937, *EP&J* 42.

'started Kung again': EP to DP, 15 Aug. 1937 (Lilly).

'got to end of Analects': EP to DP, 29 Aug. 1937 (Lilly).

'three times through': EP, 'Mang Tsze (The Ethics of Mencius)' (1938), *S Pr* 99.

an essay published in the *Criterion*: i.e. 'Mang Tsze (The Ethics of Mencius)' (1938)—details in this paragraph are drawn from this essay as printed in *S Pr* 98–9, 106–8, except for the explication of 'the character which combines the human being with the number two', which is from Eastham, 'In Pound's China', *Pai* 33.1 (2004) 97.

'a door': EP, 'How to Write' (1930), *MA* 88. For 'the sign of metamorphosis' see 57/313.

'abstracts or generalizes': EP, 'How to Write' (1930), *MA* 89.

250 'at no point': EP, 'Mang Tsze (The Ethics of Mencius)' (1938), *S Pr* 101. The whole paragraph is drawn from EP, 'Mang Tsze (The Ethics of Mencius)', 100–3.

'The "Christian virtues"': EP, 'Mang Tsze (The Ethics of Mencius)', 104.

'citizen of a chaos': EP, 'Mang Tsze (The Ethics of Mencius)', 110.

'alternating periods': EP, 'Mang Tsze (The Ethics of Mencius)', 104.

'spending my spare time': EP to Tinkham, 22 Nov. [1937], *EP/GT* 140.

'I think you are intellectually': Tinkham to EP, 10 Dec. 1937, *EP/GT* 141.

'Am only doing Mencius': EP to Tinkham, [9 Jan.1938], *EP/GT* 144.

251 'to give a few lectures': EP to Tinkham, 23 Feb. [1938], *EP/GT* 150.

'Great historical events': Tinkham to EP, 10 Dec. 1937, *EP/GT* 141.

classic anthology: see EP to Kitasono, 21 Oct. 1937, and Kitasono to EP, 15 Nov. 1937, *EP&J* 45, 50.

'a cheap edition': EP to Kitasono, 2 Mar. and 14 Aug.1937, *EP&J* 39 and 42.

Signor Mussolini speaks

Source: cutting from London *Morning Post*, 21 Aug. 1937, with EP/DP correspondence (Lilly).

To educate

251 'So much prosperity': DP to EP, 5 Sept. 1937 (Lilly).
252 'The Child': DP to EP, 8 Aug. 1937 (Lilly).
'To govern': *Confucius* 57—EP's 1945 translation is cited.
'looking at the bronze': MdR, *Discretions* 96–7. The following paragraph is drawn from *Discretions* 96–103.
253 'the charming stories': Katue Kitasono to Maria Pound, 25 Dec. 1938, *EP&J* 70. See also *EP&J* 53 and 56–7 for exchange between EP and Kitasono concerning the stories; and see Maria Pound, 'Gais, The Beauties of the Tirol', *Pai* 37 (2010) 59–151 for a reproduction of the original text in Italian, English, and Japanese.
'a swelled head': EP to Katue Kitasono, 14 Jan. 1939, *EP&J* 70–1.
'Then a huge fuss': paragraph drawn from Mary de Rachewiltz's own account, *Discretions* 107–10.
'since the days': EP, 'Tigullian Musical Life', as translated (not by EP) from *Il Mare*, 4 Dec. 1937, *EP&M* 426–7.
David Nixon was agitating: see OR to EP, 23 Oct. 1937, cited in Conover, 130.
254 'Starting [Tuesday]': most details in this paragraph drawn from 'Tigullian Musical Season' and 'February Concerts—The Pianist Renata Borgatti', as translated (not by EP) from *Il Mare*, 1 Jan. 1938, and 8 Jan. 1938, in *EP&M* 428–31.
first modern performance: see EP, 'Tigullian Musical Season. The February Concerts', as translated (not by EP) from *Il Mare*, 22 Jan. 1938, *EP&M* 432; also 'Musicians'. *Action* 16 July 1938, as in *EP&M* 441.
'wooden': EP as Atheling, 'Music', *NA* 25 Nov. 1920, as in *EP&M* 234.
'PLAN of work': EP to Gerhart Münch, 19 Nov. [1937] (Beinecke).
another image: rest of paragraph drawn from MdR, *Discretions* 119–20. See also Stella Bowen, *Drawn from Life* (1940) (Maidstone: George Mann, 1974), p. 145.
255 **the use of microfilm**: for some of EP's many calls for it to be brought into use see 'Tigullian Musical Life' and 'Tigullian Musical Season', *EP&M* 426–9; and 'Notes on Micro-Photography', *Globe* II.5 (Apr./May 1938) 29.
'enormous quantities': *EP&M* 429.
'another 600 pages': EP to AB, 29 June 1938 (Lilly).
persuaded the editor of *Broletto*: see EP, 'Notes on Micro-Photography', *Globe* II.5 (Apr./May 1938) 29.
tried to persuade Faber: details from EP to L. Pol[linger], 23 Feb. [1938] (Beinecke).
presented his microfilm copies: details from O.R.'s *Antonio Vivaldi, Quatro concerti autogafi*, and *Antonio Vivaldi, Due concerti manoscritti* (Siena: Academia Musicale Chigiana, 1949 and 1950) (HRC).
'the 100 best': EP to Kitasono, 14 May 1938, *EP&J* 63–4.
256 'since Imagism': Kitasono to EP, 26 Apr. 1936, *EP&J* 27.
'a poet can not neglect': EP to Kitasono, 24 May 1936, *EP&J* 27–8.
'neither Zen': EP to Kitasono, [13 Aug. 1936], *EP&J* 31.
'to meet any member': EP to Japanese Ambassador in Rome, 26 Dec. 1936, *EP&J* 34–5.
a three hour talk: EP to Kitasono, 1 Jan. 1937, *EP&J* 35.

'The new microphotographic': EP to Hajime Matsumiya, Secretary of the Japanese Embassy, Rome, 15 Dec. 1937, *EP&J* 248.

257 'bilingual or trilingual': 'Trilingual System Proposed for World Communications', *Japan Times and Mail*, 15 May 1939, in *EP&J* 150.
'Two young poets': Kitasono to EP,10 Feb. 1939, *EP&J* 72.
'my chinese Cantos/': EP to Kitasono, 3 Mar. 1939, *EP&J* 72.

Anschluss

Details from William L. Shirer, *The Rise and Fall of the Third Reich* (1960), pp. 322–56.

Going wrong, thinking of rightness

258 'you are NOT to concede': EP to Montgomery Butchart, 12 Dec. 1938 (HRC).
six or even eight sets: EP to DP, [? 2 June 1938] (Lilly).
'copying out': from an unpublished notebook kept by Noel Stock in the 1960s, as in Carpenter 520. About 17 July 1938 EP told DP he was 'doing Vivaldis'. In 'Muzik, as Mistaught', *Townsman* I.3 (July 1938) 8, EP wrote: 'No process with pen in hand teaches a man so much both of the thought and of the actual idiom; of the actual way to *write down* the sound desired and the durations desired as the copying out of work of genius' (*EP&M* 436).
idea of relaxing: see EP to Laurence Binyon, 8 and 12 May 1938, *L (1951)* 412 and 414.
Guide to Kulchur: the copy marked by TSE is now in HRC. Gallup: 1983, 61–2 gives details.
'Omar says': DP to EP, 7 Aug. 1938 (Lilly).

259 'not yet very grown up': DP to EP, 5 Aug. 1938 (Lilly).
'Daily Mirror': DP to EP, 20 July 1938 (Lilly).
'A consciousness': EP to DP, 26 July 1938 (Lilly).
'Is the Pope': DP to EP, 30 July 1938 (Lilly).
cutting from an Italian newspaper: enclosed with EP to DP letters (Lilly). Farrell, *Mussolini*, 309, cites *L'Osservatore romano*, 30 July 1938, and *Il Giornale d'Italia*, 20 Sept. 1938, to same effect.
the race laws: paragraph drawn mainly from Farrell, *Mussolini*, 303–11; some further details from Meir Michaelis, *Mussolini and the Jews: German–Italian Relations and the Jewish Question in Italy 1922–1945* (Oxford: Clarendon Press for the Institute of Jewish Affairs, 1978)—see particularly pp. 171–2.
'a spiritual enemy of the Fascist faith': Farrell's words, *Mussolini* 308.
'policy of segregation': Mussolini's words, cited Farrell, *Mussolini* 310.

260 'a Jew could embrace the Fascist faith': Farrell's words, *Mussolini* 308.
'excellent and sober stuff': EP to DP, 21 Aug. 1938 (Lilly).
'like it has been bottled': EP to DP, [2 Sept. 1938] (Lilly).
Waaal all yits': EP to DP, [3 Sept. 1938] (Lilly).
'the jewish Problem': Gerhart Münch to EP, 29 Aug. 1938 (Beinecke).
'Lots today': DP to EP, 2 Sept. 1938 (Lilly).
'I am sorry for you': reported by Aldo Tagliaferri, ed. *Ezra Pound Lettere* (Milan: Feltrinelli, 1980), p. 115, as cited by David Anderson in *Pai* 10.2 (1981) 440.
an earlier Fascist statement: see Farrell, *Mussolini* 306.
'where they touch Russia': EP to DP, [3 Sept. 1938] (Lilly).
'What are Jews to do?': Lina Caico to EP, 2 Aug. 1938 (Beinecke).

261 'Get down to USURY': EP to Lina Caico, [? before 10 Aug. 1938] (Beinecke). Preda, *EPEC* 215–16, prints this letter and dates it [3 Aug. 1938].

'when you have seen': Lina Caico to EP, 25 Mar. 1939 (Beinecke).

'The Revolution Betrayed': EP, *British Union Quarterly* II.1 (Jan./Mar. 1938) 36–8.

'aryio-kike': EP wrote a verse squib: 'Did I not coin the term: "Aryio-kike" | to designate just those Aryan bastards | whom, quo ante | Our eminent brother Dante | had also found need to stigmatise; sic vide: | *Che fra voi | di voi | Il Guideo non ride!*'— 'Usury', *NEW* XIV.19 (16 Feb. 1939) 292.

'It will be a great pity': EP, 'Pity', *Action* 139 (15 Oct. 1938) 16.

262   Another contribution to *Action*: 'Infamy of Taxes', *Action* 120 (4 June 1938) 13.

'could not get at the masses': Wilhelm Reich, *The Mass Psychology of Fascism* (Harmondsworth: Penguin Books, 1975), pp. 116–17.

praising Wyndham Lewis: see *GK* 134.

Leihkapital: international loan capital. In 'Symposium-I. Consegna', *Purpose* X.3 (July/Sept. 1938) EP wrote: 'Hitler's declaration on the bases of German currency, this spring (1938) was a public event, important and interesting to some people as the "axis" to others. Hitler's statement on Leihkapital in "Mein Kampf", so masterfully cited by Wyndham Lewis and used at chapter head in his "Hitler" already pre-existed as an idea in J. A. Hobson's exposition of the syphilitic venom of international lending.'

'the German terror': LZ to EP, 14 Nov. 1938, *EP/LZ* 196–7.

'Why curse Adolphe': EP to LZ, 2 Dec. 1938 (HRC).

'You know as well as any man': BB to EP, 16 Dec. 1938, as cited by A. David Moody, '"EP with two pronged fork of terror and cajolery": The Construction of his Anti-Semitism (up to 1939)', *Pai* 29.3 (2000) 78–9.

263   'Dear Zuk': EP to LZ, 7 Jan. 1939 (HRC).

'let's not correspond': LZ to EP, 18 Jan. 1939, *EP/LZ* 198–9.

'theoretical': Carlo Izzo, [Notes accompanying] 'Three Unpublished Letters by Ezra Pound', *Italian Quarterly* (Riverside, California) XVI.64 (1973) 118.

'not anti-semite': EP, 'Symposium-I. Consegna', *Purpose* X.3 (July/Sept. 1938) 167–8.

thinking of rightness: cf. 'And as to why they go wrong, | thinking of rightness' (116/797).

Czechoslovakia sacrificed

264   'the most democratic': Shirer, *Third Reich* 358. This section is based on Shirer's chaps. 12 and 13, 'The Road to Munich' and 'Czechoslovakia Ceases to Exist', pp. 357–427 and 428–54.

'a quarrel in a faraway country': Neville Chamberlain, radio broadcast to the nation, 27 Sept. 1938, as cited by Shirer, *Third Reich* 403.

'symbolic of the desire': declaration of Hitler and Chamberlain, 30 Sept. 1939, as in Shirer, *Third Reich* 419.

'peace with honour': Neville Chamberlain, 30 Sept. 1939, as reported by Shirer, *Third Reich* 420.

'under protest': Czechoslovak official statement, 30 Sept. 1939, as reported by Shirer, *Third Reich* 420.

'We have been forced': Dr Kamil Krofta, Foreign Minister, as cited in dispatch to Berlin of German Chargé d'Affaires in Prague, in Shirer, *Third Reich* 420–1.

Comings and goings

265   'Chamberlain is the FIRST': EP, 'Who Profits?', *NEW* XIV.4 (3 Nov. 1938) 55–6.

'If ever war': EP, 'A Money Is', *Delphian Quarterly* XXI.4 (Oct. 1938) 47.

'a ruler promotes': EP, 'Ubicumque lingua Romana', *Fascist Europe/Europa Fascista* (Milano), 1 (28 Oct. 1938) 41–6—this paragraph and the one following are based on this article.

267   **composition was interrupted**: EP to Willis Overholser, [after 21] Nov. 1938, 'Just home after 5 weeks in London/continuity broken' (Beinecke).

a temperature of 102°: DP, entry for 2 Oct. in her 1938 diary (Lilly). On 3 Oct. DP noted 'Olivia died' and 'four telegrams'; and on 5 Oct. 'EP returned'.

'animated and indignant': MdR, *Discretions* iii.

'gotta start': EP to OR, 13 Oct. 1938 (Beinecke/OR).

'Oh . . . Cremate' . . . 'against letters' . . . 'For goodness sake': DP to EP, 19 Oct. 1938 (Lilly).

'ridiculously generous terms': Henry Swabey, 'A Page Without Which', *Pai* 5.2 (1976) 330–1. Swabey also provides the detail about WL and a chair.

'pockets bulging': Ronald Duncan, *All Men Are Islands* (Hart-Davis, 1964), p. 197—as cited in Carpenter: 1988, 555.

'bring her back some thing': DP to EP, 16 Nov. 1938 (Lilly).

13 cases: detail from Carlo Rupnick to EP, Jan. 1939 (Beinecke).

268   **'acted as the leader'**: Swabey, 'A Page Without Which', *Pai* 5.2 (1976) 331.

a Noh play: details from Wilhelm: 1994, 139–40.

'coat-tails flying': WL, 'Early London Environment', *T. S. Eliot: A Symposium*, compiled by Tambimuttu and Richard March (Frank Cass & Co., 1965), p. 29.

what to put in on the left: see WL to EP, 17 Dec. 1938, *EP/WL* 202.

'rapturous applause': WBY to his wife, 18 Nov. 1938, as cited in Foster: 2003, 642.

'he cd/ buy': EP to Tinkham, 13 Jan. 1939, *EP/GT* 161.

not 'a moral coward': EP, 'Does the Government of England Control the B.B.C.?', *Action* 150 (7 Jan. 1939) 3.

'vivacious, bustling and practical': Oswald Mosley, *My Life* (Nelson, 1968), p. 226—as cited in Carpenter: 1988, 551.

'what he was headed for': EP, 'To Albion', *'Ezra Pound Speaking': Radio Speeches of World War II*, ed. Leonard W. Doob (Westport, Conn.: Greenwood Press, 1978), p. 397.

269   **'in 13 years'**: OR to EP, 31 Oct. 1938 (Beinecke/OR). See also Conover, 133–4.

'damn unfair': OR to EP, 2 Nov. 1938 (Beinecke/OR). See also Conover, 134.

'IN GREAT ANXIETY': OR to EP, 8 Nov. 1938 (Beinecke/OR).

'ASSURED DURABLE': EP to OR, 9 Nov. 1938 (Beinecke/OR).

'He ain't stayin'': EP to OR, 9 Nov. 1938 (Beinecke/OR).

'She breathing again': OR to EP, 10 Nov. 1938 (Beinecke/OR).

'To make up': MdR, *Discretions* iii—paragraph drawn from *Discretions* iii–14.

'projecting continuance': EP to WL, 9 Jan. [1939], *EP/WL* 204.

'deeply shaken': TSE, *The Idea of a Christian Society* (Faber & Faber, 1939) 63–4.

270   **'depression of spirits'**: TSE, 'Last Words', *Criterion* XVIII.71 (Jan. 1939) 274.

'Who killed Cock Possum': EP to Ronald Duncan, 10 Jan. 1939, *L (1951)* 415.

'Olga, scandalized': EP to TSE, [Jan. 1939] (Beinecke), cited Conover, 134. The source is an unpublished poem, 'Elegy (1936)'—though obviously written 1939—beginning 'O weep for Buck Possum | the arrow-collared Adonis' (Beinecke).

'constitute a source': EP,'Concerti Mozartiani a Rappalo, in Marzo', *Il Mare* 1561 (11 Feb. 1939) [1], translated in *EP&M* 448. For the programmes see *EP&M* 446–8.

to Washington in the spring: see EP to Tinkham, [21 Dec. 1938], *EP/GT* 160; also EP to WL, 8 Dec. [1938], *EP/WL* 200, with WL's response of 17 Dec. on p. 201.

acquired in November 1937: in a letter to W. H. D. Rouse, 1 Dec. [1937] (Beinecke), EP wrote, 'Moyriac de Mailla "Histoire de Chine" which I have just bought from continental bookseller for 200 LIRE'.

in June 1938: information from Dr Gyorgy Novak. In Jan. 1939 EP wrote to TSE, 'Took me 53 years to find out Braintree; Quincy, Merrymount wuz all on or by "a plantation named Weston's"/damn all my folks don't never stik to their real estate till it rizes' (Beinecke)—he turned 53 in Oct. 1938, and would have found that information on p. 4 of vol. i of John Adams's *Works*. EP also told Tinkham in Jan.1939,'Has taken me years to get John Adams' works' (*EP/GT* 161). Near the close of canto 62 (62/350) there is the line '(11th Jan. 1938, from Rapallo)', a misdating for '1939' originating in the notebook draft.

'Chewing thru Adams': EP to OR, 1 Feb. 1939 (Beinecke/OR).

'on vol. Ten': EP to OR, 3 Feb. 1939 (Beinecke/OR).

'got to the end': EP to OR, 7 Feb. 1939 (Beinecke/OR).

'much more the father': EP to Willis Overholser, [Jan.–Mar. 1939] (Beinecke).

'*pater patriae* U.S.A.': EP to Katue Kitasono, 3 Mar. 1939, *EP&J* 72.

'helluva time': EP to OR, 19 Feb. [1939] (Beinecke/OR).

271   **up to canto 67**: see EP to Katue Kitasono, 3 Mar. 1939, *EP&J* 72.

      polished and shined: see EP letters to TSE in Jan. 1939 (Beinecke).

      sent off to Faber: 'Cantos 52/71 to Faber', EP to AB, 4 Apr. 1939 (Lilly).

The end of Czechoslovakia

Details from William L. Shirer, *The Rise and Fall of the Third Reich* (1960), pp. 427–54.

271   **'Neither Britain nor France'**: Shirer, *Third Reich* 450.

Two books for governors: (1) cantos 52–61

This section is particularly indebted to: Carroll F. Terrell, 'History, de Mailla and the Dynastic Cantos', *Pai* 5.1 (1976) 95–121; Carroll F. Terrell, *A Companion to the Cantos of Ezra Pound*, [vol. i] (Berkeley: University of California Press, 1980), pp. 199–258; David Gordon, '"Confucius Philosophe": An Introduction to the Chinese Cantos 52–61', *Pai* 5.3 (1976) 387–403; David Gordon, 'The Sources of Canto LIII', *Pai* 5.1 (1976) 122–52; John J. Nolde, *Blossoms from the East: The China Cantos of Ezra Pound* (Orono, Me.: National Poetry Foundation, 1983); Dun J. Li, *The Ageless Chinese* (J. M. Dent & Sons, 1968).

271   **More than the history**: Marcel Granet, *Chinese Civilization* (New York: Meridian Books, 1958), p. 132. A page from the abridged version of Joseph Needham's *Science and Civilisation in China* provides further valuable background:

> Confucianism appeared in the sixth century B.C. and is named after its founder...[whose] family name was Khung...[and who] is always referred to by his title of honour as Khung Fu Tzu (Master Khung) of which Confucius is the Latinised form. Born in 525 B.C. in the state of Lu (now Shantung) he traced his descent from the Imperial house of Shang, and spent his life developing and propagating a philosophy of just and harmonious social relationships. From about 495 B.C. he spent a number of years in enforced exile from Lu, wandering from state to state with a group of disciples and conversing with feudal princes, ever hoping for a chance to put his ideas into practice. For the last three years of his life he was back in Lu, writing and instructing his students. In 479 Confucius died, his life an apparent failure; yet as it turned out his influence proved, in the end, so great that he has often been called 'the uncrowned emperor of China'.
>
> Confucianism...strove for as much social justice as was possible in a feudal-bureaucratic society. This was to be achieved by a return to the ways of 'the ancient Sage Kings'—a use of legendary historical authority that led Confucius to term himself a transmitter rather than an innovator. In a chaotic feudal society torn apart by wars between states, Confucius sought order. In a society in which human life was cheap,

where there was little law and order save what each man could enforce by personal strength, armed followers, or intrigue, Confucius preached peace and respect for the individual.... He advocated universal education and taught that diplomatic and administrative positions should go to those best qualified academically, not socially: in this sense he was revolutionary. The true aim of government, he taught, was the welfare and happiness of all the people, brought about by no rigid adherence to arbitrary laws but by a subtle administration of customs that were generally accepted as good and had the sanction of natural law. In early Confucianism, then, there was no distinction between ethics and politics... (Colin A. Ronan, *The Shorter Science and Civilisation in China: An Abridgement of Joseph Needham's Original Text*, vol. i (Cambridge: Cambridge University Press, 1978), pp. 78–9)

273 **de Mailla's translation**: to be exact, what de Mailla translated was the version in the Manchu language made for Emperor K'ang-hsi, of the most recent revision of the 'Outline and Digest of the Comprehensive Mirror', originally compiled in the mid-twelfth century under the direction of the Sung neo-Confucian scholar Chu Hsi (1130–1200), that being a condensation of 'A Comprehensive Mirror for the Aid of Government' put together in the eleventh century by a team of scholars led by Ssu-Ma Kuang (1019–1086). De Mailla's *Histoire générale de la Chine* was published in 13 vols., in Paris, between 1777 and 1783—(from Nolde, *Blossoms from the East* 25–7).
'having to do with *instruction*': see *EP: Poet I* 24.
to Italy's Il Duce: see 55/298—'put up granaries | somewhat like those you want to establish'—and 61/335 where Mussolini's Italian term is used, 'AMASSI or sane collection, | to have bigger provision next year, | that is, augment our famine reserve | and thus to keep the rice fresh in store house'.
'if you remain keen': TSE to EP, 15 July 1939 (Beinecke).

274 **so *Li Ki* goes on**: see *Li Ki: ou Mémoires sur les bienséances et les cérémonies*, Texte Chinois avec une double traduction en Français et en Latin par S. Couvreur S.J. (Ho Kien Fou: Mission Catholique, 1899), tome premier, chap. IV, article iii, §19 (p. 358). Canto 53 is drawn from IV.iii–vi (pp. 353–410).
De Mailla's history: the title and opening pages are reproduced in Terrell, 'History, de Mailla and the Dynastic Cantos', *Pai* 5.1 (1976)100, 110–21.

275 'luminous details': see *EP/Poet I* 170. Cf. *GK* 277 re picking 'the live details from past chronicle'.

277 **a song to be found in the *Shih King***: see *CA* 8 (no. 16).
two odes in *The Classic Anthology*: see *CA* 190–3 (nos. 262, 263).

279 **Ngan, the next great reformer**: see *The Shorter Science and Civilisation in China: An Abridgement of Joseph Needham's Original text*, i. 53.

280 **a gigantic encyclopedia**: see Dun J. Li, *The Ageless Chinese* 306.

281 **a Jesuit's version**: i.e. A. De Lacharme, *Confucii Chi-King*, ed. Julius Mohl (Stuttgart and Tübingen, 1830).

283 'one of [the poem's]': Robert Fitzgerald, 'Mr Pound's Good Governors', *Accent* 1 (Winter 1941) 121–2, as in Homberger: 1972, 352.
'this survey': George Dekker, *Sailing After Knowledge: The Cantos of Ezra Pound* (Routledge & Kegan Paul, 1963), p. 182.
'monotonous didacticism': Randall Jarrell, 'Poets: Old, New and Aging' (1940), *Kipling, Auden & Co.: Essays and Reviews 1935–1964* (New York: Farrar, Straus and Giroux, 1980), pp. 43–4.
'There is no alternative': Donald Davie, *Ezra Pound: Poet as Sculptor* (Routledge & Kegan Paul, 1965), p. 161.
Hugh Kenner: see 'Inventing Confucius', *The Pound Era* (Faber & Faber, 1972) pp. 445–59. On the apparent contradiction see pp. 454–8. Kenner could see why the *Comprehensive Mirror* is anti-Taoist while the other Confucian books are not, so it is

puzzling that he should not credit Pound with the same insight. Possibly it was because he did not quite fasten on the key to the paradox: that for good government the *tao*, the process of things, must be enacted by the rectified human will (Dante's *directio voluntatis*). Civilization means harmony with nature, but its root, in Pound's reading of Confucius, is volition (cf. *GK* 279). One might say that to Make It New requires Tao + Kung—*tao* alone won't do the job.

Two books for governors: (2) cantos 62–71

This section is indebted to: *The Works of John Adams*, ed. Charles Francis Adams, 10 vols. (Boston, 1850–6)—Pound's set is now in the Rare Book Room of the Library of the University of Toledo, Ohio; *Diary and Autobiography of John Adams*, ed. L. H. Butterfield, 4 vols. (Cambridge, Mass.: Belknap Press of Harvard University Press, 1961); *The Adams–Jefferson Letters: The Complete Correspondence between Thomas Jefferson and Abigail and John Adams*, ed. Lester J. Cappon (Chapel Hill: University of North Carolina, 1959, 1988); EP, 'The Jefferson–Adams Letters as a Shrine and a Monument' (1937, 1960), *S Pr* 117–28; Catherine Drinker Bowen, *John Adams and the American Revolution* (Boston: Little, Brown, 1950); Frederick K. Sanders, *John Adams Speaking* (Orono, Me.: University of Maine Press, 1975); Carroll F. Terrell, *A Companion to the Cantos of Ezra Pound*, [vol. i] (Berkeley: University of California Press, 1980), pp. 259–360; Kay Davis, chap. 5, 'Fugue', *Fugue and Fresco: Structures in Pound's Cantos* (Orono, Me.: National Poetry Foundation, 1984); Philip Furia, chap. VIII, 'The Adams Papers', *Pound's Cantos Declassified* (University Park: Pennsylvania State University Press, 1984); Jean-Michel Rabaté, chap. 3, 'Ezra Pound and Pecuchet: The Law of Quotation', *Language, Sexuality and Ideology in Ezra Pound's Cantos* (Macmillan, 1986); A. D. Moody, 'Composition in the Adams Cantos', *Ezra Pound and America*, ed. Jacqueline Kaye (Macmillan, 1992); David Ten Eyck, Introduction and chapters 1–3, *Ezra Pound's Adams Cantos* (Bloomsbury, 2012).

284 **If we are a nation**: EP, 'The Jefferson–Adams Letters as a Shrine and a Monument' (1937–8), *S Pr* 118. The paragraph in full: 'If we are a nation, we must have a national mind. Frobenius escaped both the fiddling term "culture" and rigid "Kultur" by recourse to Greek, he used "Paideuma" with a meaning that is necessary to almost all serious discussion of such subjects as that now under discussion [i.e. American civilization]. His "Paideuma" means the mental formation, the inherited habits of thought, the conditionings, aptitudes of a given race or time.'

285 **'nonsensical hurly-burly'**: Davie, *Ezra Pound: Poet as Sculptor* 161.

288 **'a society'**: the reading of the early Faber editions—the current 'of society' is an error.
 'mowed all the grass': Adams wrote 'mowed', but all editions give 'moved', due to a misreading of EP's notebook transcription where the 'w' is unclear.

289 **'before Lexington'**: see *Cantos* 32/157, 33/161.

291 **depreciation of the paper money**: for details of the depreciation and the immense profits made see Charles A. Beard, *An Economic Interpretation of the Constitution of the United States* (New York: Macmillan, 1913, 1935), pp. 32–8.

293 **THEMIS**: see *The Adams–Jefferson Letters* 378–80. See also Jane Ellen Harrison, *Themis: A Study of the Social Origins of Greek Religion* (1912, 1927; reprinted Merlin Press, 1963).

294 **'cruel war'**: Jefferson's draft of 'A Declaration [of Independence]', in his *Autobiography*, in *Thomas Jefferson: Writings* (New York: Library of America, 1984), p. 22.

295 **'re USURY'**: EP, 'Foreword', *S Pr* 6.
 Cleanthes' hymn: for EP's translation see Cantos [256]. For a full version see *Oxford Book of Greek Verse in Translation* (1938), no. 483.

296 **'governments are instituted'**: Jefferson's draft of 'A Declaration [of Independence]', *Thomas Jefferson: Writings* 19.

6. ALIEN IN AMERICA

A good deal of the detail in this chapter comes from Charles Norman's interviews with persons who saw Pound while he was in the United States between 20 April and 17 June 1939, as used in Norman's *Ezra Pound* (1960). Further details have been added to his account by Stock, Wilhelm, Carpenter, and Conover. See also Maurice Hungiville, 'Ezra Pound, Educator: Two Uncollected Pound Letters', *American Literature* XLIV.3 (Nov. 1972) 462–9.

297   'dug up for shelters': DP to EP, 19 Apr. 1939 (Lilly).
     'Dear Ezz': WL to EP, 16 Apr. 1939, *EP/WL* 209–10.
     'There SHOULD be no war/': EP to Ronald Duncan, 8 Apr. [1939] (HRC). EP had written to Senator Borah on 13 Jan. 1939, 'What every decent man in Europe WANTS is a sane Europe and NO WAR west of the Vistula' (*EP/WB* 68)—Chamberlain and Baldwin were saying much the same thing at the time (see Paul N. Hehn, *A Low Dishonest Decade: The Great Powers, Eastern Europe, and the Economic Origins of World War II, 1930–41* (New York: Continuum, 2002), p. 25).
     'the last whimper': EP, 'The "Criterion" Passes', *British Union Quarterly* III.2 (Apr./June 1939) 67.
     'to *try* to be American': EP to Hubert Creekmore, Mar. 1939 (Beinecke)—printed with deletions in *L (1950)* and *L (1951)*.

298   'manifestly honorific': EP to Tinkham, 16 Jan. [1938], *EP/GT* 148–9—most of this paragraph is drawn from this letter, and from the editor's note 1. The names of those EP nominated are from Ahearn's editorial note (s.v. 'a BODY') in *EP/EEC* 122.
     'Mr Tinkham seems to think': G. C. Hamelin, Secretary to Mr Tinkham, to EP, 19 Apr. 1938, *EP/GT* 152.
     'educated or drowned': EP to FMF, 31 Jan. 1939, *L (1951)* 416.
     'scurrilous attacks': Henry Seidel Canby to EP, 14 Mar. 1938, as in editor's note, *EP/EEC* 147.
     'a working, model': FMF to EP, 17 Feb. [1938], *EP/FMF* 153–4.
     'Does Olivet USE'... 'Will he GET': EP to FMF, [21 Feb. 1938], *EP/FMF* 155.
     'I do not approve'... 'have already a press': FMF to EP, 16 Mar. 1938, *EP/FMF* 156.

299   'they START': EP to FMF, 18 Mar. [1938], *EP/FMF* 158.
     'small Western college': EP to Kitasono, 14 May 1938, *EP&J* 64.
     'a revival': EP to John Crowe Ransom, 15 Oct. 1938, *L (1950)* 319.
     Introductory Text Book: first published following EP, 'Are Universities Valid?', *NEW* XIV.19 (16 Feb. 1939) 281–2; then privately printed as a single folded sheet broadside, 500 copies for distribution gratis by the author; subsequently reprinted in several periodicals in 1939; added as an appendix to the new edition of *GK* in 1952. (For other reprintings see Gallup: 1983, 433.)
     'Fundamentals': EP, 'Are Universities Valid?', *NEW* XIV.19 (16 Feb. 1939) 282.
     'utter treachery': comment accompanying copies of *Introductory Text Book* sent to new President of Hamilton and to the Alumni Committee, as enclosed with EP to Ibbotson, 25 Mar. 1939, *EP/Ibb* 93, 96.

300   'the PIVOT': EP, 'Communications [following 'Introductory Text Book']: I. Money', *Townsman* II.6 (Apr. 1939), 12.
     'possible to restore': EP to John Slocum, 6 Aug. 1939 (Beinecke).
     'Saw again Mongiardino': Carlo Rupnik to EP, 4 Mar. 1939 (Beinecke).
     The Globe: the relevant correspondence with James Taylor Dunn, the editor, is at Hamilton College. *The Globe* (1937–8) was published from Milwaukee, Wisconsin, as 'an intimate journal of travel . romance . adventure . world interest... a truly international magazine' (Gallup: 1983, 315).

'The "Ente Provinciale"': Rupnik to EP, 17 Mar. 1939 (Beinecke). The 'Ente' would be the Provincial Tourist Office.

'un'ottima cabine': Rupnik to EP, 21 Mar. 1939 (Beinecke).

His cheque for $299: the cheque, endorsed as cashed, is with other used cheques from EP's account no. 252 with the Jenkintown Bank & Trust Co. (Brunnenburg). A further cheque for $10 was paid to the 'ITALIA Soc. An.di Nav. —NY' on 6 June. Possibly in preparation for his trip to America, EP had withdrawn three amounts of $100 from the account on 21, 27, and 31 March; and he withdrew a further $150 from the account while in America.

'descriptive booklet': EP to Rupnik, [before 1 Apr. 1939] (Beinecke).

'an important collaboration': Rupnik to EP, 17 July [1939] (Beinecke).

'He iz feelink': EP to DP, 12 Apr. 1939 (Lilly).

301 'magnificent quarters': EP to DP, 13 Apr. (Lilly).

'Aboard in surroundings': EP to HLP, 13 Apr. 1939 (Beinecke).

'very calm trip': EP to HLP, 19 Apr. 1939 (Beinecke).

'GIVE ECONOMIC': Munson's wire, and details of the interview, are in Norman: 1960, 357–8; Wilhelm: 1994, 146–7; Carpenter; 1988, 558–9.

'literature ... is now': Edmund Gilligan, *New York Sun*, 26 May 1939, as given by Redman: 1991, 190.

'Gargling anti-semitism': Cummings to James Sibley Watson Jr, [30 May 1939], *EP/EEC* 139.

302 '10 . 11 . 12': EP to DP, 22 Apr. 1939 (Lilly). Further details in this paragraph from EP to DP, 26 or 27 Apr. 1939 (Lilly).

warned him against trusting England: according to Stock: 1970, 363.

'found Pound wandering': Paul Mariani, *William Carlos Williams: A New World Naked* (New York: McGraw-Hill Book Company, 1981), p. 428.

'I can hardly bear': WCW to JL, 5 Apr. 1939, *William Carlos Williams and James Laughlin: Selected Letters*, ed. Hugh Witemeyer (New York: W. W. Norton, 1989), p. 45.

'very mild and depressed': WCW's impression, according to FMF in a letter to Allen Tate, 3 May 1939, *The Letters of Ford Madox Ford*, ed. Richard M. Ludwig (Princeton, NJ: Princeton University Press, 1965), p. 319.

'somewhat incoherent': Mariani, *William Carlos Williams* 428.

'Bill Wms here': EP to HLP, [1 May 1939] (Beinecke).

'fed me': EP to OR, 3 May 1939 (Beinecke/OR).

'a very poor show': EP, 83/536. Copy of pass to Senate seen at Brunnenburg.

his 'catch': EP to DP, 10 May 1939 (Lilly).

'Bridges, Lodge': EP to HLP, 10 May [1939] (Beinecke).

303 'Pound seemed normal': Henry Wallace to Charles Norman, in Norman: 1960, 360.

a long article: EP, 'Ezra Pound on Gold, War, and National Money', *Capitol Daily* V.89 (9 May 1939) [1], 4–5.

Munson recalled: Norman: 1960, 364–5.

207 pounds: EP to DP, [c.18 Apr. 1939] (Lilly).

'fatigue that prevented': EP to Cummings, 13 Nov. [1946], *EP/EEC* 200.

'gallant combatant': EP, 'Ford Madox (Hueffer) Ford; Obit', (Aug. 1939), *S Pr* 431, 433.

304 'suggested to the Harvards': JL to EP, 23 Apr. 1939, *EP/JL* 104.

'the steep rows': Norman: 1960, 365–6.

'he spent 2½ hours': EP to OR, 17 May [1939] (Beinecke/OR).

His voice on the recording: for details see Gallup: 1983, 443 (E5a).

'would have been magnificent': John Holmes, as recorded by Norman: 1960, 366.

'academic world orful': EP to DP, 16 May 1939 (Lilly).

305 'across miles of Mass': EP to HLP, [13 June 1939] (Beinecke).

'letters of introduction': Tinkham to EP, 15 May 1939, *EP/GT* 170.

Corker remembered Pound: Charles E. Corker to Daniel Pearlman, 25 Aug. 1980, printed as 'Appendix B: The Meeting between the Poet and the Senator', in *EP/WB* [79]–83.

'I can still feel his hand': EP, 'On Resuming' (29 Jan. 1942), *'Ezra Pound Speaking'*: *Radio Speeches of World War II*, p. 25. See also 84/537.

306   a foreign columnist: details from EP to Ibbotson, 4 Nov. [1940], *EP/Ibb* 108, and Redman: 1991, 189–90.

should be impeached: see EP to Tinkham, 20 Jan. [1939], *EP/GT* 165.

Mary Barnard: this paragraph and the next based on her own account in *Assault on Mount Helicon: A Literary Memoir* (Berkeley: University of California Press, 1984), pp. 158–67.

'real old-fashioned': Mrs Serly, as in Norman;1960, 362.

'exchange of frankness': Louis Zukofsky in Charles Norman, *The Case of Ezra Pound* (New York: The Bodley Press, 1948), pp. 55–7; reprinted in Charles Norman, *The Case of Ezra Pound* (New York: Funk and Wagnalls, 1968), pp. 87–8.

307   Eastman's first impression: Max Eastman, 'Memorandum on Dining with Ezra Pound and E. E. Cummings', dated 24 May 1939, in *EP/EEC* 138.

'What is Money For?': reprinted in *S Pr* 260–72—citations from pp. 268–71.

308   'desperate attempt': EP to DP, [9 June 1939] (Lilly).

'keen on J. Adams': EP to DP, [9 June 1939] (Lilly).

'one of the serious characters': EP to Douglas Fox, [? 1939], as cited by Norman: 1960, 372.

an 'essential book': WCW, 'Penny Wise, Pound Foolish', *New Republic* XCIX (28 June 1939) 229–30, as in Homberger: 1972, 336–7. Homberger omits WCW's accusing EP of 'thirty years' anti-Semitism'—see Witemeyer's note in *EP/WCW* 203.

Pound had 'spread himself': WCW to JL, 7 June 1939, *William Carlos Williams and James Laughlin: Selected Letters*, p. 49.

309   'useful': EP to DP, 10 and 16 May 1939 (Lilly).

'Hamilton at least to try' . . . 'with increasing irritation' etc.: EP to Ibbotson, 17 Jan. [1939], *EP/Ibb* 87–8.

'95%': comment accompanying copies of *Introductory Text Book* sent to new President of Hamilton and to the Alumni Committee, as enclosed with EP to Ibbotson, 25 Mar. 1939, *EP/Ibb* 94, 96. See also *Ezra Pound. A Selected Catalog from the Ezra Pound Collection at Hamilton College*, compiled with notes by Cameron McWhirter and Randall L. Ericson (Clinton, NY: Hamilton College Library), p. 29—a facsimile of the copy sent to William Bristol, Jr, a member of the Alumni Committee.

'Ez axd': EP to Dr A. P. Saunders, 30 May 1939 (Hamilton).

'such an agile': Olivia Saunders (Mrs Robert W. Wood, Jr), to Charles Norman, as in Norman: 1960, 368.

'down from 207': EP to OR, [? 10 June 1939] (Beinecke/OR).

310   'if war came': Mrs Edward Root to Charles Norman, as in Norman: 1960, 367.

'Dupont (gun family)': EP to DP, 8 June 1939 (Lilly). Cp. 'Du Pont powder works to lunch', EP to HLP, 8 June 1939 (Beinecke).

'econ. & hist dept.': EP to DP, 8 and 9 June 1939 (Lilly).

'finally had to interpose': Mrs Edward Root to Charles Norman, as in Norman: 1960, 368.

the Alumni Luncheon: primary source for this paragraph is Norman: 1960, 369–71.

a gentleman's agreement: see William Hoffa, '"Ezra Pound: A Celebration", Hamilton College, April 25–26, 1980', *Pai* 9.3 (1980) 576.

'About bust the commencement': EP to OR, 13 June 1939 (Beinecke/OR).

'Hamilton OUGHT': EP to President Cowley, 28 June [1939], reproduced in facsimile in *Ezra Pound: A Selected Catalog from the Ezra Pound Collection at Hamilton College*, 26–7.

311 'I won't attempt': President Cowley to EP, 11 July 1939, *Ezra Pound: A Selected Catalog from the Ezra Pound Collection at Hamilton College*, 28.

'git over the idea': EP to Cowley, 25 July [1939] (Hamilton).

'*Ezra Pound*': the citation is as given in Norman: 1960, 369.

APPENDIX C. OUTLINE OF *CAVALCANTI*. A SUNG DRAMEDY IN 3 ACTS

321 'dramedy': 'T. J. V.', 'Dramedy', *Athenaeum* XCIV. 4688 (5 Mar. 1920) 315.

'wother hell': EP to AB, 24 Oct. 1933 (Lilly).

Decameron: see the ninth tale of the sixth day. Cited here in the translation by Guido Waldman in The World's Classics (Oxford: Oxford University Press, 2003), pp. 401–3.

323 'tour de force': EP to AB, 20 Aug. 1932 (Lilly).

'thought melody came up'...'meagre': EP to AB, 20 Aug. 1932 (Lilly).

'DULL': as echoed by EP in letter to AB, 7 June 1933, cited *CPMEP*(1) 78. Margaret Fisher reports, however, that in the Bolzano 2000 performance this aria was sung impressively and to 'mesmerizing' effect.

remarked in *The Spirit of Romance*: *SR* 116, 177, 127.

background to Sordello's song: see EP, 'Troubadours—Their Sorts and Conditions', *LE* 97; *GK* 107–8; 6/22–3, 29/141–2, 36/180. Dante placed Cunizza in the Third Heaven (under Venus)—see *Paradiso* IX, 25ff. See also Peter Makin, *Provence and Pound* (Berkeley: University of California Press, 1978), pp. 79–82 and chap. 9 (pp. 186–214) especially pp. 204–5.

'formed [Sordello's] genius': Makin, *Provence and Pound*, p. 204.

'Background': EP, as given in *CPMEP*(2) vii.

324 historical record: see Niccolo Machiavelli, *History of Florence and of the Affairs of Italy*, Bk. I, chap. 4.

'Guido turns to an intellectual sympathy': EP, 'Introduction' to *Sonnets and Ballate of Guido Cavalcanti* (1912), *T* 20, Anderson 14–15.

the cypher: see Margaret Fisher, *EPRO* 182–91 and 286–90 (n. 136). An issue for critics has been how seriously Pound took suggestions that in Cavalcanti's (and Dante's) poetry there was enciphered the 'secret language' of a mystic cult. In his 'Cavalcanti' essay he accepted as a useful 'irritant', while declaring them not applicable to 'Donna mi prega', 'Luigi Valli's theories *re* secret conspiracies, mystic brotherhoods, widely distributed (and uniform) cipher in "all" or some poems of the period, etc.' (*MIN* 375–6—see also 382–6, *LE* 173, 179–82). In a letter to OR, 6 Feb. 1928, he was, however, simply dismissive: 'a big book on Linguaggio secreto di Dante which explains a lot of things re/Guido that don't need it and...don't explain any of the ones that might stand a bit of xplaining'—'fails to fit the facts' (Lilly). In *GK* he wrote that 'Valli's wanderings in search of a secret language...are, at mildest estimate, unconvincing' (294—see also 221). Re the critics on the issue, see Colin McDowell, 'Literalists of the Imagination: Pound, Occultism and the Critics', *Pai* 28.2–3 (1999) 56ff. McDowell argues that Pound was 'questioning the whole idea of using codes for writing or interpreting poetry' (57).

325 Pound's notes: 'Notes on Act III', *CPMEP* (2) 126.

'fortune shows her power': Niccolo Machiavelli, *The Prince*, trans. George Bull (Harmondsworth: Penguin Books, 1961), p. 91.

Guido's failure: see Fisher and Hughes, *CPMEP* 113, for a somewhat different account of the failure.

ACKNOWLEDGEMENTS AND
COPYRIGHT NOTICE

When one works on Pound one does not work alone. I have enjoyed support both material and moral, together with encouragement, incitement, and provocation from many persons and institutions, and it is a pleasure to recall once again what I owe to them and to record my gratitude.

There are the great libraries which collect, conserve, and make available to researchers the vast treasury of Pound's unpublished writings and drafts. I am most grateful for the courteous welcome, the frequent kindness, and the willing and expert assistance accorded me at Yale University's Beinecke Library, at the Harry Ransom Humanities Research Center of the University of Texas at Austin, at the Lilly Library of Indiana University, Bloomington, Indiana, and at the Daniel Burke Library of Hamilton College, Clinton, New York.

Next I must thank the phalanx of scholars who have edited valuable resources from those archives, to the great benefit of other readers and researchers: D. D. Paige, Richard Reid, Noel Stock, Forrest Read, William Cookson. Eric Homberger, Michael John King, R. Murray Schafer, Leonard W. Doob, Harriet Zinnes, Vittoria I . Mondolfo, Margaret Hurley, Brita Lindberg-Seyersted, David Anderson, Donald Pearce, Herbert Schneidau, Omar Pound, A. Walton Litz, Timothy Materer, Mary de Rachewiltz, Barry Ahearn, Sanehida Kodama, Robert Spoo, Thomas L. Scott, Melvin J. Friedman, Jackson R. Bryer, Lea Baechler, James Longenbach, Richard Sieburth, Richard Taylor, Ira B. Nadel, David M. Gordon, Walter Sutton, Hugh Witemeyer, E. P. Walkiewicz, Philip J. Burns, Maria Luisa Ardizzone, Demetres Tryphonopoulos, Leon Surette, Sarah C. Holmes, Robert Hughes, Margaret Fisher, Massimo Bacigalupo, Roxana Preda, Joanna Moody, Miranda B. Hickman, and Alec Marsh. Here the late Carroll F. Terrell deserves a special honourable mention for his outstanding services to Ezra Pound scholarship, as founding editor of *Paideuma*, compiler of *A Companion to the Cantos of Ezra Pound*, animator of conferences, and generous instigator, supporter, and publisher of others' work, especially that of younger scholars. In another special category is Donald Gallup—his *Ezra Pound: A Bibliography* (1983) is an indispensable resource always at hand. I have reason to be grateful also for Volker Bischoff's *Ezra Pound Criticism 1905–1985: A Chronological Listing of Publications in English* (Marburg, 1991); and for Archie Henderson's thesaurus of 'new notes on the Pound/Agresti correspondence', *'I Cease Not to Yowl' Reannotated* (Houston, Tex., 2009).

The good and useful critics and interpreters of Pound's work are legion, and though it is invidious to single out individuals, I must name a few to whom I feel especially indebted. Foremost is Hugh Kenner, the inventor of literary modernism in his time. Then I would name as they come to mind, each for some particular donation: Donald Davie, Eva Hesse, Hugh Witemeyer, George Kearns, David Gordon, M . L. Rosenthal, Walter Baumann, Ian Bell, Guy Davenport, Christine Brooke-Rose, Jean-Michel Rabaté, Richard Sieburth, Massimo Bacigalupo, Peter Makin, Marjorie Perloff, Michael Alexander, James Longenbach, Wendy Flory, Emily Mitchell Wallace, Kay Davis, Ronald Bush, Tim Redman, William McNaughton, Christine Froula, Peter Nichols, Leonardo Clerici, Leon Surette, Demetres Tryphonopoulos, Luca Gallesi, Maria Luisa Ardizzone, Colin McDowell, Scott Eastham, Robert Hughes, and Margaret Fisher. More generally, I have enjoyed being a member of a lively, contentious, and collaborative community of scholars at the biennial International Ezra Pound Conferences, from the first in 1976, and have profited from innumerable discussions in various agreeable settings with fellow scholars and critics.

'Biography, a minor form of fiction', Hugh Kenner wrote somewhere, not altogether dismissively, though with reason; yet, as a biographer, I have been glad to be able to check out the facts of Pound's life against the biographies of Noel Stock, J. J. Wilhelm, and Humphrey Carpenter. Mary de Rachewiltz's memoir *Discretions: Ezra Pound, Father and Teacher* has been an inimitable inspiration. Anne Conover's *Olga Rudge & Ezra Pound* has been a mine of information.

I am especially grateful to the following for their generosity in providing me with books, articles, unpublished results of their own research, or critical dialogue: Michael Alexander, Massimo Bacigalupo, Stefano Maria Casella, Danilo Breschi, Bernard Dew, Scott Eastham, Margaret Fisher, Leah Flack, Luca Gallesi, Dryden Gilling-Smith, Robert Hughes, A. Walton Litz, Charles Lock, Alec Marsh, Marie-Noelle Little, Philippe Mikriammos, Alan Navarre, Catherine Paul, Caterina Ricciardi, Richard Sieburth, Richard Taylor, Noel Stock, Demetres Tryphonopoulos, Emily Mitchell Wallace, William Watt.

Poets, like those who write about them (and those who would read them), need publishers. Beyond the copyright acknowledgements below, we must be grateful to Elkin Mathews, Pound's first publisher in London; to Charles Granville, Harriet Shaw Weaver, John Rodker, William Bird, and Nancy Cunard, who brought out his early and wholly uncommercial poetry through their private presses; to Alfred A. Knopf, Boni and Liveright, and Farrar and Rinehart, his first publishers in New York; to Faber & Faber, who became his publishers in London after 1933; to Stanley Nott; and above all to James Laughlin, whose New Directions became his American publisher, and ultimately the leading publisher of his work. Other publishers helped keep his work in print in his later years, notably Peter Owen of London. In recent years we owe edited collections of his correspondence and prose to the enterprise of a number of North American and British university presses. To Garland Publishing we owe the invaluable ten-volume collection of Pound's contributions to periodicals. To the Library of America we owe Richard Sieburth's comprehensive selection of Pound's poems and translations. And to Robert Hughes and Margaret Fisher we owe the now complete series of editions of his music.

There are more personal debts. To the late Hugh Kenner for opening his personal Pound archive to me and for generous hospitality. To Hugh Witemeyer for his conversation and kindness. To the late George Kearns and to Cleo Keams, for their hospitality and conversation, and to George in particular for a gift of books from his Pound collection. To Noel Stock for his warm hospitality and informed conversation. To Geoffrey Wall, biographer and translator of Flaubert, for his close attention to my prose and for his constructive advice. To Declan Spring at New Directions for extraordinary courtesies and helpfulness. To Mary de Rachewiltz for permission to quote from Pound's published and unpublished writings; for generous practical assistance, including giving access to her library and making freely available her collection of photographs; also for her wholly Poundian principle of placing no restriction on the use of her father's work. To Elizabeth Pound and the estate of Omar S. Pound for generous and unrestricted permission to quote from Pound's published and unpublished writings and from Dorothy Pound's letters and diaries.

I owe much to the impressive expertise and enthusiasm of all who have worked on the book at Oxford University Press.

I am grateful for the skilled photographic work of Paul Shields of York University's Photographic Unit.

Visits to the archives in the United States were supported by a British Academy Leverhulme Visiting Professorship, and by two British Academy research grants. Yale University's Beinecke Library awarded me its Donald C. Gallup Visiting Fellowship, and the Lilly Library of Indiana University, Bloomington, Indiana awarded me its Everett Helm Visiting Fellowship. This book owes a great deal of its substance to those grants and awards.

COPYRIGHT

INDEX

Note: Includes writings indexed by title. Bold entries in parentheses refer to Plate numbers.